THE CULTURES OF AMERICAN FILM

Robert P. Kolker
PROFESSOR EMERITUS
UNIVERSITY OF MARYLAND

NEW YORK OXFORD
OXFORD UNIVERSITY PRESS

Oxford University Press is a department of the University of Oxford.
It furthers the University's objective of excellence in research,
scholarship, and education by publishing worldwide.

Oxford New York
Auckland Cape Town Dar es Salaam Hong Kong Karachi
Kuala Lumpur Madrid Melbourne Mexico City Nairobi
New Delhi Shanghai Taipei Toronto

With offices in
Argentina Austria Brazil Chile Czech Republic France Greece
Guatemala Hungary Italy Japan Poland Portugal Singapore
South Korea Switzerland Thailand Turkey Ukraine Vietnam

For titles covered by Section 112 of the US Higher Education Opportunity Act, please visit www.oup.com/us/he for the latest information about pricing and alternate formats.

Published by Oxford University Press
198 Madison Avenue, New York, New York 10016
http://www.oup.com

Library of Congress Cataloging-in-Publication Data
Kolker, Robert Phillip.
The cultures of American film / Robert P. Kolker, University of Maryland.
pages cm
ISBN 978-0-19-975342-0
1. Motion pictures--United States--History. I. Title.
PN1993.5.U6K575 2015
791.430973--dc23

2014008962

BRIEF CONTENTS

CONTENTS

I love in movies how our sense of things is continually contracting and expanding. The fading out of interest in one event, moving along at a sleepy rhythm, can lead abruptly to a surprised discovery of how much something related to it—perhaps sitting right next to it—suddenly *matters*. Finding our way back in after a disappointing lull often feels like the director is turning to us directly, and asking for a renewal of faith. He tells us that it is possible to go deeper in this situation, if we are willing. "Can you imagine this with the energy that I do? Are you up to the demands of seeing what is now before you?"

—GEORGE TOLES[1]

". . . We're all the children of D. W. Griffith and Stanley Kubrick."

—MARTIN SCORSESE[2]

---

1. "Rescuing Fragments: A New Task for Cinephilia," *Cinema Journal*, vol. 49, no. 2 (Winter, 2010), 164.
2. Quoted in his film *A Personal Journey with Martin Scorsese Through American Movies (1995)*.

PREFACE

The Cultures of American Film integrates a number of approaches to the study of movies. Its chronological organization provides a historical overview, a survey of films across the decades from cinema's invention to the present. Its analytical approach addresses form and content: how films work and how we respond to them. By putting films in their cultural contexts, it examines how films fit into our lives and their own: that is, the life of film itself; the technologies that made them possible; the studios in which they were made; the filmmakers' struggles with politics and censorship. *The Cultures of American Film* covers movements, directions and **directors, genres**, the structures of films and their audiences.

American film is spread across a broad canvas. Since 1893, it has developed many genres, created many stars, spoken to us in a variety of voices, and, despite fluctuations through the decades, maintained a loyal audience, almost continually excited about its images and stories. That audience—we who view and respond to films—is itself a creation of the movies. In a sense, we are what the movies make us: happy, sad, longing, aroused, frightened, delighted, disappointed, angry, accepting. These emotions and attitudes can outlast our time with any given film. They can enter our lives and, like literature or music or painting, enlarge our outlook on the world and ourselves. At the same time, much—some might say most—American film is incredibly narrow, depending on the repetition of tried and true formulae, often made up of the most obvious and conventional stories of love, death, terror, or awe in order to guarantee a response from its viewers.

American film is a mass of contradictions, but these are contradictions that can be teased apart, examined, analyzed, and made sense of. Throughout its history, film has evolved, moved forward, experimented, fallen backward, tried new visual and narrative ideas, returned to old tried and true ideas. It is, like its audience, in love with technology. Since its earliest days, when spectators peered through the eye piece of a machine and cranked a handle to move a strip of film, through the introduction of sound in the late 1920s and widescreen and 3D in the 1950s, when viewers peered through glasses at the screen, and again in the 2000s, when viewers peered through glasses at the screen, various technologies have been tried, have succeeded or been abandoned, all to increase the pleasure of our viewing. The introduction of sound created a revolution in filmmaking, resulting in the aural field becoming as important as the visual, sometimes more so when dialogue became more central than the visual articulations of a film.

Special effects have always been a part of the technology of filmmaking. Despite its claim to be a "realistic" art, film is an artificial construct, building its images from foreground to background, often piece by piece. Actors might be photographed against a movie screen with the background projected on it. They might be photographed against a **blue** or **green screen**, with the background added at a later time. Paintings and sets with false perspective are used to give the image a sense of presence and depth. **CGI**—computer-generated imagery—has merely taken the place of older processes that allow filmmakers to build the visual (and aural) content of a film, layer by layer, shot by shot, creating foreground, background, and the color tonalities of a film.

Filmmakers and their audiences are continually engaged in pushing the boundaries of content. Despite its dependence on tried and true conventions of stories and storytelling, throughout its history film has responded to and in some instances been in the forefront of changes in what are considered socially acceptable representations of sexuality, violence, and language. This apparent contradiction is important: to maintain and engage its audience, any given film may be simultaneously familiar and novel, containing its audience within recognizable boundaries while at the same time varying content and even pushing on those boundaries just enough to make things interesting.

American film and its audience engage in a process of ongoing negotiation: will a film gain an audience? What kind of audience? A broad one, consisting of ages 18–46, the demographic most desired? Will the film have "legs," bringing in more viewers by word of mouth and repeat viewers? Will a film be made for a smaller audience, made with a small budget and perhaps attempting to experiment somewhat with form and content? What do you as a viewer expect from a film? Do you want simple entertainment, an escape from the everyday? Do you want a film to engage in complex emotions or even ideas? What satisfies you most when you see a film? Do you respond most to acting and the presence of stars? Do you like digital spectacle with superheroes? Do you prefer more intimate dramas or films with sex and violence?

All of this and more make up the cultures of American film. Production and reception (that's you, the viewer, responding to a film), the history of events surrounding and sometimes absorbed by a film, the ways in which film speaks to us and we to it constitute a constellation of events and interactions that we will examine in the course of this book. In chronological order, we will analyze the ways in which films work as part of the cultures of their own making as well as the larger structures of their society. We will make general observations and close analyses of particular films, talk about how and why films are made, and investigate the kinds of responses that they require and desire. At the beginning of each chapter are some ideas of what the chapter contains and how that content may affect you, along with suggestions for further critical analysis of the issues presented in the chapter. At the end of each chapter are suggestions for further reading. The aim, finally, is not to be inclusive but rather to attempt to discover connections, interactions, even surprises when film, its makers, its audience, and the culture they are part of interact.

INTRODUCTION

The analysis of film is an intricate process. For one thing, we have to pierce through the veil of entertainment that flows over most movies. They resist being taken seriously, wanting us to be moved, amused, frightened, or thrilled. They don't, by and large, want us to ask questions of them, despite the fact that they ask much of us: they want our undivided attention and a positive response to their characters and stories. Our job then is to reverse the terms. Without losing our sense of enjoyment—in fact, adding to it—we can examine exactly what films ask of us and why. We can, as well, discover how film fits into our lives today and the history and cultures of lives past.

DEFINITIONS OF CULTURE

This book is concerned with the cultures of film. But what do we mean by the word "culture"? In its broadest sense, culture is the product of everything we do, think, create, and express. Culture is the sum total of our doing and being as human beings. But this is too broad a concept to work with. We need to break it down. We have all heard the phrase "corporate culture" and have a vague idea of what that means. It's what goes on within a corporation, the ideas and rules they work by, the moral structures (or lack thereof) that guide them, the way management treats their employees and the employees treat each other and their customers.

The major film studios—MGM, Warner Bros., Paramount, Universal, 20th Century Fox, Universal, United Artists—had a corporate culture during their period of dominance, roughly between the early 1920s and mid 1950s. This culture varied from one studio to the other but shared many elements. Most of the studios were ruled by two people (three in the case of Warner Bros.). One lived in New York and oversaw the studio finances, and the other who lived in Hollywood and supervised the actual production of motion pictures. Jack Warner at Warner Bros. and Louis B. Mayer at MGM, for example, ruled over a kingdom made up of producers, writers, directors, actors, and technical staff. The producers selected the stories and scripts that would be filmed; they chose the writers to create the screenplays, the actors and actresses who would play the roles, the director who would transfer script to screen. Each studio had a chief art director or **production designer**, the person who saw that the sets were dressed with furniture and other decorations appropriate to the time and place of the film. They had a cohort of **cinematographers**, some of whom specialized in photographing glamorous female stars. After 1927, they had sound engineers. They had a team of **editors** who worked with the film's producer—and sometimes the director—to assemble the shots made during filming into a coherent narrative. They had publicity people to create advertising campaigns. And all of these were contract employees, even the high-priced acting talent, who had to take the scripts assigned to them. In 1936, the famous Warner Bros. star Bette Davis fled to England to escape the roles she was asked to play. She sued Warners and lost, forcing her to return to Los Angeles and honor her contract.

But while corporate structures were similar across the studios, there were cultures specific to each one, cultures of form and content that drove the kinds of films they turned out. In the 1930s, for example, MGM tended to produce brightly lit entertainments, musicals, comedies, dramas that featured high production values. Warner Bros. also produced a range of **genres**, but theirs were darker, both in the visual and the thematic sense. MGM's films in the 1930s were escapist—that is, they tried to move their viewers away from the burdens of the Great Depression, of joblessness and despair, and into worlds of romance and even fantasy. *The Wizard of Oz* (Victor Fleming, George Cukor, Mervyn LeRoy, Norman Taurog, King Vidor, 1939) is an extreme example of the kind of film MGM made, in which Judy Garland's Dorothy is whisked away from her dark Kansas home to the wonderland of Oz, complete with witches, munchkins, a scarecrow, a tin man, and a cowardly lion. *The Wizard of Oz* is a road movie that travels through a magical, colorful landscape; a dreamscape, finally, that leads to the kind of sentimental conclusion—there's no place like home—that Louis B. Mayer, head of MGM, was fond of.

Warner Bros., meanwhile, was making gangster films, even musicals that were often bleak and despairing in tone, films that led its audience not out of but into the depths of the Depression. *I Am a Fugitive from a Chain Gang* (Mervyn Leroy, Warner Bros., Vitaphone, 1932) tells the story of James Allen, an architect, once jailed, who, on his escape, makes good in the world. But he is turned in by a jealous lover and, though promised clemency, is put on a brutal chain gang. He escapes once again and now lives like a criminal. The film's ending is as chilling as it gets. Allen agrees to meet his girlfriend at night. His face appears out of the dark. "How do you live?" she asks. "I steal. . . ." He disappears into the darkness and the film ends.

The culture at MGM, as far as their films were concerned, was based in sentimental uplift. Louis B. Mayer wanted his films to create a perfect alternative world. The brothers Warner, on the other hand, worked closer to the world as it was, even darker than it was, as their emphasis on gangster films and even their musicals attest. These attitudes, resulting in the production of particular kinds of films in the 1930s, represent an important aspect of culture, the creative culture of the two studios under question. Today, the studios exist pretty much in name only. They are all of them part of larger corporations for whom the production of film is only one part of their operations. The cultures of these companies are complex to say the least. Rupert Murdoch's News Corporation, for example, owns 20th Century Fox (here abbreviated to just "Fox"), but also the Fox News cable channel (among many other media holdings). The movie side of the company bankrolled and distributed James Cameron's *Avatar* (Dune Entertainment, Ingenious Film Partners, Fox, 2009), experimental in its use of 3D computer imaging and somewhat progressive in its story of an embattled tribe on a distant planet threatened with environmental devastation. The broadcasting side of the company hosts conservative commentators. It is neither progressive nor experimental.

The cultures of film viewing are as complex as those of film production. It is quite possible to say that each viewer carries with her a set of cultural values that allow her to respond to film differently than anyone else. The culture of viewing, of response to a film, is determined by personality, by taste, by gender—itself a complex mix of biological and learned responses. Can we say then, that culture is made of a set of responses? In part, yes: learned responses, innate ones, and responses that are specific to any given individual. Even economics play a part. A culture of frugality or of need may prevent someone from paying the price of admission to a first-run film in a theater. Again "culture" becomes complicated. Economic need may seem to have nothing to do with culture, but rather with the fiscal circumstances a person finds himself in. If economic need comes from a sense of frugality, of not spending money on nonnecessities, even if the money were available, we are firmly in the realm of culture, a culture of frugality. If economic hardship is part of social-economic class, we are also in the realm of culture. While a person's class is determined by economic circumstances, there are cultural aspects to it: class is as much a social-cultural phenomenon as it is economic. In fact, to make things still more complicated, the political culture of the United States tries to deny the existence of classes, assuming, instead, that the nation is made up of one large middle class, with the very poor and the very rich on either ends of the spectrum. But social-economic classes and groups do, in fact, exist. As do race and gender. There are cultural elements peculiar to social-economic groups that include religious and political beliefs, choice of entertainment, even the choice of where to live. These are cultural because, though determined in part by economics, they express beliefs that are individual, group, race, gender, and class driven and involve choices about how to live, how to express oneself, how to engage with the world.

"Engagement with the world" might constitute one useful working definition for culture. Culture, or cultures, are expressions of our engagement—individually, by group, class, race, gender, by institutions—with one another and with the world at large. "Engagement" includes the varieties of response, the way we react emotionally and intellectually to the stimuli we receive. Filmmakers engage with the world by creating movies that will, hopefully, move viewers to respond positively. We, as viewers, engage with films according to our tastes and the responses learned by seeing many other films. Together, these acts of engagement and response constitute the cultures of film, which we will examine in a variety of ways.

We will examine film as part of America's history and culture and how these have influenced film and its audiences. Our methodology will be to move chronologically from film's beginnings at the end of the 19th century until close to the time of the writing of this book. Within that chronology we will look at general issues and do close analyses of particular films. The latter is the key: by understanding the language of cinema and its evolution, looking closely at individual films and the history and cultures of their making, we can come to an understanding of how films address us and how we read that address. It is through the process of "reading" a film that we engage with it. Ordinarily, we do this unconsciously.

All of us "get" what a film is telling us. We learn to read images at an early age and even in the early age of film audiences understood what was going on before them on the screen. As films got more complicated, viewers were able to keep up with advances in visual story telling. The culture of filmgoing developed early, swiftly, and intuitively. Here it will be the job of critical inquiry into this development to replace intuitive reception with analytical thinking. We want to discover what film is telling us and how it is doing its telling. We want to understand the circumstances of a film's production and reception and talk about form itself as a cultural phenomenon.

FILM FORM

What do I mean by "form?" Allow me to ask first, what do you see when you watch a movie? Characters, scenery, action, a story unfolding before your eyes. What do you hear? Dialogue, music, sounds from various sources. All of these are elements of form, which are perceived and interpreted as ongoing story. In other words, the formal construction of American film is largely invisible. It is *there;* it makes the story you see possible, but it hides itself, makes itself invisible. From the very beginning, filmmakers and viewers joined in a compact of comprehension: early filmmakers made images, then began cutting images together, editing them into a narrative; they made **far shots** and **close-ups;** they figured out ways to move characters across a room and then cut to show them leaving the room and entering another. They alternated parts of the narrative so that one scene could take place at the same time as another, but in a different place. Every time filmmakers complicated the narrative, audiences were with them, following the story, which always emerged from the formal properties of its telling. To be sure, at many screenings of early films, there occasionally were explainers who narrated the story to the audience as they viewed the film. Sometimes, during the silent film period, there were people who stood behind the screen and spoke the dialogue the characters on the screen were mouthing.

All of this was in the service of self-education. Audiences were not aware—on a conscious level at least—of shot content, of where the camera was in relation to the characters, or how editing worked to establish narrative continuity. What they were aware of was that a story was being told in an involving and exciting way. With the advent of directors' commentaries on DVDs, viewers may today be more conscious of the formal aspects of film. But the pleasures of moviegoing, part of the *culture* of moviegoing, lies in the tacit agreement that film will overwhelm us with pleasure, thrills, fright, or uplift, without demanding that we attend to the formal mechanisms that deliver these emotions.

But attend we will. In the course of this book, we will examine the formal structures of film, how they evolved, and how they produce meaning—that is, the story you see unfolding before your eyes. We will look at those stories and question them: Why were they made? What kind of response do they demand? Why are they repeated, with variations, over and over again? That means that we will examine film genres—melodrama, the war film, the Western, science fiction, the superhero film. What is the business of making these films? How are new media impacting our viewing of film? What is the effect of film now spread across media from the big screen to the smartphone?

THE FORM OF THIS BOOK

I have chosen a chronological approach in order to see the evolution of form, meaning, and the business of making meaning. Films, filmmaking, and film viewing habits change over the course of time. It is obvious that a film made in 1912 looks different from a film made today. But a film made in 1960 also looks (and sounds) different from a film made today. By moving chronologically, we can account for these differences and understand that the way we view the world cinematically alters over the course of time.

What films will we be looking at and how will we be looking at them? The history of American film has created a small canon—that is, a list of films generally agreed upon as the best representatives of their kind. But the canon, these lists of the 10 or 100 best films, are always changing and often idiosyncratic. They reflect the opinion of people who make up the lists, and these lists differ according to those polled: a list chosen by general audiences will be different from one made up by film reviewers, which will be different from films selected by film scholars or filmmakers. (Each of these groups has their own culture of taste and criteria when it comes to choosing the films they love.) We will be following some of the accepted canon in our work. *Citizen Kane* (Orson Welles, RKO, 1941—title, director, studio, production companies, distributor, and date will be our means of citing a film) has been universally noted as the greatest American sound film. We will need to interrogate "greatest" and understand why *Kane* is so popular in critics' polls and note why in more recent critic's polls, the one conducted every 10 years by the British Film Institute, Alfred Hitchcock's *Vertigo* (Paramount, 1958) has topped *Kane*. Other films that are part of the canon—based on the American Film Institute's listings of "greatest movies"—include Victor Fleming's and David O. Selznick's *Gone with the Wind* (Selznick International, MGM, 1939—a film as much a product of its producer, Selznick, as its many directors), Victor Fleming's *The Wizard of Oz* (and its many uncredited directors listed earlier, MGM, 1939), Frank Capra's *It's a Wonderful Life* (Liberty Films, RKO, 1947), Stanley Donen's and Gene Kelley's *Singin' in the Rain* (MGM, 1952), John Ford's *The Searchers* (Warner Bros., C. V. Whitney Pictures, 1956), and Stanley Kubrick's *2001: A Space Odyssey* (Stanley Kubrick Productions, MGM, 1968). More recent films include Francis Ford Coppola's *The Godfather* (Paramount, Alfran Productions, 1972) and Martin Scorsese's *Raging Bull* (Chartoff-Winkler Productions, United Artists, 1980).

Everyone has a list of their favorite films. I have mine, and they include not only the films I love, but the films that mark important milestones in film history and films that are necessary to know in order to understand that history. For example, D. W. Griffith's *Birth of a Nation* (David W. Griffith Corp., Epoch Producing Corp., 1915) is one of the most unpleasant films ever made. Despite its excellent representation of Civil War battles, it is by turns mawkishly sentimental and ferociously racist. It is as disgraceful a film as one can imagine. But it is also one of the earliest long-form feature films that develops (not invents) a number of cinematic strategies that place it as an important milestone in film history. Griffith is such an important figure that I will devote an entire chapter to his work. The same is true for Stanley Kubrick, who is among the most remarkable of contemporary American filmmakers. Like Griffith, I devote a chapter to Kubrick's films. Martin Scorsese, the director of such films as *Taxi Driver* (Columbia, Bill/Phillips, Italo/Judeo Productions, 1977), *Raging Bull, Goodfellas* (Warner Bros., 1990), *The Aviator* (Forward Pass, Appian Way, IMF Internationale Medien und Film GmbH & Co. 3. Produktions KG, Mirimax, Warner Bros., 2004), *The Departed* (Warner Bros., Plan B Entertainment, Initial Entertainment Group, 2006), *Hugo* (Paramount, 2011), and *The Wolf of Wall Street* (Paramount, Red Granite Pictures, Appian Way, 2013) said of American filmmakers, ". . .We're all the children of D. W. Griffith and Stanley Kubrick."

It is important to note that what follows is not, strictly speaking, a history of American film. We will not discuss every film and filmmaker, but rather pick and choose among the riches of titles that are relevant to the argument at hand. At the same time, we will need to discuss a wide variety of films, some of which you know, some you may not be familiar with. In any case, most the films discussed are available on DVD (and many of the silent films discussed are on YouTube) and should be accessible for you to see.

METHODOLOGY

There are a variety of approaches interwoven in this book. We will look closely at a number of films, combining synopses with analyses, looking at what happens in the course of a film while analyzing the meaning of what happens. We will see how form and structure create a narrative which, in turn, creates a film's story, and how story affects the viewer. We will examine the culture and history of the times in which the films were made, and we will look at the business and technologies of filmmaking, at how the studios work and what happened to them during the period of conglomeration in the 1920s and the 1970s. We will look at the changing technologies of filmmaking, from the invention of film to the coming of sound to film's digitalization. All the way through our study, we will examine the role of censorship—embodied from the early 1930s to the 1960s by the Production Code—that influenced what audiences saw on the screen. In short, our method can be seen partly as a study of infiltration: how films infiltrate our consciousness; how culture infiltrates films; how business infiltrates both.

A WORD ABOUT DIRECTORS

When serious study of film began in the 1960s, it was important to give a proper name to a film. Just as we refer to a novel by its author's name—Ernest Hemingway, William Faulkner, F. Scott Fitzgerald, Philip Roth—for film to be taken seriously, it had to be given authorial authority. The French had already done this. After the embargo on American films during the Nazi occupation of France, there was a deluge of movies from the United States made during the 1940s. *Citizen Kane*, made in 1941, was seen in Paris in 1946 and reviewed by the French philosopher Jean-Paul Sartre. French critics began noting similarities across American films that had nothing to do with the studio in which they were made or who produced or wrote them, but by the director. They noted stylistic and thematic coherences that seemed to belong to the person directing the film because they could be perceived and tracked from film to film directed by the same person.

From this they developed what has come to be called the **auteur theory**, the idea that no matter who else is involved in the creation of a film, it is the director who is responsible for the overall design, the visual structure, the *vision* of the film or a body of films. This is true of a handful of American filmmakers: D.W. Griffith, Orson Welles, John Ford, Alfred Hitchcock, Frank Capra, and more recently Stanley Kubrick, Martin Scorsese, David Fincher, Steven Spielberg, Paul Thomas Anderson among others. But the auteur theory, in regard to American film, and especially during the studio period, roughly between 1915 through the early 1950s, is really something of a convenient fiction. More often than not, the director was only one person in the production line through which a film passed from inception to writing to filming to editing to previews to reediting and finally to release. But the director was and is an important figure at the crucial moment of translating the words of the script into the acting and action on the screen, and often creating the film's visual structure. That is why I keep the director's name in the reference to a film, along with the production and distribution companies responsible for getting it made and seen, even though there are so many other aspects to the creation and reception of a film that we will be discussing. (The decision to include both distributor and production company will lead to a great deal of information following the title of a film. But this is necessary to indicate, especially in recent film, the number of individuals and entities that are involved in a film's creation.) This is also why I will often devote some chapters to directors who were and are important to film's development in a particular time period. In the case of John Ford, Orson Welles, and Alfred Hitchcock, I will devote a chapter to their work before and then after World War II.

To sum up, any film is a concerted and complex effort of production and reception. Our purpose is to investigate various aspects on both sides of the equation. In each chapter we will examine some of the historical and cultural events that surrounded filmmaking of the period and look closely at particular films. Taken together, I hope to present both a large picture and a microanalysis of films in order to understand this most important form of cultural and imaginative expression.

CHAPTER 1

IN THE BEGINNING (1893–1903)

At the end of the 19th century, moving images began to appear on the screen. We examine what those early images looked like, what their history was, who made them, who saw them, and how people reacted to them; how they were a part of modernity. The film "industry" developed rapidly at the turn of the century, and film narratives became more complex, leading to storytelling techniques still used today. *The Great Train Robbery* (1903) is an example of early sophistication in film storytelling.

AFTER READING THIS CHAPTER, YOU SHOULD UNDERSTAND:

- The origins of motion pictures.
- The makeup of early film audiences.
- The role of Thomas Edison in the development of early film.
- The contribution of the French to the development of early film.
- Early film technologies and the development of the formal structures of early film.
- The commercialization of film from its beginnings.
- The concept of "modernity" and its relation to early film and its audience.

YOU SHOULD BE ABLE TO:

- Discuss the earliest moving images.
- Account for the variety and popularity of these early images.
- Understand how film form developed rapidly at the turn of the 20th century.
- Define some basic terms.
- Speculate on the immediate attraction of the moving image.
- Understand the importance of *The Great Train Robbery.*
- Place film within 19th-century technologies.

WHAT THEY SAW AT THE BEGINNING

UNCLE JOSH

We see the side seats and the screen of a moving picture house. Projected on the screen is a slide that says "The Edison Projecting Kinetoscope." Another slide takes its place: "Parisian Dancer." A man peers out of the side seat and looks at the screen, where we see the moving image of a woman lifting her skirts and beginning to dance. The man leaps out of his seat and begins dancing in front of the screen. Another slide appears on the screen, "The Black Diamond Express." A train races toward the camera. This is a **process shot**: the images on the screen that Uncle Josh reacts to appear to be projected onto that screen after the main action was photographed. In other words, the film was exposed twice: once to photograph the stage and Uncle Josh, then again to show the various images on the screen. This is an early example of a **special effect** and the result is that the train appears to run over the man, who runs back to his seat. Even as far back as 1902, film was being manipulated to create the effects the filmmaker wanted the audience to see—in this case, not only the audience watching the movie, but the audience in the movie. Uncle Josh sees various other scenes and antics on the screen: he leaps around until, in a fit of delight and confusion, he runs up and pulls down the screen. The movie theater owner appears and wrestles the man to the ground.

MCKINLEY

Under a canopy of trees, two men walk slowly from a house toward the camera. A woman can be faintly seen sitting on the porch. The man on the left holds a piece of paper that he hands to the man on the right, who puts on his hat and glasses as he looks at the document. He then hands the paper back, removes his hat, and the two continue their slow walk toward the camera and then off screen right.

The first film is called *Uncle Josh at the Moving Picture Show*. It was made early in 1902 by Edwin S. Porter for the Edison Manufacturing company and lasts about two minutes. The second is called *McKinley at Home* and was made by William Kennedy Laurie Dickson for the Biograph Company in September, 1896. It lasts just over a minute. McKinley was to become the 25th president of the United States and the first to use modern media to advertise his campaign. *McKinley at Home* was made just a few years

Uncle Josh gets ready to attack the movie screen. That screen is in fact a special effect, matted or projected separately into the shot. *Uncle Josh at the Moving Picture Show* (Edwin S. Porter, Edison Company, 1902).

The first campaign film: *McKinley at Home* (William K. L. Dickson, Biograph, 1896).

after the very first films were shown. *Uncle Josh* already demonstrates the rapid sophistication of movies at the turn of the 20th century. *McKinley* would be considered a **documentary**, that is, a film of an event that might have happened even if the camera wasn't present, or a depiction of actual people in real situations. *Uncle Josh* is clearly a **fiction film**, something made up and filmed in the studio. Not only made up but clearly depending on early special effects to achieve its images of a man looking at a movie screen.

But both films, in very different ways, demonstrate the *presence* that movies had in their early history. By "presence," I mean a number of things: most obviously, film very quickly gained presence in the culture. From the first peep shows where customers peered into a machine called a kinetoscope to look at a loop of film of prize fighters, or a dancer, or a couple kissing, or a strong man flexing his muscles, to the projection of films in vaudeville houses, in storefront Nickelodeons, and later in elaborate theaters devoted to showing movies, film made its mark on the public consciousness. Movies became *present* in the culture, a force, an object of admiration and of desire. People wanted to see movies and be entertained and informed.

THE REAL THING

The McKinley film is an example of this presence. Audiences were thrilled to see a presidential candidate on the screen. This little film was also boosted in the press—newspapers were as amazed as the audience and helped foster the novelty of the presentation. Before it was screened, a reporter for a Republican newspaper (McKinley was the Republican candidate) wrote: "The distinguished statesman will make his appearance, apparently on the lawn of his house in Canton, full life size, and in action so perfectly natural that only the preinformed will know that they are looking upon shadow and not upon substance. . . . The picture thus shown is not flat—in fact it can not be distinguished as a picture at all."[1] In other words, the representation of McKinley on the screen can be taken as the real thing.

This might be a sign of innocent naïveté or political boosterism, or perhaps more accurately as excitement over the newly discovered power and presence of the moving image. Of course, no one would be fooled into thinking that they were seeing anything but a picture, or would they? Uncle Josh is fooled. He is the country bumpkin, someone not "preinformed," who takes the moving image as an actual presence. He is a figure of fun. But *Uncle Josh at the Moving Picture Show* is itself quite sophisticated. Not only is it making fun of someone taking images literally, but, in so doing, it makes reference to Edison's own films—an early example of **product placement**—and to a famous film from France.

Arrival of a Train at the Ciotat Station (Auguste and Louis Lumière, 1895). Audiences were said to have ducked in fear as the train approached. Note how the camera is placed at an angle that captures the vanishing point of the composition, adding depth to the image.

In 1895, almost at the moment of film's invention, Auguste and Louis Lumière, brothers in the photography business in France, made a film showing the arrival of a train at the Ciotat train station (*L'Arrivée d'un train á la Ciotat*). The camera is set so that it sees the arrival of the train and the people waiting for it at the station. As it arrives, the train seems to head straight for the camera. Like Uncle Josh, people in the audience were said to have ducked in fear at the approaching train, as if it were actually headed for them.

ORIGINS IN PHOTOGRAPHY

Were the audiences for early film so gullible? Could they not tell a representation of reality for reality itself? It's hard to imagine. Photography had been available for almost half a century before cinema. As far back as the 17th century, painters were climbing into a black box, a camera obscura. Through a pinhole on one side, an image of the outside world was projected on the opposite side of the box, allowing the artist to paint directly from nature. The Civil War was documented in photographs, most famously by Matthew Brady. Popular entertainments in the 19th century included lectures, often narrated stories or travel adventures, illustrated by painted or photographed slides. But even further back, early in the 19th century, a Frenchman, Joseph Plateau, invented a gadget, the phenakistoscope, that contained, around a drum, drawings of figures in motion. The drum had slits in it through which the viewer peered. When the drum spun and was held up to the eye, it created the illusion of a figure in motion. In short, there was an almost global urge to capture images of the world and, once captured, to put them in motion.

In the late 1870s, the English photographer Edweard Muybridge made a series of photographs of animals and people in action, capturing, in still photographs, the sequence of motion. (In France, Etienne-Jules Marey was doing similar work.) In a famous wager, Leland Stanford, the former governor of California, bet that, in the course of a gallop, all four hooves of a horse left the ground. He asked Muybridge to make a photographic series of a horse in motion, which proved the point. Muybridge's work lacked only a means to set his images in motion, which he partially solved through the invention of the zoopraxiscope, which projected his images one after the other, creating the illusion of movement.

Other inventors during the late 19th century—in France, Germany, and England—were experimenting with capturing motion and making that motion visible. In a kind of harmonic convergence, the cinema

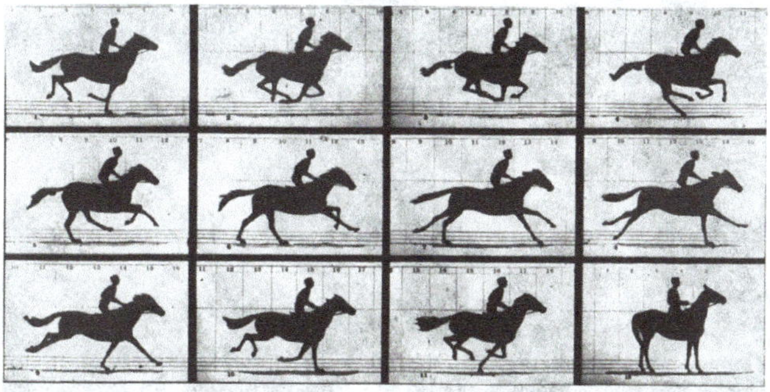

Edweard Muybridge's series photograph of a horse in motion (1878), proving that at one point in its gallop, all four feet leave the ground.

came to be. The French film critic, André Bazin, hypothesizes that the moving image lay nascent throughout history, waiting to be realized, to be invented.[2] This is a fanciful notion, but it contains the idea that I am pursuing, that the movies were less a surprise than a welcome occurrence, that many were responsible for its birth, and that audiences were not quite as gullible as Uncle Josh (if they were, there wouldn't be a film making fun of him).

EDISON

At the same time we consider that the invention of movies was inevitable, there is also a point to be made that it was incidental. Thomas Edison was looking for a way to accompany his invention of the phonograph player. Edweard Muybridge made the suggestion that exhibitions of the phonograph be accompanied by projections of his motion photographs. Edison followed a different path, and in 1888 he announced: "I am experimenting upon an instrument which does for the Eye what the phonograph does for the Ear, which is the recording and reproduction of things in motion. . . ."[3] He wanted the two to go together, that is, to have sound movies. Problems in achieving the appropriate amplification and synchronization of sound prevented this from happening until the late 1920s. But, as we will see, films were seldom shown silently.

Once Edison made up his mind to pursue the moving image and turned development over to his employee, W. K. L. Dickson, things moved very rapidly. First came the kinetograph to photograph images and the kinetoscope, the device that allowed the viewer to peer inside a box where a loop of film was turned by hand by a crank or by an electric motor and lit by a lightbulb. Patents for these inventions were applied for in 1892. To make films, Edison built a studio in New Jersey called the Black Maria that could turn to follow the sun, permitting filmmaking all day long. The first public demonstration of the movies was held in May 1893, where viewers at the Brooklyn Institute of Arts and Sciences lined up to peer at *Blacksmith Scene*, in which three Edison employees hammered on an anvil and drank beer.

Approximately 30 seconds in length, this little film establishes male, physical activity as a basic image set for films to come. It provided a baseline for the boxing films that were a mainstay of early film, for the muscle flexing of a Hungarian strongman named Sandow, who was the subject of another early Edison production. Earlier still, the French photographer Etienne-Jules Marey photographed many series of images of naked bodies. The body in stress, the body naked is a mainstay of cinematic imagery from the beginning. By 1894, after a lull in production due to a stock market crash, Dickson and his coworker William Heise were turning out more than 75 short films, and many more followed in the ensuing years—a woman dancing, a couple kissing, a man sneezing, a bucking Bronco, an Indian war council, fights, fire engines racing to a fire, wrestling matches, and reenactments of violent historical events, such as the

Blacksmith Scene (Edison, 1893). Men at work. The focus on the body in action became a template for American film to come.

Execution of Mary, Queen of Scots. Executions had some popularity. When William McKinley was assassinated in 1901, his funeral was filmed by the Edison Company. They followed this up with a reenactment of the execution of McKinley's assassin, Leon Czolgosz, a somewhat unusual film for its time, combining a panorama of the prison where Czolgosz was put to death, followed by the reenactment. The film, directed by Edwin S. Porter, was made with a minimum of sensation. The same cannot be said of Edison's 1903 film, *Electrocuting an Elephant*, a gruesome bit of footage of an animal being killed.

One theory is that because Edison was a prime mover in harnessing electricity for public and domestic use late in the 19th century and because his phonograph and cinema inventions depended on electricity (although early movie cameras and projectors had to be cranked by hand), and because he was also secretly developing the electric chair he was, unsurprisingly, a supporter of executions by electricity. Therefore, showing sensational images of electricity served the interests of his company, as well as attracting viewers who wanted sensational images. This may be the first, but certainly not the last example of exploiting the new medium for private or corporate gain.[4]

SHOW AND TELL AND SHOW MORE

The speed with which the public embraced movies is nothing short of amazing. The consumption and, therefore, the production of images grew rapidly in the early part of the 20th century. Competitors to Edison proliferated, despite his continuing efforts to exercise patent control over motion picture equipment. That equipment itself very quickly evolved from the peep show kinetoscope to projectors that could project movies on a screen for large audiences. In churches and schools, in vaudeville houses (devoted to various live musical and comedy acts) and nickelodeons devoted solely to the exhibition of films, and then in the picture palaces that began to appear in the cities in the late teens of the 20th century, audiences could see an extraordinary variety of moving pictures.

The audiences themselves were as diverse as the films they saw. The nickelodeons, often nothing more than little storefront theaters situated in diverse locations around the city, drew a wide range of viewers, and were, initially, especially attractive to immigrants and working people who could enjoy the films without facing a language barrier (which also allowed large-scale importation of foreign films, especially from France). But, at the same time, language was often supplied. "Explainers" would narrate the film and summarize its plot. Sometimes actors would stand behind the screen and supply dialogue for the silent film. And there was always music: a piano in a nickelodeon or full orchestra in a vaudeville theater or large movie house.

EARLY FILM FORM

The creation of expansive and luxurious movie theaters occurred with the expansion of the movies they showed. Until the turn of the 20th century, films were relatively short in length. Very early films consisted, usually, of one shot. Sandow, the strongman, flexed his muscles, and that was it. Uncle Josh leapt out of his seat and attacked the movie screen—although the images on that screen keep changing. But there was a growing urge to show and see more. *The Execution of Czolgosz, with Panorama of Auburn Prison* (Edwin S. Porter, Edison Manufacturing Company, 1901) is made up of four shots: two moving camera **pans** of the exterior of the prison (the first shot follows a moving train as it crosses before the camera), then a cut to a set representing a cell block where the prisoner is taken to go to his death, and finally a **dissolve** into long shot of the "execution" itself. The two shots that make up the execution sequence are shot frontally, at a **90-degree angle** to the wall along which the prisoner is taken and against which the victim sits in the chair as the guards around him stand watch and then listen to his heart to make sure he is dead. The pan of the prison at the beginning of the film is meant to lend an air of immediacy, even reality in contrast to the otherwise obvious movie set of the prison and execution chamber. The film puts together the "real" and the reenactment, the fictionalized version of what actually took place.

Sports films, especially boxing matches, were extremely popular with early filmgoers, and sometimes these too were reenactments. The early film audience took an enormous pleasure in *looking*. It was perhaps the commotion and instability of the modern world, the rush of sensation and change that was the mark of the early 20th century that made movies a source of refuge, pleasure, and the desire to see the world in the relative security of the nickelodeon or the movie theater.[5] Jonathan Crary argues that in the

Execution of Czolgosz (Edison, 1901). A reenactment of the electrocution of McKinley's assassin. The film begins with a panorama of the exterior of the prison and then moves to a standard composition (for the time) with the camera positioned 90 degrees to the scene of the execution itself. Here the prison officials feel for a pulse.

19th century, the viewing subject—the audience for still and moving images—was literally created by means of the technologies of vision suddenly made available. There were so many things available to see and this created the desire to see even more.[6] Movies supplied something of a controlled medium of the visible, a way to manage the rush of modernity while satisfying the desire to see and see some more.

Early filmmakers filled the desire to see by all available means at their disposal at the moment. Mixing what we would now call documentary footage with staged scenes, they tried, simply and directly, to thrill their audience. Their means, at first, were extremely simple. Almost all films until about 1907 were shot in a static frontal style, as if the camera were placed in front of a stage—or in front of the screen in *Uncle Josh*. It was an assured approach, not as primitive as we might think. And very effective. The frontal view was the **master shot**, *mastering* the shot, allowing both filmmaker and filmgoer to see easily and completely what was going on before the camera.

MANUFACTURING FILM

Mastering the shot was not the only goal of early filmmakers. They wanted to master it in order to sell it. Filmmaking is often referred to as an "industry." There is a historical reason for using a term that applies to a business that is less of an industry and more like the mass creation of works of the imagination. Film production then as now was operated as a business, and the job of the businessmen involved was to master the process of turning out films and getting them into places of exhibition. Edison set the model, filming "products" and selling or leasing them to exhibitors. His company attempted to bring suit against any competing manufacturer of films. But this only encouraged the competition, who won their rights to compete by means of lawsuits against Edison. Such was the case with the American Mutoscope and Biograph Company, known simply as Biograph, whose films eventually outstripped Edison in popularity. When D. W. Griffith joined the company as a director in 1908, Biograph moved to the forefront of film innovation in form, content, and technology. But it wasn't only creative talent that moved a company forward. Sometimes it was a simple technological invention. Biograph patented the "Latham Loop," a simple technology that allows film that is passing through a camera or a projector to have some slack before it reaches the shutter so that it doesn't tear. It was a simple but important innovation that, among other things, allowed Biograph to free itself from Edison's patents that were inhibiting competing film companies.

It must be emphasized that "innovation" was not foremost in the business of Biograph, the Edison Film Manufacturing Company, the Lubin Manufacturing Company, the Vitagraph Film Manufacturing Company, or any of the other "manufacturers" and distributors of early film. They were in the business of making and moving product, of feeding the insatiable demand of film exhibitors and their audiences. They worked out various deals for leasing or renting prints, of circulating the newest releases throughout the major American cities at the turn of the 20th century. And in the course of fulfilling that demand, the product went through changes.

Tracing the history of these changes is difficult. So much of early film is lost that we cannot accurately trace the evolution of cinematic style that occurred rapidly from 1900 through 1914. But even more, it is difficult to discover a reason for the changes beyond a supposition that the pressure for more and more film led to an increase in production, an increase in the length of the films that were produced, and an increase in the complexities of **narrative**. What we can say with some certainty is that a film culture rapidly developed in which viewers and producers of film were eager to see and create more and more; that the complexity in storytelling that developed in this period satisfied a desire to see more and experience more from the films that were being shown. The result of this was an urge to tell stories that were as rich and comprehensible as possible. Filmmakers had to measure narrative enrichment against what their diverse audiences would understand, and there were always critics and exhibitors who worried about films whose narratives were beyond their audience's ability to understand. But as I indicated earlier, audiences were never left far behind; they learned with the filmmakers themselves how to read and understand complex narratives.

OF TIME AND SPACE

The single shot and frontal presentation of much early film was unaccommodating and limiting. It could *show* but not easily *tell*. Narrative requires flexibility, an ability to weave a pattern of events over the course of time. Seeking this flexibility led early filmmakers to experiment with space and time. The ways they did this established the conventions of cinematic storytelling that survive to this day.

Creating a more intimate space between the spectator and the screen image was an important component of these developing conventions. We don't know who invented the **close-up**. Indeed, if we go as far back as the Lumière brothers' *Arrival of a Train at the Ciotat Station* we can see both objects (the train) and people (the passengers waiting at the station) moving close to the camera. *Fred Ott's Sneeze,* a kinetoscope film made by Edison's company in 1894, held its sneezer in midclose-up. So were the two smootchers in Edward Heise's *The Kiss,* made for Edison in 1896. But the use of the close-up in a dramatic film, to emphasize emotion or record a reaction, came gradually. There was an initial reticence based on a concern that the sudden appearance of a large head in the midst of a dramatic scene would prove disorienting. It did not, and closer views, more intimate shots of the characters onscreen, became commonplace as part of a general expansion of the formal approaches to storytelling. These included moving the camera off of the 90-degree axis so that, instead of strictly frontal views, the camera was now free to investigate other ways of filming a scene, creating a visual dynamic that was always possible—after all, the *Arrival of a Train* was filmed at approximately 45 degrees between the incoming train and the station.

Freeing up camera position and moving people and objects into the foreground was not the only change that occurred during the early development of film. Filmmakers began experimenting with the temporal structure of their films. They knew that, in literary fiction, many scenes might take place simultaneously but in different places, what might be called the "meanwhile" effect. "Meanwhile, as the robbers were attacking the train, the townspeople were enjoying a dance, unaware of what was happening." This temporal-spatial play allowed for complexity and variety in action. Film is more literal than written fiction in the sense that it must show the spaces in which the narrative takes place, and must show them linearly. This simply means that one scene has to follow another and it is difficult to imply a "meanwhile" without a title announcing this simultaneity. But, again, once filmmakers attempted to create spatial and temporal simultaneity, to imply the "meanwhile," audiences had no trouble deciphering this added narrative element.

THE GREAT TRAIN ROBBERY

The most famous early example of alternating scenes that take place at the same narrative time but at a different place, called **parallel editing**, occurs in Edwin S. Porter's *The Great Train Robbery,* made for the Edison Company in 1903. The film is just over 10 minutes in length—films were getting longer early in the century—and contains interior and exterior scenes. There are no explanatory titles. The interior scenes are shot in the standard frontal style, with the camera at a 90-degree angle to the action. What is interesting about them is that the action occurring outside the window in many of the scenes, including those in a "moving" railroad car, are created by a special effect, possibly a **rear-screen projection**, in which the action is projected on a screen behind the set, or a **matte** effect, in which the foreground is photographed with a blue or green screen over the window and the background then projected on to the unexposed film with the colored section dropped out, giving the illusion of a complete image. In the film's first scene, the robbers enter a telegraph office, forcing the operator at gunpoint to send a message to the train. The window is on the right rear of the set, and through it we can see the image of a train going by.

The scene goes on for some 60 seconds, with the stationary camera at a distance from the action. The robbers force the telegraph operator to hand someone from the train a note, a character who appears at a window to the left of the set. The robbers then knock the telegraph operator down and bind and gag him. The film then cuts to an exterior shot on location. The camera is here set slightly off the 90-degree angle and a water tower looms close to it as the robbers wait for the train, which pulls in from screen left. The robbers board the train and the film cuts to the interior of the mail car, in a far, 90-degree shot, the background whizzing by, seen through an open door in the rear. In the next shot, another exterior, the camera is mounted on the moving train, and the robbers enter from the bottom of the frame, crawling over the fuel car and entering the locomotive, though not before one of them beats one of the engineers into submission and, in an invisible cut in which a dummy is substituted for the character, is tossed off the train. The following shots are also exteriors, with the camera at an angle to the action as the robbers take over the train and empty the passengers onto the tracks. They finally disconnect the engine, speed off with their haul, and, in a following shot, wind up running through the woods.

The film then returns to the interior of the telegraph office, where a little girl finds and revives the operator bound on the floor. At this point the film cuts to an entirely different scene, a dance being enjoyed by the town folk. Again, the camera is at 90 degrees to the action, but the dancers move back and forth in the screen space. The telegraph operator rushes in and the men go in pursuit of the robbers in exterior shots in the woods. They shoot down the robbers and recover the money. Here is where the film ends. Almost. There is a cut to a medium close-up of one of the robbers, who looks straight at the camera, aims his gun at it, and fires. The distributors of the film permitted exhibitors to place this shot at the beginning or the end of *The Great Train Robbery.*

MODERNITY

In about 15 shots, *The Great Train Robbery* sums up much of what was happening in film at the turn of the 20th century and looks forward to what was to come. The complication of the narrative indicates the growing sophistication of filmmakers and film viewers. The film is also a kind of cultural container of 19th- and 20th-century technologies and attitudes. The film references three key technological events of the 19th century, the train and the telegraph, and, of course, filmmaking itself. These technologies signified a speed of travel and communication that changed the perception of the individual's place in the geographical and cultural landscape. The railroad and the telegraph signified the collapse of physical space and the telescoping of time. Distances were foreshortened; communication became instantaneous. Early cinema continually referred to both these inventions (as well as to the telephone) and in a way seemed to be a virtual summation of them. A film could take its viewers anywhere; it could elide time and space. Sitting in one place, the viewer could experience a multitude of other spaces, enter narrative worlds, and see far beyond the limits of his or her surroundings. Recall what we said about early film being a container of the overwhelming sensations of the modern world. No wonder so many films were about movement—trains, fire engines, or simply people chasing each other. *The Great Train Robbery* sums up these images and places them in the then recent past of square dances and train robbers, of pursuit on horses and gun battles. Like so much of cinema then and now, it is about the past and present and future intersecting.

Film is a product of modernity, which is partially defined by the explosion of new technologies—the railroad, the telegraph, the photograph, the electric light, the cinema—that marked the 19th century. Modernity also includes larger economic, societal, political, and cultural changes: the concentration of power in a central government—a marked result of the Civil War; the growth of factory production and the assembly line; the movement of population from the country to the city, or from Europe to America's East Coast and from the East Coast westward; a move from religion to secularization, all of which led to a growing sense of cultural unease, a loss of a stable, unambiguous, knowable center to life. The beginning of the 20th century was an extraordinarily complex time of change, and film was part of this complexity. Born of photography, illuminated by electricity, partaking in the time-space manipulations that other 19th-century inventions created, film announced modernity, made its viewers experience it, and made

The Great Train Robbery, Edwin S. Porter, 1903. The camera remains at a 90-degree angle to the action. The image of the train outside the window is matted in separate from the main action.

them comfortable with it. It also offered a refuge, a way to control the onslaught of modernity through the security of the moving image.

It is interesting to note that in 1895, at the very birth of cinema, William Röntgen, working in Germany, discovered X-rays. A year later, Edison used the discovery to develop the fluoroscope, which initiated the medical use of X-rays. As Charles Musser points out, the invention of film, the art of the visible, was accompanied by another photographic offshoot, the art of the invisible. One transformed the interior of the body into a ghostly landscape of bones and organs. The other opened the landscape of the world and its inhabitants to the full view of everyone. Not only was the exterior world made visible and available, but the interior world as well became opened to perception. Film, as it continued to develop, became its own X-ray of perception and consciousness, creating psychological portraits and examining the happiness and despair of the human spirit.[7]

In the case of film, the world was presented to the viewer, who remained in a privileged but passive position. Rather than getting on a train or talking on a telephone (two events so often depicted in film and unavailable to the poor working-class audiences of early film), the spectator could remain secure in place and have time and space manipulated for him or her in the form of images that moved effortlessly, and with greater complexity, representing virtual worlds. With few exceptions, those worlds were both exciting and comforting. The product of modernity was a defense against modernity. The train robbers are undone first by a little girl in a red dress (parts of *The Great Train Robbery* were hand tinted in various colors), who finds the telegraph worker tied up by the robbers, who then alerts the townspeople at the dance. They proceed to chase down and shoot the robbers. Yes, there is that close-up of a gunman shooting at the camera, but his very presence indicates the safety of the image. Unlike the audience who allegedly ducked in fear when the Lumière's train entered the station, 1903 audiences were sophisticated enough to get the joke and be thrilled by it at the same time. Martin Scorsese knew this in 1990, when he alluded to this shot at the end of his film *Goodfellas* (Warner Bros.).

Excitement and safety. In the increasingly complex world of the early 20th century, film provided a haven where a variety of emotions could be played out, a variety of characters and situations could be experienced in the security of a darkened hall. And though isolated in the dark, the film viewing experience also provided a community of sorts for a wide variety of people from different social and ethnic classes. Film could play to the faithful by portraying the life and death of Christ, or to the thrill seeker in recreations of boxing matches or battles in the Spanish-American War. As films got more complex themselves, got longer and more visually intriguing, their audience grew as well. The storefront nickelodeons were replaced by more luxurious theaters. The static, frontal view of the action commonplace since the invention of cinema became replaced by a more luxurious sense of what the image and the manipulations of the image could accomplish, about how the world could be seen through cinema.

And as the narrative complexity of cinema grew, so did the industry that created it. In the next chapter, we will examine the growth of the film studios, the invention of the star system, and the institutionalizing of film style itself. From there, we will go on to examine the career of one the directorial stars of early film, D. W. Griffith, followed by a discussion of silent film comedy, and conclude with an overview of silent film before the coming of sound.

SELECTED FILMOGRAPHY

(Note that most of the films listed for this chapter are available on YouTube or the website of the Library of Congress, http://www.loc.gov.)

Blacksmith Scene, Edison Manufacturing Company, 1893.

Fred Ott's Sneeze, Edison Manufacturing Company, 1894.

Arrival of a Train at the Ciotat Station (*L'Arrivée d'un train á la Ciotat*), dir. Auguste and Louis Lumière, France, 1895.

The Kiss, dir. Edward Heise, Edison Manufacturing Company, 1896.

McKinley at Home, dir. William K. L. Dickson, American Mutoscope and Biograph, 1896.

Execution of Czolgosz, with Panorama of Auburn Prison, dir. Edwin S. Porter, Edison Manufacturing Company, 1901.

Uncle Josh at the Motion Picture Show, dir. Edwin S. Porter, Edison Manufacturing Company, 1902.

The Great Train Robbery, dir. Edwin S. Porter, Edison Manufacturing Company, 1903.

SUGGESTIONS FOR FURTHER READING

Rick Altman, *Silent Film Sound* (New York, NY: Columbia University Press, 2004).

Jonathan Auerbach, *Body Shots: Early Cinema's Incarnations* (Berkeley, CA: University of California Press, 2007).

Francesco Casetti, "Filmic Experience," trans. Dafne Calgaro & Victoria Duckett, *Screen*, vol. 50, no. 1 (March, 2009), 56–66.

Jonathan Crary, *Techniques of the Observer: On Vision and Modernity in the Nineteenth Century* (Cambridge, MA: MIT Press, 1991).

Thomas Elsaesser & Adam Barker, *Early Cinema: Space-Frame-Narrative* (London, UK: BFI, 1990).

André Gaudreault, ed. *American Cinema, 1890–1909: Themes and Variations* (New Brunswick, NJ: Rutgers University Press, 2009).

Charles Musser, *The Emergence of Cinema: The American Screen to 1907, History of the American Cinema*, vol. 1 (Berkeley, CA: University of California Press, 1990).

Ben Singer, *Melodrama and Modernity: Early Sensational Cinema and Its Contexts* (New York, NY: Columbia University Press, 2001).

Kristen Whissel, *Picturing American Modernity: Traffic, Technology, and the Silent Cinema* (Durham, NC: Duke University Press, 2008).

NOTES

1. The quotation about McKinley is found in Jonathan Auerbach, *Body Shots: Early Cinema's Incarnations* (Berkeley, CA: University of California Press, 2007), 23. The discussion of the McKinley film owes much to Auerbach's essay.
2. André Bazin, "The Myth of Total Cinema," *What Is Cinema?* ed. & trans. Hugh Gray (Berkeley and Los Angeles: University of California Press, 1968), 17–22.
3. The quotations from Edison are contained in Charles Musser, *The Emergence of Cinema: The American Screen to 1907, History of the American Cinema*, vol. 1 (Berkeley CA: University of California Press, 1990), 64. Much of the information on early film comes from Musser's monumental study. The early history of the projection

of Edison's film is found in Paul Spehr, "Movies and the Kinetoscope," *American Cinema, 1890–1909: Themes and Variations*, ed. André Gaudreault (New Brunswick, NJ: Rutgers University Press, 2009), 22–44.

4. See Jean-Pierre Sirois-Trahan, "1900–1901 Movies, New Imperialism, and the New Century," trans. Timothy Barnard, in *American Cinema, 1890–1909*, 104–105.
5. Ben Singer, in *Melodrama and Modernity: Early Sensational Cinema and Its Contexts* (New York, NY: Columbia University Press, 2001), presents the argument that early cinema was a response to the chaos of the modern world.
6. Jonathan Crary, *Techniques of the Observer: On Vision and Modernity in the Nineteenth Century* (Cambridge, MA: MIT Press, 1991).
7. For cinema and X-ray, see Musser, 45. The description of modernity follows closely Singer's discussion in *Melodrama and Modernity*. See also Francesco Casetti, "Filmic Experience," trans. Dafne Calgaro and Victoria Duckett, *Screen*, vol. 50, no. 1 (March 2009), 56–66.

CHAPTER 2

THE STUDIOS AND THE STARS (1907–1928)

From manufacturing and distribution, the business of film evolved into the large, self-contained production facilities that were called studios, formed largely by Jewish immigrants. Contemporary industrial practices began to be used for the production of movies, and the so-called producer system was put into practice. Even before the studios were formed, a star system came into being as audiences became sometimes hysterically attracted to the actors they adored on screen.

AFTER READING THIS CHAPTER, YOU SHOULD UNDERSTAND:

- The origins of key Hollywood studios.
- The confluence of industry and imagination.
- The economic management of film production.
- The role of immigrants in the formation of the studios.
- The origin of the star system.

YOU SHOULD BE ABLE TO:

- Know the history of the major studios.
- Note the difference between United Artists and the other studios.
- Define the producer system.
- Understand the early development of tie-ins between film and other media.
- Account for the difference between "star" and "celebrity."
- Discuss the state of current celebrities, their rise and fall.

THE STUDIOS

In the preceding chapter, we discussed the proliferation of the film manufacturing companies in the early years of film: Edison, Biograph, Mutual, Essanay (an important film company founded in 1907 by George Spoor and Gilbert Anderson—"S and A"), Lubin, IMP (Independent Motion Pictures), and more. They operated out of New Jersey, New York, Chicago, Philadelphia, and other venues. Their business was to manufacture short films and supply them to film exchanges, who in turn sent them out to product-hungry nickelodeons and vaudeville houses. It was a ragged process, hampered by Edison's Motion Picture Patents Company, which threatened lawsuits and sometimes violent action against infringement on Edison-owned equipment while demanding that royalties be paid on the amount of film exposed and exhibited on that equipment.

As demand for product increased, this scattered model became increasingly unworkable. The entrepreneurs of the production companies wanted, indeed needed, to expand. A new venue beckoned them. Los Angeles was not a very large city in the early 20th century, and Hollywood existed only as an outpost, connected to LA first by streetcar and then in 1904 by the construction of Sunset Boulevard. But Hollywood had many advantages: good weather, cheap real estate and labor, a goodly distance from Edison, and, if his goons came after filmmakers even there, they could easily flee to Mexico. D. W. Griffith, a major director of the silent period, began dividing his production activities between New York and Los Angeles by 1910. He started by building a makeshift studio and wound up constructing a huge set for the Babylon sequence of his long, multi-narrative film, *Intolerance* (Triangle Film Corp., 1916), at the intersection of Sunset and Hollywood Boulevards. In 1913, Mack Sennett discovered Charlie Chaplin playing vaudeville in LA and signed him to his Keystone company, which was producing films in the city.[1]

These pioneers who set up production in Los Angeles and Hollywood were one-man operations and their work did not efficiently solve the problem of product demand. What followed was, in effect, an act of convergence between moviemaking and the growth of industrial production that occurred in other industries early in the 20th century. Henry Ford had established the assembly line to turn out automobiles by 1914. In 1911, Frederick Taylor wrote *Principles of Scientific Management*, which claimed to measure labor output based on the principles of time and motion, which could be controlled and optimized if labor was fragmented into smaller and smaller units. The division of labor that went hand in hand with assembly line production meant that workers would have specific tasks, tightly managed and numbingly repetitive. They needed to know only the one task that was assigned to them, and they did that task over and over again. Charlie Chaplin satirized the mechanical numbness of the assembly line in the opening sequences of his film *Modern Times* (United Artists, 1936).

HOW THE INDIVIDUAL STUDIOS CAME INTO BEING

Long before *Modern Times*, film production had rapidly converged with the principles of **Fordism** and **Taylorism**. By the middle of the teens of the 20th century, film distribution had begun to consolidate, so that three major distributors handled the films of the

Charlie Chaplin caught inside the assembly line in *Modern Times* (1936).

many production companies that remained in operation. But there were still too many individual, independent operations, and soon, out of the turmoil, mergers began and new companies emerged. These new companies became, in essence, self-contained factories whose product was not cars, but movies. More accurately, in economic terms, their ultimate product—like that of all corporations—was profit, which was made by movies, rented out to theaters, many of which were owned by the studios. Part of that profit was plowed back into the making of more films, which were financed by bank loans as well, in a process that was completely self-contained. Unlike the fragmented structure of film manufacturers and film exchanges that preceded them, the studios did everything in house. From **gaffers**, the electricians who adjusted the lights, to the stars themselves, everyone was under contract to the studio. **Producers**, **screenwriters**, **directors**, **cinematographers**, **production designers**, and **composers** all worked at the bidding of the studio head or his delegated executive producer. The studio head, in turn, answered to the studio's financial officer, usually located on the East Coast. The process became so efficient that most of the major studios could turn out a film a week to supply the enormous demand of exhibitors. It was an efficiency brought about by top-down management, who ruled their kingdoms with an iron hand.

What follows are very brief histories of the inception and development of some of the major film studios and an indication of some of their productions. In the chapters that follow, we will examine in more depth the films that came out of this amazing confluence of art and industry known as the Hollywood production system.

UNIVERSAL

Carl Laemmle, a Jewish-German immigrant, a former clothing salesman in Chicago, turned first to film exhibition and then formed the production company, IMP. In 1912, he merged IMP with a number of other companies and renamed his new business Universal Film Manufacturing Company. Universal produced a major hit, *Traffic in Souls* (George Loane Tucker, 1913), and a year later opened Universal City in California, the first major studio created on the West Coast. Laemmle was proud of his company and welcomed the public to see its work, both on screen and in production. He instituted studio tours, which remain popular to this day. He hired director Erich von Stroheim and financed his huge production of *Blind Husbands* (1919), a successful and controversial film that brought down the anger of censorship groups. A few years later, Laemmle's general manager, Irving Thalberg, fired von Stroheim because of budget and time overruns on *Merry Go Round* (1923). We will come across von Stroheim and Thalberg again as the struggle between the business and the creative poles of filmmaking became, at times, quite heated and led to the loss of control of the director over his production.

Universal produced two very popular films in the 1920s, with an actor named Lon Chaney, famous for playing grotesque characters: *The Hunchback of Notre Dame* (Wallace Worsley, 1923) and *The Phantom of the Opera* (Rupert Julian, 1925). This penchant for shock and horror served Universal well in the early 1930s, when the studio produced *Dracula* (Tod Browing, 1931), *Frankenstein* (James Whale, 1931), and *The Mummy* (Karl Freund, 1932). Universal's World War I drama, *All Quiet on the Western Front* (1930), won an Academy Award for best picture and best director, Lewis Milestone. More recently, Steven Spielberg got his start at Universal, making *Jaws* for the studio in 1975, and Alfred Hitchcock made his late films for Universal as well. Universal remained a family affair until the mid-1930s, when it was bought out by investors. Today, it is part of Comcast-NBC Universal, a communications and cable company with many media outlets.

UNITED ARTISTS

A different kind of studio was put together by four of the most important and influential figures in Hollywood at the time: film stars Douglas Fairbanks, Mary Pickford, Charlie Chaplin, and director D. W. Griffith (we will examine the work of Griffith and Chaplin in some detail in following chapters). Pickford and Fairbanks were major stars of the teens of the 20th century. Mary Pickford got her start with Griffith at Biograph and rapidly rose to be one of the most famous figures in silent Hollywood film.

Like Chaplin, she moved from one company to another in search of money and artistic control, at one point forming her own production company—the first run by a star. Douglas Fairbanks, who would become Pickford's husband, started as a stage actor and was tempted to films by a large salary offered by Triangle Pictures, which also had Griffith under contract for a time. Fairbanks began his career making light, satiric comedies, and he came into full stardom with action films made for his own production company and distributed by United Artists like *The Mark of Zorro* (Fred Niblo, 1920), *Robin Hood* (Allan Dwan, 1922), and *The Thief of Bagdad* (Raoul Walsh, 1924).

In 1919, through a mutual desire to control the distribution of their films and escape the growing power of Adolf Zukor, who was busy consolidating companies, the four joined to form United Artists, not a studio in which films would be made, but a company through which films would be distributed. Certainly a company made up of the large egos of its star owners had many conflicts, but through the management of a professional showman, Joseph Schenk, the company did well enough, even owning a chain of theaters, something that most of the larger studios did. This practice led to major legal and financial difficulties many years later when the government successfully sued the studios for holding a monopoly on production and distribution, called **vertical integration**.

United Artists struggled through complex negotiations with its signatories, its stockholders, and with other studios. But it managed to distribute important films, those of its star owners, as well as Walt Disney's animated shorts and features in the 1930s to *West Side Story* (Jerome Robbins, Robert Wise, 1961), the Pink Panther, and early James Bond films in the 1960s and 70s. In the 1960s, the company was bought by the Transamerica Corporation and went on to join with MGM (which by this time was no longer a production studio) to distribute their films. As we will note in detail in Chapter 25, the company was finally bankrupted in 1980 by a film called *Heaven's Gate* (Michael Cimino) that went enormously over budget and failed at the box office. United Artists was an important counter to the emerging power of the studios, and it finally fell because of its trust in a profligate director.[2]

PARAMOUNT

Of the four original founders of United Artists, D. W. Griffith broke with his company to sign with

D. W. Griffith, Mary Astor, Charlie Chaplin (seated), and Douglas Fairbanks at the signing of the contract creating United Artists in 1919.

Adolf Zukor, born in Hungary, and one of the wiliest and most persistent of early movie moguls. Intent on building an empire, he moved from nickelodeon owner (in partnership with Marcus Loew, who would be an important player in the formation of MGM) to film importer, to one of the earliest producers of feature-length films. Zukor started off with a notion of film as high theatrical art, and his first major effort was to import a French film, *Queen Elizabeth* (Henri Desfontaines, Louis Mercanton, 1912), with the then famous melodramatic actress, Sarah Bernhardt. Through a series of company restructurings and mergers with existing companies, he gained enough power to force the hand of Edison's Patents Company, finally putting it out of existence, a process that led to the expansion of film distribution across state lines, giving the studios access to theaters throughout the nation.

Zukor merged and brought under his leadership two large companies, Jesse Lasky's Famous-Players Lasky and Paramount. In 1916, he took the latter as the name of his company and established a large body of actors, directors, and producers, including, at one time or another, Mary Pickford, Douglas Fairbanks, D. W. Griffith, Cecil B. DeMille, Mack Sennett, and Samuel Goldwyn. It has been estimated that by the late teens of the 20th century, Zukor held 75% of the best talent in the filmmaking business.[3] In addition to owning stars and directors, his company purchased theater chains and perfected the practice of **block booking**. Simply put, theaters had to show a block of Paramount films, sight unseen, or be denied access to their profitable titles. All Paramount products, good or bad, would be forced on exhibitors, whether they liked them or not.

As part of this vertical integration of production, distribution, and exhibition, block booking would face legal challenges and ultimate defeat in the late 1940s. But long before that, Paramount pictures became a powerful major studio. Its 1927 war film, *Wings* (William A. Wellman), was the first silent film to win an Academy Award for best picture. It was home to directors as diverse as Cecil B. DeMille, maker of huge biblical epics, and Ernst Lubitsch, a German-born director of comedies, who became Paramount's production manager in 1935. More recently, Paramount has produced the television and big screen *Star Trek* and Indiana Jones franchises and has distributed films as diverse as *Anchorman 2: The Legend Continues* (Adam McKay, Apatow Productions, Gary Sanchez Productions, 2013) and Martin Scorsese's *The Wolf of Wall Street* (Red Granite Pictures, Appian Way, 2013). Adolf Zukor remained chairman of the board until his death at 103 in 1976, even as the company passed through a number of owners over the years, and is currently part of Viacom, a communications company that also owns MTV and Comedy Central.

WARNER BROS.

Warner Bros. was created a bit later than Paramount. Like Adolf Zukor, Harry, Albert, Sam, and Jack Warner—first-generation Americans—operated nickelodeons and a film exchange. After a difficult time attempting to battle the Trust Company, the brothers moved to Los Angeles. In 1918, they had a major financial success with a film about the American ambassador to wartime Germany, *My Four Years in Germany* (William Nigh), which marked the beginning of a Warner Bros. tradition of making films linked to the social and political currents of the moment. They also found success in the 1920s with a series of films starring the German shepherd Rin Tin Tin. The dog helped the studio head off financial disaster.

Like the other majors, Warner Bros. grew by acquisition. It acquired the Vitagraph Company in 1925, which gave the new studio properties and film exchanges, and in 1928 First National, the production and distribution company that was founded in 1917, in part to counter Adolf Zukor's growing monopoly. First National had employed Charlie Chaplin and D. W. Griffith before they formed United Artists. These purchases not only gave Warners more production facilities, but—with the purchase of the Stanley chain of movie theaters—the size and financial clout to compete with Paramount and MGM. However, this is only a small part of the Warner Bros. story. Throughout the early 1920s, there had been experimentation by various studios of synchronizing sound to the moving image. It was treated as a novelty by most, except by the brothers Warner.

Using the Vitagraph studios in Brooklyn as a base for experimentation, the company developed a system of recording sound on disks, synchronizing them to the film running through the projector. They released many shorts and two features with sound sequences: *Don Juan* (Alan Crosland, 1926) and *The Jazz Singer* (Alan Crosland, 1927). The latter changed the course of film history. Warner Bros. went on to establish the crime film genre with *Little Caesar* (Mervyn LeRoy, 1931), and throughout the 1930s dealt directly and darkly with social issues, in films such as *I Am a Fugitive from a Chain Gang* (Mervyn LeRoy, 1932), and the first American film to expose the Nazi takeover of Germany, *Confessions of a Nazi Spy* (Anatole Litvak, 1939). Warner Bros. was an important part of the new Hollywood renaissance of the late 1960s and early 1970s, releasing such groundbreaking films as Arthur Penn's *Bonnie and Clyde* in 1967 and Martin Scorsese's *Mean Streets* in 1973.

Warner Bros., like the other majors, went through many corporate changes during the 1960s and 70s and is now part of the giant media conglomerate Time Warner.[4]

MGM

What would become the biggest and most famous studio during the 1920s and 30s started as a chain of theaters owned by Marcus Loew. In 1919, Loew bought out Metro Pictures Corporation, a company that ran theaters and production studios. The purchase offered Loew the opportunity to go into production himself. One of Metro's associates was the theater owner, Louis B. Mayer, an immigrant from Minsk, who had made a fortune as the New England distributor of Griffith's *The Birth of a Nation* in 1915. Loew merged Metro with Goldwyn Pictures Corporation. Samuel Goldwyn (born in Warsaw, Poland as Schmuel Gelbfisz, which he then changed to Samuel Goldfish, and finally to Goldwyn) was originally a founder and chairman of Famous Players-Lasky, one of the companies bought out by Adolf Zukor. Goldwyn was no longer head of the company that bore his name, nor was he involved in Metro-Goldwyn-Mayer. He would, however, go on to a distinguished career as an independent producer. Marcus Loew brought in Louis B. Mayer to run his new studio in Los Angeles. Loew died in 1927, and Nicholas Schenck, brother of United Artist's Joseph Schenck, took over operation of the whole organization from New York.

This completed the complicated process of forming MGM, both a studio and a subsidiary of a larger corporation, Loew's Incorporated. The power of MGM came not merely from its stable of stars but from its method of operation. When Mayer took charge of production on the West Coast, he brought with him a young man named Irving Thalberg, who was working for Carl Laemmle at Universal, making him, along with Irving Rapf, head of production. Thalberg rapidly became the brains of the studio, backed up by Mayer's brawn. The **producer system** that emerged from this combination became the model for every other studio, not merely in their financial structure, in which the business would be run on the East Coast and production on the West, but in the core methodology of filmmaking, the convergence of mass production of goods with the work of the imagination.

One of the first things that Thalberg did at MGM was take away a film made by one of the foremost directors of the silent period, Erich von Stroheim. Von Stroheim was a director of obsessive detail. He paid little attention to what was fast becoming the rule at the new studios: producers and directors had to bring films in on time and on budget. You may recall that Thalberg had fired von Stroheim once before, when both were at Universal and von Stroheim was going over budget on a film called *Merry Go Round* (1923). Just before the merger that would create MGM, von Stroheim began work on an adaptation of a novel by Frank Norris, *McTeague*, at Goldwyn Pictures. He wanted to film the novel almost page by page and in exquisite detail, and he was doing so as MGM was taking shape. He created a film that was 42 reels in length, at a running time of more than 8 hours. Thalberg removed the film, called *Greed*, from Stroheim's control, had it cut to 10 reels, or about 2 hours running time, destroyed the cut footage, and fired the director again.[5]

Von Stroheim's career tanked, but MGM went on to great fame and fortune in the 1930s and 40s, known for its optimistic and sentimental story lines, its bright collection of stars, such as Clark Gable and Greta Garbo, and its musicals, including perhaps the most famous musical film, *Singin' in the Rain* (Stanley Donen, Gene Kelly, 1952). In recent years, MGM has become a greatly diminished entity, though it has had some success with films like the

James Bond *Skyfall* (Sam Mendes, Eon Productions, Danjaq, co-distributed with Columbia Pictures, 2012) and *The Hobbit: An Unexpected Journey* (Peter Jackson, New Line Cinema, WingNut Films, 2012). For a time it distributed films with another diminished company, United Artists, both a shadow of their former greatness.

FOX

William Fox was an immigrant from Hungary who began his career first as a newsboy and then working in the garment industry. He started in film as an exhibitor and owned the Greater New York Film Rental Company in addition to some vaudeville houses. Like so many of his peers, he needed product for his various venues and started film production in 1914. This provoked conflict with the Motion Picture Patents Trust (Edison's attempted monopoly on film equipment). Fox sued the Trust and won, which, along with Adolph Zukor's fight against the Trust, further helped to break Edison's stranglehold.

Along with Warner Bros., Fox was a pioneer in sound. Unlike Warners and like RKO, Fox used a **sound-on-film** optical process called Movietone and with it produced newsreels that became a staple of an evening out at the movies. He also, along with Paramount, worked on big screen processes, developing 70 mm, wide-screen techniques still in use today. Fox enlarged his holdings by building movie houses—some of them grand palaces—and a movie studio for the production of sound films, as well as purchasing a large amount of stock in the Loews Corporation, which, in effect, gave him controlling interest in MGM. This was all classic overreaching, and the reach brought William Fox down. In 1929, the stock market crashed. The Justice Department brought an anti-trust suit against Fox (instigated by Louis B. Mayer, upset about the takeover of MGM), and an auto accident removed him from supervision of his company. The financial meltdown of the company took Fox out of the picture. In 1933, Fox's management bought out 20th Century Pictures and brought in Darryl Zanuck, a Nebraska native, from Warner Bros. to run the company. 20th Century Fox was born.

During his heyday, William Fox produced some of the most important films of the late silent period, including John Ford's *The Iron Horse* (1924), Frank Borzage's *7th Heaven*, and the German director F. W. Murnau's *Sunrise* (both 1927). We will examine the latter two films in Chapter 6. During the 1930s, 20th Century Fox had successes with the child star Shirley Temple and the director John Ford, whose *The Grapes of Wrath* (1940) is one of the most important films about the Great Depression. In the late 1940s, Zanuck distinguished his studio with a series of socially relevant films: an attack on anti-Semitism in *Gentleman's Agreement* (Elia Kazan, 1947); a grueling drama on mental institutions, *The Snake Pit* (Anatole Litvak, 1948); and race relations in *Pinky* (Elia Kazan, 1949). More recently, 20th Century Fox has held the *X-Men* franchise and the huge hit, James Cameron's *Avatar* (Dune Entertainment, Ingenious Film Partners, 2009).

20th Century Fox is now owned by Rupert Murdoch's News Corporation, which also runs Fox television.

COLUMBIA

The other studios fell quickly into place. Columbia pictures, headed by the brothers Harry and Jack Cohn, first-generation Americans, set itself up as a low-budget outfit, though it met with great success through the films of Frank Capra in the 1930s, such as *It Happened One Night* (1933) and *Mr. Smith Goes to Washington* (1939). Harry Cohn was notorious for his domineering, autocratic management style. Today, Columbia is owned by the Japanese company Sony. They have distributed the recent *Spider-Man* films and the Tom Hanks vehicle, *Captain Phillips* (Paul Greengrass, Scott Rudin Productions, Michael De Luca Productions, Trigger Street Productions, 2013). Their subsidiary, Sony Pictures Classics, is a major distributor of independent and foreign films.

RKO

RKO came together later and more slowly than the other studios, but in a technical sense had an important stake in the filmmaking business. Its initials stand for "Radio-Keith-Orpheum" because the company is a result of the merging of RCA, the Radio Corporation of America, through its president, David Sarnoff, and the Keith-Albee-Orpheum vaudeville houses. Another stakeholder was the small production company the Film Booking Office, run by Joseph Kennedy, the father of President John F. Kennedy. This all came to pass in 1928, a year before the Great Depression, and the company immediately ran into hard financial times, despite commercial successes like *King Kong* (Marian C. Cooper, Ernest B. Schoedsack, 1933), the Fred Astaire–Ginger Rogers musicals, and Walt Disney's *Snow White and the Seven Dwarfs* (1937). But the studio survived into the 1940s and produced one of the most important American sound films, Orson Welles's *Citizen Kane* (1941), a film that did poorly on its initial release (we will look at *Citizen Kane* in Chapter 13). Howard Hughes, the financier and dabbler in movies, took control in 1948, starting a long decline that led to the studio's demise in the late 1950s.

David Sarnoff was interested in owning a movie studio because he wanted to demonstrate his optical sound system. Early sound film used Western Electric's sound-on-disk process, which created problems in synchronizing sound and image since the discs ran separately from the film strip running through the projector. The problem was somewhat mitigated by driving the disk player and the projector together, but it still was not an elegant method. As we noted, Fox had developed a sound on film process called Movietone and produced newsreels with this technology in 1926. Sarnoff, with the Edison Company and General Electric behind him, developed his own sound on film process, called Photophone, in which, like Movietone, the soundtrack is actually printed alongside the image track on film. The optical track provided perfect synchronization between image and sound and had better fidelity than the sound-on-disk process.

THE IMMIGRANT'S LEGACY

What is clear from this brief survey of studio history is that most all of the pioneers were either Jewish immigrants or the first-generation children of Jewish immigrants (a fact that led to no little anti-Semitism in regard to the entertainment field). Neal Gabler writes that in the film business, these men found opportunities closed to them in other occupations, and that "having come from fashion and retail," they had a particular understanding of public taste. As immigrants, "they had a peculiar sensitivity to the dreams and aspirations of other immigrants and working-class families." They created factories of the imagination; their studios turned out narratives of hope and despair, of comic antics and melodramatic yearnings. They were tough and sentimental men, who had an uncanny ability to gauge what audiences wanted, or, perhaps more accurately, to create an audience who would want their product. They ruled their studios with an iron will and sometimes a heavy hand. They ruled their audience by guiding their films within the bounds of public taste—as they understood it—and by pushing the envelope of that taste in ways that enabled them to innovate just so much as to keep their audiences both satisfied and wanting more. They created not only desire for their films but also the expectation that desire would be fulfilled in ways both novel and familiar. From humble backgrounds they produced—or had produced for them by means of the talent they fostered—an incredible variety of fictional worlds.[6]

THE PRODUCER SYSTEM

We will look more closely at the films produced by the various studios as we continue examining their output across the decades. Here it is important to note how filmmaking was changed by the introduction of the producer system adopted by MGM and the other studios. In the pre-studio days, the director—D. W. Griffith, Charlie Chaplin, Buster Keaton, Thomas Ince, Cecil B. DeMille, and others—controlled their work. Early film was a director's medium. The studios, in effect, demoted the director to one of the many persons on the assembly line of film production. A film would now originate with a producer, who would oversee production in the name and under the control of the studio. The producer would set budget and schedule, select the screenwriters, the actors, the crew, and the director, all of whom were under contract to the studio. Occasionally, a star or director would be lent out to another studio, but the practice was to keep things in house as much as possible. With all the cast and crew in place, the producer would keep tabs on the production, visit the set, guide the director, chastise him if things went over budget or time, and then supervise the editing of the film, recutting and even reshooting scenes if the film played poorly in previews.

The creation of the studio system was all about new processes: technical, managerial, and artistic. The phenomenon was the result of a desire—perhaps not always consciously or logically thought out—to overcome the seat-of-the-pants production and distribution methods that existed before the studios were formed, with their multitude of producers, distributors, and exhibitors. That was the point and the result: to consolidate production, systemize financing, guarantee distribution through studio-owned theater chains, and to rationalize filmmaking along the lines of other industries. The question, of course, is how one industrializes the imagination. By the late 20s, the studios were cranking out close to a film a week to meet the demands of their audiences and to keep their bottom line strong. The circulation of product in return for profit drove everything the studios produced, and this created the urge—as it did in other industries—to normalize if not homogenize the product, to make it simple, palatable, familiar, to create desire for films by making the films as desirable as possible. There were and are many means of realizing this. One was through the attraction of stars. Movie stars early on became the cultural capital of filmdom, what the studios could bank on and audiences would want to see over and over again.

STARS

> The fabrication of stars is the fundamental thing in the film industry.
>
> —CARL LAEMMLE

In the beginning, the players in film were anonymous. Whether it was the film producers, who believed they would not have to pay their actors a lot of money if they remained nameless, or the players themselves, who were somewhat embarrassed by appearing in this new, vaguely disreputable medium (some of them were forbidden by their theatrical and vaudeville employers to reveal their identities), the faces on the screen were not connected to a name. But in about 20 years, this changed dramatically. In 1926, the New York funeral of film star Rudolph Valentino drew some 100,000 people. There were riots in the streets.

The rapid development of star and celebrity culture might seem to be counterintuitive to the formation of the studios, based as it was on the rapid and anonymous production of films for a quickly growing and anonymous audience. The fact was that, once established in the minds of the audience, stars became part of the production process, fabricated, in the words of the head of Universal Pictures, for an audience that wanted to know the names and lives of their beloved actors.

There was a lapse in star recognition between old and new entertainments. Audiences knew the names of theatrical and vaudeville players, who were the major popular entertainers before the advent of movies, and this seemed early on to satisfy audiences and divert their curiosity about the faces on the screen. At the same time, viewers did recognize the names of the production companies. Biograph, for example, was particularly popular. But their players, even the regulars in D. W. Griffith's Biograph films—Lillian Gish, Blanche Sweet, Mary Pickford, and Mae Marsh—while familiar to audiences were not identified. It did not take long, however, for these and other faces to intrude more and more on viewers' consciousness. The extravagant gestures of early film along with the advent of close-ups created a growing feeling of proximity, even intimacy between viewer and image, viewer and player. Intimacy breeds desire (and vice versa), and viewers began to identify with and then wanted to know the identity of the faces on the screen. Writing to the producers (or "manufacturers," as they were called before the studios), they attempted to make contact with the players, sometimes addressed simply to the "Biograph Girl," "The Vitagraph Girl," or simply "Dimples."

It wasn't long before the manufacturers yielded, under pressure from exhibitors and the public. The Edison Company announced its players to exhibitors in 1909. Kalem, a production company, placed photographs of their players in theater lobbies in 1910. Also in 1910, Carl Laemmle, then head of IMP, in one of the first publicity stunts in film celebrity history, took an advertisement denying that one of their players, Florence Lawrence, had been killed by a streetcar.

She hadn't, but, since it is difficult to prove a negative, the notice got a great deal of attention. In any case, Florence was already recognized by her fans: "We do not know the lady's name," wrote a reviewer of Florence Lawrence in a 1909 Griffith Biograph film, "but certainly she seems to us to have a very fine command of her emotions."[7] By 1911, the value of named stars was clear to all concerned. The manufacturers produced slides of their players for the exhibitors to show between films. Soon, credits began to appear on the films themselves, often in the **intertitle** that introduced the appearance of a key player. Product tie-ins were developed: star images on postcards or pillows, for example. The fan magazine was invented around the same time, expanding the recognition of players, doing the work of publicity for the studios, turning stars into celebrities, and filling the public appetite for proximity to their favorites.

STAR AND CELEBRITY

Within a few years, the apparatus of presentation, representation, recognition, and response was in place. The film companies and the studios that succeeded them presented and promoted their players,

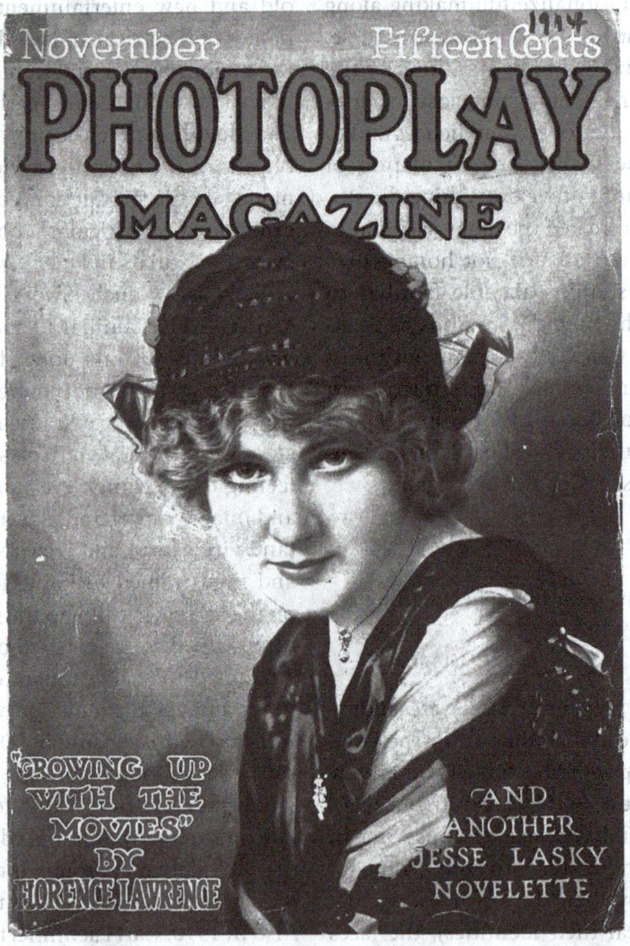

Florence Lawrence, one of the first movie stars to receive major studio publicity, appearing on the cover of the early fan magazine *Photoplay* in 1914.

who represented characters on the screen and who, in turn, would be recognizable in two ways: the actor or actress would be familiar to the viewer, while the characters they created would either intrigue the viewer with their novelty or reassure her with their familiarity. Players became typecast so that the presentation and the representation—the actor and the role—would be more comforting than surprising, and the viewer could respond with pleasure and the security born of repetition. Charlie Chaplin's Tramp is a perfect example. His adventures and misfortunes might change from film to film, but the character's appearance, his responses, actions, and reactions would be recognizable and dependable from film to film. Indeed, late in his career, when Chaplin stepped away from the character to play a wife murderer in *Monsieur Verdoux* (Charles Chaplin, Charles Chaplin Productions, United Artists, 1947), the public responded by not going to see the film. And, as we will see, Chaplin's "private life," his love affairs, his politics, became an active part of his celebrity narrative.

This is an important step in the process: the actor or actress moving from star to celebrity. When this happens, multiple narratives or stories form around the actor. Added onto the roles the star plays, celebrity layers on another story, this one of the personal life of the star that exists outside of the films themselves. When Carl Laemmle took out his advertisement denying rumors about the death of Florence Lawrence, he was creating a story. There were reports of the star's death in some newspapers, but it is quite possible that those reports were planted in the first place. As the studios grew, so did their publicity departments, busily writing stories about their stars for the general press as well as the fan magazines published for an eager public anxious to move beyond the films they loved by learning about the stars that played in them. The magazines even extended the viewing experience by publishing novelizations with stills of current films, or novelizations of films that were themselves originally based on novels![8] Later, in the 1920s, radio became an important instrument for broadcasting the voices and the stories about the stars. Then followed tabloids, television, and the Internet, expanding the networks for gossip about celebrities and their adventures—some real, many, to use Laemmle's word, fabricated.

VALENTINO

What remains difficult to explain in all of this is yet another narrative, that of the extravagance of

Rudolph Valentino in *The Sheik* (George Melford, 1921). His bug-eyed posing looks odd to us today. In his time, he was a major object of desire.

audience response. What brought out 100,000 people to gawk at and fight over the funeral of actor Rudolph Valentino? When we look back at Valentino's films today, especially his most famous, *The Sheik* (George Melford, Paramount, 1921), we find a very unlikely heartthrob. For the first part of the film, he plays a lecherous Arab, staring with bulbous eyes at the white woman who has fallen into his clutches. In the second part, having fallen under the woman's spell, he becomes an ardent protector, eventually revealed not to be an Arab at all, but of British descent. This does little to dispel the orientalism of the film—its representation of the Arab as an erotic object of desire and a threat simultaneously. In short, watching *The Sheik* today gives us some information about the racial views of the early 1920s, but only a little information about how its star became so popular.

One possibility is that in many of his films, the Valentino character was simultaneously threatening and threatened, sexually aggressive and recessive. This may have contributed to his incredible appeal to women during the 1920s, when the women's liberation movement was strong in the wake of their winning the right to vote in 1920. Valentino's onscreen image, the representation of his various characters, the celebrity publicity surrounding them that hinted at the sexual ambiguity of his private life, allowed full expression of female sexual desire to be projected on him. It was as if Valentino belonged to them, becoming, in one critic's words, a fetish, something almost tangible that they could grasp, certainly with their eyes, something they might grasp physically on his death (fans tried to rip the buttons off the suit that clothed his corpse).[9] Men found Valentino a sexual threat; women found him an erotic fascination.

FLAPPERS AND VAMPS

There were, of course, female stars who attracted a great deal of attention. We've already noted that Florence Lawrence was the first film actress identified by name. Mary Pickford, who started work under the direction of D. W. Griffith, became widely known for the films in which she played vivacious young girls and as the celebrity wife of action star Douglas Fairbanks. With her husband, and along with Griffith and Chaplin, she was one of the cofounders of United Artists. Clara Bow represented the liberated "flapper" of the decade, called the "It Girl," which she played in a film called *It* (Clarence G. Badger, Josef von Sternberg, Paramount, 1927) and in William Wellman's famous World War I fighter pilot film, *Wings* (Paramount, 1927). We will revisit these

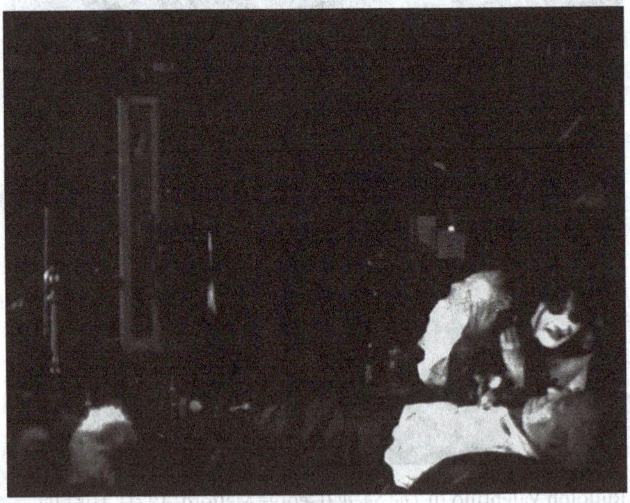

Theda Bara, the Vamp, destroyer of men, takes pleasure in the destruction of her victim in *A Fool There Was* (Frank Powell, 1915).

characters in Chapter 6. Earlier, Theda Bara—a star of Fox Film Corporation—was publicized as the "Vamp," short for "vampire"—a seductive and presumably dangerous female. In *A Fool There Was* (Frank Powell, 1915), where she is identified in the cast list simply as "The Vampire," she seduces an American diplomat away from his family and destroys him. He is left a ruined corpse while the Vamp kneels and drops flowers on him. Her heartlessness became part of her appeal—sexuality and threat were an unbeatable combination then as now. The Vamp was an early version of the killer woman, the "femme fatale," who we will meet again when we come to film noir in the 1940s.

THE STORIES WE TELL ABOUT STARS

Like American culture as a whole, American film, then and now, is deeply conflicted about sexuality and the role of women in particular. Silent film developed a range of representations of female stereotypes, from the virgin to the vampire, in an attempt to exploit the conflicts rather than resolving them. The star and celebrity system as a whole was and remains a way to exploit the audience and satisfy its desire for proximity to the people whose images they see on the screen. Perhaps "exploit" is too strong a word, suggesting as it does that the star system takes advantage of a weakness or pushes us to places we don't wish to go. Keep in mind that, in the beginning, it was the audience that wanted to know about the players they saw on the screen. We still do.

Like everything else in our relationship to film, stardom and celebrity are complex. As audience members we must *want* to see actors on the screen and read or view their celebrity lives in fan magazines and now on television or the web. The "red carpet" is one of the most popular parts of the Academy Awards show. Stars and their extracurricular lives may be fabricated by studio publicity or by their agents. Today we have celebrities who are not stars but only celebrities—famous, as the saying goes, for being famous, or perhaps only because they appear on a "reality" TV show. While some actors and actresses use their celebrity status for charitable work or to adopt babies from struggling countries, many just work to keep their name in the public eye. The narrative then and now is basically unchanged. Studios, publicity agents, and now bloggers promote stars by telling stories about them or making up stories about them. Audiences, segmented by age and gender, lap up the stories, embracing with some passion the celebrities they love.

The embrace of celebrity also comes with its opposite, the pushing away of the star who falls from grace. As much as audiences follow with pleasure the rise of celebrity, so do we revel at scandal that leads to a celebrity's disgrace. One of the earliest involves the silent film comic Roscoe "Fatty" Arbuckle, who early in his career worked with the comedian Buster Keaton, and in 1921 signed a million-dollar contract with Paramount. He celebrated at a party where a young girl died amidst the festivities. Arbuckle was charged with rape of the girl, and even though he was exonerated after three trials, the sensational and lurid newspaper reporting of his alleged actions caused him to be blacklisted, and his career came to an end. Still today we take odd pleasure in the antics, the bad behavior, and the downfall of celebrities that were once admired.

Divorces, murders, suicides, drug overdoses, and plain bad behavior litter the celebrity narrative. They seem to have more currency, more impact, more emotional resonance than the similar events that occur among the general population. This is the stuff of sensationalism, of *schadenfreude*, the strange pleasure we take from the misery of others, especially when that misery is visited on someone who was once a figure of admiration and wealth. I am tempted to say that such events signal the fragility of celebrity, but I think in fact that they are a necessary part of the celebrity narrative, the story of rise to success and hard fall to failure. This narrative becomes more pressing and more relevant when the celebrity fall is the result of politics. In 1934, the political power of the studios—MGM in particular—was such that they could help bring down political figures, as happened when the socialist novelist Upton Sinclair ran for governor of California. MGM produced fake newsreels that frightened viewers over what might happen if Sinclair were elected. He lost.

Political power could move from the studios to the federal government. In the 1950s, his celebrity life near its end and his progressive politics on the rise, Charlie Chaplin was denied entry into the United States, the country that once celebrated him as the king of comedy. Chaplin was not alone. During the late 1940s and early 1950s the government's House Committee on Un-American Activities, in league with the studios, held show trials in Hollywood, forcing celebrities to incriminate themselves and others for what were essentially crimes of political belief. Hundreds were blacklisted; many left the country.

We will examine the witch hunt for communists in the film business in Chapter 15. But we should emphasize again how rapidly the organization of the studios and their celebrity stars occurred. By the 1920s, a strong, demanding audience was met by a strong, productive industry which produced movies and personalities, satisfying what seemed to be an endless desire to see and to know more.

SELECTED FILMOGRAPHY

Traffic in Souls, dir. George Loane Tucker, Universal, 1913.

A Fool There Was, dir. Frank Powell, Fox, 1915.

Blind Husbands, dir. Erich von Stroheim, Universal, 1919.

The Mark of Zorro, dir. Fred Niblo, Douglas Fairbanks Pictures, United Artists, 1920.

The Sheik, dir. George Melford, Paramount, 1921.

Robin Hood, dir. Allan Dwan, Douglas Fairbanks Pictures, United Artists, 1922.

Merry Go Round, dir. Erich von Stroheim, Universal, 1923.

The Hunchback of Notre Dame, dir. Wallace Worsley, Universal, 1923.

The Thief of Bagdad, dir. Raoul Walsh, Douglas Fairbanks Pictures, United Artists, 1924.

The Iron Horse, dir. John Ford, Fox, 1924.

Greed, dir. Erich von Stroheim, MGM, 1924.

The Phantom of the Opera, dir. Rupert Julian, Universal, 1925.

It, dirs. Clarence G. Badger, Josef von Sternberg, Paramount, 1927.

All Quiet on the Western Front, dir. Lewis Milestone, Universal, 1930.

Frankenstein, dir. James Whale, Universal, 1931.

The Mummy, dir. Karl Freund, Universal, 1932.

King Kong, dirs. Marian C. Cooper, Ernest B. Schoedsack, RKO, 1933.

Confessions of a Nazi Spy, dir. Anatole Litvak, Warner Bros., 1939.

SUGGESTIONS FOR FURTHER READING

Tino Balio, *United Artists: The Company Built by the Stars.* Madison, WI: University of Wisconsin Press, 1976.

Eileen Bowser, *The Transformation of Cinema, 1907–1915, History of American Cinema,* vol. 2 (Berkeley, CA: University of California Press, 1990).

Richard Dyer, *Stars* (London: BFI Publishing, 1998).

Lucy Fischer & Marcia Landy, eds., *Stars: The Film Reader* (New York, NY: Routledge, 2004).

Neal Gabler, *An Empire of Their Own: How the Jews Invented Hollywood* (New York: Doubleday, 1988).

Christine Gledhill, ed., *Stardom: Industry of Desire* (London, UK: Routledge, 1991).

Sumiko Higashi, *Cecil B. DeMille and American Culture: The Silent Era* (Berkeley, CA: University of California Press, 1994).

Richard Koszarski, *An Evening's Entertainment: The Age of the Silent Feature Picture, 1915–1928, History of American Cinema,* vol. 3 (Berkeley, CA: University of California Press, 1990).

Marsha Orgeron, *Hollywood Ambitions: Celebrity in the Movie Age* (Middleton, CT: Wesleyan University Press, 2008).

Nick Roddick, *A New Deal in Entertainment: Warner Brothers in the 1930s* (London, UK: The British Film Institute, 1983).

NOTES

1. For the settling of Hollywood by the film community, see Kenneth Starr, *Inventing the Dream: California through the Progressive Era* (New York and Oxford: Oxford University Press: 1985). Some of the material for this chapter was drawn from Richard Koszarski, *An Evening's Entertainment: The Age of the Silent Feature Picture, 1915–1928, History of American Cinema,* vol. 3 (Berkeley, CA: University of California Press, 1990) and

Douglas Gomery, *The Hollywood Studio System* (London, UK: MacMillan Publishers, 1986).

2. For an in-depth study of United Artists, see Tino Balio, *United Artists: The Company Built by the Stars* (Madison, WI: University of Wisconsin Press, 1976). The material on United Artists draws on Balio's work.
3. Neal Gabler writes about Zukor's power in *An Empire of Their Own: How the Jews Invented Hollywood* (New York, NY: Doubleday, 1988). Gabler's book is an important source for this chapter on the development of the studios.
4. A thorough study of the company, which I have drawn on, is Nick Roddick, *A New Deal in Entertainment: Warner Brothers in the 1930s* (London, UK: The British Film Institute, 1983).
5. A detailed history of MGM can be found in Gomery, 51–75, and of RKO, 124–146. Information on von Stroheim and *Greed* can be found in Arthur Lennig, *Stroheim* (Lexington, KY: University of Kentucky Press, 2000).
6. The quotations come from Neal Gabler, 5.
7. Quoted in Eileen Bowser, *The Transformation of Cinema, 1907–1915, History of American Cinema*, vol. 2 (Berkeley, CA: University of California Press, 1990), 110. See p. 108 for nicknames of early stars. Bowser's book is an important source of information for the section on stars.
8. See Sumiko Higashi, *Cecil B. DeMille and American Culture: The Silent Era* (Berkeley, CA: University of California Press, 1994), 32.
9. The notion of Valentino as an erotic fetish is from Miriam Hansen, "Pleasure, Ambivalence, Identification: Valentino and Female Spectatorship," *Stardom: Industry of Desire*, ed. Christine Gledhill (London, UK: Routledge, 1991), 259–282.

CHAPTER 3

THE HOLLYWOOD STYLE AND THE PRODUCTION CODE (1903–1922)

Economies of industrial production constituted one element in the development of the studio system. Economies of style were another. Even though the films of each studio developed their own personality, there grew a uniformity of narrative and visual elements across the board. Part of this uniformity was created by the Production Code—censorship that assured that some things were never to be seen on the movie screen.

AFTER READING THIS CHAPTER, YOU SHOULD UNDERSTAND:

- How the "Classical Hollywood Style" evolved.
- The importance of shot-reverse shot editing.
- How formal elements and production processes were linked to each other.
- The development of film genres.
- The early history of the Production Code.

YOU SHOULD BE ABLE TO:

- Account for formal elements in film, like the over-the-shoulder style of dialogue scenes.
- Describe "three-point lighting."
- Discover exceptions to the 180-degree rule.
- Describe the contours of typical film genres, such as the Western or gangster film.
- Understand how Charlie Chaplin became his own genre.
- Discuss the early history of film censorship.
- Ask if censorship is necessary and why.

FILMMAKING AS AN INDUSTRY

The economics of stardom are different today. Players are no longer under contract to their studios because the studios no longer exist as self-sufficient production and distribution entities—as we will see in later chapters. But as the studios formed and their stars were celebrated in the early part of the 20th century, a unique relationship formed between viewer and the figures on the screen and between the figures on the screen and the roles they played and the celebrity lives that were rumored and fabricated around them. These relationships were emotional and sexual, even at the mediated distance between viewer and movie screen or fan magazine. The star system was a sign of how quickly and closely the movies and their audience cleaved in an embrace, even as the moviemakers themselves were organizing a structured economic system, rationalizing production in an attempt to maximize their profits. Indeed, as early as 1916, *The New York Times* was claiming the motion picture industry ranked fifth among all the other industries in the country.[1]

Industries, as we pointed out in the previous chapter, require rationalized, structured, predictable modes of production. We saw how the studios achieved this through the producer system; the contractual obligations of writers, directors, technicians, and players; the ownership of theaters that guaranteed distribution of films the studios produced. There was another kind of "rationalization" that occurred with the formation of the studios that had as much to do with the internal structuring of films that were created as with the processes of their creation and reception. An economics of production went hand in hand with an economics of style and content. The result was a style of filmmaking, a *culture* of filming, that with variations, transcended directors and studios and has come to be known as the **Classical Hollywood Style**.

THE CLASSICAL HOLLYWOOD STYLE

It is difficult if not impossible to trace the origins of the style, given the number of early films that have been lost. It emerged in the late teens of the 20th century and while undergoing many variations has survived to this day. It includes the basic components of a film—the shot and the cut—the construction of a film's narrative, the formation of genres, and the expectations of how an audience will respond.

THE SHOT

As far back as Edwin S. Porter's *The Great Train Robbery* and D. W. Griffith's Biograph films (discussed in the following chapter), we can see the formation of some basic elements of film form that become normative by the 1920s. Framing and composition, lighting and editing, and the arc of the narrative itself achieved an amount of standardization. We noted that in very early cinema, the camera was rooted and unmoving in front of its subject. Later, it became more flexible, but only to a degree. Silent filmmakers would occasionally use a **tracking shot** as a way to follow rapid action, or a **dolly** as a way to move close to a character at a moment of stress or surprise. King Vidor's *The Crowd* (MGM, 1928) contains an unusual sequence of shots in which the camera seems to twist around city buildings, pan and then track up the front of a skyscraper, track through a window and then track above what looks like hundreds of people sitting at desks, doing their daily labor, before coming to rest on John Sims (James Murray), the film's central character. But the vast majority of shots, even in this imaginative film, are stationary, frontal, composed with the main characters shot from the knees up, with closer shots used for emphasis.

Within the shot, lighting conventions are clearly mandated. **Three-point lighting** is the norm, with a **key light** illuminating the faces of the characters, **backlighting** setting off the actors from the background, and **fill lighting** controlling and creating the shadows around the characters. In the hands of creative directors, this lighting pattern can be altered to create dramatic effects. In *Citizen Kane* (RKO, 1942) (briefly leaping ahead in our chronology), Orson Welles might cut off the key light on a character, placing him or her in shadow, even if that character was important in the scene. Film noir, the style that swept over American cinema in the 1940s, depended on deep shadows to create its **mise-en-scène** of threat and violence. But these are exceptions to the rules of lighting, which is conventionally used to set off the characters from the backgrounds.

Another element of the shot that was noted earlier is the layering effect: the building up of elements through optical printing, rendering unnecessary the building of complete sets. The very nature of the shot lies in its artificiality, in which the various parts, from characters acting in the foreground to painted backdrops are made to look like an integrated whole. The Classical Hollywood Style depended on a sense of integration, of seeing the elements of the shot as whole and "real," despite the optical tricks that went into their creation.

Some directors are very conscious of the ways in which elements in the shot are composed, making

In this image from *Citizen Kane* (Orson Welles, 1941), we see an example of three-point lighting. Note the key light reflected in the actress's eyes, as if it were coming from the lamp beside her. We can see the backlighting behind her and the fill lighting shining from the various lamps around the room.

In the second image from *Citizen Kane,* Welles has placed his character in shadow, denying him a key light, backlighting him only. Note the composition of the shot: the low camera angle taking in the ceiling that looms over the characters. The position of Kane's body puts him forward in the frame, while the gaze of the other characters directs our own gaze to him.

them articulate and occasionally eloquent. But, as with lighting, most compose their shots in the most proficient way, framing the scene so that our attention is on the most important characters, without drawing attention away from them to their surroundings.

EDITING

In the Classical Style, editing emphasizes continuity from shot to shot. This is of particular importance. Film, then and now, is shot in short, discontinuous sequences, usually out of sequence. That is, shooting does not follow the events of the narrative as they will appear in the finished film. If, for example, a particular set or location is needed in various parts of the story, all the sequences that require that set may be filmed together, with the resulting footage edited into their narrative place in the finished film. Editing is the way filmmakers give narrative form to the shots that are made during filming.

The editing process became standardized early on. For example, cutting between characters taking part in a dialogue scene became the norm in silent film, setting in motion a style of editing that would become all but universal when sound arrived. A dialogue sequence will begin with a **two shot** of the participants, and then begin cutting over the shoulder of one of the participants while the other is talking and then a **reverse shot** looking over the shoulder of the second participant while the first is talking. The pattern is varied as we look over the shoulder of the character who is speaking while the other is listening. There may be inserts of one participant listening or talking.

This pattern became part of the economy of narrative creation. There is nothing realistic about the way dialogue sequences are composed, and there is no clear reason as to why the style developed as it did. But once established, it became a default, an economical means to a simple end on both sides of the equation. On the production side, a director or producer could make many takes of each camera setup—two shot, **over-the-shoulder** of one participant, over the shoulder of the other, etc.—and edit together the

In a dialogue sequence, cutting over the shoulder from one speaker to a shot over the shoulder of the second speaker is the most conventional editing sequence in American film. Even the most contemporary filmmakers use it, as in these images from Christopher Nolan's *Inception* (2010).

best takes in the relative peace and quiet of the editing room, without the expense of actors and crew hanging around. On the audience side, there is the comfort of repetition and comprehension. The viewer is privileged to both an inclusive view of the participants in the dialogue and a close-up view taking him or her into earshot (literally, since the camera is placed near one character's ear in the over-the-shoulder shot) of the characters.

SHOT-REVERSE SHOT

The construction of a dialogue sequence depends on a **shot-reverse shot**, another staple of the continuity style. We look at a character looking at another character or at an object and then cut to a shot of what or who that character is looking at. **Eyeline matches** must be perfectly aligned so that the space covered by the reverse shot is matched closely with the direction in which the character is looking. The manipulation of narrative space is key to all of this. The viewer must be assured where his own gaze is located at any given point. The editing must not confuse the viewer; the camera must remain in front of the action, on one side of an imaginary **180-degree line** cutting across the picture plane.

Cutting must be done on the gaze, or on motion (a character leaves the room and in the next shot we see her exiting the door she went through in the previous one). All these "musts," passed on from one generation of filmmakers to the next, creates the Hollywood continuity style—an illusion of an ongoing story told through the construction of fragments made to appear as a seamless whole to the viewer's eye.

NARRATIVE RESOLUTION

Sequences in film had to follow a logical narrative order, easily followed: "Continuity of events is a feature of the best pictures ever made," wrote a columnist in a 1912 issue of *Photoplay* magazine.[2] That continuity included the arc of the story as well. Every narrative must have a resolution. No matter how chaotic the comedy or how emotionally upsetting the melodrama, some harmony must prevail. An evil character will die and another be redeemed by love; battles may rage in wartime; Buster Keaton may be pursued by dozens of would-be wives but find his true love at the end; Chaplin's Little Tramp may lose the woman he loves but persevere nonetheless. In almost every instance, some peace and reconciliation must occur, even

In this sequence from Frank Capra's *American Madness* (1932—a film we will discuss in detail in Chapter 8)—a married woman is forced into an unwanted embrace.

Another character enters the room and sees them.

Capra cuts back to the couple acknowledging the appearance of the character at the door.

if it is the image of Charlie Chaplin, the plucky Tramp, kicking up his heels and walking down a dusty road.

GENRES

Genres, or *types* of film, are as old as the movies themselves. Comedy, melodrama, gangster films, Westerns, horror movies (the Edison company made a 13-minute version of *Frankenstein* in 1910), and documentary (although the term did not come into existence in the late 1920s, documentaries existed since the beginnings of film—recall the image of McKinley taken in 1896) all established themselves by the turn of the 20th century.[3] To be sure, in many cases, generic properties flowed into film from the 19th-century stage. This was particularly true of melodrama, whose broad emotions and gestures, cruel villains and virtuous heroines, and last-minute rescues were taken over by the movies and given greater presence and immediacy.

But then, a few shots later, he cuts 180 degrees behind the couple to show their point of view.

Here is a contemporary example of breaking the 180-degree rule. In these shots, two young men confront each other in a school hallway. Director Derek Cianfrance cuts to the opposite side of the two in the course of their confrontation (*The Place Beyond the Pines*, 2012).

Genres are predictive and prescriptive. A moviegoer at a Western film knows exactly what to expect: cowboys, wide-open desert spaces, threats from outlaws and Indians, perhaps a schoolteacher from the East who is trying to tame the frontier town. Filmmakers must meet the audience's expectations or risk disappointment. At the same time, the generic properties must be altered enough to keep audience attention and approval. In every film, Charlie Chaplin's Tramp becomes a comic/melodramatic genre unto itself. He goes through the same slapstick gestures: he falls down and causes others to fall down; he kicks people in the pants and gets kicked in the pants in return; he pines after a lovely girl and sometimes gets her, sometimes not. These are predictive elements that the audience expects to see and they prescribe what Chaplin must deliver. At the same time, he invents different narrative containers for these generic elements. In *The Kid* (Charles Chaplin Productions, First National, 1921) he looks after an abandoned child. In *The Gold Rush* (Charles Chaplin, Charles Chaplin Productions, United Artists, 1925) he is a prospector, starving in the Alaska wilds. The different situations allow him to invent new gags and comic routines while remaining within the comic parameters viewers expect. Even in contemporary film, we expect the bickering couple in a romantic comedy to come together in love at the end. We want the rowdy, misbehaving male character to find some redemption. We demand that the villain be punished. We demand plenty of shooting in an action film, with guns held sideways and characters flying through the air while firing away.

Expectation is what genres are about; it is what American film as a whole is about. Filmmakers from the head of the studio or the producers through the writers, the director, and the actors create stories, genres, characters, actions, reactions, drama, comedy, and narrative lines with ascending emotional curves and a satisfying closure in which good and endurance triumph. They create these stories by means of a narrative construction that erases its means of creation, rendering itself invisible through continuity cutting and a narrative drive that carries the viewer to an end that is simultaneously expected and surprising. These expectations and satisfactions make up the structure of American film to this day, and we will be examining them in more detail as we proceed.

THE CODE

A major force in shaping Hollywood and its products from its earliest days to the present is the Production Code—now known as the MPAA ratings

Charlie Chaplin as the little tramp, walking resolutely down the road with his girl (Paulette Goddard). Chaplin became a genre unto himself. *Modern Times* (Charles Chaplin, 1936).

system (as in "PG 13" or "R"). In one form or another, the code has influenced the stories films have told. It has had periods of strong and weak enforcement since 1909, and it has been involved in the politics of filmmaking and film distribution. The mayor of New York attempted to close down the city's nickelodeons in 1909, partly because of the content of films, partly because of the fact that the nickelodeons were open on Sundays. In response, a group of progressive education, church, and women's organizations put together a Board of Censorship of Motion Picture Shows in an attempt to review films for immoral content and therefore prevent the theaters from being closed down. Their arguments became part of a larger social discussion about protection of the family and the film business's desire to situate its product as a socializing force for good. There were even arguments that the nickelodeons would take the place of the saloon and would be a safe place for families to gather.

The New York Board became a national organization, but it ran into criticism from other states and faced the imposition of a bill to form a federal censorship board in 1914, caused by an uproar over prize fight films as well as films about birth control and white slavery, especially *Traffic in Souls* (George Loane Tucker, Universal, 1913) and *The Inside of the White Slave Traffic* (Frank Beal, Moral Feature Film Co., 1913). Those films mixed sensationalism and sexuality with morality, the latter gaining the support of progressive reformers. Censorship groups fought back and the bill to form a federal censorship board almost passed, until the appearance of *The Birth of a Nation*. Various states attempted to ban that film because of its racist content and their fear that it would cause rioting. The Supreme Court upheld the state of Ohio's suit to ban the film in 1915, and the ruling by the court, written by Justice Joseph McKenna, said a lot about how film was viewed then and now:

> It cannot be put out of view that the exhibition of moving pictures is a business, pure and simple, originated and conducted for profit, like other spectacles, not to be regarded, nor intended to be regarded by the Ohio Constitution, we think, as part of the press of the country, or as organs of public opinion. They are mere representations of events, of ideas and sentiments published and known; vivid, useful, and entertaining, no doubt, but, as we have said, capable of evil, having power for it, the greater because of their attractiveness and manner of exhibition.[4]

Film exhibition is a business "pure and simple," "capable of evil," not subject to free speech liberties. The justice even indulged in some advanced film criticism, saying that films "are mere representations of events, of idea and sentiments. . . ." Apparently he believed that the business of film was a separate entity than the events, ideas, and sentiments represented by the films. One part was imagination, the other commerce. The part that was imagination was capable of causing harm, and it had to be controlled like any offending business operation. The notion of filmmaking as an "industry" is implicit in the justice's ruling.

THE 13 POINTS

In the face of this, various state and local censorship boards flourished, but the push for a National Board of Censorship lost support. In the meantime, filmmakers began self-censoring their own work. Clearly some order had to come from these conflicting forces, especially in the midst of growing scandals: the trial of comedian Fatty Arbuckle for rape; the murder of a film director, William Desmond Taylor; the release of Erich von Stroheim's *Foolish Wives* (a transgressive film, perverse and without sentimentality—we will discuss it more fully in Chapter 6). In 1922, the studios put together their own censorship board: The Motion Picture Producers and Distributors of America (MPPDA), headed by Will Hays, and therefore known as "The Hays Office." Hays set out 13 points that filmmakers needed to avoid. They included any films that

1. dealt with sex in an improper manner
2. were based on white slavery
3. made vice attractive
4. exhibited nakedness
5. had prolonged passionate love scenes
6. were predominantly concerned with the underworld
7. made gambling and drunkenness attractive
8. might instruct the weak in methods of committing crime

Erich von Stroheim in his transgressive film, *Foolish Wives* (1922). The film was a factor in the creation of the Hays Office.

9. ridiculed public officials
10. offended religious beliefs
11. emphasized violence
12. portrayed vulgar postures and gestures
13. used salacious subtitles or advertising.[5]

The studios were asked to submit reader's reports on all scripts being considered for production to make certain they did not transgress any of the "points."

The studios, in effect, put into practice a guide for creating films that would offend no one; but at the same time, if followed strictly, would constrain the narrative limits of the films they made. The 13 points, by turns vague and proscriptive, were created as much to quiet public opinion as they were to control filmmakers. The result was a kind of culture of constraint, if not restraint. Filmmakers would still emphasize violence, exhibit almost naked bodies, portray vulgar postures and gestures, even make vice attractive, as long as the offending characters were either punished or shown the error of their ways. Filmmakers in the 1920s were as smarmy in their depictions of sexuality as they were in their moralizing about the effects of bad behavior. The code and its "points" served as a kind of cultural mask, hiding, protecting, but quite porous nonetheless. Like the films made under its aegis, it had a calming effect for both the studios and the audiences for their films.

The MPPDA code lost much of its effectiveness throughout the 1920s and into the early sound period. The resurgence of gangster films in the early 1930s and some witty attempts at portraying sexuality led to an even stricter set of prohibitions during that decade, and we will examine those later on. What needs emphasis at this point is that the early cultures of American film involved a complex interweaving of stardom, of formal properties of narrative creation, of rules and regulations that attempted to control the kinds of stories films told, and the reaction of audiences to all of this. The latter remained steadfast and growing. The movies, no matter what internal turmoil they went through or how standardized their production methods became, only grew in popularity.

We need to turn our attention to the contours of filmmaking in the 1920s to get an idea of what was happening before the coming of sound. We will first look at the work of D. W. Griffith, then at the silent comedians, and finally at some important films made in the late silent period.

SELECTED FILMOGRAPHY

The Kid, dir. Charlie Chaplin, Charles Chaplin Productions, First National, 1921.

Foolish Wives, dir. Erich von Stroheim, Universal, 1922.

The Gold Rush, dir. Charlie Chaplin, Charles Chaplin Productions, United Artists, 1925.

The Crowd, dir. King Vidor, MGM, 1928.

Citizen Kane, dir. Orson Welles, RKO, 1942.

SUGGESTIONS FOR FURTHER READING

David Bordwell, Janet Staiger, Kristen Thompson, *The Classical Hollywood Cinema: Film Style and Mode of Production to 1960* (New York, NY: Columbia University Press, 1985).

Lee Grieveson, *Policing Cinema: Movies and Censorship in Early-Twentieth-Century America* (Berkeley, CA: University of California Press, 2004).

Richard Koszarski, *An Evening's Entertainment: the Age of the Silent Feature Picture, 1915–1928, History of American Cinema*, vol. 3 (Berkeley, CA: University of California Press, 1990).

NOTES

1. Information about the ranking of the film industry is from Richard Koszarski, *An Evening's Entertainment: The Age of The Silent Feature Picture, 1915–1928, History of American Cinema*, vol. 3 (Berkeley, CA: University of California Press, 1990), 93.
2. The quotation from *Photoplay* magazine is from David Bordwell, Janet Staiger, Kristen Thompson, *The Classical Hollywood Cinema: Film Style and Mode of Production to 1960* (New York, NY: Columbia University Press, 1985), 195.
3. The history of the word "documentary" comes from Koszarski, 241.
4. Information on the early formation of the code comes from Lee Grieveson, *Policing Cinema: Movies and Censorship in Early-Twentieth-Century America* (Berkeley, CA: University of California Press, 2004), 92–94. The quotation from the Supreme Court ruling is in Grieveson, 201.
5. The 13 points of censorship are listed in Koszarski, 206–207.

CHAPTER 4

THE DISTRESSING LEGACY OF D. W. GRIFFITH (1908–1925)

David Wark Griffith was a towering figure in the development of American cinema in the first part of the 20th century. His work drew together the various narrative, generic, and formal elements that other directors were developing piecemeal. But at the same time, his major work, *The Birth of a Nation*, was a racist film that caused a backlash. An African American filmmaker, Oscar Micheaux, made films to counteract *Birth*'s racism and became part of what would become a tradition of filmmaking by and for African Americans.

AFTER READING THIS CHAPTER, YOU SHOULD UNDERSTAND:

- Early cinematic pantomime.
- Griffith's work at Biograph.
- Griffith's use of parallel editing and the close-up.
- The basic narrative structures developed in the Biograph films and realized fully in *The Birth of a Nation*.
- The history of post–Civil War racism that fed into *The Birth of a Nation*.
- Contemporary reactions to the film.
- Oscar Micheaux and the origins of African American cinema.

YOU SHOULD BE ABLE TO:

- Trace the development of Griffith's work from the Biograph shorts through the long-form films.
- Discuss the cinematic innovations in *The Birth of a Nation*.
- Consider how the narrative techniques Griffith used are still employed in today's films.
- Discuss the racism inherent in that film.
- Compare *The Birth of a Nation* with Steven Spielberg's *Lincoln*.
- Discuss Griffith's films after *The Birth of a Nation*.
- Ask whether a work can be formally innovative yet promote a reactionary content.
- Ask if we can separate the aesthetic from the political.

BEGINNINGS

THE TRUST

Early in the 20th century, the Edison Company held patents on motion picture equipment and tried to corner the market on the production and distribution of films. To do this, they brought suit against any company that tried to work independently, the upshot being that many companies worked under license to Edison. One of the companies that bucked this trend and produced films on its own was the American Mutoscope and Biograph Company—Biograph, for short. Biograph did reach an agreement with Edison, and together they formed the Motion Picture Patents Company, which licensed other film producers and exchanges, the middlemen who received films from the producers and rented them out to distributors.

W. K. L. DICKSON

W. K. L. Dickson, Edison's filmmaker and inventor, the man who created the kinetoscope and the use of 35 mm film stock (the film gauge that remains the standard today), pushed for further refinements in film cameras and projectors. This put him at odds with Edison, who held fast to his inventions, and this forced Dickson to leave the company and become one of the founders of Biograph. There he continued exploring, inventing, and refining filmmaking techniques (partly as a means of dodging Edison's patents). This included a camera that used 68 mm film, similar to what IMAX uses today, and that produced a sharply defined image. Even more important than the refinements of equipment were the refinements in the cinematic narratives that the equipment recorded and reproduced. Dickson and his colleagues created an enviable team of filmmakers.[1] There was also a stock company of players (whom Biograph kept anonymous for as long as possible): Lillian Gish, Mary Pickford, Henry B. Walthall, Lionel Barrymore, and Florence Lawrence, who, when the studio relented and began publicizing its players, became known as "the Biograph Girl." There was the cameraman or **cinematographer**, Billy Bitzer, and, perhaps most important of all, the director with whom Bitzer worked so closely, David Wark Griffith.

GRIFFITH AT BIOGRAPH

Why is Griffith considered so important a figure in the development of silent film, especially since he did not exactly *invent* any specific narrative technique? One reason is that, given the enormous number of films from the early silent period that are lost, we have a great number of films by Griffith that have survived. Many of these are among the 450 films that he directed for Biograph between 1908 and 1913. And there is *The Birth of a Nation* (David W. Griffith Corp., Epoch Producing, 1915), the first American long-form narrative film, a monumental work of cinematic invention, and the most racist work in the history of American film.

Griffith's legacy is extraordinary, especially given the fact that he had no training in film when he came to Biograph. He was an out-of-work actor and a failed writer who had crisscrossed the country in search of a living. He stumbled into Biograph on the recommendation of a friend and started there as an actor. But when he began directing, he drew upon a fertile imagination that began molding the language and the look of film, reimagining filmic space itself in ways that continue as the foundational conventions of filmmaking. He was as much responsible for defining the **Classical Hollywood Style** as any other contemporary filmmaker; he also demonstrated that the style could be varied in imaginative ways. He brought to his filmmaking a high seriousness of purpose. After all, Griffith came to film thinking it was beneath him. He wanted to act and to write; that he could do neither very well did not lessen his desire to bring to his directing the notion that movies could be better than they were.[2]

PANTOMIME

As we discussed in the previous chapters, the movies before Griffith were a grab bag of chase films, fight films, Passion Plays, slapstick comedies, "actualities" (what we would call documentaries today), and broadly acted melodrama. "Broadly acted" is an understatement. Silent film was pantomime. Emotions and states of mind had to be communicated through facial expressions and physical gestures. Given the paucity of close-ups during the early silent period, the body was the medium of expression. And that expression was imported from the 19th-century stage and strictly codified. There were prescribed positions, largely influenced by the work of a Frenchman named François Delsarte, who wrote manuals demonstrating and illustrating the various positions that would signify specific emotions. Here, from a follower of Delsarte, is a description of how to act out a scene in which "continued disbelief in your truth and innocence enrages you. You make, however, one final effort for self-control, but show extreme anger in bearing and face":

> . . . Right hand sweeps to left moral zone of torso. Hand clenches in conditional attitude, . . . concentrated passion, wrists turning in. At the same time, left elbow sinks, bring wrist to level of hip. Hand clenched, wrist turned in [showing] vital energy in concentration. Right knee has stiffened, marked attitude of legs [showing] defiance. Head has sunk in opposition to attitude [showing] hate. A half spring on to right leg, as if to advance on object, is checked, resulting in a quick stamp only; then you recoil into attitude of legs. . . . At the spring, the hands have unclenched convulsively and rotated slightly, only to reclench at the recoil. Head has risen and sunk in opposition. The face expresses menace. The brows are lowered, the nostrils dilated, jaws clenched, etc.[3]

This narrative of gestures constitutes a kind of drama in itself. In other words, no matter what particular melodrama is being staged or filmed, the actors are required to perform from a manual of gestures and poses, a script that underlies the script of the play or film itself. In the very first film that Griffith made for Biograph, *The Adventures of Dollie* (1908), a slim film about a child stolen by Gypsies, who lock her in a barrel and throw her in the river until a little boy saves her, contains elements of the melodramatic script, as the characters run around raising their arms in anger or victory. *The Usurer* (1910) is one of a group of films Griffith made about the rich taking advantage of the poor. In this case, a moneylender causes grief by repossessing the property of a poor woman with a sick child. When the dispossessed woman comes to beg for her property back, she is told the moneylender is gone. She falls backward, arms on her head, and in the act, closes the door of the safe, locking the usurer inside. When his wife and clerk discover him the following morning, the wife rears back, arms extended, mouth open as the clerk leans slightly forward with one hand extended, the other held to his chest—both poses signifying shocked surprise.

The melodramatic gesture. Discovering the usurer's body in D. W. Griffith's *The Usurer* (1910).

NATURALISM

It must be noted that, when Griffith began his work at Biograph, the Delsartean directives for melodramatic poses were already out of fashion. New modes of more "realistic" and restrained acting had taken to the stage just as they had in the naturalist school of fiction. One of the most prominent authors of the naturalist school, Frank Norris, whose novel *McTeague* (1899) would be adapted by Erich von Stroheim into one of the most important films of the silent period, wrote that the new school of fiction would concern itself with "the smaller details of everyday life, things that are likely to happen between lunch and supper."[4] For Norris and others of his school, those details were likely to be sordid if not downright lurid—as we will see when we look at von Stroheim's *Greed* (1924). For Griffith, attending to the "smaller details" meant a calming down of the most egregious of melodramatic poses, even reframing the action of his films so that his compositions might move characters from the center of the shot to the edges, inviting the viewer to visually investigate the various elements within the frame. Within the frame, Griffith's actors moved more slowly than those in older melodramas, and with his reliance on the close-up, the face played an important role in expressing thought and emotion, "the smaller details of everyday life."

PARALLEL EDITING AND SCREEN SPACE

Griffith extended the **parallel editing** that we saw in its early stages in *The Great Train Robbery*, and that became an important part of the Hollywood style, complicating narrative by interlocking scenes taking place at different places at the same time. He extended his narratives, so that a number of events and characters are involved even in the simplest story. *The Usurer* contains sequences of the moneylender's high life with rich people at a fancy meal; a title card, stating "Meanwhile," followed by a scene of his repo men removing the furniture of a poor woman, an action that itself is interrupted by returning to the celebrations of the moneylender; and then to a scene of a ruined husband committing suicide, an act itself interrupted by another shot of the moneylender celebrating. The film cuts back to the repo men taking the bed out from under a sick child. And so forth as the narrative proceeds to the inevitable just reward of the moneylender dying in his locked vault.

"Meanwhile" is the operative adverb that signals an important advance in the formal structure of film

D. W. Griffith experimented with composition. The opening of his Biograph short, *The Unchanging Sea* (1910), breaks the frontal position of the camera and its subject by placing the figures at a diagonal to the picture plane.

narrative. "Meanwhile" something else is happening while you, the viewer, are watching the scene in front of you. Both, or more, events are occurring concurrently, and by alternating from one scene to another, a simultaneity effect is achieved. Porter did it in *The Great Train Robbery*, Griffith perfected it in his Biograph films. Time and space, the two basic components of cinematic construction, were enriched by Griffith's experiments. He made cinematic and narrative time flexible and made the space encompassed by his shots expressive and painterly. He often placed his camera in other than the simple, eye level, 90-degree position that ruled throughout the early silent period. He found that placing figures to the side of the frame enriched the picture plane by allowing inventive compositions that directed the spectator's eyes off the simple dead center. He would use the diagonal line as a compositional anchor, as in the opening shot of *The Unchanging Sea* (1910), which shows characters coming out of their houses at a diagonal to the center of the frame. He would permit characters to move close to the camera: in the same film, the figures walk directly toward the camera, moving forward and off to screen left. In *The Unseen Enemy* (1912), he focuses tightly on a gun held by a hand poking through a hole in the wall, threatening two sisters, crouching in terror in a room.

GRIFFITH'S STORIES AND THE CRITICS

Making cinematic time and space flexible and expressive enabled Griffith to undertake large themes and complicated narratives, many of which became, like the formal elements of the films themselves, turned into conventions that have become the basis of many films to come. His melodramas of vulnerable women held captive by dangerous men and rescued by righteous heroes remains, despite all the variations played on it, a basic narrative device, a simple premise that still calls forth a response from viewers. Contemporary viewers and reviewers understood, almost instinctively, the power of Biograph shorts. According to Griffith biographer Richard Schickel, Griffith's film of the play by poet Robert Browning, *Pippa Passes* (1909), was the first film to be seriously reviewed in *The New York Times*. Previously, when film was noticed at all in newspapers (and newspapers were the main information media at the turn of the 20th century), the emphasis was on the business of film. Now, the *Times* took notice of the imaginative, indeed the artistic element of this new form of entertainment. The review compared its cinematography—by Arthur Marvin and Griffith's main director of cinematography, Billy Bitzer—to contemporary art photographers. The review did condescend to movie audiences, and recognized that film censorship was partly responsible for the appearance of literary adaptations. In other words, to escape the condemnation by censorship groups, Griffith and his contemporaries would turn to literary works as an example of their high-mindedness. The *Times* review noted as well that the film, and by extension many of the Griffith Biographs, along with the productions of other companies, were moving away from broad melodramas to more subtle representations:

> That this demand for the classics is genuine is indicated by the fact that the adventurous producers who inaugurated these expensive departures from cheap melodrama are being overwhelmed by offers from renting agents. Not only the nickelodeons of New York but those of many less pretentious cities and towns are demanding Browning and the other "high-brow" effects.[5]

There is no question that Griffith considered his work high minded, if not "highbrow." With the exception of very few comedies, his Biograph films, and the feature films he made when he struck out on his own, were serious and, no matter how restrained, melodramatic. He dwelt upon women in distress and men who were heartless, rich, and immoral or strong-hearted individuals, who overcame odds to save frail women. Occasionally, he would reverse the gender stereotype and present vulnerable and sensitive male characters, as in a Griffith favorite, *Enoch Arden*, a costume drama made from a Tennyson poem in 1911 (a remake of his earlier film, *The Unchanging Sea*, 1910), where the male characters suffer a loss and grieve, sacrifice, and renounce their love. Later, in *Broken Blossoms* (D. W. Griffith Productions, United Artists, 1919), he creates an Asian character—played by a white actor, Richard Barthelmess—who is a gentle, peace-loving, lost, and finally destroyed soul.

By and large, Griffith's was a conservative view of human relations and of American culture. His films long for an imaginary simpler time but are aware of the rapid urbanization of the country. He was generous and sympathetic when he made films about Native Americans. *The Redman's View* (1909) alludes to the "Trail of Tears," President Andrew Jackson's forced removal of the Cherokee from their native lands in 1838. At least until *The Birth of a Nation*, when Griffith's view of history turned reactionary, he was able, in the Biograph films, to balance conservative with vaguely populist views. He was sensitive to the dangers posed by the moneyed class and could demonstrate an awareness of the growing corporate structure in American life at the turn of the 20th century in the wake of America's "Gilded Age." One of his most famous Biographs is *A Corner in Wheat* (1909). The film was based on a short story by Frank Norris and its bucolic images of sowing the fields are influenced by the painting *The Gleaners* by Jean-François Millet. These scenes alternate with sequences of the "the wheat king," who is cornering the market and artificially driving up prices. Griffith creates sequences in the stock market, banquet scenes of the rich celebrating at lavish parties (that he would repeat in *The Usurer*), intercut with poor people unable to purchase bread because of the rise in prices. But the wheat king meets his just rewards. Visiting his grain elevators, he slips and falls into a pit. His wheat pours over him, and, while poor folk come to the bakery, demanding their bread in the face of the police who try to hold them off, he dies. The film ends with the image of the farmer, laboriously sowing his crop. The image slowly fades to black.

The Griffith Biograph films limbered up the movies, made them flexible in the ways their stories were told, and added a bit of complexity to the stories that were being told. More subtle acting styles, emotions suggested as well as exaggerated, and a widening array of genres were just some of the elements that Griffith explored during his Biograph apprenticeship. Along with other pioneers, Griffith established film as a serious medium; the films he and his colleagues made broadened the audience, making films acceptable to middle-class patrons, who could, by the mid-teens of the 20th century, visit well-appointed movie palaces instead of the crowded and stuffy nickelodeons.

THE LONG FILM

Griffith ultimately felt stifled by the constraints placed on him by Biograph. He began advocating for the long-form film. The one reelers he made ran only about 10 minutes or so. He wanted more; Biograph resisted. *His Trust* (1911) was made as a two reeler, running over 20 minutes. Biograph broke it up into two parts for exhibition, much to Griffith's displeasure. But the urge for longer films was there, and audiences were ready for it. Other film companies were making and distributing longer films, as well as serials, which extended their narratives from week to week. There were "epics" coming in from Europe, most spectacularly two films from Italy, *Quo Vadis* (Enrico Guazzoni, 1912), running at 2 hours, and *Cabiria* (Giovanni Pastrone, 1914), running almost 2 ½ hours.

There was also the urge to broaden the locations for the shooting of films. New York and Chicago were the main production centers up until 1910, but the weather and the limited locations—the New Jersey suburbs served as background for Westerns, for example—began to constrain production possibilities. As did Edison's patent spies, who tried to find out who was using equipment without paying a fee to the Patents Company. Various companies tried filming in Florida and Texas, but the West beckoned. As we pointed out earlier, Los Angeles in particular offered a wide variety of locations, from ocean to desert, which, along with its relatively inexpensive real estate and its distance from New York and Edison, made it ideal. In addition, audiences responded well to films advertised as made in California.[6] Film companies began working in Los Angeles around 1907, and Griffith began filming there in 1910, moving back and forth from New York.

The last years at Biograph were strained for Griffith. He made some of his best films during this period—*The Battle of Elderbush Gulch* (1913), for example, and *Judith of Bethulia* (1914), which would eventually become part of the successor to *Birth of a Nation*, the huge, multinarrative film *Intolerance* (Triangle Film Corp., Wark Producing, 1916)—but he was eager to move on to bigger things and, not the least of his issues, to receive greater recognition of his talents. Biograph, the company that thrived on the films Griffith made for them, did not publicize him or his players. They were kept anonymous. As we saw in the previous chapter, it took all of the film manufacturing companies some time to publicly recognize their "stars," preferring to brand themselves by their own company's name—Vitagraph, Essanay, Lubin, Edison, Biograph—rather than by the players in them or the directors who made them.

Biograph held out a long time, refusing to recognize their stars or their star director, despite the fact that he made the company's fortunes, and the company went into decline when Griffith left. Leave he did, and on leaving took out an ad in *The New York Dramatic Mirror* on December 3, 1913, in which he took full credit for his Biograph films and claimed that he was responsible for "revolutionizing Motion Picture drama and founding the modern technique of the art." He claimed invention of the close-up, the fade out, and the alternation of scenes and "the raising [of] motion picture acting to the higher plane which has won for it recognition as a genuine art."[7] As I pointed out earlier, Griffith invented very little, but he did take the rudiments of film form available to him when he began his work at Biograph and elaborated on them. He may not have single-handedly raised film to the status of "genuine art," but the 450 films he made during this period refined cinematic form. They may not have greatly expanded film's thematic reach, but they did help create the cinematic structures, the *means* of creating stories. In them, as Tom Gunning points out, Griffith developed a system of narration, of telling film stories across time and space that remain vital to this day.[8] The film that enlarged upon the stories told was soon to come. It did "revolutionize Motion Picture drama," and it did place film squarely within the cultural turmoil of its nation.

THE BIRTH OF A NATION

Griffith left Biograph for a company named Majestic, a film exchange (they gathered films from producers and rented them to distributors) run by Harry and Roy Aitken. Majestic was notable for fighting the Edison-Biograph patents trust and setting up independent production companies to supply. At Majestic, Griffith was allowed to make multireel, long-form films. While he was at work on these, he formed the idea for what would become, at that time, the most important film yet made: a film about the Civil War and the horrors (from the point of view of the South) of Reconstruction. Griffith had already made a few shorts at Biograph about the Civil War, mostly sympathetic to the South. But the immediate influence on what would become *The Birth of a Nation* was a work that had appeared in both novel and theatrical form, Thomas Dixon Jr.'s *The Clansman*. Published as a novel in 1905 and a play in 1906, *The Clansman* became the source for Griffith's film. It was a violently racist work that turned the Ku Klux Klan into a force of righteous southern anger against the perceived wrongs visited on it first by the Civil War and then by Reconstruction.[9]

RACE IN THE EARLY 20TH CENTURY

A number of other influences—personal, cultural, and historical—were at work in the creation of *Birth*. Griffith was born and raised in Kentucky, and he considered himself a southerner, with roots in the Confederacy. Even though Kentucky was not a secessionist state, Griffith's father fought for the South in the Civil War, and his father's stories stayed with him. Griffith also retained racist notions of African American inferiority and servitude, but this was not a wholly personal belief. His was a kind of everyday racism shared by many, perhaps a majority of people, a holdover from the period of Reconstruction and sealed by the Jim Crow laws that ruled the South. During Reconstruction, the United States took control of the former Confederate states, backed by federal troops. African Americans—former slaves—were permitted to vote. They held political office in southern states, and they gained a measure of economic and political freedom they had never known. This all came to an end in 1877, when a compromise was reached with the former Confederate states. Republican Rutherford B. Hayes became the 19th president of the United States, and the Democrats (at that time the party of reaction) were promised that the remaining 3,000 federal troops would be withdrawn from the southern states. The result was a rapid reversal of the gains African Americans had achieved during Reconstruction. They were reduced to second-rate status and treated appallingly.[10]

THE KLAN

The theory and practice of white supremacy returned with a vengeance. By the 1880s, poll taxes, literacy laws, and the requirement to own property served to disenfranchise African Americans. They lost the ability to vote. Share cropping and tenant farming replaced slavery. Jim Crow laws and segregation returned African Americans to the inferior status they held before the Emancipation Proclamation. Lynchings occurred with horrible frequency. African Americans were no longer slaves, but they were forced to live in a condition of poverty and submission in an atmosphere of violence and terror, one manifestation of which was the Ku Klux Klan.

The first incarnation of the Klan occurred in 1865, organized by former Confederate officers in Tennessee, who were now college students. They looked at it as a kind of fraternity and played around, wearing disguises and riding through town scaring people, especially freed slaves. During Reconstruction, the Klan spread across the South from a prank to a terrorist force. It drew on the resentment and fear of poor whites, who transformed the organization into sheet-covered night riders, burning crosses and committing violence against African Americans and northern whites. The Klan fell apart from internal dissension and was disbanded in 1869, and its remnants were brought to heel by federal sanctions. In 1915, an Atlanta man named William J. Simmons saw *The Birth of a Nation*. Excited by the prospects of a renewed organization, Simmons ran an ad for the Klan next to an ad for the movie. The Klan was reborn at Stone Mountain, Georgia.[11]

I think it is safe to say that what Griffith did *not* have on his mind when creating *The Birth of a Nation* was the making of a racist scandal. He was thinking of a long film that would honor the South, and, just as important, a film that would be the culmination of the narrative techniques he had been developing throughout his Biograph films. He was thinking as well of promoting himself. Chafing under the anonymity forced upon him by Biograph, Griffith wanted to be known to the world as the person who turned film into an art form. That was the reason for the advertisement citing his Biograph accomplishments. To that end, he created his own production company, Epoch Films, and with the help of the Aitkin brothers and a variety of investors, raised the money necessary to make *The Birth of a Nation*. Every title card in the film contains Griffith's signature and initials, and, more important, every shot and edit bears the visual signatures of Griffith's work. The film turned out to become the highest grossing film of the silent period, holding that honor until dethroned by Walt Disney's *Snow White and the Seven Dwarfs* (RKO) in 1937.

FORMAL METHODS

In a film of this length, with as many sequences and characters as it contains, continuity is a major issue. As we have seen, throughout the early silent period filmmakers were working toward a narrative form that could contain alternating scenes—occurring at different places but at the same time. What Griffith and other filmmakers were adding to this process was the act of cutting into a scene to the various characters who were in it, so that various points of view could be incorporated within a given sequence. The results of these efforts was that cinematic space and time become even more malleable and responsive to the director's desire to communicate the emotions and ideas he wants to share with the audience. In *The Birth of a Nation* this complexity of narrative is handled with remarkable fluidity. Its multiple characters and locations are handled in counterpoint with each other, their lives intermingling with disastrous results.

Griffith is so confident with this method that he can play with his audience and sometimes make a joke about something serious. When we are introduced to Dr. Cameron (Spottiswoode Aitken), the patriarch of the southern family at the center of the film, Griffith's camera tilts down to observe the puppies at his feet. At one point, Cameron drops a cat onto the dogs. "Hostilities" reads the title card, in a playful foreshadowing of a grim future. A bit later, after the Stonemans have left—the Stonemans are members of the Abolitionist family who begin as friends but become enemies of the Camerons during the war and

A quiet moment in *The Birth of a Nation* (D. W. Griffith, 1915). Ben Cameron, The Little Colonel (Henry B. Walthall), pauses and reflects.

its aftermath—Griffith creates a subtle piece of action without cutting. The Cameron family waves goodbye to the Stoneman sons and go inside their house, while Flora Cameron (Mae Marsh), in love with one of the sons, lags behind, making a small gesture, placing her hand to her mouth before going into the house. In the same shot, Ben Cameron ("The Little Colonel" played by Henry Walthall) and his brother (Robert Harron) walk in from screen right. Ben is in love with Elsie Stoneman (Lillian Gish) but also has larger historical issues on his mind—the upcoming war between the states. He pauses before entering the house, places his hand below his heart, and stares off into the distance. The scene fades to black, and in the next sequence we see a tableau in which Abraham Lincoln signs a proclamation calling up troops to fight the war.

Small gestures and restrained acting mark much of the first part of the film—at least those sequences involving the Camerons. The ensuing battle scenes are spectacular, and Griffith concentrates not only on large, wide scenes of explosive fighting but on the individual struggles on both sides. At one point, early in the war, one of the Stonemans and one of the Cameron sons fall in battle. When they fall, they move toward each other and die in what is almost a sexual embrace. "War's Peace" reads a title card, an ironic comment because what follows are tableaux of dead bodies. There are moving scenes in an army hospital, where The Little Colonel is recuperating and where, as in so much of the film, scenes are articulated with fine details. The Little Colonel's mother pushes past a guard, daring him to shoot her as she makes her way to her recuperating son. She goes to President Lincoln to plead for his release. At the hospital, another guard comically flirts with Elsie Stoneman, the Little Colonel's love, who has been looking after him.

But it is just here that the tone of the film changes. Battlefield heroics and its aftermaths, along with cute flirtations, turn to ugly racism when Griffith creates representations of Reconstruction. The full racist poison of the film bubbles up. There had been hints in the first part of the film. Stoneman's "mulatto" servant (played by a white actress, Mary Alden) goes into sexual paroxysms in a sequence apparently trimmed in response to the outpouring of complaints from the National Association for the Advancement of Colored People (NAACP). It is a curious scene because she seems to go mad because she's asked to see to the door one of Stoneman's colleagues. But in the second part of the film, it becomes clear that she is Stoneman's lover, and she takes great pleasure in her man's postwar rise to prominence and his promise to

War's Peace—the embrace of dying friends in *The Birth of a Nation.*

put freed slaves in positions of power, under his henchman, another "mulatto," the ironically named Silas Lynch (George Siegmann, also a white actor).

The flirtations continue. Stoneman's son tries to rekindle the affection of Margaret Cameron (Miriam Cooper). She has a memory—represented in an insert to show her thoughts—about her brother's death and turns away. The Little Colonel seems on his way to consummate his love with Elsie Stoneman, represented by his kissing a dove. Elsie expresses her love in a close-up in which she caresses a bedpost. But Griffith is playing a melodramatic diversion here. These scenes of innocent love and budding sexuality are muddied by the images of Stoneman's evil machinations to give African Americans power, which the film sees as a travesty of postwar justice. The threat of interracial sexuality leads, almost inevitably, to an African American's attempted rape of the Cameron's youngest daughter, an act which sends her literally over the edge. She jumps off a cliff to escape his animal-like advances.

The racist calumny is laid on thick. The South Carolina legislature is depicted as a bunch of unruly, drunken, chicken-eating louts. Their most desperate measure is passing legislature to permit miscegenation. The quiet domesticity of the old South has been trampled by the power-hungry Stoneman, played by Ralph Lewis and roughly and inaccurately modeled on Thaddeus Stevens, a congressman who supported the strongest methods of Reconstruction in order to destroy southern white supremacy. (At a later time, Stevens would be played by Tommy Lee Jones in Steven Spielberg's *Lincoln* [Dreamworks SKG, 20th Century Fox, 2012].) Stoneman puts African Americans in power and allows his henchman, Lynch, to run rampant.

THE CAPTIVITY NARRATIVE

What emerges is a large version of the captivity narrative on which so much of Griffith's work, and the work of many other filmmakers, depended. The American version of the captivity narrative originated in the 17th century and, in its earliest forms, involved a white woman taken prisoner by Indians. The racial factor was well established in these early tales. In Griffith's hands, captivity is paralleled by rescue, as the heroic male character rides to save the captive woman in a series of parallel scenes that are cut in decreasing lengths to increase the visual rhythm and heighten tension.

In *The Birth of a Nation*, Griffith would have us believe that an entire people were held captive by black freedmen and white carpetbaggers from the North. But, like all filmmakers, he needs to put a more personal face on the issue. He needs to see the large social issues in intimate, melodramatic terms. There is the death by suicide of "the Pet Sister," escaping the clutches of the rapacious Gus, an African American soldier, played by white actor Walter Long in blackface. Griffith draws out this sequence and plays it against a beautiful landscape of tall trees and mountains. The Little Colonel tries to rush to his sister's rescue, but he is too late to keep her from leaping to her death. This being melodrama, that death is drawn out, as she is held in The Little Colonel's arms. When he brings Flora's body home to her grieving family, Griffith does two interesting things. One is visual: he either lowers the lighting or closes down the aperture of the camera lens so that the light fades and the characters are seen only in dimly lit highlights. He follows this with a kind of retraction of the outrage he has just committed as the director of the film, the suggestions that African Americans are voraciously lusting after white women. "And none grieved more than these," reads the title card, followed by a brief shot of the household servants weeping. As far back as the Biograph shorts, *His Trust* and *His Trust Fulfilled* (1911), Griffith's expressed his naïve belief in the loyalty of African Americans toward their owners.

Things go from bad to worse. The Cameron family and Stoneman's son are taken prisoner by rampaging African Americans. They take shelter in the hut of friendly Union veterans. Reflecting the racial language of the time, a title card reads, "The former enemies of North and South are united again in common defence [sic] of their Aryan birthright." The hut is surrounded. Meanwhile, Silas Lynch, Stoneman's henchman, proposes marriage to Elsie. He promises to "build a Black Empire and you as a Queen shall sit by my side." Stoneman's liberal view of race doesn't extend to his daughter, and he rebuffs Lynch's desire. Lynch's response is to take Elsie prisoner.

But something else—"meanwhile"—has occurred. Sitting by a river, The Little Colonel, lamenting the treatment that white people are receiving, observes a group of children hiding under a sheet. A group of African American children come by, the children under the sheet jump up and scare them away. "The result," reads the title card, "The Ku Klux Klan, the organization that saved the South from the anarchy of black rule, but not without the shedding of more blood than at Gettysburg. . . ." Following the card we see the clansman in full sheeted regalia, spikes on their heads, frightening black people. Gus is captured by the Klan after he shoots a white man, and he is

The Ku Klux Klan returns Elsie Stoneman (Lillian Gish) to the arms of her father (Ralph Lewis), saving her from the mulatto Silas Lynch (George Seigmann) at the end of *The Birth of a Nation*.

held for trial by the hooded Klan in a scene tinted red, a color often used in silent film to indicate violence. They dump his body in front of Silas Lynch's house. It is in retaliation for this that Lynch captures the Cameron family. As this is happening, according to a title card, "crazed negroes" have taken over the town. The Klan races to the rescue, managing the resolution of two captivity narratives: the Camerons and the Stoneman son in the Union soldiers' shack and Elsie Stoneman being held by Lynch and his cohorts.

There is of course the implied larger rescue of the South itself from its captivity by "crazed negroes." The film ends with the Klan threatening African Americans into not voting, with the Stoneman and Cameron children united, Jesus appearing to The Little Colonel and Elsie, sitting by the ocean, which dissolves into a vision of the City of Peace. This egregious final spectacle is at least less obnoxious than the conclusion that both Griffith and Dixon had wanted, which was to solve the problem of race by having African Americans returned to Africa—a popular solution to the race issue proposed during Reconstruction.

THE BIRTH OF A NATION AND WOODROW WILSON

Did D. W. Griffith purposely set out to make a racist diatribe, whose melodramatic climax is the attempted rape of a white girl by an African American and whose grand climax is the ride of the Klan to rescue the South from the predations of African Americans? Was he merely reflecting the reigning cultural racial prejudices and beliefs in white supremacy? A title card in the film quotes from Woodrow Wilson's *A History of the American People* that "at last there had sprung into existence a great *Ku Klux Klan*," an "Invisible Empire of the South . . . to protect the southern country from some of the ugliest hazards of a time of revolution." In his book, Wilson does go on to modulate his view, speaking of the violent excesses of the Klan and going so far as to call its actions a "reign of terror."[12] When, as 28th president of the United States, Wilson saw the film, he said, "It is like writing history with lightning, and my only regret is that it is all so terribly true."

THE NAACP

The problem, of course, is that it is all so terribly false and defamatory, however in tune with the view of race in the early part of the 20th century. The film's representation of African Americans was taken for granted by contemporary audiences (this despite the fact that all the major African American characters in the film were played by whites in blackface). Jim Crow and segregation, fears of immigration, and theories of white racial superiority were so prominent at the turn of the 20th century, and Griffith's film fit in so well with the anxieties and prejudices of his white audiences, that the majority of them took no offense. But offense was taken by some, and the film's view of race did not go unchallenged. The NAACP was founded in 1909 "to ensure the political, educational, social and economic equality of minority group citizens of the United States and eliminate race prejudice."[13] When the group saw *The Birth of a Nation*, they realized that "race prejudice" was indeed an issue in this film and they launched a years' long campaign to ban its exhibition. They went to every city and state where the film was exhibited but were largely unsuccessful in getting it shut down.

Not that they did not have some precedent that gave them hope. Dixon's play, *The Clansman*—the source for Griffith's film—was banned in some localities where riots had occurred over its racist content. The NAACP did manage to get Griffith to trim some scenes; he added a prologue title card, "A Plea for the Art of the Motion Picture. . . . We do not fear censorship, for we have no wish to offend with improprieties or obscenities, but we do demand . . . the liberty to show the dark side of wrong, that we may illuminate the bright side of virtue—the same liberty that is conceded to the art of the written word. . . ." This high mindedness and the appeal to free speech seemed to have worked. Along with a short film (which no longer exists) called *The Hampton Epilogue* that was screened following *Birth* and presumably showed the progress African Americans had made, most localities allowed the film to be exhibited. The attempt to ban it succeeded only in Ohio and Kansas, whose Republican governors were courting the African American vote. And, as we noted in the previous chapter, the Ohio victory led to an important ruling about the status of film and free speech. Elsewhere, even in the face of fistfights that occasionally broke out after screenings of the film, Griffith and his people were able to mount effective counterattacks against censorship. *The Birth of a Nation* thrived despite its appalling content and because of its aesthetic triumph, thereby creating the question of form versus content—whether a work can be formally innovative yet promote a reactionary content—that has remained a point of controversy to the present day.[14]

OSCAR MICHEAUX

The reaction to *The Birth of a Nation* took place, on a much smaller scale, in film itself. African Americans began making films for black audiences in 1913, when William A. Foster founded the Foster Photoplay Company in Chicago. By 1927, there were more than half a dozen African American film production companies serving a growing ghetto audience in the North and all-black theaters in the South, making what were called at the time "race movies." There was even an attempt on the part of a major production company, Carl Laemmle's Universal Film Manufacturing Company—soon to become Universal Pictures—to find a script for a film that would counter Griffith's view of Reconstruction. Laemmle reached out to the NAACP for financial assistance and offered them help in writing the scenario. The NAACP went so far as to form a "scenario committee" to help finance the film through production. But 1915 was a year of great economic and political turmoil. World War I was raging in Europe. German U-boats were sinking American ships. Backing for a film project for African Americans was not a high priority and the project did not garner financial support. Universal dropped the project.[15]

Attention turned to Booker T. Washington, founder and head of the historically black Tuskegee Institute. His secretary, Emmett Scott, was putting together a film called *The Birth of a Race* (John W. Noble, Birth of a Race Photoplay Corporation, Frohman Amusement Corp.). Minimum financing was procured from both white and African American investors, including the Selig company, a major producer at the time. But despite the financing and good intentions, the film that emerged in 1918 was a failure. Financial fraud and loss of creative control caused the film to be largely stripped of its original intentions to celebrate the rise of African Americans: it started out at 6 hours in length and was whittled down to an hour of indifferent footage (the original version of the film is lost). What remains is, in Thomas Cripps's words, "a pastiche of two movies edited into one pictorial, rambling, falsely pious mélange that ignored its racial premises. . . ."[16] The film begins with the Creation and the story of Adam and Eve and leaps through history in an attempt to depict slavery, intolerance, and the growth of racial understanding through the ages. Some of its images are interesting, but they are interrupted by huge intertitles, and the little acting that occurs between the titles is mostly old school melodramatics.

One filmmaker managed to work through all the obstacles set in the path of African American cinema to produce a body of work beginning in the silent period and continuing until 1948. The child of former slaves, starting his creative career as a writer and eventually deciding to turn his stories into films, Oscar Micheaux has become the most recognized and celebrated figure among African American filmmakers in the field of "race" movies—that is, films made especially for African American audiences. His work parallels the outpouring of imaginative energy in literature, music, and painting that were part of the movement in the 1920s and 30s called the Harlem Renaissance. Micheaux worked independently of that movement, creating his own company to finance production and control distribution, and he was largely successful within the nationwide community of African American audiences.

WITHIN OUR GATES

His second film (the first, *The Homesteader*, made in 1919, is lost) is, in effect, a response to *The Birth of a Nation*. The very title of this film, *Within Our Gates* (Micheaux Book & Film Company, 1920), comes from a title card in Griffith's film, *A Romance of the Happy Valley* (1919):

> Harm not the stranger
> Within your gates,
> Lest you yourself be hurt.[17]

Within Our Gates is not a historical melodrama, but a melodrama of the moment—many moments, in fact. The film moves from the present to the near past in drawing its complex canvas of racial prejudice and violence, while responding to Griffith's racial calumnies almost point by point. The central character of the film, Sylvia Landry (Evelyn Preer), is a "mulatto." But unlike the mixed race caricatures of *The Birth of a Nation*, Sylvia is an educated woman whose goal in life is to help the poor students in her southern town of Piney Woods. Micheaux chronicles her difficulties in romance and life, including the revelation of her childhood that comes during a violent scene of attempted rape, not by an African American character as in Griffith's film, but by a white man who turns out to be Sylvia's father (the discovery is made by means of a scar on her chest, an old literary trope by means of which the parents of estranged children are discovered by means of a scar or birthmark).

Along the path of his narrative, Micheaux represents a spectrum of African American characters, types, and classes. Sylvia is herself identified as "typical of the intelligent Negro of our times" (it should be noted that the intertitles of the films are translated from the Spanish, since the only existing print of the film came from Spanish archives). But Micheaux also presents us with a variety of characters: a black thief and murderer; black card sharps and a white philanthropist; a preacher who guiltily submits to the prejudices of white men; a tattletale, who spreads a false rumor that Sylvia's adoptive father shot a rich man and who winds up beaten and lynched for his pains. Her kindly adoptive family are themselves lynched and burned, while her well-read supporter, Dr. Vivian (Charles D. Lucas), urges her to recognize the greatness of her country beyond its obvious racism. He recounts the triumphs of African American soldiers in wartime, including the just concluded World War I. These complicated narrative strains are packed into a film that runs only about 1 hour and 18 minutes. It depends heavily on intertitles—as do so many of the films of the period—but also on a compact visual style that communicates a great deal by means of sequences nested within sequences, on flashbacks and flash forwards, and the viewer's ability to remember a large cast of characters and events that happen early in the film and are not fully explained until the end.

The film not only presents African American culture as a rich mix of characters of various temperaments and occupations, from all strata of society, but understands that its audience is ready to see a response to the racist stereotypes created by Griffith (and not only by Griffith) in films made for white audiences. Micheaux is unsparing in his depiction of the indignities and violence committed by whites against African Americans as he is of the vices of

A lynch mob in Oscar Micheaux's *Within Our Gates* (1920).

some members of the black community themselves. There is a tough-mindedness embedded in his melodramatic framework that is in many ways more sophisticated than Griffith's sentimentality, even if Micheaux's cinematic style is less inventive. *Within Our Gates* is also firmly embedded in its time. The references to the country's wars, to the liberal North and the segregated, violent South, do not idealize or sentimentalize race by placing it in an imagined past. For this, his film underwent censorship that was more successful than that aimed at *The Birth of a Nation*. It was banned by many states and localities. It was deemed lost for many years. But its rediscovery lets us know of a nascent and powerful African American film culture that served an audience ready to see some truths of their lives.[18]

GRIFFITH AFTER *THE BIRTH OF A NATION*

INTOLERANCE

The Birth of a Nation was an enormous critical and commercial success. But Griffith was astonished by the negative reaction to its racism and the persistent call for it to be censored. By way of response, he made a gigantic spectacle of a film, *Intolerance: A Sun-Play of the Ages* (Triangle Film Corporation, 1916). At almost 3 hours in length, it is made up of four narratives, each of which, according to an opening title card, "shows how hatred and intolerance, through all the ages, have battled against love and charity." The narratives concern the fall of ancient Babylon, the story of Jesus, the persecution of the Huguenots in late 16th-century France, and a modern story of a young man falsely accused of a crime. The stories are interwoven and linked by the image of actress Lillian Gish (who plays Elsie Stoneman in *Birth*, and was one of Griffith's favorite actresses) rocking a cradle bathed in sunbeams, with the words, taken from Walt Whitman: "Out of the cradle endlessly rocking."

Intolerance is an audacious work, not least for the demands it makes upon its audience, requiring a persistent engagement with four distinct narratives, each with many characters, but audacious as well for Griffith in calling forth enormous production requirements with gigantic sets, requiring his cinematographer, Billy Bitzer, to go to extraordinary lengths to create a **mise-en-scène** of great depth and detail. It is, in fact, the visual detail and the booming camera movements of this film that hold attention across its expanse of stories. But at the same time, its insistence on size and scope and its attempt to bring a unified theme to narratives that are not at all similar undermine the film's intent. Spectacle has a way of swallowing meaning, and Griffith's *Intolerance* may absorb the

The Babylon sequence in Griffith's *Intolerance* (1916). Giganticism replaces—or magnifies—melodrama.

spectator in its images but does not successfully deliver a message of tolerance.[19]

The historical tales are spectacular, but banal in their message of tolerance. Only the modern-day narrative, *The Mother and the Law* (an idea for a film that preceded and was then enfolded into *Intolerance* and then unfolded as a stand-alone feature) expresses a strong message of moral responsibility. A tale of rapacious capitalists, "moral uplifters," and the struggle of labor, is resolved in a typical Griffith chase. A young man, "the boy" (Robert Harron), is sentenced to death for a murder and must be saved by those who know his innocence. Even here, "message" is outstripped by the suspense of the boy's last-minute rescue. As the Russian filmmaker and theorist Sergei Eisenstein pointed out many years ago, the editing of the last-minute rescue so beloved by Griffith neutralizes any progressive ideas. Its outcome is already always determined. We know that the innocent will be rescued just in time. Griffith and his contemporaries who used this technique set a pattern for film in which the suspense is generated by the ride to the rescue, the release from captivity, the saving of the innocent, resulting in an easily managed emotional response. They do not enlighten us at all because the moments of suspense contain within them the certainty that the captive will be saved.[20]

BROKEN BLOSSOMS

Griffith did make one film in which no one was rescued at the end, and it was once more a film about race. *Broken Blossoms* (D. W. Griffith Productions, United Artists, 1919) is, unlike *The Birth of a Nation* or *Intolerance*, a small-scale chamber piece, delicate and mostly restrained in its cinematography and its acting. The narrative is about a man from China, referred to as "The Yellow Man" (played by the white actor Richard Barthelmess), who settles in London to bring a message of peace. Contrasted with the "The Yellow Man" is "Battling Burrows" (Donald Crisp), a sadistic boxer who profoundly abuses his daughter, Lucy (Lilian Gish). She finds solace with The Yellow Man, who idealizes her as a kind of asexual fetish object, laying her out on a bed on a pedestal and worshipping her. Perverse in its depiction of erotic longing and fetishization, it can only end in extreme violence when Battling Burrows discovers the odd relationship between his daughter and The Yellow Man. The cruelty is enormous and threatening, as Griffith presents Battling Burrows in huge close-ups that threaten the very bounds of the screen. He beats her to death after using an axe to smash through a closet where she has been hiding. This is a scene that communicates the woman's frenzied terror so powerfully that it influenced Alfred Hitchcock's *Psycho*

Sexual perversity. The Yellow Man (Richard Barthelmess) worships Lucy (Lillian Gish) in D. W. Griffith's *Broken Blossoms* (1919).

(Paramount, 1960) and Stanley Kubrick's *The Shining* (Warner Bros., Hawk Films, Peregrine, 1980). The Yellow Man shoots Battling Burrows and then himself. Forbidden desire and miscegenation, Griffith seems to say, can end only in the death of all its participants. In the course of reaching that conclusion, Griffith makes one of his most restrained and lyrical films, as well as his most violent.

A CAREER IN DECLINE

Griffith's output was strong during the late teens and early 20s of the 20th century. *Hearts of the World* (D. W. Griffith Productions, Famous Players-Lasky, Paramount, 1918) took World War I as its theme. We will look more closely at this film in Chapter 6. He went on to make domestic melodramas, such as *Way Down East* (D. W. Griffith Productions, United Artists, 1920), and a large-scale historical melodrama, *Orphans of the Storm* (D. W. Griffith Productions, United Artists, 1921), in which the French revolution is equated rather oddly with the Russian Revolution of 1918. Both are built toward a climax of last-minute rescues, with *Way Down East* concluding famously with the rescue of Lillian Gish's Anna on an ice flow headed toward a waterfall.

But by the mid-1920s, Griffith's time had passed. His creative energies were flagging and his financial difficulties were expanding. Moviemaking styles—those styles that he had helped so much to develop—were, in the hands of other filmmakers, outstripping Griffith's own sense of invention. Rescue melodramas were certainly still in fashion, but Griffith's infatuation with virginal young girls at the mercy of brutal men, his attacks on the "moral uplifters," the older women do-gooders who populate many of his films, his sentimental, Victorian outlook on a world that had changed radically after World War I were no longer what many filmgoers wanted to see. Griffith faded into financial straits and cinematic oblivion. But not before he was involved in the early formation of the Hollywood studio system—in the creation of United Artists and his work with Paramount—that institutionalized filmmaking into something analogous to a mass production assembly line. He made a few sound films, including *Abraham Lincoln* (D. W. Griffith Productions, United Artists, 1930). But he did not survive the studio system because he was of the old school in which the director ruled the production. He could not survive the increasingly byzantine world of film finance because of his own ineptness at working through an economic maze. Ironically, American filmmaking has not surpassed Griffith. The style he helped develop became institutionalized as the Classic Hollywood Style. And the narrative content of American film has not gone very far from Griffith's melodramatic sensibility.[21]

SELECTED FILMOGRAPHY

D. W. Griffith

(Note that many of Griffith's Biograph shorts are available on various DVD collections and on YouTube.)

A Corner in Wheat, Biograph, 1909.
The Adventures of Dollie, Biograph, 1909.
Pippa Passes, Biograph, 1909.
The Usurer, Biograph, 1910.
The Unchanging Sea, Biograph, 1910.
The Unseen Enemy, Biograph, 1912.
The Battle of Elderbush Gulch, Biograph, 1913.
The Birth of a Nation, David W. Griffith Corp., Epoch Producing, 1915.
Intolerance, Triangle Film Corp., Wark Producing, 1916.
Hearts of the World, D. W. Griffith Productions, Famous Players-Lasky, Paramount, 1918.
Broken Blossoms, D. W. Griffith Productions, United Artists, 1919.
Way Down East, D. W. Griffith Productions, United Artists, 1920.
Orphans of the Storm, D. W. Griffith Productons, United Artists, 1921.

Oscar Micheaux

Within Our Gates, Micheaux Book & Film Company, 1920.
Body and Soul, Micheaux Film, 1925.

SUGGESTIONS FOR FURTHER READING

Pearl Bowser, Jane Gaines, & Charles Musser, eds., *Oscar Micheaux and His Circle: African-American Filmmaking and Race Cinema of the Silent Era* (Bloomington, IN: Indiana University Press, 2001).

Thomas Cripps, *Slow Fade to Black: The Negro in American Film, 1900–1942* (New York, NY: Oxford University Press, 1977).

J. Ronald Green, *Straight Lick: The Cinema of Oscar Micheaux* (Bloomington, IN: University of Indiana Press, 2000).

Tom Gunning, *D. W. Griffith and the Origins of American Narrative Film: The Early Years at Biograph* (Urbana, IL: University of Illinois Press, 1991).

Jackson Lears, *Rebirth of a Nation: The Making of Modern America, 1877–1920* (New York, NY: Harper Collins, 2009).

Roberta E. Pearson, *The Eloquent Gesture: The Transformation of Performance Style in the Griffith Biograph Films* (Berkeley, CA: University of California Press, 1992).

Richard Schickel, *D. W. Griffith: An American Life* (New York, NY: Proscenium Publishers, 1996).

Melvyn Stokes, *D. W. Griffith's The Birth of a Nation: A History of The Most Controversial Motion Picture of All Time* (New York, NY: Oxford University Press, 2007).

NOTES

1. For Dickson and Biograph, see Charles Musser, *The Emergence of Cinema: The American Screen to 1907, History of the American Cinema*, vol. 1 (Berkeley CA: University of California Press, 1990), 92, 145–147.
2. Information on Griffith comes from Richard Schickel, *D. W. Griffith: An American Life* (New York, NY: Proscenium Publishers, 1996). On his work at Biograph see Tom Gunning, *D. W. Griffith and the Origins of American Narrative Film: The Early Years at Biograph* (Urbana, IL: University of Illinois Press, 1991).
3. Genevieve Stebbins, *Delsarte System of Expression*, 2nd ed. (New York, NY: Edgar S. Werner, 1887), 181–182. For a critical discussion of pantomime and Griffith's use of it, see Roberta E. Pearson, *The Eloquent Gesture: The Transformation of Performance Style in the Griffith Biograph Films* (Berkeley, CA: University of California Press, 1992).
4. The quotation from Norris is in *The Apprenticeship Writings of Frank Norris*, ed. Joseph R. McElrath, Jr., Douglas K. Burgess, vol. 1 (Philadelphia, PA: The American Philosophical Society, 1896).
5. Quoted in Schickel, 141–142.
6. Schickel points this out, 147.
7. Griffith's ad proclaiming his place as an innovator is quoted in Melvyn Stokes, *D. W. Griffith's The Birth of a Nation: A History of "The Most Controversial Motion Picture of All Time"* (New York, NY: Oxford University Press, 2007), 74–77.
8. See Gunning, 10–28.
9. Schickel supplies the details of Griffith's move from Biograph to Majestic, 212–250.
10. There are many histories of Reconstruction and race after the Civil War. See Jackson Lears, *Rebirth of a Nation: The Making of Modern America, 1877–1920* (New York, NY: Harper Collins, 2009). See also the website "Race, Voting Rights, and Segregation," http://www.umich.edu/~lawrace/vote.htm.
11. History of the Klan can be found in Stokes, 202–204, and at the website of the Anti-Defamation League, http://www.adl.org.
12. The quotation from Woodrow Wilson is from *A History of the American People*, vol. LX (New York, NY: Harper & Brothers, 1918 [originally published 1901]), 60–65.
13. The statement of the NAACP is found at their website, http://www.naacp.org/pages/naacp-history.
14. Much of the material on the attempts to censor *Birth of a Nation* is drawn from Stokes, *D. W. Griffith's The Birth of a Nation*, 129–170.
15. For the attempt of Universal to fund a filmed response to *Birth*, see Stokes, 165–166.
16. Thomas Cripps, *Slow Fade to Black: The Negro in American Film 1900–1942* (New York, NY: Oxford University Press, 1977), 75. Cripps provides much of the material on the early history of African American film developed here. An excerpt from *Birth of a Race* can be found on YouTube.
17. The reference to Griffith's *A Romance of the Happy Valley* is in J. Ronald Green, *Straight Lick: The Cinema of Oscar Micheaux* (Bloomington, IN: University of Indiana Press, 2000), 1.

18. See also Pearl Bowser, Jane Gaines, Charles Musser, eds., *Oscar Micheaux and His Circle: African-American Filmmaking and Race Cinema of the Silent Era* (Bloomington, IN: Indiana University Press, 2001); and Pearl Bowser and Louise Spence, *Writing Himself into History: Oscar Micheaux, His Silent Films, and His Audience* (New Brunswick, NJ: Rutgers University Press, 2001).
19. Information on the production of *Intolerance* is in Schickel, 303–339.
20. Sergei Eisenstein's theories of Griffith's editing style are in his essay "Dickens, Griffith, and the Film Today," *The Film Form*, trans. Jay Leyda (New York, NY: Harcourt, 1977), 195–255.
21. Schickel details Griffith's decline, 560–609.

CHAPTER 5

SILENT COMEDY (1903–1936)

Among the most enduring films from the silent period are its comedies. Charlie Chaplin is still revered as one of the masters of comic cinema, while his rival, Buster Keaton, continually amazes with his physical daring and his inventive use of cinematic devices.

AFTER READING THIS CHAPTER, YOU SHOULD UNDERSTAND:

- The origins of silent film comedy.
- The elements of film comedy.
- The relationship of comedy and modernity.
- Parody as a form of comedy.
- How editing effects comic style and timing.
- The cultural forces that formed Chaplin's character, "The Little Tramp."

YOU SHOULD BE ABLE TO:

- Discuss the ways in which silent comedy evolved.
- Understand the differences between the comedy of Charlie Chaplin and Buster Keaton.
- Trace the changes of comedy from the silent to the sound eras.
- Understand silent comedians other than Buster Keaton and Charlie Chaplin.

ORIGINS

In 1902, Uncle Josh, in *Uncle Josh at the Moving Picture Show*, did battle with the movie screen. He believed that what he saw projected on it was somehow real. He mistook illusion for the material world. We find it funny because the character is so foolish. He is the country bumpkin, stereotyped for his simplemindedness, comic because he takes everything literally. He is the object of laughter, and we feel superior to him. Uncle Josh's antics with intractable material, his confrontation with the objects projected on the movie screen, form the basis of silent comedy, a rich vein of material that sustained the movies from their inception.

Like melodrama, some silent film comedy had its origins on the stage, vaudeville in particular. Vaudeville was essentially a variety show, consisting of singers, dancers, jugglers, acrobats, performing animals, minstrel acts (in which white and even African American performers appeared in black face), comics, and, eventually, movies, which, for a brief period, were shown between the live acts. Some vaudeville comedy was verbal, obviously not suitable for silent film. But some of it was knockabout slapstick—the word derives from a flat, two-pronged stick with which one comic would whack another, resulting in a loud slap. It was first used in the Italian *Commedia dell'arte*, popular during the 16th–17th centuries, and it made its way into modern vaudeville. Slapstick is unsophisticated entertainment, based on motion, surprise, and no little amount of mock violence. It formed the basis of almost all film comedy to come in the silent era and beyond, and especially in two of the most famous comics of the period who came from vaudeville: Buster Keaton and Charlie Chaplin.

COMEDY AND MODERNITY

Live vaudeville comedy was only a small part of comedy's genesis. Comedy is as old as the classic Greeks, but silent film comedy is *sui generis*: it is a native cinematic form. You will recall our earlier discussion of film as the art of modernity. Like the other technologies of the 19th century, film transports the viewer into different spaces, imaginary ones in its case. Like those other technologies, film is about movement. A strip of film moves through the camera and the projector, carrying its images to the eye to create a sense of movement before it. At the same time, it captures the movement of the world in front of it, and silent comedy is the art of motion.[1] Film melodrama tends to pull the viewer away from the world of forward propulsion into a static space of large emotions contained in rituals of redemption. Even in D. W. Griffith's rides to the rescue, the dynamics of the action—think of the ride of the Klan in *The Birth of a Nation*—are in the service of stasis, that is, of returning the world to a balanced, often regressive state, of white supremacy in the case of *Birth*.

Classic comedy, Shakespearean comedy, for example, also resolves itself, usually in the marriage of the couple who, along with their families, are at odds throughout the duration of the play. But so much of silent comedy emphasizes the restless, often lunatic carryings on of its characters, in which resolution is sometimes an afterthought, simply a way of ending the craziness. There are important exceptions to this, especially in Charlie Chaplin's films, but even here, the resolution is often about the difficulty in making one's way in an upside down world. Even Chaplin, who went some distance in sentimentalizing comedy, focused the body of his films on interactions of his body with an intractable world. Silent comedy is about disruption and chaos. It reflects the disordered world of the spectator and makes her feel at home in its chaos.

THE CHASE

Intractability and chance, crazy interaction with the material world surrounding the comic, along with often incessant movement, characterize the body of silent film comedy. Among the most popular and resilient of the earliest silent film comedies was the chase. In 1903, Biograph released *The Escaped Lunatic*. It was so popular that it was almost immediately remade as *Maniac Chase* by Edwin S. Porter for the Edison Company the following year. Porter's film starts with a setup typical of the time: a stationary camera situated at a direct, 90-degree angle to a set, in this case the interior of a jail cell, in which a man dressed like Napoleon (it was something of a cultural comic cliché that lunatics thought they were Napoleon) paces up and down. One of the guards comes in with a bowl of food, which our comic Napoleon tosses in his face. Two other guards arrive to beat and club the poor lunatic. Undaunted, he gets up, smashes the furniture in his cell and uses a table leg to pry open the bars of the window and escapes. He runs, the guards pursue. He crosses a creek; he hides in a barrel and rolls down hill; through a bit of trick photography, he leaps high into a tree; his pursuers follow him. The camera pans along the countryside as he magically reappears, jumping down from another tree his guards following him. And so on, until the end, when he manages to leap back up a wall and return to his cell. He puts his furniture back together and sits down to read the paper, much to the astonishment of the bedraggled guards.

The emphasis in the chase film is on seemingly unstoppable movement, the rush of the body through various landscapes echoing the rush of the real world around the spectator. The focus is on the male character, either going mad, or in a state of panic and escape. In his movement is the narrative of the film, which, like the modern world, is in perpetual motion.[2] He needs to get away, sometimes just for the hell of it, sometimes because he is pursued by a crowd of women!

One of the most popular varieties of chase comedy involved the bachelor who puts an advertisement for a wife in the newspaper. The result is that dozens of women appear and give him chase. Once again, Edwin S. Porter and the Edison Company copied a film made by Biograph. Porter's is about a French nobleman who puts his ad in the papers, announcing that he will be waiting at Grant's Tomb at 10 A.M. (*How a French Nobleman Got a Wife through the* New York Herald *Personal Columns*, 1904). On location, in front of the tomb, he prances about, and the ladies begin to appear. He bows deeply to each, until the crowd of interested women grows so large that he is frightened off and takes flight. The would-be brides pursue through varying landscapes—beachside, woods, over a country fence. Only when the nobleman walks into the middle of a pond do his 10 pursuers pause, until one bravely goes into the water and claims her husband to be.

These chase films focus not only the image of a man frightened by too many women, but on a kind of tumbling landscape through which the running man flees. The chase films are travelogues of a kind, representing movement for its own sake, giving the spectator a safe place for a wild ride. The wildness emerges from the desperate desire of the women to catch their man. Perhaps the growing strength of the woman's suffrage movement, which resulted in the passage of the 19th Amendment in 1920, giving woman the right to vote, created a backlash. In the chase films, women are depicted as a kind of faceless mob of insatiable characters with only one obsession in mind, allowing no obstacle to stand in the way of getting a man.

SEVEN CHANCES

Films of women chasing a man held the interest of filmmakers through the mid-1920s, well past the passage of the 19th Amendment. Buster Keaton, at the peak of his career, made *Seven Chances* (Buster Keaton, Buster Keaton Productions, Metro-Goldwyn Pictures, 1925), in which he is willed a fortune from a dead relative if he gets married by 7 o'clock on his 27th birthday—that being the exact day that the will is read. He is too shy to directly tell his girlfriend, and the first part of the film, made in an early two-color **Technicolor** process, consists of a **montage** of the two of them by a garden gate as the seasons pass, his dog growing from a pup to an adult, while he is unable to announce his love. When he gets news of his inheritance and what he needs to do to get it, he manages to insult his girlfriend by telling her he needs to marry "someone" by the allotted time. Though she relents, she cannot communicate her decision to him because she can't reach him by telephone and a messenger (a servant in blackface, who rides a horse too slowly to reach him—the film is marred by a number of racial and ethnic stereotypes) fails to deliver the message. Failure of communication is an important catalyst to movement in *Seven Chances*.

Buster tries to approach various women with a proposal of marriage, and all turn him down, many with comic effect. His business partner decides to put an announcement in the paper . . . and by now you know the results. Buster waits in the church for someone to answer the ad. He falls asleep, and the church fills with women dressed in bridal gowns. They come by foot and by horseback; they come on roller skates; they fill the church to overflowing. Buster escapes the church in time to receive the message from his beloved, but it is too late, even as he tries to find out how much time he has left, a process that includes many gags, including a watchmaker who cannot give him the time of day.

Inevitably, as Buster is walking down the middle of the street, the camera tracking him at a high angle, the would-be brides appear. Hundreds of them. They run down a football field full of players. Buster has himself lifted up in a crane to escape them, but the women take over the crane and twirl him around until he drops in a train yard. The brides think they have killed him, until he reappears and the chase continues. Even when, like his distant relative, the French nobleman in *Personal*, he jumps in a pond, the would-be brides continue their pursuit. Through it all, Buster runs and runs, the camera in pursuit—the film is a study in moving camera, creating the kinetics of attempted escape. He arrives, at last, at his true love's door, dragging the garden gate with him. For a moment, it seems that he has arrived too late, but not quite; his watch has the wrong time, and at the last moment marriage and riches are his.

Seven Chances is based on a play produced by David Belasco in 1916. Belasco was a famous theatrical producer active from the late 19th century until around 1930, and many of his plays were adapted for film. But it is hard to imagine the connection between Keaton's film and a stage presentation, because *Seven Chances* epitomizes the elements of the chase film as well as the physical comedy prevalent during the silent era. This is a film about open spaces filled with people in motion, overcoming obstacles, moving like a tide through the countryside. It is cinematic to its core, alive in its energies of movement and accident and the interaction of people—mainly Keaton—and objects. This is how film embraced its own modernity, of perpetual motion and chance, of unexpected encounters that played jokes on the comic's body, of a rush of events that threaten always to get out of control.

KEATON AND CHAPLIN

THE THREE AGES

All of Buster Keaton's films, from the earliest shorts to his longer works, involved Buster in contention with the things of the world. He sometimes interacted, via parody, with the cinematic world itself, playing with the movies around him or with the very illusion-making apparatus of film. *The Three Ages* (Edward F. Cline, Buster Keaton, Buster Keaton Productions, Metro Pictures Corp., 1923) is a parody of Griffith's *Intolerance* (and the Italian epics that in their turn influenced Griffith). In place of Griffith's gigantic film set in ancient Babylon, Biblical times, 17th-century France, and the modern era, Keaton's film is located in the Stone Age, in ancient Rome, and in the present. Like Griffith, Keaton moves back and forth among the sequences, but in each Buster tries to get the same girl, battling against the same suitor. Only the costumes, backgrounds, and gags change. Parody is typically the art of deflation by means of exaggeration. The parodist takes elements of the target work, picks out elements from it and makes fun of them by blowing them out of proportion. In contemporary film, we see parody at work in Mel Brooks's *Blazing Saddles* (Warner Bros., Crossbow Productions, 1974),

Buster, pursued by a throng of suitors in *Seven Chances*, attempts an escape (Buster Keaton, 1925).

where Western conventions are exploded and racial stereotypes are turned upside down. Cowboys sit around a campfire, eating beans and breaking wind. A cowboy punches out his horse.

Keaton, in his parody, deflates by deflating instead of inflating. He miniaturizes Griffith's gigantisms and his overblown sets (in the Babylon sequence) and over-the-top melodrama. Even though in the opening caveman sequence Buster rides in on a gigantic lizard (in a neat bit of special effects), most of the film depends on clever gags typical of Keaton's style. There are small jokes, like his wearing a wristwatch sundial in the Roman sequence; bigger ones, like playing golf with a big wooden club and rocks; being dragged along the ground by an elephant; or having himself catapulted to a hilltop to get his girl (whom he drags off by her hair) in the Stone Age sequence. He gives a manicure to a lion (someone dressed up in a lion suit) in the Roman sequence.

The end of the modern day sequence is more complicated. The year 1923 was early in the period of Prohibition, that ill-considered law that made alcohol illegal. In *Three Ages*, Buster's rival gets Buster sent to jail by planting a liquor bottle in his pocket. In the police station, he discovers that his rival is wanted by the cops. What follows is a typical Keaton maneuver. He steps into a phone booth to make a call—presumably to his girlfriend—and some moving men arrive and replace the phone booth, carrying off the one with Buster in it. He falls out of the booth when it is loaded on a truck and is pursued by the police to the top of a building. He tries to jump from one building to another, falls down the side of the building into a firehouse, lands on the back of a fire truck, which promptly leaves for a fire. Speeding fire trucks were a staple of film from its earliest days, climaxing in Edwin S. Porter's 1903 *Life of an American Fireman* (Edison Manufacturing Company), and continuing throughout the silent period. In 1916, Charlie Chaplin made a short film called *The Fireman* (Lone Star Corporation, Mutual Film). Buster reaches the church where his beloved is marrying the wrong man and, in a scene that would be repeated 44 years later in *The Graduate* (Mike Nichols, Embassy Pictures, 1967), grabs his girlfriend and runs from the church.

Buster's comedy is based on the kind of perpetual motion we see in *Seven Chances* and *Three Ages*. Heir to the chase films, his work depends on perpetual motion in a world of hostile things. The world plays tricks on him and he in turn plays tricks on his environment. The emphasis throughout is on his deadpan confrontation with things that seem to have no other purpose but to get in his way, and his stoic purpose to overcome that intent. Keaton is a kind of everyman with extraordinary physical prowess that he himself seems unaware of. He simply presses on, undaunted.

THE PLAY HOUSE

Keaton was enamored of the cinema and the ways in which film changes perceptions, creates illusions, and allows the human body to interact in crazy ways with world around it. In *The Play House* (Buster Keaton, Joseph M. Schenck Productions, First National Pictures, 1921), Buster dreams himself into a vaudeville show (Keaton began his career as a child, performing knockabout slapstick with his family in vaudeville shows). Everyone in the show, in the orchestra, and in the audience is Buster. Using carefully calibrated multiple exposures, in which a strip of undeveloped film is exposed multiple times to different images, Keaton is able to create wonderful illusions, interacting with himself in a hilarious variety of ways, including an ingeniously synchronized dance number between himself and himself.

SHERLOCK, JR.

Sherlock, Jr. (Buster Keaton, Buster Keaton Productions, Metro Pictures Corp., 1924), goes one step further—or perhaps backward, rethinking *Uncle Josh at the Moving Picture Show* (and looking forward to Woody Allen's *The Purple Rose of Cairo*, Orion Pictures, 1985) by putting Buster literally inside a movie. He plays a projectionist who wants to be a private detective. Falling asleep in the projection booth, he dreams himself walking into the movie on the screen. Because Buster is angry that a rival is sneaking his way into Buster's girlfriend's heart, the dreaming Buster is angry at the characters in the film within a film because they look like his girlfriend and his rival. In his dream, they become them. He jumps into the screen to break them up, but, unfortunately, due to the nature of film editing, he gets caught up in changing locations. He tries to get into the door, but finds himself facing a garden wall. He sits down on a stool, only to fall down, because he is suddenly out on the street in the middle of traffic. Then he is teetering on the edge of a cliff. He is in the jungle surrounded by lions; then he is in the middle of a desert as a train goes by behind him. He sits down to find himself in the ocean, and so on, until he is returned to the movie, in which his rival steals his girlfriend's pearls. In the dream Buster becomes a famous detective and, after many gags, including a hair-raising ride to the rescue on the handlebars of a runaway motorcycle, he solves the case and gets the girl in the film within the film and in the film itself. When he wakes up, he learns how to embrace his girlfriend by looking at the screen and imitating the movements of the characters in the film-within-a-film. That film ends with the couple dangling babies on their knee. In our film, Buster looks and scratches his head in perplexity.

We have seen how film from its earliest period moved quickly from single shot presentations of events to edited narratives that turned time and space into malleable objects under the control of the filmmaker. *Sherlock Jr.* indicates another side of the equation where the film viewer is at the mercy of the filmmaker's manipulation. By 1924, the institutionalizing of film production and film form had been cemented into place. Keaton himself would suffer from the process when he moved from relatively independent production to MGM, a studio that from its start did not honor directors and instead practiced corporate control over its productions. Buster's travails and antics inside the film-within-a-film of *Sherlock Jr.* indicate, in a comic way, that filmmaking was trapping the filmmaker. Buster, to his detriment, would have to follow the rules. But, at the same time, what's going on in *Sherlock Jr.* also demonstrates the growing sophistication of the filmgoing audience. The jokes played upon Buster by editing him around various disconnected spaces paradoxically indicates the viewer's comfort with the **continuity editing** that had by this time become the norm. Buster is confused; the audience understands the jokes.

Continuity editing is the opposite of the fragmented editing that bedevils Buster. The continuity style allows fragments of film, the various shots that are taken of characters in action, to be seamlessly edited together. Early in the film, Buster comes bounding to his girlfriend's house with a box of candy. He reaches the front door and there is a cut to the interior of the house, as his girlfriend runs to the door. Just before she gets there, there is a return to the original camera position outside the house as she opens the door. Another cut shows the two of them inside the house, walking side by side, back to the camera. This little sequence serves no other purpose but to make a transition from one part of the film's narrative to the other. It does not serve the larger purposes of showing actions occurring at two different places occurring at the same time. But it is necessary to get Buster in the door, and the continuity of this simple action confirms the fact that editing had, by this date, become supple and invisible. Therefore, by paying obeisance to the continuity style, Keaton can then turn the tables on that style, on himself, and on the audience by literally showing editing at work and its comic effects when it is rendered visible.

STEAMBOAT BILL, JR.

With the exception of transition sequences like Buster entering the house, or sequences where cutting was necessary to keep up with the action, as in Buster's mad ride on the handlebars of a motorcycle, Keaton liked to film his gags in single shots. This is nowhere more effective than in *Steamboat Bill, Jr.* (Charles Reisner, Buster Keaton, Buster Keaton Productions, Joseph M. Schenck Productions, United Artists, 1928), the last film before Keaton joined Metro Goldwyn Mayer and got lost in the grind of studio production. In this film, Buster is the son of a steamboat captain, who tries to win the hand of his father's rival's daughter. Much of the film is unusually slow moving for Keaton until he gets caught in a windstorm. Once again, Buster faces the hostile elements of the world. An entire building is lifted off a hospital where Buster is lying after being slugged by a cop. His bed is blown through the streets and then through a horse barn as buildings crash around him. As he hides under the bed, in the middle of the street, the front of a

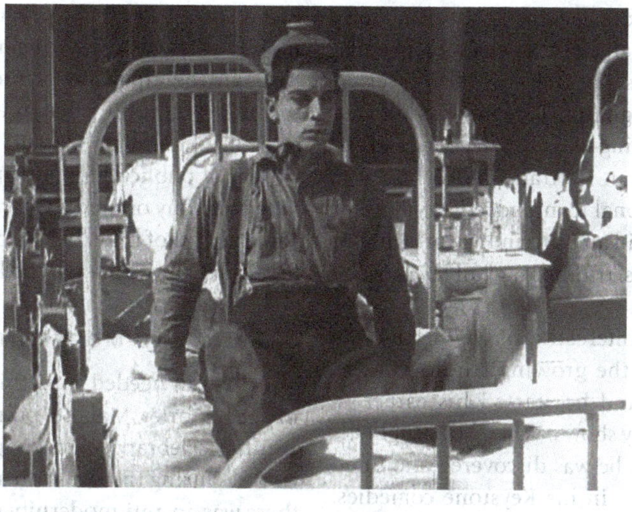

Buster in the hospital for a bump on the head has the building blown away on top of him during a storm in *Steam Boat Bill, Jr.* (Charles Reisner, Buster Keaton, 1928).

building begins to give way. An occupant jumps from a window onto Buster's bed. The bed blows away and Buster slowly gets up. There is a cut to a long shot in which Buster stands in front of the building, which proceeds to fall on him. There is no cut to a closer shot, no cutaway to indicate that this is a trick shot: we see the building fall and we see Buster saved because he stands precisely at the spot where the open window of the second story of the building falls around him. It is a breathtaking stunt.

CHARLIE CHAPLIN

Buster Keaton's unsmiling face throughout the chaos around him marks him as a kind of comic stoic. Despite his perpetual motion, he becomes, in effect, the still point in a turbulent world, constantly surprised but unperturbed, resourceful without having many resources other than his body and its good luck in overcoming circumstances. He rides with the turbulent currents, flying debris, hundreds of would-be marriage partners, in a large locomotive in *The General* (Clyde Bruckman, Buster Keaton, Buster Keaton Productions, Joseph M. Schenck Productions, United Artists, 1926)—a Civil War film, in which Buster plays a train man, driving his locomotive for the Confederacy. A commercial failure, it was partly responsible for the loss of independent control of his films. In the face of all of the elements, objects, and people thrown in his path, he is unbowed and unsentimental, though occasionally in a state of temporary sadness when he thinks he's lost his girl.

There were other important comedians during the silent period: Fatty Arbuckle, with whom Keaton got his start and whose offscreen behavior led to one of Hollywood's earliest sex scandals; Harry Langdon, who created a peculiar character, an adult with a little boy's face; Harold Lloyd, a middle-class version of Buster Keaton, whose mild demeanor belied his prowess in physical stunts; and Stan Laurel and Oliver Hardy, who started late in the silent period. Each had a particular inflection on the ways they dealt with the physical world, and they supplied useful antidotes to the melodramas that filled the screens. They each had a measure of fame, but none, Keaton included, compared in renown to Charlie Chaplin.

Chaplin's creation, "The Little Tramp," was a deeply sentimental figure, a persona who remained basically unchanged from the late teens of the 20th century through the early sound period. The derby hat, the moustache, the too-small, too-tight jacket, the baggy pants, the oversized shoes, the cane, and the duck-like walk became instantly recognizable and carefully crafted. Like Keaton before he joined MGM, and long after, Chaplin was in charge of his persona and knew how to fashion it to his advantage. Keaton received some international recognition; Chaplin was beloved and celebrated by working-class moviegoers and intellectuals the world over. He transcended his films to become an international icon, indeed a symbol of the poor man's striving in an unfriendly world, bereft of love, living by his wits, triumphing only because of his will to endure.

Chaplin's career is interesting as well in the way it followed the arc of the growing studio system. Chaplin was British, and he started his career in British music hall variety shows. When he brought his act to the United States, he was discovered and hired by Mack Sennett to play in his Keystone comedies. Sennett started his career working for D. W. Griffith at Biograph and from there went on to establish Keystone, which in turn became part of Triangle Pictures Corporation. Chaplin's Keystone comedies—he was there only for a year in 1914 and made 35 short films—are mostly knockabout slapstick and chase comedies. He tries out his tramp costume in his second Keystone short, *Kid Auto Races at Venice* (Henry Lehrman, 1914), in which he continually walks in front of newsreel cameras trying to photograph the races. It is as if Charlie, in his new incarnation as the Tramp, just wants to be seen, to be glimpsed at first by his new audience.

The year at Keystone included a feature-length film, *Tillie's Punctured Romance* (Mack Sennett, Keystone Film Company, Mutual Film, 1914) in which Chaplin plays second fiddle to Marie Dressler, a full-bodied comedienne, who mugs her way through the film. Here Charlie plays a scheming fortune hunter, who pursues Tillie from the farm to the city. The film is slapstick at its most annoyingly obvious: bricks are hurled, kicks are delivered, people fall down, and the mayhem concludes with the inevitable chase, as the Keystone cops pursue Tillie, Charlie, and his girlfriend (Mabel Normand) until Tillie winds up falling into the ocean. Clearly, Chaplin was not in complete control of his image at this point in his career. Or his salary. But his popularity was growing, and, as it grew, he demanded more money and artistic control. Mack Sennett could not meet his demands, and Chaplin moved on for a year to Essanay. Even before the move, his persona was outgrowing his films. That is, Charlie, through the character of the Little Tramp, was becoming a cultural phenomenon, far exceeding his roles in films. Articles were written about him in a variety of publications. He appeared in comic strips. One company offered a Charlie costume for sale. In a short period of time, he had become a celebrity of the first order, a world renowned figure.

CHAPLIN AND MODERNITY

But Chaplin needed something more to enhance his image. Charles Maland points out that amidst the cultural celebrations of Chaplin there were negative voices. During the late 19th and early 20th centuries, there was an anti-modernity movement known as the "Genteel Tradition," which argued against the raucous progress of industry and culture and the gritty realism of much of American fiction. The Genteel Tradition constituted, in Jackson Lears's words, an "escape from the economic realm of strife and struggle . . . an overall pattern of evasion in the dominant culture." In a word, it was conservative and sentimental about a lost time of simplicity and privilege. Chaplin's critics looked upon the movies and Chaplin as too "vulgar" for their tastes and (as always is the case with conservative critics) a threat to their status quo.[3] Chaplin looked for a way to navigate between the shoals of modernity's chaos, the rough and tumble of underprivileged working people versus the luxuries of the rich, and the dreams of gentility existing in the lost world of the collective imagination. He understood his critics and played them.

THE TRAMP

Chaplin's sixth short film for Essanay, *The Tramp* (Charles Chaplin, 1915), is filled with the usual knockabout slapstick of kicks and punches, of falling down and running. But at the end, two interesting things happen. Charlie, chasing a bunch of bandits who have tried to rob the farm where he is staying, falls off a fence and gets hurt. It is the unspoken rule of slapstick that no one appears to get actually hurt in the knockabout. But here, Charlie is in pain and has to be carried back into the house, where he passes out.

Of course, he revives and does a funny routine with a seltzer bottle. And then something else happens. The girl he is sweet on (played by Edna Purviance, who would become his main leading lady) meets up with her boyfriend, and Charlie leaves the farm. The last shot, which will become something of a signature image for Charlie, shows him from behind, kicking up his heels and duckwalking down the road. An **iris shot** closes off the film. Chaplin, the figure of cinematic modernity, was now reaching out toward the gentleness of sentiment and pathos. In many of his films, the Little Tramp dreams of an unobtainable gentility, a world of calm and even riches. He never quite gets there, but his sentimental yearning was part of his appeal.

In 1916, Chaplin moved studios again, this time to the Mutual Film Corporation. Not only did his salary grow, but so did his fame. He was emboldened to continue experimenting with his character. He played an upper-class, falling down drunk in *One A.M.* (Charles Chaplin, Lone Star Corp., Mutual Film, 1916), and then reverted back to his tramp character, this time with a more romantic turn in *The Vagabond* (Charles Chaplin, Lone Star Corp., Mutual Film, 1916) and *The Immigrant* (Charles Chaplin, Lone Star Corp., Mutual Film, 1917), with its famous opening shot of Charlie from the rear, leaning over the side of the ship as if throwing up, only to turn around and reveal that he's been fishing. Many of the Mutual films explored a peculiar romance of poverty and continued to extend the sentimental streak developed in the Essanay films.

A DOG'S LIFE

Chaplin moved once again, this time to the First National Exhibitors Circuit, a company formed to compete with Adolf Zukor's Paramount Pictures Corporation. Paramount would become one of Hollywood's biggest film studios, combining production, distribution, and exhibition in its own theaters. First National would eventually merge with Warner Bros. But in 1917, First National was still a relatively small company and in offering Chaplin complete control over his films, he was guaranteed not only a healthy salary, but a chance to further hone his art, which continued to focus on the Tramp and his travails in poverty and the city, especially in *A Dog's Life* (Charles Chaplin, First National Pictures, 1918). This film has the usual gags of kicking and punching, but it uses a dog to increase the sentimentality of the Tramp's life. Sharing film space with a dog is always precarious, because a cute animal will upstage an actor. But Charlie is as cute as any dog, and a dog in Charlie's hands becomes an extension of his personality; better, their personalities merge and expand in a bubble of sentiment, especially in the final sequence where Charlie and his girl (Edna Purviance) have settled in the country and Scraps the dog is shown in a basketful of puppies.

THE KID

The same gambit is played out in *The Kid* (Charles Chaplin, Charles Chaplin Productions, First National Pictures, 1921), "A picture with a smile—and perhaps a tear," to quote its opening title card. Charlie finds an abandoned child (Jackie Coogan) and brings him up to age 5. In *The Kid* pathos is doubled as Charlie, in effect, doubles himself by matching the mischievous but ultimately innocent tramp with an innocent, mischievous little boy. There is yet another doubling of a kind going on in the film, this time a doubling of the opposing forces of rich and poor. This is something that Chaplin toys with in a number of his films and which is partly responsible for his international fame: he pits the poor Tramp with the rich who try to undo him. The Tramp is on the side of the downtrodden and often has to confront the inhospitable or downright nasty well-to-do in order to prevail. In *The Kid*, class difference is ameliorated. The child's mother (Edna Purviance) has become a wealthy actress and a social worker who discovers her child's identity. When things are finally resolved, she accepts Charlie and the kid.

UNITED ARTISTS AND *THE GOLD RUSH*

Chaplin does not necessarily indulge in class criticism. *The Kid* ends in a final reunion of Charlie, the child, and the mother. But in this and other films, he does seem to represent himself as a voice of the poor and afflicted, even as he was one of the highest paid stars of his time. It was a successful gambit that he further exploited in a book and essays that he wrote in the early 1920s. He clearly had a well-honed sense of self-promotion. In 1919, he became one of the founders of United Artists, along with D. W. Griffith, and two of the major stars of the silent era, Douglas Fairbanks and Mary Pickford. United Artists was set up as a distribution company for the films made by its founders. Its purpose was to allow a modicum of artistic freedom that was being squelched by the growth of the other film studios. Chaplin used this freedom through the 1920s to create some of his most important films, including *The Gold Rush* (Charles Chaplin Productions, United Artists, 1925), which contains two of Chaplin's most inventive and hilarious routines, both involving food and deprivation. In one scene, Chaplin skewers a dinner roll on each of two forks and creates a little ballet. In the other, in a dream delirium brought on by hunger during a snowstorm, Charlie cooks his shoes, carefully

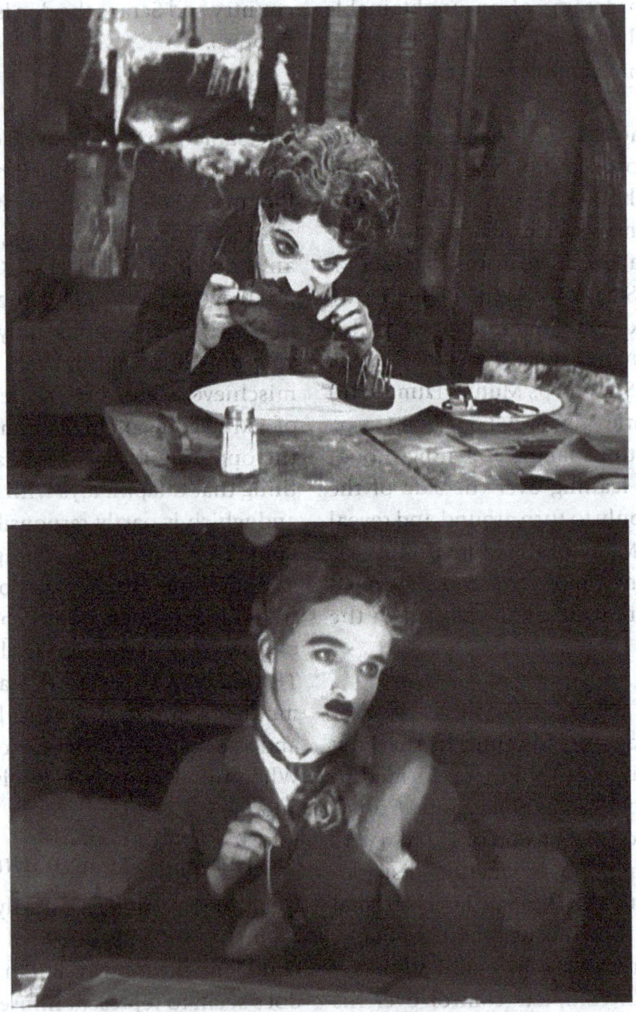

The Little Tramp eats his shoe and does a dance with dinner rolls in *The Gold Rush* (Charlie Chaplin, 1925).

separating the soles from the nails and eating the remainder, twirling the laces around his fork like spaghetti. He also made a serious melodrama, *A Woman of Paris* (Charles Chaplin Productions, United Artists, 1923), which he directed but did not play in.

A WOMAN OF PARIS AND CHAPLIN'S SERIOUS FILMS

A Woman of Paris is an interesting work in the Chaplin canon. Chaplin directs Edna Purviance, but he is not himself in the film, which is quiet and restrained. Gone is the frenetic activity, the pratfalls and kicks that mark his comedies. There are lighting and compositional effects that borrow from **German expressionism**, a movement that was having a marked influence on the appearance of films made in America. Chaplin would attempt serious films throughout his career, especially after the coming of sound. *The Great Dictator* (Charles Chaplin Productions, United Artists, 1940) is a seriocomic satire on the fascist leaders in Europe; *Monsieur Verdoux* (Charles Chaplin Productions, United Artists, 1947) is a curious work about a wife murderer, in which Chaplin turns on his comic persona and emerges as the dark side of the loveable tramp, happily killing the women he woos, rather than sadly giving up to rejection.

THE SOUND FILMS

Chaplin's two early sound films mark the climax, though not the end of his career. The figure who stood for the struggle between modernity and a vague longing for a simple, sentimental time, who used film to create an internationally recognized and admired persona, felt himself trapped by the coming of sound. He depended on the silent articulation of his character and the way that silence focused viewer attention on the tramp's antics. He could not conceive of the tramp talking, and he had the authority and control to keep him from doing so. *City Lights* (Charles Chaplin Productions, United Artists, 1931) and *Modern Times* (Charles Chaplin Productions, United Artists, 1936) have a **music and effects track**, and *Modern Times* allows some characters to talk and even has Charlie sing a nonsense tune at the end, but they are, in effect, silent films which enlarge somewhat on the gags and the pathos Chaplin had developed in his earlier work.

MODERN TIMES

Modern Times was Chaplin's most political work up to that point. Lauded as a representative of the poor, the Tramp had used his status in film after film as a means to focus sentimental emotions on that singular figure. At least part of *City Lights* focuses on class differences as the tramp wanders through the modern city, wondering at its riches. At the beginning of the film, the city fathers unveil a fancy statue, only to find the Tramp sleeping in its lap. But the central narrative of Charlie and the blind girl he falls for deflects the social commentary onto the usual pathos of Charlie the plucky loser. Much of the film involves his searching for money to cure the girl's blindness. When she is finally cured and recognizes her benefactor, the film ends on the pathetic note that this recognition may not be to the Tramp's benefit.

Modern Times in part avoids the sentimental trap of unrequited romance. The film directly confronts factory assembly line production—in one of Chaplin's most famous gags, where he gets caught in factory machinery—and the Great Depression. (See the image from *Modern Times* in Chapter 2.) In this film, people are out of work and desperate. The Tramp needs to save himself from mechanical labor and from jail (he's mistaken for a Communist sympathizer at one point) and then win the heart of a poor girl out to steal food. The sentimentality is still there, and some gags are repeated from earlier films. Charlie still falls down a lot and gets hit on the head (he takes a hit of cocaine at one point). But the underlying current that catches the political upheaval of the Depression is strong. The film ends on an upbeat note. Charlie's girl is on the run from the law, and the two escape to the country. The film ends on Charlie's favorite image of the Tramp on the road, seen from behind, this time arm in arm with his girl, walking off into the **fade out**. Once again, the urge for a mythical simpler time is fulfilled.

And so the end of the Tramp, a creature of silent film who survived only so long into the sound period.

Chaplin himself grew more political, directly addressing the perilous situation of fascist dictators in *The Great Dictator* (where his famous brush mustache allows him to play both a Jewish barber and Hitler), and himself getting caught up in the anti-Communist hysteria that gripped the United States after World War II. The celebrity, who had the admiration of the whole world in the 1920s and 30s, found himself locked out of his adopted country. The man whose cinematic character spoke to the poor and downtrodden was, in 1952, called by the attorney general "an unsavory character . . . making statements that would indicate a leering, sneering attitude" toward the United States.[4] Having left on a trip to Europe to celebrate his film *Limelight* (Celebrated Productions, United Artists, 1952), he was denied the right to return. He stayed away from his adopted country for 20 years and made a film mocking his situation, *A King in New York* (Attica Film Company, 1957).

Silent film comedy was an extraordinary genre. Keaton, Chaplin, Harold Lloyd, Harry Langdon, and many others cavorted in pantomime and did battle with the physical world. They spoke silently and physically to the anxieties of their audience, who were themselves facing a world of rapid change, of an enormous burst of technology, of political upheaval that led to the first World War, and of economic insecurity (there were three recessions and stock market failures during the early part of the 20th century before the crash of 1929). They spoke to these anxieties by absorbing them into their resilient bodies; they got hit and hit back in return; they fell down and had things fall on them. They hung from buildings and fell in the water. They were chased, they turned around and chased their foes in turn. They fell in love, a state that often put them into worse circumstances than when they were lonely, and won the hand of their loves after going through a hilarious number of obstacles. More than anything else, they proved the ability of silent film to embrace its audience in dynamic movement and the intimate relationship of the body and the world around it. Chaplin mixed slapstick with pathos; Keaton deadpanned his way through the most outlandish events, like a house falling on top of him. But they all prevailed, which is, of course, a generic necessity of comedy. No one must die or fall into despair, which is why, with or without the girl of his dreams, Charlie will kick up his heels and duck step down the road.

Among other silent comedians was Harold Lloyd, who, like Keaton, did physical stunts. *Safety Last!* (Fred C. Newmeyer, Sam Taylor, 1923).

SELECTED FILMOGRAPHY

Life of an American Fireman, dir. Edwin S. Porter, Edison Manufacturing Company, 1903.

Maniac Chase, dir. Edwin S. Porter, Edison Manufacturing Company, 1904.

How a French Nobleman Got a Wife through the New York Herald *Personal Columns*, dir. Edwin S. Porter, Edison Manufacturing Company, 1904.

Buster Keaton

The Play House, Joseph M. Schenck Productions, First National Pictures, 1921.

The Three Ages, Buster Keaton Productions, Metro Pictures Corp., 1923.

Sherlock, Jr., Buster Keaton Productions, Metro Pictures Corp., 1924.

Seven Chances, Buster Keaton Productions, Metro-Goldwyn Pictures, 1925.

The General, Buster Keaton Productions, Joseph M. Schenck Productions, United Artists, 1926.

Steamboat Bill, Jr., codir. Charles Reisner, Buster Keaton Productions, Joseph M. Schenck Productions, United Artists, 1928.

Charlie Chaplin

Kid Auto Races at Venice, dir. Henry Lehrman, 1914.

Tillie's Punctured Romance, dir. Mack Sennett, Keystone Film Company, Mutual Film, 1914.

The Tramp, Essanay Film Manufacturing Company, General Film Company, 1915.

One A.M., Lone Star Corp., Mutual Film, 1916.

The Vagabond, Lone Star Corp., Mutual Film, 1916.

The Immigrant, Lone Star Corp., Mutual Film, 1917.

A Dog's Life, First National Pictures, 1918.

The Kid, Charles Chaplin Productions, First National Pictures, 1921.

A Woman of Paris, Charles Chaplin Productions, United Artists, 1923.

The Gold Rush, Charles Chaplin Productions, United Artists, 1925.

City Lights, Charles Chaplin Productions, United Artists, 1931.

Modern Times, Charles Chaplin Productions, United Artists, 1936.

The Great Dictator, Charles Chaplin Productions, United Artists, 1940.

Monsieur Verdoux, Charles Chaplin Productions, United Artists, 1947.

Limelight, Celebrated Productions, United Artists, 1952.

A King in New York, Attica Film Company, 1957.

Other Silent Comics

Harold Lloyd, *Safety Last!*, dirs. Fred C. Newmeyer, Sam Taylor, Hal Roach Studios, Pathé Distributors, 1923.

Harry Langdon, *The Strong Man*, dir. Frank Capra, Harry Langdon Corporation, First National Pictures, 1926.

SUGGESTIONS FOR FURTHER READING

Charles Chaplin, *My Life in Pictures* (New York, NY: Grosset & Dunlap, 1974).

Kenneth S. Lynn, *Charlie Chaplin and His Times* (New York: Simon & Schuster, 1997).

Charles J. Maland, *Chaplin and American Culture: The Evolution of a Star Image* (Princeton, NJ: Princeton University Press, 1989).

Joan Mellen, *Modern Times* (London, UK: BFI, 2006).

David Robinson, *Buster Keaton* (Bloomington, IN: Indiana University Press, 1969).

———, *Chaplin: His Life and Art* (London, UK: Collins, 1985).

Joanna E. Rapf and Gary L. Green, *Buster Keaton: A Bio-Bibliography* (Westport, CT, 1995).

Andrew Horton, ed., *Comedy/Cinema/Theory* (Berkeley, CA: University of California Press, 1991).

———, *Buster Keaton's Sherlock Jr.* (Cambridge, UK: Cambridge University Press, 1997).

NOTES

1. The analogue of narrative movement and the movement of film through the projector is suggested by Devin Orgeron in *Road Movies: From Muybridge and Méliès to Lynch and Kiarostami* (New York, NY: Palgrave MacMillan, 2008).
2. A discussion of *The Escaped Lunatic* can be found in Jonathan Auerbach, *Body Shots: Early Cinema's Incarnations* (Berkeley, CA: University of California Press, 2007), 85–103.

3. For the negative reactions to Chaplin, see Charles J. Maland, *Chaplin and American Culture: The Evolution of a Star Image* (Princeton: Princeton University Press, 1989), 14–20. Much of the history of Chaplin's career is drawn from Maland's excellent study. The quotation about the Genteel Tradition is from T. J. Jackson Lears, *No Place of Grace: Antimodernism and the Transformaton of American Culture, 1880–1920* (New York: Pantheon Books, 1981), 17.
4. Quoted in Maland, 289.

CHAPTER 6

BETWEEN WORLD WAR I AND THE COMING OF SOUND (1913–1927)

In the years before sound, silent film became a sophisticated and technically proficient form of visual expression. Whether its subject was the Jazz Age and "flappers" or the horrors of World War I, film expressed itself with an inventiveness that reflected its many years of development. Cecil B. DeMille began his long career of films exploiting both the lurid and religious aspects of the culture. Women filmmakers briefly held important positions in early and late silent film. Some of the most interesting films of the period demonstrated the influence of German Expressionism. One director, Erich von Stroheim, showed that silent film could divest itself of sentimentality and embrace an ugly and fascinating naturalism.

AFTER READING THIS CHAPTER, YOU SHOULD UNDERSTAND:

- The large variety of styles and themes in late silent cinema.
- Representations of youthful exuberance in the 1920s.
- How World War I was constructed in contemporary film.
- How the film *7th Heaven* successfully manages war and romance.
- The influence of Cecil B. DeMille on 1920s melodrama.
- How DeMille's films interacted with changing American taste.
- The function of women filmmakers in the silent period.
- The influence of naturalism on the films of Erich von Stroheim.
- The influence of German expressionism.

YOU SHOULD BE ABLE TO:

- Address the varieties of gender representation in early film.
- Compare World War I films with war films from later decades.
- Compare DeMille's 1923 *The Ten Commandments* with his 1956 version.
- Think through the ways melodrama functions in silent and later sound films.
- Discuss European influences on early film.
- Discuss the growing technical sophistication of late silent film.
- Understand the significance of Murnau's *Sunrise*.
- Trace the influence of German expressionism throughout the history of American film.

POLITICS, THE WAR, PROHIBITION, AND RADIO

Decades rarely present themselves in rounded numbers. The important events that mark them are often longer or shorter than the nominal 10 years. So the period of the 1920s can be said to start with America's entry into World War I in 1917, and end with the beginning of the Great Depression in 1929. It was a period of great historical and cultural change. The war was brutal. Trench warfare and hand-to-hand combat, along with Germany's use of poison gas, resulted in massive casualties—dead, wounded, and disfigured. Four million Americans were called up when the United States entered the war in 1917. One hundred and twenty-six thousand were killed and 234,000 wounded. On the home front, there was a severe crackdown on dissenters. With the advent of the war and the success of the Russian Revolution in 1917, the forces of reaction in the United States came out in force. The so-called Palmer Raids, carried out by Attorney General A. Mitchell Palmer in 1919 and 1920, rounded up some 16,000 presumed radicals, Communists, and labor leaders. They were held without trial for many months and some who were immigrants were deported. A bomb was exploded at Palmer's house in 1919, which led to a redoubling of efforts to crack down on Communists and "anarchists." Two Italians, Nicola Sacco and Bartolomeo Vanzetti, were arrested for robbery and eventually tried as anarchists. Their trials and appeals lasted for 6 years and caused an international, political uproar. The two were executed in 1927. Bomb-throwing "anarchists" were the occasional targets of fun in some comedies, but little of the political current flowed through the films of the time. It took the Great Depression to trigger a direct response in film to contemporary life and politics. Even the silent films about World War I evaded the politics of the war to concentrate on the spectacle of battle and the sentimentality of romance.

After World War I, in 1919, a nationwide prohibition against alcohol, the Volstead Act, went into effect, as a result of decades-long lobbying by, among others, women's temperance groups. Prohibition resulted in nationwide law breaking—the culture did not easily or willingly give up the universal drug of choice—and the rise of gangsterism, violently cashing in on the illegal manufacture and trade of liquor, would have a great effect on movies in the early 1930s.

During the 1920s, radio became a major competitor to the movies. Here was a medium of entertainment and information that did not require people to leave their homes. True, radio was sound without pictures, but movies were pictures without sound, or at least without spoken dialogue. A curious gulf existed, for a time, between the two most popular forms of mass media in the decade. This gulf seemed to be echoed in late silent films where characters talk and talk; the films built around conversations, with the result that intertitles presenting their dialogue proliferate throughout, bringing the visual action to a halt every few minutes, in some cases every few seconds. Some late silent films require as much reading of intertitles as looking at images. Characters were anxious to be heard, and their words are displayed at length. But movies were fast playing catchup with the urge to talk. There had been experiments with synchronized sound throughout the twenties, though it would not be until 1927 when two films for Warner Bros., *Don Juan* (Alan Crosland, 1926), which had a synchronized music track, and *The Jazz Singer* (Alan Crosland, 1927), which contained sequences with dialogue and singing, marked the beginning of the sound era.

Despite the reliance on intertitles, silent cinema in the mid- and late-1920s reached a maturity of cinematic expression. In many cases, directors allowed their cameras to become unmoored from their stationary position and become more mobile; they experimented with composition and lighting, some of this under the influence of European and Russian filmmakers. **German expressionism**, with its deeply shadowed **mise-en-scène**, and **Russian montage**, with its rapid collision of shots, were noticed by American filmmakers and, in some instances, absorbed into their films. American film was also influenced, as it always is, by the culture around it. The culture of the Jazz Age and the horrors of World War I were incorporated into the cinema of the 1920s.

THE JAZZ AGE

OUR DANCING DAUGHTERS

Despite the political turmoil of the decade, or perhaps in the face of it, there emerged a culture of brightness and gaiety. Universal suffrage went into effect in 1920. Women had the vote. This empowerment led to a period of political and sexual liberation—for those women who had the means to be liberated—and introduced the figure of the "flapper" and the "It" girl to the culture. The 1920s were dubbed "the roaring twenties" and named "The Jazz Age" by novelist F. Scott Fitzgerald. Some movies reflected this. *Our Dancing Daughters* (Harry Beaumont, MGM, 1928) opens with the image of a statue of a naked woman frozen in a position of dancing. The image dissolves to a pair of shoes, which dissolves again to fill those shoes with a pair of woman's legs, bare and dancing like mad, reflected in a three-way mirror. Holding on this shot, we see the woman bend down to put on her underclothes and then, fully clothed, we see her complete, dancing in front of her mirror until in a **far shot**, we see her in a large, fancy art deco bedroom with curved walls and glossy surfaces. The woman, Diana (Joan Crawford), is a self-centered "flapper," whose wild ways are contrasted with Ann (Anita Page), who, like Diana, is introduced by her legs, as she pulls on her stockings. Diana may be wild, but she holds a tender heart. In the midst of a wild party, filled with balloons, and dancing, she falls in love with the millionaire Ben (John Mack Brown). He stares at her legs and they exchange glances in what was already an essential part of the Hollywood style—the locking of glances indicating the transfer of potent emotion.

But the gaze is stolen by Ann, the fortune hunter, and the film devolves into a melodrama. At a crucial point, the location changes from art deco party scenes to a romantic ocean setting, where Diana and Ben talk about life and Diana's desire to capture all of it. Diana is a good girl at heart and refuses to make love with Ben. In an odd sequence, he "sees" two versions of Diana, one madly dancing, the other kissing him. He returns to the romantic seascape, this time with Ann, who convinces him that she wants a home and children. They embrace and a **dissolve** out from them indicates that, unlike the romantic interlude with Diana, Ben and Ann consummate their lovemaking.

Our Dancing Daughters is a melodrama with something of a social conscience. It wants to celebrate the wildness of the "roaring twenties" and condemn it at the same time. Ben and Ann marry and, of course, are unhappy. Ann cheats. At a drunken party Ann and Diana confront each other and, in a long, tight, tear-stained close-up, Ben and Diana proclaim their undying love. Conveniently—in melodrama coincidence and convenience push narrative in the direction it needs to go—Ann falls down the stairs and dies. Before the fall, there is a remarkable moment in which the drunken Ann, at the top of the stairs, looks down at the washerwomen below and proclaims (in an intertitle), "Women—Women—*working*!" She asks if they haven't any pretty daughters to help them; they return an unsmiling look, one shakes her head in pity. For an instant, the film recognizes the external world beyond its own frame, beyond the "roaring twenties" of movies and magazine articles, a world of poverty and hard work.

Our Dancing Daughters is typical in its mixture of sophistication, exploitation, eroticism, and melodramatic punishment and redemption. It allows us an amazed gaze at "liberated" women, free with their sexuality and often manipulating men and one another, and then assures us that too much liberation will lead to disaster and that there is an essential moral goodness in at least one of the women in the film. It is hardly unusual for film then and now to have things many ways at once.

IT

Diana is a flapper and has "It," a term invented by a writer of romance fiction, Elinor Glyn, who wrote the story on which the screenplay is based and appeared in a film called *It* (Clarence Badger, Josef von Sternberg, Famous Players-Lasky, Paramount, 1927). There are definitions of "It" throughout the film. An opening title defines "It" as "a quality possessed by some which draws all others with its magnetic force." Later in the film, Glyn herself appears to define her own term as "self-confidence and indifference as to whether you are pleasing or not." The film itself stars Clara Bow, a famous young player of the decade, called the "It" girl. In the film she plays a shop girl, poor but with a big heart. She looks after her roommate (Priscilla Bonner) and her roommate's baby. She goes to the Ritz to meet her boss's friend and, as in *Our Dancing Daughters*, the viewer is treated to a scene of her dressing, complete with close-ups of her legs. At the restaurant, there is a rapid **track** in to her boss (Cyrus Waltham), indicating

Clara Bow, the It girl in *It* (Clarence Badger, 1927).

that Betty Lou, the Clara Bow character, is immediately attracted to him. The camera movement is indicative of the chances that filmmakers were taking in the late silent period, unmooring the camera from its fixed position, putting a bit of dynamism into their compositions. The two characters exchange glances, and it is clear that they both have "It."

But "It" is not without its melodramatic complications. Lady social workers—a target of many a silent film—attempt to take away the roommate's baby, who Betty Lou has claimed as her own. The usual complications arise—the boss misunderstands Betty Lou's protection of the baby—and there is a climactic scene on the boss's yacht in which everyone falls in the ocean. Betty Lou is redeemed.

Once again, the film exemplifies certain trends in the developing Hollywood style, specifically the redemption of the central character. Joan Crawford in *Our Dancing Daughters* and Clara Bow in *It* are presented as objects of the audience's gaze; we are asked to look at them as erotic objects. They are also presented as women of the age—or at least the age as constructed in the popular media: newspapers, magazines, radio. These "flappers," according to the cultural discourse surrounding them, should be carefree, sexually liberated, and active partygoers. But the movies could not leave them at that. Partly as a result of the Production Code, partly as a result of a seemingly inescapable sentimentality that needed to discover a pure heart above the dancing legs, Betty Lou and Diane must reveal a caring, and, in Betty Lou's case, a nurturing side. *Our Dancing Daughters* goes so far as to propose two kinds of flappers, a fortune-hunting drunk and a carefree young lady who really wants to settle down.

WORLD WAR I

WINGS

Redemption and settling down have become the most conventional narrative solutions in film. No matter how outrageous a character's actions, or even a character's *character*, might be, in the end that character must understand the better part of his or her nature and find a domesticating solution to excessive behavior. This holds true even in the films of World War I made in the teens and 1920s. In these films, the war is often presented as an imposition on a love affair, even as filmmakers outdid themselves in representing the spectacle of battles and wartime destruction. It sometimes seems as if the war was fought for the affirmation of the romantic couple rather than the political turmoil of revolution, collapsing empires, and ancient border disputes.

Clara Bow makes her appearance in William Wellman's *Wings* (Paramount, Famous Players-Lasky, 1927) peering through a pair of bloomers hanging on a clothesline. The "It" girl has to be presented as an erotic character, even though it is not the character she will play in the course of the film. In fact, she bears a great deal of responsibility as a member of the ambulance corps. As Mary, Clara Bow is transformed from "It" to responsible, and *Wings* becomes a cautionary tale about the "roaring twenties," despite the fact that it is set in 1917. The film's spectacular aerial battles helped win it the first Academy Award for Best Picture. Its romantic tale, and the sacrifices of its leading characters in war and love, placed the battle sequences within familiar contexts. War's violence, at least in so many of the films about World War I made in the 1920s, is always tempered by familiar conventions that might calm audiences and perhaps make them forget the horrors of the past.

HEARTS OF THE WORLD

D. W. Griffith's *Hearts of the World* (D. W. Griffith Productions, Famous Players-Lasky, 1918), a film made in small part on location in Europe during wartime, announces itself with a title card that reads, "An old fashioned play with a new fashioned theme." It is an "old fashioned" melodrama that focuses on the agonized suffering of the two lovers, Griffith regulars, Lillian Gish, playing Marie, "The Girl," and John Harron as Douglas, "The Boy." The "new fashioned theme" is the war. The "old fashioned" **mise-en-scène** of the film is an idyllic French village, home to two American families, filmed with great visual delicacy, painterly in composition and lighting. But once battle commences, Griffith piles on atrocities. The boy is presumed dead in battle, and the girl wanders the battlefield clutching her wedding dress, falling asleep by his side in the open field and then wandering off again. She becomes enslaved to a Prussian soldier and almost raped. (Prussians were portrayed as monsters throughout popular culture during World War I.) The "old fashioned" melodrama wins out as The Girl and The Boy are reunited. She stabs a Prussian soldier threatening The Boy, while another young woman, the village waif, known as "The Little Disturber" (Dorothy Gish), throws a grenade at the oncoming Prussian mob. As in *Wings*, the women prove their heroism on a footing almost equal to their men.

THE BIG PARADE

The melodramatic urge cannot be overcome, even in a film like King Vidor's 1925 *The Big Parade* (MGM), which has some antiwar pretentions. Vidor is concerned with the pain inflicted by the war and the lessons it teaches. The film takes a somewhat distanced perspective, seeing war as both patriotic fervor and mass slaughter. It sees the troops as a massed parade of men as well a collection of individuals. The film focuses on Jim (John Gilbert), a privileged boy from the upper class, and the two friends he makes in the service, Slim (Karl Dane), a riveter, and Bull (Tom O'Brien), a barkeeper—the convention of representing a group of soldiers from a variety of backgrounds will be carried over into World War II films. The movie follows them from boot camp to battle, pausing to establish Jim's love for the French girl he meets in a long sequence in which he is wearing a barrel over his head—an example of what was already a Hollywood cliché, known as the "meet cute."

The cuteness and pleasantry of Jim's and Melisande's (Renée Adoré) courtship is viewed in a long medium **close-up** of the couple attempting to communicate with each other over the language barrier. This is an interesting attempt on Vidor's part to overcome the lack of audible dialogue, even while the conversation between the two characters is *about* dialogue—the fact that they don't understand each other. Vidor repeats this setup later, when the lovers discuss Jim's American sweetheart, Justyne (Claire Adams). The long **two shot** creates a sense of intimacy between the Jim and Melisande and the viewer, an intimacy that remains even when Jim is torn away by the war. Jim and Melisande attempt to hold on to each other, even at a distance. Caught in the rush of soldiers heading for the front, they spot each other, embrace, and Jim is pulled away and put in a truck. She clings to the truck as long as she can, dragged along until she falls. He throws his watch, his dog tag, and his shoe at her as parts of him she can hold on to. The loss of the shoe is prophetic of what is to come.

Once in the trenches, the violence of war, especially as it affects individuals, takes on another sort of intimacy. From the "big parade" of soldiers moving through the woods and fields, encountering the enemy, Vidor moves back to the three principles and their suffering in battle. As his friends in battle suffer, Jim gets absolutely hysterical with fear and anger, winding up shot in the leg in a foxhole with a wounded German, who looks ghastly with a death's grin. In another long two shot, Jim aids the dying soldier, giving him a cigarette in a sequence that, like the one with Jim and Melisande, emphasizes the pathos of lost communication. Vidor heightens the emotional temperature of the film by concentrating on Jim's ability to overcome his wartime misfortune. He is wounded twice and loses a leg as he tries to find his Melisande. The massive battles and the individual torments of war reduce the individual figuratively and literally. On his return home, he discovers that he has even lost his hometown sweetheart. Cradled in his mother's arms, in another long two shot, he is convinced to return to France to find Melisande. He does, and, back in France, from Melisande's **point of view**, we see him, a small figure, coming over the rim of a hill. Now with a prosthetic limb, he hobbles to his love, and the last two-shot of the film has them embrace.

The long two-shots of *The Big Parade* are a far cry from the static, frontal shots so common in the early years of film. There is a degree of intimacy that indicates that both filmmaker and audience were comfortable with a prolonged gaze at characters in deeply emotional states. And because of that intimate gaze, the melodrama of the film is moderated. There is, here, no need for exaggerated expression or gesture; or, more accurately, the extravagance of gesture is transferred to the battlefield, where large movements and individual agonies are used to represent the enormity of the war's grueling spectacle and pain.

7TH HEAVEN

Not all World War I films balanced out war and romance with such delicacy. In *The Four Horseman of the Apocalypse* (Rex Ingram, Metro Pictures, 1921), tango-dancing Rudolph Valentino must prove his worth in battle in a complex narrative in which different family members take different sides in the war. Charlie Chaplin's *Shoulder Arms* (Charles Chaplin Productions, First National Distributors, 1918) takes a comic look at life in the trenches, with the Tramp becoming a soldier and a hero, capturing the Kaiser himself—though his heroism turns out to be a dream. Frank Borzage's *7th Heaven* (Fox Film Corporation, 1927) reaches an epitome of romantic longing mixed with battle, as a lowly Parisian sewer cleaner, Chico (Charles Farrell), a poor working man, falls in love with a poor girl, Diane (Janet Gaynor), whom he saves from a sadomasochistic relationship with her sister, a drunken prostitute who beats her with a whip.

The entire film is made on studio sets that are marked in their artificiality, but suggestive enough to lend almost a fairy-tale quality to the images. There is a lightness to *7th Heaven* as well. These are particularly dark lives we are asked to look at, but Borzage and his players manage to express them with an understanding and even a tenderness of touch that renders them playful in the midst of their poverty—at least until the outbreak of the war. Before going off to battle, Chico, a nonbeliever, gives God "one more chance" and marries Diane by giving her a religious medallion that was given to him by the priest. He asks her to see him even when he's gone and to imagine a visit with her at the 11th hour of every morning. This would have been significant to contemporary audiences, who remembered that the war ended at the 11th hour of the 11th day of the 11th month, November 11, 1918.

The scenes of battle are as ferocious as the earlier scenes were fanciful. But the melodramatic turn is inevitable. Chico is blinded in the war, and it seems that he is lost to his love. But the fairy-tale aura of the film returns at its end. Everyone believes Chico dead; the priest comes to Diane with his medallion, and she loses hope and her faith, even as everyone celebrates the Armistice. But suddenly Chico is seen pushing through the crowd; he mounts the seven flights to their garret, seen in a **90-degree shot** looking down at him mounting the spiral staircase and appearing almost as an apparition to his adoring Diane (earlier, the camera had craned up seven flights as the lovers climbed to their garret). He feels his religion returning, promises her he will see again, and their embrace is bathed in heavenly light, the priest looking on.

The cauldron of World War I as represented in Frank Borzage's *7th Heaven* (1927).

Chico (Charles Farrell) climbs the staircase to reunite with his love in *7th Heaven.*

Made almost 10 years after the fact, the war fading from the memory of contemporary audiences, Borzage could turn the turmoil of battle into a romantic, quasi-religious fantasy of the war that remained in American memory. The film was honored with Academy Awards, and it remains a moving work, lightly marked by German expressionism, but even more with a lightness of emotional touch that makes its melodrama tolerable.

DEMILLE AND MELODRAMA

The delicacy and relative restraint of *7th Heaven* was somewhat unusual for silent cinema, even this late. Audiences and the filmmakers who served them still enjoyed blood and thunder melodrama, often with a large dollop of moralism that seemed to make the exaggerated emotions and gratuitous immorality of the characters acceptable. We have seen this at work in the "flapper" films, but it is nowhere more obvious than in the films of Cecil B. DeMille, a Hollywood pioneer who made films from 1914 to 1956. DeMille moved west in 1913 to be director general of Jesse L. Lasky's Feature Play Company, which would soon merge with Adolf Zukor's Famous Players Films Company and adopt the name of its distribution company to become Paramount Pictures. DeMille began his filmmaking career with a Western, *The Squaw Man* (Famous Players-Lasky, 1914), and, to satisfy Zukor's ideal of making high-class entertainments to lure in a more culturally substantial audience, directed the opera *Carmen* in 1915 (Famous Players-Lasky). It is a silent opera, starring a famous opera singer of the day. It sounds (or rather doesn't sound) ludicrous to us today, but, accompanied by an orchestra when projected in large venues, the film was quite successful. Successful enough that someone indeed found it ludicrous: Charlie Chaplin immediately filmed a parody, *A Burlesque on Carmen* (Essanay Film Manufacturing Co., 1916).

THE CHEAT AND *MANSLAUGHTER*

The fact is that DeMille is easy to parody. Many of his silent films are salacious and moralistic at the same time. He knew well how to please an increasingly sophisticated audience with audacious movies such as *The Cheat* (Paramount, 1915), in which a white woman (Fannie Ward) is actually branded by her would-be Asian lover (Sessue Hayakawa). But this audaciousness always comes with the price of redemption. His flaunting of the assumed excesses of the Jazz Age is, in the end, countered by the humiliation and contrition of the offenders. In *Manslaughter* (Paramount, 1922), the rich party girl Lydia (Leatrice Joy) assures us and her disapproving boyfriend that "modern girls don't sit by the fire and knit." He is a district attorney and condemns the excesses of "1922—with its debauches of Speed, and carelessness of Human life. . . ." He finds that Lydia's parties (at one such, everyone jumps around on pogo sticks) are like Roman bacchanals, and this gives DeMille the excuse to create a tableaux of a Roman bacchanal with many drunken revelers in togas writhing about until, exhausted, they lie around as the Goths enter the hall to take over the Empire.

None of this is intentionally tongue in cheek, and as the film proceeds its narrative gets quite complex. Its heroine goes to jail for killing a policeman; her boyfriend tries to defend her. But redemption is always at hand. Her maid, who winds up in jail with her, teaches Lydia morality and common sense. O'Bannon (Thomas Meighan), stricken with guilt over prosecuting his beloved, quits his job and becomes a drunkard, going into a speakeasy to buy illicit booze. Lydia comes out of jail a changed woman and brings O'Bannon back to his senses. He even reaches a point where he is ready to run for governor, but he must give it up because of Lydia's past as a convict.

THE TEN COMMANDMENTS

These wild swings of events, of coincidences and changes in fortune and even personality, are typical of melodrama, where the outrageous and improbable are made to appear commonplace. DeMille was not the only director of the period to indulge in these exaggerations, but the ways in which he intertwined his melodramas with religiosity and morality, while not unique, were certainly a trademark. His lighting style as well was noted as a departure from the usual high-key lighting of the time. He employed shadow and a painterly style that his production company advertised as "Rembrandt lighting."[1]

But the formal elements of DeMille's films are not as complex as their stories, and his stories are complex to the point of being absurd. DeMille expanded the lurid aspects of melodrama, but not the way melodrama is expressed. His camera setups are frontal and stationary, his compositions wide. He likes to emphasize small and large groups rather than close-ups and often allows his actors to indulge in big melodramatic gestures common to an earlier period.

But despite this, DeMille always had his eye on the present and the mood of the moviegoers he wanted to reach and uplift. His first attempt at *The Ten Commandments* (Paramount, 1923; he remade it in 1956) announces its timeliness in the first title card: "Our modern world," it claims, has "laughed at the Ten Commandments as OLD FASHIONED. Then, through the laughter, came the shattering thunder of the World War. And now a blood-drenched, bitter world—no longer laughing—cries for a way out."

The way out for DeMille was to link biblical spectacle with a modern day story. The first part of the film is painted on a broad canvas—indeed painted in color: DeMille used a hand-tinting process on some of the sequences.[2] The Jews enslaved in Egypt, the parting of the Red Sea, Moses receiving the commandments, the worship of the golden calf, and, always, writhing bodies, are set as trademarks of DeMille's representation of the Old Testament. The modern day story is somewhat more restrained and linked more to the New Testament than the Old. It is a by now familiar tale of sin and redemption, this time focused on a male character, a builder, Dan (Rod La Rocque), who disrespects the Bible and his religious mother (Edythe Chapman). He mocks both by pretending to worship a gold coin. He builds a church with adulterated concrete, which fails, bringing down the building on his mother. Dan's brother, John (Richard Dix), is—significantly, obviously—a carpenter, who tries to set Dan on the right path. John takes in a homeless woman, Mary Leatrice Joy, but she falls for Dan and marries him, rapidly assuming his irreligious ways and becoming an "It" girl: "Nobody believes in these Commandment things nowadays—and I think Elinor Glyn's a lot more interesting!"

Money, dancing, excitement, acquiring "It" are, according to DeMille, the sins of the modern world of the 1920s, and they lead to worse excesses. Woven into the modern story, running parallel with Dan's cost-cutting and disastrous building methods, is a strand of Orientalism that DeMille had already toyed with in *The Cheat* and that infuses the orgy sequences in *Manslaughter* and Egyptian sequence of *The Ten Commandments*. Orientalism involves a distorted and exaggerated view of Asian or Middle-Eastern culture, usually emphasizing an imagined sexuality that is strange and destructive. It is an ideology of the "Other," in which the Asian, Arab, or Persian is a figure of strangeness, of physical, often sexual threat.[3] In the case of *The Ten Commandments*, it appears when Dan smuggles inferior material from Asia for the church he builds. Slicing out of a sack of this material is a woman with leprosy. We see her sinuous hands, pushing aside the sack as she emerges from the dark like a serpent. It is the most arresting image in the film. Somehow, she represents the infection of immorality that is eating away at Western culture. What is interesting is that DeMille and his screenwriter, Jeanie MacPherson, cannot themselves take all of this with total seriousness. On a few occasions, there is a cut to a newspaper with a story about the search for the leprous woman. The newspaper item states that the search is "almost worthy of a movie plot"—a bit of reflexive self-commentary that winks at the viewer, seeming to acknowledge that the filmmakers might just have been aware of how ludicrous their story is. (Another wink occurs a bit later when Dan confronts his wife, demanding that she stay with him, even though he is a murderer. "You're branded, the same as I am," he says, the reference going back to the infamous branding scene in *The Cheat*.) Redemption comes, as it must, when evil is destroyed and a modern day Jesus, in the form of John the Carpenter, brings Mary to the Bible. The film ends with a tableau of Christ curing a leper and Mary, feeling cleansed, resting on John's knee.

This seems ludicrous today, but the film was a big success in 1924, and audiences took it very seriously. One newspaper reported:

> At several of the performances hundreds were turned away. The enthusiasm is such as has never been witnessed before for the so-called silent drama, with the possible exception of "The Birth of the Nation."
>
> The hurricane of emotions—awe, horror, majesty, reverence, fear, hope, exultation, mirth, sex feeling, covetousness, adventure, thrill, jealousy, love and hate, worship and spiritual passion—is unparalled in its power and complexity.[4]

The elements of self-parody that seem obvious to a modern viewer and create a kind of leavening for

Dan (Rod La Rocque) at the knee of the leprous woman from the Far East (Nita Naldi) in the modern sequence of Cecil B. De Mille's 1923 version of *The Ten Commandments.*

the absurdity of the film's plot were apparently invisible to contemporary audiences. Or if visible, they did not detract from audience response. What appears to us as overblown spectacle and melodramatics that were already going out of fashion by the mid-1920s were accepted by a contemporary audience as expressions of religious and moral passion. Some modern critics find praise for DeMille's formal and technical prowess, illustrated, for instance, by the shot in which Mary ascends in an elevator to the top of John's construction site, the movement photographed from her point of view. And there is that extraordinarily effective sequence in which the leprous Sally Lung (Nita Naldi) uses her sinuous hands to slice her way out of a sack.

Sumiko Higashi, in her book-length study of DeMille's silent films, points to the exaggerations and downright corniness of the modern section of *The Ten Commandments.* She indicates how the culture in which DeMille's films had thrived was changing in the late 1920s." . . . The antimodernist tradition that DeMille represented was ultimately subverted by its internal contradictions, but its legacy of spectacle as the ultimate form of commodification still reverberates in today's postmodern culture."[5] DeMille had, early in his career, supplanted D. W. Griffith because he struck a chord with contemporary audiences. But his excessive moralizing split audiences who had themselves fragmented into different religious affiliations. It is difficult to understand, from our perspective, the way audiences responded to films that, in our cultural milieu, appear somewhat ludicrous. But at the same time, we must admit that contemporary films still moralize, are still largely conservative in their cultural view, and in many instances, depend on spectacle to hold our attention. Steven Spielberg's science fiction films, and films that depend on large digital effects, are heirs to DeMille. At one point in *Close Encounters of the Third Kind* (Spielberg, Columbia, EMI Films, Julia Phillips and Michael Phillips Productions, 1977), the characters are watching on television the 1956 version of DeMille's *The Ten Commandments.*

THE WOMEN

ALICE GUY BLACHÉ AND LOIS WEBER

Women held a number of important positions in pre-sound film. There were prominent writers: Jeanie MacPherson, who wrote scripts for DeMille; June Mathis, who wrote some of Rudolph Valentino's movies and did the screen adaptation for Erich von Stroheim's *Greed.* Women were editors, and there were even a few women cinematographers. And, of course, there were the actresses, who won audiences' hearts and became the major attractions of viewers to film. But what of directors? There were up to 30 women directors during the silent period. Among the most famous of these were Alice Guy Blaché and Lois Weber, and another, who spanned the movement from silent to sound, Dorothy Arzner. And then there were none until the 1950s, when actress Ida Lupino became a director for a short period of time.[6]

MATRIMONY'S SPEED LIMIT

Alice Guy Blaché is considered the first woman director and the first woman to run a movie studio. She began her work in France in 1896 and then came to the United States, where she wrote, directed, or produced over 1,000 films until 1920. She even experimented with synchronized sound before it became the norm in 1927, and in the course of her career directed a number of genres. One of her short films, *Matrimony's Speed Limit* (Solax Film Corporation, 1913), takes up and reverses an idea that Buster Keaton would use 12 years later. A young man gets a telegram telling him that he will come into a fortune if he marries by noon. In Keaton's case, he is pursued by dozens of women. In Blaché's film, the young man pursues the various women he meets, including—in a racist moment all too common at the time—an African American woman, from whom he flees. He finally finds his fiancée, and they are married in the back of a car while pursued by a steam roller—perhaps an indication of trouble to come.

THE BLOT AND TOO WISE WIVES

Lois Weber was another talented and prolific filmmaker, something of an anti-DeMille in that she focused on contemporary issues in a rather calm and restrained style. She began her career working for Paramount and Universal, and in 1917 formed her own production company. As befitted a strong female director, her films focused on women and on pressing social issues. She made films about abortion and birth control, and about hypocritical religiosity. *The Blot* (Lois Weber Productions, 1921) is a film that dramatizes the poverty that results from the low salary paid to college professors, perhaps the only film to take up an issue affecting this rather small part of the population. *Too Wise Wives* (Lois Weber Productions, 1921) starts with a couple walking into the sunset, the conventional ending of a romantic melodrama. But the film is in fact an interrogation of romance and married love. Two women work their marriages in different ways. One, Mrs. David (Claire Windsor), tries too hard to please her husband (Louis Calhern), "the martyred kind of wife who lives only for her home and husband." The other, Sara (Mona Lisa), is a bad housekeeper. She calculates ways to please her own husband while scheming to capture Mrs. David's. All of this is filmed, quite simply, keeping the women central to the mise-en-scène and using intertitles that are mostly descriptive and informative rather than transcribing dialogue. Weber speaks directly to the viewer through her intertitles, in a genial, gentle, sometimes quietly moralizing, sometimes bemused tone. When the women admire each other's clothing, an intertitle reads "(As women will!)."

The film does not end on a feminist note, at least by today's standards. The wives learn lessons about marriage and the pleasure that comes from a well-tuned domesticity. The "woman's touch" of Lois Weber is felt through the gentleness of her approach and the simplicity of her style. Her films addressed a broad range of issues left untouched by most filmmakers. She was a potent figure in her time, which did not survive the coming of sound. Her and Blaché's careers indicate that, despite the growing control of the male-dominated studio system, there was room for women to work, though two women out of dozens of male filmmakers is hardly impressive. The sad fact is that even today few women are offered the chance to direct a film. Between these two women and the 1950s, there were, as I noted, only two more active women directors: Dorothy Arzner from the 1930s through the early 1940s and Ida Lupino in the 1950s. We will return to this problem in Chapter 20, but we need to keep in mind that issues of gender are either at the forefront or in the background of almost any film we see. We must keep in mind as well that American film (like American culture) is largely male dominated, and that this has a real effect on what we see.

ERICH VON STROHEIM

We have briefly touched on the career of one filmmaker, Erich von Stroheim, who was born in Austria, and who had been around Hollywood since 1913. He worked for a time for D. W. Griffith and appeared in small roles in *The Birth of a Nation*, *Intolerance*, and *Hearts of the World*. He played in other directors' films as well, sometimes as a World War I German army officer, gaining him the title "the man you love to hate." But it was through the films he directed, in which he often played a leading role, that von Stroheim's talent is best on display. These were often troubled productions, since von Stroheim was obsessive about detail and rather less obsessive about budget and schedule. The debacle surrounding his film *Greed* (MGM, 1924), which we discussed in Chapter 2, stands as an object lesson to any filmmaker about the power of the studio and its ability to take over a director's work. However, *Greed*, even in its truncated version, stands as one of the monumental films of the silent period, more important, in certain respects, than *The Birth of a Nation*.

Most of von Stroheim's films take place in a small, exotic European country, peopled by aristocrats and army officers, with von Stroheim himself playing a cad, who uses women to bad advantage. These films are anti-melodramas: they play against sentimentality and are often perverse and downright ugly in their portrayal of unpleasant people doing unpleasant things to each other. Unlike the general run of silent melodramas, von Stroheim's work, with the exception of *Greed*, is alien in place and format, and the characters he plays are arrogant, sour, and sadistic. His hair close cropped, he dresses up in stiff, high-collared uniforms, somewhat campy and repulsive. He loved to play the anti-hero, drinking ox blood for breakfast, seducing wives and daughters, and, in *Foolish Wives* (Universal, 1922), getting killed for his pains and stuffed down a sewer. *Foolish Wives* was advertised as "The Most Wonderful Picture in America. Written and Directed by von Stroheim, 'The Man You Will Love to Hate.'" It seems to have fared fairly well in a year of major melodramas like D. W. Griffith's *Orphans of the Storm*, which indicates that audiences, then and now, were hardly monolithic in their tastes.

But, as we have seen in our discussion of DeMille, it is notoriously difficult to gauge then or now how audiences respond to a film. We can be more accurate in gauging how von Stroheim reacted to the reigning melodramatic structures of the 1920s. He deliberately set out to sabotage them and, in effect, to swing his camera around to view a world in which morality is skewed, where people act upon their own worst instincts, and where cruelty and deceit are at work among sadomasochistic characters. With the possible exception of *The Wedding March* (Paramount Famous Lasky Corp., 1928), where some sentiment creeps in—von Stroheim's stiff-necked soldier, Nikki, is promised to a physically disabled woman (Zazu Pitts), while his true love (Fay Wray) is carried off by an abusive butcher (Matthew Betz)—von Stroheim keeps the emotional temperature low. As a corrective to the melodramas of the period, they introduce into film the naturalism school that was a mark of literary fiction at the turn of the 20th century.

NATURALISM REVISITED

In the chapter on D. W. Griffith, we briefly discussed the naturalism movement in literature, a movement of concentrated realism that focused on the underbelly of life. Its subjects were poor or lower-middle-class characters fated to do damage to one another in a futile attempt to live out a blighted life in blighted surroundings. The majority of von Stroheim's films, with their fake aristocrats and stiff-necked soldiers seducing unsophisticated women in middle-European countries, don't quite fit the naturalist mode, though their focus on sadomasochistic behavior comes close. It is unsurprising, given his aesthetic proclivities, that von Stroheim would at a crucial point in his career turn to an undisputed naturalist source, Frank Norris's 1899 novel of cruelty, avarice, and murder in San Francisco, *McTeague*.

GREED

He was so taken by the gritty malevolence of Norris's work that he wanted to film it almost page by page. The result was a film—the screen adaptation and dialogue of which was written by June Mathis—that ran over 8 hours. MGM would not, indeed could not distribute it at that length. Under Irving Thalberg's supervision, it was cut to 2 hours, eliminating subplots and much detail. The cut footage has never been found, though there are stills that indicate what that footage contained. Even in its truncated form, the film has enormous power. The story of a poor, working-class, unlicensed dentist, McTeague (Gibson Rowland), who marries and murders a psychotically miserly woman is a far cry from the high-society melodramas of *It* and *Our Dancing Daughters* and contains none of the heavy-handed moralizing of DeMille's spectacles or the rural simplicities of D. W. Griffith. Von Stroheim casts a cold eye on his characters, viewing them most often in a **midshot** against their surroundings, themselves actual locations in San Francisco and, in its unsettling conclusion, Death Valley.

His characters, like their originals in Norris's novel, have low expectations. "Let's go over and sit on the sewer," McTeague's beloved Trina (Zazu Pitts) suggests when they meet for a date. And so they do, amid the garbage and dead rats along an industrial river bank. When they marry, a funeral procession is seen passing by through the window, a quiet, if not quite subtle, visual anticipation of the outcome of their marriage. McTeague is a coarse but well-meaning oaf at the start. He is beaten down by Trina's obsessive-compulsive miserliness—at one point she goes to bed and covers herself with her hoarded coins—which puts them into poverty, despite the money they have won in the lottery (they are informed of their winnings by a man with a horrible sore on his face). They are further ruined by Mac's friend Marcus (Jean Hersholt), who, jealous of their marriage and fortune, denounces Mac to the authorities so that he loses his dental practice.

The downward spiral of these characters is extreme, though they don't fall far from where they begin. The extremity lies in the intensity of their fall caused by Trina's greed and Mac losing his job. She buys rotten meat for their dinner. Mac becomes a drunkard, seething with anger and resentment. He bites her hand and, finally, kills her in the schoolhouse where she cleans rooms. The grueling conclusion of the film has Mac and Marcus doing battle with each other in the desert of Death Valley. McTeague beats Marcus to death and, in the process, finds himself handcuffed to the body. In the closing shots of the film, Mac frees the canary that he has been carrying around with him in its cage, first clutching the bird in his bloody hand. When he releases it, it falls dead on his empty canteen. The film ends with a **far shot** of McTeague, held fast to Marcus's body, and a dead mule in the endless stretch of desert.

In retrospect, it is amazing that MGM released this film at all. Presumably, they hoped that they might recoup some of its expense. But the film was

The power of location shooting. McTeague (Gibson Rowland) and Trina (Zazu Pitts) have a date by going to sit on the sewer. *Greed* (Erich von Stroheim, 1924).

a commercial failure, which is no surprise. Its unremittingly bleak view of human behavior is pretty strong even by today's standards. After *Greed*, von Stroheim returned to his middle-European milieu and his character of stiff-necked princes and soldiers. He continued having struggles with his studios and barely survived the coming of sound as a director. He finished his career as an actor, most famously as a film director named Max Von Mayerling in Billy Wilder's *Sunset Boulevard* (Paramount, 1950)—a film in which Cecil B. DeMille also makes an appearance.

I noted earlier that *Greed* is a more important film of the silent period than *The Birth of a Nation*. This is because the problems of its production are a lesson about the growing power of the studios and the **producer system** of filmmaking that is the Hollywood norm. But more, because it is one of the only noncomedic films to shed the reigning melodramatic conventions of the time, it stands as a model for filmmaking that goes against the grain, against the Production Code, against audience expectations. There are few films that are like *Greed*, but there *are* films made in its spirit of defiance and imagination. Von Stroheim was a brave filmmaker and paid for that bravery. His films stand as an example that the Hollywood style was not monolithic, that at least one filmmaker could take an artistic stand against it.

THE EUROPEAN INFLUENCE

From the start, American film was enormously popular the world over. Also from the start, it was subject to influence from film abroad. Films of the Lumière Brothers (we discussed *The Arrival of a Train at the Ciotat Station* earlier) and the magician Georges Méliès were popular in the United States during the pre-studio era. But by far, the greatest influence on American cinema came from Germany. Even before the rise of fascism in Germany that led to the emigration of German filmmakers to the United States, their experiments in mise-en-scène, acting, and narrative techniques were beginning to have an effect on some American filmmakers.

EXPRESSIONISM

Erich von Stroheim came to Hollywood early on, and his Germanic roots developed into his imaginary worlds of Prussian soldiers and fake aristocrats, preying on innocent Americans. But there is another Germanic influence that shows up in von Stroheim's work. There are some strange images in *Greed*, a film that otherwise takes a rather cold and almost objective gaze at its miserable characters. To signify Trina's soul-destroying avarice, von Stroheim cuts in images of grotesquely elongated arms, their hands playing with coins. An image of hands toying with McTeague and Marcus occurs during their dance of death in the desert. Trina's murder takes place in a dark space, penetrated by shafts of light. These images owe something to a movement in the arts that flourished right after World War I and that had an enormous influence on American film: German expressionism. Expressionism can be found in painting and theater, in literature and film of the time. But it is through film that it passed on its most enduring features.

THE CABINET OF DR. CALIGARI

Expressionism is marked by the creation of a dark, shadowy, uncomfortable mise-en-scène that reflects the disturbed state of mind of the characters. The expressionist world collapses onto its characters, confining them in states of madness or extreme threat. In its earliest appearance in Germany, in films like Robert Wiene's *The Cabinet of Dr. Caligari* (1920), the mise-en-scène is entirely artificial, created in the studio. Sets are built off kilter, distorted and angular. Light and shadows are literally painted on the set rather than coming from actual lights. Characters scuttle around like insects. *Caligari* is a dream film, in which the inmates in an asylum imagine the evil Caligari (Werner Krauss) and his Frankenstein-like monster Cesare (Conrad Veidt, who went on to play the German Major Strasser in *Casablanca*), terrorizing a town.

An early example of the horror film genre, *Caligari* set the conventions for a lasting influence on cinema, most notably in the United States. This influence came not only from American filmmakers watching German films but also from a stream of German filmmakers who fled Germany after the Nazis took over. Directors such as Fritz Lang, Billy Wilder, and Douglas Sirk made an important mark on American film in the 1930s, 40s, and 50s. One German filmmaker, F. W. Murnau, who came over before the Nazi

The expressionist mise-en-scène: distorted buildings in a dreamscape as the monster carries off the woman In *The Cabinet of Dr. Caligari* (Robert Weine, 1920).

takeover, made four films in the United States: *Sunrise: A Tale of Two Humans* (Fox Film Corp., 1927), *4 Devils* (Fox, 1928, now lost), *City Girl* (Fox, 1930), and *Tabu: A Story of the South Seas* (Murnau-Flaherty Productions, Paramount, 1931). Of these, *Sunrise* is the most important film and one of the glories of the late silent period.

MURNAU AND *SUNRISE*

F. W. Murnau was an heir to the expressionist movement. He made the very first Dracula movie, *Nosferatu*, in 1922, a film that had a profound influence on the first American Dracula film, made by Universal in 1931 (*Dracula*, Tod Browning), which in turn set off a seemingly unending series of films playing variations on the blood-sucking undead. Murnau made other films in Germany, most notably *The Last Laugh* (*Der letzte Mann*, 1924), about a doorman of a fancy hotel who loses his job and his self-esteem, until he is left a fortune. It is a study in the use of shadow and moving camera to create mood and define character. A commercial failure in the United States, *The Last Laugh* was a very important film in Hollywood, whose filmmakers were intrigued by its style. It appeared at a time when William Fox was anxious to add some artistic class to the films his company was making. He invited Murnau and allowed him a great amount of freedom and a considerable budget. Fox had already promoted the work of his talented directors. Frank Borzage's *7th Heaven*, which appeared the same year as *Sunrise* and is in some ways a similar film, demonstrates the studio's desire to experiment with styles and subjects that were more adventurous than the usual run of silent melodramas. Murnau's work would burnish that desire to experiment.

Sunrise: A Song of Two Humans is a transnational film. Its geographical location is unstated. The characters have only generalized names—the Man (George O'Brien), the Wife (Janet Gaynor), the Woman of the City (Margaret Livingston). The narrative itself is generalized and deceptively simple. The film takes place in an unnamed countryside and in an unnamed city. In the country, a simple peasant couple are broken up by the Man's love for the Woman of the City, a Vamp, dressed in black, who insinuates herself into this garden of Eden, almost convincing the man to drown his wife. What follows is an imaginative journey of the Man and the Wife into a fantastic city, where they renew their love. Few films better indicate the difference between a story abstracted from the film—its plot—and what actually goes on in the mise-en-scène of the film itself. The world of *Sunrise* is a self-contained fantasy created entirely in the studio. By means of lighting and shadow and a massive amount of special effects, Murnau defines his characters by the artfully created world that surrounds them. There are some overtly expressionist effects (the scenario of the film was written by *The Cabinet of Dr. Caligari*'s Carl Mayer). The Woman of the City upsets the calm of the simple country life, and Murnau visualizes this by showing a peasant couple—perhaps the Wife's mother and father—sitting at a table that is tilted almost 45 degrees against the horizontal of the composition, literally visualizing a world set off kilter. When the woman enters the room, she makes the elderly lady clean her shoes. When she leaves to call on the Man, Murnau follows her in the dark with a long, leisurely **tracking shot**. They meet in the depths of the country, near a swamp. The camera follows the man as he walks by a gate, tracks right and then left as he comes to another gate and climbs it; he moves toward the camera, which then moves away from him, **pans** to the left, moves through some foliage, revealing the Woman of the City standing with a full moon (created by a studio spotlight); the camera holds on her as she puts on her makeup until the Man reenters the frame from the left; they embrace.

In a 1 minute and 28 second shot, Murnau indicates just how far film had come from the simple one-take setup of a simple scene that was the norm in the early silent era. His mobile camera and use of shadow and light go beyond their expressionist roots to indicate a vigorous cinematic imagination and an ability to tell a story with a minimum of intertitles and a maximum of lyrical, visual sophistication. Murnau's imaginative vision grows with each successive sequence, some of which approach what we would today call "magical realism." When the Man and wife ride the trolley to the City, a trip that covers many miles in under a minute, the landscape outside subtly and fantastically turns from rural to urban. The City itself is a complex, studio-made series of sets using **matte paintings**, **forced perspective**, double exposures, and other optical tricks—including small people placed in the background to create a sense of a receding space. Here a series of comic adventures bring the couple back together until, on the return to the country, the Wife is feared drowned in a storm. The mix of comedy and melodrama is nicely balanced, and the redemption of the Man is expressed in the context of the fantasy of a simple life regained.

In the end, *Sunrise* is a triumph of form over content. The story of lust, temptation, attempted murder, reconciliation, and redemption is a constant over the course of American film's history and a staple of silent film, as we have seen. Murnau reimagines the narrative through an expressionist mise-en-scène and an abstraction of the narrative into general, even

The Man and The Wife (George O'Brien and Janet Gaynor) ride the trolley to the fantastic city of *Sunrise* (F. W. Murnau, 1927).

universal principles. Perhaps too general and abstract for contemporary audiences, the film's critical success was not matched by a commercial one. It won three Academy Awards, for its actress, Janet Gaynor, its cinematographers, Charles Rosher and Karl Struss, and for "Best Picture, Unique and Artistic Production," the only such Academy Award ever given. William Wellman's World War I fighter pilot film, *Wings*, won the award for best picture. Four years later, Murnau died in a car crash. He never again achieved the imaginative vision of *Sunrise*.

THE END OF THE SILENT ERA

In his *New York Times* review of *Sunrise*, on September 24, 1927, Mordaunt Hall noted that before the film, there were some short subjects with sound, including an address by the Italian Fascist leader, Benito Mussolini, saluting "the noble Government of the United States." Mussolini would soon join with Hitler in a war against the rest of Europe and later the United States. This historical incongruity notwithstanding, it is important to note that the studios were experimenting with sound, trying it out, adding, as Fox did with the release of *Sunrise*, a **music and sound effects track** to their new films. There were numerous short films that had synchronized sound tracks. Warner Bros.' *The Jazz Singer* (Alan Crosland, 1927), usually credited as the first feature film with spoken dialogue, premiered in New York just a month before *Sunrise*. The silent film was silenced by sound.

SELECTED FILMOGRAPHY

Matrimony's Speed Limit, dir. Alice Guy Blaché, Solax Film Company, 1913.
The Squaw Man, dir. Cecil B. Demille, Famous Players-Lasky, 1914.
The Cheat, dir. Cecil B. Demille, Paramount, 1915.
Hearts of the World, dir. D. W. Griffith, D. W. Griffith Productions, Famous Players-Lasky, 1918.
The Cabinet of Dr. Caligari, dir. Robert Weine, Germany, 1920.
The Blot, dir. Lois Weber, Lois Weber Productions, 1921.
Too Wise Wives, dir. Lois Weber, Lois Weber Productions, 1921.
Nosferatu, dir. F. W. Murnau, Germany, 1922.
Manslaughter, dir. Cecil B. DeMille, Paramount, 1922.
Foolish Wives, dir. Erich von Stroheim, Universal, 1922.
The Ten Commandments, dir. Cecil B. DeMille, Paramount, 1923, 1956.
The Last Laugh, dir. F. W. Murnau, Germany, 1924.
The Big Parade, dir. King Vidor, MGM, 1925.
It, dir. Clarence Badger, Josef von Sternberg, Paramount, Famous Players-Lasky, 1927.
7th Heaven, dir. Frank Borzage, Fox Film Corp., 1927.
Wings, dir. William A. Wellman, Paramount, Famous Players-Lasky, 1927.
Greed, dir. Erich von Stroheim, MGM, 1924.
Sunrise, dir. F. W. Murnau, Fox Film Corp., 1927.
Our Dancing Daughters, dir. Harry Beaumont, MGM, 1928.
The Wedding March, dir. Erich von Stroheim, Paramount,1928.

SUGGESTIONS FOR FURTHER READING

Leslie Midkiff DeBauche, *Reel Patriotism: The Movies and World War I* (Madison, WI: University of Wisconsin Press, 1997).
Lotte Eisner, *The Haunted Screen*, trans. Roger Greaves (Berkeley, CA: University of California Press, 1969).
———, *Murnau* (Berkeley, CA: University of California Press, 1973).
Paul Fussell, *The Great War and Modern Memory* (New York, NY: Oxford University Press, 2000).
Sumiko Higashi, *Cecil B. DeMille and American Culture: The Silent Era* (Berkeley, CA: University of California Press, 1994).
Michael T. Isenberg, *War on Film: The American Cinema and World War I, 1914–1941* (Rutherford, NJ: Fairleigh Dickenson University Press, 1981).
Richard Koszarski, *The Man You Loved to Hate: Erich von Stroheim and Hollywood* (New York, NY: Oxford University Press, 1983).
Arthur Lennig, *Stroheim* (Lexington, KY: University Press of Kentucky, 2000).
Edward Said, *Orientalism* (New York: Vintage Books, 2003).
Anthony Slide, *Lois Weber: The Director Who Lost Her Way in History* (Westport, CT: Greenwood Press, 1996).

Herman G. Weinberg, *Stroheim: A Pictorial History of His Nine Films* (New York, NY: Dover Publications, 1975).

NOTES

1. Sumiko Higashi, *Cecil B. DeMille and American Culture: The Silent Era* (Berkeley, CA: University of California Press, 1994), 3.
2. See Higashi, 184–185.
3. The best study of Orientalism is Edward Said's *Orientalism* (New York: Vintage Books, 2003).
4. John J. Daly, "'Ten Commandments' Starts Second Week at National," *The Washington Post*, Oct. 5, 1924, 10.
5. Higashi, 188, 191, 194.
6. Information on women in early film, on Alice Guy Blaché and Lois Weber, is from Anthony Slide, *Lois Weber: The Director Who Lost Her Way in History* (Westport, CT: Greenwood Press, 1996).

CHAPTER 7

THE COMING OF SOUND (1927–1931)

Wait a minute . . . Wait a minute. You ain't heard nothin' yet!

—AL JOLSON, *The Jazz Singer*

The advent of sound caused the most radical change in the cultures of American film since the first strip of images ran through Edison's Kinetoscope. The way films were made changed; the ways audience responded to them changed; the stories they told changed.

AFTER READING THIS CHAPTER, YOU SHOULD UNDERSTAND:

- The early experiments in sound recording.
- The relationship between aesthetics and technique.
- How blackface played a role in early sound film.
- How sound created new film genres.

YOU SHOULD BE ABLE TO:

- Consider the change in narrative and acting styles after the coming of sound.
- Ask whether silent film had run its course by the coming of sound.
- Discuss your own response to silent vs. sound film.

EARLY TECHNOLOGIES OF SOUND

The conventional wisdom is that sound film began with *The Jazz Singer* (Alan Crosland, Warner Bros., 1927). As so often in the history of the film, the conventional wisdom is wrong. Sound and film went together in a variety of ways before the popular entertainer, Al Jolson, uttered his famous words. Live piano or orchestral accompaniment was almost universal in the exhibition of silent films. In some venues, there were explainers, who talked the audience through a film. Sometimes, actors would stand behind the screen and speak dialogue for the characters who were pantomiming on it. Edison hoped from the start that he could synchronize recorded sound with the moving image, that film would in fact be an adjunct to his phonograph. Into the 1920s, his laboratory experimented, unsuccessfully, with connecting sound and image. Even earlier, in 1907, the French production company headed by Herbert Blaché and Alice Guy Blaché experimented with a mechanically amplified system called the chronophone.[1]

The problem for Blaché, Edison, and the other scientists and inventors was twofold: how to synchronize sound and image so that there was no lag between one and the other, and how to amplify the sound so that it would efficiently and without distortion fill an auditorium. The last problem was solved early on with invention of the vacuum tube, a device in which an electronic signal was bumped up in power as it passed through a grid in a gas-filled container. The vacuum tube had many inventors and it made radio possible. One of its inventors, Lee De Forest, an important radio pioneer, took an active interest in film sound, promoting the sound on film technology.

The problem of synchronization was solved in two ways: sound on film and sound on disc. Like so many of the other technologies that brought in the talkies, sound on film had many fathers, going as far back as the Edison laboratories at the turn of the 19th century and the Biograph Company. Two varieties of sound on film—**optical tracks**—were developed, one called "variable density," the other "variable area." The technological differences are less important (the variable area optical track became the dominant technology) than the often complicated jockeying for position that went on between the various stakeholders in the technologies. General Electric went into competition with Western Electric while RCA held the patents on the vacuum tube amplification processes. Western Electric was also experimenting with sound on disc.

William Fox adopted a version of sound on film for his Fox Movietone newsreels, and we have noted the appearance of the Italian dictator, Benito Mussolini, speaking in a Fox newsreel that accompanied *Sunrise,* a silent film with a music and sound effects track in 1927. Fox was not only interested in fascists. The Irish playwright George Bernard Shaw made an appearance and talked on film, as did Charles Lindbergh after his famous flight from Long Island to Paris (Fox recorded the takeoff from Long Island as well). The newsreel was an important part of the filmgoing experience well into the 1950s, and the early addition of sound made it a lively supplement to newspapers and more vital than radio, which at the time was restricted in the depth of news reporting it was permitted to broadcast so as not to compete with newspapers.[2]

Fox's sound on film system did not prevail in the early sound period. The Western Electric Company and AT&T pushed their sound on disc technology, and Warner Bros.—in the 1920s a relatively small studio, whose fortune came largely from films starring the dog Rin Tin Tin—decided to make a push for expansion by adopting Western Electric's sound on disc. They purchased the Vitagraph studio in New York, changed its name to Vitaphone, and began sound film production in 1926. They made short films of vaudeville acts, singers, comics, and orchestral music, both serious and popular. The stage and vaudeville star, Al Jolson, was especially popular in *A Plantation Act*, a short film where he not only sang in blackface but also delivered a few lines of dialogue. Early in 1927, Warners released a costume drama/action film, *Don Juan* (Alan Crosland), starring a famous stage performer, John Barrymore. The film had a full orchestral score and sound effects—especially the sounds of swordplay. Though a failure with the critics, *Don Juan* was a commercial success and spurred Warner Bros. to increase sound production with more short films and features with recorded music and sound effects. But none of these had the wide-ranging, game changing effect of *The Jazz Singer.*

THE JAZZ SINGER

The Jazz Singer premiered in New York on October 6, 1927. It was not an all-sound film, but rather a silent film with musical numbers and a brief stretch of dialogue. Its popularity was as much due to its star, Al Jolson, as to its use of sound. But, as much as one tries to put this film in its historical context, to downplay its originality or place it in the history of early sound cinema, it remains an extraordinarily interesting piece of work. It originated as a popular stage play by Samson Raphaelson about the son of a Jewish cantor, who is ostracized by his father because he wants to sing popular music. He is redeemed when he returns to his father's death bed and agrees to leave his show on the Jewish holiday of Yom Kippur to sing Kol Nidre during the service. After that redemptive act, he can return to his singing career and his non-Jewish girlfriend.

JEWISHNESS AND BLACKFACE

As the critic Michael Paul Rogin points out, there are multiple narratives at work in *The Jazz Singer.* There is the overriding technological narrative about the arrival of sound film. But there is also the story of the assimilation of immigrants, Jews in this instance, in a film that is as steeped in Jewish culture as any work produced by the Jewish immigrants who founded the film studios. In a way, as Rogin suggests, the film stands as a kind of autobiography of the Warner Bros. Just as Jack, Harry, Albert, and Sam Warner overcame their roots as sons of Jewish immigrants to become successful producers of popular entertainments, so Jakie Rabinowitz, the Al Jolson character in *The Jazz Singer*, overcomes his background in order to become a popular entertainer. The films made by the studio heads suppressed their origins because they wanted total assimilation into American culture and, even more, wished their films to speak to an assimilated nation. But in this groundbreaking work, the brothers Warner decided to speak directly to their religion and culture and, at the same time, tell a story about a man who breaks with both. They decide to speak out, literally, by having their main character talk and sing in their film.[3]

Along with the narrative of religion is the narrative of race: the African American race in particular and its soul-destroying mimicking by white entertainers. Jolson, the stage performer, and the character he plays in *The Jazz Singer*, both perform in blackface. Blackface had a long tradition going back to slavery, when white men blacked their faces to mock their slaves. The tradition evolved into minstrel shows, which continued the mockery long after slavery ended and continued into vaudeville. Blackface was so popular that black performers put on blackface themselves to appeal to white audiences and, perhaps, to mock the mockers.

Blackface merged with radio to create one of the most popular programs in broadcasting history, *Amos 'n' Andy*, a comedy series about African Americans trying to get by in the city. Created and played by two white actors, Freeman Gosden and Charles Correll, the show originated in Chicago in 1926, just a year before *The Jazz Singer*, and lasted on network radio in one form or another until 1960. Their performance could be called "black voice," since the invisible actors could only imitate African Americans by creating an outlandish dialect. Gosden and Correll appeared in blackface when they performed their act on stage. There was a television version of the radio program in the early 1950s with, finally, black actors playing the roles. Complaints from the NAACP took it off the air after only a few years. *Amos 'n' Andy* played upon racial stereotypes, but with a certain geniality that made it popular with African American as well as white audiences.

Jolson's blackface in *The Jazz Singer* is not calculated to insult or disrespect a race. It is an act, a mode of performance, which during its time was perfectly acceptable in a cultural moment that is now foreign to us. It is also a way for the character, Jakie Rabinowitz, to become the performer Jack Robin. It is his method of assimilation—his way of defying his father and the demands of his father's religion, partly by hiding under the mask of another race. This all seems somewhat perverse to us, but the logic of the film is clear: Jakie escapes his past by disguising himself in his performance as Jack Robin, donning blackface as a way to both hide his old and reveal his new identity.

I pointed out earlier that there is an overriding narrative of technological change in *The Jazz Singer*, of the movement out of the silent period into sound that runs parallel to the narrative of assimilation and defiance. In fact, as Rogin points out, the filmmakers themselves seem as reluctant as Jakie's father to allow the conversion to be complete. The film is, after all, only partly in sound and there is only one passage of dialogue, between Jakie, sitting at the piano, singing "Nothing but blue skies, from now on" to his mother. The sequence—wonderfully spontaneous and playful—occurs almost in the middle of the film after Jakie's conversion to a jazz singer and his return home. He sings to his mother and tells her how the money he earns as an entertainer will make her wealthy and happy. He returns to his song, and his father enters and calls out "Stop!" There is no more verbal dialogue after this point.[4]

Here is a curiosity: MGM's first all-talking release, *Broadway Melody* (Harry Beaumont, 1929)—a backstage melodrama—contains a character who stutters. Did the filmmakers believe that this was a comic effect that could only be achieved in sound film? Does it somehow express the studios own halting efforts, their uncertainty concerning the conversion

Jackie Rabinovitz talks with and sings to his mother in *The Jazz Singer* (Alan Crosland, 1927).

Al Jolson in blackface, singing his signature song "Mammy" in *The Jazz Singer* (Alan Crosland, 1927).

to sound that was occurring slowly but inexorably at this point? Jakie's father calls out "stop." The character in *Broadway Melody* has trouble getting his words out. Hollywood sputtered into sound, was nervous about what changes it would bring, but could not stop its audience's demand to hear their stars speak.

CONVERSION TO SOUND

The conversion to sound film moved sporadically during 1928–1929. After a short period of denial—a belief that sound film was just a passing fad—the studios were convinced by audience response that the days of the silents were over. They made films that, like

The Jazz Singer, were part sound, part silent. They added sound to silent films that were already in the can. And they made all-talkies. The technical process of conversion was a complex business as competing communications companies with competing sound technologies vied for the studios' business. Western Electric's sound-on-disk competed with General Electric, AT&T, and RCA's sound-on-film formats. At first, the studios seemed to line up with sound-on-disc, until Joseph Kennedy, father of future President John F. Kennedy, joined forces with David Sarnoff, head of RCA and the NBC radio network, who held the patents on sound amplification systems. By the end of 1928, after buying out the theaters and production facilities owned by Kennedy, Sarnoff formed RKO Radio Pictures.[5]

Competition and patent wars occurred between the two systems: sound-on-disc and sound-on-film. The latter slowly won out, partly because of the persistence of its owners, but mostly because it was easier to edit broken film. If a film using the sound-on-disk system broke, it was difficult to patch it up without losing synchronization with the disk. But because the sound track was next to the image track in the sound-on-film system, breakage and splicing did not cause the film to go out of sync with the dialogue.[6]

As systems became standardized and the studios came to realize that sound was not only here to stay, but the only way movies would be made in the future, conversion moved more rapidly. Of the 21,739 movie houses that existed in the United States early in 1931, more than 13,000 were wired for one sound system or the other. By the mid-1930s, all theaters were set up for sound-on-film.[7]

THE CULTURES OF SOUND

Based on seeing the early sound short subjects, called "Prologues," a columnist in the *The New York Times* wrote in 1926: ". . . No single word, however compounded, is quite adequate to suggest the amazing triumph which man has at last achieved in making pictures talk naturally, sing enthrallingly and play all manner of instruments as skillfully as if the living beings were present instead of their shadows." The writer imagined sound as one of the great inventions that would "minister to the enlightenment or entertainment of the world in the larger leisure which the labor-saving machine has brought to its millions." Sound film—at least those films with high-culture content, like opera singers and symphony orchestras—would improve the culture of the masses, appeal to the "higher reaches of the human spirit, if they are not to become as mere machines themselves."[8]

That wish did not quite work out, and it could be argued that sound did not change the form and content of film that had become set by the late silent period. There is a certain truth to this: the formal structures and the generic content that we described in previous chapters evolved with the coming of sound but maintained many of their roots in the silent period. The editing of dialogue sequences that were established in the 1920s remained largely the same after the characters actually talked to each other. But sound had the effect of tightening up narrative structure and creating a new kind of relationship between the audience and the onscreen events. Gone were the long stretches of **intertitles** that interrupted the pantomime of silent film, often every few seconds. Acting styles were very much toned down as dialogue and music carried off some of the emotional expressiveness of pantomime. While it is true that, with sound, some films concentrated more on dialogue than on the image, it is equally as true that very soon after the introduction of sound, the camera limbered up. After a very brief period of remaining immobile, as sound technicians worked out ways to muffle the sound of the camera's machinery, filmmakers began to explore cinematic space with as much energy as they did in the late 1920s.

A new genre, sound dependent, was created: the musical. The gangster film that had its origins in the silent era quickly became a major genre in the 1930s. Tough talk, screeching tires, and the blast of machine gunfire launched gangsters from newspaper headlines onto the screen, where they have remained as part of the most enduring of film genres. In general, it might be said that sound film was itself a new genre that subsumed the other genres within it, which then reemerged, changed by the ability of characters to talk. Sound film created not only new technologies but also a new kind of contract with the audience, an intimacy and involvement with the images on the screen and the sound emanating from it that the silents could not provide.

Sound changed the personnel of filmmaking. Filmmakers had to create spoken dialogue, a fact that made reluctant studio heads import New York writers and treat them badly, forcing them to sit in an office from 9 to 5 and churn out scripts. It was a situation that earned the enmity of screenwriters and led to the formation of a strong union, the Screenwriters Guild in 1933, which is still active in adjudicating screenwriting credits. (The Screen Actors Guild and the Screen Directors Guild were also formed during this period. The union for stagehands and technicians, the International Alliance of Theatrical Stage Employees, and Moving Picture Technicians, IATSE, was already formed late in the 19th century.)

Acting styles changed, and many silent film stars were unable or, in the case of Charlie Chaplin, unwilling to make the transition. Chaplin did not make a talking picture—that is a film in which he spoke extensively—until *The Great Dictator* in 1940. As they did with writers, studio heads began importing actors from New York. In some early sound film, one can detect the theatrical diction of some of the actors against a more natural speech, even more rapid than normal speech, that was developing as a result of new actors emerging within the studios as sound film evolved. See, for example, the Warner Bros., First National, Vitaphone newspaper drama, *Five Star Final*, directed by Mervyn LeRoy in 1931. Edward G. Robinson's rapid-fire delivery is matched against the more deliberate speech of the other actors.

Even the methods of recording the actors' voices had to be worked out. Should the sound of a voice diminish as the angle on the action or the distance of the actor from the camera changed, or should the volume remain the same? How many cameras should be used to record a scene? The traditional method of cinematography is to use a single camera, photographing every scene from various angles and in multiple takes that would be edited into a single scene during the editing process. But in the early days of sound, with the cameras locked in soundproof booths and the need for coverage of a scene from multiple angles, multiple cameras were used.[9]

The coming of sound was a massive event in which aesthetics and technology, production and reception were joined in something like a concerted effort. Audiences wanted sound; the studios and their technicians, producers, actors, writers, and directors worked to create a process that finally made sound and image seamless, as if they had always existed together. The result of all this was a change in how films were made, in what viewers saw on the screen, as well as what they heard and how they responded. New sounds, new stars, new genres, a new way of relating to the moving image—all of which came crashing down with a new and ugly reality: The Great Depression.

SELECTED FILMOGRAPHY

The Jazz Singer, dir. Alan Crosland, Warner Bros., Vitaphone, 1927.

Broadway Melody, dir. Harry Beaumont, MGM, 1929.

Five Star Final, dir. Mervyn LeRoy, Warner Bros., Vitaphone, 1931.

SUGGESTIONS FOR FURTHER READING

Scott Eyman, *The Speed of Sound: Hollywood and the Talkie Revolution* (New York, NY: Simon & Schuster, 1997).

Douglas Gomery, *The Coming of Sound: A History* (New York, NY: Routledge, 2005).

Donald Grafton, *The Talkies: American Cinema's Transition to Sound, 1926–1931, History of the American Cinema*, vol. 4 (Berkeley, CA: University of California Press, 1999).

James Lastra, *Sound Technology and the American Cinema: Perception, Representation, Modernity* (New York, NY: Columbia University Press, 2000).

Michael Paul Rogin, *Blackface, White Noise: Jewish Immigrants in the Hollywood Melting Pot* (Berkeley, CA: University of California Press, 1996).

NOTES

1. Donald Grafton, *The Talkies: American Cinema's Transition to Sound, 1926–1931, History of the American Cinema*, vol. 4, (Berkeley, CA: University of California Press, 1999), 55–56. Grafton's book is a trove of information on early sound experiments which informs the discussion here.

2. For early sound newsreels, see Grafton, 96–100.
3. Michael Paul Rogin, *Blackface, White Noise: Jewish Immigrants in the Hollywood Melting Pot* (Berkeley, CA: University of California Press, 1996), 79–90. The correlation between the Warner brothers' biography and the film is in Rogin, 84.
4. Rogin points out the significance of Jakie's father calling out "stop," 83, 102, 105.
5. See Grafton, 136–142.
6. Grafton, 239. Crafton discusses the competition of sound-on-disc vs. sound-on-film, 146–148.
7. These figures come from Crafton, 155–160.
8. "Audible Pictures," *The New York Times*, August 8, 1926, E6.
9. Crafton, 244–246.

CHAPTER 8

AMERICAN FILM AND THE GREAT DEPRESSION (1931–1935)

The Depression was a cultural as well as an economic event. While most films tried to create a diversion from the enormous suffering of people during the Depression, a few took an unflinching look at the times and its turmoil. The musical flourished during this period, and Warner Bros. turned many of its musicals into topical reflections of hard times.

AFTER READING THIS CHAPTER, YOU SHOULD UNDERSTAND:

- The effect of the Depression on the movie studios.
- How films directly addressed the Depression.

YOU SHOULD BE ABLE TO:

- Discuss how various genres responded to the Great Depression.
- Understand how Warner Bros. musicals reflected the darkness of the era.
- Compare the Warner Bros. Depression musicals with the 1950s MGM musicals such as *Singin' in the Rain* and *It's Always Fair Weather.*
- Discover what contemporary films address social issues as powerfully as *Wild Boys of the Road* and *Heroes for Sale.*

THE GREAT DEPRESSION

Just as the studios were making their adjustments to the transition to sound in 1929, the national economy collapsed. The stock market crashed. Banks failed. Industrial output diminished drastically. By 1932, an estimated 34 million people were without work. Among the very poor there was famine. Men wandered the country looking for work or setting up shanty towns called "Hoovervilles" after Herbert Hoover, the 31st president, who, during the early years of Depression when his administration was in power, seemed unwilling or unable to do anything to mitigate the national suffering. In 1932, thousands of World War I veterans and their families set up a camp in Washington, DC, demanding early payment of their service benefits. Hoover ordered the army to clear them out, which they did, using fixed bayonets and gas.

Such was the state of things when Franklin Delano Roosevelt assumed the presidency in 1933 and tried to bring the full force of the federal government to bear on alleviating the Depression. Through a series of presidential and congressional acts, the creation of departments, and initiatives, he attempted to get people to work and promote fair practices in business, like eliminating child labor and promoting fair competition. One of these initiatives, the National Recovery Administration, or NRA, developed to encourage industrial recovery and unionization, was adopted by some of the movie studios, and the NRA logo can be seen at the beginning or end of their films. These efforts created a brief surge in the economy, but it sank again, only to be revived by America's entry into World War II in 1941.[1]

THE DEPRESSION IN HOLLYWOOD

In Hollywood, the Depression hit hard. Costs associated with the production of sound films went up and ticket sales went down. People stayed at home and listened to the radio. Profits fell and many of the studios filed for bankruptcy or went into receivership. These failures occurred largely on the exhibition side of the business. It was the studio-owned theaters that went under because of lack of attendance. The only studios that managed to avoid economic disaster were United Artists, Columbia, Warner Bros, and Loew's, Inc., parent company of MGM. Warners had made a lot of money with its sound films and purchased the First National chain of theaters. It had gone into debt in the 1930s, but survived by cutting salaries and lowering production costs. The other studios did the same. Many changed management and enforced **block booking**, compelling exhibitors to take all of their films if they wanted to show the best of them. Some others sold off their theaters. On the exhibition side, theater managers cut ticket prices and offered incentives to bring back patrons, offering drawings for cash prizes or giving away dishes. They also began showing two films for the price of one. The advent of the double feature not only made an evening out at the movies more attractive but opened up the market for independent production and increased the production of "B" or low-budget movies produced by the major studios to fill out the bottom half of a double bill.[2]

Most interesting is the ways in which the films made by the studios confronted the Depression, though perhaps "confront" is not quite accurate. It might be more appropriate to say that most films of the period sidestepped or only alluded to the troubles of the time. After all, in the realm of entertainment, diverting the public is the rule. But at the same time, as we have seen and will continue to note, entertainment is impossible to separate completely from the culture it is part of. The Depression influenced films across almost all generic boundaries, even if it was not directly confronted. We will examine those inflections and those genres in a moment. But first I want to look at two films that took the Depression head on, took it as its subject and were unflinching in their gaze at history unfolding at the moment of their making.

HEROES FOR SALE AND *WILD BOYS OF THE ROAD*

The films are *Heroes for Sale* and *Wild Boys of the Road.* Both appeared in 1933 and were directed by William A. Wellman for Warner Bros-First National-Vitaphone. We looked at Wellman's World War I film *Wings* (Paramount, Famous Players-Lasky, 1927) in the previous chapter. Wellman had already made an important early sound gangster film for Warner-Vitaphone, *Public Enemy* (1931). But his two films about the Depression are marked by a tone of despair and the recognition of social injustice that are unusual for film of any era. The despair is evidenced in the cold eye the films cast on the social, economic, and cultural realities of the period. The recognition is of the apparent hopelessness of lives caught up in a pitiless system aggravated by officials who prey on the helpless or, in the case of *Heroes*, on the helpful. It is against the grain of the Hollywood style to present helplessness unleavened by some ray of hope; but there were few such rays in the 1930s, and these two films look squarely at the darkness.

The narrative of *Heroes for Sale* begins in World War I, continues into the 1920s, and pivots on an act of cowardice and the complications that occur when one of its characters, Roger Winston (Gordon Westcott), claims credit for a military mission actually led by Tom Holmes, who is played by Richard Barthelmess, a former silent film actor, perhaps best known for his role as the "Yellow Man" in D. W. Griffith's *Broken Blossoms*, and who made a briefly successful transition to sound. The events that follow mix an unlikely stew of drug addiction, revolutionary thought, successful capitalism, and ultimate failure. In simple, stark images, Wellman incorporates contemporary events: the red scare that was sweeping the country in the 1920s, the fear of revolutionary anarchists, the fantasy of creating a successful business. Tom takes a room in a rooming house in Chicago, falls in love with and eventually marries a beautiful boarder, Ruth (Loretta Young), and listens to the rantings of another boarder, Max Brinker (Robert Barratt), a German Communist, "a red" as he is identified in the film. This character is played mostly for laughs, as he spouts ideas about class oppression while making funny noises with his mouth. "When you get to be my age," he says, recalling memories of the bomb-throwing activists and the labor uprisings throughout the country, "you'll have a bomb in every pocket." The Depression was a seed bed for radical thought, but Hollywood would not entertain these seriously. (When the left-wing novelist Upton Sinclair ran for governor of California in 1934, MGM actively campaigned against him by creating fake newsreels to frighten viewers. It worked, and Sinclair was defeated.) Red Max eventually changes his ways. Tom has taken a job in a laundry, where he works his way up by devising a plan to get new customers. Max invents a new factory process to speed up the laundry's operations.

The turn comes when the new owners of the laundry cut their work staff, and the workers riot in the street. Hollywood filmmakers have always shown an aversion to mass action, most often depicting an angry mob as dangerous and bloodthirsty. But *Heroes for Sale* is different in its creation of a riot scene where the police are as aggressive as the mob. Wellman creates a sequence of extraordinary chaos and violence, in which Tom's wife is killed by a blow to the head. The film doesn't show whether it comes from a police baton or one of the workers, though it has shown the police viciously gassing and clubbing the mob. Wellman is unsparing in his condemnation, allowing a rare image of violent death, allowing us to see Mary's bloody corpse lying in the street. Tom tries to stop the mob as they get gassed and beaten by the police, but is arrested and jailed until 1932, which brings the film's narrative into the present moment when the Depression has struck. Despite the fact that he comes out of jail a rich man, due to Max's invention, he is still hounded for his politics and is picked up by the Red Squad, an actual police unit set up in Chicago to root out political "radicals." The film digresses into a brief **montage** of police picking up foreigners, before returning to Tom, who is exiled from Chicago.

The irony is strong: a rich man, who tried to prevent worker unrest, is made poor because of the misguided zeal of anti-Communist crusaders. Tom goes on the road, and Wellman creates another montage of Tom crisscrossing the country looking for work where none exists. In St. Louis, he passes a huge Chamber of Commerce billboard that reads "Jobless Men Keep Going. We Can't Take Care of Our Own." On a freight car, among a bunch of other jobless men rounded up by the police, he meets up with Roger, the coward, who we discover helped his father embezzle bank funds. Sitting in the dark in the freight car, the rain coming down, the two of them worry that the state of the nation means the "end of America." Tom is optimistic; he believes Roosevelt will help them out of the Depression. "It takes more than one sock in the jaw to lick 120,000,000 people." The cops return and send them off on their marching in the dark to nowhere. The film ends with an even more bitter irony, as Tom's son says he wants to grow up to be just like his dad.

Wellman's *Wild Boys of the Road*, his follow-up to *Heroes for Sale*, attempts to bring those suffering from the Depression out of the dark, but this optimism is bought at the price of laying salvation at the feet of a single virtuous character, which is typical of the Hollywood style. When the "wild boys" of the title hit the rails because their parents can no longer afford to care for them, one loses a leg when he is run over by a train. The others steal a prosthetic limb for him. They are forced to set up a shantytown near the railroad tracks where they are attacked by the police using water hoses. The shocking last image of this rout is the prosthetic limb lying in the rubble.

The boys cross the country again (a map montage tracing the journeys of hapless characters is typical of

Tom (Richard Barthelmess) attempts to talk an angry mob of workers from rioting in *Heroes for Sale* (William Wellman, 1933).

Boys on the run, battling the police in William Wellman's *Wild Boys of the Road* (1933).

films of the period), finally setting up camp in a trash dump in New York. Captured by the police for being tricked into a robbery, they appear before an understanding judge, who sets them free and promises to set them up with work. Usually, when such a figure appears in films of the decade—as he does again in the form of a friendly migrant camp manager in John Ford's *The Grapes of Wrath* (20th Century Fox, 1940)—he is a surrogate for Franklin Delano Roosevelt. A majority of Americans looked to Roosevelt to save them from the ravages of economic collapse, and he became represented in film as the protective father figure.

The happy ending of *Wild Boys of the Road* posits that such a protector can be found and offer individual help to a lucky few. This was not what President Roosevelt offered. His job was to administer programs that tried to lift the country out of the economic doldrums. But his style, especially as communicated through his radio "fireside chats," suggested that he was personally connected to each person's suffering. The film, however, works its way out of the dead end it posits for its characters simply because they are children. In *Heroes for Sale*, Tom Holmes goes off into the oblivion of poverty and the endless road. The wild boys are allowed to celebrate their good fortune.

AMERICAN MADNESS

Warner Bros. was not the only studio to address the Depression. Frank Capra, one of the most important directors in 1930s Hollywood, made a remarkable film in 1932, called *American Madness* (Columbia). The film is of interest on two levels: it shows the great flexibility that the camera gained shortly after the introduction of sound. Capra tracks and dollies, photographs his characters from various angles other than the eye-level frontal style, and even violates the **180-degree rule**, cutting from one side of an imaginary line across the horizontal of the composition to the other (you can see examples of this in Chapter 3). The film moves with the assurance of a filmmaker fully at ease with the new technologies of sound and able to put them at the service of an expressive cinematic style.

The film is also prophetic of the cultural rawness of the time. Although it is cloaked in a melodrama concerning a wife's presumed infidelity and a gambler who, in order to pay off his debts, allows crooks to rob the bank he works for, *American Madness* is essentially about the massive financial insecurity that marked the early years of the Great Depression. Its core sequence is a massive run on a bank. Its president, Thomas Dickson (Walter Huston), is a strong figure who fights his board of directors over his belief that money should be loaned to those who are the most needy and deserving, based on his "hunches" about their credit worthiness—a typical gambit of Capra. He believes that money has to stop being horded by the banks and by individuals and put back in circulation to return the country to prosperity. Dickson speaks to the fears of the moment, and when word gets out that the bank has been robbed, people pour in by the hundreds to pull their money out.

Bank failures began in earnest late in 1932, about the time that *American Madness* was released. They grew in intensity throughout the end of the year and into 1933, forcing state after state to declare "bank

A run on the bank in Frank Capra's *American Madness* (1932).

holidays" and close the banks down. When Franklin Roosevelt took office in March, 1933, he declared a national bank holiday so that the temperature of fear that was gripping the country and despoiling the economy could cool down. The run on Dickson's bank—started by rumors that keep escalating the amount that was actually stolen from its vault—is a mirror of that fear. As is Capra's wont (and we will examine his other films in detail in Chapter 10), the run is stopped when the sturdy souls to whom Dickson loaned money come to the bank's rescue and the board has a change of heart and contributes to the bank's funds. In other words, *American Madness* does not propose government solutions to the problem, but the goodness of the people. Typical of Hollywood film, *things work out*, whether or not they were working out in fact.

THE 1930s MUSICAL

THE FORGOTTEN MAN CHOREOGRAPHED

The Forgotten Man, alluded to in *Heroes for Sale* and directly referenced in Warner Bros.-Vitphone's grim film, *I Am a Fugitive From a Chain Gang* (Mervyn LeRoy, 1932), was a phrase used in a radio address by Franklin Delano Roosevelt in 1932, referring to the poor and unemployed who were "at the bottom of the economic pyramid."[3] The term became associated with World War I veterans who could not find work and became a symbol of the suffering of the Depression. The Forgotten Man appeared in the most curious of places, a 1933 Warner Bros.-Vitaphone musical, *Gold Diggers of 1933* (Mervyn LeRoy, musical numbers directed by Busby Berkeley). To get to the "Forgotten Man" sequence in *Gold Diggers*, we need to look very briefly at the musical in the 1930s.

Love Me Tonight

As noted, the musical was a genre invented by the coming of sound, and in some instances filmmakers used the new technology as an imaginative device to create the very rhythm of a film's editing and visual structure. Such was the case with Rouben Mamoulian's 1932 film, *Love Me Tonight* (Paramount). Set in Paris, the film begins with an aural and visual montage, lovely images of the city in early morning, church bells determining the cuts from one shot to another. A street repair man throws down his tools and, taking up a pick axe, rhythmically chops at the pavement. A man sleeping in the street adds his snoring to the sound of the axe. A woman comes out of her house and begins sweeping the street, the rhythm of her broom joining the other sounds. A visual element is added as the camera zooms in on three smokestacks belching smoke. The visual and sound montage continues as people awake, shake their laundry, saw on lumber, nail shoes, grind knives, beat rugs, until the camera finally tracks into a window where the film's star, the French singer Maurice Chevalier, sings along with and about the rhythm of the city. The musical as genre is interlaced with the formal rhythms of film editing.

ASTAIRE-ROGERS

A subgenre of musicals was constituted by the films made for RKO by Fred Astaire and Ginger Rogers. These films leave the Depression behind, creating instead a fantasy world of the well-to-do in which Fred Astaire dances and sings, eventually meeting up with Ginger in graceful routines that their director, Mark Sandrich, photographs at a comfortable distance with few camera movements that quietly capture the grace of their dancing. *Top Hat* (1935) is typical of the Astaire-Rogers musicals. Two Americans in Paris meet cute and continue dancing and singing through the film, culminating in a big number, "The Piccolino," with dancers choreographed on a huge set, bedecked with ribbons and ending with Astaire and Rogers doing their final number in a rhapsodic dance. The narratives in these films are thin; they supply a simple ground for the high energy of the dancing and singing.

BUSBY BERKELEY

Gold Diggers of 1933

But even the most extravagant of the Astaire-Rogers routines pale in comparison to the massive choreographies created by Busby Berkeley for the Warner Bros. musicals of the 1930s. Like many musicals of the decade, these were backstage stories about putting on the show. Working under deadlines, feeling the pressure of developing last-minute routines, the actors

Fred Astaire and Ginger Rogers Dance "The Piccolino" in *Top Hat* (Mark Sandrich, 1935).

and producers in *42nd Street* (Lloyd Bacon, 1932) and *Footlight Parade* (Lloyd Bacon, 1933) feverishly, sometimes depressingly, push to get their shows onstage. But once onstage, once "produced" and in front of the camera, once Berkeley takes charge, cinematic space becomes a fantasy **mise-en-scène**, a spectacle of women, scantily clad, photographed from every possible angle, in obsessive symmetrical shapes, in spatial configurations that can exist only on film.

Gold Diggers of 1933 is a Depression-era musical with the Depression as its theme. It opens with a song and dance number, "We're in the Money," with chorus girls in skimpy costumes made up of gold coins: "Old Man Depression, you are through/You done us wrong" they sing. But Old Man Depression isn't through, and the number is interrupted by the police, who close down the show because of overdue bills. We see a list of shuttered theaters that might just as well be a list of closed movie houses that brought so many of the studios to the brink of ruin. But Barney the producer (Ned Sparks) is undaunted, as are the bevy of chorus girls whose domestic life makes up something of a plot for the film. Brad and Polly—Dick Powell and Ruby Keeler, two of the stalwarts of the 1930s Warner Bros. musicals—provide a love interest. But the Depression remains central. "That's it. That's what this show's about," cries Barney when he hears Brad play the "Forgotten Man" song. "The Depression. Men marching, marching in the rain. . . . Men marching, marching. Jobs, jobs. . . . The big parade of tears."

When the show finally goes on, the numbers begin in stage space—that is, they appear to be performed in a theater. But as they progress, the theater space is replaced by Busby Berkeley space, filled with dancing women in geometric choreographies. The second number (after the opening "We're in the Money") is "Petting in the Park." It is fairly tame, except for the end, when Polly appears dressed in armor and Brad borrows a can opener from a small person dressed as a baby and pries her open. It is an extremely perverse routine.

The climactic Forgotten Man number is somewhat subdued as befitting the film's downbeat subject. The song is performed by various women singing in stylized sets. As the number grows in complexity—as Berkeley's always do—soldiers march, crowds wave. They march in the rain, bearing stretchers. A **wipe**, in which one scene replaces another in a kind of fanlike motion, shows the men now beggars in a bread line, the camera tracking along an endless row of men, their collars turned up against the weather. Then, in a stage tableau, the soldiers walk backlit over three concentric overhead bridges, while the homeless men walk forward toward the camera, women waving at

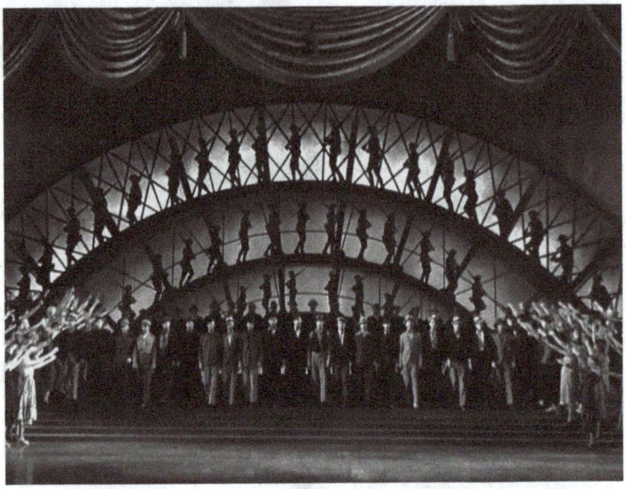

The Forgotten Man number choreographed by Busby Berkeley in *Gold Diggers of 1933* (Mervyn LeRoy). This image is typical of the huge geometric compositions Berkeley created in his song and dance sequences.

them from the side as the solo singer completes her lament. The Forgotten Man is turned into a musical spectacle of romantic longing.

But there was no romance to the Depression. Things did not work out in the culture at large as they often did in film. The Depression got worse going forward from 1932. Banks continued to fail. Roosevelt tried various programs to stimulate the economy and create jobs. The right wing rose up to attempt to block the initiatives, and was largely successful. Meanwhile, another right wing was expanding in Europe, far more malevolent than the one at home. The growth of fascism in Italy and Nazism in Germany eventually led the world to war in Europe in 1939. The United States joined the fight after the attack on Pearl Harbor in 1941. It was World War II that ended the Great Depression as businesses revived for wartime production.

The Depression haunted American film as it did the culture until the war. More often than not, it acted as a kind of reflection, with films playing against the sadness of the times. A new comic genre, the screwball comedy, emerged as the Depression's glittering opposite. Yet another genre formed, embracing the Depression, in a sense paralleling it: Depression's mirror, the gangster.

SELECTED FILMOGRAPHY

Heroes for Sale, dir. William A. Wellman, Warner Bros., Vitaphone Corp., 1931.

Wild Boys of the Road, dir. William A. Wellman, Warner Bros., Vitaphone Corp., 1931.

American Madness, dir. Frank Capra, Columbia, 1932.

Love Me Tonight, dir. Rouben Mamoulian, Paramount, 1932.

42nd Street, dir. Lloyd Bacon, Warner Bros., 1932.

Footlight Parade, dir. Lloyd Bacon, Warner Bros., Vitaphone Corp,, 1933.

Gold Diggers of 1933, dir. Mervyn LeRoy, Warner Bros., Vitaphone Corp., 1933.

Top Hat, dir. Mark Sandrich, RKO, 1935.

SUGGESTIONS FOR FURTHER READING

Andrew Bergman, *We're in the Money: Depression America and Its Films* (New York, NY: Harper, 1971).

Tino Balio, *Grand Design: Hollywood as a Modern Business Enterprise, 1930–1939, History of the American Cinema*, vol. 5 (Berkeley, CA: University of California Press, 1995).

Steven Cohan, ed., *Hollywood Musicals, The Film Reader* (London, UK: Routledge, 2002).

Jane Feuer, *The Hollywood Musical* (Bloomington, IN: Indiana University Press, 1982).

Lucy Fisher, "The Image of Women: The Optical Politics of Dames," *Film Quarterly*, vol. 30, no. 1 (Fall, 1976), 2–11.

Greg Mitchell, *The Campaign of the Century: Upton Sinclair's Race for Governor of California and the Birth of Media Politics* (Sausalito, CA: PoliPoint Press, 2010).

NOTES

1. For material on the Great Depression see, for example, William E. Leuchtenburg, *Franklin Roosevelt and the New Deal* (New York, NY: Harper Torchbooks, 1963).
2. For the studios that survived bankruptcy see Tino Balio, *Grand Design: Hollywood as a Modern Business Enterprise, 1930–1939, History of the American Cinema*, vol. 5 (Berkeley, CA: University of California Press, 1995), 14–18.
3. The quotation from Roosevelt is found at http://newdeal.feri.org/speeches/1932c.htm.

CHAPTER 9

THE DEPRESSION-ERA GANGSTER FILM (1931–1939)

The gangster film is the most enduring genre to emerge from the early sound period and the Great Depression. Providing an antidote to helplessness, the gangster offered a mythology of violent action, of working men breaking out of their constraints and taking control of their lives and their "territory." But the genre was also about inevitable failure. The gangster's rise and fall drew the attention of the censors, and it was the gangster film that helped created the Production Code.

AFTER READING THIS CHAPTER, YOU SHOULD UNDERSTAND:

- The rise of the gangster film.
- How gangster films contributed to the creation of the Production Code.
- The difference between "the gangster" and "the criminal."
- The meaning of the "places" of the gangster film: the car, diner, and nightclub.
- The narrative construction of the first three major gangster films.
- What is "tragic" about the gangster.

YOU SHOULD BE ABLE TO:

- Continue discussion of the Production Code and its influence on films from the 1930s on.
- Consider how the code created a more imaginative cinema.
- See the relationship between the gangster and the Depression.
- Discuss the role of power and sexuality in the gangster film.
- Apply Robert Warshow's essay "The Gangster as Tragic Hero" to current gangster films.
- Compare the original *Scarface* with the 1983 remake.
- Discuss what makes the gangster such an attractive figure.

THE GANGSTER

In 1970, the US Congress passed an anti-crime bill, "The Racketeer Influenced and Corrupt Organizations Act," known as RICO. The acronym is based on a character, Caesar Enrico Bandello, otherwise known as Rico, in a 1931 film, *Little Caesar* (Mervyn LeRoy, Warner Bros., First National). The fact that this film remains in our cultural and political memory after so much time speaks to the power of the gangster genre and its lasting influence. The genre began with a literal bang, with three films, one after the other—*Little Caesar, The Public Enemy* (William A. Wellman, Warner Bros., Vitaphone Corp., 1931), and *Scarface* (Howard Hawks, Howard Hughes [producer], United Artists, 1932)—celebrating the modern outlaw, cautioning against him and his way of life, admiring his macho daring, recoiling before his moral degradation.

Chronologically, the narrative of the early 1930s gangster film takes place in the 1920s, during Prohibition, when mobsters, especially Chicago's Al Capone, became something of folk heroes. Capone was finally imprisoned in 1932 on tax evasion—he was never brought to justice on racketeering or murder. The 1920s were not immune to the making of myths of thugs, or was this the first time in history when it happened. Admiration of the outlaw has a long history in American culture (think of the Western outlaws Billy the Kid and Jesse James). Audiences in the early 1930s could think back with a kind of nostalgia to the recent past and see the gangster as heroically triumphing over the cruelty of the capitalist system that was oppressing them during the Great Depression. The outlaw hero of the 1920s became a kind of forbidden model of success in the face of the Depression. But his was a success that was always tempered by failure: gangsters always die at the end of their film. The gangster film therefore provided a kind of push and pull on the sentiments of their audience. Both attractive and repulsive, the exploits of the gangster were always thrilling, as was his bullying his way to success. But his success could never succeed; it contains always the seeds of his failure.

"THE GANGSTER AS TRAGIC HERO"

In an essay written in 1948, Robert Warshow, a young critic who was an important forerunner of popular cultural criticism, talks about the gangster as a kind of avatar of the moviegoer's worst and best instincts. Warshow points out that the gangster is a creature of the movie-made city. "The real city . . . produces only criminals; the imaginary city produces the gangster: he is what we want to be and what we are afraid we may become." During the Great Depression, we can imagine that this fear might have been quite real. For people in great want, living near or below the poverty level, criminality might have been a tempting alternative. We have already noted the grim end of Warner Bros.'s 1932 film *I Am a Fugitive from a Chain Gang* (Mervyn LeRoy), in which James Allen (Paul Muni), a successful architect wrongly committed to jail, escapes. At the end of the film, he meets his girlfriend, who asks how he lives. He calls out to her from the darkness: "I steal." That the great majority of people did not steal is not only a testament to a significant moral structure in the culture but also to the moral code that supported the great gangster films of the period. The gangster always dies, these films told us over and over. Failure is always an option. "At bottom," Warshow writes, "the gangster is doomed because he is under the obligation to succeed, not because the means he employs are unlawful."

> In the deeper layers of the modern consciousness, *all* means are unlawful, every attempt to succeed is an act of aggression, leaving one alone and guilty and defenseless among enemies: one is *punished* for success. This is our intolerable dilemma: that failure is a kind of death and success is evil and dangerous, is—ultimately—impossible. The effect of the gangster film is to embody this dilemma in the person of the gangster and resolve it by his death. The dilemma is resolved because it is *his death*, not ours. We are safe; for the moment, we can acquiesce in our failure, we can choose to fail.[1]

What are we to make of this? Is there a deep-seated cultural, even personal belief that we will fail in exact measure that we succeed? Does the gangster embody all our wishes to succeed and our deepest fear that, no matter what we do, we will fail? Is this what the gangster films of the early 1930s told its audience? Or was there a dialogue carried back and forth, between the violent, preening figures viewers saw on the screen and the viewers' own constricted lives? The dilemma of the Depression was that fantasies of success were squelched by the economic realities of a destroyed economy, of hunger and breadlines, of joblessness, and downright despair. The gangster represented that despair in his rise and fall. Few members of the filmgoing audience wished to emulate the gangster; most understood the despair of his failure. Some, perhaps, identified with his meteoric rise and bloody fall.

THE GANGSTER AND THE CODE

Gangster films played a large role in toughening the censorship of films. To understand this, we need a bit of history. The coming of sound brought more attention to the content of film and more calls for censorship. There were a number of contributing reasons for this. One was technical. It was a notorious fact that local distributors and exhibitors of silent film felt free to cut sequences and even rearrange the editing structure of the films they were showing. This allowed censorship after the fact of a film's production. Of course, this was no longer possible when film came with a synchronized sound track. With the coming of sound, there were odd fears among exhibitors and moviegoers outside of major cities that sound film would bring a greater sophistication, would carry the values and morals of the city to the country, would consider subjects—in the words of MGM production head Irving Thalberg—"the silent picture was forced to shun." This fear of moral corruption was coupled with a certain amount of anti-Semitism and anti-Catholicism aimed at what middle-American audiences perceived as the "foreign" influence of Hollywood and urban centers. Church and women's groups protested against the movies they saw as dangerous. States and municipalities tried to enforce stronger censorship on films.[2]

Despite attempts to stiffen and enforce the code in the early 1930s, there remained enough representations of sexuality and violence in early sound film to continue irritating and worrying the conservative groups and small-town exhibitors who feared the influence of the movies on the morals of their customers. With a growing conservative mood in the country, with the appearance of the gangster film and popular films by a particularly risqué performer named Mae West, who was arrested on indecency charges for her stage performances *before* she even appeared in films such as *I'm No Angel* (Wesley Ruggles, Paramount, 1933) and *She Done Him Wrong* (Lowell Sherman, Paramount, 1933), the calls for stricter censorship became louder. The Catholic Legion of Decency joined the chorus, claiming "those salacious motion pictures . . . are corrupting public morals and promoting a sex mania in our land."[3]

Will Hays, president of the Motion Picture Producers and Distributors of America, the MPPDA, who, as we saw in Chapter 3, administered an early round of film censorship, hired Joseph Breen to head the Production Code Administration (PCA) in 1931. A strict Catholic, Breen set himself up as America's moral conscience, and by 1934—under threats of boycotts of films led by religious groups—he set up a new, stronger code. The PCA vetted every script headed or being considered for production by the studios. It carried out ongoing negotiations with the studios about what could and could not be shown, and at times, it supervised the editing of a film. By code rules, sexual and political content was strictly controlled. Only twin beds could be shown in bedrooms, even of married couples. The human body needed to be decently covered. No crime or infraction, no broken law, "natural" or human, could go unpunished. No profanity could be used. Breen could be both blunt and accommodating—on his terms—in dealing with filmmakers. Josef von Sternberg was an important director of the 1930s, the creator of sensual, visually intricate films. He approached Breen about creating a sequence of a "brief romantic interlude." When Sternberg refused to clarify what he meant, Breen is reported to have said "stop the horseshit and face the issue. We can help you make a story about adultery, if you want, but not if you keep calling a good screwing match a 'romantic interlude.'"[4] The censor could be as crude as he wished in the cause of censoring what he might consider to be crude.

The code was deeply paternal and, given the influence of church groups, Catholic. It worried over the fact that film is a universal art that appeals to all classes of people, who, it assumed, needed protection. At first, some leeway was provided, again in a highly paternal tone. As early as 1927, a member of the MPPDA, stated that the studios must be allowed some leeway, to show or narrate events "from which conclusions might be drawn by the sophisticated mind, but which would mean nothing to the unsophisticated and inexperienced."[5] While this attitude recognized, in however elitist a manner, that it would be impossible to strip film of all "adult" content, the code did enfold film production within a cocoon of puritanical rules that, if followed to the letter, would result in the most banal and irrelevant movies. The code had some immediate and some far-reaching results: it squelched some of the more blatant sexual innuendo that was apparent in the early 1930s and kept actresses more covered up than they had been. Less skin and more gowns. Sexuality of any kind needed to be controlled: "Adultery and illicit sex, sometimes necessary plot material, must not be explicitly treated or justified or presented attractively."[6] Such rules allowed enough wiggle room to allow a burst of creativity on the part of screenwriters and directors. If they couldn't portray sexuality directly, they would do it indirectly, via discreet comments or looks, by a **quiet fade out** or a noisy storm or a **pan** to a roaring fireplace to indicate lovemaking. The code did not do away with sexuality in the movies; it made its representation more subtle, coded—indeed, coded against the code—to replace blatancy with suggestion. Neither the "sophisticated" nor the "unsophisticated" would miss the cues.

Censors are notoriously stupid; they go after the obvious and are oblivious to subtleties. Screenwriters would often write outrageous sequences to throw them off track. Orson Welles and Herman Mankiewicz allegedly wrote a sequence in a brothel in the original script for *Citizen Kane* (Orson Welles, RKO, 1941) that they knew would not pass PCA scrutiny. But it diverted attention from the film's mature treatment of infidelity and spousal abuse, issues that Breen and his censors would probably condemn were they not diverted and were the film less sophisticated than it is.

What they were not diverted from in the early 1930s was the violence of the gangster films. Despite the inevitable death of the gangster at film's end, despite the occasional moralizing about the gangster as a product of his environment and the need for public vigilance, the almost constant gunplay, the bombing of rival gang headquarters and saloons, the cocky preening of the early gangster films got on the censors' nerves. Along with the overt sexuality of early 1930s films, the gangster genre was responsible for the outcry against what film was allegedly doing to the country's morals. Gangsters were violent and immoral. They might influence viewers or at least upset their moral equilibrium. The formation of the Production Code was created to save them. It remained in effect until the early 1960s.

THE GANGSTER FILMS

LITTLE CAESAR

Mervyn LeRoy's 1931 film, *Little Caesar*, provides the model that most gangster films would follow throughout the decade. Though still showing some signs of the careful, static **mise-en-scène** of early sound films, there is a dynamic at work that flows mainly from the performance of the central character, Caesar Enrico Bandello, played by Edward G. Robinson, one of the sturdiest actors in Warner's stable. Performance is a key concept here, and it is more complex than an actor performing a role. Movie gangsters perform their own roles in that they are highly self-conscious, well attuned to their status, or lack of it, and their desire to improve it. Director LeRoy presents his gangster's status literally by viewing him from high and low positions, according to the power he holds at any moment in his career. At the peak of his success, Rico dresses for his meeting with the "Big Boy" (Sidney Blackmer), who will hand over to him a large part of the city as his territory. We see Rico reflected in a mirror, standing on his bed, attended to by his admiring second, Otero (George F. Stone). He is fidgeting in his tuxedo, but he ends up preening and mincing. Earlier, we had seen Otero ministering to Rico in bed, and there is a strong suggestion that Rico is either gay or asexual. We will see again in *Scarface* hints that the gangster's sexuality is part of his outlaw behavior. Rico's fall is precipitous after the sequence with "Big Boy," and by the end of the film, we see him laid low, groveling in a flophouse, pursued by the cops through shadowy streets that, in their darkness, preview the look of film noir that will develop in the 1940s. Preening or groveling, the gangster is always self-conscious, always the center of attention. He is the narcissist of crime.

Little Caesar opens quietly enough, with a car silently driving into the parking lot of a diner. The automobile becomes one of the most important icons in the gangster film: a conveyance; a means of arriving at and fleeing from a crime scene; a symbol of mobility and power; a place in which the gangster may be hunted down and killed. The diner is also a recurring image in the genre, along with the bar and the nightclub, it is a place of meeting, refuge, comfort, and confrontation. Once inside the diner, in the film's opening sequence, Rico sets the hands of the clock back to hide the time of the robbery. It is a means for Rico to buy time, setting the clock to begin his climb to the top.

Rico sits at the counter with his friend, Joe (Douglas Fairbanks, Jr.), a dancer, who is uncertain about his role of gangster's best man. Like Rico, he wants to get to the city, but to find excitement, women, great clothes. Joe will eventually sell Rico out to the cops, preferring his girlfriend and his dancing to a life of crime. "Dancin'! Women!" Rico responds contemptuously to Joe in the diner. "Where do they get you? I don't want no dancin'. I figure on making other people dance." He wants to be somebody; more than just make money, he wants to "look hard at a bunch of guys and know that they'll do anything you tell 'em. Have your own way or nothin'. Be somebody!"

Rico makes his violent impulses clear, but LeRoy holds off the gunplay for a while. He doesn't even show the robbery of the diner. He moves quickly with Rico and Joe into the city, where Rico edges his way into Sam Vettori's (Stanley Fields) mob, looming in the frame in a way that defies his small physical stature. Again, LeRoy frames him in a way that indicates his rise to power. He is introduced to the mob, as the camera circles the table, each gangster looking up in recognition. Almost 60 years later, Martin Scorsese would pay homage to this scene in *Goodfellas* (Warner Bros., 1990), in a scene where Henry Hill (Ray Liotta) introduces his mob, seated around a bar, to the audience. Rico pushes his way up through the mob hierarchy and the film makes it clear that his goal is—as Rico stated—status rather than money. When he meets Pete Montana (Ralph Ince), a higher up in the mob, who warns Rico to not be trigger happy, there is a cut to a shot from Rico's point of view gazing at Montana's fancy tie pin and ring. Rico is a man interested in self-display, wanting to dress and perform the role of rich man as much as he wants to play tough.

LeRoy presents Rico's first big job, knocking over a night club on New Year's Eve, in the form of a rapid **montage** of **dissolves** from one part of the robbery to another, one gangster to the next. Rico manages to kill the crime commissioner, who didn't know he was patronizing a mob run club. Rico's criminal courage

The threatening gangster. Rico (Edward G. Robinson) looms in the frame in *Little Caesar* (Mervyn LeRoy, 1931).

continues to give him an edge over the old mob bosses. "You can dish it out, but you're gettin' so you can't take it no more" is his favorite retort to all he considers cowards. And that includes members of his own gang. When one of its young members, Tony (William Collier, Jr.), falls to pieces after the night-club robbery and goes for comfort to his Italian mother and his priest, Rico shoots him down on the church steps and then gives him a big funeral. Rico grows in pride and circumstance. And that, of course, is his downfall, which is less a fact of Rico's brutality as his overweening vanity. At a banquet the mob throws in his honor, Rico allows his picture to be taken by the press, and his chutzpah gets him shot by a rival gang. The cop, Flaherty (Thomas E. Jackson), moves closer on his tail.

His rise is noted by, of all things, a title card—a holdover from the silent days—that reads: "Rico continued to take care of himself, his hair and his gun—with excellent results." He sets himself up in fancy digs. But Rico's fate is sealed. Trailed by the cops, falling into the life of a bum, living in a flophouse, Little Caesar winds up literally in the gutter. The cops close in. Caesar crawls under a billboard advertising the dancing duo of Joe and his partner, Olga (Glenda Farrell)—a billboard that calls them a "Laughing, Singing, Dancing Success." The cringing failure that Rico has become is mown down by the cops' machine gunfire. "Mother of mercy, is this the end of Rico?" His last words are uttered in disbelief that someone gone so high can fall so low.

SCARFACE

Rico's last words could well echo the dispirited state of the country in the early 1930s. Substitute "prosperity" for "Rico" and there is a sense of the disbelief and despair gripping Depression America. But Rico's pathetic fall might also account for the immediate popularity of the gangster genre. Here was a surrogate for the Forgotten Man, someone who came from anonymity to attain at least an outlaw version of fame and fortune. The gangster took what he wanted, lived well, but, unfortunately, was killed at the end. "Do it first, do it yourself, and keep on doing it" is the motto of Tony Camonte, the title character of Howard Hawks's *Scarface*, produced by the millionaire aircraft tycoon, Howard Hughes. It speaks to an urge for quick relief and to the reality that such relief may be fleeting or, finally, nonexistent. Such was the ambiguity of the gangster film's mixed messages: succeed and fail. At least succeed. What is unambiguous is the dynamism of these films, no more obvious than *Scarface*.

Tony Camonte (Paul Muni) is a more vicious version of Rico Bandello, more feral and bloodthirsty. *Scarface* itself is more ornate, more given to rhetorical and visual flourishes provided by its director, Howard Hawks. Almost every time a murder occurs, there is, somewhere in the frame, a cross or an X sign to match the cross-shaped scar on Camonte's face. Someone is shot down in the street under the sign of an undertaker. From a high angle, the sign makes the shadow of a cross across the dead man's body. Hawks stages the infamous St. Valentine's Day massacre of 1929, in which Al Capone's gang machine-gunned an opposing gang in a warehouse used to store contraband liquor. The camera tracks away from a ceiling beam made up of crosshatches in the shape of Xs. It pans down to the silhouettes of the mobsters lined up for execution. They are mowed down by machine gun fire and the camera pans back up to the beam of Xs. We hear a dog howl and bark off screen.

There is a tension between a certain coolness of approach and the heat of the violence in *Scarface*. The 3 ½ minute take—long by any standards, but unusual for this early in the sound era—that begins the film almost casually introduces us to the central character: the camera pulls away from a street sign to the exterior of a club, where gangsters have been celebrating all night. It follows a milkman making his delivery and then picks up a handyman, who moves inside, sweeping up the garbage from the night's festivities and pauses at a table where three gangsters are talking about their territory. The camera tracks one of the men, Big Louis (Harry J. Vejar), as he walks toward a phone booth. In the far distance, a shadow of a man can be seen entering the hallway. The camera pans around and tracks into Louis, but then pulls away and tracks to the shadow of the man who just entered. The man whistles as his shadow moves behind a screen with a cross silhouetted over it. He calls "hello" to Louis and shoots him, whistles, throws the gun down, and moves off. The camera tracks to Louis's body on the floor, as the cleanup man walks in, looks, and hurries off.

In the body of the film, Hawks appears confident in the genre and presents its elements in what amounts to a series of blackouts: sequences that end in fades to black. It was as if he were chronicling the rise and fall of a vicious thug with the detachment of an objective reporter, albeit one who likes to look long and close at the actions of his subject, though without much interest in his motive. Camonte wants money and power; he defies the cops; he takes over Johnny Lovo's crew, who are introduced to us by the camera panning around their faces, as was done in *Little Caesar*. He has a sidekick, Little Boy (George Raft), paralleling Rico's friend Joey. When Camonte takes over from Lovo (Osgood Perkins), he also takes Lovo's girlfriend, Poppy (Karen Morley). At the same time, he keeps control over his sister in what amounts to an incestuous relationship—the sexual "flaw" in his character that parallels Rico's implied homosexuality. But above all, he is ruthless, even more than Rico. Camonte hurls bombs and kills a rival who survived his first assault and is lying in a hospital. In what quickly became a movie cliché, the pages of a calendar fly off as a machine gun rips bullets across the screen. When he gets his hands on a new machine gun, he yells, "Some little typewriter, eh? I'm gonna write my way all over this town with big letters. Get out of my way. . . . I'm going to spit!"

The mayhem is briefly interrupted by scenes of moralizing: the cops talk about the way the public is romanticizing gangsters, which in fact they were. A newspaperman gives a speech about the need for government control over the sales of machine guns. He calls for tougher laws to deport the Italian mobsters. "They bring nothing but disgrace to my people," says a man with an Italian accent. This interlude interrupts a montage of violence, which climaxes with Camonte beating up his sister when he catches her dancing in a nightclub and an attempt on Camonte's own life. As we noted, such interludes of preaching about controlling the mob did nothing to placate the moral outrage over this and other gangster films that led to the strict restructuring of the Production Code.

Tony's fall begins when he kills Little Boy, his sidekick and bodyguard, whom he finds living with his sister. The cops soon close in and Tony goes mad with fear when his sister, who stands by him in his fortress apartment, is killed, appalled at the fear shown by her brother. The gangster, as Warshow pointed out, is doomed to fail and fall. Camonte goes down in a fog of tear gas and a hail of bullets. The film ends with a shot of the advertising sign that

"Get out of my way . . . I'm going to spit." Tony Camonte (Paul Muni) gets his gun in *Scarface* (Howard Hawks, 1932).

Camonte looked to as his motto: "The World Is Yours."

Scarface is, finally, a film without the courage of its convictions. Perhaps by 1932 the two Howards, Hughes and Hawks, as well as the film's screenwriters, were beginning to feel the pressure of censorship and therefore created the sequences in which the police rail against the romanticizing of gangsters and newspaper men call for government control. Perhaps that's why they have Tony Camonte turn craven lunatic at the end. At least Rico in *Little Caesar* maintains some of his tough dignity, some astonishment at how far he has fallen when he is shot down, some gangster self-possession. *Scarface* is a much more violent film than *Little Caesar* but oddly more conservative. The explosive dynamism of the gangster finally implodes and renders him mad and helpless.

THE PUBLIC ENEMY

In *The Public Enemy*, the middle entry in the trilogy of early gangster films, Tom Powers is all self-possession. Played by James Cagney, one of Warner Bros.'s original and premier tough guys, Powers combines a rough-hewn elegance with his thuggish endeavors. He has a dancer's grace, and in fact James Cagney would go on to play the song and dance man George M. Cohan in Warner Bros.' *Yankee Doodle Dandy* (Michael Curtiz, 1942). It is a grace that combines with the character's pugnaciousness to create a curious mix of attraction and repulsion. Tom Powers is not the power and celebrity mad gangster in the mode of Rico and Tony Camonte. He comes from a warm, loving family, with a brother devoted to work and study to improve himself. But from an early age, Tom is seduced by a life of crime (the film moves from 1909 to the late 1920s and begins with an almost documentary use of footage of Chicago at the turn of the 20th century). From an early age, Tom steals, and he grows up to steal some more, guided first by a cheap hood named Putty Nose (Murray Kinnell) and later by the big boss, Paddy Ryan (Robert O'Connor).

We have already seen William Wellman's work in *Heroes for Sale* and *Wild Boys of the Road*. His style in *The Public Enemy* is just as stark and immediate. He presents a particularly dynamic sequence that takes place between Tom and his brother, who enlists to fight in World War I. There is a sharp confrontation between the two that Wellman films by **dollying** in to a close, low-angle two shot of the men. As their argument and accusations mount, the camera pulls back. Tom accuses his brother of being a thief, and Wellman moves to quick over-the-shoulder shots as brother Mike (Donald Cook) knocks Tom down. Tom takes out his frustration by kicking the door.

Tom Powers is both killer and lover. He is ruthless enough to kill Putty Nose, who brought him into a life of crime and then double-crossed him, and to kill a horse who threw and killed his gangster friend, Nails Nathan (Leslie Fenton). He is also misogynist enough to push a grapefruit in the face of a girlfriend who gets on his nerves, but gentle enough to gain the affections of a high-class prostitute, Gwen. She is played by Jean Harlow, a major star in the early and mid-1930s (she died in 1937 at the age of 26). Platinum blond, with an odd stage accent that sounds like a cross between Brooklyn and British, Harlow's appearance in *The Public Enemy* almost brings the film to a halt, as if Wellman were suddenly going in a new direction. In a sequence that takes place in Gwen's apartment, a film whose style is as rough as its character, with a mobile camera, rapid cutting, and occasional location shooting, suddenly moves to static, eloquently framed compositions. The love scene between Tom and Gwen is played against a statue in the background, a white marble figure, turned sideways, hiding her eyes with her right arm, as if turned away from something she doesn't want to see. The statue appears in almost every shot in the scene (one of the few that has music accompanying it) and seems to represent our own reticence in viewing this intimate moment.

This odd sequence is surrounded by another domestic dispute between Tom and his brother and by Tom and Matt (Edward Woods) killing the horse that killed Nails. The love scene serves to introduce a bit of contemporary elegance and offer an alternative view of Tom Powers, the "bashful boy," as Gwen calls him. But it is the only scene of relief from Tom's life of crime. And it is at the apex of his career from which, like all gangsters, he must fall. We do not see Gwen again. Gang warfare breaks out. Tom and Matt are shot at in the street. Tom tries to take over

An intimate moment in *The Public Enemy* (William Wellman, 1931). Tom Powers (James Cagney) and Gwen (Jean Harlow).

his rival's gang and gets gunned down. "I ain't so tough," he cries as he falls in the rain in the gutter—an echo of Rico's "Mother of mercy." He is taken to the hospital and then kidnapped by the rival gang, who return him to his mother's door dead and wrapped up like a mummy. It is a gruesome end to a violent life.

THE GANGSTER IN ECLIPSE

THE ROARING TWENTIES

Since the gangster genre was one of the targets of Breen and the PCA, the studios began to tone down the genre—at least a bit. At Warners, they simply reversed the roles their gangster actors played. In *'G' Men* (William Keighly, 1935), *The Public Enemy*'s James Cagney becomes an FBI man, battling the mob. By the end of the decade, it looked like the gangster might be in eclipse. Raoul Walsh's *The Roaring Twenties* (Warner Bros., 1939) is a kind of history of the decade and a valedictory to the gangster as tragic hero. The film begins by moving backward, with a montage of faces familiar to moviegoers at the time: Franklin Roosevelt, Adolf Hitler, Benito Mussolini, Herbert Hoover. It comes to rest with explosive images of World War I and Eddie Bartlett (James Cagney), who leaps into a foxhole with George Halley (Humphrey Bogart), who will play a role in leading Eddie into a life of crime.

After the war, Eddie becomes a "forgotten man," unable to find work, finally turning to a life of crime with the coming of Prohibition. "And so the Eddie of this story," the narrator tells us, "joins the thousands and thousands of other Eddies throughout America. He becomes a part of a criminal army, an army that was born of a marriage between an unpopular law and an unwilling public. . . . The public is beginning to look upon the bootlegger as something of an adventuresome hero, a modern crusader. . . ." The images beneath the narration show an ever more smartly dressed Eddie delivering liquor to a host of clients. The film offers us a neatly told summary of the 1930s gangster film, with all the implications of what drove the censors to do their work. The gangster is reviled and admired. He works in the face of an unpopular law to serve the public with the alcohol they crave. Most important of all, he is represented on screen by actors who may not be attractive in the usual movie-star way, but who are full of explosive energy and take a manic delight in their work.

Eddie has the added advantage of a heart of gold. He is a criminal in spite of himself. Unlike Tom

Powers in *The Public Enemy,* Eddie doesn't barrel into crime, he does it out of need. He is a romantic in an unlawful business that he undertakes against his better judgment. Murder and violence escalate into gang warfare, and Eddie loses his girl. The gangster and the sweetheart can't be reconciled, and Eddie's inevitable decline begins. The moral imperative that forces the gangster's fall is drawn all the more clearly in this film of the post-code era. As Eddie rises in his role of violent criminal, the possibility of simple affection diminishes, and when it does, his end is assured. Eddie's decline is matched by the decline of the country as a whole. A montage sequence of 1929 shows crashing piles of money and skyscrapers seeming to melt under the pressure of falling stocks. Franklin Roosevelt is elected, the narrator tells us, largely because of his opposition to Prohibition. "After thirteen years, Prohibition is dead, leaving in its wake a criminal element used to wealth and power, but unable . . . to cope with the new determination by an aroused public that law and order should once more reign." We see Eddie, who was forced to sell off everything, shabbily dressed, living in a flophouse, driving a cab. His bad luck has turned him into an alcoholic (during Prohibition, he only drank milk). When he picks up his old flame, Jean (Priscilla Lane)—now married to an attorney and with a child—and comes face to face with the domesticity that is denied him, he falls to pieces.

Here the code can be seen working in full force. The gangster has fallen from grace but can regain it by saving Jean and her husband from the mob, giving up his own life in the process. In an extraordinary sequence, Eddie, drunk and disheveled, goes to George's mansion. It is New Year's Eve, the end of the old decade. In a swift set of maneuvers, he shoots George and pushes most of his gang down the stairs or over the railing. Of course, he gets shot himself, and director Walsh executes a long tracking shot as the wounded Eddie runs down the snowy street. He winds up on the steps of a church, dying in the arms of the woman, Panama Smith (Gladys George), who has held her affection for him through it all, in a composition that brings to mind a Pietà (the traditional painting showing the dead Jesus in the arms of his mother). Her last words to the cop who asks who Eddie is: "He used to be a big shot." The camera pulls back, isolating the figures on the snowy church steps. The 20s gangster and the 30s films about him are over.

The gangster genre, however, was far from over. It remains one of the strongest and longest lived of

The end of the 1920s gangster—"He used to be a big shot." Panama Smith (Gladys George) holds the body of Eddie Bartlett (James Cagney) at the end of *The Roaring Twenties* (Raoul Walsh, 1939).

all film types. Brian De Palma's remake of *Scarface* (Universal, 1983), for example, with Al Pacino's Tony Montana playing a vicious Cuban immigrant version of Tony Camonte, was enormously popular. We will come across the gangster film again many times, especially as it mutates into film noir in the mid-1940s. The attraction to the gangster's rise and fall is irresistible. As Robert Warshow wrote, "He is what we want to be and what we are afraid we may become."

SELECTED FILMOGRAPHY

Little Caesar, dir. Mervyn LeRoy, Warner Bros., First National, 1931.

The Public Enemy, dir. William A. Wellman, Warner Bros., Vitaphone Corp., 1931.

Scarface, dir. Howard Hawks, prod. Howard Hughes, United Artists, 1932.

I Am a Fugitive from a Chain Gang, dir. Mervyn LeRoy, Warner Bros., 1932.

I'm No Angel, dir. Wesley Ruggles, Paramount, 1933.

She Done Him Wrong, dir. Lowell Sherman, Paramount, 1933.

'G' Men, dir. William Keighly, Warner Bros., 1935.

The Roaring Twenties, dir. Raoul Walsh, Warner Bros., 1939.

SUGGESTIONS FOR FURTHER READING

Tino Balio, *Grand Design: Hollywood as a Modern Business Enterprise, 1930–1939, History of American Cinema,* vol. 5 (Berkeley, CA: University of California Press, 1995).

Hardy, Phil, ed. *The BFI Companion to Crime* (Berkeley, CA: University of California Press, 1997).

Alain Silver & James Ursini, *The Gangster Film Reader* (Pompton Plains, NJ: Limelight, 2007).

Robert Warshow, "The Gangster as Tragic Hero," *The Immediate Experience,* (Cambridge, MA: Harvard University Press, 2001).

NOTES

1. Robert Warshow, "The Gangster as Tragic Hero," *The Immediate Experience,* (Cambridge, MA: Harvard University Press, 2001), 97–104.
2. Information on how sound film brought greater calls for censorship comes from Richard Maltby, "The Production Code and the Hays Office" in Tino Balio, *Grand Design: Hollywood as a Modern Business Enterprise, 1930–1939, History of American Cinema,* vol. 5 (Berkeley, CA: University of California Press, 1995), 37–72. The quotation from Irving Thalberg is from Maltby, 45.
3. Quoted in Maltby, 60.
4. The comment of Breen to Sternberg is from Maltby, 64.
5. The 1927 comment of the MPPDA is from Maltby, 40.
6. Quoted in Lea Jacobs, "Hollywood Institutions: Industry Self-Regulation and the Problem of Textual Determination," *The Velvet Light Trap,* vol. 23, no. 4, 9.

CHAPTER 10

COMEDY, CAPRA, AND MONSTERS (1931–1944)

Two genres that emerged during the 1930s could not be more different. Unlike the gangster film, screwball comedy presented an alternative universe of the rich and sophisticated. The monster film represented the dark side of the Depression-burdened imagination—a world of threatening creatures and frightened women. In this chapter, we also consider the films of Frank Capra, whose *It Happened One Night* (1934) starts the screwball genre and whose later films touch broadly on the culture and politics of the decade.

AFTER READING THIS CHAPTER, YOU SHOULD UNDERSTAND:

- Different generic responses to the Depression.
- The origin of screwball comedy.
- Frank Capra's response to the culture of the 1930s.
- The birth of the modern horror film.
- Why we like to be scared by monster and horror movies.

YOU SHOULD BE ABLE TO:

- Consider the ways screwball comedy beat the censors.
- Understand the changes comedy went through from the 1930s to the early 1940s.
- Trace the variations on "the forgotten man."
- Consider how the monster film became as enduring a genre as the gangster film.

SCREWBALL COMEDY

The gangster film was one response to the Great Depression. It was a genre that confronted a bad situation with images of murder and mayhem, of success outside of the law and inevitable, violent failure. But there was another, opposite cinematic response, not of poor men working their way to the top through gunplay and explosives, but of upper-class couples, in luxurious settings. The settings are complemented by the characters that are smart, rich, and incredibly witty. They are often married, and at such odds with each other that they get divorced, only to discover that, in the end, they are the only two people meant for each other. This is a cinema of affirmation at a time when audiences needed some notion that there might be alternatives to the hard lives they were living. Screwball comedy indicated that in a desperate time, it was possible to laugh at the rich and take amused comfort in their problems.

MY MAN GODFREY

The scene is a huge rubbish dump under a bridge in Manhattan at night. Garbage is pouring down. Fog horns are heard in the distance. At the base of the pile are mean little huts made out of packing boxes. Men are gathered around a fire. Two of them talk about hard times. One of them, Duke, quotes Herbert Hoover, the 31st president, in power when the Depression started: "Prosperity is just around the corner." "Yeah," Mike (Pat Flaherty) says, "it's been there a long time. I wish I knew which corner." A fancy car pulls up at the edge of the dump and a man and two well-dressed women jump out. They tell Duke that they are on a scavenger hunt to find a Forgotten Man and offer him five dollars to come with them to a hotel so they can show him off to a party. Duke, whose real name is Godfrey (William Powell), gets belligerent and threatens them. One of the women, Irene Bullock (Carole Lombard), stays behind and, in a long two shot, explains to Godfrey just what a scavenger hunt for a human being is—an entertainment for the rich. Out of curiosity, Godfrey goes with her.

So begins the 1936 film *My Man Godfrey* (Gregory La Cava, Universal) on a serious, downbeat note, reflecting the huge class differences opened by the Depression. The tone shifts quickly, though, when the film cuts to the party of the rich people, who have started the scavenger hunt. Someone suggests to Alexander Bullock (Eugene Pallette), the heavy-set, gravel-voiced patriarch of the Bullock family drinking at the bar, that the place resembles an insane asylum. "Well," says Bullock, "all you need to start an asylum is an empty room and the right kind of people." A woman pushes through the crowd with a goat on a leash—another trophy from the scavenger hunt. "Take a look at the dizzy old gal with the goat," the man says. "I've had to look at her for 20 years," Bullock replies, "that's Mrs. Bullock." So the "screwball" dialogue that marks these films picks up speed and propels the film through a series of witty remarks, sharp exchanges, and mistaken identities.

Based on the character she played in *My Man Godfrey*, Carole Lombard, at the time a very famous star, was referred to as a "screwball dame" in the show business newspaper, *Variety*. That comment might be the origin for the term "screwball comedy," which has since been used to refer to that body of films, mainly from the mid- and late-1930s, that focus on rich people, their marriages, divorces, and, sometimes, remarriage.[1] *My Man Godfrey* veers crazily from the screwball and sometimes offensive antics of the Bullock family and the self-possessed, mostly sane behavior of Godfrey, who Irene—madly in love with him—takes on as the family's butler.

Despite its downbeat opening, Godfrey, it turns out, is no "Forgotten Man," but rather a member of a rich Boston family, who, disappointed in love, drifted from suicidal despair into the life of the men close to despair but surviving it on the peripheries of society, the forgotten men. Godfrey is therefore in a position to do the best for both worlds, in control the way no one in the crazy world that surrounds him is. He puts the rich in their place. He cures Irene, who is madly in love with him, of her "spells" by shoving her fully clothed into the shower. He saves Mr. Bullock's fortune from bankruptcy and builds a nightclub on the city dump and gives his hobo friends jobs. The film ends, as comedy must, with marriage, of Godfrey and Irene.

My Man Godfrey works by diversion. It calls attention to the plight of the poor and then offers a fantastic method of helping them—at least a few of them. At first downbeat, it turns on its heel and presents us with a family of unattractive rich people who need to be brought around by another rich man who has been sobered by living among the poor. In short, the film tries to have it all ways. Screwball comedy did not in general skitter along the peripheries of Depression reality. It avoided the Depression entirely, substituting for the poverty and grime of people out of work a sparkling upper-class world whose inhabitants vie with each other for who can act crazier.

BRINGING UP BABY

The craziness almost always emerges from sexual tension between the central characters of the film. *Bringing Up Baby* (Howard Hawks, RKO, 1938) creates a three-way

Godfrey (William Powell) plays a Forgotten Man picked up by Irene (Carole Lombard) on a human treasure hunt. *My Man Godfrey* (Gregory La Cava, 1936).

Screwball behavior. Cary Grant and Katherine Hepburn in *Bringing Up Baby* (Howard Hawks, 1938).

affair between Dr. David Huxley (Cary Grant), a zoologist, looking for an "intercostal clavicle" bone to finish the construction of a Brontosaurus; the free-spirited and slightly loopy society woman, Susan Vance (Katherine Hepburn); and Baby, a leopard. Hawks does away with any sense of logic or narrative coherence for the sake of rapid-fire verbal humor and slapstick comedy. The jokes, verbal and visual, come at a rapid pace. Within the first 15 minutes of the film, David and Susan meet by chance on the golf course. Susan plays David's ball and then mistakes his car for hers, practically wrecking it in the process. Then David, in top hat and tails, enters a cocktail lounge, only to find Susan playing with olives, letting one slip to the floor, on which David—of course—falls down and crushes his hat. A series of mishaps continues until the sequence finishes with Alice, her underwear showing, clinging close to David, who walks pressed up against her, waddling out of the nightclub.

And then Baby is introduced. How does a leopard get into the picture? It doesn't matter. Susan's brother just happened to send it to her. What does matter is that David, who is about to be married to his rather uptight assistant, is introduced to anarchy, in the person of Susan. She does everything in her power to turn his ordered life into chaos, fall in love with him, make his life miserable, and eventually bring him around to her way of not thinking. In the interim, she sends off his clothes to the cleaners, leaving him dressed in her bathrobe. When her Aunt comes to call and asks why he is dressed that way, he leaps in the air and declares: "Because I just went gay all of a sudden." Susan further overturns gender conventions, saying that David looks handsome without his glasses (a clichéd line usually aimed at a woman). All the while, David keeps worrying about his bone (which Aunt's dog has stolen and buried). The double entendre is certainly not coincidental.

Everything and everybody gets mixed up, and inevitably, David gives in to Susan's persistent lunacy and falls in love with her. The film ends with the two of them precariously perched on top of the Brontosaurus. David realizes that the day spent with Susan was the best he's ever had. A freewheeling madness overcomes reason. But one more lunatic thing must happen to complete the chaos. Susan's shenanigans break the Brontosaurus apart, and David's bones come tumbling down.

The sexual innuendo embedded in *Bringing Up Baby* is part of its screwball charm and indicates how much fun the writers, Dudley Nichols and Hagar Wilde, and director Hawks had playing tag with the Production Code. By turning things upside down and replacing order and logic with comic chaos, the film can stand as something of a model for screwball comedy and as a way of playing with gender that would be unacceptable in melodrama. There is yet another mode of screwball called the comedy of remarriage, which takes the genre to a higher mode of sophistication.[2] Cary Grant, the actor who plays David in *Bringing Up Baby*, rarely played such a geeky role as he does in this film. He specialized in playing much more knowing, sophisticated, and perceptive characters that nonetheless get caught up in the craziness resulting in divorce and the eventual discovery that the couple, no matter how much they fight and disagree, are the only ones meant for each other.

THE AWFUL TRUTH

A wonderful example of this—quite possibly the most perfect of the screwball comedies—is *The Awful Truth* (Leo McCarey, Columbia, 1937). Rich New Yorkers Jerry and Lucy Warriner (Cary Grant and Irene Dunne) decide to divorce because they believe each is cheating on the other. Jerry probably. Lucy maybe. The trajectory of the film leads them to grow closer, no matter what they do to the contrary. And they try hard. Lucy takes up with a slightly goofy Oklahoman rancher, Dan Leeson (Ralph Bellamy). Jerry goes out with a nightclub dancer, Dixie Belle Lee (Esther Dale). Jerry teases Lucy about her impending marriage to Dan and their move to Oklahoma City. Screwball comedies are profoundly urban. Despite the fact that the films are made in Hollywood, their characters always live in New York (and probably have another home in Connecticut). They are creatures of the city; but unlike gangsters, they live at the top of the social scale. They don't have to violate the law to be known; they are at ease in their world and own it as well. Jerry's mockery over Lucy's impending move is quite funny, given that he knows she could not exist outside of New York. "Lucy, you lucky girl," he mocks. "No more running around the night spots. No more prowling around in New York shops. (McCarey cuts to a close-up of Lucy with a slightly pained expression.) "I should think of you every time a new show opens and say to myself, 'She's well out of it.'" "I know I'll enjoy Oklahoma City," Lucy responds somewhat meekly. "But of course," Jerry says. "And if it should get dull, you can always go over to Tulsa for the weekend."

It is difficult to imagine how this kind of New York snobbery went over with a Depression-era audience, except that the mockery is so good natured and both parties get their share of embarrassment. Certainly,

"I know I'll enjoy Oklahoma City. . . . And if it should get dull, you can always go over to Tulsa for the weekend." Jerry Warriner (Cary Grant) is smug. Dan Leeson (Ralph Bellamy) and Lucy Warriner (Irene Dunne) are not amused in *The Awful Truth* (Leo McCarey, 1937).

Will Hays, head of the Motion Picture Producers and Distributors of America and overseer of the Production Code Administration, was not concerned. "Apparently Main Street and Park Avenue are sisters under the skin insofar as appreciation of truly great pictures is concerned," he said in 1937, shortly before the release of *The Awful Truth*.[3] Apparently, fears of urban contamination of middle America had eased by the late 1930s. *The Awful Truth* proved to be an enormous hit. Perhaps it was the presence of an adorable dog, Mr. Smith, over whose custody Jerry and Lucy fight. More likely it is the good naturedness of the film, leavened with just enough slapstick and sight gags to make it available to a wide variety of viewers. For the movie wise, there are even inside jokes. Lucy pretends to be Jerry's loud-mouthed sister and imitates Katherine Hepburn, with whom Cary Grant would star in *Bringing Up Baby*. In the end, of course, the couple wind up back together—in a cabin in the country, trying to sleep in separate rooms until the wind blows open the door and they are brought back together again. They appear, finally, as little live figures in a cuckoo clock, following each other into the clock door.

The Awful Truth is a very cuckoo film. And nothing is more amusing about it than the conclusion that Jerry and Lucy are a perfect match, no matter their infidelities. These comedies of remarriage are different than contemporary romantic comedies, where young couples meet cute and go through a series of trials before finally coming together. The screwball comedies were about adults, often acting like kids, but mature enough to understand where their ultimate joy lies. They were also a way of evading the code. Jerry and Lucy should be punished for having sex outside of marriage. That they get back together in the end makes up for their transgressions and kept the censors mollified if not happy.

THE PHILADELPHIA STORY

Screwball comedy had a relatively short life, starting with Frank Capra's *It Happened One Night* (Columbia, 1934)—a film and director we will discuss in a moment—and pretty much ending with George Cukor's *The Philadelphia Story* (MGM, 1940). This film opens on an astonishing note as Katherine Hepburn's Tracy Lord throws her husband, C. K. Dexter Haven (Cary Grant), out of the house. She breaks his golf clubs and he, first clenching a fist as if to hit her, throws her down on the floor. Spousal abuse is not the same as the verbal sparring that is the basis of

Screwball comedy grows dark. C. K. Dexter Haven (Cary Grant) pushes Tracy Lord (Katherine Hepburn) to the ground in *The Philadelphia Story* (George Cukor, 1940).

screwball comedy. *The Philadelphia Story* has its share of comic moments, and Tracy and Dexter do get remarried at the end (actually they remarry before just before their divorce is final); but there is much anger and bitterness in between. Gone is the zaniness of Hepburn and Grant carried in *Bringing Up Baby*.

THE MARX BROTHERS, PRESTON STURGES, ERNST LUBITSCH

With the onset of the 1940s, with Europe at war, the Depression still raging, the complexion of comedy was changing. Perhaps the audience's delight in the exploits of the wealthy was on the wane. "You and your whole rotten class. . . . You're on your way out, the lot of you, and good riddance," cries George Kittridge (John Howard), Tracy's would-be fiancé in *The Philadelphia Story*. "Class, my eye," Dexter responds. But there might be something to it. After all, some 1930s comedy that was not screwball was based on skewering the upper class. (Donald Ogden Stewart, who wrote the script for *The Philadelphia Story*, was a leftist who was later blacklisted for his views; his take on class structure in the film is not surprising.) The Marx Brothers, in films like *Duck Soup* (Leo McCarey, Paramount, 1933) and *A Night at the Opera* (Sam Wood, MGM, 1935), played anarchic pranks on stuffy matrons, turning common sense upside down, with Harpo Marx leering and lewdly lifting up people's legs in ways that must have particularly annoyed the censors. For the Marx Bros., the rich were a source for creating chaos.

As the early 1940s moved into war, comedy as a genre changed. The brightness of the screwballs faded into something a bit darker, as the films of Preston Sturges attest. *Sullivan's Travels* (Paramount, 1941) concerns a director who wants to make a socially conscious film, *O Brother, Where Art Thou*. His producers are asking for *Ants in Your Pants of 1941*. They relent and Sullivan (Joel McCrea) heads out on the road to find out how the poor live. He is followed by a huge trailer with his cook, butler, and various hangers on. Like James Allen in *I Am a Fugitive from a Chain Gang*, Sully gets caught and sentenced to a chain gang, and the film goes quite bleak and violent. Before his release, Sully winds up sitting with his fellow inmates laughing at a Disney cartoon. He comes to understand that people need to laugh. . . . "It's all some people have in this crazy caravan."

Sturges's films are the tail end of the screwball genre. Some, like *The Lady Eve* (Paramount, 1941) and *The Palm Beach Story* (Paramount, 1942), are very

The Marx Brothers (and friend)—Harpo Marx, Alan Jones, Chico Marx, and Groucho Marx—pensive on a park bench in *A Night at the Opera* (Sam Wood, 1935).

much in the screwball tradition. Others, like *The Miracle of Morgan's Creek* and *Hail the Conquering Hero* (both Paramount, 1944), satirize home life during wartime, heroism, and outrageous sexuality. The pregnant young lady of *Miracle of Morgan's Creek* finds herself unable to remember who the father is. Her name is Trudy Kockenlocker.

Ernst Lubitsch was another important comic director of the period. A German émigré, he was briefly head of production at Paramount during the late 1930s and made sophisticated comedies, different from the screwballs because of the way they treated sexuality—frankly and obliquely at the same time. Lubitsch was sly and witty. In films like *Design for Living* (1933), *Trouble in Paradise* (Paramount, 1934), and *Ninotchka* (MGM, 1939)—the latter with Greta Garbo, one of the great stars of the late silent, early sound period—Lubitsch combined subtlety with broad humor. He could create great comedy and innuendo by simply filming a scene in front of a closed door while allowing the viewer to imagine what was going on inside.

CAPRACORN

Frank Capra is best known for a film he made in 1946. *It's a Wonderful Life* (Liberty Films, RKO) was not a commercial success when it was released but has become the beloved Christmas film for later generations. However, it is Capra's films of the 1930s that are among the most interesting barometers of the cultures of the decade. Capra, a Sicilian by birth, started his career in the silent period and worked during the 1930s for Harry Cohn's Columbia Pictures, among the poorest of the major studios. Capra was Cohn's star director and perhaps the only person Cohn treated with some respect. This was only because Capra kept turning out hits for the studio and because he showed little fear in the face of the man he called "his crudeness."[4]

IT HAPPENED ONE NIGHT

We have already noted Capra's *American Madness* (Columbia, 1932), a film that addressed the bank failures that occurred in the pre-Roosevelt years of the Great Depression. We can begin here with *It Happened One Night* (Columbia, 1934), a film many see as the first screwball comedy. The film features two major stars of the decade, Claudette Colbert and Clark Gable, the latter on loan from MGM. Loaning out a star was a common practice where artists under contract could be traded from one studio to another for a one-picture deal. In this instance, the trade was made as punishment

On the road, trying to hitch a ride. Peter and Ellie (Clark Gable and Claudette Colbert) in Frank Capra's *It Happened One Night* (1934).

for Gable's having turned down a role in an MGM film. Going to work for Harry Cohn's Columbia Pictures was considered a punishment.

It Happened One Night plays out as a road movie and a comedy of *un*marriage. It pits a spoiled rich girl, Ellie (Colbert), who jumps a marriage—literally by jumping off her father's yacht (indeed, from the silent period on, jumping in the water seems to be a ready way for a filmmaker to get a laugh)—and meets up with Peter Warne (Gable) on a bus to New York. Peter is an out-of-work journalist. In the course of their adventures they grow fond of and dependent on each other. The film's comedy is drawn on the couple's encounters with the characters they meet on the road as well as their interactions with each other. In a famous sequence, they try to thumb a ride on the road. Peter goes through elaborate variations of thumbing, none of which work. Ellie steps out and lifts her skirt and gets a ride immediately. Unfortunately, it is with a thief who takes their suitcases and leaves them stranded.

The film had a major impact on the national economy and dress codes. On the road, in their motel room—where Peter strings a blanket between them, calling it the "wall of Jericho," which comes down when they finally consummate their relationship—Peter takes off his shirt. He isn't wearing an undershirt. Legend has it that men across the country, struck by Gable's physique, stopped buying and wearing undershirts.

MR. SMITH GOES TO WASHINGTON AND *MEET JOHN DOE*

While *It Happened One Night* deftly demonstrates Capra's comic touch and class consciousness, it is his political films that are the most revealing about the culture of his time. They pit individuals—innocent loners—against seemingly insuperable odds, institutions that seem to move under their own power to crush individual will. I want to consider two of these films, one of which, *Mr. Smith Goes to Washington* (Columbia, 1939), was made late in the decade, and the other, *Meet John Doe* (Frank Capra Productions, Warner Bros., 1941), was made when Capra left Columbia early in the 1940s. Even though it comes after our period, *Meet John Doe* very much reflects the political turmoil of the late 1930s.

Mrs. Smith is a study in contrasts, of innocence vs. corruption, of the politics of the people vs. the entrenched machinations of power. Jefferson Smith (James Stewart) is a typical Capra hero: simple, unaffected, unworldly, the leader of the "Boy Rangers"

Facing overwhelming odds, Jefferson Smith (James Stewart) almost gives up his filibuster in Frank Capra's *Mr. Smith Goes to Washington* (1939).

in a small city run by a corrupt newspaper tycoon, Jim Taylor (Edward Arnold). Capra fleshes out a simple, basic narrative—Smith fills a Senate seat and faces down the corrupt forces of his state—with lessons in legislation and a rich array of incidents expressed through a busy visual palette that turns simplicity into a complex battle of good and evil.

Jeff comes to Washington wide eyed and full of patriotic admiration for its institutions. He escapes his handlers and tours the city. Capra and editor Slavko Vorkapich create a stirring **montage** of monuments, waving flags, and patriotic words meant to convince the viewer that Jeff is a blank slate on which is imprinted the noblest of democratic intentions. He even convinces his hard-nosed aide Clarissa Saunders (Jean Arthur) to help him get through his bill for boys' camps—until it comes up against Taylor's plan to buy up all the land for his dam. The filibuster that ensues carries the thrust of the film's drama, as Jeff Smith attempts to talk his bill past its detractors. Typical of Capra, boss Taylor is presented as an all but insuperable foe: he tries to smear Jeff; he floods the Senate with mail against the bill; his goons attempt to beat up the Boy Rangers back home. All seems lost as Jeff falters after many hours on the Senate floor. Capra builds dramatic tension by intercutting the increasingly fatigued and hoarse Jeff with the smug Senator Paine (Claude Rains), the indulgent president of the Senate, and Clarissa, who prompts him from the gallery. In the last minutes of the film, Senator Paine attempts suicide and admits to the corruption behind the attempt to kill Jeff's bill.

Jeff loses his innocence but the viewer gains a renewed faith in government, or some individuals in government. At least that is the film's intent. In the late 1930s, viewers needed some renewal. The Depression, somewhat alleviated for a few years by Roosevelt's New Deal, returned at the end of the decade. Fascist dictators in Germany and Italy had gained power and were waging war on much of Europe. The Japanese had invaded China and were moving against the whole of the Pacific, joining in an alliance with Germany and Italy. World War II pulled America in after the Japanese bombed Pearl Harbor on December 7, 1941. Frank Capra joined the army and produced a series of wartime propaganda films under the title of *Why We Fight* and *Know Your Enemy*. He also made a fiction film about fascism at home and the uneasy alliance of journalism, a restless public, instant celebrity, and exploitation. *Meet John Doe* is an uneasy film that tries to be comic, succeeds in being scary, and proves that a hoax can lead to dictatorship.

The film returns to the "forgotten man" theme we have seen play out in previous Depression-era movies. Here, a newspaper reporter, Ann (Barbara Stanwyck) writes a fake column about a forgotten man who is planning to jump from a building to protest his condition as well as national unemployment and the general state of the world. The newspaper's editor decides to make it all come true, and they audition a number of hobos until they decide on Long John Willoughby, who just happens to be played by Gary Cooper, one of the most recognized faces in the 30s American film. Capra, working again with Slavko Vorkapich—who created many of the montage sequences in 30s and 40s films—creates a montage of John Doe crossing the country, building John Doe Clubs, frustrating politicians, preaching neighborliness. The populist hero and his followers claim to eschew politics and, in doing so, make themselves the unwilling tools of someone with politics, especially with the power to influence and herd the innocent. In this case it is the home-grown fascist D. B. Norton (Edward Arnold), who gets the idea to have John form a third party and nominate Norton himself for president. Norton organizes a troop of Blackshirts, fashioned after the Italian dictator Benito Mussolini's paramilitary forces.

In a long, inebriated speech to John, the newspaper editor, Connell (James Gleason), warns John about the fifth column—a term used in the late 1930s and early 1940s to refer to subversive, mainly fascist, groups—that Norton is attempting to create. When John attempts to break with Norton, the would-be dictator breaks up a huge John Doe rally, using his Blackshirts to foment a riot. Broken and dispirited, John attempts to go through with his Christmas Eve suicide, saved only by a chastened Norton, the rousing of the John Doe clubs, and Ann, who compares John to Jesus. Bells ring and the chorus of Beethoven's Ninth Symphony plays on the soundtrack.

It is all utterly unconvincing. There were fifth column fascist movements in the United States in the late 1930s, but they did not get much traction. Who did get traction was a radio preacher by the name of Father Coughlin, an anti-Roosevelt, anti-Semitic agitator, who gained millions of followers. America's entry into World War II in 1941 briefly put an end to such right-wing agitation, but not as cleanly or simply as Capra's characters do by their professions of faith and love. As in *Mr. Smith Goes to Washington*, John Doe is too easy a dupe and too easily dissuaded from his stupidity at the very last minute. Capra's evil characters are too strong to be so easily turned away from their villainy. But Capra's heart, if not his brain, was in the right place. He was closely in tune with the cultural and political currents of the 1930s and proposed that the "people" would always make the right choices and pull together. It was a misguided optimism, and it has been argued that Capra's populism is basically a conservative and anti-intellectual ideology, cocooning its characters in an unworldly fantasy. But at the same time, it is a fantasy that makes his films charming and disarming.[5] They offer a vision that is inviting within the context of the films' own fiction, but just a little scary in their portrayal of gullibility and simplemindedness that are improbably saved from ruin at the very last moment.

MONSTERS

FRANKENSTEIN AND *DRACULA*

The 1930s were a rich decade of film genres. On the opposite pole of the screwball comedy and Frank Capra's comedies and melodramas were horror films, narratives of monsters and bloodsuckers that fed an audience's desire for shock and fear. In a period of war and Depression, these films provided a different kind of escape than gangsters and screwballs, an escape into the comfortable darkness of fear of things that go bump in the night, of creatures too fantastic to be real; too real to be easily dismissed.

The Edison Company made the first movie adaptation of Mary Shelley's 1818 novel, *Frankenstein*, in 1910 (directed by J. Searle Dawley). It is just over 10 minutes long. The monster is reasonably scary, appearing first as a burning skeleton emerging from a cauldron in Dr. Frankenstein's laboratory and then as a hulking figure dressed in rags. Most interesting is the way the film uses mirrors. The monster is appalled at his own appearance in the mirror. In two scenes the mirror is prominent in the right side of the frame: we see its reflection before we see the monster himself. At the end of the film, confronting his image, the monster disappears, leaving only his reflection, which is in turn banished by Dr. Frankenstein. In the later Dracula films, it is the vampire who is afraid of mirrors.

These images of terror proved irresistible. Horror, the ability of threatening figures, grotesque and monstrous, to throw a fright into filmgoers, to become a mirror of our fears of the unknown, grew into one of the sturdiest of film genres. **German expressionism**, as we noted in Chapter 6, was the early 20th-century aesthetic movement in which the **mise-en-scène** of a film reflected the stressed, sometimes psychotic state of mind of the characters and was an important breeding ground for horror films. In 1920, *The Cabinet of Dr. Caligari* (Robert Wiene) created a monster in a box—a sideshow attraction created by Dr. Caligari. The monster is a sleepwalker who murders people in the night. He moves through fantastic sets of distorted buildings and lighting patterns that emphasize shadow and dread.

The great German director, F. W. Murnau, whose American film *Sunrise* (Fox, 1927) we looked at in Chapter 6, made the first vampire film in 1922. His *Nosferatu* creates a thin, hook-nosed Dracula, bald, with long fingers and pointy ears, bat-like teeth, and a hideous face. The film is reasonably faithful to the 1897 novel by Bram Stoker and emphasizes the voyage to Transylvania, the fear of the villagers, the visit to Dracula's castle, the vampire's voyage to England, and his destruction by sunrise.

These European productions set the stage for what would be the start of a genre that would prove among the most durable of all—even more than the gangster: the horror and monster film. Following on Edison's *Frankenstein*, the horror genre started in American cinema in earnest during the late silent period, with expressionist-influenced films, often with German immigrant directors, such as *The Cat and the Canary* (Universal, Paul Leni, 1927). It reached its maturity at Universal with its versions of *Dracula* (Tod Browning, 1931) and *Frankenstein* (James Whale, 1931), followed by a series of sequels: *Bride of Frankenstein* (James Whale, 1935), *Son of Frankenstein* (Rowland V. Lee, 1939), *Dracula's Daughter* (Lambert Hillyer, 1936), and onward into the 1940s, when *The Wolfman* (George Wagner, 1941) was added to the gallery. Over at RKO, a giant gorilla (actually a small model made to look like a giant gorilla) horrified and captivated audiences. Like Universal's *Frankenstein* and *Dracula*, *King Kong* (Merian C. Cooper and Ernest B. Schoedsack, RKO, 1933) became a major success. It has been remade a number of times, spawned other giant beast films, and met its Japanese cousin, Godzilla, in 1962 (*King Kong vs. Godzilla*, Ishirô Honda). *Frankenstein* has had many remakes as well, and in contemporary film it has often morphed into the form of robots and computers. The computer HAL in Stanley Kubrick's *2001: A Space Odyssey* (MGM, 1968) is a distant relative of Frankenstein's monster. But Frankenstein's monster hardly approaches the fascination with vampires who have made their appearance in countless films and in television series.

This fascination has a number of origins. Our shear love of fright, of being startled while being safe in the confines of a movie theater or in front of the television is perhaps the greatest attraction. But, at the same time, these films speak to our desire to cheat death and, in the Frankenstein movies, to cheat birth itself—at least the organic human kind of birth. This was the drive of Mary Shelley's original novel, in which a scientist makes a man, only to discover that this patchwork of organs has consciousness and questions about who he is. Dracula has a more intimate attraction. After all, the bite on the neck is both a destructive and a sensual act, a way of entering another body and transforming it.

Transformation is itself a principal element in these films, and it may have been what attracted Depression-era audiences to them. They took viewers to mysterious foreign lands where horrible creatures are made or attach themselves to unsuspecting humans. In *King Kong*, foreign lands reveal a beast who becomes a victim of civilization. A creature at home in its environment is taken to New York and turned into a theatrical attraction. Hopelessly attracted to—in his hands—a tiny woman, an attraction so graphically expressed when the gorilla scratches at her clothes and sniffs his fingers that the censors demanded the scene be cut (it has since been restored). Kong's famous last stand on top of the Empire State Building proves that nature's monster is no match for civilization's weapons.

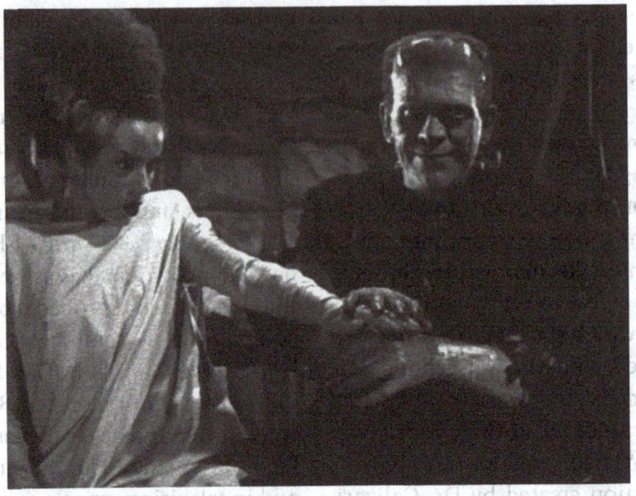

The monster and his bride (Boris Karloff, Elsa Lancaster). *The Bride of Frankenstein* (James Whale, 1935).

Bela Lugosi as *Dracula* (Tod Browning, 1931).

Frankenstein's monster and Dracula are of another order of fright. The first films in the series are slightly comical in retrospect. *Dracula* in particular is a bit awkward and stiff, showing its derivation not from Bram Stoker's novel, but from a stage play that was the film's origin. But at the same time, Bela Lugosi's Dracula is a more menacing figure than Boris Karloff's monster in *Frankenstein*, who comes off as vulnerable as he is threatening, despite the fact that he drowns a child in a fit of glee. Frankenstein's monster is a misunderstood freak, the cause of anger in the villagers, who succeed in burning down the castle. In *Bride of Frankenstein*, a sequel superior to the original, more clearly demonstrating its expressionist roots, the monster has great sensitivities, learns language, befriends a blind man, and thoroughly disgusts the bride Dr. Frankenstein has made for him.

Frankenstein's monster is a forlorn figure, childlike and uncomprehending of his brutal strength. King Kong, the giant gorilla, seems mainly to want his freedom and some affection. Dracula is pure malice, undead, unloving, a spreader of pestilence, a bloodsucker, part bat, part demon lover. Dracula is imprisoned only by sunlight or a stake through the heart; otherwise, he is free to roam and suck, hover in the dark and seduce. He becomes the most popular of the 30s monsters, an intriguing figure who has populated countless films, in enumerable guises, including, in the popular *Twilight* series, as a lovelorn adolescent in the 2010s—"the children of the night," as Lugosi's Dracula calls his fellow creatures. In the 1930s, these monsters were projections of an instability in the culture, wracked by economic despair, the threat of war, and the memories of the monstrosities of a war just over.[6] They entertained fear and were fearsomely entertaining.

SELECTED FILMOGRAPHY

Dracula, dir. Tod Browning, Universal, 1931.
Frankenstein, dir. James Whale, Universal, 1931.
King Kong, dirs. Merian C. Cooper and Ernest B. Schoedsack, RKO, 1933.
Duck Soup, dir. Leo McCarey, Paramount, 1933.
Design for Living, dir. Ernst Lubitsch, Paramount, 1933.
Trouble in Paradise, dir. Ernst Lubitsch, Paramount, 1934.
It Happened One Night, dir. Frank Capra, Columbia, 1934.
Bride of Frankenstein, dir. James Whale, Universal, 1935.
Dracula's Daughter, dir. Lambert Hillyer, Universal, 1936.
A Night at the Opera, dir. Sam Wood, MGM, 1935.
My Man Godfrey, dir. Gregory La Cava, Universal, 1936.
The Awful Truth, dir. Leo McCarey, Columbia, 1937.
Bringing Up Baby, dir. Howard Hawks, RKO, 1938.
Ninotchka, dir. Ernst Lubitsch, MGM, 1939.
Mr. Smith Goes to Washington, dir. Frank Capra, Columbia, 1939.
The Philadelphia Story, dir. George Cukor, MGM, 1940.
The Wolfman, dir. George Wagner, Universal, 1941.
Meet John Doe, dir. Frank Capra, Frank Capra Productions, Warner Bros., 1941.
Sullivan's Travels, dir. Preston Sturges, Paramount, 1941.
The Lady Eve, dir. Preston Sturges, Paramount, 1941.
The Palm Beach Story, dir. Preston Sturges, Paramount, 1942.
The Miracle of Morgan's Creek, dir. Preston Sturges, Paramount, 1944.
Hail the Conquering Hero, dir. Preston Sturges, Paramount, 1944.
It's a Wonderful Life, dir. Frank Capra, Liberty Films, RKO, 1946.

SUGGESTIONS FOR FURTHER READING

Stanley Cavell, *Pursuits of Happiness: The Hollywood Comedy of Remarriage* (Cambridge, MA: Harvard University Press, 1981).
Wheeler W. Dixon, *A History of Horror* (New Brunswick, NJ: Rutgers University Press, 2010).
David J. Skal, *The Monster Show: A Cultural History of Horror* (New York, NY: Faber and Faber, 1993).
Robert Spadoni, *Uncanny Bodies: The Coming of Sound Film and the Origins of the Horror Genre* (Berkeley and Los Angeles, CA: University of California Press, 2007.
Gerald Weals, *Canned Goods as Caviar: American Film Comedy of the 1930s* (Chicago, IL: University of Chicago Press, 1985).
Mark Winokur, *American Laughter: Immigrants, Ethnicity, and 1930s Hollywood Film Comedy* (New York, NY: St. Martin's Press, 1996).

NOTES

1. *Variety,* September 23, 1936, p 16, cited by Patience Wieland, "Screwball Comedy," *Noir Dame Blog,* http://www.noirdame.com/blog/screwball-comedy.
2. The term "comedy of remarriage" is from Stanley Cavell, *Pursuits of Happiness: The Hollywood Comedy of Remarriage* (Cambridge, MA: Harvard University Press, 1981).
3. The quotation from Will Hays comes from Nelson B. Bell, "Let There Be Rejoicing and Dancing in the Streets Urges Will H. Hays in Forecast of New Film Season," *The Washington Post* (October 4, 1937), 14.

4. See Frank Capra, *The Name Above the Title: An Autobiography* (New York, N.Y.: Da Capo Press, 1997).
5. For a negative reading of Capra's populism, see Jeffrey Richards, "Frank Capra and the Cinema of Populism," reprinted in Bill Nichols, *Movies and Methods*, vol. 1 (Berkeley, CA: University of California Press, 1976), 65–77.
6. David J. Skal in *The Monster Show: A Cultural History of Horror* (New York: Faber and Faber, 1993) makes the point that the disfigurements suffered by soldiers in World War I may have played into the construction of monsters in the early 1930s.

CHAPTER 11

1939

Considered by some to be one of the great years of Hollywood production, 1939's films offer an opportunity to look at some specific film genres and four films that remain classics of their kind: *Stagecoach, Dark Victory, Gone with the Wind,* and *The Wizard of Oz.*

AFTER READING THIS CHAPTER, YOU SHOULD UNDERSTAND:

- The continuing pressure on the studios regarding the code and the ownership of theaters.
- How four very different films spoke to their times.
- *Stagecoach* as the classic Western film, setting the generic pattern for Westerns to come.
- The evolution of melodrama.
- The enduring stature of John Wayne.

YOU SHOULD BE ABLE TO:

- Consider how the melodrama and the monster movie share some common traits.
- Define the lasting popularity of *Gone with the Wind.*
- Study *Gone with the Wind* in light of *The Birth of a Nation.*
- Discuss how a film like *The Wizard of Oz,* not a commercial success in its time, reaches a state of permanent popularity.

THE CODE, FILMMAKING, AND POLITICS

The end of the 1930s was a complicated period in Hollywood and in the culture at large. Economic conditions were becoming dire once again. Abroad, the Spanish Civil War, in which the progressive forces of the loyalists battled the fascist army of Francisco Franco, was lost in 1939. Franco's government, backed by Nazi Germany and Fascist Italy, further aggravated the growing threat in Europe. Germany invaded Poland, and England declared war on Germany, beginning World War II. At home, isolationism was rampant, with many conservatives in denial about the growing threat abroad.

In Hollywood, in 1938, the Department of Justice began antitrust proceedings against the studios. The process would conclude some 10 years later when the studios were ordered to divest themselves of their exhibition outlets, bringing **block booking** to an end and hastening the decay of the studio system. As part of its investigations during the late 1930s, the Justice Department found that the Production Code was too restrictive of controversial material in films. While maintaining its moral basis, the investigation concluded, it was still possible for the code to allow filmmakers to deal with "controversial" subjects. Ironically, this was just the kind of governmental intrusion that was one of the reasons for setting up the code in the first place.[1]

The studios had been particularly reluctant to take on political subjects, especially the growing conflict in Europe. It was a question of not wanting to give offence at home and abroad. As always in American business practice, fear of giving offence was actually fear of losing money. The studios depended, as they still do, on income from overseas markets. Paramount, for example, had a financial interest in the largest German studio, UFA. When Walter Wanger, an independent producer, was planning a film about the Spanish Civil War, Joseph Breen, head of the Production Code, wrote, "Your picture is certain to run into considerable difficulty in Europe and South America if there is any indication in the telling of your story, that you are 'taking sides' in the present unfortunate Spanish Civil War."[2] The resulting film, *Blockade* (William Dieterle, Walter Wanger Productions, 1938), despite the fact that it was written by a left-wing screenwriter, John Howard Lawson, barely mentioned Spain and did not identify the sides the antagonists were fighting for or against. It is an amazing example of a political film from which politics have been wiped clean.

However, the Justice Department's comments on the code's restrictive policies helped loosen up things a bit. In 1939, Warner Bros. produced *Confessions of a Nazi Spy* (Anatole Litvak), a film about "fifth columnists"—Nazi sympathizers—in the United States. Like *Blockade*, it caused much concern at the Breen office; there were fears raised that it would make Hitler angry! The concerns of what was called "premature anti-fascism" and the isolationist spirit of the country presented strong obstacles to the film. But Jack Warner prevailed, and *Confessions of a Nazi Spy* became the first film explicitly to address the Nazi threat.[3]

Despite the appearance of some very few politically minded films, the major output of the major studios remained in the rarified realm of "entertainment"—films apparently unconnected to the serious issues of the individual and the world and instead aimed at distracting an audience from them. 1939 turned out to be an exceptional year for such films, some believe one of the most exceptional years in Hollywood history. I have chosen four films as a kind of cross section of Hollywood output at the end of the decade. They are a Western, *Stagecoach* (John Ford, Walter Wanger Productions, United Artists); a melodrama, *Dark Victory* (Edmund Goulding, Warner Bros.); a southern Civil War film, one of the most famous of Hollywood films, *Gone with the Wind* (David O. Selznick, Victor Fleming, George Cukor, Sam Wood, Selznick International Pictures, MGM); and a musical fantasy, *The Wizard of Oz* (Victor Fleming, George Cukor, Norman Taurog, Richard Thorpe, King Vidor, MGM). The films are analyzed in terms of their genre, their narrative structure, and their relationship to the culture of the period in which they were made and seen.

STAGECOACH

With *Stagecoach*, John Ford became the master of the Western, the genre that celebrated a mythic past of open spaces, inhabited by Indians and outlaws who were confronted by lone heroes, fighting to make the land safe for "civilized" habitations. The Western was about frontiers, boundaries—both geographic and cultural—being pushed further and further westward, with white Europeans displacing Native Americans. Its key figure is the cowboy, riding the desert and the mountains, seeking peace for himself and for the easterners trying to settle a savage land that was given away before them.

John Ford's Westerns are complex meditations on the genre. His films are sensitive to the kinds of characters that populate the western landscape, a landscape that, in Ford's films, was almost always Monument Valley, with its long horizons broken by craggy towers of rocks. His characters are sometimes in contention with that landscape, sometimes comfortable in it, always at odds with each other, sometimes with themselves. But *Stagecoach* is in some ways an indoor Western. Although there is the requisite battle against marauding Apache warriors, led by the Native American Chief, Geronimo, the real drama of the film takes place inside a stagecoach and the places it stops to rest its travelers. Within the coach is a variety of character types: a bank president, who embezzles funds and rails against the government; a southern gambler; a liquor salesman; a pregnant gentlewoman off to meet her soldier husband; a drunken doctor; and a prostitute, driven out of town by, as the doctor says, "social prejudice," practiced by the "law and order league" of do-gooders, shown as sour-faced old ladies (Ford taking his cue from D. W. Griffith, who often parodied social workers as mean-minded women.)

The most interesting passenger is Ringo, an outlaw and escaped prisoner, played by John Wayne, here early in his career and in his first starring role with the director. John Ford created John Wayne. Although the actor played in many films, under many directors, it was Ford who, over the course of a number of films, honed Wayne into the laconic and tough hero who is still held by the culture as the image of a no-nonsense fighter for just causes. Wayne is the hero of the West, the loner who brings the peace necessary for settlement and civilization. In *Stagecoach*, he is the outsider who falls in love with another outsider, Dallas, the prostitute (Claire Trevor). Society's castoffs win the day in this film. Doc Boone (Thomas Mitchell), the drunk, safely delivers Lucy Mallory's (Louise Platt) baby. But Ringo is the major hero of the piece. He helps the hapless travelers survive an Indian attack with, of course, the help of a last-minute cavalry charge.

Stagecoach contains almost all the elements of the classic Western, including a carefully staged and shot shootout on the main street of the town, in the dark of night, between Ringo and three men out to kill him. Ford emphasizes the dark spaces between the hero and the killers that grows smaller as the group walks toward each other in shadow. Ringo drops to the ground and fires; Ford cuts away to Dallas as screams are heard. We then see the killer stagger into the bar and fall dead (Ford doesn't show us what happened to the other two). Ringo and Dallas are reunited. Doc Boone and the sheriff allow them to ride off to freedom. "That saves them the blessings of civilization," Doc says. But the fact is that "civilization" for Ford is the town set free from outlaws, a job that Ringo finishes and in so doing gives him freedom to live as he pleases.

Stagecoach set the generic patterns for so many Westerns to come and raised the genre's cultural status. Ford's visual style—the carefully photographed interiors; the wide open Monument Valley landscapes—and his painstaking but seemingly effortless editing style that drives the narrative forward were extraordinarily influential. When Orson

In a dramatic dolly shot, John Wayne is introduced as The Ringo Kid against the background of Monument Valley in John Ford's *Stagecoach* (1939).

Welles came to Hollywood shortly after the release of *Stagecoach* and before he filmed *Citizen Kane*, he said the film was his textbook, and he ran it over and over to learn how Ford constructed shots and edited them together. Ford's films continued to influence successive generations of filmmakers and the culture's notions of the West, which encompassed the myth of the open frontier and fantasies of individual freedom in virgin spaces. We will return to him again when we look at the films of the 1940s and again in the 1950s when we examine his great revisionary work about the Western hero, *The Searchers* (Warner Bros., C. V. Whitney Pictures, 1956).

DARK VICTORY AND MELODRAMA

Melodrama lives at the heart of cinema. As we saw in our first chapter, the exaggerated emotions, the great gestures of desire and despair, longing and loss entered film from the Victorian stage and, however modified, have remained ever since. During the 1930s, melodrama was as strong an escapist form as screwball comedies. The gangster film allowed the audience a parallel experience to the Depression, an experience of clawing one's way to fortune and notoriety, outside the law, only to fall hard at the end. Melodrama allowed a kind of emotional complicity with the suffering of the characters onscreen. Much like the monster in a horror film, the melodramatic hero or heroine is misunderstood or constrained, unable to express herself (or himself—there are the occasional male-centered melodramas), trapped in an untenable situation, suffering and the cause of suffering in others.[4]

The melodramatic character becomes a kind of avatar, a version of ourselves posited on the screen, filled with more pain and passion than we might ever experience in our lives, achieving in the end some release, always within boundaries that still contain them—even if that boundary is death itself. Melodrama is about desire and sacrifice, loss, gain, and loss some more. It is a genre that seeks balance and finds it at the expense of its central character and the viewer, who is left saddened, perhaps uplifted, but not necessarily wiser.

Dark Victory has a simple plot and a rich **narrative**. A wealthy young woman, Judith Traherne (Bette Davis), goes blind from a disease that will eventually kill her. After a period of denial, she accepts her fate and settles in marriage with her doctor. She keeps the extent of her blindness from him, sharing it only with her close friend, Ann (Geraldine Fitzgerald), and her housekeeper. The film's richness derives from its cast, the relative complexity of its narrative—which is more than its plot—and the shamelessness of its play on the viewer's emotions. Bette Davis was Warner Bros. star actress in the 1930s and early 1940s. She played an array of types from scheming women to rich, but sensitive souls, whose better nature—as in *Dark Victory*—had to be discovered through adversity. Humphrey Bogart, also a Warner's contract player since the 1930s, relegated to gangster types before breaking out as a private detective in *The Maltese Falcon* (John Huston, 1941) and as a romantic lead in *Casablanca* (Michael Curtiz, 1942), has a role as the keeper of Judith's horses. Ronald Reagan, the Warner's player who would go on to become the fortieth president of the United States, has a small role as one of Judy's partygoing friends. George Brent, a frequent Bette Davis costar, plays the doctor who diagnoses her illness and marries her.

The narrative structure of the film plays the ups and downs of Judith's condition, beckoning us through careful compositions and well-timed **close-ups** into the spaces of her denial, her despair when she discovers her condition by accidentally coming across the doctor's files, her discovery of a strength she didn't know she had. The film plays on the intensity of the characters' gazes and reactions, the swelling **music track**, the rapid changes in editing rhythms and shot length as Judy goes through the turmoil of her self-discovery and her decision, in the end, to hide her deteriorating condition from her husband. At the end, with only her friend and housekeeper aware, the latter clasping her hands in a gesture reminiscent of silent film melodrama, Judy goes to bed alone to die. The music swells in a heavenly choir and the camera **defocuses**, leaving us to imagine the misery of her husband when he returns to find his beloved is dead—in fact transferring that misery to us. The vicarious experience of loss is a major event in melodrama. The sufferer must transfer his or her suffering onto us, completing the melodramatic

A melodramatic death, Judy (Bette Davis) in her final moments, looked over by her housekeeper in *Dark Victory* (Edmund Goulding, 1939).

bond that holds us in thrall in a kind of airless place of identification.

Melodrama depends on our passive identification with its characters and our active participation in their emotional turmoil. If we don't feel with or for the characters, the melodrama fails. If we refuse to believe in the coincidences of events on which a melodrama narrative is built, the genre's structure collapses. In that sense, melodrama is rather fragile—like its tormented characters—depending on our allegiance to its movements of emotion.

GONE WITH THE WIND

A melodrama can end with sacrifices made and the hero or heroine enduring in the face of adversity. Such is the case with one of the most famous films of 1939, *Gone with the Wind*. The film is based on what was a widely read novel by Margaret Mitchell, published in 1937. The novel was such a success that independent producer David O. Selznick optioned it immediately and set out to film it almost page by page. Selznick was an extremely controlling producer, who needed to be involved in every aspect of the film he was making. That is the reason there are three directors listed for the film. Victor Fleming is the director of record, but George Cukor and Sam Wood, each important filmmakers in their own right, had some hand in the making of the film. Ultimately, Selznick was the director of the film, calling the shots, making sure the directors he hired were doing what he wanted done and firing them when they didn't. He succeeded on the commercial level. *Gone with the Wind* was the most popular film and the biggest moneymaker up to that time.

But he failed on the level of great, or even good, filmmaking. *Gone with the Wind* is lavish and long, but it is, at this distance at least—and from the point of view of this author—an exasperating narrative about a narcissistic character, who floats through the Civil War, stopping only to care for the wounded of Atlanta, flapping around her various "beaux," and mourning the death of the Old South. The film is ideologically contorted. There is barely a reference to slavery throughout its length. And though praised by some for its use of African American actors, especially Hattie McDaniel as Mammy and Butterfly McQueen as Prissy, the film portrays them as loyal retainers, not slaves, who dutifully continue their service after the Civil War. Under one of the opening title cards that reads "Margaret Mitchell's Story of the

Old South," we see a group of slaves toiling in the fields. As the music of "Look Away Dixie Land" plays, and horseback riders and farm workers are seen in silhouette, the titles read: "Here was a land of Cavaliers and Cotton Fields called the Old South. . . . Here in this pretty world Gallantry took its last bow. Here was the last ever to be seen of Knights and their Ladies Fair, of Master and of Slave. . . . It is now more than a dream remembered. A Civilization gone with the wind."

Indeed. Master and slave and knights and ladies fair. A dream world, Mitchell and Selznick want us to believe, not, as one contemporary African American reviewer of the film wrote, a world "built on the rape of Negro women, the hellish exploitation of black men, the brutalities of overseers, and the bloodhounds that tore human beings to pieces."[5] *Gone with the Wind* is not as virulently racist as *The Birth of a Nation* (perhaps sensitive to what happened to Griffith, Selznick cut references to the Ku Klux Klan that were in the novel), but like that film it idealizes and fantasizes a culture that was in fact built on people owned as property to be used and abused at their masters' whims.[6] Like its predecessor, it glorifies the Civil War as a tragedy for the South, punctuated by the famous shot where the camera cranes up over the ground littered by dead and wounded Confederate soldiers. The carnage does not even allow for a redemptive act on Scarlett's part, as she flees from the wounded in horror.

Scarlett is a difficult character to take, simpering in a fake southern accent (Vivien Leigh was British). Rhett Butler (Clark Gable) is the film's only figure with some authenticity. He sees through Scarlett's irritating posing and pining for Ashley Wilkes (Leslie Howard), and he voices one of the few words that express some historical truth: "Look at them," he says, when lists of the dead in the battle of Gettysburg is passed around, "all these poor, tragic people. The South sinking to its knees. It'll never rise again. The cause! The cause of living in the past is dying right in front of us. . . . That's what all of this is, sheer waste." Not a word, though, of what that "cause" is about. And when the "cause" is lost, Rhett decides to join the Confederacy.

During the siege of Atlanta, slaves are shown marching to dig trenches for the South, guarded, of course, by Confederate soldiers. (There is one brief reference in the film that alludes to slaves who have escaped after the Confederacy loses the war.) When the battle is over, Scarlett refuses to aid the wounded troops, opting instead to deliver Ashley's baby, though not before she beats her simpleminded household slave for lying about her midwife skills. The long, last part of the film follows Scarlett's attempt to save herself and Tara, her plantation, from the northern armies and the carpetbaggers (northerners who came to work the defeated South). There is an appalling scene that occurs as Scarlett is leaving Rhett, who has been jailed by the Yankees. She walks through the streets of Atlanta, now occupied by freed slaves and northerners. She passes a man promising a group of former slaves "forty acres and a mule," the reparation of land offered to freed African Americans after the Civil War. But the man is a slimy type, grinning with malice as he says, "'cause we're your friends, and you're going to become voters and vote like your friends do." She continues on, passing a group of shuffling and dancing blacks. Reconstruction, as Selznick sees it, was a means of fooling African Americans into believing they could take part as equals in American society. Perhaps, in retrospect, he was right.

Some have argued that the film's popularity rests on Scarlett's determination to overcome all the odds against her, that her cry "As God is my witness, I'll never be hungry again," silhouetted against the red sky of the ruined South, was a full-throated response to Depression weariness.[7] Like James Allen in *I Am a Fugitive from a Chain Gang*, she vows to "lie, steal, cheat, or kill" to feed herself and her "folk." But Allen's despair was a cry against the injustice of southern prison camps, the voice of one man against systemized injustice. Scarlett's is one of selfishness and endurance—perhaps a winning combination. But her irritation factor can't be overcome, and Rhett's famous line, "Frankly, Scarlett, I don't give a damn," not only struck a blow against the censor's prohibition against cursing, but gave voice to what must be the viewer's own fatigue at her fussing, flouncing, and phony tears. The melodramatic contrast between Scarlett's undying devotion to Ashley and Rhett's cynicism and violence is marked. But the

Rhett and Scarlett O'Hara (Clark Gable and Vivian Leigh) in *Gone with the Wind* (David O. Selznick and others, 1939).

film is clever enough to soften his violence with his devotion to his daughter, who dies trying a jump on her horse, and his misery when Scarlett falls down the stairs and loses their second child. The character of Rhett emerges as the strong, suffering figure of the film; while Scarlett remains only suffering, her claim of strength mitigated by her childishness.

This is the stuff of melodrama, and it seems to me that it becomes almost comically excessive in this film. When melodrama begins to exceed its limits, when in the last reels of the *Gone with the Wind* deaths pile up—children, born and unborn, the death of Melanie (Olivia de Havilland), Scarlett's cousin who marries Ashley—we are back in the territory we last explored in Cecil B. DeMille's 1920's spectacles and tend to find the loss and the tears more risible than provoking of sadness. But it is certainly this melodrama's excess that has maintained its popularity over the years. Scarlett's near redemption at film's end, her promise to go on despite her losses, may not mitigate her consuming narcissism, but it allows the viewer to connect to her in ways that her irritating traits prevent in the course of the movie's 4 hours. Perhaps the film's popularity must remain a mystery. Its pining for a lost cause that deserves to be lost and its central figure of a largely unsympathetic woman, along with its extravagant production design, seem to hit some chord of response. Perhaps there remains a perverse need to maintain the popularity of *Gone with the Wind*. If we should admit how flawed it is, how deeply racist its treatment of its African American characters, it would somehow finally destroy the myth of the chivalrous Old South. In other words, the film is a kind of inoculation against the loss of our most conservative fantasies of "a pretty world [where] Gallantry took its last bow." But it also allows us to understand what a lie it is.

THE WIZARD OF OZ

There is no mystery to *The Wizard of Oz*. Though it was not a big hit at the time, it has become among the most loved of films and an inseparable part of the culture. It is broadcast on television regularly. The line "We're not in Kansas anymore" has become a commonplace; the song "Over the Rainbow" has become a standard. The place names, such as "the Emerald City," echo through our discourse. Dorothy's ruby slippers are in the Smithsonian Institution. It is the great escape film that, in its time, addressed the Depression and the war in Europe by offering a dreamscape alternative and, at the same time, indicating that there was no escape from where one is.

The frame narrative of the film (which, like *Gone with the Wind*, had multiple directors) takes place in a

The Tin Man, Dorothy, the Scarecrow, and The Cowardly Lion (Jack Haley, Judy Garland, Ray Bolger, Bert Lahr) in *The Wizard of Oz* (Victor Fleming and others, 1939).

barren, sepia-toned, Dust Bowl Kansas, a place from which thousands of people attempted to escape the depths of the Depression. Dorothy (Judy Garland) escapes by means of a dream brought about by a tornado and a knock on the head. The world she escapes to is a bright Technicolor realm of magic and creatures both good and evil, ruled by a charlatan Wizard (Frank Morgan). The heart of the film is a road movie along the yellow brick road, with the Cowardly Lion (Bert Lahr), the Scarecrow without a brain (Ray Bolger), and the Tin Man without a heart (Jack Haley). The journey is itself circular. Despite the characters they meet and their destruction of the Wicked Witch of the West (Margaret Hamilton), the characters learn commonplace wisdom and the need of home. They leave home in order to find it. Dorothy discovers that staying in one place is safer than moving on.

Is the message of the film isolationist? Is it telling us to remain close to the familiar and ignore "foreign entanglements"? "If I ever go looking for my heart's desire again," Dorothy tells the Good Witch Glinda (Billie Burke), "I won't look any further than my own backyard." The film leaves us with a message of containment and contentment with what we have—in spite of the fantasy world that enthralled us throughout the body of the film. It is as if *The Wizard of Oz* were contradicting its own creativity and the imagination of its viewers, cautioning them perhaps to travel in their dream world only through the safety of cinema. There's no place like home or the movie house. At the end of the 1930s, the real world was about to explode into a global war. In the film world, at least in the world of *The Wizard of Oz*, people were warned to stay close to the familiar and to ignore the conflagration raging outside their borders.

SELECTED FILMOGRAPHY

Stagecoach, dir. John Ford, Walter Wanger Productions, United Artists, 1939.
Dark Victory, dir. Edmund Goulding, Warner Bros., 1939.
Gone with the Wind, dirs. David O. Selznick, Victor Fleming, George Cukor, Sam Wood, MGM, 1939.
The Wizard of Oz, dirs. Victor Fleming, George Cukor, Richard Thorpe, King Vidor, MGM, 1939.

SUGGESTIONS FOR FURTHER READING

Edward Buscombe, *Stagecoach* (London, UK: BFI Publishing, 1992).
Christine Gledhill, *Home Is Where the Heart Is: Studies in Melodrama and the Woman's Film* (London, UK: British Film Institute, 1987).

Barry Keith Grant, ed., *John Ford's Stagecoach* (Cambridge, UK: Cambridge University Press, 2003).

Aljean Harmetz, *The Making of the Wizard of Oz* (New York, NY: Knopf, 1977).

———, *On the Road to Tara: The Making of Gone with the Wind* (New York, NY: Abrams, 1996).

Ina Rae Hark, ed., *American Cinema of the 1930s: Themes and Variations* (New Brunswick, NJ: Rutgers University Press, 2007).

Richard Harwell, ed., *Gone with the Wind as Book and Film* (Columbia, SC: University of South Carolina Press, 1983).

Molly Haskell, *Frankly, My Dear: Gone with the Wind Revisited* (New Haven, CT: Yale University Press, 2009).

Steven J. Ross, "*Confessions of a Nazi Spy*: Warner Bros., Anti-Fascism and the Politicization of Hollywood," *Warners' War: Politics, Pop Culture & Propaganda in Wartime Hollywood, http://www.learcenter.org/pdf/WWRoss.pdf.*

David Welky, *The Moguls and the Dictators: Hollywood and the Coming of World War II* (Baltimore, MD: Johns Hopkins University Press, 2008).

Garry Wills, *John Wayne's America: The Politics of Celebrity* (New York, NY: Simon & Schuster, 1997).

NOTES

1. On the Justice Department and the code, see Richard Maltby, "The Production Code and the Hays Office" in Tino Balio, *Grand Design: Hollywood as a Modern Business Enterprise, 1930–1939, History of American Cinema*, vol. 5 (Berkeley, CA: University of California Press, 1995), 69–71.
2. Quoted in David Welky, *The Moguls and the Dictators: Hollywood and the Coming of World War II* (Baltimore, MD: Johns Hopkins University Press, 2008), 74.
3. A good history of the film can be found in Steven J. Ross, "*Confessions of a Nazi Spy*: Warner Bros., Anti-Fascism and the Politicization of Hollywood," *Warners' War: Politics, Pop Culture & Propaganda in Wartime Hollywood, http://www.learcenter.org/pdf/WWRoss.pdf.*
4. For an interesting discussion of gender and genre, see Linda Williams, "Film Bodies: Gender, Genre, and Excess," *Film Quarterly*, vol. 4, no. 44 (Summer, 1991), 2–12.
5. Melvin B. Tolson, quoted in Charles Maland, "1939: Movies and American Culture in the *Annus Mirabilis*," in Ina Rae Hark, *American Cinema of the 1930s: Themes and Variations* (New Brunswick, NJ: Rutgers University Press, 2007), 250–251.
6. Maland points out that Selznick cut out references to the Klan, 250.
7. Maland, 242–243.

CHAPTER 12

HOLLYWOOD AND WORLD WAR II (1942–1949)

Important changes occurred in filmmaking with the onset of the 1940s. Something as simple as the change in film stock helped create a new genre—film noir. Directors, such as Orson Welles and Alfred Hitchcock, began their work in Hollywood. The nation's entry into World War II changed the nature of the war film genre. The beginning of the decade saw the production of *Casablanca,* one of the most enduring of American films. In this chapter we concentrate on the changes in Hollywood filmmaking in the early 1940s and the war effort.

AFTER READING THIS CHAPTER, YOU SHOULD UNDERSTAND:

- The changes that occurred in Hollywood filmmaking at the turn of the decade of the 1940s.
- How film acting in the 1940s differed from the 1930s.
- The changes in lighting in the 1940s.
- The difference between films of World War I and World War II.
- The continuing popularity of *Casablanca.*

YOU SHOULD BE ABLE TO:

- Consider how filmmaking evolves from decade to decade.
- Begin thinking about the emergence of new directorial talent.
- Think about Frank Capra in his role of World War II documentarian.
- Place *Casablanca* in its historical context.
- Untangle the complexities of Bogart's character Rick in *Casablanca.*
- Consider whether the enduring popularity of *Gone with the Wind* and *Casablanca* may have to do with individuals who overcome difficult circumstances and broken love affairs.

PART ONE: THE REEMERGENCE OF HOLLYWOOD CINEMA

While some argue that 1939 was the apex of Hollywood production, and we have noted some of that year's most famous films, there is a way to understand that American film came fully into its own during the decade of the 1940s. It was during the 1940s—at least until 1946—that the American studio system, along with some independent filmmakers, produced more creative, inventive, even complex films than in the preceding decades. Many things happened and changed in American culture and American film early in the 1940s that brought this change about. They ranged from the shattering, global experience of World War II, to small technological changes in filming, to the emergence of strong directorial voices, and the unexpected appearance of a style of film called film noir.

This was the period of maximum audience attendance. By 1946, everyone who was able to go to the movies did. The total box office gross in 1946 was $1.7 billion! It was an astronomical figure for the time.[1] Hollywood was at the peak of its powers and the movies it created expressed an extraordinary imaginative variety.

ACTING

The changes in filmmaking in the early part of the decade were subtle. Film acting became somewhat more restrained. More than during the 30s, actors seemed to be talking to one another rather than declaiming for the microphone and the audience. They talked more slowly as well. Even though some directors, like Howard Hawks, favored rapid fire dialogue, in general, acting became calmer. There was a sense of internalizing roles, even before the influx of "method" actors that occurred in the late 1940s and early 1950s. "The Method" acting style stressed that an actor must call upon his or her deepest emotions in order to inhabit a role. (We will discuss the "Method" in Chapter 18.) But before that, beginning in the early 40s, actors seemed to more intensely realize their characters. Gone were the holdovers of silent film melodramatic gestures that were still occasionally seen in the 1930s. The result was that the fictional worlds of 1940s film became more deeply articulated, the **mise-en-scène** created around the actors became more subtle, **production design** more detailed as acting became more integrated within the larger design of a film.

LIGHTING

Lighting changed drastically from the generally **high-key lighting** of the 1930s to a more subtle use of light and shadow. Most films of the 1930s—with exceptions such as the Universal horror films of the early part of the decade and the films of the director Josef von Sternberg—were evenly and brightly lit. This changed in the early 40s. One reason was the development of a faster **film stock**. The "speed" of film has to do with the amount of light it takes to create a usable image. The faster the film, the less light is required, and the development of a fast stock allowed **directors** and **directors of cinematography** to take advantage of the dark, emphasizing shadow and creating a mise-en-scène that was much more richly sculpted in light and dark than many films of the 30s. Orson Welles and his cinematographer Gregg Toland took full advantage of the change in film stock in the creation of *Citizen Kane* (RKO, 1941). One end result of this was the appearance of film noir in the middle of the decade (though film stock was only one part of the development of noir), a style of film that has had a lasting influence on film and film criticism.

DIRECTORIAL VOICES

A number of directors came to the fore in the early 1940s who went on to dominate American and international film each in different ways for decades to come. There were, of course, important directors in the 1920s and 30s—Frank Borzage, William A. Wellman, Frank Capra, to name but a few—and we have spoken of them in earlier chapters. One major director to emerge fully in the 1940s was John Ford. Ford had been making films since the late 1900s, but it was *Stagecoach* in 1939 (the film we discussed in the previous chapter) that set the tone for the Western genre and helped bring John Wayne and his director to stardom. In the early 1940s, Ford went outside the Western with an adaptation of novelist

During the 1930s, MGM was known for bright, high-key lighting, as in this image from *Dinner at Eight* (George Cukor, 1933).

Orson Welles and cinematographer Gregg Toland used low-key lighting to bathe characters in shadow in *Citizen Kane*, 1941.

John Steinbeck's *The Grapes of Wrath* (Fox, 1940), a dark melodrama about a destitute Depression-era family and their trek to California, and a film about a Welsh mining family, *How Green Was My Valley* (Fox, 1941). After World War II—during which he made propaganda films for the government—he returned to the Western with *My Darling Clementine* (Fox, 1946), *Fort Apache* (Argosy, RKO, 1948), and *She Wore a Yellow Ribbon* (Argosy, RKO, 1949). Together, these films established him as a major figure in Hollywood filmmaking, a position he held until his death in 1973.

Alfred Hitchcock began his directorial career in England in 1922. He came to America at the invitation of David O. Selznick, the producer of *Gone with the Wind*, and spent a large part of the 1940s getting out from under Selznick's suffocating wing. His first American film, the Selznick-produced *Rebecca* (1940), was set in England. It was not until his fifth film in Hollywood, *Shadow of a Doubt* (Universal, 1943), that he found his footing and began realizing a cinematic style and a thematic intensity that would blossom fully in the mid-1950s.

Orson Welles was the most influential figure to emerge from the decade. Welles came to film from a distinguished career in New York theater and radio, climaxing in the famous (or infamous) 1938 broadcast of H. G. Wells's *War of the Worlds*, that frightened people into believing the Earth was being attacked by Martians. When RKO offered Welles a contract, with the right to final cut (that is, the film he edited would be the film that the studio would distribute, without interference), Welles arrived with plenty of resentment on the part of the film community. When he made *Citizen Kane*, which was—among many other more important things—a thinly disguised biography of the media baron William Randolph Hearst, the film got into immediate trouble. In its time, *Citizen Kane* did not turn a profit. After its moment of creation, it became the most famous and influential American sound film ever made. In the following chapter, we will discuss the work of these three directors in some detail.

PART TWO: THE WAR FILM

Much more momentous events were occurring in the culture at large. The isolationist resistance to the growing war in Europe and Asia came to an end when the Japanese attacked Pearl Harbor, Hawaii, on December 7, 1941. America joined the war and the immediate growth of war-related industry and their need for workers finally put an end to the Depression. But the end of one wrenching national experience signaled the beginning of a new 4-year struggle abroad and at home. The war sent hundreds of thousands of young men abroad into strange, hostile lands. Women were in demand to take their place in the workforce, an event that gave them economic power they never had before. There were large migrations of women and African Americans northward to where the jobs were, resulting in further, lasting changes in the makeup of American culture and geopolitics.

Hollywood was hardly immune from these changes. The studios backed both the war effort and President Franklin Delano Roosevelt. Advertisements for war bonds accompanied an evening's show. The war film was revived, but this time under government censorship. What the studios had feared for so long now came to pass under the rubric of a national emergency. The Office of War Information was set up to be sure that, among other things, films, and war films in particular, upheld the wartime ideology of communal activity in which the country and the troops all fought together for the common cause of defeating fascism in Europe and Japanese imperialism in Asia.

Along with battleground films, there were sentimental melodramas about the homefront, such as *Since You Went Away* (John Cromwell, David O. Selznick, Selznick International Pictures, 1944), a film that traces the attempts of a middle-class family to hold their lives together while the husband is away at war. At home or at the front, wartime films held out an optimism that was often difficult to maintain in the face of the struggles on the battlefield. Since the national consensus was forcefully behind the war effort—as it was not before the attack on Pearl Harbor—these films were embraced and well attended. We will look at some of them next.

As we saw in Chapter 6, World War I films tended to emphasize the romantic engagements of one or more of its characters, interspersed with scenes of battle. The 1927 film, *Wings*, a World War I film about flyers and the "It" girl, Clara Bow, contains exciting aerial dog fights throughout the film interspersed with the romances of the various male characters. D. W. Griffith's *Hearts of the World* (1918) and King Vidor's *The Big Parade* (1925) also focus on the love affairs of their central characters. Although Vidor's film is very much concerned with the pain inflicted on the battlefield, the love affair between Jim and Melisande is central to the **narrative**. In contrast, World War II battle films emphasized men in groups, themselves made up of a cross section of America: a Texan, a midwesterner, a guy from Brooklyn, a Catholic, a Jew. They played and joked together and fought the war selflessly. And the emphasis was always on the strain toward victory or the defeat of battle. Men were killed in the films of World War II, but their deaths were always an encouragement for those who fought on.

AIR FORCE

In Howard Hawks' *Air Force* (Warner Bros., 1943), women appear only peripherally: a crewman's mother and the captain's wife, who are seen briefly as they send their men off on their mission; nurses take care of the wounded. The film pivots on the need for male cohesion aboard the diverse crew of the fighter plane "Mary-Ann," heading for Hawaii on the eve of the Pearl Harbor attack. Aboard are a midwesterner, a Jew from New York, a Texan, etc. While airborne, the crew hears the noise of the attack and the sound of Japanese pilots over their radio. "Who you got tuned in, Orson Welles?" jokes Winocki (John Garfield), in a reference to Welles's 1938 *War of the Worlds* radio broadcast.

Winocki is the odd man out. Disappointed because he washed out as a pilot, he is the angry member of the crew, who needs to be brought into line so that they can all fight as a unit. Still listening to the plane's radio, they hear President Roosevelt declare a state of war against Japan, which further galvanizes the crew. History and personalities mix in a drama of men in groups, fighting for a just cause and proving their worth. Winocki finally comes around, landing the battered "Mary-Ann" after Captain Quincannon (John Ridgely) has been shot. Quincannon's death bed scene (written by the novelist William Faulkner) further unites the crew in a common cause, and they proceed to put together their shot-up plane from spare parts, defend themselves against a Japanese air and ground attack, and get back in the air in time to spot the Japanese fleet headed for Australia. A stirring **montage** of men and machines getting ready for battle and a climactic fight over the South Pacific allows the film to create a surrogate revenge for the attack on Pearl Harbor. The film ends as the crew prepares for an attack on Tokyo and the voice of Roosevelt promises to bring the battle to an end on the enemy's home ground.

Like so many early films about World War II, *Air Force* is a call to solidarity in which the flyers are a microcosm of America and their bravery a mirror to be held up to the viewers of the film to hang together in the face of the enemy. The World War II film, made as the war itself was being waged, served as a mediation between the people at home and those at the front. It was meant to propagate the idea that "we are all in this together," that the homefront was as important to the effort as the soldiers fighting overseas.

The cohesive fighting unit could be figured through the strength of a single individual, particularly when that individual was played by John Wayne. Wayne's appearance in John Ford's *Stagecoach* put him in the forefront of early male action heroes both in the Western and in war films. He was a commanding presence, tough, but understanding of the needs of his men. He was indestructible. Even if he was killed in battle, his indefatigable spirit lived on. Wayne the man never saw battle. John Wayne the movie star helped to define the idea of heroism in wartime. Wayne the celebrity became a figure of national admiration and a proponent of right-wing political views, supporting American wars wherever they were fought, especially, and most controversially, the war in Vietnam.

BACK TO BATAAN

Two films made at the end or right after World War II show Wayne at his most heroic and, in a way, his most restrained. This is particularly true of *Back to Bataan* (Edward Dmytryk, RKO, 1945), a film that is essentially about the Philippine resistance to the Japanese, who had driven the Americans out of the country early in the war. Wayne's Colonel Madden is the leader of the Americans, who are aiding the resistance and a comforter of those who would lose their lives to the merciless Japanese. The film does contain a romance, of sorts, though this doesn't involve Colonel Madden—Wayne's characters were usually too busy being tough and singleminded to be distracted by romantic involvements. Here a leader of the resistance, Andrés Bonifácio (Anthony Quinn)—playing the grandson of an actual Philippine nationalist and independence fighter—is in love with a woman who is a double agent: she does propaganda broadcasts for the Japanese (or the "Japs" as they are referred to in the film and by most every American during the war) in which she delivers coded messages to the resistance.

Back to Bataan is a variation on the theme of cohesion, in this case arguing for the support of foreign forces—Philippine guerillas, in this case—fighting on our side. The film is something of a counterbalance to some unpleasant events that occurred at home during the war, namely the imprisonment of Japanese Americans after the attack on Pearl Harbor. Imprisoned in the American version of concentration camps were 120,000 people, most of them children, living on the West Coast.[2] The Philippine resistance fought the Japanese, and their depiction as heroes was important in representing Southeast Asians in a positive light, an indication that all "foreigners" were not enemies.

Colonel Madden acts as the backbone to the resistance. When the final battle occurs, the colonel and his band of fighters hide underwater, breathing through reeds, to fool the Japanese, who they attack with bravery exceeding their numbers. The film ends with the American force landing on the island, using stock newsreel footage, something that was common in World War II films. A voiceover announces that "Freedom is on the march again," as documentary footage of marching soldiers ends the film as it had opened it, while the narrator reads off the names of soldiers from all over the country. But at the end, over the "real" soldiers, we see the actors superimposed, ending with Wayne marching and smiling broadly.

SANDS OF IWO JIMA

Films that looked back at World War II after it was over brought a touch of nostalgia to an already war-weary society, and Wayne was ready to remind viewers of past heroism. In *Sands of Iwo Jima* (Allan Dwan, Republic, 1949), Wayne's Marine Sergeant Stryker is a no-nonsense squad leader, tough, steely-eyed, unsparing in his devotion to their training. He must push against the sometimes bitter disharmony of his squad, against the antagonism of one marine, Conway (John Agar), who sees in Stryker an implacable substitute for his father. There is an intense sequence in which Stryker and Conway face each other on the battlefield, Conway wanting to save a fallen colleague, a friend of Stryker's. Stryker is determined to shoot him if he does this because he will jeopardize the mission. Dwan holds a long close-up on Stryker's face as we hear the voice of the wounded soldier calling in the distance—a powerful moment of duty versus moral need.

Stryker is given a backstory. Embittered because his wife abandoned him, he is an alcoholic, who must face action and be strong for his men despite his

The steely-eyed look of duty. John Wayne as Sgt. Stryker puts on his war face in *Sands of Iwo Jima* (Allan Dwan, 1949).

sadness and addiction. But these personal touches are merely glosses on the battles. As always in World War II films, they are fierce and unrelenting; many men die, especially those that have most gained our sympathies. "Lock and load!" yells Stryker as the troops ready to land at Iwo Jima. The phrase has become a cliché in war movies ever since. Reaching the top of Mount Suribachi, Stryker says, "I never felt so good in my life," and is immediately killed. The film ends with the reading of a sentimental letter that Stryker wrote to his child and with a reenactment of the raising of the flag at Iwo Jima. This famous image, which was turned into a war memorial statue in Washington, DC, became a symbol of American victory in World War II. In fact, the image taken at the site by a journalist, was itself a reenactment of the flag raising that occurred before the photograph was taken. The image is so ingrained in the national consciousness that it keeps reoccurring in film. Clint Eastwood made a sort of sequel to *Sands of Iwo Jima* in his 2006 film, *Flags of Our Fathers* (DreamWorks, Warner Bros.), and paired it with a film that tells the story of the battle of Iwo Jima from a Japanese point of view, *Letters from Iwo Jima* (DreamWorks, Warner Bros., 2006).

FRANK CAPRA: *WHY WE FIGHT*

In addition to fiction films of battle, there were documentaries. Among the most famous and influential of these were a series of films that Frank Capra supervised for the US Government War Department, some aimed at a military audience, others for the general public. These were propaganda films in the fullest sense of the term, meant to propagate a particular political and ideological point of view. Making use of a variety of documentary footage, animations provided by the Walt Disney studio, rapid and forceful montages, and stirring voice-over narration, often by the actor Walter Huston, these films provided bite-sized bits of historical background and full-throated patriotic fervor in the cause of affirming America's role in the conflict.

One film, *Know Your Enemy: Japan*, which was not released until 1945, just as the war ended, is, from our perspective, incredibly racist. It fits well with the anger at the Japanese that permitted the government to intern Americans of Japanese descent at the beginning of the war. The Japanese are represented as an almost subhuman "other," so alien, so despicable that they need eradication. It is not too much of a stretch to see in this film a stereotyping of a race similar to how the Germans stereotyped the Jews. The difference is that Capra's film focuses on an enemy that was causing widespread destruction, and whom we destroyed by dropping two atomic bombs on their country. The stereotyping was meant to compensate for the destruction that our country, in its turn, visited on the Japanese.

Despite the occasional racist bombast, the Capra war documentaries are a rare instance of how cooperation between the government and the forces of American film production worked well together. They reflect a moment in the culture where there was an all but universal support of a national undertaking: the war against fascism. Between the documentaries and the war-themed fiction films—films about combat, films about the home front and personal sacrifice for the war effort—Hollywood and the country were in equanimity. American film reemerged as a national force, even stronger than it had been in its earliest days.

CASABLANCA

This rousing patriotism marked not only the combat film of the 1940s, but many other genres popular at the time. Domestic melodramas about the home front showed families keeping together in the face of privation as their men were fighting overseas. There were service comedies that presented a lighter side of military life. There were romantic melodramas that tested loyalties in the face of a dangerous world at war. The most famous of these is *Casablanca* (Michael Curtiz, Warner Bros., 1942). *Casablanca* is a film, like *It's a Wonderful Life*, or even *Citizen Kane*, that has consistently gained popularity over the course of time. Unlike those two films, *Casablanca* was successful when it first opened in 1942. It was an important film for Humphrey Bogart, a Warner's contract player since the early 1930s, who was given his first important romantic lead. Previously, Bogart mostly played "heavies," gangsters, who got shot by the end of the film. His breakthrough was *The Maltese Falcon* (Warner Bros., 1941), a detective film based on a novel by

Dashiell Hammett and directed by John Huston and often considered a predecessor of film noir. But it was in *Casablanca* that Bogart came into his own as a serious dramatic player.

In its time, *Casablanca* was important in the way it integrated wartime politics within an exotic, romantic melodrama. Audiences then and now respond to the bittersweet romance between Ilsa (Ingrid Bergman) and Humphrey Bogart's Rick. But contemporary audiences had the added advantage of understanding the references to global politics and a world at war. From the very opening of the film, the turmoil of a disrupted world is made clear. As part of the film's opening montage, which represents the migration of fugitives from Nazi rule in Europe to Casablanca, Morocco, a man is shot by the police and falls under a large poster. The image on the poster is of Marshall Pétain, the leader of the southern part of occupied France. In return for his promise of obeisance to the Nazis, the Germans allowed Pétain a very small amount of leeway in ruling the Vichy government—named after its capital city. Vichy is also the origin of a famous bottled water, which is important to know to get the reference at the end of *Casablanca* when Captain Renault (Claude Rains) tosses a bottle of Vichy water into the trash before he decides to go off with Rick.

The slogan on the poster, in French, can be translated as "I keep my promises as I do those of others," the others being the Germans. It is a grim reminder to contemporary audiences of the precarious state of wartime Europe. A card in the wallet of the man shot down under the poster reveals him to be a member of the Resistance, the large underground of the anti-Nazi forces who, in the film, are represented by the character of Victor Laszlo (Paul Henried). The first few minutes of the film, therefore, condense an important part of the history of the moment, providing the context, the shell of *Casablanca* into which the romantic and heroic elements are arranged, and out of which emerges the figure of Rick, the would-be isolationist, who, he says, sticks his neck out for nobody.

Rick is emotionally wounded; a former fighter for leftist causes, like the loyalists in the Spanish Civil war, he is now withdrawn and depressed because of his aborted love affair with Ilsa, Victor Laszlo's wife. We are introduced to him deep within the inner sanctum of his café, where he stands for all Americans who will not engage with the world. The camera prowls though the café, like one of its patrons, pausing from table to table, picking up conversations of people desperate to leave the country. It moves through the gambling area, deeper into the heart of the place where Rick keeps tabs on everyone. Literally, since the first we see of him is his hand signing an advance for one of his gambling patrons. The date on the check is December 2, 1941, 5 days before Pearl Harbor and America's entry into the war. The camera reveals Rick first by those who surround him, then as the dispenser of money to gamblers in his establishment, then by the accoutrements that define him: a cigarette burning in an ashtray, a chessboard, a glass holding his drink. Finally, the camera pans up to reveal Bogart's face.

The body of the film proceeds to push Rick slowly out of his shell, forcing him to relive his romance with Ilsa, via a flashback, and by means of a song, "As Time Goes By." The romantic Paris of Rick's and Ilsa's romance comes to an end with the German occupation. When she and Victor show up in Casablanca, Rick is forced to confront the past in light of the politics of the present. Every melodrama ends in sacrifice, a kind of payment that the characters must put down for the amount of freedom they gain, or the amount of pain they must pass through in order to come out more complete than they were when they started. For Rick, the price is giving up his love for Ilsa and his life as a self-pitying drunk. Even Ilsa has to sacrifice, by making love to Rick one more time to convince him that he must give her and Victor the means to leave Casablanca for freedom. Rick comes to the agonizing conclusion that "the problems of three little people don't amount to a hill of beans in this crazy world." Ilsa and Victor escape. Rick and Renault join the Resistance.

The rebirth of the hero is an old mythological event, an archetype, which may explain the enduring popularity of *Casablanca*. Rick's move from self-indulgence to self-sacrifice, from self-pity to heroic endeavor is irresistible, no matter what the historical context. But the historical context of *Casablanca* is of particular interest because the pressure of the moment—America's entry into World War II—was a

A brooding Rick (Humphrey Bogart). Depressed over his lost love, he will have to learn the necessity of engaging the enemy at the beginning of World War II. *Casablanca* (Michael Curtiz, 1942).

turning point, a movement away from an isolationist stance to a strong, indeed by war's end, the strongest national force in the world.

Casablanca is also an excellent example of the multiple cultures of Hollywood filmmaking. On the basic level of production, it stands as one of many wartime films made by Warner Bros. in the early 1940s, in this instance using their company of contract players; a contract director, Michael Curtiz (a Hungarian, who came to Hollywood in the 1920s and never gained a strong command of English); and four screenwriters (Julius and Philip Epstein, Howard Koch, and Casey Robinson), who it is said were writing pages well into the shooting of the film. In terms of its own **textuality**, that is, how the film can be understood as a complex interaction of narrative and character, it stands as a political melodrama in which personality and contemporary history mix. The tensions between the personal and the political, figured through the love affair of Rick and Ilsa and the marriage of Ilsa and Victor, constitute a struggle that must be resolved in melodramatic fashion, in which the lead character (unusual for melodrama, a man) must sacrifice his desire for a higher purpose, in this case engagement with a world in crisis. But long after its historical relevance, the attraction of Bogart and Bergman in *Casablanca* remains strong, as does the incredibly seamless direction of Curtiz, who weaves the topical and the emotional aspects of the story into one of the great political melodramas to come out of Hollywood. *Casablanca* is 1940s studio filmmaking at its best.

SELECTED FILMOGRAPHY

Casablanca, dir. Michael Curtiz, Warner Bros., 1942.
Since You Went Away, dir. John Cromwell, David O. Selznick, Selznick International Pictures, 1944.
Air Force, dir. Howard Hawks, Warner Bros., 1943.
Back to Bataan, dir. Edward Dmytryk, RKO, 1945.
Know Your Enemy: Japan, dir. Frank Capra, U. S. War Department, 1945.
Sands of Iwo Jima, dir. Allan Dwan, Republic, 1949.

SUGGESTIONS FOR FURTHER READING

Marc Augé, *Casablanca: Movies and Memory*, trans. Tom Conley (Minneapolis, MN: University of Minnesota Press, 2009).

Thomas Patrick Doherty, *Projections of War: Hollywood, American Culture, and World War II* (New York, NY: Columbia University Press, 1999).

Robert Eberwein, *The Hollywood War Film* (Malden, MA: Wiley-Blackwell, 2009).

Howard Koch, et al., *Casablanca: Script and Legend* (Woodstock, NY: Overlook Press, 1973).

Lawrence W. Suid, *Guts & Glory: The Making of the Military Image in Film* (Lexington, KY: University Press of Kentucky, 2002).

Frank J. Welta and Stephen J. Curley, *Celluloid Wars: A Guide to Film and the American Experience of War* (New York, NY: Greenwood Press, 1992).

NOTES

1. Box office figures come from Thomas Schatz, *Boom and Bust: American Cinema in the 1940s* in *History of the American Cinema*, vol. 6 (Berkeley, CA: University of California Press, 1997), 291.
2. A good, brief history of the internment of Japanese Americans is at http://www.pbs.org.

CHAPTER 13

DIRECTORS OF THE FORTIES: JOHN FORD, ORSON WELLES, AND ALFRED HITCHCOCK (1941–1946)

This chapter focuses on three of the most important directors of the 1940s: John Ford, Orson Welles, and Alfred Hitchcock. By examining their work, we understand how individual talent creates films that speak to contemporary culture, speak to us now, and express personal style.

AFTER READING THIS CHAPTER, YOU SHOULD UNDERSTAND:

- How to tell when a personal style emerges from a body of a director's work.
- How *The Grapes of Wrath* differs from earlier Depression-era films.
- The right to final cut.
- The technical and narrative achievements of *Citizen Kane* and how it broke with Hollywood conventions.
- Why Welles could not accommodate himself to the Hollywood system.
- The McGuffin.
- How Hitchcock's *Shadow of a Doubt* is a narrative of the country's coming to terms with World War II.

YOU SHOULD BE ABLE TO:

- Define auteurism.
- Describe the nonlinear narrative of *Citizen Kane*.
- Try to answer the question, "Who is Charles Foster Kane?"
- Explain why depth of field composition is rarely used.
- Understand Welles's fall from grace at RKO.
- Understand Hitchcock's ability to merge sexual politics with larger political power plays.
- Compare the work of Ford, Welles, and Hitchcock for similarities and differences.

THE AUTEUR

The study of the auteur, the idea that the director is the driving imaginative force of a film, is a highly contested critical endeavor. It was developed by the French in the 1950s, when a number of young critics, seeing many American films that had been embargoed during the Nazi occupation, began to discover coherent patterns of form and content in films made by particular directors. No matter who wrote the films, no matter what studio produced them, these critics saw in the films by such directors as Howard Hawks, Alfred Hitchcock, Orson Welles, and John Ford a particular way of seeing the world in cinematic terms, specific to their own cinematic vision.

The "**auteur theory**," as it was called, was adopted by American film critics from the French as a way to give the subject of their study respectability. If a film could be credited with single authorship, like a novel, there might be an opportunity to take it seriously. The early days of modern film scholarship in the 1960s, spurred by the work of *Village Voice* film critic Andrew Sarris, were steeped in the study of particular directors and their work. But a counter argument to the auteur approach emerged. American film is a collaborative art, with many people contributing to its content and structure. The structure of Hollywood filmmaking is team based, with a **producer** at the top of the creative group, with the the actors and actresses, the screenwriters and **director**, art director, **cinematographer**, **editor**, **composer**, and a host of crafts people working together to create the matrix of the finished product. It would not be enlightening to call *Casablanca*, for example, "a Michael Curtiz film" because it is, in fact, an extraordinary example of an entire studio working at the peak of its powers, with many contributors forming this near perfect example of early-1940s Hollywood filmmaking.

But, as we have seen in previous chapters, directors can make a mark on their films in the form of stylistic and thematic continuities that continue throughout the body of their work. D. W. Griffith is an early example of a director who not only established a style of his own, but influenced all American filmmaking to come. It is useful, therefore, to examine the films of directors who not only have developed a particular style in their films, but who have had a lasting influence on other filmmakers as well as film viewers. Here we will highlight the work of three important directors of the 1940s. Their work is representative of the best filmmaking of the decade, while at the same time pointing to individual talent that went beyond the usual Hollywood output. Orson Welles and Alfred Hitchcock both, in very different ways, used the camera as an investigative extension of their imaginations and therefore redefined the way film addresses us and the ways we respond to it. John Ford made one of the most potent films about the Great Depression and then went on, after World War II, to make extraordinary Westerns. We will have the opportunity to revisit the Western, as well as the postwar work of these filmmakers again in a later chapter, but here we continue with the 1940s and analyze the work of three of its greatest filmmakers.

JOHN FORD AND *THE GRAPES OF WRATH*

John Ford made a number of non-Western films in the early 1940s, the most important of which are *The Grapes of Wrath* (Fox, 1940), an adaptation of John Steinbeck's famous novel about the Depression, and *How Green Was My Valley* (Fox, 1941), a film about the decay of a Welsh mining town. *The Grapes of Wrath* is one of the most uncompromising of Depression-era films. Although it is less bleak than its source novel, and offers a ray of hope as the Joad family finds refuge in a government camp for displaced migrant farmers in California, it remains a stark and sometimes painful film to watch. It is a film of great visual presence, photographed by Gregg Toland (who went on to shoot *Citizen Kane*). Many of the compositions, made in a stark black and white, have the look of 1930s Depression-era photographs and documentaries. Toland alludes to the style of such photographers as Walker Evans, Gordon Parks, and Dorothea Lange, much of whose work was sponsored by the government and appeared in magazines like the widely read *Life*. This visual style gave Ford's film an immediacy that a contemporary audience could readily respond to.

Along with the strength of its images, *The Grapes of Wrath* generates a powerful **narrative** of poor

Faces of hunger and despair: Casy and Tom Joad (John Carradine and Henry Fonda) in John Ford's *The Grapes of Wrath* (1940).

Oakies—uprooted farmers from Oklahoma and the Dust Bowl, the drought-stricken area of the Midwest—mistreated, left homeless and struggling. Their homes repossessed and without money, the Joads travel Route 66 in search of work. Along the way, family members die. Corrupt police and angry townspeople pursue them. They are offered work picking fruit, but only as scabs to break a striking union. They are red-baited (accused of being Communists), hounded, and hurt. Tom Joad (Henry Fonda) is pushed to killing a company thug. He is hunted even within the security of the government-run migrant camp, whose director (Grant Mitchell) looks and sounds like Franklin Roosevelt. Tom disappears and becomes the spirit of survival, a lone figure silhouetted on a hill. A film so full of despair needs to hold out some hope, in this case—and this is so very rare in American film—the hope of collective action. Both the film's director, and its producer, Fox studio head Darryl F. Zanuck, were able to overcome their basic conservative leanings in order to portray a class of people usually ignored by American film. "We're the people that live," says the family matriarch (Jane Darwell) at the end of the film. "They can't wipe us out, they can't lick us." This is vague enough, and hardly promoting of class struggle, but the film remains at least a liberal view of the hardships of the 1930s and the Great Depression, and was strong enough for its time.

Compared to the Depression-era films of William Wellman, *Heroes for Sale* and *Wild Boys of the* Road (both Warner Bros-First National, 1933), *The Grapes of Wrath* has a broader vision, a sense of the scope of hardship and struggle that may have been possible only in retrospect, looking back at an earlier period. Ford, working from Steinbeck's novel, is able to visually encompass the pain of peoples' loss of livelihood and hope and capture even more painfully than had Wellman the brooding violence that broke out of the people's desperation.

ORSON WELLES AND *CITIZEN KANE*

Orson Welles had already gained nationwide fame when he played on the country's war fears in his 1938 radio broadcast of *War of the Worlds*. A nation on edge because of the unrest and violence swirling in countries across the seas was ready to respond fearfully to the fake news-documentary style of the show. Welles constructed the first part of the broadcast as a program of music interrupted by news flashes about a Martian landing. Thousands took it for the real thing and fled their homes. The notoriety of the event, along with Welles's career as a theatrical actor and director during the 1930s, brought him to the attention of RKO Radio Pictures, whose executive, George Schaefer, offered Welles—who was not yet in his mid-twenties—an unheard of 3-year contract. He was to make a film a year and have the right to final cut. This meant that the film he made would be the film that got distributed, without interference from the studio. Very few directors, then and now, have such control because, in the Hollywood system, producers, the studio head, the people with the money always want to have a say in the way a film will look, and they make their mark, hovering around the shooting of the film, interfering in the editing. Welles maintained this extraordinary control for precisely one film. He didn't regain it again until the 1960s, when he worked in Europe and was constrained only by lack of sufficient funding.

Citizen Kane was not the first film Welles wanted to make, or the first experiment he wanted to try. He considered an adaptation of Joseph Conrad's novella, *Heart of Darkness*, which he planned to create as a first-person narrative. That is, the film would be told and "seen" by a single character. The camera would only present the character's point of view. Welles quickly understood that this technique could not work. It was tried a few years later by actor Robert Montgomery, who directed an adaptation of a Raymond Chandler detective novel, *Lady in the Lake* (MGM, 1947). We only see the main character when he looks in a mirror; otherwise everything was seen from his/the camera's eyes. When he gets beat up, the fists of his assailant hit the camera. When he has a cup of coffee, a cup is lifted to the camera lens. The film is an absurd exercise, and Welles wisely realized early on that his idea for a first-person narrative wouldn't work.

Instead, he and co-screenwriter Herman J. Mankiewicz went in an opposite direction. They fragmented point of view into a **nonlinear narrative** so that the film they made is, in effect, told from the perspective of five characters that knew or are trying to find out just who Charles Foster Kane was. *Citizen Kane* is in part a detective film. Not the traditional kind, but rather a quest to uncover the character of a powerful and wealthy man, a media baron, largely patterned on a contemporary, extraordinarily powerful media mogul, William Randolph Hearst, and a larger than life narcissist, who coveted other people but gave little of himself. To achieve the fragmentation of points of view, yet create a narrative that provided some continuity, if not answers to the questions it poses, Welles employed a variety of techniques. The film starts with a warning: a "No Trespassing" sign on the fence of Xanadu, the castle that Kane built for himself and the treasures he bought or looted from Europe. Ignoring this warning, the camera cranes up the fence and Welles edits a montage of the castle and its grounds, coming to rest, by means of a daring 180-degree cut on the dying Kane, who, in an extraordinary close-up of his mouth, utters the word "Rosebud." A snow globe he holds in his hands falls to the floor and shatters.

This opening section, like much of the film, is deeply shadowed, photographed in the **expressionist** style in which the spaces surrounding the characters and the lighting reflect their state of mind. It is brooding and foreboding, a mood heightened by the score, composed by Bernard Herrmann. And it ends abruptly. From the deathbed scene, we are suddenly confronted with a newsreel of Kane's life. "News on the March" a narrator calls out, as loud music blares. The newsreel sequence is a parody of *The March of Time*, a newsreel produced by the company owned by Henry Luce, another media baron, and a competitor to William Randolph Hearst. *The March of Time*, with its loud booming narrator and occasionally staged sequences, was a regular part of the moviegoing experience for years. Contemporary audiences watching *Citizen Kane* might actually have thought that the film was being interrupted by the newsreel (Welles was playing the same trick as he had in *The War of the Worlds* broadcast). The newsreel conveniently moves through all of the events of Kane's life that will be detailed in the film to come. It ends as abruptly as it begins: the screen on which we see the newsreel suddenly becomes the screen in a projection room on which the newsreel is being projected.

These quick changes in mode, mood, and tone of the film's narrative indicate a restless cinematic imagination, eager to stretch the limits of its medium and its audience. *Citizen Kane* is about the quest for the meaning of a complex character; it is also a quest for a flexible, vital cinematic language that would break from the straightforward **continuity style** of the 1930s into something resembling the visual complexity of modern literature and painting. But Welles understood that, in a commercial medium, experimentation had to grow out of something stable and easily grasped by the viewer. So, he invents a hook. The newspaper men gathered in the projection room are told to find out the meaning of "Rosebud," Kane's dying word. Alfred Hitchcock called such a gimmick a "McGuffin," something that occupies the characters in the film but has no real narrative importance other than propelling the characters through the plot. "Rosebud" turns out to be the name of a sled that Kane had as a child, and which we see go up in flames at the end of the film, when Kane's belongings in the enormous basement of Xanadu are weeded out. "I don't think any word can explain a man's life," says Thompson (William Alland), the reporter, who acts as our surrogate into the investigation of Kane.

But the search for "Rosebud" drives the film and, after the projection room sequence, there are six parts, based on the memories of the people who knew Charlie Kane, as told to or discovered by Thompson:

His second wife, Susan (Dorothy Comingore)
Kane's guardian, Mr. Thatcher (George Coulouris)
Kane's childhood protector and retainer, Mr. Bernstein (Everett Sloane)
Kane's friend, Jed Leland (Joseph Cotton)
Susan, again
Kane's butler, Raymond (Paul Stewart)

In each of these sections, we learn as much about the informant as we do of Kane himself. The first meeting with Susan, the camera booming down through the skylight of the nightclub where she works as a singer, reveals nothing. In a drunken stupor, she refuses to talk. Thompson's visit to Thatcher's library, where he reads the guardian's diary, is more revealing. Welles creates another extraordinary transition, this time from the black ink handwriting on the white paper of the diary to the figure of young Charlie Kane in his black clothing against a snowy white background. Welles cuts to the interior of the Kane cabin, where his mother (Agnes Moorehead) signs over guardianship of the young boy to Mr. Thatcher. In an unbroken shot that is about 2 minutes long, Welles uses the tight quarters of the cabin's interior to indicate the shifting allegiances between mother, son, father, and Thatcher.

Here and throughout the film, Welles uses a technique called **deep focus** or **depth of field**, an optical property of a camera lens that allows everything in the field of vision, from up close all the way to the back of the composition to be equally sharp. In this sequence, as in so many others, Welles asks us to be aware of many different things in the frame. Not only do we see Mrs. Kane, Thatcher, and Kane's father (Harry Shannon) move in shifting positions from behind the cabin to a table in front, where the papers will be signed, but we see as well young Kane (Sonny Bupp) playing in the snow outside the window. We not only see him, but hear him as well, calling out "the Union forever," as the adults talk about breaking up the union of their family. Welles uses and transcends his theatrical and radio experience to create a visual and aural field that is not "realistic" but purely cinematic. He combines a variety of effects to represent a way of seeing that is only possible through film, showing much but hiding what everyone wants to know: who is Charles Foster Kane?

The quest for the meaning of "Rosebud" and the truth of Kane's character is, therefore, also a quest for a cinematic language that is up to the task—that *creates* the task and shapes our response. Welles seeks to redefine cinematic space and time. He asks us to look deeply into the frame, but the more we look, the more we see, the less clear Kane's character becomes. Deep focus engages our gaze; it can trick it as well. Seeing everything in the frame does not necessarily mean that we see beyond the frame or within the characters that populate it. Because Welles covers long periods of time in a flash does not mean that we know what took place during the time covered—though sometimes we have a good idea.

One of the most famous passages in *Citizen Kane* is the breakfast table sequence between Kane and his first wife that occurs in the section narrated by Kane's embittered friend, Jed Leland. "It was a marriage just like any other marriage," he says, as the background fades out to reveal the interior of Kane's dining room.

Deep focus in *Citizen Kane* (Orson Welles, 1941). Kane's mother (Agnes Moorehead) signs away her son (who can be seen outside the window) to Mr. Thatcher (George Coulouris), while his father (Harry Shannon) looks on.

Kane brings Emily (Ruth Warrick) breakfast at a small table. He tells her how much he adores her and offers to stay home to be with her during the morning. Then the camera seems to swirl around the room, coming to rest on Emily, complaining about how long Kane has kept her waiting. The table has become larger; they sit farther apart. Kane assures her that there is no other woman in his life, only his newspaper. Another flash pan (as Welles called it) around the room reveals the couple sitting at opposite ends of the table. She complains about what he prints about the president. He hints that he may run for president someday. Another swift pan comes to rest on an older Emily, complaining about Kane's friend Mr. Bernstein. She does not want him not to visit their child's nursery; Kane insists that he will. Another pan: "Really Charles," says Emily, "people will think." Cut to Kane: "What I tell them to think." The final pan ends without dialogue. Emily is reading Kane's rival paper, the *Chronicle*. Kane reads his *Enquirer*. The camera tracks around and pulls back to reveal them sitting at either end of a long table, surrounded by shadows: scenes from a marriage that tell of its dissolution in a few short minutes.

Welles is a master of the quick stroke, the telling movement of the camera, the power of light and shadow, the subtlety of perspective. Kane demands that his second wife, Susan, be an opera singer, despite her utter lack of talent. Her sad story is told by Jed Leland and by Susan herself. Welles isn't strict in holding onto a point of view. In other words, the narrative shows us more than the teller could have seen, though perhaps what he might have heard about. Obviously Jed was not present at the breakfast table during the years of a decaying marriage. Nor would he have been present when Kane met Susan on a rainy night and she invited him up to her room. He could not have seen the snow globe on her shelf—the very globe that Kane would find when he wrecks Susan's room when she leaves him and that drops from his hands at his death.

But we do see Kane's election campaign from Jed's point of view, though not the confrontation of Kane, Emily, Susan, and Jim Gettys (Ray Collins), the politician Kane is smearing in an attempt to win the election. Gettys reveals Kane's "love nest" with Susan, and the revelation brings down his bid to be a political leader. The confrontation of Jed and Charlie, after the election is lost, is photographed from an extreme low angle, the figures looming over the camera, in a disorienting display of a friendship broken and an ego—Kane's—that cannot see what led to his electoral defeat and the loss of his friend.

When Susan performs in public, in her opera debut, we see the stage from the audience's side, where Jed would be sitting. Perhaps he could not see the stagehands, visible as the camera cranes up and up from the stage, one of them holding his nose at the sound of Susan's terrible voice. When it is Susan's turn to tell her story, we see her opera debut from the stage looking out, facing a vast, dark hall whose hostile, bored faces are invisible to her. Only Kane maintains a steady gaze, turning away only when someone in the audience calls out "perfectly dreadful." Susan's story becomes a dying fall, as she loses to Kane's domineering personality. Shrieking at him in her pain of embarrassment over her bad reviews, she says she won't go on singing. Kane literally casts his shadow over her, demanding that her job is to satisfy him. She sings until she can no longer. Welles creates a **montage** of *Inquirer* headlines praising Susan's singing until the light goes out. Sound and lighting fall as if life itself goes down the drain, and Susan tries to commit suicide. In one of the film's startling deep focus shots we see close-up a glass and bottle of medication; in the middle field, Susan lying in bed breathing heavily; in the background, the door of her bedroom, burst open by Kane.

The end of Kane and Susan's relationship is violence: first, Susan attempts to kill herself; then, exiled to Xanadu, in a tent surrounded by guests on an outing, Kane slaps Susan, and Welles does an interesting displacement of sound. Susan barely reacts to the slap, except to warn him not to say he's sorry. The reaction to this act of violence is a scream from off screen, from someone else in the party who we do not see. The final act of violence is again committed by Kane. Susan's story ends with her leaving him. The last perspective on Kane's life is provided by Raymond, the butler, and his memory begins where Susan's left off. Susan has left. Kane is alone in her room, which he destroys in a fit of hysterical anger. He breaks it to pieces, leaving with the snow globe in his hands and the word "Rosebud" on his lips. He walks past a mirror that reflects his image into infinity—a man whose entire world revolved around an image of himself.

The film ends in Xanadu's basement, where Thompson and the other reporters from the "News on the March" team are finishing their investigation. Thompson looks at the pieces of the jigsaw puzzle that Susan had played with to pass the hours at Xanadu, and the symbolic connection to his quest is clear. Thompson—and we—have tried to fit together the puzzle of a man's life, and failed. Workmen toss a sled into the fire and it is revealed to have the name "Rosebud" on it. Was Kane's lifelong grief and egomania based on memories of a lost childhood? That answer is too simple. The sled was a McGuffin, and it goes up in flames; the camera tracks the smoke out of the chimney and comes to rest where it began, on the chain link fence and the sign reading "No Trespassing."

Welles, then, brings all the cinematic tools of his imagination to bear on an enigma. The more we learn about Kane, the less we know, the less the film *wants* us to know. This may be *Citizen Kane*'s greatest triumph: creating an intricate visual and narrative structure that becomes a labyrinth of false leads and an ultimate dead end. The film asks us to look, but warns us against trespassing. Welles moves against most of the conventions set up in 1930s film. He refuses a happy ending; he clouds the transparency of the Hollywood style by drawing attention to his cinematic means. Depth of field compositions are purely the function of camera lenses. The human eye does not see in deep focus. The rapid, startling transitions and multiple points of view, while not confusing, work against the smooth continuity that American film had been developing since the teens. It would be fair to say that *Citizen Kane* is a film about *discontinuity* and therefore of a piece with modernity. It reflects the uncertainties, the lack of a secure center, the uneasiness of the country on the eve of World War II. It exposes, even while it complicates, the life of a man with too much power and too little self-understanding. It also represents Welles's own involvement with the politics of the 1930s and 40s. As an attack on wealth and power, the film reflects the left-leaning movements that gave rise to much theater and literature of the period, like the theatrical performances of Welles's Mercury Theater and Steinbeck's *The Grapes of Wrath*.[1]

It is therefore possible to understand *Citizen Kane* as a film both of and outside its time and culture. While it partakes of the left-leaning liberalism of the moment and speaks to the power of the news media in the person of William Randolph Hearst, it also, as a work of cinema, transcends its moment. *Kane* is unlike films that became before and after. Welles sees the world with a strong, piercing cinematic gaze; and while the film has influenced many filmmakers, none have been able to imitate it.

WELLES AFTER *KANE*: *THE MAGNIFICENT AMBERSONS*

At the same time, the film reflected the insecurities of the film business itself. Any large corporate undertaking depends upon stability and continuity and it fears disruption. The disruption caused by *Citizen Kane* within the Hollywood bubble had nothing to do with its style and everything to do with its content. The cinematic life of Charles Foster Kane was too close to the real life of William Randolph Hearst. The media tycoon did everything he could to destroy the film, including an attempt to convince MGM—a studio to which Hearst was closely connected, and that had his girlfriend Marion Davies under contract—to buy the negative of the film from RKO and destroy it. Short of that, he did not allow the film to be advertised or reviewed in any of his many newspapers across the country. Although the film was a critical success outside of Hearst's newspapers, it did not do well commercially. Though widely seen and admired within the Hollywood community, it was not widely seen in the country at large.

Then Welles fell victim to his own studio and his propensity to take on many projects at once. He shot his second film for RKO, *The Magnificent Ambersons* (1942), a few months after *Kane* premiered. (The third film on his contract, *Journey into Fear* [1943], was directed by a Welles associate, Norman Foster.) What we have of *Ambersons* is a dark, brooding melodrama about the decay of a once rich and powerful midwestern family, much more somber in tone than *Citizen Kane*. "What we have" is the operative term. As Welles was completing *The Magnificent Ambersons*, he was invited by the government to shoot a documentary film in Latin America, a film that would indicate the close relationship between America and its neighbors. Welles and his editor, Robert Wise, did a rough cut of *Ambersons*, and RKO promised that they would allow Welles to continue editing long distance while he was preparing his Latin American film in Brazil.

Perhaps Welles was naïve in his trust of the studio, because things rapidly fell apart. The studio previewed an initial cut of the *Ambersons*, and it was received very badly. Audiences were unprepared for its dark vision of a family in decay, especially after the shock of Pearl Harbor and America's entry into the war. Whatever the reasons, the studio was unhappy and they recut it. Meanwhile, Welles was sending back footage of Carnival in Brazil, with many images of people of color dancing in the streets. This offended the racist sensibilities of the RKO executives, who were afraid that the film would not play well in the South. The executives were also concerned about the cost overruns being incurred by the Brazilian film. And finally, George Schaefer, Welles's defender at the studio, was fired. "Showmanship in place of genius at RKO" was the slogan of the new management in a direct swipe at Welles. *The Magnificent Ambersons* was taken from his hands, recut from 2 hours to 88 minutes, scenes not directed by Welles were added, and the ending became a happy reconciliation of characters rather than the bleak emptiness that Welles had envisioned.[2] The fragments of the Brazilian footage were not assembled and distributed until 1993, under the title *It's All True*.

Welles never again had the financial freedom he enjoyed with *Citizen Kane*, and a cruel legend grew that he never surpassed his first film. The truth is more complex. Welles certainly did not comfortably fit within Hollywood culture. He was too independent, too insistent on having his own way, too *sensitive* to the impositions imposed by the Hollywood system to get along within the confines of the studios. Whenever he did work for the studios, his films were taken away from him and reedited. But he continued a distinguished filmmaking career as an actor, taking on roles in order to finance his films, but especially as a director, filming as the income from his acting became available, regaining creative control on some of his later films made in Europe: *The Trial* (Paris-Europa Productions, Astor Pictures Corp., 1962), *Chimes at Midnight* (Alpine Films, International Films, Peppercorn-Wormser, 1965), and for French television, *The Immortal Story* (1968). During the rest of the 1940s, after the debacle with RKO, Welles was able to direct three films.

THE STRANGER

For independent producer Sam Spiegel, he directed a postwar spy film, *The Stranger* (International Pictures, 1946). Welles plays a Nazi, Charles Rankin (whose real name is Franz Kindler), who passes as a college professor in a small New England town while being pursued by a Nazi hunter, Wilson, played by Edward G. Robinson. The film has much melodrama and some striking imagery. At its end, Welles's character is impaled on the sword of a statue that rotates around the town clock. But the real climax of the film occurs when the Nazi hunter shows footage of the liberation of the concentration camps. These horrific images would not have been new to the audience; but this would have been the first time they were inserted into a fiction film. They are there to convince the family about the monster in their midst. The flickering shadows of the film within a film play upon the faces of Wilson and the shocked family. The sequence recalls the projection room in *Citizen Kane,* where the brightness of the screen accentuated the shadows of the reporters in the room. Here, film becomes a means of revelation; it wants to imprint its images on the viewers' faces with the horrors that were close in the memories of a 1946 audience and remain haunting reminders of one of the darkest periods in modern history.

Welles's most important post-*Kane* 1940s film was *The Lady from Shanghai* (1947), made for Harry Cohn's Columbia Pictures. This is a film noir, and as such will be discussed more fully in Chapter 14, devoted to the noir style. Here, it is important to note that Welles was comfortable in a number of genres, that *Citizen Kane* was not a one-off, but a film that was one of a kind. It's not that Welles never did better than *Kane,* but that he made films different than *Kane.* He loved Shakespeare, for example, and his last film in the 1940s was an adaptation of *Macbeth* (1948), which he made on the cheap for Republic, a low-budget studio that mainly produced Westerns. In 1952, he finished an adaptation of *Othello,* which he made in Europe. The last, full-length narrative film that was released before his death in 1985 was the independently produced *Chimes at*

Images of the concentration camps projected on the face of Nazi hunter Wilson (Edward G. Robinson) in Welles's *The Stranger* (1946).

Midnight, a version of the Shakespeare plays that feature the character Falstaff. It is, arguably, Welles's greatest achievement.

In the end, 1940s Hollywood proved too inhospitable for the kind of films Welles wanted to make. When not making or playing in movies, he busied himself with work in liberal politics, speechmaking for Franklin Delano Roosevelt and getting involved in civil rights causes.[3] After making *Macbeth*, he left the country and pursued a lifelong career of acting and filmmaking as money became available. He returned to the United States in 1955 and made one of the most important films of that decade, *Touch of Evil* (Universal, 1958). Because he is such a major figure, we will have cause to return to Welles more than once in our discussion of American film.

ALFRED HITCHCOCK

Alfred Hitchcock's career was very much the opposite of Welles's. Welles completed 10 feature-length films, one short narrative film, two documentaries, some television programs, and a few unfinished projects. Hitchcock directed some 53 films and some television shows. Welles was in contention with the studio system throughout his career; Hitchcock worked comfortably within it. Welles only occasionally had control over his projects; Hitchcock almost always had full control from inception to editing. Hitchcock's control is demonstrated in the tight, focused structure of his films. Welles is an exuberant filmmaker of extravagant images; Hitchcock calculates his films carefully; Welles is a showman in love with the dynamic possibilities of cinematic image making. Hitchcock, no less intrigued by the powers of the image, used it to probe the psychology of his characters and his audience. Welles wanted to see and define those characters by the environment that surrounded them. However, they were similar in that their best films are intricate and complex investigations of the ways cinema imagines the world and expresses a particular filmmaking intelligence. And they crossed paths—at least their films did—at a crucial point. Welles's *The Stranger* is very much a piece with Hitchcock's *Shadow of a Doubt* (Universal, 1942) and *Notorious* (RKO, 1946). *Touch of Evil* was very much an influence on Hitchcock's *Psycho* (Paramount, 1960). But that is for a later chapter.

Here, I want to focus on two Hitchcock films that are tied into the culture of their time, films that manifest the Hitchcock style as well as making use of contemporary history. They are among the films that Hitchcock made when he was able to break away from the smothering hand of David O. Selznick, the producer (most famous for his 1939 film, *Gone With the Wind*), who was responsible for bringing Hitchcock to the United States and for his first U.S. film, *Rebecca* (Selznick International Pictures, 1940). Hitchcock made a number of films in the 40s with wartime themes. *Saboteur* (Universal, 1942), for example, concerns the sabotage of military installations. *Lifeboat* (Fox, 1944) places a group of survivors of a shipwreck on a raft in the middle of the ocean. One of them is a Nazi, and the interactions of the group reveal many of the tensions that existed in the United States during the war. *Shadow of a Doubt* seems to ignore the war entirely. There are some soldiers seen on the street and, at a climactic moment, a newspaper headline can be seen mentioning Tojo, the prime minister of our World War II enemy, Japan.

SHADOW OF A DOUBT

But *Shadow of a Doubt* is about the war by inference and suggestion. Its primary subject is a serial killer, named Charlie, played by Joseph Cotton (Jed Leland in *Citizen Kane*), who flees the East Coast to hide out among his family in Santa Rosa, California. The film becomes a study in the disruption of a small town domesticity—the chaos that evil brings when it infiltrates a place that believes it is innocent and separated from the troubles of the rest of the world. Hitchcock visualizes this almost literally, as Uncle Charlie steams into town on a train belching black smoke. He emerges from the train hunched and menacing, only to stand up and assume the guise of a friendly family member as he approaches his sister (Patricia Collinge), brother-in-law (Henry Travers), and their children. One of these, a young woman whose name is also Charlie (Teresa Wright), becomes her uncle's double. She doesn't kill defenseless widows, but she stalks, is tempted and threatened by

The menacing close-up. Uncle Charlie (Joseph Cotton) threatens the very boundaries of the frame in Hitchcock's *Shadow of a Doubt* (1942).

her evil other, and comes to learn about fear. "You're just an ordinary little girl, living in an ordinary little town," he tells her as they sit in a shadowy, noirish bar. "You wake up every morning in your life and you know perfectly well there's nothing in the world to trouble you. You go through your ordinary little day, and at night you sleep your untroubled, ordinary little sleep filled with peaceful, stupid dreams. And I brought you nightmares." The words could make up an allegory about America and the advent of the war and America's awakening to the nightmares of fascism.

Hitchcock does his best to localize his narrative, that is, to present a story of a serial killer who finally gets his comeuppance. The film's larger implications are left to be understood by the viewer. In the end, Uncle Charlie attacks young Charlie on a moving train, and she manages to get the better of him so that he falls off the railroad car into the path of an oncoming train. The film ends with the calm of Charlie and the FBI agent she has fallen in love with. At Uncle Charlie's funeral, her FBI boyfriend (Macdonald Carey) tells her that sometimes the world "needs a lot of watching. It seems to go crazy every now and then, like your Uncle Charlie." The closing words of the film, spoken by the priest at Uncle Charlie's funeral service, are "the sweetness of their character lives on with us forever." This is an ironic counterpoint to the real character of Uncle Charlie and his corrosive effect on the world around him. It is too optimistic an assessment of the character of a world at war. At this point in his career, Hitchcock still had to supply a soothing ending to a film that otherwise ruptured the quiet of his audience. But there is no doubt that *Shadow of a Doubt* is about the dissolution of American innocence. Young Charlie becomes the mirror of American isolationism that was shattered with the bombing of Pearl Harbor. She is, in a sense, invaded by her uncle, who casts his shadow over the pleasant, sleepy ordinariness of small town America.

NOTORIOUS

Hitchcockian irony has a way of enveloping the world at large within a compelling narrative of individuals caught up in unexpected chaos. He is fascinated by psychological and sexual power plays between men and women that reflect larger political power plays between governments or within cultures. This is nowhere more evident than in his post–World War II film *Notorious* (RKO, 1946). The film covers the same moment (and was released the same year) as Orson Welles's *The Stranger*. The war just ended, the search for Nazi spies still going on, the Cold War against the

Soviet Union just beginning—everyone was on edge. A global chess game was being played to see what nation would emerge as the most powerful. *Notorious* plays this global conflict against an interpersonal relationship that has sadomasochistic overtones between characters played by two of the biggest stars of the decade, Ingrid Bergman and Cary Grant.

A government agent named Devlin (Grant) is put on the trail of an escaped Nazi, Alexander Sebastian (Claude Rains), suspected of smuggling uranium. The smuggling of uranium is the film's McGuffin, the least important element of the plot. The most important element of the narrative is the way Devlin manipulates Alicia Huberman (Bergman), the daughter of a convicted Nazi spy, into marriage with Sebastian to spy on him. Devlin is introduced as a dark intruder into the drunken, dissolute world that Alicia inhabits. He carefully manages this intrusion in order to get her trust and, quickly, her love. He then, acting in his role as a government agent, forces her into marriage with Sebastian, in effect turning her into a prostitute in the cause of his and his country's political righteousness. The result is that he comes to hate her, while she is slowly poisoned by her husband and his evil mother (Leopoldine Konstantin).

There is a remarkable little sequence near the end of the film. Devlin has not seen Alicia for days (she is near death, imprisoned in her husband's house), and he goes to visit his handler, Prescott (Louis Calhern). Prescott is lying on his bed, eating cheese and crackers, oblivious to Devlin's concern and Alicia's predicament. He assumes that Alicia is on another drunken spree. Power and its abuse, Hitchcock suggests, is a product of willful ignorance and an uncomplicated desire to use people when their use is more important than they are. People become pawns in a global power game.

People are diminished by power and the threat it causes, which is why Hitchcock loves to use a very high-angle shot when his characters are in trouble. He does this in *Shadow of a Doubt* when young Charlie goes to the library to read about her uncle's crimes in the newspaper. When she realizes who he is, the camera **cranes** up and up, leaving her small and vulnerable in her painful revelation. In *Notorious*, Hitchcock uses the opposite motion. Alicia gets the key to Sebastian's wine cellar, where the uranium ore that the Americans are after is hidden in a bottle of wine. At a party where she will meet Devlin, the camera begins at an enormously high angle, looking down at Alicia and the party guests. It slowly glides down to a tight close-up of her hand holding the key. Alone amidst the crowd, Hitchcock marks her vulnerability by the high-angle shot, craning down to see the key to that vulnerability, the object that will get her deeply into trouble and nearly killed.

Devlin (Cary Grant) saves Alicia (Ingrid Bergman) from the Nazis at the end of Alfred Hitchcock's *Notorious* (1946).

As noted, in the 1940s, Hitchcock was obligated to provide a happy ending to his films. Young Charlie is told by her boyfriend that the world simply has to be looked after because it goes crazy once in a while. Alicia is almost killed by her Nazi husband and his mother until Devlin, realizing what he has done, comes to her rescue. The ending of *Notorious* turns into a kind of fairy tale with Devlin as the prince saving the maiden from the evil castle. He carries her down a long flight of steps, exchanging looks with Sebastian, his mother, and their Nazi pals. It is a carefully edited orchestration of gazes and a moment of victory as Sebastian is now faced with the wrath of his colleagues. And a fairy tale is what the film, in retrospect, turns out to be, a fantastic tale of a time gone by.[4] While Nazi hunting went on for many years after World War II, Nazis quickly faded into the background as the "Communist threat" and the McCarthy witch hunts overtook the national political and cultural consciousness. *Notorious* is a powerful meditation on patriarchy and its manipulations of women; about the callousness of governments in their quest for information and power; and—from our perspective—a look back at a period just after the Second World War before attention shifted from Nazis to the scurrilous investigations into Americans' "loyalty."

SELECTED FILMOGRAPHY

John Ford

The Grapes of Wrath, Fox, 1940.
The Long Voyage Home, Argosy Pictures, Walter Wanger Productions, United Artists, 1940.
How Green Was My Valley, Fox, 1941.

Orson Welles

Citizen Kane, RKO, 1941.
The Magnificent Ambersons, RKO, 1942.
The Stranger, International Pictures, 1946.
The Lady from Shanghai, Columbia, 1947.
Macbeth, Republic, 1948.

Alfred Hitchcock

Rebecca, Selznick International Pictures, 1940.
Shadow of a Doubt, Universal, 1942.
Saboteur, Universal, 1942.
Life Boat, Fox, 1944
Notorious, RKO, 1946.

SUGGESTIONS FOR FURTHER READING

Simon Callow, *Orson Welles: The Road to Xanadu* (New York, NY: Penguin, 1995).
———, *Orson Welles: Hello Americans* (New York, NY: Viking, 2006).
Catherine L. Benamou, *It's All True: Orson Welles's Pan-American Odyssey* (Berkeley, CA: University of California Press, 2007).
Marshall Deutelbaum & Leland Pogue, eds., *A Hitchcock Reader*, 2nd ed (Malden, MA: Wiley-Blackwell, 2009).
Joseph McBride, *Searching for John Ford: A Life* (New York, NY: St. Martin's Press, 2001).
James Naremore, ed. *Orson Welles's Citizen Kane: A Casebook* (New York, NY: Oxford University Press, 2004).
Andrew Sarris, *American Cinema* (New York, NY: Da Capo Press, 1996).
François Truffaut, *Hitchcock*, rev. ed. (New York, NY: Simon & Schuster, 1984).
Robin Wood, *Hitchcock's Films Revisited*, rev. ed. (New York, NY: Columbia University Press, 2002).

NOTES

1. See Michael Denning, "The Politics of Magic: Orson Welles's Allegories of Anti-Fascism" and Paul Arthur, "Out of the Depths: Citizen Kane, Modernism, and the Avant-Garde Impulse, in James Naremore, ed. *Orson Welles's Citizen Kane: A Casebook* (New York, NY: Oxford University Press, 2004), 185–216, 263–284.
2. On the reception at RKO of the footage Welles shot in Brazil, see Simon Callow, *Orson Welles: Hello Americans* (New York, NY: Viking, 2006), 96–97. See also Catherine L. Benamou, *It's All True: Orson Welles's Pan-American Odyssey* (Berkeley, CA: University of California Press, 2007).
3. For Welles's political career in the 1940s, see Callow.
4. See Richard Abel, "*Notorious*: Perversion par Excellence," in Marshall Deutelbaum and Leland Pogue, eds., *A Hitchcock Reader*, 2nd ed. (Malden, MA: Wiley-Blackwell, 2009), 164–171.

CHAPTER 14

FILM NOIR (1944–1950)

How did film noir, a French term, become common currency for a style or genre of film that today almost everyone recognizes? We attempt to understand how this style or genre appeared without filmmakers knowing that they were creating it and how film noir emerged from the culture of postwar America. We speculate on why more books and articles have been written about film noir than just about any other facet of American film.

AFTER READING THIS CHAPTER, YOU SHOULD UNDERSTAND:

- How film noir grew out of the culture of the 1940s.
- How to account for the elements of its construction.
- How noir got its name.
- The role of gender in noir.
- The lighting styles of noir.
- Noir and the domestic scene.

YOU SHOULD BE ABLE TO:

- Describe, define, and classify film noir.
- Consider whether noir is a genre or a style.
- Discuss the role of women in noir and the notion of the femme fatale.
- Discover other noir films than those discussed below.
- Speculate on noir's lasting popularity.

THE QUESTIONS OF NOIR

There are differing theories about how to define film noir and even address noir. When did noir start? Is it strictly a post–World War II, 1940s, phenomenon, or can we trace it to earlier films? Many critics say that John Huston's detective film with Humphrey Bogart, *The Maltese Falcon* (Warner Bros., 1941), is the first film to show the traits of noir. Jonathan Auerbach goes a bit further back, pointing to the first American anti-Nazi film, Warner Bros.'s *Confessions of a Nazi Spy* (Anatole Litvak, 1939) and a strange expressionist film, *Stranger on the Third Floor* (Boris Ingster, RKO, 1940).[1] James Naremore looks abroad, finding the roots of American noir in a 1930s movement in

French cinema called poetic realism.[2] There is disagreement about whether noir is a distinct genre of film. While there is general agreement about the conventions of noir—a dark, **expressionist mise-en-scène**; seedy rooms and nightclubs; tough, often murderous female characters, often referred to as "femmes fatales"; weak, vulnerable men; a general aura of threat and paranoia—it is not clear whether these and other noir attributes cohere into one genre or are spread across a number of genres: the detective film, the gangster film, domestic melodrama, even science fiction. Naremore attempts to solve the problem, pointing out that film noir transcends a particular type of film and even a particular moment in film history. Noir, he says, has become a way of thinking about film and culture in general: "We might say . . . that film noir has become one of the dominant intellectual categories of the late twentieth [and early 21st] century, operating across the entire cultural arena of art, popular memory, and criticism."[3]

In a sequence in *The Terminator* (Hemdale, Pacific Western, Euro Film Funding, 1984), James Cameron names a nightclub "Tech Noir." Around the same time, television listings of films began using the term "film noir." Contemporary filmmakers began making movies dubbed "neonoir." Book after book, article after article appeared in the ensuing years. The name became part of the cultural discourse. We speak not only of film noir, but of noirish attributes in the other arts and even in day-to-day experience. Noir has become part of our way of seeing the world.

WHERE DID FILM NOIR GET ITS NAME?

As we noted earlier, between 1940 and 1944, the Germans occupied France and, among many more heinous acts, they embargoed American films from appearing on French screens. After the war, from 1945 to 1946, these once forbidden films flooded into France, and critics noted changes. There seemed to be a darkening of the mise-en-scène of many of these films, a heightened use of shadow, dark rooms, and threatening side streets slick with rain. The content of what they saw was changing as well. There was more violence; women characters were emerging as strong and dangerous; men somehow weaker and vulnerable; the thugs that populated the films were scarier and even psychotic. Searching for a way to classify the films, the French borrowed a title from a series of detective fiction called *Série noire*. The film critics adapted the name to film noir and eventually it was taken by the Americans who had invented it.

HOW DID NOIR DEVELOP IN HOLLYWOOD WITHOUT ANYONE KNOWING ABOUT IT?

Until the 1970s, when new directors emerged from film school with a knowledge of film history, Hollywood filmmaking was largely an intuitive and an internally self-perpetuating process. Directors moved up through the studio ranks and learned their trade by watching and listening to their studio colleagues. Some directors were German émigrés, bringing with them the expressionist style of filmmaking developed in their country. And perhaps more important than anything else, filmmakers watched *Citizen Kane* and took note of its use of shadow and deep focus, its fractured narrative, its refusal to draw a conclusive explanation of its central character. They also took note of that film made in 1941 by John Huston. It was the third adaptation of a novel by the detective fiction writer, a member of the so-called hard-boiled school, Dashiell Hammett, called *The Maltese Falcon*. This film starred Humphrey Bogart in a role that was different from the craven thugs he was mostly playing up to the time, and came just before his big breakthrough in *Casablanca*. Huston's version of *The Maltese Falcon* was a dark and, for its time, violent film about corruption and detection, in which the detective has to enter a moral swamp, full of suggestions about a variety of sexual activity that just managed its way past the Production Code.

All of this had an influence on the style of films being made, but the influence was largely unconscious. True, some filmmakers tried to imitate the visual style of *Citizen Kane*. They were influenced by the expressionist style of the German directors coming from abroad as well as French cinema of the 1930s. They were intrigued by the "tough guy" elements of *The Maltese Falcon* and the fiction of Dashiell Hammett, Raymond Chandler, and James M. Cain. There was the development of a faster film stock that allowed filmmakers to darken the general mise-en-scène of their work. There was also a great deal going on in the culture at large that was influencing the content of film as it was developing in the middle of the 1940s. But were the filmmakers aware that a new style was being created? Not until the end of the decade did they begin to notice that something had radically changed in the form and content of the films they were making.

NOIR AND AMERICAN CULTURE

We have been insisting throughout this book that American film responds to or even creates changes in the culture that surrounds it. One of the great arguments about film noir is just why it appeared at the time it did. What was going on that helps us account for the darkening of tone and content that marks noir? One answer, at least *an* answer, has to do with World War II and the anxieties and uncertainties it created. Despite the calls for unity of purpose and the war films and documentaries that portrayed a nation at one with the war effort, the strains on the society were great. There were wartime shortages of gasoline and rubber tires and rationing of sugar, coffee, meat, and other basics. There were population shifts, with African Americans moving to the North to find work and women taking the place of men in the workforce. Women gained economic power of the kind they had never before experienced. This was great for the women but anxiety producing for the fighting men, who were worried about their jobs, indeed their sense of place and patriarchal authority when they returned. There was the basic horror of the war itself that no amount of patriotic war films could communicate. Fought on two fronts, in the Pacific against the Japanese and in Europe against the Nazis, the war was a terrifying experience for all concerned. Coming home did not ease the anxiety.

The servicemen who return from war in *The Blue Dahlia* (George Marshall, written by Raymond Chandler, Paramount, 1946) are tortured by their experiences abroad and at home. One has a metal plate in his head from a war wound and suffers from what we now know as post-traumatic stress. He is hypersensitive to loud music—"monkey music," he calls it in a barely disguised racial slur. Another finds his wife, who claims her liberation and has been unfaithful: his young son died because of her drinking, and she is murdered. Through the dark and the rain, in the nightclub (there is always a nightclub in a noir film) that gives the film its name, peopled by shady characters, the former soldiers find no rest as accusations of guilt pursue them. Suspicions about who murdered the wife fall on the troubled Buzz (William Bendix), the most likely suspect, though he is proven innocent. The postwar atmosphere, the cultural mise-en-scène, was—at least as configured in film noir—oppressive and dangerous. Everyone bears some guilt, though often unaware of what they are guilty of.[4]

The contemporary director and screenwriter, Paul Schrader, points to the fact that as noir progressed through the late 1940s and early 1950s, there was the frequent appearance of a psychotic character, someone who enjoys inflicting violence for the fun of it—like Richard Widmark's Tommy Udo in *Kiss of Death* (Henry Hathaway, Fox, 1947), who giggling crazily ties an old lady to her wheelchair and pushes her down a flight of stairs. This sadism grew out of the dark violence boiling out of noir, but it grew as well from the anxious responses to the knowledge of Nazi atrocities committed in World War II. This background is sometimes represented literally. In Jules Dassin's *Brute Force* (Universal, 1947), a sadistic prison warden wears a Nazi-like uniform and listens to the music of Wagner, one of the Nazi's favorite composers. The noir psychopath is a kind of sublimation, a way of handling the enormity of history by funneling it into the recognizable representation of a single brutal individual.[5]

There were other forces at work on noir. Along with the anxieties of the war and its aftermath was the growth of the national security state. Beginning in the 1930s, the FBI was given powers to spy on US citizens to root out Nazi and communist sympathizers. In 1938, the House Committee on Un-American Activities was formed, and it would wreak havoc on Hollywood beginning almost immediately after the war. Jonathan Auerbach argues that noir is partially born out of and addresses the paranoia of the national security state and is a response to the Cold War and the deep fears embedded in a culture that came to believe it was being infiltrated by a dark, alien enemy.[6]

We need to be clear that there was no simple one-to-one case of cause and effect in the evolution of film noir. It is not as if producers, screenwriters, and directors suddenly, in the mid-1940s, said that the culture was in an anxious state, so we should make films that reflect that anxiety. Rather, many individuals at different studios seeking a means of expression that differed from the major formats and genres of the 1930s began creating dark films. Some sensed the changes in the culture; some wanted to experiment with new forms and themes. And there was the constant desire to push against the confines of the Production Code, to attempt a greater "realism," which in Hollywood terms in the 1940s meant more violence, more overt, even more perverse sexuality. The result was a radical change in the way many films looked and the stories many films told.

WHAT IS FILM NOIR?

LIGHTING

Film noir is easy to describe, difficult to define, and even more difficult to classify. One element of noir is evident and omnipresent: darkness. With a few notable exceptions, such as Warner Bros.'s early gangster films, Universal horror films, and the work of Josef von Sternberg, the films of the 1930s were mostly bright and **high-key** (see an image of this in Chapter 12). That is, they were evenly lit, with shadows used as accents or to indicate a suspenseful or threatening moment in the film. This began to change in the early 1940s, partly as a result of the faster **film stock** that became available, allowing lower light levels to be used during filming, and partly because of a desire to experiment with lighting on the part of some filmmakers. For example, John Ford worked with cinematographer Gregg Toland on *The Long Voyage Home* (Argosy, Walter Wanger Productions, United Artists 1940) to create a shadowed, deeply focused mise-en-scène with the action restricted mostly to a ship on the high seas. Toland went on to photograph *Citizen Kane,* and it was that film that changed the lighting conventions of film for good.

Instead of sculpting with light, Welles sculpted with shadow, in many instances using light to accent elements in an otherwise dark shot. He went so far as to put characters in shadow when they spoke, denying them a **key light** (see an image of this in Chapter 3). This radical change in style gave other filmmakers the opportunity to experiment on their own with low-key lighting and begin the darkness of the image that would mark the noir style. Shafts of light coming through the slats of venetian blinds would soon become a central image—along with the dark, rain-soaked streets, apartments, bars, and lounges—that became the visual conventions of film noir.

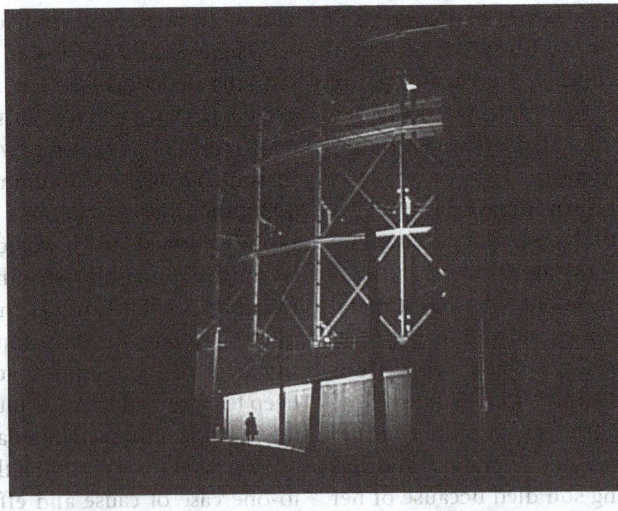

The shadowy mise-en-scène of film noir. *T-Men* (Anthony Mann, 1947).

THEMES AND CONTENT

Noir explores paranoid and threatening worlds. Noir characters hurt each other, cause emotional and physical damage. The men are weak or brutish; the women often murderers. The landscape they inhabit is urban, the city at night after a rain. Reflecting on his own detective fiction and screenplays, Raymond Chandler wrote:

> Their characters lived in a world gone wrong, a world in which, long before the atom bomb, civilization had created the machinery for its own destruction, and was learning to use it with all the moronic delight of a gangster trying out his first machine gun. The law was something to be manipulated for profit and power. The streets were dark with something more than night.[7]

That "something more" is the sense of menace and dread, of dark figures lurking and nefarious plans being hatched that usually involved murder, of driving down a dark road and getting beaten up or killed at the end of the ride.

GENDER IN FILM NOIR

At the beginning of *The Blue Dahlia*, Helen (Doris Dowling) is caught by her husband, Johnny (Alan Ladd), with her lover. Drinking heavily, she tells him: "I take all the drinks I like. Any time, any place. I go where I want to with anybody I want. I just happen to be that kind of a girl." It sounds like a clarion call of freedom by the new postwar woman. Indeed, some have found in noir a voice of the recently liberated woman, breaking free of domestic ties. But in their freedom, these women turn unfaithful at best and murderous as worst. "Liberation" seems to mean, for the noir woman, a freedom to commit mayhem and murder. For Helen, her drinking led to the death of their child.

There is no liberation offered to the noir male. He is an oppressed figure, undone by the woman who infiltrates herself into his life; pursued by shadowy, brutal men who want to beat him up. The noir male may be psychotic or the victim of someone else's psychosis. He is not—even if he is a detective attempting to solve a complex case of murder and seduction—the least bit heroic, and redemption is always beyond his reach.[8]

FILMS NOIR

MURDER, MY SWEET

Citizen Kane is not a film noir, although it contains the stylistic seeds of noir. *Murder, My Sweet*, made by Edward Dmytryk at RKO in 1944, three years after *Kane* and for the same studio, is. *Murder, My Sweet* is a detective film, an adaptation of a novel, *Farewell, My Lovely*, by Raymond Chandler. Dark and violent, its detective bears the brunt of the intrigue he tries to solve. The film starts with the camera at a 90-degree angle, tracking downward on a pool of light shining on a table. Detective Philip Marlowe (Dick Powell) is undergoing an interrogation by the police. He sits in the dark and is blindfolded, narrating the film that, in effect, is told in flashback. Marlowe wanders through a dark, forbidding world, full of odd and dangerous characters as a large man named Moose (Mike Mazurki) sends him on a search for a killer woman named Velma (Claire Trevor) and a mysterious jade necklace. In the course of his detection, he is knocked out by a blackjack and the screen goes black with a spot of light as he "falls through a dark hole." Later, he is strangled, beaten, drugged, and has an expressionist hallucination of a never-ending hallway filled with doors. He ends up getting his eyes scorched by a gun blast. This was as great an amount of screen violence that an audience would have seen outside of a war movie.

". . . I'm just a small businessman in a very messy business" is how Marlowe defines himself as he wanders through a world where the darkness of violence and corruption all but engulf him. One of the villains of the piece—an evil psychiatrist, of the kind often portrayed in 1940s film—calls him a "dirty stupid little man in a dirty stupid world." He can't really solve anything in this dirty stupid world, although he discovers the sources of the various mysteries and the bad guys and woman get killed by the time the film is over. The film ends in an embrace with the one woman Marlowe discovers he can trust. But he is left with his eyes bandaged and the world not much better than when he began his quest.

A pool of light surrounding by darkness sets the noir mise-en-scène in Edward Dmytryk's *Murder, My Sweet* (1944).

THE BIG SLEEP

Another version of Marlowe, this one played by Humphrey Bogart in Howard Hawks's version of a Chandler novel co-scripted by William Faulkner, *The Big Sleep* (Warner Bros., 1946), is somewhat less put upon than his earlier incarnation, though he does take the requisite beating. Hired by a rich old man to find out who is blackmailing his daughter, he discovers what is clearly (though because of the Production Code unstated) a pornography racket. He gets caught up in a series of murders that take place on dark Los Angeles streets and gloomy warehouses. He is himself responsible for at least two deaths, even as he gets involved in a romance with Vivian Sternwood (Lauren Bacall). But romance for the noir detective is always fraught with danger, because the women of noir are highly aggressive, calculating, and many times more dangerous than the men.

The narrative complexities of *The Big Sleep* are legendary. Supposedly the filmmakers couldn't figure out who committed one of the murders and had to contact Chandler for the answer. But this complexity is part of the noir style. Its plots are often labyrinthine; they suck the characters in and leave the audience with a sense of loss and being lost. But it is precisely a sense of loss and being lost that noir seeks to impart. Its world is one of confusion and hurt, of a bad past that keeps intruding on a troubled present in face of an uncertain future. By the end of *The Big Sleep*, Marlowe and Vivian sit in the dark, a corpse on the floor, the sounds of police sirens in the distance. Though the film offers the notion of romance between them, the dangerous world around them intrudes and threatens.

The detective film is a genre well established before the advent of noir. It can be seen operating in the lighthearted *Thin Man* series produced by MGM in the 1930s that mixed screwball comedy with detection. I noted that *The Maltese Falcon* was made twice by Warner Bros. in the 1930s—unmemorable films that needed the darker tone provided by John Huston and the brooding presence of Humphrey Bogart. Noir infiltrated the detective and the gangster genre right into the 1950s.

DOUBLE INDEMNITY

In 1944, the same year as *Murder My Sweet*, the German émigré director, Billy Wilder, took a script by Raymond Chandler, based on a book by James M. Cain, who wrote raw novels about lower middle-class people visiting corruption on one another, and made *Double Indemnity* (Paramount), a film that has little to

The detective, Marlowe (Humphrey Bogart), in the dark, a suspect tied up on the floor behind him, in Howard Hawks's *The Big Sleep* (1946).

do with detection and everything to do with noir. It should be noted that two other of Cain's novels were turned into noirish films in the 1940s: *Mildred Pierce* (Michael Curtiz, Warner Bros., 1945); and *The Postman Always Rings Twice* (Tay Garnett, MGM, 1946—a book that had already been filmed in France in 1939, in Italy in 1942, and was remade as a Jack Nicholson vehicle in 1981).

Double Indemnity is about a universe of self-destructive people: a weak-willed insurance agent named Walter Neff (Fred MacMurray), who comes under the spell of a homicidal woman, Phyllis Dietrichson (Barbara Stanwyck). Neff is not an innocent. He is willingly lascivious in his gaze at Phyllis, marked by the camera assuming his point of view when he comes to her house to sell her insurance. He sees her coming down the stairs and fixates on her anklet as she descends. Neff is full of himself, no matter that he is a small man in a small job. He willingly joins in a plot with Phyllis to sell her husband insurance that will pay double for accidental death, kill him, and make it look like an accident. All this is grim enough, but the narrative of these unpleasant killers is enclosed first of all in a flashback—the story is told by a dying Neff. He dictates it from his office, late at night, deep in shadow. Second, the story is told with a great deal of wit. This might seem counterintuitive given the bleakness of the noir mise-en-scène and the content of the film's narrative, but it works to the film's advantage, as an ironic contrast to its quiet brutality.

Walter Neff comes to Phyllis Dietrichson's house in an LA suburb, its hazy interior lit through the slats of the venetian blinds—an image that would become a convention in 1940s cinema. "The windows were closed and the sunshine coming in through the venetian blinds showed up the dust in the air," Walter narrates, doubling what we see. Walter ogles Phyllis's anklet and they sit down to talk, Phyllis comfortable in an armchair, Walter sitting on the arm of the couch. Neff tries to tell her about the insurance he's selling. Phyllis tries to divert him, telling him to come back and talk to her husband. Walter gets more and more intrigued with Phyllis and her anklet and comes on strong:

PHYLLIS: There's a speed limit in this state, Mr. Neff, 45 miles an hour.

WALTER: How fast was I going, officer?

PHYLLIS: I'd say around 90.

WALTER: Suppose you get down of your motorcycle and give me a ticket.

PHYLLIS: Suppose I let you off with a warning this time.
WALTER: Suppose it doesn't take.
PHYLLIS: Suppose I have to whack you over the knuckles.
WALTER: Suppose I bust out crying and put my head on your shoulder.
PHYLLIS: Suppose you try putting it on my husband's shoulder.
WALTER: That tears it!

Neff goes off, promising to return in the evening when Phyllis's husband is at home. He wants to know if she'll be there.

WALTER: Same chair, same perfume, same anklet?
PHYLLIS: I wonder if I know what you mean.
WALTER: I wonder if you wonder.

Film noir as downscale screwball comedy. But this couple is not sparring playfully over Martinis. This couple plans and executes the murder of Phyllis's husband. Neff has an affair not only with Phyllis, but with her daughter. They get entangled in a domestic mess so sordid that the only way it can end is with the death of both of them. Even the moderating presence of Neff's boss and friend, Keyes (Edward G. Robinson), who acts as the film's sole voice of reason, cannot save Neff.

Keyes is a fascinating character. A claims investigator for the company—Pacific All Risk—he says that he can spot a phony claim by listening to "the little man" in his belly. He is an obsessive little blowhard, but his faith in Neff is touching. There is almost a father-son relationship between the two, which, of course, Neff betrays by writing a policy and killing the man he insured. Keyes cannot bring light into the darkness of this world despite his dedication and friendship. These are qualities that can't survive in the noir universe, which in this film does not have to play out entirely in the dark. There is a key sequence in which Walter and Phyllis make their plans in the baby food isle of a supermarket. Ordinary domesticity becomes the backdrop to the dark parody of domesticity represented by this couple, just as the honest, straightforward Keyes is played a fool by his favorite coworker.

Phyllis Dietrichson is hardly a domesticated woman. Walter Neff is helpless in the face of Phyllis's lurid and murderous charms. Only at the end of the affair, her husband dead, her daughter compromised, does Neff recognize that she is in fact a serial killer of wives and husbands. She admits that she is "rotten to

Walter Neff (Fred McMurray) and Phyllis Dietrichson (Barbara Stanwyck) playfully planning for murder in the venetian blind shadows of *Double Indemnity* (Billy Wilder, 1944).

the heart," and they shoot each other. The narration comes full circle as Neff returns to his office and, while bleeding to death, dictates the story we have been seeing for the duration of the film. (Billy Wilder liked this idea so much that he took it one step further in *Sunset Boulevard* that he made for Paramount in 1950. In this film, the narrator is already dead when the film begins.)

As we noted, one of the most controversial elements of noir is the role of women. Phyllis Dietrichson is, by any measure, a strong female character. She uses her sexuality as a weapon. She has a power over Walter Neff that reduces him to murder. The domestic scene over which she rules is a ruthlessly ugly parody of the sweetness of family life so many films of the 1920s and 30s liked to portray. Did this mark an important change in the representation of women in American film or was it misogyny in a different form? The question becomes even more interesting when the evil noir woman is paired with a weak male. Walter Neff is a willing victim of lust and avarice. Other noir males are seduced for no other reason than that they appear at the wrong place.

THE WOMAN IN THE WINDOW AND *SCARLET STREET*

There were many films of the 1940s that promoted the old conventions of the happy home and the docile female, but noir put its teeth into these conventions and pulled out its banal core. Two such films were made by Fritz Lang, films that explored the destruction of a middle-class, mild-mannered man who falls under the spell of an amoral woman, liberated to the point of heartlessness. Lang was yet another German émigré, who fled when the Nazis took over his country and was asked by Joseph Goebbels, the Nazi Minister of Propaganda, to lead the German film industry. He was a prolific filmmaker before coming to the United States. *Metropolis* (1927), a monumental science fiction film, is a hallmark of European silent cinema as *M* (1931), a disturbing film about a child killer, is of early sound film. Once in America, Lang exercised his imagination in a number of genres, including two Westerns: *The Return of Frank James* (Fox, 1940) and *Rancho Notorious* (Fidelity Pictures, RKO, 1952). But he was at his best making dark melodramas, two of which, made back to back in 1944 and 1945, each starring Edward G. Robinson, who we saw in *Little Caesar* (Mervyn LeRoy, Warner Bros., 1930), *The Stranger* (Orson Welles, 1946), and *Double Indemnity*, are among the best of the early noir films.

The Woman in the Window and *Scarlet Street* (both made as independent productions; *The Woman in the Window* was distributed by RKO, *Scarlet Street* by Universal) are about middle-aged men who fall in love and in trance to younger women, much to their regret. Richard Wanley in *The Woman in the Window* is a professor of criminal psychology. His name, based on the word "wan," means tired and washed out. He lives a simple, contained life. When his wife and children go off for summer vacation, he spends his evening at his club with two friends—"three old crocks" as he refers to their group. But the imagination and the id are stirring, and after leaving his friends, he falls under the spell of a painting of a woman in an art gallery window. The woman in the painting suddenly appears "in the flesh," and the result is a nightmare of murder and guilt, moving through the dark, almost expressionist streets outside the woman's apartment through the daylight world of Wanley's attempts to cover the tracks of his crime. Wanley sinks under the downward spiral of the noir male's inevitable guilt, saved from suicide only when he is abruptly awakened from his bad dream.

The Woman in the Window is a dream film. It represents an eruption of the unconscious of a plain man who needed a touch of darkness in his life, a spark of erotic excitement (he falls asleep reading the biblical *Song of Songs*). The noir world he dreams himself into is like a collapsing room, a space that becomes more constricted with each step Wanley takes, until it threatens to overcome him, a common fate of the noir male. But if *The Woman in the Window* is a dream film, the work that followed it, *Scarlet Street*, is a nightmare. Three actors from *The Woman in the Window*—Edward G. Robinson, Joan Bennett, and Dan Duryea—return, but their class, their place in life, are brought down considerably. The Bennett character, Kitty, is clearly a prostitute (though because of the code, not named as such) and Johnny (Duryea) is her pimp. They live in a sadomasochistic relationship. When Christopher Cross (Robinson) comes across them, on a dark, rain-soaked street, Johnny is beating up Kitty. Chris in turn beats Johnny down with his umbrella, and with this act of courage falls into a bottomless pit.

Chris is crossed at every turn. A lowly bank cashier, his domestic life is dismal beyond belief. His only refuge from a nagging wife is to escape into the bathroom to paint strange canvases of snakes in the subway and huge psychedelic flowers. His art becomes his downfall; his paintings are stolen by Johnny, who pretends they were painted by Kitty. Chris is reduced to stealing his wife's insurance and embezzling from his bank to keep Kitty, who he believes is in love with him. He loses all sense of perspective, in his painting and his life: "That's one thing I never could master—perspective," he says.

In the great tradition of melodrama, coincidence plays a cruel and ironic role in *Scarlet Street*, and humiliation seems to drive Chris, even when his wife's supposedly dead husband returns, freeing him to be with Kitty. He discovers her making love to Johnny, and stabs her to death with an ice pick. Double crossed and hung out, Chris Cross does not get convicted of his crime. Johnny is sentenced to death for Kitty's murder. Chris's only punishment is his guilt, and he wanders the city tortured by hearing the love-making and taunting words of Kitty and Johnny. Sleepless in his hotel room, with the blinking neon light outside—so much part of the noir nightscape—he tries to hang himself. Failing that, he wanders the city. It is Christmastime. He passes a gallery where his portrait of Kitty is being carried out. The camera cranes up to find Chris in the crowd, which dissolves away. Everyone around him disappears. He wanders alone, the only man on earth, Johnny's and Kitty's voices echoing in his head.

American film does not get any darker than *Scarlet Street*; there are few screen characters as abused and unredeemed as Chris Cross. Certainly there are characters treated with greater physical violence than he receives, but few so morally compromised and wracked by guilt, left so radically alone. The darkness that swallows Chris only deepens as noir expands its reach across studios and directors in the mid- and late-1940s. And this leads us to some conclusions about whether noir is a style or a genre. I am inclined to believe the former. Since the attributes of noir spread across different genres, we can think of them as a flexible set of stylistic formats: a dark, urban mise-en-scène, dark apartments with light streaming through venetian blinds, light from a single source, like a bare bulb, and, as the writer and director Paul Schrader points out, characters composed within "odd shapes—jagged trapezoids, obtuse triangle, vertical slits," that is when they are not obscured completely by the dark. There are the inevitable scenes in ratty hotels and bars and lounges.[9] The noir style spread across genres from the detective and gangster film to the prison film like *Brute Force* referred to earlier, into the boxing films,

Alone and guilt ridden, Chris Cross (Edward G. Robinson) wanders the streets in Fritz Lang's *Scarlet Street* (1945).

such as Robert Wise's grim *The Set-Up* (RKO, 1949), and domestic melodrama.

NOIR AND MELODRAMA: THE CASE OF *MILDRED PIERCE*

Film noir is essentially melodramatic. Like all melodrama, it puts characters in emotional or physical danger; it demands emotional response from its viewers; it tries to reach some sort of closure, however violent; and it certainly allows its mise-en-scène to reflect the emotional turmoil its characters are suffering. Domestic melodrama focuses on its female character. During the 1940s, there were straightforward melodramas of the classic kind, in which a woman, constrained and living in unhappy circumstances, is offered a momentary release into a world of self-expression and sexual liberation.

In 1945, Warner Bros. made a woman's melodrama in a film noir wrapper. *Mildred Pierce* (Michael Curtiz) is based on a novel by James M. Cain, whose influence on the noir movement we have noted in the discussion of *Double Indemnity*. Curtiz's film resets the novel—which was set in the Depression-era 1930s—into wartime 1940s Los Angeles, and begins the film in strong noir fashion: in the dead of night, at a fancy beachfront house, the sound of gunshots, and a man falling dead. The man's last words are "Mildred," but we do not see the fleeing shooter as she drives away into the night. In the next sequence, the camera cranes down on a rain-soaked pier, as Mildred (Joan Crawford), dressed in furs, walks in the night to the railing, ready to jump until stopped by a cop. The noir cloak remains as Mildred traps her one-time friend Wally (Jack Carson) in the beach house with the body. But once Mildred is picked up by the police and begins telling her story, the film moves to flashback, and the noir atmosphere is replaced by a high-key lighted narrative of Mildred's rise from waitress to riches as a restaurant owner. Her melodrama involves the breakup of her marriage, the death of one daughter as a "punishment" for her having an extramarital affair, and the rise to power of her older daughter Veda (Ann Blyth), who turns into a kind of monster.

Here is where noir infiltrates the film again. We have seen the destructive noir woman—the "femme fatale"—in *Double Indemnity* and in *Scarlet Street*, and she reappears many times across the noir spectrum. Veda is a particularly virulent form of this misogynist figure, a creation by male writers and directors of a despicable woman who more than anything seems to reflect a fear of the feminine out of control. She acts as a counterirritant to her mother. As Mildred

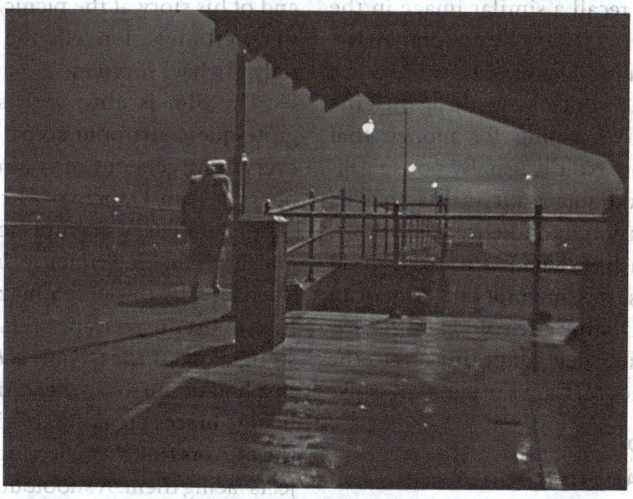

In the noirish opening of *Mildred Pierce* (Michael Curtiz, 1945), the title character (played by Joan Crawford) contemplates suicide.

gets more successful and independent, Veda gets more poisonous. She fakes a pregnancy to blackmail a rich boyfriend. She sleeps with her mother's husband Monty (Zachary Scott), a ne'er-do-well who takes Mildred's money and sells out her business. The men in this film do not come off much better than the women—except for Mildred, who remains strong in face of all her reversals, even the knowledge that Veda shot Monty. We see a repeat of the shooting near the end of the film, as the police get the whole story about the incident. The film ends on an odd note. Mildred leaves the police detective's office with her first husband, and, as they do, we see two washerwomen scrubbing the floors. That Mildred had to be brought back to where she came from is partly a necessity of the Production Code. But the washerwomen indicate as well that she needs to be close to the bottom of the ladder, to the working class from which she came.

Mildred Pierce was a wartime diversion. There are only the briefest and joking references to the war in the course of the film and a maximum of sensation derived from the thrill of seeing a woman succeed and fail because of a pathological daughter. This film does not have the intensity of corruption found in most noir or the bleakness of noir's worldview. In fact, the curious closing images of the film bring it quite down to earth. The washerwomen are always with us, and we might recall a similar image in the film *Our Dancing Daughters* (Harry Beaumont, MGM, 1928) that we discussed in Chapter 6. They provide a kind of continuity of the workaday world against the sporadic couplings and grasping for money that *Mildred Pierce* focuses on. Noir is usually not so cautionary; domestic melodrama is. It insists that its characters and by extension its audience come down to earth—with the washerwomen. (In 2011, Todd Haynes, one of the best of contemporary American directors, made an HBO miniseries of *Mildred Pierce*. It is an extraordinary film that is faithful not to the 1945 movie, but to James M. Cain's original novel.)

ORSON WELLES AND *THE LADY FROM SHANGHAI*

Orson Welles's films are never down to earth. They are exuberant flights of visual imagination and, no matter how constrained they might have been by studio interference, always transcend their limitations. Welles's 1947 entry into the 40s noir universe, *The Lady from Shanghai*, plays an interesting turn on the killer woman. The film stars Rita Hayworth, one of the biggest stars of the late 1940s and certainly the most important actress in Harry Cohn's studio, Columbia Pictures. She was also, for a time, Welles's wife. The film was made after their separation. This adds an extra level of perversity as Welles creates Hayworth's character, Elsa Bannister, as a killer with a face as blank as a mask. She lures Welles's innocent Irish seaman, Michael O'Hara, into the world of corrupt lawyers out to murder each other and leads him on a dizzying journey by boat to South America.

On the beach in Mexico, Elsa, her crippled husband Arthur (Everett Sloane), and his mad partner, Grisby (Glenn Anders), have a drunken picnic. Standing over them, Michael tells them a story about sharks. "A shark it was," he says, cutting to Elsa's face. He proceeds to tell a grisly tale of the sharks turning and eating at each other and themselves. "You could smell the death reeking up out of the sea. I never saw anything worse until this little picnic tonight." The image of underwater carnage is repeated later in the film when Elsa and Michael meet in an aquarium, Elsa telling Michael more lies, the marine animals gigantic behind them. And Michael's caution at the end of his story at the picnic, that none of the sharks were left alive, foretells the end of the film, where only Michael survives.

The film is alive with such great set pieces: a grotesque courtroom scene in which everyone and everything gets out of control; a scene at a Chinese opera in San Francisco where a doped Michael escapes Bannister's attempts to frame him for murder; and a climactic sequence in a carnival funhouse. Michael falls through a maze of tunnels and an expressionist dreamscape of shadow and distorted lines straight out of *The Cabinet of Dr. Caligari*. He winds up in a hall of mirrors, where Arthur Bannister appears, his leg braces creaking, his image multiplied across the mirrors that are reflecting each other and the subjects facing them. A shootout occurs with great shards of glass shattering and falling as the images of Elsa and Arthur fall to pieces. They kill each other.

Shootout in the hall of mirrors. Arthur Bannister and Michael O'Hara (Everett Sloane and Orson Welles) in Welles's *The Lady From Shanghai* (1947).

The Lady from Shanghai adds a touch of the grotesque to noir, turning its already nightmarish dreamscape into a surreal one. Welles seems already conscious of the style and plays with it and with the audience, burying plot with his extraordinary images, and narrating a tale that is both banal and profound in its portrayal of weakness and betrayal.

ANTHONY MANN AND *T-MEN*

By the late 1940s, the stylistics of noir were becoming evident to filmmakers and audiences alike. What had started as a disconnected collection of dark films became something of a movement. Some filmmakers pushed the limits of the style into idiosyncratic forms that exaggerated mise-en-scène and raised violence to unprecedented levels. Anthony Mann, working with cinematographer John Alton, created some of the most intense noirs of the style's late middle period.

T-Men (Eagle-Lion, 1947) sets out as a pseudo-**documentary** about treasury agents. A number of films of the late 40s adopted this style to tell patriotic stories about the FBI or other governmental and local law enforcement outfits. But any pretense to documentary-style filmmaking vanishes as Mann and Alton present us with the dark streets of Los Angeles, as an agent walks through a desolate industrial landscape, shot on location, past a huge gas tank, shot from a distance so that his small, dark figure can just be seen against a partly lighted background. (See the image from *T-Men* above.)

Location shots lit in an expressionist fashion predominate the film, and it is worth noting that shooting on location became more common in the late 1940s, partly as a result of the loosening grip of the studios, partly as a result of the influence of **Italian neorealism**. This was a movement that occurred in Italy after World War II, when filmmaking facilities were in ruins and filmmakers, anxious to capture the devastated state of their country and the poor people attempting to reconstruct their lives, took to the streets with nonprofessional actors. Films like *Rome, Open City* (Roberto Rossellini, 1945) and *Bicycle Thieves* (Vittorio De Sica, 1947) were influential this side of the Atlantic in urging filmmakers out of the confines of the studio and onto the streets. Location shooting became mostly the province of low-budget crime films and noirs, as we see in *T-Men*. But Mann's exteriors are not realistic. Night scenes are lit to emphasize shadow and photographed from odd and disturbing angles. The evident "there-ness" of the location and the expressionist distortion of the locations create intriguing, disturbing images. German expressionism and Italian neorealism join to create landscapes of dread.

A droning voice-over continues throughout the film, but this documentary pretense continues to be countered by the visuals that become darker and darker. Rooms are lighted with bare lightbulbs; characters are seen deeply focused and in shadow, punctuated by spots of light. Faces appear close to the camera, slightly distorted. In one shot, the top of a man's head is foreground in the frame, talking on the phone, with two characters and a hanging light fixture behind him. There is a **montage** sequence in which one of the agents looks for a suspect in various steam baths. The images are appropriately dark and smoking, bodies appearing out of the steamy haze. One character is cooked to death.

What plot there is in *T-Men* involves counterfeiting. But as in many of Mann's (and other directors') noir films, plot disintegrates beneath the darkness and violence. There is something almost abstract about Mann's films, a foregrounding of image over narrative. His work consummates the modernist influence on noir with its emphasis on the image itself in which shadow, light, and composition diminish the human figure. Fully self-conscious of the noir style, Mann is one of the first group of directors who would later reflect back on the noir style. In films like Robert Aldrich's *Kiss Me Deadly* (United Artists, 1955) and Orson Welles's *Touch of Evil* (Universal, 1958), the first phase of noir was brought to a close with films that are fully aware of their 40s forebears.

NOIR AND THE PRODUCTION CODE

Anthony Mann himself shifted to Westerns in the 1950s. In his first, *The Furies* (Paramount, 1950), he used the style of his 40s noirs. A film noir Western! Then he dropped the style entirely. His approach to his 1950s films was more straightforward, less dependent on the shadowy, distorted compositions that marked his late 40s work. Meanwhile, in the late 1940s, people were beginning to take notice of the change that was occurring in American film. John Houseman, a former associate of Orson Welles, who went on to be an important producer, wrote about the state of film and, in particular, *The Big Sleep* and a noir film produced at MGM in 1946, based on a James M. Cain novel, *The Postman Always Rings Twice*:

> What is significant and repugnant about our contemporary "tough" films is their absolute lack of moral energy, their listless, fatalistic despair.
>
> One wonders what impression people will get of contemporary life if *The Postman Always Rings Twice* is run in a projection room twenty years hence. They will deduce, I believe, that the United States of America in the year following the end of the Second World War was a land of enervated, frightened people with spasms of high vitality but a low moral sense—a hungover people with confused objectives groping their way through a twilight of insecurity and corruption.[10]

Houseman is not far off in observing the anxieties and insecurities suffered in the culture after the war being reflected in the culture's films. As to the "low moral sense," this might be considered in another way. Filmmakers began to break through the strict "moral" codes of the censors and viewers took it in stride, indeed wanted more. Noir can be understood, in part at least, as a rebellion on the part of filmmakers and audiences alike against the Production Code. (In fact, censors in Atlanta, Georgia, tried and failed to ban *Scarlet Street*.) Where Houseman is correct is his observation of "confused objectives." The end of World War II, the shock of the atomic bombs dropped on Japan, the horror of the revelations of the Nazi death camps, the incipient and insidious rise of anti-Communism led to a culturewide confusion and a sense of confused dread. These led, in short, to the difficult decade of the 1950s and some of the greatest films Hollywood produced.

Film noir, meanwhile, has become the most commented-upon style in American film. A never-ending source of interest to film scholars and filmgoers, there are more books and articles written about it than any other topic in film. This speaks to an ongoing fascination with that period in Hollywood when filmmakers broke rules, defied the censors, spoke to fear rather than optimism, and used their medium in a most articulate manner, eschewing the conventions of Hollywood realism developed in the 1920s to find new means of expression on the screen.

SELECTED FILMOGRAPHY

Confessions of a Nazi Spy, dir. Anatole Litvak, Warner Bros., 1939.

The Maltese Falcon, dir. John Huston, Warner Bros., 1940.

Murder My Sweet, dir. Edward Dmytryk, RKO, 1944.

Double Indemnity, dir. Billy Wilder, Paramount, 1944.

The Woman in the Window, dir. Fritz Lang, Christie Corporation, International Pictures, RKO, 1944.

Scarlet Street, dir. Fritz Lang, Fritz Lang Productions, Diana Production Co., Universal, 1945.

Mildred Pierce, dir. Michael Curtiz, Warner Bros., 1945.

The Big Sleep, dir. Howard Hawks, Warner Bros., 1946.

The Postman Always Rings Twice, dir. Tay Garnett, MGM, 1946.

The Blue Dahlia, dir. George Marshall, Paramount, 1946.

Kiss of Death, dir. Henry Hathaway, Fox, 1947.

Brute Force, dir. Jules Dassin, Universal, 1947.

The Lady from Shanghai, dir. Orson Welles, Columbia, 1947.

T-Men, dir. Anthony Mann, Eagle-Lion, 1947.

The Furies, dir. Anthony Mann, Paramount, 1950.

Kiss Me Deadly, dir. Robert Aldrich, United Artists, 1955.

SUGGESTIONS FOR FURTHER READING

Jonathan Auerbach, *Dark Borders: Film Noir and American Citizenship* (Durham, NC: Duke University Press, 2011).

E. Ann Kaplan, ed., *Women in Film Noir* (London, UK: BFI, 2008).

Frank Krutnik, *In a Lonely Street: Film Noir, Genre, Masculinity* (London, UK: Routledge, 1991).

James Naremore, *More Than Night: Film Noir in Its Contexts* (Berkeley, CA: University of California Press, 2008).

Paul Schrader, "Notes on Film Noir," *Schrader on Schrader*, ed. Kevin Jackson (London, UK: Faber & Faber, 2004).

Alain Silver & Elizabeth Ward, *Film Noir: An Encyclopedic Reference to the American Style*, 3rd ed. (Woodstock, NJ: Overlook Press, 1992).

Vivian Sobchack "Lounge Time: Postwar Crises and the Chronotope of Film Noir," *Refiguring American Film Genres: History and Theory*, ed. Nick Browne (Berkeley, CA: University of California Press, 1998), 129–170.

J. P. Telotte, *Voices in the Dark: The Narrative Patterns of Film Noir* (Urbana, IL: University of Illinois Press, 1989).

NOTES

1. Jonathan Auerbach, *Dark Borders: Film Noir and American Citizenship* (Durham, NC: Duke University Press, 2011), 27–55.
2. James Naremore, *More Than Night Film Noir in Its Contexts* (Berkeley, CA: University of California Press, 2008), 11–27.
3. Naremore, 2.
4. Frank Krutnik makes a similar argument about *The Blue Dahlia* is his book, *In a Lonely Street: Film Noir, Genre, Masculinity* (London: Routledge, 1991), 56–72. See also Paul Schrader, "Notes on Film Noir," *Schrader on Schrader*, ed. Kevin Jackson (London, UK: Faber & Faber, 2004), 80–94.
5. Schrader, "Notes on Film Noir," 80–94.
6. Auerbach, 1–26
7. Raymond Chandler, *Trouble Is My Business* (New York, NY: Vintage Books, 1992), 1.
8. For gender in film noir, see Krutnik, *In a Lonely Street*; Sylvia Harvey, "Women's Place: The Absent Family of Film Noir" and Janey Place, "Women in Film Noir," in E. Ann Kaplan, ed., *Women in Film Noir* (London, UK: BFI, 2008).
9. Schrader, 84. For the settings of noir, see Vivian Sobchack "Lounge Time: Postwar Crises and the Chronotope of Film Noir," *Refiguring American Film Genres: History and Theory*, ed. Nick Browne (Berkeley, CA: University of California Press, 1998), 129–170.
10. John Houseman quoted in Elizabeth Cowie, "Film Noir and Women," *Shades of Noir*, ed. Joan Copjec (London, UK: Verso, 1993), 187. The quotation comes from two separate essays written by Houseman.

CHAPTER 15

HOLLYWOOD AFTER WORLD WAR II (1946–1960)

Postwar America was riddled with doubts and anxieties that flowered into the virulent anti-Communist movement spearheaded by Joseph McCarthy and carried on as well by the House Committee on Un-American Activities (HUAC). This group invaded Hollywood with the blessing of the studios, who instituted the blacklist and turned colleagues into informers on one another. But even as this oppression was carried out, some filmmakers bucked the tide to make progressive works.

AFTER READING THIS CHAPTER, YOU SHOULD UNDERSTAND:

- How *The Best Years of Our Lives* tries to reclaim soldiers back into civilian life.
- The technologies and aesthetics of screen size.
- The various events that led to the decline of Hollywood.
- The history of postwar anti-Communism.
- The causes of the blacklist.
- How and why the blacklist was ended.
- How Hollywood dealt with issues of race in the late 1940s and early 1950s.
- How American film is so intimately tied to the national consciousness.

YOU SHOULD BE ABLE TO:

- Differentiate the way Gregg Toland uses deep focus in *The Best Years of Our Lives* and *Citizen Kane.*
- Account for the return of 3D, which was first used in the 1950s.
- Discuss why HUAC chose Hollywood for the focus of its investigations.
- Discuss why individuals turned on one another and informed on their colleagues.
- Describe how the divestiture affected the studios.
- Understand why the studios bent under the pressure of HUAC.
- Consider the irony of Hollywood under siege by the government it had tried to appease by means of the Production Code.
- Decide whether, in the words of blacklisted writer Dalton Trumbo, regarding the blacklist, "we are all victims."
- Speak to the importance of *Salt of the Earth.*

PART ONE: *THE BEST YEARS OF OUR LIVES*

In 1946, a year before financial disarray and the red scare hit Hollywood, the last year of great profit and something remotely approximating innocence in the film business, there were two films about three servicemen returning home to reclaim their lives. *The Blue Dahlia* (George Marshall, Paramount) is, as we have seen, a dark film in which postwar America was viewed as damaged and murderous. But there was also an independent production from Samuel Goldwyn, directed by William Wyler, *The Best Years of Our Lives.* This film tries nothing less than to signal and move the country's moral and cultural state from a wartime to a peacetime footing. It is a film about change and reclamation—reclaiming the family, changing men from battlefield groups into responsible domestic partners, proclaiming a world set right by America's winning the war. It is the optimistic response to *The Blue Dahlia*, creating a microcosm of white America in which servicemen, representing three branches of the military—the air force, the navy, and the army—come home to Boone City, the fictional representative middle-American town, and successfully reclaim their lives.

The three represent distinctive social classes. Homer (Harold Russell), the navy man who has lost his hands in battle, is from the lower middle class, with a humble, loving family and a loyal fiancée. Fred (Dana Andrews), the air force captain, is a working-class guy who lives literally on the other side of the tracks. He was a soda jerk before the war and married to a not very faithful woman (Virginia Mayo) who has taken up with a gangster in his absence. Al (Fredric March), the army sergeant, is a banker, a man of the upper middle class, who lives in a fancy apartment and is welcomed home by a loving family. Wyler stages his homecoming as if it were an actual stage, his children stand on either side of the entranceway while Al's wife, Milly (Myrna Loy), is seen in **deep focus** in the rear. (*Best Years* was photographed by Gregg Toland, who shot *Citizen Kane* 5 years earlier. He uses many of the deep focus techniques he employed for Welles, but, with a few exceptions, not to such radical effect.) The result is to present the almost perfect family framed perfectly: husband and wife, bookended by their son and daughter.

Framed perfectly, but not yet perfect. There is much work to be done. The returning soldiers need to acclimate themselves, break the male bond, and renew the family. As the film presents it, it is the role of the women to accomplish this. The narrative goes through a series of maneuvers in which the men

Al (Fredric March) and Milly (Myrna Loy) greet each other when Al returns from war. *The Best Years of Our Lives* (William Wyler, 1946).

attempt to avoid the realities of home life while the women see that they do not. Homer, who seems to be the hardest case, given that he has hooks for hands, proves the easiest. After some clumsiness and embarrassment at home, his sweetheart, Wilma (Cathy O'Donnell), accepts him as he is, and in a tender (and chaste) sequence helps him get ready for bed when he is at his most helpless without his prostheses.

Milly has a slightly more difficult task. Al is an alcoholic, and during their first evening together, he insists on going out with Milly and his daughter Peggy (Teresa Wright) to various nightclubs. There is a cute montage triggered by Al's saying that he has been around savages for so long, he wants to get back into civilization. The **montage** of jazz clubs and teenage dancing indicates that "civilization" is not as civilized as Al thinks; postwar life has become more brazen in the intervening years. His wife and daughter in tow, they reunite with Fred and Homer at Butch's place, owned by Homer's uncle, played by a popular singer-songwriter of the decade, Hoagy Carmichael, a calming and centering figure in the film.

Butch sends Homer home. Milly and Peggy take the drunken Al and Fred back to their apartment. Peggy puts Fred to bed; Milly puts Al to bed. The women reclaim their dominion, but the domestic scene is not quite settled.[1] Al has to make peace with himself and his job at the bank. Only after getting drunk at a company dinner is he able to pull himself together and make a Capraesque speech about the necessity of taking chances on loans to small business people. Fred is the most at odds of the three returning veterans. Peggy falls in love with him, but he remains married to his unsavory wife and is without a job. When he returns to the drugstore where he used to work, he finds it has been taken over by a chain. The postwar world of industrial expansion hits close to home, and he is overwhelmed by the huge store and an unsympathetic manager. He is offered a menial job back at the soda fountain. There the postwar world of paranoia and hatred appears full blown.

Throughout the film, there are references to the changed, even alien world that greets the homecoming veterans: the black market for hard-to-get items; taxes; the economy, all receive some recognition in the film. When Al first greets his son, he gives him his wartime souvenirs of a samurai sword and a Japanese flag. The son is unimpressed and asks his father if he noticed the effects of radiation at Hiroshima as a result of the atomic bomb dropped on the city. Al answers that he hadn't. The son goes on to tell his father about what he has learned in school that the world has to learn to live in peace because modern technology has increased the dangers of destruction. Al seems befuddled by this and so it seems is the film. The son represents too much of an intrusion of the modern world—an infiltration of realities the film is not interested in or cannot manage—and he soon disappears entirely. An even more potent figure of disruption appears at the soda fountain where Fred works and where Homer has come by for a visit.

At the lunch counter, a man with an American flag pin in his lapel tells Homer that the war was a mistake, that we were pushed into it by a bunch of radicals in Washington. The Germans, he says, would have beat "the limeys and the reds" if we stayed out of it. His is the voice of the isolationist who existed before the war, who has morphed into the paranoid right winger whose voice would grow louder in the public sphere after it. But just now, in a film devoted to healing and amelioration, such reactionary ideas have no place. Homer threatens the man, rips off his pin and puts it in his own pocket. Fred jumps over the counter and slugs the guy. The result, of course, is that he loses his job.

Fred is now the odd man out. He sends Homer into Wilma's arms, but he is in a loveless marriage and at the same time in love with Peggy. He is also unable to shake his old military identity. Director Wyler solves the dilemma with two set pieces. The first is a figurative rebirth. Fred breaks up with his wife and in a state of depression goes to a field where hundreds of decommissioned planes are stored. He jumps into the nose of one of the aircraft and effectively relives his wartime fears that have led to what we would now call posttraumatic stress. As the camera **dollys** in to simulate the plane in motion and the score on the soundtrack simulates the revving up of engines, Al goes through a reemergence into the postwar world. Fate steps in as a man calls up to Fred from the ground. It breaks the spell. The man is in the construction business and gives Fred a job breaking up

Fred (Dana Winters) knocks down the right winger in *The Best Years of Our Lives.*

the old planes and turning them into prefab housing. It is a last-minute rescue from Fred's fears and an affirmation that the postwar world is full of opportunity—especially the opportunity to break with the wartime state of mind.

The finale of the film is the marriage of Homer and Wilma. During the ceremony, Fred and Peggy are framed in deep focus behind the bride and groom. They exchange glances, indicating that their union is not far off. They finally embrace and the film ends on the appropriately optimistic note. *The Best Years of Our Lives* is a grand affirmation, a film that insists that America will be reborn after World War II into a nation of self-sufficient families where love and generosity reign. The reality was somewhat different, because the angry voice of the man at the lunch counter became a dominant voice in the culture at large. Hollywood itself became the target of what it had so long feared: the wrath of the government.

PART TWO: HOLLYWOOD UNDER SIEGE

On August 6, 1945, the United States dropped an atomic bomb on the Japanese city of Hiroshima, followed on August 9 with another atomic bomb dropped on Nagasaki. The Japanese surrendered, and the Second World War came to an end. Franklin Delano Roosevelt had died in April of 1945. The Germans surrendered in May. Harry S. Truman was the president who elected to use the bomb to end the war in the Pacific. Truman also initiated the Cold War against the Soviet Union and Communism. The Cold War was an overriding ideology that mixed fear and threats with calls for military competition with an enemy state. Anti-Communism became an obsessive-compulsive cultural and political disease that dominated most of the public and many of the private lives in the United States for over 50 years. The United States may have emerged from the Second World War richer and more powerful, but Cold War culture was filled with anxiety and uncertainty, with individuals and groups more ready to strike out at and attempt to destroy enemies more imagined than real.

THE DIVESTITURE

Profound changes were under way in business and politics of Hollywood. A number of events set the American motion picture business back on its heels after World War II. During the full flower of the studio system, the studios not only owned the means of production, they owned the outlet of their production as well, the theaters in which their films were shown. That meant, given the number of people who went to the movies on a regular basis and patronized the studio's theaters, they practically owned their audience. This so-called **vertical integration** constituted a clear monopoly, and beginning in 1938, the courts went after it. In 1946, the lower courts rendered a split decision against the studios. The government persisted, and in 1948, the Supreme Court ruled that the studios had to divest themselves of their distribution outlets, thereby drastically reducing their income. It was the beginning of the end of Hollywood's golden age.[2]

The divestiture ruling was only a part of the process that led to the dissolution of the studios as independent, self-sufficient entities. The studio heads were aging. The contracts that held their stars, producers, and directors under near bondage to them were running out and the employees began moving on, some of them, like Humphrey Bogart and Kirk Douglas, setting up independent production companies of their own. Attendance, after reaching an all-time high in 1946, began falling off. Television, a technological novelty before the war, began to take hold after the war, and by the mid-1950s more than half of American homes had a television set. By the end of the decade anyone who could afford a television had one. Despite the low resolution of the early black and white television signal, people could now enjoy the moving image at home rather than going out to see images on the big screen. Hollywood, for the first time since the advent of radio, had a major rival for viewer attention.

SIZE MATTERS

The movie business was in trouble. It attempted to counter television on a physical and optical basis by making the movie screen bigger. The thinking was if audiences could be convinced that they were seeing bigger, higher definition images than what they saw at home, they would leave their television sets and go out to movie theaters. The **standard (or academy) ratio** of films from the coming of sound up to the early 1950s was 4x3 or 1.33:1. That is, the screen was four units in width to three units in height. Widescreen formats had been tried out as early as the 1920s and were quickly abandoned. But in the early 1950s, anxieties over television's impact on attendance led to the desperate measures of increasing screen size. The most extreme was "Cinerama." Here, three synchronized cameras photographed a huge horizontal panorama, which was then projected by three projectors on a curved screen. The process was ungainly, expensive, and you could always see the lines that separated the three parts of the image.

Cinerama was too ungainly and too wide to be useful for narrative films. Its brief life was devoted mostly to travelogues, and it rapidly disappeared to be replaced by various anamorphic wide-screen processes. **Anamorphic** processes squeeze the image onto a 35 mm or 65 mm strip of film and when unsqueezed by a special lens on the projector create an image of 2.35:1—or wider when a larger gauge film is used. Twentieth-Century Fox introduced their anamorphic process, **CinemaScope**, in 1953, and all their subsequent films were shot in this proprietary process (which had in fact been invented back in 1926) well into the 1960s. **Panavision**, the company that manufactured and leased cameras to filmmakers, developed their own version of the anamorphic process that produced less distortion of the image and was not proprietary.

Beginning in the early 1950s, even films that were not shot in an anamorphic process created a widescreen effect simply by masking off the top and bottom of the image in the camera or the projector. The result of all of this was a permanent change in the moving image, which caused filmmakers to think about the width of the composition and reorient viewers to a wider cinematic space. Paradoxically, by the 1960s and the advent of mall multiplexes, theater screens began getting smaller, despite the fact that the image was wider. Today, yet another change is occurring as increasingly films are seen via DVD or Blu-ray on large screen television monitors, or on small-screen computer monitors, or even smaller screen smartphones. On one end, the film image has maintained its resolution, even though reduced in size. On the other, the smartphone image or images seen on YouTube only suggest the visual information the image contains.

Stereoscopy, or 3D, which was used to create the illusion of depth in photographic images as far back

In *Citizen Kane* (1941), Orson Welles uses all of the standard ratio frame, filling not only edge to edge, but in depth as well.

In this CinemaScope film, *Bad Day at Black Rock* (1955), director John Sturges takes full advantage of the wide screen. But compare this composition with the still from D. W. Griffith's *The Unchanging Sea* (1910) in Chapter 4.

as the 19th century, had a brief run in films of the 1950s, with its fuzzy image and headache-inducing glasses, consisting of one red and one blue lens to fuse the color-coded dual images made by two cameras and projectors that created the illusion of depth. These were supplanted by a polarizing process that filters the two images according to how the light is allowed to come through each lens, and was further refined so that the illusion could be created using a single camera and, today, by digital filming and projection. 3D was always something of a novelty, with objects and faces seeming to poke out of the screen. There was a 3D jungle adventure film, *Bwana Devil* (Arch Oboler, United Artists, 1952), a musical based on Shakespeare's *Taming of the Shrew, Kiss Me Kate* (George Sidney, MGM, 1953), and a horror film, *The House of Wax* (André de Toth, Warner Bros., 1953). Even Alfred Hitchcock experimented in 3D with *Dial M for Murder* (Warner Bros., 1954), though by the time it was ready for release, the fad had ended. The early 21st century has seen a brief upsurge in 3D films, and it remains to be seen how long the new fad will last—though its aesthetic possibilities, a novel and expressive use of three-dimensional space, has been realized in at least one film: Martin Scorsese's *Hugo* (Paramount, GK Films, Infinitum Nihil, 2011). We will have the opportunity to discuss more about screen size and other technological developments in film in Chapter 21.

ARE YOU NOW OR HAVE YOU EVER BEEN A MEMBER OF THE COMMUNIST PARTY?

HUAC

Screen size and 3D were something of a refuge for Hollywood, attempts to lure audiences back into theaters to make up for the income lost by divestiture and television, as well as a diversion from the rot that was eating away at the film community. The House Committee on Un-American Activities (HUAC) was established in 1938, under the leadership of Martin Dies and later John E. Rankin, both anti-Semites and the latter a supporter of the Ku Klux Klan. The "un-Americans" of choice for the Committee were Communists, or Communist sympathizers, or left-leaning liberals, or perhaps anyone that the right wing disapproved of, especially such as might be involved with the arts. They investigated the Federal Theatre Project and the Federal Writer's Project, set up by the Roosevelt administration as part of the Works Progress Administration (the WPA), intended to support and celebrate the arts in the United States. They came to Hollywood in 1939 to find Communists in the movies, but no one was interested at the time. After the war, a lot of people were interested. The real threat of fascism faded and political hay could be made by scaring people about a new enemy, the "Communist threat" and "Communist infiltration."

That the country itself was under a cloud of fear in the late 1940s was without doubt. Russia tested its first atomic bomb in 1949. A few months earlier, Mao Zedong consolidated Communist control of China. In 1948, at home, Alger Hiss, who had worked for Roosevelt, the United Nations, and the Carnegie Endowment for International Peace, was, on the testimony of an ex-Communist, charged with spying. After a second trial, when incriminating microfilm was found hidden in a pumpkin on a farm, he was sentenced to 5 years in jail. The trial elevated the career of Richard Nixon, who would go on to be the 37th president of the United States. In 1950, Ethel and Julius Rosenberg were arrested and charged with spying for the Russians in 1950. They were executed in 1953.

Early in 1950, a Senator from Wisconsin named Joseph McCarthy, searching for an issue to burnish an undistinguished career, stood up before a crowd in Wheeling, West Virginia, and said he had a list of 205 members of the Communist Party at work in the Department of State. It was a sensation, despite the fact that the number of names kept changing every time he gave the speech and no one in the State Department was ever discovered to be a Communist. McCarthy and his Senate committee (not to be confused with HUAC) went on a Communist-hunting spree, investigating innocent people and institutions and ruining careers. Almost everyone was afraid of him. He finally met his comeuppance when he took on the army in 1953. In 1954, Edward R. Murrow, a famous and influential radio and television newsman, did a television program denouncing McCarthy. And, during the army-McCarthy hearings, an unprepossessing attorney for the army, Joseph Welch, stood up to an attack by McCarthy by saying the words many people were afraid to utter: "Have you no sense of decency sir, at long last? Have you left no sense of decency?" McCarthy was censured by the Senate in 1954 and died of alcohol-induced cirrhosis of the liver in 1957.

THE HOLLYWOOD TEN

In Hollywood, the second round of witch hunts were fomented by the Motion Picture Alliance for the Preservation of American Ideals, a right-wing group formed by director Sam Wood, and whose members included Walt Disney, John Wayne, Ronald Reagan, and other actors, screenwriters, and directors. They, along with HUAC, now headed by J. Parnell Thomas, and backed by the FBI, pressured the studio heads to weed out Communists from their ranks and investigate their influence on the movies they made. The studio heads had been frightened by union activity in the 1940s and frightened even more by the loss of revenue following divestiture. They were nervous about losing their standing as upholders of American values, since the anti-Communists convinced them that the public would boycott their films if they thought they were infiltrated by "Communists." They caved in to the committee, which held hearings in Hollywood beginning in 1947. Many Hollywood personnel—actors and actresses, writer, producers, directors—were called to testify. Ten of them were cited for contempt. They shouted their defiance to the committee and refused to answer its questions, and they were sent to jail: director Edward Dmytryk, director and screenwriter Herbert Biberman, screenwriters Alvah Bessie, Ring Lardner, Jr., John Howard Lawson, Dalton Trumbo, Samuel Ornitz, Albert Maltz, Lester Cole, and producer Adrian Scott.

In jail, Lester Cole and Ring Lardner, Jr. happened upon none other than J. Parnell Thomas, the former head of HUAC, who had been convicted of misappropriation of funds. Thomas was tending the prison chicken coop when Cole came by and offered a political comment. Thomas presumably said, "I see that you are still spouting radical nonsense." Cole responded, "And I see that you are still shoveling chicken shit."[3] But there was not much humor in what was going on in the HUAC hearings and their repercussions. Following the indictment of the Ten in 1947, a group of liberal and left-wing Hollywood luminaries, including Humphrey Bogart, formed The Committee for the First Amendment, to defend the Ten and condemn the HUAC hearings. They marched on Washington. When they returned, the studios took them to task. Bogart was forced to write a magazine article, "I'm No Communist."

THE BLACKLIST

The studio heads were preparing something more potent than an article. They gathered in the Waldorf-Astoria Hotel to create a blacklist, and in November, 1947, issued this statement:

> Members of the Association of Motion Picture Producers deplore the action of the 10 Hollywood men who have been cited for contempt by the House of Representatives. We do not desire to prejudge their legal rights, but their actions have been a disservice to their employers and have impaired their usefulness to the industry.
>
> We will forthwith discharge or suspend without compensation those in our employ, and we will not re-employ any of the 10 until such time as he is acquitted or has purged himself of contempt and declares under oath that he is not a Communist.
>
> On the broader issue of alleged subversive and disloyal elements in Hollywood, our members are likewise prepared to take positive action.
>
> We will not knowingly employ a Communist or a member of any party or group which advocates the overthrow of the government of the United States by force or by any illegal or unconstitutional methods. . . .

Despite the fact that the Waldorf Statement claimed that there was "a danger of hurting innocent people,"[4] the result was that dozens of Hollywood professionals—actors and screenwriters in particular, including television personnel—lost their jobs. Many fled the country. Some screenwriters went to England or to Mexico and continued to write scripts under assumed names at a fraction of the salary they had previously earned. Some Hollywood figures bent to the will of the committee and named names—that is, they gave the names of people and friends they knew who had briefly been members of the Communist Party of the United States or held left-wing views. It was, in effect, a humiliation ritual. HUAC had all the names. The individuals who informed did so to save their careers. Among the most infamous of the informers was director Elia Kazan, who followed his performance on naming names in front of the committee with a full-length newspaper advertisement defending his actions and then made a film, scripted by Budd Schulberg, another informer, that defended informing. The film was *On the Waterfront* (Columbia, 1954), in which the character played by Marlon Brando, Terry Malloy, informs on the corrupt leadership of his union.

All of this did not placate the studios or the committee. Mechanisms were set in place to insure compliance. There was a Hollywood psychiatrist and a lawyer who specialized in preparing people to testify and name names to the committee. The head of a major union worked with the committee to get names named. There was a film script, *I Married a Communist*, which was sent around to various directors. If they turned it down, they were blacklisted. It was eventually made in 1949 by Robert Stevenson for RKO—then owned by the staunchly anti-Communist Howard Hughes—renamed *The Woman on Pier 13*.

From one perspective, the collusion of the studios and the committee roughly parallel the circumstances that brought about the Production Code in the early 1930s. Fear! The code was created when the studio heads feared that the public and, even worse, the government would force a boycott of their product or, in the case of the government, meddle with it and take away their control. But the fear-induced events of the late 1940s were of a greater order of magnitude than the outcry against immoral movies in the early 1930s. The Production Code had a long-lasting effect on the content of movies. HUAC and its aftermath had a briefer but more corrosive effect. And, while the code may have squelched or redirected some creativity in the making of films, the blacklist served to ruin careers, make filmmakers fearful, and allow the studio heads to pander to the very worst that the political culture of the time had to offer.[5]

Between HUAC and McCarthy, the country was in a fit of anti-Communist hysteria, but, somewhat surprisingly, overtly anti-Communist films had a mixed performance at the box office. The infamous *Woman on Pier 13* was a flop. *My Son John* (Leo McCarey, Paramount, 1952), a bizarre domestic melodrama in which a mother is driven to a nervous breakdown because her son is a Communist, was pummeled by reviewers, though—as a sign of Hollywood's state of mind—received an Academy Award nomination for best screenplay. At the same time, there were some films that overtly or covertly attacked McCarthyism and the blacklist. There were, as well, and somewhat ironically, a number of "socially conscious" films made just as the blacklist got started, and many of the makers of those films came under attack at the very moment those films were released.

THE END OF THE BLACKLIST

Dalton Trumbo, one of the Hollywood Ten, wrote scripts under various pseudonyms and borrowed names. The writer Ian McLellan Hunter loaned Trumbo his name for the film *Roman Holiday* (William Wyler, Paramount, 1953). Hunter/Trumbo won an Academy Award for best screenplay. Writing under the pseudonym Robert Rich, he won another Oscar for his screenplay for *The Brave One* (Irving Rapper, King Brothers Productions, RKO, 1956). The ironies are bitter, and the farce of the blacklist would be amusing if so many people hadn't suffered because of it. Trumbo won awards, but he was getting paid a fraction of what he would have been worth under his real name.

The Academy of Motion Picture Arts and Sciences repealed its blacklist provision in 1959. But it took the work of two brave men to break the blacklist for good. Director Otto Preminger hired Trumbo to write, under his own name, the script for *Exodus* (Carlyle-Alpina, United Artists, 1960), a film about the founding of the state of Israel. In the same year, after Preminger's announcement, the actor/producer Kirk Douglas announced that Trumbo would, again under his own name, write the script for *Spartacus* (Stanley Kubrick, Universal, 1960). Because *Spartacus* appeared a few months prior to *Exodus*, Douglas claimed credit for breaking the blacklist.

One can suppose that the end of the blacklist was a victory for all who suffered under it. Dalton Trumbo said, "In the final tally, we are all victims because almost without exception each of us felt compelled to say things he didn't want to say." Albert Maltz, another one of the 10, disagreed. "To say we're equally without sin—what does that mean? What did we fight for? What did people suffer for?"[6] I tend to agree with Maltz. People did fight against victimhood; they largely lost, but at least stood for the principle that one was free to choose political affiliation. A counter argument could be made that the very idea of "principle" in Hollywood is a joke. The lasting truth about the blacklisted screenwriters, directors, producers, and actors is that they never were able to put the "subversive" messages in their films that HUAC tried to accuse them of doing. The studio bosses would never have permitted it. The Production Code would not have allowed it. They themselves wouldn't have done it because they knew it would never pass through unchanged. There was a Communist Party active in Hollywood and there were some screen people who were members of it in the 1930s. Why the fuss? Much of the political life of the Communist Party in

Hollywood had to do with arguing about purity of ideology that, pure or not, none of its members could practice in their work. The truth lay in the fact that embedded in the political culture of postwar America was a fear that created anxiety and produced hardship over nothing. It happened, in part, because the culture was left with an enemy vacuum after the defeat of fascism. Into that vacuum stepped a number of intellectually and morally corrupt politicians who filled the public with fears of Communism. The results were hysteria, humiliation, and censorship of an economic kind.

SOCIALLY CONSCIOUS CINEMA

Grasping at straws, HUAC went after what it considered to be "Un-American," pro-Russian films, conveniently forgetting that the Soviet Union was our ally during the war. They and their informers complained about Samuel Goldwyn's *The North Star* (Lewis Milestone, Samuel Goldwyn Studios, 1943), which had the presumption to show Ukrainian peasants happy with their lot before being attacked by the Nazis; *Song of Russia* (Gregory Ratoff, MGM, 1944), which the novelist and anti-Communist Ayn Rand said "was pro-soviet propaganda because it showed so many smiling Russian children"; and Warner Bros.'s *Mission to Moscow* (Michael Curtiz, 1943), a film supported by Franklin Roosevelt that approved of Stalin's show trials.[7] But the curious fact is that, even as HUAC was doing its dirty work, "socially conscious" films—that is, films that took on serious cultural and political issues—were being made.

ANTI-SEMITISM: *CROSSFIRE* AND *GENTLEMAN'S AGREEMENT*

Two films took on the issue of anti-Semitism—a subject considered taboo by the largely Jewish executives of the film companies. They did not want to draw attention to their ethnicity. But after the war, after the attempted extermination of the Jews in Europe, it was difficult to ignore the subject. *Crossfire* (Edward Dmytryk, RKO, 1947) involved the anti-Semitic murder of a returning serviceman and the pursuit of his killer. It is somewhat noirish in style, not surprising given that its director and John Paxton, its screenwriter, had made *Murder My Sweet* (RKO, 1944) a few years earlier. However, with an irony that only that particular moment in American history could

In film noir style, an anti-Semitic murder is seen in shadow. *Crossfire* (1947) was produced by Adrian Scott and directed by Edward Dmytryk, both of whom became members of the Hollywood Ten shortly after the film was released. After his imprisonment, Dmytryk informed on his colleagues, including Scott.

provide, both its director, Dmytryk, and its producer, Adrian Scott, became part of the Hollywood Ten and were blacklisted while the film was still in distribution. After his release from jail, Dmytryk turned informer. *Gentleman's Agreement* (Elia Kazan, Fox, 1947) was a glossier production, with actor Gregory Peck playing a non-Jewish journalist who pretends to be Jewish in order to write about anti-Semitism. Whenever he is overwhelmed by the prejudice he meets, he is reminded that he is not really Jewish. The film, therefore, pulls its punches whenever the manifestations of its subject become too intense.

POSTWAR FILM AND RACE: *PINKY* AND *NO WAY OUT*

Elia Kazan also directed *Pinky* (Fox, 1949), a film about a light-skinned African American woman who "passes" as white. Played by a white actress, Jeanne Crain, the film confronts issues of racism, but, like *Gentleman's Agreement*, it skirts around the real issues, creating a safety valve of sorts in its use of a white actress in the leading role. However, the issue of race became surprisingly prominent in the 1950s, with many films taking a liberal, sometimes even radical view of race relations, while the government and the culture as a whole were confronting a civil rights revolution. President Truman had ordered the armed forced integrated in 1948, though it would be many years before the order became fact. In 1954, the Supreme Court ruled in *Brown v. the Board of Education* that "separate but equal" segregation was illegal. In 1955, the murder of Emmett Till, a young African American boy, and the refusal of Rosa Parks to sit in the back of the bus, gave energy to the burgeoning movement. The work of Martin Luther King and a host of brave individuals enduring beatings and jail time led finally to the passage of the Civil Rights Act in 1964. This energy seemed to infuse some 1950s films.

A few African American actors emerged in 1950s film, led by Sidney Poitier, whose handsome and calm demeanor was relatively unthreatening. His first major role was as a young doctor in *No Way Out* (Joseph L. Mankiewicz, Fox, 1950), a film that comes close to being overtly radical in its depiction of racial hatred. A crazed racist thief, played by Richard Widmark, accuses Poitier's Dr. Biddle of killing his brother. In the complications that follow, there occurs a full-scale racial uprising, in which the African American participants are shown to be in the right to protect themselves against an angry white mob. The film was

Racial harassment. "Pinky" (Jeanne Crane) plays a light-skinned African American, who returns to her home town in the South and faces the potential of violence from local bigots. (*Pinky*, Elia Kazan, 1949).

African American uprising against white bigotry. *No Way Out* (Joseph L. Mankiewicz, 1950).

strong enough for its time to have some of its sequences trimmed after a threatened ban in Chicago. It remains a powerful piece of filmmaking, indicating that Darryl F. Zanuck, head of Twentieth Century Fox, was, for a time at least, interested in putting his films into the mix of cultural turmoil.

ANTI-MCCARTHY, ANTI-HUAC FILMS: *STORM CENTER* AND *SALT OF THE EARTH*

In 1956, a film called *Storm Center* (Daniel Taradash, Phoenix Productions, Columbia) was made as a kind of antidote to the hysterical anti-communism of *My Son John*. Bette Davis plays a librarian who refuses to remove a book called *The Communist Dream* from the shelves. She is redbaited by a McCarthy-like member of the city council and hounded by the community out of her job. A young boy, who is entranced by reading, is driven mad by what he sees as her betrayal of him and by the anti-intellectual abuse of his father. He burns the library down, and the film looks with horror while books of all kind go up in flames, reminding the audience of the book burnings undertaken by the Nazis. The film ends with the Bette Davis character returned to her position, acknowledging that her biggest mistake was not fighting back from the beginning.

Storm Center was not the only anti-McCarthy film of the period. There were Westerns, such as Fred Zinneman's *High Noon* (Stanley Kramer Productions, United Artists, 1952) and Nicholas Ray's *Johnny Guitar* (Republic, 1954) that allegorized the crowd mentality and cowardice that marked the period. But perhaps the most remarkable film that countered the anti-Communist hysteria of the 1950s was an independent production made by various blacklisted personnel and members of the Hollywood Ten: *Salt of the Earth* (Herbert Biberman, International Mine, Mill & Smelter Workers, Independent Production Company, 1954). Biberman was one of the Ten, and the film's writer Michael Wilson, producer Paul Jarrico, and actor Will Geer were blacklisted. The film was made on location in New Mexico and its narrative focus is a strike by copper mine workers. But more than that, the film enunciates its left-liberal views in stark and moving images, reminiscent of the government-sponsored documentaries of the 1930s. *Salt of the Earth* addresses class inequality, the difficulties faced by immigrant workers, and the strength of women in the face of economic and social adversity. Its feminist position is striking for the time and looks forward to the organized feminist movement of the late 1960s.

The face of an angry wife of a mine worker in the one film took a radical stand during the 1950s. *Salt of the Earth* (Herbert J. Biberman, 1954).

The film met with the full fury of anti-Communist hysteria while it was being made. Hollywood unions railed against it. Hollywood laboratories refused to process the footage. Its Mexican star, Rosaura Revueltas, was arrested and returned to Mexico before production was completed. Local townspeople beat up members of the cast and crew and burned down the local union hall. But the film got completed and received a very limited release. It remains, in all its rough-hewn frankness, a striking contrast not only to the general slickness of Hollywood filmmaking, but to the political cowardice that shivered through Hollywood during the period of the blacklist.[8]

At the same time, we have to recognize that political oppression sometimes does, particularly in a society like ours, permit the imagination to work freely. Hollywood was cruel to its most politically outspoken or most craven figures. But there were filmmakers who quietly managed to create some of the most important films not only of the decade of the 1950s, but of the entire history of American film. John Ford and Alfred Hitchcock made their best films during the decade, and Orson Welles returned from exile to make a film that observed his native country from a mad and vertiginous perspective.

SELECTED FILMOGRAPHY

Mission to Moscow, dir. Michael Curtiz, Warner Bros., 1943.

The North Star, dir. Lewis Milestone, Samuel Goldwyn Studios, 1943.

Song of Russia, dir. Gregory Ratoff, MGM, 1944.

The Best Years of Our Lives, dir. William Wyler, Samuel Goldwyn Co., 1946.

Crossfire, dir. Edward Dmytryk, RKO, 1947.

Gentleman's Agreement, dir. Elia Kazan, Fox, 1947.

The House of Wax, dir. André de Toth, Warner Bros., 1953.

Dial M for Murder, dir. Alfred Hitchcock, Warner Bros., 1954.

The Woman on Pier 13, dir. Robert Stevenson, RKO, 1949.

Pinky, dir. Elia Kazan, Fox, 1949.

No Way Out, dir. Joseph L. Mankiewicz, Fox, 1950.

My Son John, dir. Leo McCarey, Paramount, 1952.

High Noon, dir. Fred Zinneman, Stanley Kramer Productions, United Artists, 1952.

Roman Holiday, dir. William Wyler, Paramount, 1953.

Johnny Guitar, dir. Nicholas Ray, Republic, 1954.

Salt of the Earth, dir. Herbert Biberman, International Mine, Mill & Smelter Workers, Independent Production Company, 1954.

Storm Center, dir. Daniel Taradash, Phoenix Productions, Columbia, 1956.

The Brave One, dir. Irving Rapper, RKO, 1956.

Exodus, dir. Otto Preminger, Carlyle-Alpina, United Artists, 1960.

Spartacus, dir. Stanley Kubrick, Universal, 1960.

SUGGESTIONS FOR FURTHER READING

Larry Ceplair & Steven Englund, *The Inquisition in Hollywood: Politics in the Film Community, 1930–1960* (Berkeley, CA: University of California Press, 1983).

J. Hoberman, An Army of Phantoms: American Movies and the Making of the Cold War (New York, NY: New Press, 2011).

Frank Krutnik, Steve Neale, Brian Neve, & Peter Stanfield, eds., *"Un-American" Hollywood: Politics and Film in the Blacklist Era* (New Brunswick, NJ: Rutgers University Press,2007).

Jon Lewis, "'We Do Not Ask You to Condone This': How the Blacklist Saved Hollywood," *Cinema Journal*, vol. 39, no. 2 (Winter, 2000), 3–30.

Victor S. Navasky, *Naming Names*, 3rd ed. (New York, NY: Hill and Wang, 2003).

Thomas Schatz, *Boom and Bust: American Cinema in the 1940s, History of the American Cinema*, vol. 6 (Berkeley, CA: University of California Press, 1997).

NOTES

1. Robert Warshow talks about how the women are always putting their men to bed in *The Best Years of Our Lives* in his essay "Anatomy of a Falsehood," *The Immediate Experience* (Cambridge, MA: Harvard University Press, 2001), 125–132.
2. See Gorham Kindem, "The Postwar Motion Picture Industry," in Thomas Schatz, *Boom and Bust: American Cinema in the 1940s, History of the American Cinema*, vol. 6 (Berkeley, CA University of California Press, 1997), 323–328.
3. Quoted in Larry Ceplair and Steven Englund, *The Inquisition in Hollywood: Politics in the Film Community, 1930–1960* (Berkeley, CA: University of California Press, 1983), 356. See also Neal Gabler, *An Empire of Their Own: How the Jews Invented Hollywood* (New York, NY: Doubleday, 1988), 351–386.
4. The full Waldorf Statement can be found at http://cobbles.com/simpp_archive/huac_nelson1947.htm
5. For a good summary of the studios and the blacklist, see Jon Lewis, "'We Do Not Ask You to Condone This': How the Blacklist Saved Hollywood," *Cinema Journal*, vol. 39, no. 2 (Winter, 2000), 3-30
6. Quoted in Victor S. Navasky, *Naming Names*, 3rd ed. (New York, NY: Hill and Wang, 2003), 391.
7. The quotation from Ayn Rand is in Navasky, 224.
8. A good summary of the production history of *Salt of the Earth* can be found in the entry in the American Film Institute Catalogue, http://www.afi.com.

CHAPTER 16

FORD, WELLES, AND HITCHCOCK IN THE 1950s (1948–1960)

The interesting fact about the period of the anti-Communist witch hunts, the career-destroying blacklists, and the decay of the studio system is that none of this dampened the creativity of Hollywood film. To be sure, there were any number of banal films produced during the 1950s, but there were also intelligent films, socially conscious films, films that began pecking away at the Production Code. There was the reblossoming of the Western and science fiction genres, and some of the best films of the three directors that we highlighted in Chapter 13. We will look here at some of their work during the decade.

AFTER READING THIS CHAPTER, YOU SHOULD UNDERSTAND:

- John Ford's treatment of Native Americans.
- Ford's use of the western landscape.
- How some Westerns allegorized McCarthyism.
- Orson Welles's critique of America in *Touch of Evil*.
- How mise-en-scène functions in *Touch of Evil*.
- How Welles and Hitchcock dealt with the Hollywood studio system, and it with them.
- How Hitchcock manipulates his audience.
- Why Hitchcock's *The Wrong Man* is an allegory of the blacklist.
- The relation of *Psycho* to the Production Code.
- How films like *Vertigo* and *Psycho* spoke to Cold War issues, even though they do not directly address politics.

YOU SHOULD BE ABLE TO:

- Examine how the Cold War was a cultural as well as a political issue and infiltrated the discourse of the culture as a whole.
- Discuss the difference between the pre- and postwar films of Ford, Welles, and Hitchcock.
- Account for the lasting influence of Ford's *The Searchers*.

- Discuss why Westerns were so popular in the 1950s.
- Discuss how John Ford's Westerns are about postwar America.
- Discuss how Welles understands 1950s American culture.
- See the connection between *Touch of Evil* and *Psycho*.
- Consider how Bernard Hermann's scores work with Hitchcock's images.
- Explain how the images of *Psycho* are tied together.
- Analyze how *Psycho* and *Vertigo* work on multiple levels of perception.

JOHN FORD AND THE WESTERN

FORT APACHE

Among John Ford's postwar productions was a trilogy of films, starring John Wayne, about the cavalry. They are *Fort Apache* (Argosy, RKO, 1948), *She Wore a Yellow Ribbon* (Argosy, RKO, 1949), and *Rio Grande* (Republic Pictures, Argosy, 1950). *Fort Apache* is the most interesting of the group, and it poses what would become a Fordian problem in the 1950s: what do you do with the misfits of the West, the characters that don't fit comfortably into the generic mold? Do you condemn them, show the results of their errors, or somehow embrace them and find a way to embed them into the larger mythology built by films about the West and the even larger myths in the culture as a whole?

Fort Apache is a godforsaken outpost surrounded by hostile Indians (for Ford, Native Americans were always "Indians," and no matter how much sympathy he was able to muster for them, they remained "savages"). Captain Kirby York (Wayne) keeps peace with the Indians through an understanding of their culture, and the fort itself is a peaceful community in the desert wilderness surrounded by Apaches, domesticated by the soldiers' wives.

Into this environment comes an embittered Lieutenant Colonel Owen Thursday (Henry Fonda—playing against the type he had cultivated of a good-natured, easygoing man). A stickler for rules, he is uncomfortable with the community of the fort and despises his new assignment. On his arrival, he breaks into a community dance, disrupting what for Ford is always a sign of harmony. There are two dance sequences in the film. The second is interrupted by York, who tells Thursday that Cochise has come to talk peace. But Thursday is a figure of disharmony and is unhappy with Captain York's relationship with the Indians. He once again interrupts the dance, this time to lead the men to slaughter by breaking the bond that York has formed with Cochise.

Ford's mythical western space, Monument Valley, provides refuge for the Indians. It is their native soil and they are comfortable within its landscape while the cavalry troops are exposed, both physically and culturally through Thursday's refusal to deal with the Indians on their terms. In the inevitable battle, Thursday and his men are wiped out, with the exception of York and a small contingent that Thursday had banished from the fight. The historic parallel is, of course, Custer's Battle of Little Big Horn, and Ford is clear in condemning the stupidity of bad leaders. But he refuses to go all the way with this condemnation. The film has a coda in which Ford presents a somewhat different story. York is gathered with a group of newsmen, who talk of Thursday's gallantry and his heroic charge against the Indians. "Correct in every detail," York lies. For Ford, the lie is important in order to keep the reputation of the military strong. "When the legend becomes fact, print the legend" a newspaperman says at the end of Ford's *The Man Who Shot Liberty Valence* (Paramount, John Ford Productions, 1962). Myths have a stronger hold on the culture than any historical reality might. Ford banked his reputation as a maker of Westerns on that assumption.

THE SEARCHERS

But there are moments when truths intervene. In 1956, Ford made a Western that became one of the most admired and influential films since *Citizen Kane*. *The Searchers* (Warner Bros., C.V. Whitney Pictures) examines some truths about heroism hiding behind movie legends. John Wayne plays Ethan Edwards, a racist outlaw and former Confederate soldier, who launches a 5-year quest to kill his niece Debbie (Natalie Wood), who has been taken by the Comanche Indians who destroyed her family. This slim summary does not do justice to the complexity of the film. Obsession is the key to its narrative movement. Ethan is driven by racial hatred, blinded by his revulsion at the thought that Debbie has become a wife to his enemy, Chief Scar (played by a white actor, Henry Brandon). His enemy and his double. Scar also bears hatred against the white men who have slaughtered his people. Ethan's pursuit, accompanied by his nephew, Marty (Jeffrey Hunter), who is part Cherokee, and therefore despised by Ethan, takes him through the wilderness of Monument Valley and takes the viewer to a place where heroism and morality are uprooted and put into question.

When John Ford introduces John Wayne in *Stagecoach,* it is by means of a rapid tracking shot to his heroic, smiling, rifle-wielding figure. The track is so rapid and energetic that the camera goes momentarily out of focus as it approaches Wayne's Ringo Kid (see an image of this in Chapter 11). Late in *The Searchers,* Ethan and Marty come upon a cavalry outpost. The soldiers have taken a group of white women from the Indians and are holding them in a room so that the two searchers might discover whether any one of them is Debbie. The women, torn twice from their homes—once by the Indians, then by the soldiers—are hysterical. Debbie is not among them. One of the soldiers comments, "It's hard to believe they're white." Ethan turns to look at them once more, "They ain't white. They're Comanche." The camera tracks into his face, partly shadowed by his hat. He has a look of hatred, confusion, and a certain amount of fear.

This is very far from the vigorous, exciting figure that was introduced in *Stagecoach* and it indicates the complexity of character that has made *The Searchers* such a potent film. Perhaps because of his complexity, Ethan does not survive his quest, at least in the way he intended when he set out. He is given his moment of redemption and loss. The Indians are wiped out by the cavalry and Debbie is freed not by Ethan, but Marty, and Scar is killed not by Ethan, but also by Marty. When Ethan confronts Debbie, he does not kill her—as he had tried to do once before—but instead swoops her up into his arms, as he had at the beginning when she was just a small child. He brings her home, but he cannot enter the sanctuary of the domestic place. At the beginning of *The Searchers,* a door opens onto the desert, and we look with Martha, Ethan's sister-in-law, and the rest of the family, as Ethan approaches. At the end of the film, Debbie delivered safely back to her home, Ethan stands at the door, which is closed against him.

"They ain't white. They're Comanche." Ethan Edwards (John Wayne) looks with disgust and apprehension at the white women taken from their Indian captives in John Ford's *The Searchers* (1956). Compare this with the image of Wayne as the Ringo Kid in Ford's *Stagecoach* in Chapter 13.

The domestic space of western expansion, the taming of the western wilderness that Ethan works so obsessively to create, has no room for him. He is too much the outlaw, too crazed by his own sense of racial righteousness. The door closes him out of the comforts that he, in fact, could probably not enjoy. And this is what makes *The Searchers* so fascinating. The western hero has become, in Ford's hands, a rootless figure in perpetual search for something that, even when found, will not satisfy him. It puts into question the assumptions of the simple western myths of good guys and bad guys, of savage Indians and strong-willed settlers. In their place is the huge landscape of the West, peopled by threatened homesteaders and an obsessed wanderer.

The Searchers is a film of such power that it has influenced a diverse variety of filmmakers. In the first *Star Wars* (*Episode IV—A New Hope*, Fox, 1977), George Lucas depicts a scene in which Luke Skywalker (Mark Hamill) returns to see his aunt's and uncle's burning home. It is an almost shot-by-shot duplicate of the scene in *The Searchers* where Marty comes home to his relative's house after the Indians have torched it. Martin Scorsese bases the narrative of *Taxi Driver* (Columbia, Bill/Phillips, Italo/Judeo Productions, 1977) on *The Searchers*, which is itself, in turn, based on the old American captivity narrative, stories told about women abducted by Indians. We discussed the captivity narrative in relation to D. W. Griffith's *Birth of a Nation*. It remains a potent fiction that still forms the basis of film narratives today.

OTHER WESTERNS

HIGH NOON

The 1950s was the decade of the Western. Many filmmakers tried their hand at the genre, and the genre was able to incorporate many of the cultural currents of the time. There were, as we pointed out in the previous chapter, some Westerns that addressed the fear and the crowd mentality of the anti-Communist witch hunts. The most famous of these is *High Noon* (Fred Zinnemann, Stanley Kramer Productions, United Artists, 1952). The film's script was by Carl Foreman, who was also its associate producer. Foreman had been called before HUAC, refused to name names, and was blacklisted. He somehow managed to keep his name on *High Noon*. However, countering Foreman was the film's star, Gary Cooper, a member of the pro-HUAC Motion Picture Alliance for the Preservation of American Ideals.

The film concerns a sheriff waiting for the return of an outlaw he had sent to prison, who is returning for vengeance along with three of his gang. The townspeople, fearful, angry, and resentful, are unwilling to help Cooper's Sheriff Kane. The narrative is told in real time, the events taking up roughly 90 minutes, as the clock ticks to the arrival of Kane's nemesis. The townspeople flee from assisting Kane until his pacifist Quaker bride (Grace Kelly) takes up a gun to save him from the bad guys. The film aims for high moral purpose: a lone righteous figure facing the cowardice of the mob; the passive and quiescent woman who must overcome her reticence and come to his aid. This is just barely an allegory of the political moment and, as so often in American film, the outcome is based not on the act of the community (which is put in bad light), but on the actions of a single individual. The craven townspeople may represent those who remained silent during the McCarthy and HUAC witch hunts, but there were only a few individual heroes or heroines who stepped forward to stop the process. Certainly the film's star, Gary Cooper, was no heroic figure. He stood up, but for the wrong side.

JOHNNY GUITAR AND *SILVER LODE*

Nicholas Ray was an important new director in the 1950s, and we will discuss his work in more detail later on. Within the context of the 1950s Western, we need to note one of the most unusual entries into the genre, *Johnny Guitar* (Republic, 1954). The film centers on a strong woman, the owner of a gambling casino, Vienna, played by Joan Crawford. Her nemesis is a jealous rabble rouser, Emma Small (Mercedes McCambridge), who forces a young man to accuse Vienna of complicity in a robbery. Emma's hectoring of the mob brings to mind the whining accusatorial voice of Joe McCarthy, who makes another not-so-subtle appearance in an obscure Western called *Silver Lode*, directed by a Hollywood veteran, Alan Dwan (Pinecrest Productions, RKO, 1954). Here, a character named McCarty (Dan Duryea) pretends to be a

A woman as Western heroine. Joan Crawford as Vienna in Nicholas Ray's *Johnny Guitar* (1954).

US Marshall, bribing and terrorizing a town, accusing one its inhabitants of shooting his brother.

In both cases, the contemporary political scene of accusation, of faked or shaky evidence, of downright bullying by HUAC and Joseph McCarthy, are filtered relatively safely through the conventions (not so conventional in the case of *Johnny Guitar*) of the Western genre. Ray's film plays out largely indoors and, filmed in a two-color process that renders its tonalities in odd greens and reds. It is almost an abstract idea of a Western film, a commentary on the genre, a glancing critique of contemporary politics.

THE WESTERNS OF ANTHONY MANN: *THE MAN FROM LARAMIE*

We looked at the noir films of Anthony Mann in Chapter 14. In the 1950s, after he made *The Furies* (Paramount, 1950), a film that, like *Johnny Guitar*, features a strong female lead, and has an unusually dark **mise-en-scène** for a Western, Mann gave up the highly stylized black and white lighting and camera work of his noir films to concentrate on the distress of his heroes and their attempts to find peace within the western landscape. He directed a series of films, many of them with James Stewart, like *The Man from Laramie* (William Goetz Productions, Columbia, 1955), that rings changes on the Oedipus story, of fathers and sons, of questions of masculinity and its role not only in the Western landscape but, by extension, in the landscape of the 1950s. The men in Mann's Westerns often try to prove their worth or try—contrary to the conventions of male heroism—to refrain from proving it.

Although he eschews the visual darkness of his noir films, Mann's Westerns probe the restlessness and insecurity of their heroes, and they are punctuated by outbursts of violence. At one point in *The Man from Laramie*, the James Stewart character is crippled by being shot in the hand. Yet despite such violent acts, Mann's Westerns are quieter than Ford's, more apt to investigate character psychology. In fact, the genre as a whole came to be known as "the psychological Western" during the 1950s. *The Searchers* might well fit into this category, but in most cases, Ford remained intent on presenting his characters in action and, in part, defined by the landscape that surrounds them. His characters are made as much by their history than by their internal drives. But when those drives are exposed, as they are in *The Searchers*, the result is a film that swirls in and around a troubled character, whose actions result in a domestic harmony that can only ostracize him and his obsessive behavior. At the same time, Ford was able suggest the aura of contemporary culture enveloping the mythos of the West. The past, in Ford's hands, is a blueprint of the present. The racism inherent in Ethan Edward's character speaks to the civil rights movement of the middle 1950s when the film was made. As the critic Brian Henderson suggests, if we substitute "black" for "red," African American for Native American, *The Searchers* becomes an interesting gloss on the struggles against racism that wracked the decade and beyond.[1]

ORSON WELLES AND *TOUCH OF EVIL*

Orson Welles's Hollywood-made film of the 1950s also addressed racism. In 1948, Welles directed a version of Shakespeare's *Macbeth* for Republic Pictures, a low-budget studio, best known for its Westerns in which the good guys wore white hats and the bad guys black. *Macbeth* was the studio's attempt at prestige. It was the last film that Welles would direct in the United States until 1958. Shortly after filming *Macbeth*, he left the country, escaping a failing career and HUAC. He did a great deal of acting, most notably as Harry Lime, the American black marketeer in postwar Vienna in Carol Reed's British production, *The Third Man* (London Film Productions, Selznick Releasing, 1950). He spent a number of years filming Shakespeare's *Othello*, which was finished in 1952 and released by United Artists in 1955. *Mr. Arkadin* (Filmora, Cervantes Films, 1955) was another European production, a kind of parody of *Citizen Kane*, in which a rich and corrupt European hires an American to discover the secrets of his past so that he can destroy the people who hold them whenever they are revealed. *Mr. Arkadin* is a gloriously strange film, full of loony, grotesque characters, a kind of orphan child of the director, a film that was taken away from him and edited into at least three different versions.

In 1955, he returned to the United States, acted in a number of films and on stage, and managed to get a film of his own to make. *Touch of Evil* (Universal, 1958) is one of the most remarkable films of the decade, a culmination of Wellesian visual ideas to date, a reflection on film noir, the style that Welles helped create with *Citizen Kane*, and a critique of racial attitudes and McCarthyism. Ostensibly about a corrupt law enforcement official locking horns with a Mexican anticrime official in a border town with Mexico, like all great films, *Touch of Evil* is much more than the sum of its plot. In its deeply shadowed, deeply focused mise-en-scène, shot in remarkably long takes, it is a film about an out-of-kilter world, teetering on the edge of dissolution, where boundaries are as fluid as loyalties and cheating justice by planting evidence is the rule.

Hank Quinlan (Welles), the bloated, alcoholic police captain of Los Robles, has a history of planting evidence on accused criminals. He is the film's McCarthy figure, a racist lawman who manipulates the law to fit his twisted conception of it. He is paired against Mike Vargas (Charlton Heston), a Mexican law-enforcement official, who enters Quinlan's dark domain when a car blows up as he and his American wife, Suzy (Janet Leigh), cross the border to get an ice cream soda. The banality of this is intentional. The darkness is as well, through which Welles's fluid camera moves its sinuous way, attempting to see into the bizarre characters that people the border. The opening of the film is a long take just over 3 minutes in length. The camera begins with a close-up of a man setting the timer on a car bomb, tracks him to the trunk of the car in which he places the bomb, cranes high up and across the roofs of buildings, ending on the other side of the border, observing various pedestrians coming and going, including a man with a donkey and a pushcart, and picking up Mike and Suzy as they pass the car with the bomb, which stops at the crossing guard, the woman passenger complaining about a ticking noise in her head; the camera returns to Mike and Suzy: they kiss, the car explodes.

Such dark humor infuses the film. Welles simultaneously takes his material very seriously and realizes that it's all pulp fiction into which he can suffuse a political and cultural charge. Keep in mind that Welles had been away from his native country for many years and returned to find it a place of political fear and racial turmoil. Welles had been active in liberal politics in the 1940s and could quite possibly have been caught up in the HUAC hearings had he remained in the country. *Touch of Evil* gave him the opportunity to reflect on an America gone politically insane during the period he was away. Hank Quinlan is a disgusting character, but Welles endows him with very human traits. Quinlan believes that planting evidence is the best way to get his man because a long time ago he let the man who murdered his wife get away. Indeed, the person responsible for setting off the car bomb does prove guilty. Quinlan's nemesis, Vargas, turns out as ready to plant evidence as is Quinlan, following him through the swamps with a recording machine to tape his confession. He does this with the help of Quinlan's partner and closest friend, Menzies (Joseph Calleia). Like the border, loyalties are porous.

At the end, Quinlan is shot by Menzies and falls like a whale into an open sewer. The town madam, Tanya (Marlene Dietrich), an old friend of Hank's, comes by and offers the final judgment. "Hank was a great detective, alright," says the assistant district attorney, standing next to Tanya. "And a lousy cop," she says. "Is that all you have to say for him?" asks the D.A. "He was some kind of a man. What does it matter what you say about people?"

Welles has a deeply humane streak, and he saw if not the good, at least the human in even the most despicable of his characters. Quinlan is a murderer and a fraud as a cop; he is a gross parody of a McCarthy-like figure. But Welles is willing to allow sympathy for the devil. Tanya says, "He was some kind of man," but not what kind. From the dark, grotesque, garbage-strewn world that Welles creates in *Touch of Evil* there emerge many kinds of men, and even the most moral of them are tainted. Everyone is tainted to some degree in the Wellesian universe, which means either that the universe is corrupt, or it is necessary to at least find some mitigation, some human characteristics in its inhabitants—even if those characteristics are completely unacceptable. Welles may be wrong in his offering of sympathy. It does matter what you say about people.

Touch of Evil was taken away from Welles during the editing stage. Universal didn't like the film he had made and recut some sequences and shot new ones. Since the advent of DVDs, Universal has attempted to make good on its original travesty by releasing some three different cuts of the film. This happened much too late to do Welles any good. He left the United States again (not returning again until the 1970s), made two extraordinary films in Europe, an adaptation of Franz Kafka's *The Trial* (Paris-Europa Productions, Astor Pictures Corp., 1963) and the Shakespearean *Chimes at Midnight* (Alpine Films, Internacional Films, Peppercorn-Wormser, 1965). He never made another Hollywood studio film that was completed and released.

ALFRED HITCHCOCK

Touch of Evil had an unexpected influence on what could be considered the last major film of the 1950s and the first influential film of the 1960s, Alfred Hitchcock's *Psycho* (Paramount,1960). Both films star Janet Leigh, and more important, both films feature the actress trapped in an out-of-the-way motel run by a crazy man. This is a remarkable example of **intertextuality**,

Hank Quinlan (Orson Welles) in the garbage-strewn border town of *Touch of Evil* (Welles, 1958).

the seeding of one work by another so that they carry on a kind of conversation with each other. It is a remarkable example of influence given how different the two directors were. Welles was the perpetual outsider, Hitchcock the consummate insider, who learned how to manipulate the studio system to his best advantage. He made, for the most part, commercially successful films that also contained levels of complexity that went far beyond the usual Hollywood movie. Hitchcock made films that were available on a number of levels of response and analysis.

Hitchcock reached his full maturity as a director in the 1950s with a string of films that probed ever more deeply into character psychology and, even more important, audience psychology. Many of these films demonstrate an extraordinary control of imagery and narrative construction that seals the viewer into the film while at the same time allowing a space for critical observation. When Bernard Herrmann joined Hitchcock as his composer, starting with *The Trouble with Harry* (Paramount, 1955), and including *The Wrong Man* (Warner Bros., 1956), *Vertigo* (Paramount, 1958), *North by Northwest* (MGM, 1959), and *Psycho,* music became integral with the images Hitchcock created; it deepened their resonance, so much so that hearing Herrmann's music by itself can call up the emotions generated by the films.

In the discussion that follows, I will be taking Hitchcock's films out of chronological order so that they can be grouped thematically to better understand how they are interconnected with each other and with the culture they reflect.

NORTH BY NORTHWEST AND *THE WRONG MAN*

Hitchcock had been making films about men who are mistaken for someone else at least since his *The 39 Steps* (Gaumont, 1935), made while he was still in England. In his 1950s version, *North by Northwest,* he added a dash of comedy as Cary Grant's Roger O. Thornhill is chased cross-country by spies who believe he is a CIA agent. *North by Northwest* is a Cold War thriller in which politics are buried (the McGuffin is a strip of microfilm hidden in a statue—a reference to the pumpkin microfilm in the Alger Hiss case) and spectacle is foregrounded, most famously in the sequence in which Roger is dive-bombed by a plane in a cornfield. *North by Northwest* posits the potential of disorder within public spaces, a theatricality of false accusation and mistaken identity that uses the public sphere as its playing field. The climax of the film takes place as Thornhill and his double agent lover, Eve (Eva Marie Saint), are pursued by the spies over the Mt. Rushmore memorial. The monument to American presidents becomes the location of Cold War violence.

Hitchcock made one Cold War mistaken identity film that had no comic relief and hid its politics in allegory. *The Wrong Man* ostensibly concerns an ordinary man, a bass player in a nightclub, who is arrested for a robbery. The body of the film follows in an almost **neorealist** style (though a style darker and more forbidding than any other neorealist film) the processing of Manny Balestrero (Henry Fonda) from arrest to interrogation to imprisonment and trial. In the course of his ordeal, his wife goes mad. There is a particularly grueling sequence in which Manny is paraded before witnesses who claim that he is in fact responsible for the crime he did not commit. The humiliations suffered by Manny parallel those suffered by the men and women paraded before HUAC. His helplessness echoes the powerlessness of people who, in their lives as screenwriters and actors, had considerably more power in the world than Manny. But this lower middle-class man, tormented by a system over which he has no control, becomes a kind of avatar for the threat posed to almost everyone by the witch hunt for Communists that was sweeping the country.

The Wrong Man is intense and grueling. There are a few rhetorical flourishes: the one moment in the film when Manny shows a brief sign of rebellion in the face of the relentless interrogation of the police, the camera pulls back to the typical Hitchcock high-angle shot that he uses whenever a character is vulnerable. When Manny is thrown in a cell, the camera inscribes a widening, dizzying movement around him, indicating his disorientation and panic. Manny is a man trapped by suspicion and the arrogance of the law, contained and restrained, accused as were so many innocent people during the witch hunts.

Mistaken identity. Isolated in the Hitchcockian high-angle shot, Manny Balestrero (Henry Fonda) is accused in Hitchcock's *The Wrong Man* (1956).

VERTIGO

Vertigo is also about containment, in this case a man held victim to his own obsessions. It is a film that examines the intensity and tragedy of willful misperception. A weak man, suffering from dizziness at high places, is tricked into believing that another man's wife has been taken over by the spirit of a long-dead woman. Scottie Ferguson (James Stewart) is a man at odds with himself. A police detective, his vertigo caused a colleague to fall to his death during a rooftop chase. Hitchcock depicts Scottie's vertigo by a neat camera trick, zooming in one direction while simultaneously tracking the camera in the opposite. The result is that the space around Scottie seems to slip away without actually moving. This movement and its cause express much about this character, whose world slips around him as he tries to balance his precarious emotional state. He is a wanderer in the city of San Francisco. A man with no center, he moves in a world that drifts from his grasp.

Scottie believes what he thinks he sees; and what he thinks he sees is a delusion, a willful mistake fostered by his own narcissism and sexual peculiarities. There is something wrong with Scottie beyond his vertigo. Early in the film, he visits his old friend, Midge (Barbara Bel Geddes). She is an industrial designer, secure in her work and herself, framed against the San Francisco skyline outside her window. She is a woman who loved Scottie and to whom she was once engaged. When Scottie mentions this in the course of their conversation, something interesting happens. "How's your love life, Midge?" he asks her as he moves to the couch. "Following a train of thought," she replies. "Normal." "Aren't you ever going to get married?" he asks. "You know there's only one man in the world for me, Johnny-O." "You mean me," he responds, half reclining on the couch. "We were engaged once, weren't we?" On these words, Hitchcock cuts to a high-angle close-up of Midge. She is leaning over her desk, but she is looking slightly upward. "Three whole weeks," she answers, and we cut back to Scottie on the couch. "Yes, good old college days. But you were the one who called off the engagement, you remember. I'm still available . . . available Ferguson." Again Hitchcock cuts to that peculiar close-up of Midge, smiling painfully.

These brief, subtle shots of Midge's gaze suggest that there were many reasons the engagement was called off, that Scottie's "love life" might not be "normal," that Midge knows more about Scottie (or Johnny, as she calls him) than he can let on even to himself. The film is constructed of these moments, small and large, in which the look, the gaze, the way people, Scottie in particular, regard themselves and each other. The gaze becomes more important than a plot which is driven by a fundamental lie. The plot of *Vertigo* is manufactured within the film's narrative. In other words, what happens, at least in the first part

Scottie (James Stewart) stares into the abyss at the end of Hitchcock's *Vertigo* (1985).

of the film, is the result of one character, Gavin Elster (Tom Helmore), plotting the murder of his wife and sending Scottie on a false trail, following a woman, Judy (Kim Novak), whom Elster says is his wife, Madeleine, who he claims is haunted by the ghost of a woman who died at the end of the 19th century.

None of this makes much sense, even Elster's ultimate goal, which is to have Scottie chase Judy/Madeleine up a Mission tower, depend upon his vertigo to keep him from getting to the top, while Elster throws his actual wife to her death. But it is not logical sense that Hitchcock is after. It is rather the focus on Scottie and the ease with which he is manipulated into Elster's plan and how it brings about the ruin of himself and the woman, Judy, who plays Madeleine. In some ways, *Vertigo* is also about the ease with which we, as movie viewers, are manipulated by what we see on the screen and were manipulated as well by the external political pressures of the Cold War. Scottie is a victim of others and of his own credulity, so much so that it drives him mad and turns him into a hapless, predatory, broken man, pursuing the woman of his imagination long after we, as viewers, understand the folly of his pursuit. In his pursuit, he finally devours himself.

The last image of the film—after Madeleine/Judy actually does fall to her death from the Mission tower—is of Scottie, his arms held away from his body, staring from the tower down at the abyss of his own emptiness. His imagined perfect love gone, his imagination is now empty of possibilities. He is left one of the most alone and isolated men in film, more so even then Chris Cross as the end of *Scarlet Street* (Fritz Lang, Fritz Lang Productions, Diana Production Company, Universal, 1945), a figure of damaged masculinity, of reduced agency. He becomes in many ways a representative postwar male, insecure, vulnerable, without secure footing in the world. The perverse love story that *Vertigo* tells is a twisted reflection of a postwar world torn by anxiety and able to be led down false paths by untrustworthy men.

PSYCHO

Vertigo was not as successful as Hitchcock had hoped. It was too dark, too complex for contemporary audiences. But it has gained in reputation. In the British Film Institute's most recent poll of international film critics, *Vertigo* has replaced *Citizen Kane* as the most important film ever made. As he was now the producer of his films, and depended on commercial success to continue making the films he wanted to make, he was more than ever obliged to please an audience, even while making multivalent films, instantly exciting, but resonant with a certain complexity. He followed *Vertigo* with *North by Northwest,* and then came *Psycho,* a film that operates on so many levels that, like *Vertigo*, it yields up more on each viewing.

Psycho is a horror film and a cautionary tale that tells us that madness is profound and ultimately unknowable. *Psycho* is a practical joke, a twice-told tale that gives up its meanings even as it tries to hide them. *Psycho* is the film that helped to put the final nail in the coffin of the Production Code.

The Production Code began to show signs of crumbling by the early 1950s. The reasons were as ridiculous as the code itself. In 1953, the director Otto Preminger made an innocuous comedy called *The Moon Is Blue* (Otto Preminger Films, United Artists). On the basis of the script, Joseph Breen wrote on behalf of the Production Code of America: "This unacceptability arises from the fact that the humor in this play stems, almost entirely, from a light and gay treatment of the subject of illicit sex and seduction. While there is no actual seduction in the story, the general attitude towards illicit sex seems to violate that Code clause which states: 'Pictures shall not infer that low forms of sex relationship are the accepted or common thing.'"[2] Besides this nonsense, the dialogue contained such words as "virgin" and "seduce." Preminger went ahead and made the film; the morality of the country was unaffected. But it was from such banalities that the code began to come apart. In 1959, the year *Psycho* was filmed, there were some squawks about its content, some edits that Hitchcock made to throw the PCA off the scent, but it was by far the bloodiest film ever made; it contained the first shot of a flushing toilet bowl in film history; and most important, its intertwining of sexuality and violence were more extreme than anything an American film had done before.

Psycho calls upon a huge and dependable response from its viewers, and it does this by carefully pulling the rug out from under our expectations from moment to moment. But while doing this, it becomes a kind of practical joke, putting us on, teasing us, delivering its series of shocks while winking at us at the same time. There is a core sequence in the film that takes place just before the infamous murder of Marion Crane (Janet Leigh) in the shower—a **montage** sequence of a knife stabbing a naked torso while violins shriek on the soundtrack. Norman Bates (Anthony Perkins), who runs the motel where Marion has stopped for the night, has invited her into the back parlor to have a sandwich. Norman, we discover, has a hobby. He stuffs dead animals. We see him in an unnerving composition, a stuffed owl hovering over his head. He talks about his mother, who "goes a little mad sometimes." But, he assures Marion and us, "she's as harmless as one of those stuffed birds." Quite. Because Mother is a stuffed corpse; Mother is Norman and Norman is Mother. He killed her, stuffed her, and became her. The sequence, with its intimations of madness, motherhood, and taxidermy, when seen a second time, reveals *Psycho*'s "secret," but does not diminish its shocks and surprises. Hitchcock is able to have things all ways at once.

Near the end of the film, after the discovery of Mother's rotting corpse in the basement of the house, a psychiatrist delivers a long analysis of Norman's condition (he delivers it in a police station, a place where law and order should reign, but where chaos is barely contained). It sounds quite convincing and would have ended the film on a perfectly unsatisfying note. Instead, Hitchcock returns us to Norman, sitting in a bare prison cell, wrapped in a blanket, one hand lying on his lap. The camera tracks slowly toward him as Mother's voice tells us that the only thing she could do is "just sit and stare like one of his stuffed birds." A fly lands on Norman/Mother's hand: "I hope that they are watching. They will see. They will see and they will say, 'Why she wouldn't even harm a fly.'" Norman/Mother lifts his head and offers us a mad, deadly grin. Under his face mother's skull appears, and then a chain, as if emerging from his neck, pulling the car with Marion's body out of the swamp.

Psycho is a cautionary tale. It insists that we cannot put a name on madness and cannot tell when its chaos will be unleashed. It leads us from the darkness into the darkness and makes us look hard and with disbelief. Eyes are a prominent image throughout the film: Norman's eye staring at Marion through a hole in the wall; Marion's dead eye staring uselessly at the money she stole from her boss; "Mother's" hollowed-out eyes glaring at Marion's sister (Vera Miles) when she discovers the body in the cellar; Norman's crossed eyes as he grins at us at film's end. We look on helplessly and knowingly at the same time.[3]

Psycho is something akin to an abstract expressionist painting. It is designed—with the help of the graphic artist Saul Bass—on a grid of horizontal, vertical, diagonal, and circular lines. This grid serves to tie the images together and to tie us to them. It allows Hitchcock to work in short, bold strokes (or strikes),

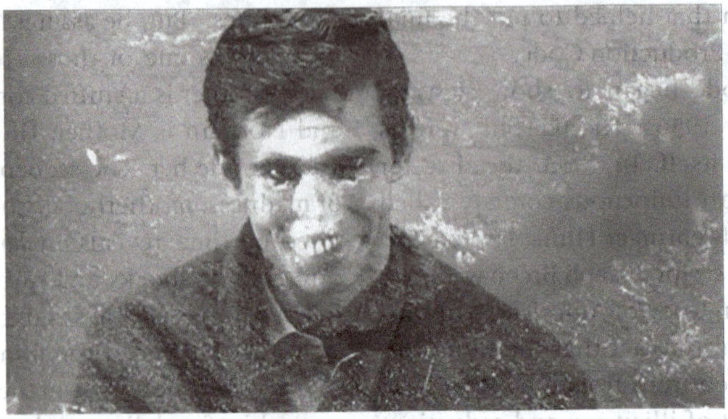

The face of madness: mother's skull and the chain pulling the car out of the swamp are superimposed over Norman's (Anthony Perkins) manic grin at the end of Alfred Hitchcock's *Psycho* (1960).

to grab and maintain attention by the almost subliminal pull of an image pattern that strengthens the film's hold on itself and on us. It allows for an economical narrative, a precise one where no shot, no camera movement goes to waste, where meaning is implied by the way an image is composed and the viewer's gaze held close.

There are few films as meticulously thought out and constructed as *Psycho*, few with such clear and deadly (and funny) designs on its viewers. Hitchcock brought all his powers and all his celebrity to bear on the film. He was probably the best known director of the time, due to his appearances on his *Alfred Hitchcock Presents* television show and the cameo appearances in his films—his means of "signing" his canvas. There are also few films that so adequately sum up a decade and look forward to the next. *The Best Years of Our Lives* did that for the 1940s on an optimistic note. *Psycho* prepares the way for the violence that would flood over American film starting in the late 1960s while at the same time being the sum of all fears of the 1950s. It is deeply pessimistic and misanthropic, as unnerving as the period it looks back on.

SELECTED FILMOGRAPHY

John Ford

Fort Apache, Argosy, RKO, 1948.

She Wore a Yellow Ribbon, Argosy, RKO, 1949.

Rio Grande, Republic Pictures, Argosy, 1950.

The Searchers, Warner Bros., C.V. Whitney Pictures, 1956.

The Man Who Shot Liberty Valence (Paramount, John Ford Productions, 1962.

Other Westerns

High Noon, dir. Fred Zinnemann, Stanley Kramer Productions, United Artists, 1952.

Johnny Guitar, dir. Nicholas Ray, Republic Pictures, 1954.

Silver Lode, dir. Alan Dwan, Pinecrest Productions, RKO, 1954.

The Man from Laramie, dir. Anthony Mann, William Goetz Productions, Columbia, 1955.

Orson Welles

The Third Man, dir. Carol Reed, London Film Productions, Selznick Releasing, 1950.

Mr. Arkadin, Filmora, Cervantes Films, 1955.

Touch of Evil, Universal, 1958.

The Trial, Astor Pictures Corp., Paris-Europa Productions, 1963.

Chimes at Midnight, Alpine Films, Internacional Films, Peppercorn-Wormser, 1965.

Alfred Hitchcock

The Trouble with Harry, Paramount, 1955.

The Wrong Man, Warner Bros.,1956.

Vertigo, Paramount, 1958.

North by Northwest, MGM, 1959.

Psycho, Paramount, 1960.

SUGGESTIONS FOR FURTHER READING

Richard Allen & S. Ishii-Gonzalès, eds., *Hitchcock: Past and Future* (New York, NY: Routledge, 2004).

Robert J Corber, *In the Name of National Security: Hitchcock, Homophobia, and the Political Construction of Gender in Postwar America* (Durham, NC: Duke University Press, 1993).

Raymond Durgnat, *A Long Hard Look at "Psycho"* (London: British Film Institute Publishing, 2002).

Robert Kolker, *Alfred Hitchcock's Psycho: A Casebook* (New York, NY: Oxford University Press, 2004).

James Naremore, *The Magic World of Orson Welles*, rev. ed. (Dallas, TX: Southern Methodist University Press, 1989).

Jonathan Rosenbaum, *Discovering Orson Welles* (Berkeley, CA: University of California Press, 2007).

William Rothman, *Hitchcock: The Murderous Gaze* (Cambridge, MA: Harvard University Press, 1982).

Gaylyn Studler & Matthew Bernstein, *John Ford Made Westerns : Filming the Legend in the Sound Era* (Bloomington, IN: Indiana University Press, 2001).

NOTES

1. Brian Henderson, "*The Searchers*: An American Dilemma," *Film Quarterly*, vol. 34, no. 2 (Winter, 1980–1981), 9–23.
2. The quotation from Joseph Breen is found in the entry for *The Moon Is Blue* in the American Film Institute Catalogue of Feature Films, http://www.afi.com.
3. For a fascinating discussion of *Psycho* and the gaze, see George Toles, "'If Thine Eye Offends Thee . . .' *Psycho* and the Art of Infection," in Robert Kolker, ed., *Alfred Hitchcock's Psycho: A Casebook* (New York: Oxford University Press, 2004), 120–145.

CHAPTER 17

SCIENCE FICTION IN THE 1950s (1950–1956)

Science fiction flourished in the 1950s. Fears of atomic energy and Communist infiltration were easily transformed into mutant monsters and aliens from outer space come to take over our minds. The "Communist threat" from the Soviet Union became the threat of creatures from outer space.

AFTER READING THIS CHAPTER, YOU SHOULD UNDERSTAND:

- What it is about the science fiction genre that makes it a vehicle for contemporary ideologies.
- How the culture of fear led to the science fiction films of the 1950s.
- The relationship of science fiction to the Cold War.
- The conservative nature of most 1950s science fiction.
- The Shakespearean connection to *Forbidden Planet.*

YOU SHOULD BE ABLE TO:

- Discriminate between horror science fiction and speculative science fiction.
- Explain the anti-intellectualism inherent in the genre.
- Account for the various remakes of *The Thing, The Day the Earth Stood Still,* and *Invasion of the Body Snatchers.*
- How science fiction has changed in contemporary film.

POSTWAR FEARS FROM OUTER SPACE

The first postwar flying saucer sighting in the United States occurred in 1947, 2 years after atomic bombs were dropped on Japan. In the same year, reports began to surface of a downed spaceship and bodies of aliens found near the army air field at Roswell, New Mexico. Atomic bomb detonations continued throughout the period, and in 1954, the "Super" hydrogen bomb was exploded. Science and fiction stirred up the culture. In 1950, Joseph McCarthy started his claims about the infiltration of a Communist (that is, alien) ideology. Nuclear fears and the conviction that alien forces were infiltrating the country haunted the decade. The culture was uncertain about the effects of atomic and hydrogen bomb testing—indeed, before the first test of the hydrogen bomb, there were predictions of a chain reaction that would destroy the world. Fears of the atom, fears of Communism somehow got spliced into beliefs that aliens were circling the planet in disc-shaped flying machines. It was all too good for Hollywood to pass up.

There were earlier science fiction films. Fritz Lang's German expressionist *Metropolis* (1927) set the standard for spectacular visions of a future dystopia, complete with a mad scientist and a fantastic robot. William Cameron Menzies' *Things to Come* (London Film Productions, United Artists, 1936) was equally spectacular, envisioning a future of great scientific promise. But these films hardly prepared for the often rough-hewn, low-budget groundswell of science fiction films that appeared during the 1950s, with their creatures from outer space and nuclear spawned monsters from under the sea. The monsters were always threatening, and the army almost always arrived to intervene and save the planet. Many of the films, especially the lowest budgeted of them, were filmed in the gray California desert and had an air of fear and despair about them.[1] In their dreariness and atmosphere of anxiety, science fiction films in the 1950s were imaginative surrogates for the Cold War anxieties.

I want to examine four specimens of 1950s science fiction, each quite different from the other, by way of indicating that there was a range of approaches even within this narrow genre. One of them is as much a monster film as science fiction, three address the Cold War, and one is, of all things, an adaptation of a Shakespeare play. They are *The Thing*, also known as *The Thing from Another World* (Christian Nyby, Howard Hawks, Winchester Films, RKO, 1951); *The Day the Earth Stood Still* (Robert Wise, Fox, 1951), *Forbidden Planet* (Fred Wilcox, MGM, 1956), and *Invasion of the Body Snatchers* (Don Siegel, Allied Artists, 1956).

THE THING FROM ANOTHER WORLD

The Thing from Another World is one of the first of the 1950s cycle of science fiction films. Though the director of note is Christian Nyby, Howard Hawks, who we previously looked at when we analyzed *The Big Sleep* (Warner Bros., 1946), had a strong hand in its making, and it bears the Hawks trademark of competent men in groups facing adversity with a strong woman allowed to enter their ranks. A flying saucer lands in the Arctic, its enormity marked when the air force men and scientists stand in a circle around the shadowy ship buried under the ice. A saucer and its inhabitant have been discovered! Thawed out, the monster turns out to be a huge, human-shaped, blood-sucking vegetable (played by James Arness, who went on to television fame in the Western series *Gunsmoke*) that proceeds to terrify the small Arctic base, the corridor of which becomes a kind of crossroads of men and monster, chasing one another until the latter is destroyed.

There is much comic and romantic byplay in the film—including the captain (Kenneth Tobey) being tied up and fed drinks by his girlfriend, Nikki (Margaret Sheridan)—and a wise-cracking newspaper reporter (Douglas Spencer), who never manages to get a picture of the monster. The head scientist of the expedition, Dr. Carrington (Robert Cornthwaite), is the odd man out of the group who wants to confront rather than destroy the monster. His very appearance marks him as different: tall with shocks of gray hair, he wears a Russian-style fur hat. He is an intellectual, and therefore, in the cultural haze of the 1950s, different, dangerous, and probably left wing. He admires the creature because of its perceived perfection: "No pain or pleasure as we know them, no emotions, no heart. Far superior . . . in every way." Pure rationality becomes a hallmark of science fiction aliens, and in a culture taught to fear the intellect because intellectuals were often branded as Communists, a danger. Dr. Carrington does not care about the hazards posed by the creature. He grows its seedpods using blood from the base medical supplies. He stands in the way of the creature's destruction by attempting to communicate with it. "Knowledge is more important than life," he says. "We split the atom . . . ," he argues. "And that sure made the world happy, didn't it," responds one of the men. The creature returns Carrington's attempt to communicate with it by sending him flying with one swoop of its vegetable arm.

And the creature is, of course, destroyed. It is Nikki who supplies the answer to their problem. "What do you do with a vegetable?" she is asked. "Boil it, stew it, bake it, fry it." Setting it ablaze doesn't work, so they rig up wires in the base corridor and electrocute it, with electronic arcs shrinking the creature to pigmy

The intellectual scientist, Dr. Carrington (Robert Cornthwaite), confronts the monster (James Arness) in *The Thing from Another World* (Christian Nyby, Howard Hawks, 1951).

size and finally to a pile of ash. The film ends with the reporter sending in his story and warning the world to "watch the skies."

THE DAY THE EARTH STOOD STILL

As a vehicle of postwar paranoia, *The Thing* contains all the prerequisites of 1950s science fiction contained in one compact, scary little film—an alien, an untrustworthy intellectual, a unified band of military men. Many of the films that followed it incorporated the horror and monster conventions into their narratives of alien invasion. *The Thing* was remade in 1982 by John Carpenter (Universal) with much more overt bloodletting and mutating of men and creatures. Made early in the HIV-AIDS epidemic, it focused on alien diseases of the blood. Yet another remake appeared in 2011, directed by Matthijs van Heijningen, Jr. (Morgan Creek Productions). But the original remains a kind of time capsule of post World War II fears, as does *The Day the Earth Stood Still*, the only science fiction film of the decade that presents its extraterrestrial visitor in a positive light. Klaatu (Michael Rennie) comes to Washington, DC, in a flying saucer to warn the earth to give up its "petty squabbles" and join an intergalactic union of planets watched over by giant robots, which will incinerate any planet that steps out of line.

The Day the Earth Stood Still is a rare liberal take on the alien invasion genre in that the space visitor is on a mission for the good of humankind. He is not out to destroy Earth but to save it. His role as savior is none too subtly noted in the name he assumes: Carpenter. This Christ-like figure is crucified for his pains. His first appearance is greeted by gunshots from the military, and, after he stops all electricity-driven activity in the world and is betrayed by the boyfriend of the woman (Patricia Neal) who is protecting and helping him, he is shot down once again. With the help of his robot, Gort, Klaatu is resurrected, and he gives a parting warning to a gathering of world leaders. He tells them that the other planets have eliminated all forms of aggression and offers a remarkable notion of how to maintain intergalactic peace: "The test of any such higher authority is, of course, the police force that supports it." Of course. Klaatu is offering a one-sided version of "mutually assured destruction" that became part of the game of nuclear chicken that constituted a major part of the Cold War. The United States and the Soviet Union would have enough nuclear capability to destroy the

Klaatu (Michael Rennie) and Gort, the destroyer of worlds, in *The Day the Earth Stood Still* (Robert Wise, 1951).

other. The terror generated by this fact was meant to keep each side from making a first strike. Klaatu makes this a little more streamlined by providing giant, metallic robots with laser beams emanating from their heads in place of nuclear armaments, and giving them absolute control. Not mutually assured destruction, but only the destruction of Earth itself should it continue its quarrelsome ways.

Like so much of 1950s science fiction, *The Day the Earth Stood Still* takes a dim view of contemporary life on Earth. Humans are portrayed as scared and vulnerable, almost always needing the protective hand of the military or some miracle to save them from the invaders. *The Day the Earth Stood Still* is the unusual film in which the invaders are trying to save us from ourselves. It is also the rare science fiction film of the decade with a relatively high budget and high production values, including a terrific score by Bernard Herrmann, complete with the electronic musicmaker of unearthly sounds, the Theremin (invented by a Russian), which became a staple of science fiction music.

FORBIDDEN PLANET

There were many lower budget science fiction/horror films during the decade of the 1950s that bear an imaginative mark, especially those directed by Jack Arnold for Universal. Their titles pretty much sum them up, though they don't give an indication of the understated power of their visuals: *It Came from Outer Space* (1953, based on a story by science fiction author Ray Bradbury and filmed in 3D), *The Creature from the Black Lagoon* (1954, also filmed in 3D), and an almost metaphysical meditation on physical size and the universe, the infinitely small and the infinitely large, *The Incredible Shrinking Man* (1957).

When a big studio went all out for a big budget science fiction film, the result was a highly influential work that traces its roots all the way back to Shakespeare. *Forbidden Planet* takes place in the future and in a galaxy far, far away. A delegation from Earth lands on the planet Altair and discovers a scientist, Dr. Morbius (Walter Pidgeon), living alone with his beautiful daughter, Altaira (Anne Francis), and their servant robot, Robby. Morbius is the survivor of a group of colonists who were destroyed by a mysterious force, "creatures from the Id," who also wiped out the planet's original inhabitants, the Krel. Morbius is roughly analogous to the magician Prospero in Shakespeare's *The Tempest*; Altaira is an outer space version of Prospero's daughter, Miranda; Robby is the metallic version of Ariel; and the monsters from the Id parallel the monster, Caliban—though in the play, Caliban is Prospero's slave, not his destroyer.

Dr. Morbius (Walter Pidgeon) shows off Robby the Robot in *Forbidden Planet* (Fred W. Wilcox, 1956).

This image from Forbidden Planet was imitated by George Lucas in *Star Wars, Episode IV—A New Hope* (1977) below.

The Shakespearean connections fall apart when the film moves into a familiar theme of 1950s science fiction, intellect versus emotions. The Krell, and then Dr. Morbius, tried to be too smart for their own good. They valued intellect over emotion, which returned in a monstrous form to destroy first the Krel and then Dr. Morbius, who dies from an excess of brain power and unleashes the creatures on the visiting crew. The film calls them "creatures from the Id"; Freud called it the return of the repressed. *Forbidden Planet* again gives voice to 1950s anti-intellectualism, the fear and resentment of knowledge and thinking, which was used as an attack by right-wing politicians. *Forbidden Planet* substitutes Freud for anti-communist sentiment, but it is clearly in line with the fear of intellect that flowed throughout the culture and which is here manifested in the return of the repressed in the form of monstrous creatures out to destroy those who bring them forth.

Forbidden Planet is able to rise above its conventional thematics through its unconventional visual brilliance—rare for a 1950s science fiction film. It is made in color and **anamorphic** wide screen. Extraterrestrial exteriors are rendered in beautifully imaginative paintings. The underworld spaces of the Krel are detailed and meticulous in their speculative representation of advanced technology, and they influenced two important science fiction films of later decades. When Morbius takes the crew down to the subterranean laboratories and energy plant of the Krell, the light show we see is a precursor of the "journey "beyond the infinite" in the greatest film of the science fiction genre, Stanley Kubrick's *2001: A Space Odyssey* (MGM, 1967)—a film we will discuss in Chapter 23. There is a holographic image of Morbius's daughter that foreshadows the hologram of Princess Leia in George Lukas's first *Star Wars* (Fox, 1977). Once underground, the group crosses a catwalk, with the camera looking down high above them, the futuristic machinery of the Krel below, in a composition that George Lukas would again imitate in his film.

INVASION OF THE BODY SNATCHERS

Forbidden Planet is an almost intelligent and completely entertaining film about the dangers of intelligence. It avoids some of the commonplaces of 1950s alien invasion films by means of its imaginative visuals and its curiosity about what an advanced culture might look like. Robby the Robot is an amusing version of what is usually a frightening figure in other science fiction films. The same cannot be said of Don Siegel's *Invasion of the Body Snatchers*, which summarizes the conventions of the genre and places itself squarely within the Cold War anti-Communist mood of the decade. Here, in a drab, gray world, the invaders float down to Earth as seedpods. When people sleep, the pods regenerate their bodies into mindless, emotionless pod people, whose sole job seems to be to discover those not yet taken over and convince them to enter the sleep of the untroubled.

The silliness of the plot is more than overcome by the tension developed through the film's often dark and creepy **mise-en-scène**. There are some fine set pieces. Dr. Miles Bennell (Kevin McCarthy), the lone holdout against the pod people, comes to his friend's house, where he finds lying on the pool table the simulacrum of his friend's body, its features in the process of being formed. Above the pool table is a poster, reading "Mirror Noir"—dark mirror—exactly what is happening to his pod body. As the friend and his wife sleep, the creature on the table takes on more of his features. At his girlfriend's house, Miles finds her partially formed body in the basement. Later, the pods themselves are found in the friend's greenhouse, popping open, extruding foaming slugs of human forms.

By this point, the film becomes a narrative of paranoia as Miles and his girlfriend, Becky (Dana Wynter), flee and attempt to keep awake. The pod people take over the police force and give pursuit. From Miles's office window, they see pod people converging on the town center. Trucks arrive, filled with pods. They manage an escape from town, the warning siren bleating the air. Hearing a woman singing—a siren's song—Miles comes to a farm where the seedpods are grown. But leaving Becky in the abandoned mine tunnel where they've been hiding is a mistake. She has fallen asleep, and Miles returns to the ghastly sight of his love turned into a pod person. Huge close-ups of both show the surprise and horror of Miles's discovery. "A moment's sleep," Miles says in voice-over, "and the girl I love was an inhuman enemy, bent on my destruction."

Miles winds up on the highway, screaming hysterically, "They're coming, you're in danger." Trucks speed by, loaded with seedpods. In startling close-up, Miles yells directly at the camera, "They're here already! You're next!" He continues in the middle of traffic, yelling hopelessly. And here the film should have ended. But a queasy studio insisted on a more hopeful ending, and Siegel created a wraparound narrative, so that at the beginning and end of the film, we see Miles in a hospital telling his story to doctors who finally believe him and call the FBI. The film becomes, in effect, an unconvincing flashback.

What is convincing about the film is its Cold War slant. Few alien invasion films of the 1950s were as explicit in their parallel of mind control and the "Communist threat." Listen to the conversation of Miles and Dr. Dan Kauffman (Larry Gates), the town psychiatrist, who was once Miles's colleague and is now one of the pod people, bent on getting Miles and Becky to sleep so they can join the others. "Less than a month ago," Dr. Kauffman says, "Santa Mira was

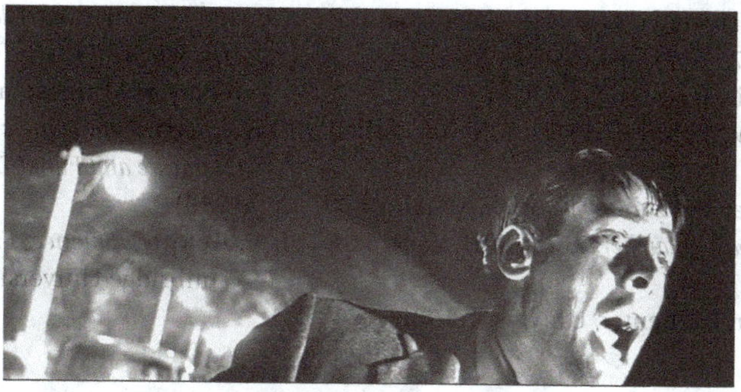

"They're here already! You're next!" Miles Bennell (Kevin McCarthy) warning the world as trucks full of seed pods speed by in *Invasion of the Body Snatchers* (Don Siegel, 1956).

like any other town. People with nothing but problems. Then, out of the sky, came a solution. Seeds drifting through space for years took root in a farmer's field. From the seeds came pods, which had the power to reproduce themselves in the exact likeness of any form of life. . . . Suddenly, while you're asleep, they'll absorb your minds, your memories, and you're reborn into an untroubled world." "Where everyone's the same?" asks Miles. "Exactly." Miles wonders if he will still love Becky after he's been taken over. "There's no need for love." "No emotions?" asks Miles, "then you have no feelings? Only the instinct to survive." Dan replies, "Love, desire, ambition, faith, without them life's so simple, believe me."

Becoming one of the pod people relieves one of human emotions; everyone becomes the same. This is not far from the language used to describe the dangers of Communist infiltration and the manufactured fears that Communism meant giving up individuality and becoming a kind of ideological automaton. "Communism," FBI Director Edgar J. Hoover wrote in 1958, "is more than an economic, political, social, or philosophical doctrine. It is a way of life; a false, materialistic, 'religion.' It would strip man of his belief in God, his heritage of freedom, his trust in love, justice, and mercy. Under communism all would become, as so many already have, twentieth-century slaves."[2] Such foolishness was obviously not only the province of the movies. It was rampant throughout Cold War culture.

Perhaps the most remarkable thing about *Invasion of the Body Snatchers* is the way it outlived the discourse of its time. It has been remade three times: once under its original title by Philip Kaufman in 1978 (Solo Film, UA), then as *Body Snatchers* by Abel Ferrara in 1993 (Dorset Productions, Robert H. Solo Productions, Warner Bros.), and more recently as a 2007 Nicole Kidman vehicle, *The Invasion,* directed by Oliver Hirschbiegel (Warner Bros.). Each of the remakes works variations on the theme of aliens taking over unsuspecting humans, which perhaps makes this something of a general fear across the years and in the face of changing ideologies. Perhaps it addresses a secret wish to believe in Dr. Dan Kauffman's assurance: "Love, desire, ambition, faith, without them life's so simple, believe me."

SELECTED FILMOGRAPHY

Metropolis, dir. Fritz Lang, Germany, 1927.

Things to Come, dir. William Cameron Menzies, London Film Productions, United Artists, 1936.

The Thing from Another World, dir. Christian Nyby, Howard Hawks, Winchester Films, RKO, 1951.

The Day the Earth Stood Still, dir. Robert Wise, Fox, 1951.

It Came from Outer Space, dir. Jack Arnold, Universal, 1953.

The Creature from the Black Lagoon, dir. Jack Arnold, Universal, 1954.

The Incredible Shrinking Man, dir. Jack Arnold, Universal, 1957.

Forbidden Planet, dir. Fred Wilcox, MGM, 1956.

Invasion of the Body Snatchers, dir. Don Siegel, Allied Artists, 1956.

2001: A Space Odyssey, dir. Stanley Kubrick, MGM, 1967.

Invasion of the Body Snatchers, dir. Phil Kaufman, MGM, 1978.

The Thing, dir. John Carpenter, Universal, 1982.

SUGGESTIONS FOR FURTHER READING

Annette Kuhn, ed., *Alien Zone II: The Spaces of Science-Fiction Cinema* (New York, NY: Verso, 1999).

Patrick Lucanio, *Them or Us: Archetypal Interpretations of the Fifties Alien Invasion Films* (Bloomington, IN: Indiana University Press, 1987).

Vivian Sobchack, *Screening Space: The American Science Fiction Film*, 2nd ed. (New York, NY: Ungar, 1987).

Constance Penley, ed. *Close Encounters: Film, Feminism, and Science Fiction Film* (Minneapolis, MN: University of Minnesota Press, 1991).

David Seed, *American Science Fiction and the Cold War: Literature and Film* (Chicago, IL: Fitzroy Dearborn, 1999).

J. P. Telotte, *Science Fiction Film* (New York, NY: Cambridge University Press, 2001).

NOTES

1. Vivian Sobchack talks about the desolate mise-en-scène of many 1950s science fiction films in *Screening Space: The American Science Fiction Film*, 2nd ed. (New York, NY: Ungar, 1987).
2. Quoted in Stephen J. Whitfield, *The Culture of the Cold War* (Baltimore, MD: Johns Hopkins University Press, 1991), 68.

CHAPTER 18

NEW METHODS IN ACTING AND NEW DIRECTIONS IN FILMMAKING (1950–1959)

The 1950s saw the advent of a new style of film acting, imported from New York and originating in Russia called "The Method." Method actors changed the way films sounded and helped create the juvenile delinquent movie. In addition to discussing the changes in film acting, we will analyze the work of some of the major filmmakers of the decade: Nicholas Ray and Samuel Fuller.

AFTER READING THIS CHAPTER, YOU SHOULD UNDERSTAND:

- How acting styles change across the decades.
- How the Method differs from other acting styles.
- What makes Marlon Brando and James Dean such important, popular, and influential actors.
- The cult status of actors and actresses who die young.
- The place of directors Nicholas Ray and Samuel Fuller in the pantheon of 1950s filmmakers.

YOU SHOULD BE ABLE TO:

- Trace the development of the Method.
- *Hear* the difference in film acting in a 1930s film and one from the 1950s.
- Define "performance" in film.
- Compare Marilyn Monroe, James Dean, and Marlon Brando.
- Consider the influence of 1950s directors on European filmmakers, such as Jean-Luc Godard.
- Summarize the films of the 1950s.

FILM ACTING

One of the most striking developments in the films of the 1950s had to do with acting styles. Each of the preceding periods had a distinctive style: the grandiloquent, melodramatic pantomime of the silent period; the often broad and artificial address of the early sound period; the more intimate, conversational style of the 1940s; and then the "Method" of the 1950s.

These changes need to be seen in the context of film acting in general. A "performance" in any film is not an ongoing process of character development of the kind that you would see in live theater.

Film acting is done in bits and spurts, often out of sequence, and the actor is tasked with maintaining his or her character throughout this disjointed process, depending very much on the director (and, in post-production, the editor) to maintain continuity. But even given this process, certain styles of acting come through, and certain actors have made their mark and have their fans, mostly through a continuity of roles and screen presence that go largely unchanged from film to film. Humphrey Bogart is a good example of the "old school" of Hollywood acting, playing, essentially, two kinds of roles: the tough guy, with lips drawn tight, arms held close to his side; or the tough but weary romantic, with eyes wide and sad. John Wayne developed his persona of a tough, no nonsense hero with some soul and the potential for redemption—laconic, but with a strength that would overcome any obstacle. Today Leonardo DiCaprio often acts with a constricted, pained expression, often seeming uncomfortable in his character, or playing a character uncomfortable in his skin.

THE ACTORS' STUDIO

In the late 1940s and early 1950s, a new acting style drifted from New York to Los Angeles. The "Method" can trace its lineage back to early 20th-century Russia and the work of actor and director Constantin Stanislavski. The Stanislavski system called upon actors to exercise "emotional memory" and the physical actions that resulted in order to create characters that drew not only on what was written in the play or script, but on the actor's own personal life experience. Transported to America, the Method, as it came to be called, was practiced in the Group Theater in New York, where Lee Strasberg brought Stanislavskian techniques to play during the 1930s, influencing such future directors as Elia Kazan. Kazan and others established The Actors' Studio in 1947, with Lee Strasberg as its lead teacher. A West Coast studio was formed in 1967. Strasberg was a Freudian, who took Stanislavski's method and turned it into a set of tools for actors to call on their memories and deepest emotions, to create characters, who, the theory went, were somehow more "realistic" than more conventional memorization and recitation of lines because they took their souls from the life of the actor portraying them.[1]

"Realistic," of course, is a loaded word, and the work of Lee Strasberg's students—and there were many of them who came to the screen from the 1950s to the present—James Dean, Paul Newman, Jack Nicholson, Al Pacino, Robert De Niro, Dennis Hopper, Marilyn Monroe, Shelley Winters, Jane Fonda, to name just a few—was in fact just an alternative kind of character representation. Many method actors brought an intensity that was unusual to screen acting, but it was an intensity that was mannered and sometimes forced. The Method created an artificial style, not a natural one, a New York style as opposed to Hollywood—more introverted, self-involved, even narcissistic, a pulling of attention to the actor acting at the expense of the ensemble. You will recall our discussion of silent screen acting and its schematic gestures used to represent common emotions. The rules of The Method do not depend on external, codified gestures, but the results, while different, are nonetheless artificial. Any acting is, by definition, an artifice, a character created by the art of the actor. But method acting became, in the 1950s, a recognizable style, almost detachable from the particular actor employing it. Its process of externalizing internal emotions leaked its way into film acting as a whole and changed the way most actors worked in film.

MARLON BRANDO AND JAMES DEAN

Two of the most famous method actors of the 1950s were Marlon Brando and James Dean. Even though Brando did not work with Lee Strasberg, his most important director in the 1950s was Elia Kazan, a founder of the Actors' Studio. Brando had a long and varied career, but his most famous roles came early on with *A Streetcar Named Desire* (Elia Kazan, Warner Bros., 1951) and *On The Waterfront* (Elia Kazan, Columbia, 1954) and later in *The Godfather* (Francis Ford Coppola, Paramount, Alfran Productions, 1972). It is interesting to note that his very best role—his most intense, even autobiographical performance—was in a foreign film, the Italian Bernardo Bertolucci's *Last Tango in Paris* (United Artists, 1973). James Dean made only three films before his early death: *Rebel without a Cause* (Nicholas Ray, Warner Bros., 1955), *East of Eden* (Elia Kazan, Warner Bros., 1955), and *Giant* (George Stevens, Warner Bros., 1956).

To understand Brando, I want to look at one of his lesser films of the 1950s, a motorcycle gang movie called *The Wild One* (Laslo Benedek, Columbia, 1953), and pair that with Nicholas Ray's *Rebel without a Cause*. The reason is twofold: these films are part of a cycle of films about rebellious adolescents, known at the time as "juvenile delinquents." Although there had always been films about young people living outside the law—we looked at *Wild Boys of the Road* (William A. Wellman, Warner Bros., 1931) in Chapter 8—the 1950s were particularly obsessed with adolescents gone wild. The fear of children out of control was part of the general anxiety of a world out of control. It was also part of the fear of some kind of alien invasion. Wild adolescents, the music they listened to (rock 'n' roll came to prominence in the 50s), the comic books they read, were part of an alien culture adults could not understand. Countless articles were written about juvenile delinquency, comic books were investigated in Congress, and concerns that rock 'n' roll was corrupting teenage morals was rampant. Films about adolescents in trouble—*Blackboard Jungle* (Richard Brooks, MGM, 1956), *Crime in the Streets* (Don Siegel, Allied Artists, 1956), even a Jerry Lewis movie, *The Delicate Delinquent* (Don McGuire, Paramount, 1957)—were common.[2] We look at *Rebel without a Cause* first and within the context of other films by its director, Nicholas Ray.

NICHOLAS RAY: *IN A LONELY PLACE*, *REBEL WITHOUT A CAUSE*, *BIGGER THAN LIFE*

The choice of *Rebel without a Cause* is based on the fact that it is a movie about troubled adolescents, because it stars James Dean, a method actor whose early death made him one of the cult figures of the 1950s, and because its director, Nicholas Ray, was one of the important filmmakers of the decade. We have already looked at Ray's Western, *Johnny Guitar* (Republic, 1954). He was also responsible for films that painfully examined the role of masculinity in a postwar world. *In a Lonely Place* (Columbia, 1950) stars Humphrey Bogart—not a method actor—as a screenwriter whose violent temper isolates him from the world of domesticity. Unable to maintain emotional stability, Bogart's Dixon Steele loses his friends and his love. The film is a study in the turmoil of contending pressures—to be tough like the culture demands that a man should be; to be so tough that violent actions begin to border on the sociopathic; to be unable to maintain a romantic relationship because the woman involved is in constant fear of male violence that might turn on her.

The face of pent-up rage. Humphrey Bogart in Nicholas Ray's *In a Lonely Place* (1950).

Jim (James Dean) and his parents (Jim Backus, Ann Duran) argue on the staircase that becomes the dynamic fulcrum of discontent in Nicholas Ray's *Rebel without a Cause* (1955).

In a Lonely Place is the rarest of films that end sadly, with Dix and his would-be fiancée (Gloria Graham) parting because she cannot overcome her fear of him, despite the fact that he has been cleared of an alleged murder. Lovers don't often part at the end of a film, but Ray's observation of passions that cannot be contained or understood, even by the person experiencing them, is strong enough to allow an unexpected unhappy ending, in which no one, least of all the lead male character, is redeemed.

Redemption is at issue in *Rebel without a Cause*, a film deeply involved with the 1950s concept of the American family. Jim Stark (Dean) is the rebellious son of a weak father and a domineering mother. The family is constantly on the move and Jim is constantly in trouble, even though his deepest instincts are to settle down. Jim is violent, but it is a violence that hides a more gentle nature, which leads to Dean's performance: explosive and tender, introverted and caring. It is a mannered performance, as if Dean were thinking carefully about every line and every emotion to be expressed. As we noted, the Method calls for a performance that externalizes the inner emotions of the actor. In practice, the performance tends to be highly stylized. In this case, the style fits Ray's somewhat stylized direction, which moves from violent outbursts of action, as in the famous "chickie run" sequence, where Jim and his rival, Buzz (Corey Allen) race their cars to the edge of a cliff. Buzz can't get out in time and plunges to his death.

Jim returns home and lies on the couch, his head leaning over the cushions. The camera assumes his point of view as his mother comes up the stairs, seen upside down. The camera then revolves 180 degrees to an upright position, creating a vertiginous effect across the expanse of the **CinemaScope** screen. In the sequence that follows, Jim and his parents argue at the foot of the stairway of their house, the camera assuming off-centered, canted angles, as Jim begs for some moral guidance. The staircase becomes the fulcrum for the disequilibrium of the family, as Ray edits the scene from a variety of angles, emphasizing the family's disorientation. His mother (Ann Doran) too domineering, his father (Jim Backus) too weak, Jim can only find refuge in a parallel family that he forms with two other misfits, Judy (Natalie Wood), whose father masks his sexual attraction to his daughter with abusive behavior, and a young gay adolescent, Plato (Sal Mineo), whose parents have abandoned him completely.

Plato is the mascot of the family group, his sexual attraction to Jim masked by sadness and anger. Pursued by Buzz's gang, Plato's anger overwhelms the momentary calm of their domestic scene. He shoots one of the gang and the police close in. The film ends at the Griffith Park Observatory, where Plato is shot dead by the police. This seems to galvanize Jim's father, who had been caricatured throughout the film, wearing an apron around the house, and he finally stands up for his son.

The lack of sentimentality that marked *Johnny Guitar* and *In a Lonely Place* is replaced here by an urge toward some sort of redemption and reconciliation. *Rebel without a Cause* is, in the end, a conservative film, arguing for a reconstruction of a patriarchal family structure. In that respect, it is quite different from the film Ray made the following year, *Bigger Than Life* (Fox, 1956). Dealing with an adult rather than a teenager, Ray is back in the territory of *In a Lonely Place*, that is, the interrogation of the function of masculinity and patriarchy. Here, Ed Avery (James Mason), a suburban school teacher, crazed on a "miracle drug," tries to destroy his hopelessly middle-class family. There is no method acting here. The film gets its strength from Ray's keen eye for the commonplaces of 1950s life and the ease with which its fragile shell could be pierced. The frightening domination of the psychotic Avery is carried on, as is the family antagonism in *Rebel*, around the staircase of the suburban house. Again it is a place of threat and fear. Holding a knife on his young son (Christopher Olsen), he threatens to carry out the Biblical story of Abraham and Isaac. Ed's wife (Barbara Rush) pleads, reminding him that God did not allow the sacrifice of Isaac to take place. Ed, in his madness, replies, "God was wrong!"

Ray made a number of important films in the 1950s, but *Rebel without a Cause* remains his best-known. Perhaps its mixture of teenage recklessness, its quest for secure domesticity, and the raw artifice of James Dean's performance—as well as the celebrity aura that has surrounded him long past his death—has kept the film vital in the public eye. It is one of those films whose visual and performative vitality has outlived its roots in anxieties of 1950s culture—or perhaps because those anxieties remain with us still.

THE WILD ONE

MILDRED: *Hey, Johnny, what are you rebelling against?*
JOHNNY: *Whad 'ya got?*

In 1956, the author Norman Mailer wrote an essay called "The White Negro," in which he talked about the desperate urge in a deadened society to be alive to experience, especially the experience of the outsider:

> A stench of fear has come out of every pore of American life, and we suffer from a collective failure of nerve. The only courage, with rare exceptions, that we have been witness to, has been the isolated courage of isolated people. It is on this bleak scene that a phenomenon has appeared: the American existentialist—the hipster, the man who knows that if our collective condition is to live with instant death by atomic war, relatively quick death by the State, . . . or with a slow death by conformity with every creative and rebellious instinct stifled . . . then the only life-giving answer is to accept the terms of death, to live with death as immediate danger, to divorce oneself from society, to exist without roots, to set out on that uncharted journey into the rebellious imperatives of the self. . . . The unstated essence of Hip, its psychopathic brilliance, quivers with the knowledge that new kinds of victories increase one's power for new kinds of perception. . . . One is Hip or one is Square.[3]

The Brando gesture in *The Wild One* Laslo Benedek (1953). Compare with the image of Brando in Chapter 25.

The juvenile delinquent movie played up the antisocial energy of the dispossessed—the hip in a square world—and this is nowhere more evident than in *The Wild One*. Marlon Brando's Johnny is the head of a motorcycle gang that zooms into a small, conservative town, meeting his rival gang, and causing havoc and romance. Brando plays his role with masculine bravado and a feminine reticence. It is his peculiar turn on the Method to introduce a kind of delicacy into his performance, a gesture that calls attention to itself and defines an uncharacteristic passivity in an otherwise blustering role. Early in the film, when a cop orders the gang out of town, Johnny puts on his aviator sun glasses. He sets them around his ears, and then pushes the right lens gently with his fingers, after which he looks at his fingers and delicately rubs them together for a second. It is at once a gesture of defiance—he takes his time obeying the cop—and it is a clue to his more fastidious self. Johnny plays the tough guy, divorced from society (in Mailer's terms). But like James Dean in *Rebel*, the toughness is a veneer over a sensitive soul. At one point in the film, abandoned by his gang, alone with his bike, Johnny looks up with a stricken face and weeps.

The Wild One is filled with hipster talk. The bikers are similar to the "white negro" that Mailer would write about in his essay, acting "the unstated essence of Hip." They are rude, rambunctious, and sometimes violent (violent enough to bring down the ire of the Production Code).[4] But the film seems to insist, like so many of the juvenile delinquent movies of the decade, that they are really just misunderstood, just looking for ways to act out undirected energies. With Brando's Johnny in their lead, they seem, in the end, less than threatening, perhaps themselves threatened by the square world that boxes them in. The struggle against "a slow death by conformity with every creative and rebellious instinct stifled" seems all but hopeless in these films. It took the cultural turmoil of the 1960s to more fully realize Mailer's call for "new kinds of victories [to] increase one's power for new kinds of perception." But even then, the "victories" were temporary and painful.

MARLON BRANDO AND MARILYN MONROE

The critic James Naremore describes Brando's performance in *On the Waterfront* in a way that applies to his role in *The Wild One* as well: his "every look, movement, and gesture is keyed to the essentially adolescent confusion of the character."[5] This statement could be applied to all the confused adolescents in 50s films: they may behave badly, but they are essentially hurt and confused at their core. They are very young and sometimes childlike at heart, an approach taken even by some of the actresses of the time. Marilyn Monroe, the great sex object of the 1950s, who had a very brief stint at the Actors' Studio, often played characters who had a

The vulnerable gaze of Marilyn Monroe in *Some Like It Hot* (Billy Wilder, 1959).

childlike sensibility and sexuality and who, like Brando, always displayed a deep vulnerability. Unlike Brando, Marilyn took this vulnerability into her nonacting, celebrity life. She never made a truly exceptional film, perhaps with the exception of *Some Like It Hot* (Billy Wilder, Ashton Productions, Mirisch Corporation, United Artists, 1959). But her multiple marriages and affairs, her breakdowns and suicide pushed her into the national consciousness as the representative image of the sensitive feminine soul unable to bear the weight of the world. Like James Dean, her early death made her into a cult object. We have seen this phenomenon in early cinema history with the death of Rudolf Valentino. There may not have been the mass hysteria over Dean's and Marilyn Monroe's death as there was over the earlier star, but the latter two entered the public consciousness more deeply and lastingly.

As to the Method, it became fairly well embedded in Hollywood acting styles by the late 1950s. Its lasting influence could be detected in the softening of male characters across a spectrum of films and can be seen as a set of contradictions expressed by those characters: toughness vs. vulnerability; belligerence vs. weakness; arrogance vs. fear; masculinity vs. femininity. Come to think of it, we see these contradictions evidenced in film noir and even embodied by John Wayne himself in his role of Ethan Edwards in *The Searchers*. The Method may be specific to actors trained in the Actor's Studio, but its attributes are present across the screen of the 1950s.

EPILOGUE TO THE 1950s

The 1950s are alternately sentimentalized as some kind of innocent period where life was simple and popular culture was uncomplicated, or demonized as a politically oppressive decade where terrible punishments were visited on innocent people. I have tended toward the latter view, but need to leaven that with the acknowledgement that this was a decade of enormous creativity. After all, rock 'n' roll made its appearance during the decade; abstract expressionist painting thrived; and American film resonated with the best work of some its finest directors, the introduction of a new acting style, as well as new actors and directorial talent.

SAM FULLER

THE NAKED KISS

We have spoken about Nicholas Ray, whose interrogations into the nature of masculinity and domesticity made for some of the most intriguing films of the decade. And there was Samuel Fuller, the rough-hewn filmmaker, who made his mark with pulp-fictional war movies, Westerns, and gangster movies during the decade. Fuller's films are direct, unsubtle, often vulgar—his 1964 movie, *The Naked Kiss* (F & F Productions, Allied Artists), opens with a handheld sequence in which a bald prostitute beats up her client with her shoe. His male characters—often named Griff—don't suffer the insecurities and psychoses

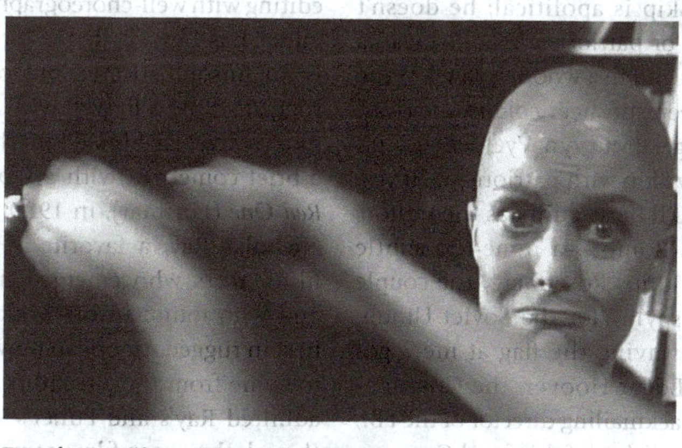

Female rage: the opening sequence of Samuel Fuller's *The Naked Kiss* (1964).

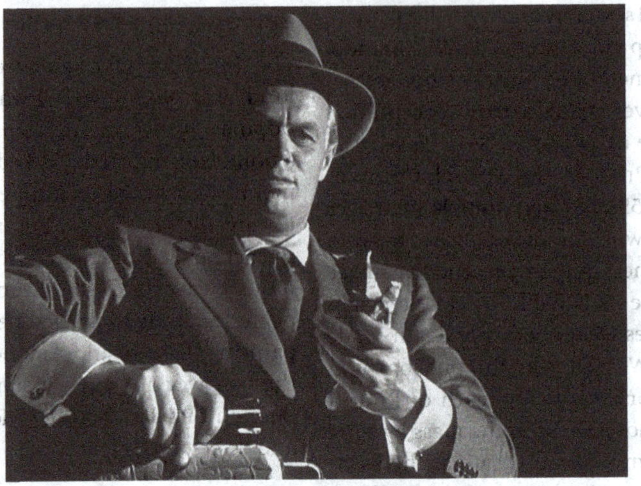

Skip (Richard Widmark), the pickpocket who helps thwart the Commies in Samuel Fuller's *Pickup on South Street* (1953).

that inflict Ray's; and his women—more likely than not named Candy—are tough and sentimental at the same time.

PICKUP ON SOUTH STREET

Pickup on South Street (Fox, 1953) is Fuller's odd Cold War film, which conveniently brings together a number of contradictory elements contained within the framework of a cops and criminals noir. In the subway, Skip McCoy (Richard Widmark) lifts microfilm destined for Communist hands from a doll named Candy (Jean Peters). Skip is apolitical; he doesn't care about "Commies" or patriotism. He just wants to pick pockets and hide out in a wooden shack at the end of pier where he keeps his beer cold in the river. When a cop named Tiger (Murvyn Vye) catches up with him, he tries to ply Skip with patriotism: "If you refuse to cooperate, you'll be as guilty as the traitors that gave Stalin the A-Bomb"—a none-too-subtle reference to Ethel and Julius Rosenberg, the couple executed for allegedly spying for the Soviet Union. Skip's reply, "Are you waving the flag at me?" got Fuller into trouble. J. Edgar Hoover, the Commie-hunting, file-keeping, blackmailing director of the FBI, was displeased with the elision of thief and Communists, and by the anti-American stance taken by Skip. Fuller joined the ranks of those who had an FBI file kept on them.[6]

It is difficult in the end to neatly categorize *Pickup on South Street* or any other Fuller film, for that matter. Skip will slug Candy one minute and then embrace her the next. An old woman named Moe (Thelma Ritter), who snitches to the cops, asks Skip, "What's the matter with you, playin' footsie with the Commies?" and winds up getting shot by one of the spies. There is a crudeness at the base of all this, but at the same time a rugged cinematic style that combines sharp editing with well-choreographed, long-take sequences. Fuller has been called a "primitive." More aptly he is an unsophisticated but canny filmmaker whose rugged silliness fit well with the 1950s, when he was most active. He filmed into the early 1960s and made a brief comeback with a World War II film, *The Big Red One* (Lorimar), in 1980. He became, along with Nicholas Ray, a favorite of the new generation of filmmakers who emerged in Europe in the 1950s, and who found in his work a representative of the best in rugged American moviemaking that appeared to come from the gut rather than the intellect. They admired Ray's and Fuller's stylized bluntness, even though their own films came from a much more cerebral place. "Film is like a battleground," Fuller says in a cameo appearance in the French filmmaker Jean-Luc Godard's 1965 film, *Pierrot le fou*. "Love. Hate. Action. Violence. In one word, emotion." Method filmmaking!

A NEW WAVE

A new wave in filmmaking was starting in Europe at the end of the 1950s, influenced to a large part by the European's love of American film. The films of Alfred Hitchcock, Howard Hawks, Orson Welles, John Ford, Nicholas Ray, and Samuel Fuller, among others, became models for the work of these young directors, who recognized, more than filmgoers in the United States, that the director is the driving imaginative force of the films that bore their names. Out of this love of American film came the **auteur theory**, the notion of the director as the imaginative center of a film. It came to change American film and inaugurated film studies as an academic discipline. Before all that, however, the studio system itself underwent major changes.

SELECTED FILMOGRAPHY

In a Lonely Place, dir. Nicholas Ray, Columbia, 1950.
A Streetcar Named Desire, dir. Elia Kazan, Warner Bros., 1951.
Pickup on South Street, dir. Samuel Fuller, Fox, 1953.
The Wild One, dir. Laslo Benedek, Columbia, 1953.
On the Waterfront, dir. Elia Kazan, Columbia, 1954.
Rebel without a Cause, dir. Nicholas Ray, Warner Bros., 1955.
East of Eden, dir. Elia Kazan, Warner Bros., 1955.
Giant, dir. George Stevens, Warner Bros., 1956.
Bigger Than Life, dir. Nicholas Ray, Fox, 1956.
Blackboard Jungle, dir. Richard Brooks, MGM, 1956.
Crime in the Streets, dir. Don Siegel, Allied Artists, 1956.
The Delicate Delinquent, dir. Don McGuire, Paramount, 1957.
Some Like It Hot, dir. Billy Wilder, Ashton Productions, Mirisch Corp., United Artists, 1959.
Pierrot le fou, dir. Jean-Luc Godard, France, 1965.
Last Tango in Paris, dir. Bernardo Bertolucci, United Artists, Italy, 1973.
The Naked Kiss, dir. Samuel Fuller, F & F Productions, Allied Artists, 1964.

SUGGESTIONS FOR FURTHER READING

Cynthia Baron, Diane Carson, & Frank P. Tomasulo, eds., *More Than a Method: Trends and Traditions in Contemporary Film Performance* (Detroit, MI: Wayne State University Press, 2004).

Samuel Fuller with Christa Lang Fuller & Jerome Henry Rudes, *A Third Face: My Tale of Writing, Fighting, and Filmmaking* (New York, NY: Alfred A. Knopf, 2002).

James Gilbert, *A Cycle of Outrage: America's Reaction to the Juvenile Delinquent in the 1950s* (New York: Oxford University Press, 1986).

———, *Men in the Middle: Searching for Masculinity in the 1950s* (Chicago, IL: University of Chicago Press, 2005).

Darryl Jones, Elizabeth McCarthy, & Bernice M. Murphy, eds., *It Came from the 1950s!: Popular Culture, Popular Anxieties* (New York, NY: Palgrave Macmillan, 2011).

W. T. Lhamon, Jr., *Deliberate Speed: The Origins of a Cultural Style in the American 1950s* (Cambridge, MA: Harvard University Press, 2002).

R. Barton Palmer, ed., *Larger Than Life: Movies Stars of the 1950s* (New Brunswick, NJ: Rutgers University Press, 2010).

J. David Slocum, ed., *Rebel without a Cause: Approaches to a Maverick Masterwork* (Albany, NY: State University of New York Press, 2005).

NOTES

1. See Perviz Sawoski, *The Stanislavski System: Growth and Methodology*, http://homepage.smc.edu/sawoski_perviz/Stanislavski.pdf; www.theactorsstudio.org; James Naremore, *Acting in the Cinema* (Berkeley, CA: University of California Press, 1988), 193–212.
2. On the fears about juvenile delinquency, see James Gilbert, *A Cycle of Outrage: America's Reaction to the Juvenile Delinquent in the 1950s* (New York, NY: Oxford University Press, 1986).
3. "The White Negro" first published in *Dissent* IV (Spring, 1957), republished in *Advertisements for Myself* (Cambridge, MA: Harvard University Press, 1992), 337–358.

4. See Jerold Simmons, "Violent youth: The censoring and public reception of *The Wild One* and *The Blackboard Jungle*," *Film History: An International Journal*, vol. 20, no. 33 (2008), 381–391.
5. *Acting in the Cinema*, 206.
6. Samuel Fuller with Christa Lang Fuller and Jerome Henry Rudes, *A Third Face: My Tale of Writing, Fighting, and Filmmaking* (New York, NY: Alfred A. Knopf, 2002), 291–306.

CHAPTER 19

DECLINE AND RENEWAL (1960–1967)

The 1960s saw major changes in what had been the stable studio system that was established in the 1920s. In the face of new owners, changing audiences, and influences of new filmmaking talent in Europe, American film and film culture changed radically. These changes caused the demise of the Production Code and the brief rise of a new American cinema.

AFTER READING THIS CHAPTER, YOU SHOULD UNDERSTAND:

- The changes in filmmaking across the decade of the 1960s.
- What happened to the studios during this period.
- How the studios went through a reverse process of formation compared to what happened in their early period of consolidation.
- New film movements in Europe and their influence on American filmmaking.
- The demise of the Production Code.

YOU SHOULD BE ABLE TO:

- Discuss the difference between the studios during the classic period of Hollywood production and today.
- Understand how the studios became merged into conglomerate corporations.
- Create a case history of the changes undergone by one of the studios in the course of the 1960s.
- Understand the rise of the auteur.
- Think about the influences of European cinema on American film.
- Discuss the efficacy and logic of the MPAA ratings system.
- Do your own rating of a movie you have seen.

EPIC DECLINE

The early 1960s were a period of radical change in Hollywood. Old studio heads died, retired, or were fired. Movie attendance fell. Confusion reigned over what kind of film would take audiences away from their television sets and back into the theaters. Often, the decision was made to create big-budget blockbusters. In the 1950s, some big-budget films did well, especially biblical "epics." Cecil B. DeMille remade his 1923 film *The Ten Commandments* (Paramount, 1956),

Stanley Kubrick took over direction of *Spartacus* (1960) when its star and producer, Kirk Douglas, fired Anthony Mann. Douglas also hired Dalton Trumbo to write the screenplay under his own name, thus helping to break the blacklist.

this time without a "modern" section, but with an introduction by the director that gives the film an anti-Communist slant. In color, widescreen, and with state-of-the-art special effects, the film remains an overlong, stilted study in bombast and bad acting. But it did well, remains popular, and encouraged the studios to do more. Nicholas Ray directed a life of Christ called *King of Kings* (MGM, 1961—a film made in Europe, a common occurrence in the 1960s when studio funds were held abroad or when producers wished to avoid union costs in Los Angeles); George Stevens made *The Greatest Story Ever Told* (United Artists, 1965), and, perhaps most famously, Stanley Kubrick took over the direction of *Spartacus* (Universal, 1960) when its producer, Kirk Douglas, fired its original director, Anthony Mann. *Spartacus* was not a biblical epic; it tells the story of a slave revolt in Ancient Rome. And despite Kubrick's direction (he had little control over the production), it maintains the overblown conventions, the ponderous acting, and gigantic sets that mark the genre.

What is notable about *Spartacus* at this point in our discussion is that it was produced by its star, Kirk Douglas. During the studio period, actors had almost no say over the roles they played, no say over the film in which they were in. But in the changing power structure that occurred in the 1960s, some actors and their agents began taking control of the business of filmmaking. As early as 1951, John Wayne formed the Batjac Production Company to oversee his films. Kirk Douglas created Bryna Productions, which, among other films, backed Stanley Kubrick's *Paths of Glory* (1958) as well as *Spartacus*. Actor Burt Lancaster, with his partners, formed Hill-Hecht-Lancaster, which produced a number of films, perhaps most notably a film noir about a brutal, reptilian anti-Communist gossip columnist, *Sweet Smell of Success* (Alexander Mackendrick, United Artists, 1958).[1]

PARAMOUNT

Meanwhile, the studios themselves were changing—changing ownership to be precise. As the old moguls—Jack Warner, Harry Cohn, Louis B. Mayer—died or retired, individuals and corporations with little or no experience in filmmaking took over. Paramount Pictures is an interesting example. In Chapter 2, we looked at the origins of the studio, how Adolf Zukor merged with Famous-Players-Lasky to form a large, powerful operation that produced films and owned the theaters in which they were shown. So many theaters, in fact, that Paramount was the main target in the government's anti-trust suit that led to the divestiture of the theater chains once owned by the studios. Despite its star power, famous directors such as Cecil B. DeMille, and a strong management that made it among the most profitable studios in the 1940s, it became the target of a major takeover in the 1960s. Gulf + Western, which began as an auto parts company and grew into a giant corporation whose specialty was acquiring other companies, purchased Paramount in 1966. Charles Bludhorn took over as

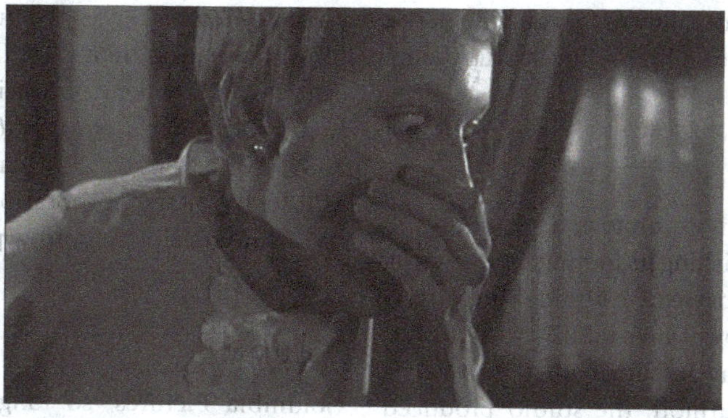

The Devil's spawn. Rosemary (Mia Farrow) sees her devil's child in Roman Polanski's *Rosemary's Baby*, a big hit for Paramount in 1968.

chairman of the board, and the company produced a number of hit films, most notably (and quite different from one another) *Rosemary's Baby* (Roman Polanski, 1968) and *Love Story* (Arthur Hiller, 1970). Gulf + Western rapidly became an early example of a media conglomerate, adding a publishing house, *Esquire* magazine, and the New York Nicks basketball team to their portfolio. It was a process of merging and acquisition that would spread across the media landscape.

In the early 1990s, Paramount was bought by Viacom, a communications company, which counts among its holdings MTV, Comedy Central, and Nickelodeon, among other cable channels. The studio remained successful, producing the *Star Trek* series, Francis Ford Coppola's *Godfather* films (1972, 1974), and co-producing with Fox the biggest grosser of its time, *Titanic* (James Cameron, 1997). But it is no longer a standalone studio, with a roster of stars, directors, cinematographers, production designers, editors, and the rest of studio personnel under contract. It acts, as do most of the "studios" that retain their original names, as a partial funder of projects and a distributor of finished films.[2]

UNIVERSAL

While he ran Gulf + Western, Charles Bludhorn joined with Lew Wasserman, head of the talent agency MCA (Music Corporation of America), in a deal for overseas distribution of films by Paramount and Universal Pictures. Wasserman had already engineered a deal to acquire Universal, and he expanded the studio's production to television, becoming, in the process, a very powerful player in the Hollywood universe. He became a kingmaker. During the 1950s, there was a popular television series sponsored by General Electric. The host of the series was Ronald Reagan, a client of Lew Wasserman's. MCA-Universal's television subsidiary, Revue, supplied the production and distribution for the show, and Reagan's popularity on the program gave his political career a push. During this period, Reagan was also president of the Screen Actors Guild and a member of the Motion Picture Alliance for the Preservation of American Ideals, which fed friendly witnesses to the HUAC investigations. Reagan began to give political speeches around the country, traded information on "leftists" with the FBI, and in the process became a prominent conservative spokesman. The government brought an antitrust suit against MCA for being a talent agency and a production company, which resulted in MCA severing its ties to its talent agency. Reagan survived the investigation, continued his path as an anti-government conservative, and ended up as 40th president of the United States.[3]

General Electric was also not diminished by these legal problems. It eventually became an owner of Universal until 2011, when it was bought out by the cable company, Comcast, together taking stewardship of Universal and its many subsidiaries, including the NBC network of on air and cable outlets.

Universal is the studio for many of Steven Spielberg's films and, of course, runs a highly successful theme park.

WARNER BROS.

Warner Bros. presents an example of a strong studio breaking down, reestablishing its footing, and moving again into the forefront of creative filmmaking. Growing old, Jack Warner slowly gave up direct control of the studio, selling it to a company named Seven Arts in 1967. Despite the turmoil, the studio produced *Bonnie and Clyde* (Arthur Penn, 1967), one of the most important and influential films of the decade. We will discuss it in Chapter 25. A few years later, the company was sold again, this time to Kinney National, a corporation that ran funeral homes and parking lots. Once again, a company inexperienced in filmmaking owned a filmmaking studio. In 1989, one of the most extraordinary series of mergers in media history occurred. Warner Bros. merged with Time Inc., the publishers of *Time* magazine, *Sports Illustrated*, and *Life*. In its time, Time Inc. was a powerful media organization, but, with the exception of its *March of Time* newsreels, not much involved in film production. In 2000, during the peak of the dot com bubble, Time Warner merged with AOL (America Online), at the time a major gateway to the Internet. The marriage failed. Old media and new did not get along well together, and AOL was dropped.

Time Warner now owns—among many other holdings—Warner Bros. film studios, CNN, HBO, all the Turner cable channels, and the vast film libraries of MGM and RKO. Those two studios did not quite survive the mergers and acquisitions of the 1960s and 70s. MGM went through a number of hands until it became mainly a hotel in Las Vegas and a codistributor of films with United Artists. RKO has, for all intent and purposes, vanished.

20TH CENTURY FOX

Twentieth-Century Fox survived for some time under Daryl Zanuck's leadership, until he produced a series of flops in the late 1950s and early 1960s. He recouped his position with *The Longest Day*, a World War II film released in 1962, with four directors credited (Zanuck was the ultimate director of the film). The studio then went through a number of executives and owners, producing its share of hit films, such as *The Sound of Music* (Robert Wise, 1965). In 1985, 20th Century Fox was purchased by Rupert Murdoch's News Corporation, yet another example of a film studio becoming part of a large international media conglomerate.

COLUMBIA

Columbia Pictures, so long the fiefdom of Harry Cohn, went through some churn after his death. It managed, during this interim, to co-produce some important films like Martin Scorsese's *Taxi Driver* (Bill/Phillips, Italo/Judeo Productions, 1976) and Steven Spielberg's *Close Encounters of the Third Kind* (EMI Films, Julia Phillips and Michael Phillips Productions, 1977)—the latter a huge moneymaker. In 1982, the studio was purchased by Coca-Cola and just 7 years later acquired by the Japanese company, Sony. Filmmaking became a matter of content production for Sony's electronic devices.[4]

EXPLOSION

In general, during and after this period of churn, various executives and studio heads took turns guiding the companies and filmmaking subsidiaries, trying to produce hit films, sometimes succeeding, often failing, getting fired, and then moving on to another filmmaking subsidiary in a Hollywood version of musical chairs. The result is that the studios went through a kind of reversal of what happened in the early teens of the 20th century. There we saw how many small film companies merged into what would become the major studios that were the heart of Hollywood film production for five decades. They were run by men who, despite their limitations, loved movies and knew how to make them, at least under the strict conditions and in the somewhat uniform styles that they created. Beginning in the later years of the 20th century, we see a kind of explosion, in which the studios blew apart to become holdings of large corporations, for whom making movies is not always the first order of business. The studios have also increasingly become distributors rather than originators of many of the films bearing their logo. They partner with small independent companies and independent producers and directors—and sometimes the stars—in putting together financing for individual films. During the studio period, financing was an automatic part of the production process. Even though the studio heads fought constantly with their financial officers (sometimes, as in the case of the Warner Bros., their relatives) on the East Coast, films got financed and made quickly. Today, films take a long time to get made, and a good bit of that time is taken up with finding the money for the production from a variety of sources—a fact reflected in the long list of producers, co-producers, and associate producers that are lined up in the film's credits. We get a sense of this in the list of production companies following the title and director of the films cited in this book.

Money was not the only problem for filmmakers beginning in the 1960s. Television continued to be a huge siphon of viewers away from movie theaters. And the demographics of the audience, particularly toward the end of the decade of the 1960s, was skewing younger. The rise of the counterculture, of the civil rights movement, of anti-Vietnam War protests, of singer-songwriter rock music, changed younger viewers' expectations of what they wanted to see on the screen. The old conventions and genres no longer satisfied. And new filmmakers, with new ideas, were emerging in Europe.

THE NEW WAVE

In 1959, a group of young French film critics turned filmmakers released their first films. François Truffaut made *The 400 Blows,* a film about a young boy adrift in Paris. Jean-Luc Godard made *Breathless,* about a gangster and his American girlfriend suffering existential angst in Paris. Their early films were marked by a loose, seemingly improvisational structure. Their characters moved within their environment with a sense of youthful exuberance. Although their early films owed much to American low-budget genre movies—especially gangster films—they demonstrated a burst of creative manipulation of their generic sources. What's more, unlike the invisible continuity editing of the **classical Hollywood style,** the films of these new directors were deeply self-conscious, often foregrounding their formal properties. In *Breathless,* for example, Godard employed **jump cuts,** the cinematic equivalent of ellipses, in which continuous actions are cut into, creating a

The French influence. Jean-Luc Godard's homage to the gangster film. Jean-Paul Belmondo as a small-time Parisian hood in *Breathless* (1959).

jarring, fragmented editing style. Along with the handheld camera they preferred over the mostly static camera of the Hollywood style, these filmmakers generated a nervous, arrhythmic, energized **mise-en-scène**, full of youthful exuberance. Truffaut, Godard, and their colleagues became known as the **French New Wave** and, throughout the 1960s, they made adventuresome, groundbreaking films. In the early 60s, two Italian directors, Federico Fellini and Michelangelo Antonioni, filmmakers who began their work in the 1950s in the **neorealist** movement, developed more complex creative approaches. Strong imagery, a powerful sense of how mise-en-scène defines character, and themes of alienation infused films like Fellini's *La dolce vita* (1960) and *8½* (1963), and Antonioni's *L'avventura* (1960) and his English language film, *Blow-Up* (MGM, 1966). These films, along with the work of Ingmar Bergman in Sweden, came as a revelation to those viewers who saw them in the United States. They were distributed as "art films," available mostly in urban areas and college towns. Their films helped create a vital film culture in the United States and were a cause of confusion to producers of American movies, who did not understand them or their popularity.

THE AUTEUR REVISITED

We return to our discussion of the auteur that we began in Chapter 13. The New Wave films coming out of Europe made it clear that movies were changing. They made clear as well that the director—traditionally considered by American producers as the person who just translated script to screen in Hollywood—was completely in charge of production. French filmmakers like Jean-Luc Godard left no doubt about who was in fact in charge of a film from inception through editing. More confusing still, European film critics began pointing to American directors, such as Alfred Hitchcock, Orson Welles, Howard Hawks, Nicholas Ray, Sam Fuller, and others as "auteurs," the driving creative force of their films. Suddenly films had a proper name. This recognition of authorship, recognizing the director as the creative principal, allowed film studies to emerge. A proper name lent gravitas to a film, making it serious enough to study. It also provided an alternative to the star system—or, perhaps more accurately, allowed another star system to emerge. In 1970, Joseph Gelmis published a book of interviews called *The Film Director as Superstar*.[5] It was one manifestation of a new film culture that was beginning to form both in the audience and for the studios that made the films they watched.

In the early 1960s, Hollywood believed it could remain oblivious to what was happening to film abroad and to their audience at home. Many of the films of that period were bland and ingratiating. Movies with singer-actress Doris Day were popular. *The Sound of Music* (Robert Wise, Robert Wise Productions, Argyle Enterprises, Fox, 1965) was a huge success (and remains popular to this day). Overblown, overlong, and overhyped "epics" were still

Compare the overcrowded spectacle of *Cleopatra* (played by Elizabeth Taylor, directed by Joseph L. Mankiewicz, 1963) with the spare, almost abstract mise-en-scène of Michelangelo Antonioni's *L'avventura* (1960) below. (Also, compare the *Cleopatra* image with that from D. W. Griffith's 1916 *Intolerance* in Chapter 4.)

made, the most notorious being Fox's *Cleopatra* (Joseph Mankiewicz, Darryl Zanuck, Rouben Mamoulian, 1963), a film that was a commercial hit because of its celebrity stars, Elizabeth Taylor and Richard Burton, and tabloid stories about its troubled production. Though a hit, it lost money because of its cost. The times were changing, the studios were changing, and films were about to change as well.

THE END OF THE CODE AND THE BEGINNING OF THE RATINGS SYSTEM

Earlier, we noted that Alfred Hitchcock's *Psycho* (Paramount, 1960) helped put the nail in the coffin of the Production Code. The full story of the decline and rise of film censorship in the 1950s and 1960s is quite interesting, particularly as it demonstrates the studios' unceasing desire to keep outsiders from applying their morality to the movies while being sure that "morality" would remain the province of the studios themselves. It is interesting as well as an example of the changes that were occurring across the spectrum of American film culture: the studios' losing battle with censorship, their declining finances, and changing audience expectations. To understand what happened to the code, we need to recover some ground.

The MPAA (The Motion Picture Association of America), the parent of the Production Code Administration, came into being in 1945, taking the place of the Motion Picture Producers and Distributors of America. MPAA's president, Eric Johnston, took an active role cooperating with the HUAC investigations and the ensuing blacklist. The result was a vicious

The graphic violence of Hitchcock's *Psycho* (1960) transgressed the Production Code and helped put an end to it.

form of political and intellectual censorship. Because of its cooperation with the government investigating body, the MPAA went beyond controlling the content of Hollywood film and attempted to control the political and, because of the blacklist, the economic lives of the people working to make films. Throughout its history, the studios tried to avoid government interference in its work. Now, during the anti-Communist frenzy, it welcomed the government's help in purging its ranks.

Joseph Breen continued overseeing the code itself. But lapses and gaps were beginning to show. As we noted in Chapter 14, during the birth of film noir in the mid-1940s, there were complaints about the violence and (for its time) open sexuality inherent in the noir style. The chief censor of Atlanta, Georgia, banned Fritz Lang's *Scarlet Street* (Fritz Lang Productions, Universal, 1945), an uncompromisingly dark film we analyzed in Chapter 14. ". . . Licentious, profane, obscene, and contrary to the good order of the community," she raged. She ordered it banned in Atlanta. The producer and distributor of the film took the censor to court. Breen, always sensitive to "outside interference," supported the studio: "to deprive art of dramatic license in choosing its own punishment [of characters who commit crimes], so long as the punishment is morally adequate, would be to rob art of its contribution to progress. . . . All other ages have conceded art this prerogative." Atlanta got to see the film.[6]

Imagine the censor-in-chief referring to the movies (or "pictures" as they were commonly referred to in the business) as "art"! But Breen did not have a sudden epiphany about the artistic aspirations of American movies, or the inherent power of Fritz Lang's film. He just didn't want someone outside of the business poking around and threatening revenue. It was *his* job to warn the studios of excessive sex and violence in their films. But clearly filmmaking and the role of the PCA was changing. Being chipped away, more accurately, despite the shameful role the MPAA played during the HUAC hearings. During the early 1940s, there was the notorious case of Howard Hughes's film *The Outlaw*, which prominently featured actress Jane Russell's partially covered breasts. Made in 1941, held from distribution by the censors until 1943, and then rereleased in 1947, Hughes played fast and loose with the demands of Breen's office to trim what Breen considered the salacious parts of the film. Hughes tried to defy the PCA by distributing the film independently and it made a lot of money. He then allowed a code-approved version to play in the studio-affiliated theaters. It took a rich, quirky millionaire outsider to play the PCA and further weaken it.[7]

An Italian film, *The Miracle*, directed by Roberto Rossellini and part of a trilogy of films, *Ways of Love*, released in 1948, created yet another blow. The film portrayed a poor peasant woman who thinks she has been impregnated by St. Joseph. It was shown in New York City without a PCA seal of approval, and the Catholic Church and other groups were incensed and tried to get the film banned. Lawsuits went all the way to the Supreme Court, which rendered a remarkable decision. You may recall our discussion in Chapter 3 of the birth of film censorship and the Supreme Court decision in 1915 that film distribution was "a business pure and simple." This time, the ruling was quite different. In 1952 the court ruled "that motion pictures are a significant medium for the communication of ideas. . . . We conclude that expression by means of motion pictures is included within the free speech and free press guaranty of the First and Fourteenth Amendment."[8] Film was suddenly given a freer voice. The end of the code was in sight.

As were at least some aspects of American attitudes toward sexuality. Two books by sex researcher Alfred Kinsey shook up conventional attitudes and long-held misconceptions. *Sexual Behavior in the Human Male* (1948) and *Sexual Behavior in the Human Female* (1953) laid out in statistical fashion the facts about the wide diversity of human sexual behavior. Kinsey's findings had an enormous cultural impact and were subjects of much discussion and controversy. Attitudes toward sexuality were indeed shaken up, though perhaps not immediately changed. The effect was more subtle, allowing for references to sexuality to become more explicit in daily conversation and in film. Sex was always the subject of Hollywood filmmaking. Post-Kinsey it could become more overt, more direct, and allowed to burrow further into the foundation of the code.[9]

Joseph Breen stepped down as head of the PCA in 1954. Film after film began defying the conventions of the code. The MPAA itself ruled against the PCA in a number of instances, and when Jack Valenti assumed leadership of the MPAA in 1966, he made the decision, in the words of Thomas Doherty, "to rate rather than regulate."[10] So was born the MPAA rating system. Instead of submitting scripts in advance to the PCA, a near final version of the film is screened before members of the Code and Rating Administration, who decide whether to give it a G, PG, PG-13, R, or NC-17 rating. The Code and Rating Administration suggests trims, often of a few frames, in order to apply the rating that the filmmakers want or, in the case of NC-17, that they never want. Recommending that a film not be seen by anyone under 17 would severely affect ticket sales. The ratings contain brief descriptions of what might be offensive in the film: "Rated R for language, some sexuality, violence and brief drug use." Just what "some sexuality" means is unclear—images of people making love? And how much is "some"? And "language"? A few curse words? "Violence"—a gunfight, a dismemberment? There are even warnings that a film contains images of people smoking, a sure sign of the times. Drinking and smoking were standard occupations of movie characters until relatively recently. Film noir would not exist without alcohol and cigarettes. Now smoking is usually confined to a villain or to a character under stress. Once again, the MPAA has joined with the government in warning the public, this time not about Communist subversion, but about the dangers of tobacco.

The real meaning of the ratings system is that many filmmakers still run scared, still believe that their public needs protection—or guidance as they might put it, lest some group apply censorship from outside. The MPAA ratings are, basically, a joke; but so was the Production Code. Filmmakers—producers, writers, directors—were always in on the joke and found their various ways around it. For all the years of the code, the joke was also on the audience, who were deprived of a certain depth of insight into human behavior because so much of that behavior was forbidden to be represented. The current ratings system is merely a fig leaf, a screen you need to get through in order to get to the film. It is vague, often silly, and it obfuscates more than it clarifies. It allows the studios to pretend that they are looking after the public morality while they notoriously let extraordinary amounts of violence past the MPAA screeners. *The New York Times* film critic A. O. Scott likes to make fun of the ratings in his reviews. For a film named *Mud* (Jeff Nichols, Lionsgate, Roadside Attractions, 2013) he noted: "*Mud* is rated PG-13 (Parents Strongly Cautioned). Cussin', fightin' and other bad stuff."[11]

The fact was that by the 1960s, "public morality" was changing; or, more accurately, filmmakers and public alike were changing in what they wanted to show on the screen and what the public was willing to accept on the screen. Along with the structural changes occurring within and to the studio system, and the rise of the director as a new force in filmmaking culture, movies themselves were changing irrevocably.

SELECTED FILMOGRAPHY

Sweet Smell of Success, dir. Alexander MacKendrick, Norma Productions, Curtleigh Productions, Hill-Hecht-Lancaster Productions, United Artists, 1958.

The 400 Blows, dir. François Truffaut, France, 1959.

Breathless, dir. Jean-Luc Godard, France, 1959.

Spartacus, dir. Stanley Kubrick, Universal, 1960.

L'avventura, dir. Michelangelo Antonioni, Italy, 1960.

La dolce vita, dir. Federico Fellini, Italy, 1960.

King of Kings, dir. Nicholas Ray, MGM, Samuel Bronston Productions, 1961.

8½, dir. Federico Fellini, Italy, 1963.

Cleopatra, dir. Joseph Mankiewicz, Darryl Zanuck, Rouben Mamoulian, Fox, 1963.

The Greatest Story Ever Told, dir. George Stevens, United Artists, 1965.

The Sound of Music, dir. Robert Wise, 20th Century Fox, 1965.

Blow-Up, dir. Michelangelo Antonioni, Italy, MGM, 1966.

Rosemary's Baby, dir. Roman Polanski, William Castle Productions, Paramount, 1968.

Titanic, dir. James Cameron, Fox, Paramount, 1997.

SUGGESTIONS FOR FURTHER READING

Christopher Anderson, *Hollywood TV: The Studio System in the Fifties* (Austin, TX: University of Texas Press, 1994).

Richard Brody, *Everything Is Cinema: The Working Life of Jean-Luc Godard* (New York, NY: Metropolitan Books, 2008).

Jerome Christensen, *America's Corporate Art: The Studio Authorship of Hollywood Motion Pictures* (Stanford, CA: Stanford University Press, 2012).

Thomas Doherty, *Hollywood's Censor: Joseph I. Breen & the Production Code Administration* (New York, NY: Columbia University Press, 2007).

Joseph Gelmis, *The Film Director as Superstar* (New York, NY: Doubleday, 1970).

J. Hoberman, *The Dream Life: Movies, Media, and the Mythology of the Sixties* (New York, NY: New Press, 2003).

NOTES

1. See Paul Monaco, *The Sixties, 1960–1969, History of the American Cinema,* vol. 8 (Berkeley, CA: University of California Press, 2003), 21–22.
2. A detailed history of Paramount is in Douglas Gomery, *The Hollywood Studio System* (Houndmills, Basingstoke and London, England: MacMillan Publishers, 1986), 26–50.
3. For information on MCA and Ronald Reagan, see William L. Bird, "General Electric Theater," *The Museum of Broadcast Communications*, http://www.museum.tv, and Dan E. Moldea, "Finding Gold in Los Angeles," http://www.moldea.com/Four-12.html and Moldea, *Dark Victory: Ronald Reagan, MCA, and the Mob* (New York, NY: Viking, 1986).
4. For a useful history of Columbia Pictures, see http://www.filmbug.com/dictionary/studios/columbia-pictures.php.
5. Joseph Gelmis, *The Film Director as Superstar* (New York, NY: Doubleday, 1970).
6. Quoted in Thomas Doherty, *Hollywood's Censor: Joseph I. Breen & the Production Code Administration* (New York, NY: Columbia University Press, 2007), 249.
7. See Doherty, 251–263.
8. Quoted in Doherty, 302.
9. See, for example, Linda Ruth Williams, Michael Hammond, eds., *Contemporary American Cinema* (Maidenhead, Berkshire, England: Open University Press, McGraw-Hill, 2006), 5–6.
10. Doherty, 333.
11. A. O. Scott, "Hiding from Trouble, Found by Innocents," *The New York Times* (April 26, 2013), C10.

CHAPTER 20

WOMEN, MEN, AND SUPERHEROES (1980–2012)

The 1970s and 1980s saw the beginning of special effects spectaculars: blockbuster films, superhero films, but also films that examined more intimate subjects such as masculinity and feminism, as well as films that responded to the era of Ronald Reagan, the 40th president of the United States, whose conservative ideology created a culture of aggressive political action and fantasies of heroic action in the world. This chapter covers some important cultural and cinematic events of the 1980s to the present with an emphasis on the ways gender is portrayed on screen and how our attraction to male action figures has given rise to the superhero genre.

AFTER READING THIS CHAPTER, YOU SHOULD UNDERSTAND:

- The rise of the modern feminist movement and how it influenced film.
- The gaze and gender.
- The difference between the male and the female gaze; and the homosocial as opposed to homosexual.
- The concept of the "monstrous feminine."
- The use of computer-generated imagery to create a fantastic mise-en-scène.

YOU SHOULD BE ABLE TO:

- Analyze the representation of gender in a particular film.
- Trace this representation across a number of decades.
- Understand the rise of women's films in the 1980s.
- Question what happens when the camera gazes on the male body.
- Address films that express an antifeminist backlash.
- Explain the spiritual angst of the superhero.
- Discuss the standard superhero "formula."
- Think about why we cannot seem to ignore the superhero and his antics.

VISUAL PLEASURE

The modern feminist movement could be said to have begun during World War II, when women moved into the workforce to take the place of men who had gone to war. Women gained, for the first time, economic freedom, which is the root, in our culture, of freedom in other areas of daily life. When the war was over, women were sent back into the home as part of a large ideological effort across media and politics to convince them that their function was to raise a family and be subservient to men. But things had changed too much: while the cultural and political work of the 1950s attempted to put women back in their place in the home, this proved only a temporary setback. By the end of the 1950s and during the cultural and political turmoil of the 1960s there emerged a strong feminist movement. Women reclaimed themselves as free agents, as equals to men, as having a will of their own, demanding recognition. The publication of Betty Friedan's groundbreaking book, *The Feminine Mystique*, in 1963, and her cofounding of The National Organization for Women (NOW) in 1966, gave the movement a great deal of energy.

A lot of that energy was generated by scholarly work that investigated the ways in which women have been represented in works of the imagination. Since women were most visibly represented in the visual arts, and in film in particular, feminist critics scrutinized the ways women are seen in film. Their findings led to surprising revelations. One of the most influential analyses occurs in Laura Mulvey's essay, "Visual Pleasure and the Narrative Cinema," published in 1975. Mulvey understands that gender is built into the very formal construction of film: the ways in which a film is planned and executed, shot and cut; the way the gaze is directed—that is, where the characters look and where the spectator is asked to direct his or her own look at the characters. What Mulvey discovers is that in the overwhelming majority of American films, the gaze is directed from the male character to the female, and the gaze of the audience is filtered through the male character so that a triangle is formed from the gaze of the viewer through the gaze of the male character on the screen to the female character on the screen. She is at the apex of gaze. The male character is the bearer of the look, the woman his object. Mulvey writes:

> In a world ordered by sexual imbalance, pleasure in looking has been split between active/male and passive/female. The determining male gaze projects its fantasy onto the female figure, which is styled accordingly. In their traditional exhibitionist role women are simultaneously looked at and displayed, with their appearance coded for strong visual and erotic impact so that they can be said to connote *to-be-looked-at-ness*. Woman displayed as sexual object is the *leitmotif* of erotic spectacle: from pinups to strip-tease, from Ziegfeld to Busby Berkeley, she holds the look, and plays to and signifies male desire.[1]

We have seen this dynamic at work throughout our study. Even in a film noir like *Double Indemnity* (Billy Wilder, Paramount, 1944), where the woman turns out to be a strong-willed murderer, we encounter her first through the gaze of the hapless insurance agent, Walter Neff, who sees Phyllis Dietrichson descending the stairs and fixates on the anklet she is wearing. Certainly in the Busby Berkeley musicals of the 1930s, the geometric patterns of women dancers indicated that the woman not only carried the condition of "to-be-looked-at-ness," but were turned into organic objects, women seen as abstract erotic shapes.[2] Mulvey's analysis of the gaze is acute and incontrovertible. The question we need to ask is how the feminist movement and the theories of the gaze laid out in Mulvey's essay were realized in American film as it went through important changes in the 1980s and beyond.

NORMA RAE AND *SILKWOOD*

There were films that attempted to openly acknowledge the women's movement by creating strong female characters. Martin Ritt's *Norma Rae* (Fox, 1979) has its protagonist, played by Sally Field, come to understand the importance of solidarity in the workplace and become a union organizer, albeit under the guidance of a union man from the North. The sequence in which Norma stands on top of a table on the textile factory floor, holding up a handwritten sign that simply reads "Union," while the rest of the workers slowly take cognizance of what her action means and turn off their machines, is a powerful image of workers learning their rights from a woman. Mike Nichols's *Silkwood* (ABC Motion Pictures, Fox, 1983) recreates the true story of Karen Silkwood (played in the film by Meryl Streep) who pursued the illegal contamination practices of a nuclear plant. She dies under suspicious circumstances—a strong suggestion that the owners of the facility engineered her contamination and ultimately her death. Both films place their women in domestic as well workplace settings, and in *Silkwood* the home itself becomes unsafe when the plutonium company destroys the domestic space to prove that Karen has been contaminated. While the films create some tension between home and work lives, the emphasis is on women in the workplace and their desire to better working conditions, in the case of *Norma Rae*, or expose corporate malpractice in *Silkwood*.

In rare films like these, the women are central to the events of the films' narrative. They are not filtered through the male gaze, but rather direct our gaze to them and from them to the events that they attempt to control. Even more important, these are portrayals of working women in rural settings, unglamorous by the usual conventions of film women, stronger than the usual conventions of romantic heroines.

BY AND FOR WOMEN

As part of the response to the feminist movement of the 1970s and 1980s, there were a very few films directed by women. We saw that in the early days of film, there were two prominent women directors: Alice Guy Blaché and Lois Weber. From the 1920s through the early 1940s, another woman, Dorothy Arzner, directed some 20 films. And then there were none until the 1950s, when the actress Ida Lupino formed her own production company (as Weber had done), called The Filmmakers, and directed a number of films, one of which, *Outrage* (RKO, 1950), dealt with the heretofore forbidden topic of rape. Other Lupino-directed films, such as *The Hitch-Hiker* (RKO, 1950) and *The Bigamist* (The Filmmakers, 1953), portrayed their male characters as less than heroic individuals—quite ordinary, in fact, and subject to normal fears and loneliness. After directing some six films—as well as working on Nicholas Ray's *On Dangerous Ground* (RKO, 1952)—Lupino left feature films for television, where she directed episodes for many TV series.

In the 1980s, there was a brief surge of women filmmakers. Amy Heckerling made the raucous *Fast Times at Ridgemont High* (Universal, Refugee Films, 1982), something of antidote to the sentimentality of *American Graffiti* (George Lucas, Universal, 1973), and a precursor to *Ferris Bueller's Day Off* (John Hughes, Paramount, 1986), all films that respond to the juvenile delinquent movies of the 1950s by showing high schoolers as irascible but ultimately lovable kids. The actress Penny Marshall directed the Tom Hanks vehicle, *Big* (Gracie Films, Fox, 1988), and, among others, another Tom Hanks film, *A League of Their Own* (Columbia, Parkway Productions, 1992). Julie Dash, an African American filmmaker, made *Daughters of the Dust* in 1991 for PBS (American Playhouse, Geechee Girls, WMG Film), a film of magical realism—combining "reality" and fantasy—that is also an anthropological study of the Gullah, the people of the islands off of South Carolina. Among the most celebrated women filmmakers of the 1980s was Susan Seidelman, who made five films in the 1980s, including *Desperately Seeking Susan* (Orion, 1985), written and produced by women—Leora Barish wrote the film; Sarah Pillsbury and Midge Sanford produced it.

DESPERATELY SEEKING SUSAN

Desperately Seeking Susan is essentially a mistaken identity film, though not of the usual kind that Hollywood is so fond of. In our lives, identity is a slippery thing—as we have seen in our discussion of Hitchcock's films of the 1950s in Chapter 16. All of us show various facets of our selves depending on the context in which we find ourselves. We tend to be slightly different people to the different people we know. On the screen, men often change or trade identities, sometimes because of amnesia, sometimes because of magic, sometimes because of a wager, as in John Landis's *Trading Places* (Cinema Group Ventures, Paramount, 1983). That film has a racial component, played for

Women victorious. Susana Arquette and Madonna in *Desperately Seeking Susan* (Susan Seidelman, 1985).

comedy, as Eddie Murphy's street person, Billy Ray Valentine, is turned into a rich man and winds up working with Dan Ackroyd's Louis Winthrope to thwart the owners of a brokerage firm. *Trading Places* is a slickly made film, with impeccable comic editing and a failure-proof narrative of a poor man getting rich and a rich man learning humility. In Penny Marshall's *Big*, a 12-year-old boy takes on the identity of an adult, with the amusing and sometimes embarrassing results of a child finding himself in a grownup body. *Desperately Seeking Susan* is not as slick as its companion big-budget identity shifters of the 1980s. It has the attributes of an independent production, lacking the gloss we expect from a studio product. What it strongly communicates is a feeling for the seedier parts of Manhattan that owes a lot to the early films of Martin Scorsese; a distinctive foregrounding of its female characters; and most important, an expression of desire that is markedly feminine.

Not merely sexual desire. In fact, hardly that, but rather a desire for adventure by women without men. While the initial cry, "desperately seeking Susan," is printed by a man in the personals column of the newspaper, it is Susan herself—played by the provocative pop star Madonna—and Roberta (Rosanna Arquette), whose activities are marked by curiosity, adventure, and a desire to see and do more than is usually assigned to feminine roles. Roberta, living in suburbia and married to a husband who sells swimming pools, is intrigued by the "desperately seeking Susan" classified ad. Susan herself is first seen happily escaping a one-night stand in Atlantic City, taking with her a pair of rare Egyptian earrings. Roberta's curiosity and Susan's nonchalant attitude collide when Roberta decides to answer the advertisement and find out who Susan and her desperately seeking friend actually are. Roberta gets knocked on the head and becomes, willingly and not, Susan. It is a magical, impossible transformation that the film admits by setting some of its sequences in a seedy magic club where Roberta/Susan allows a tacky magician to saw her in half.

Perhaps the point is that Roberta, before Susan, is less than half a woman and perhaps Susan without Roberta is too free, too irresponsible, too apt to get into serious trouble. Roberta needs Susan more than the other way around. As Susan, Roberta is freed up, sexually—she sleeps with Susan's friend Dez (Aidan Quinn)—and even her husband is briefly drawn into the mix-up when he finds the real Susan in the magic club. Susan and Roberta finally meet up at the club, where Roberta bashes the guy who has been pursuing them. Dez, a movie projectionist, gets Roberta—they literally stop the film with their embrace, falling on a running projector, causing the film to melt—and Jim (Robert Joy), who placed the original "desperately seeking" ad gets Susan. A perfect Hollywood ending. But most important, Susan and Roberta get each other. As the film suggests, they were two parts of the same person all along. One inhibited and one uninhibited woman find one another and reintegrate, while the men keep bumbling around.

All of this occurs with a great deal of good humor. There is a lightness to the film that allows its narrative to move from one ridiculous episode to the next without trying our patience or our credulity. *Desperately Seeking Susan* confronts in a direct way the complex notion of women as adventurous and curious, as more than equal to their men in their ability to freely enjoy the silliness of their lives.

The men of *Desperately Seeking Susan* are recessive and fairly passive. Even the creep (played by Will Patton) who stalks Susan and Roberta in search of the earrings turns out to be a bumbler, easily subdued by Roberta. But perhaps the strongest feminist mark on the film is the ways in which the male characters are considered as ordinary people, while the women, though not quite extraordinary, are the active agents. This rebalance is played quietly and persistently throughout the film. But it is such a rebalance of forces—of male and female gender roles—that American film cannot seem to support for long. Susan Seidelman went on to make other women-centered films, most interestingly *Making Mr. Right* (Orion, 1987), but found fewer opportunities by the end of the decade and turned to directing for television. There were other films during this period that attempted to raise their female characters above their usual passive roles, most notably *Thelma and Louise*, written by a woman, Callie Khouri, and directed by Ridley Scott (Pathé, MGM, 1991). The women of this film, played by Susan Sarandon and Geena Davis, are tough and unwilling to allow men to take advantage of them. Louise kills a man who attempted to rape Thelma, and they take to the road in what becomes a female version of the road movie with roots going so far back in film history. The film seemed threatening enough at the time that members of Congress denounced it!

THE MALE AS OBJECT OF THE GAZE

TOP GUN

As interesting and important as those films about active, courageous women, there are a larger number of films in which we can detect a backlash against the feminist movement. *Top Gun* (Paramount, 1986) is an instructive case in point. This is a Tom Cruise vehicle, directed by Tony Scott, who worked often with *Top Gun*'s producers, Don Simpson and Jerry Bruckheimer, on such films as *Days of Thunder* (Paramount, 1990), *Crimson Tide* (Hollywood Pictures, Buena Vista, 1995), and *Enemy of the State* (Touchstone, 1998). Scott went on to form his own production company with brother Ridley Scott and directed some intriguingly edited action films like *Domino* (New Line, 2005) and *Unstoppable* (Fox, 2011) until his death in 2012.

Top Gun is a male-dominated film about hotshot pilots with macho nicknames like "Maverick" (the Cruise character), "Viper," and "Merlin." A good part of the film is made up of aerial dog fights, culminating in a battle with Russian MIG jets (in 1986, the Cold War still raged, and the film imagines it heating up). When not in the sky, the pilots joke around with each other, attend training school, go to bars, and are observed dressed only in towels in their locker room.

The film is male centered and the gaze is markedly homosocial, a term that refers to men in intimate

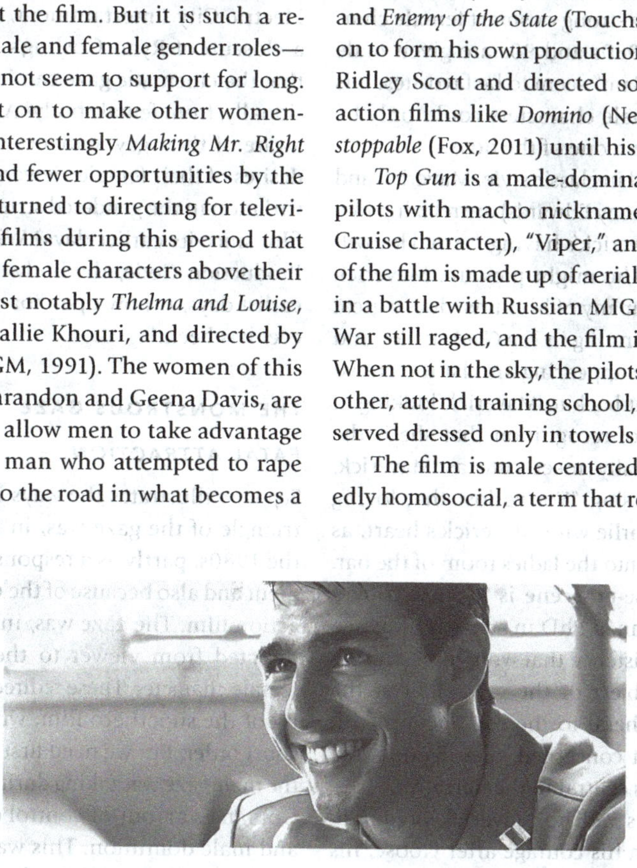

The male gaze (or smirk). Tom Cruise as "Maverick" in *Top Gun* (Tony Scott, 1986).

circumstances that preclude women and pretend to preclude homosexual contact as well. Homosocial bonding is a strong patriarchal imperative based on an assumption that the intimate and the sexual are mutually exclusive. The homosocial cements the patriarchal order, the domination of men, by constructing an all-male cohesive bond, woman not allowed.[3] The question then is where does Mulvey's theory of the male gaze enter a film in which the male body is the main focus of the audience's gaze? Can we speculate that a film like *Top Gun* allows the female to be the bearer of the look and the male its object? The problem is that too intense a concentration on the male and the homosocial group threatens to leak into the homoerotic, a place that *Top Gun* threatens to go until a woman enters Maverick's life, in the person of "Charlie" (Kelly McGinnis), a flight instructor. It is interesting that so many strong or smart female characters in films of the 1980s and 90s are given male names: "Sydney" and "Sam" seem to be favorites. It is as if recognition of female characters could only be achieved by making them one of the boys.

Charlie is introduced in classic style. Maverick and his buddy "Goose" (Anthony Edwards) are relaxing in a bar, making bets on Maverick's having "carnal knowledge" of some woman he might pick up. Maverick smirks (Cruise, as in so many of his films, does a great deal of smirking and grinning in *Top Gun*), looks, and there is a cut to Charlie appearing amidst the crowd at the bar. There is a cut back to Maverick looking at Charlie with the glint of recognition that she is the one for him. They finally meet cute as Maverick, Goose, and their crew sing "You've lost that loving feeling" to her, and Charlie wins Maverick's heart, as he bravely pursues her into the ladies room of the bar. The male-centered **mise-en-scène** is infiltrated by a woman—a smart woman, a PhD in astrophysics, in a nod to the feminist insistence that women be seen as more than only the object of the gaze—but at the same time she is peripheral to the male action with which the film is most concerned. She disrupts the gaze but never becomes central to the narrative.

She is peripheral as well to Maverick's redemption, his need to regain his courage after Goose, his copilot, dies. She tries to coax him not to be a quitter, using their intimacy by referring to his real name, Pete Mitchell. True to his machismo, Maverick has to regain his courage on his own, aided only by his superior officer, who reminds him of his father's heroism. Of course, he manages to overcome his doubts, shoots down MIGs in a dogfight, and after many manly hugs among his fellow pilots, returns to base and the arms of Charlie.

It is interesting to note that, as in *Top Gun*, the male body can indeed become the object of the camera's and the viewer's gaze. For example, the camera glides over John Travolta's all but naked body, lying in bed in *Saturday Night Fever* (John Badham, Robert Stigman Organization, Paramount, 1977)—a leisurely gaze at the male figure. Many superhero movies are entranced by the musculature of their male characters. The very first shot of *The Place Beyond the Pines* (Derek Cianfrance, Sidney Kimmel Entertainment, Electric City Entertainment, Verisimilitude, 2012) is a closeup of Ryan Gosling's bare torso. Can we say that the cinematic gaze can in fact shift, if only occasionally, from female body? Are filmmakers becoming aware of their gay audience or more sensitive to the desires of their female viewers? Or is this just a minor variation in the gendered structure that has buttressed film since its earlier days? With the relaxation of the Production Code, the body, cinema's focus since its earlist days, is now open for closer inspection than it ever has been.[4]

THE MONSTROUS GAZE

FATAL ATTRACTION

Top Gun illustrates the ways in which the traditional triangle of the gaze was, in fact, shifting slightly in the 1980s, partly as a response to the feminist movement and also because of the rise of the male-centered action film. The gaze was, in various films, being redirected from viewer to the male rather than the female character. These redirections led to the popularity of the superhero film, which we will examine in short order. But we need first to see another direction the male gaze was taking during the 1980s, a gaze at the woman as an out-of-control destroyer of domesticity and male dominion. This was certainly not new. We have seen the destructive female, the "femme fatale," thriving in film noir. Her revival during the 1980s

The monstrous female gaze. Glenn Close as Alex in *Fatal Attraction* (Adrian Lyne, 1987).

reflected a feminist backlash. One of the tenets of the feminist movement is that women have control over their bodies and their sexuality, and this was seen by some as a direct assault on patriarchal domination. A response to this can be detected in films like *Body Heat* (Lawrence Kasdan, The Ladd Company, Warner Bros., 1981) and a little later in *Basic Instinct* (Paul Verhoeven, Carolco Pictures, 1992). It is present in full horror mode in *Fatal Attraction* (Adrian Lyne, Paramount, 1987), a film in which the entire domestic order is threatened by a woman who is driven mad by being scorned by her lover.

The film is set up to make Alex (again a female character with a male name, played by Glenn Close) into a monster, and her onetime weekend lover, Dan (Michael Douglas), into an all but innocent victim of her growing, psychotic rage. She is such a monster that even though she claims that Dan has impregnated her, sympathy is drawn toward him and the family Alex threatens with assault, kidnapping, and boiling the family's pet rabbit. She becomes the monstrous female, an ancient figure of misogyny, and our gaze is riveted on her as she grows more menacing and violent, until we finally look at her staring back at us from beneath the water of a bathtub in which Dan has tried to drown her. Like a good modern movie monster, she refuses to die, rises from the tub, only to be shot dead by Dan's wife.

Film critic Linda Williams has argued that the woman and the monster both share the attributes of *difference*, that is, like the monster, women are subject not only to the erotic, but to the frightened gaze of the male character. "The horror film," Williams writes, "may be a rare example of a genre that permits the expression of women's sexual potency and desire and that associates this desire with the autonomous act of looking, but it does so . . . only to punish her for this very act, only to demonstrate how monstrous female desire can be."[5] *Fatal Attraction* marries the domestic melodrama with the horror film and creates a woman as scary as any movie monster. At the beginning, Dan can't keep his eyes or hands off of Alex. By the end, her gaze threatens not only disruption and chaos, but the destruction of the family itself. Sexual liberation, the film tries to convince us, means the liberation of jealous violence at the heart of women and the disintegration of the domestic unit.

STRONG MEN IN THE AGE OF REAGAN

RAIDERS OF THE LOST ARK

Despite the occasional foray into films about women, Hollywood remained focused on the male gaze directed at attractive women and the audience's gaze directed at the male body in action. There were any number of male buddy cop films—the Mel Gibson, Danny Glover vehicle, *Lethal Weapon* (Richard Donner, Warner Bros., Silver Pictures, 1987), is a good example—films that marginalized women and focused on male homosocial camaraderie in the face of danger. Together or alone, the male figure dominates and invites our admiring look. In a remarkable moment in Steven

Spielberg's *Raiders of the Lost Ark* (Paramount, Lucasfilm, 1981), Indiana Jones (Harrison Ford) is chasing Nazis throughout the Middle East, searching for the Ark of the Covenant and for Marion (Karen Allen), his tough female companion, who is caught in the middle of a throng of people. Indy is suddenly confronted with a giant Arab, dressed in black, with a red sash and huge sword. The Arab makes threatening swings of his sword toward our hero, who gives him a look both quizzical and disgusted, pulls his pistol, and shoots him dead.

In 1979, the new revolutionary government of Iran took 60 Americans hostage and held most of them for 444 days. The day that Ronald Reagan assumed the presidency from Jimmy Carter in January 1981, the Iranians let the hostages go. *Raiders* opened that June. Iranians, of course, are not Arabs; but in popular culture the Middle East is often imagined as an undifferentiated desert of radical Islamists out to harm Americans. The frustration that many Americans felt about the Iranian hostage crisis was immediately, imaginatively answered by Indy's shooting the giant Arab. It was a cathartic moment, and it heralded in the decade of Reagan, the tough-talking president who was both sentimental and no nonsense, a strong paternal figure that people of like political mind looked up to as a leader and guide.

And so did the movies. Tough guys and Reagan surrogates, like Indy shooting the Arab, appeared in various films in various guises. The superhero movie, which is an outgrowth of the male adventure film, became a staple by the end of the 1980s. Of course, there had been many tough guys in films before the 1980s, and comic book superheroes like Flash Gordon and Superman had appeared in afternoon serials in the 1930s and 40s. The first modern Superman film (Richard Donner, Warner Bros.) appeared in 1978, with Christopher Reeve playing the man of steel. As he developed through the 1980s and up to the present day, the superhero has taken on a number of forms. On one end of the scale is the obsessive tough guy, impervious to normal punishment that would fell an ordinary person. This character is often obsessed with a job that needs to be done and pursues it at all costs. On the other end is the genuine, comic book derived superhero, a man of extraordinary powers, a savior of the earth, who is often oppressed, either by an insuperable villain or by the very powers that make the superhero super. From Batman to Spider-Man to X-Men to Hancock to Iron Man to Captain America, and their many sequels, these figures have extraordinary powers that tend to overwhelm them.

RAMBO

We can start with the tough guy hero in one of his most popular and politically fraught manifestations, *Rambo: First Blood Part II* (George P. Cosmatos, Anabasis Investments, TriStar, 1985). The first Rambo, *First Blood* (Ted Kotcheff, Anabasis N. V., Orion, 1982), was a relatively constrained film about a restless Vietnam veteran, played by Sylvester Stallone, bullied and arrested by the town sheriff, and who goes on a rampage until he is reined in by his commander, Colonel Trautman (Richard Krenna). The sequel, the best known of the Rambo films, is involved with a thorny issue that marked the end of the Vietnam War in 1975. Many on the right, uneasy over the fact that the United States had lost a war, glommed on to the possibility that soldiers were left behind as Vietcong captives after American troops left the country. The MIA (Missing in Action) issue served to keep the cultural wound of Vietnam alive, and Rambo appeared as the imaginary figure that could single-handedly solve the problem. Embodied by a bulked-up Stallone, Rambo is a grown-up toy soldier figure, all muscle and all bent on single-minded action. Despite resistance from a government agent, and under the paternal eye of Colonel Trautman, Rambo fights the one-time enemy, the Vietnamese and their Russian leader—who bear a strong resemblance to the way Japanese and Germans were represented in World War II movies—and saves the captive soldiers.

There is an interesting nonaction sequence in the film that occurs between Trautman and the government bureaucrat who tries to stop Rambo's mission. The bureaucrat, Murdoch (Charles Napier), wants to keep the existence of MIAs from the public. Overseeing their confrontation is a photograph of Ronald Reagan, the antigovernment president. The editing of the sequence favors compositions in which the photograph and Trautman are together in the frame. The effect is

Sylvester Stallone, bulked up, taking on everyone with his bow and arrow in *Rambo, First Blood Part II* (George P. Cosmatos, 1985).

that Trautman channels Reagan as Rambo's paternal guide, and Rambo serves his country as the obedient soldier, doing its necessary dirty business, violently and selflessly. "Do we get to win this time?" is his operative question. As a result of his cinematic exploits, Rambo became an international cultural icon, so much so that he was ripe for parody.

DIE HARD

"Who are you, just another American who's seen too many movies . . . ? Do you think you are Rambo or John Wayne?"

The Bruce Willis film *Die Hard* (John McTiernan, Fox, 1988) creates a Rambo-like tough guy—a tough guy who is asked by the bad guys if he thinks he is Rambo or John Wayne—the New York cop John McClane, who single-handedly saves a group of people held hostage by foreign thieves in a Los Angeles office building. Barefoot and stripped almost naked in the course of his struggle, John travels through the airshafts of the half-finished building, walks on broken glass, dodges bullets and fists, and emerges bloodied but unscathed and, under the guidance of an African American cop (Reginald VelJohnson), achieves a reconciliation with his wife (Bonnie Bedelia). As yet another sign of the uneasy alliance of Hollywood and the women's movement, John comes to LA not to fight bad guys, but to attempt to get back together with his wife, who has assumed her maiden name and taken a corporate job. His exploits confirm his standing as a strong man, who can reclaim his wife's affections. But, interestingly, only through the mediation of a black man, and only after his wife proves her mettle by punching out an obnoxious TV newsman.

The attraction of *Die Hard* is that it does not take itself seriously. The characters refer to themselves as movie heroes. The action is so over the top that clearly no actual flesh and blood person could survive it. The film, like so many action films that follow it, is a particular, peculiar pleasure because of its self-conscious, self-parodying jokiness, and for the physical spectacle of bodies in violent motion. Like horror films, which give us permission to be scared while knowing we are just watching a movie, such action films allow us to be amazed at physical stamina, knowing it could only exist on the screen.[6]

THE SUPERHERO AND THE DIGITAL DOMAIN

The superhero movie is a different kind of spectacle. Many of them originate as comic book characters, smaller than life on the page, large than life on the screen. Superheroes create about them a sense of seeing double, of static figures coming to life from comic book into environments that are increasingly created by CGI. In other words, these characters exist first as drawings on paper and are then transferred to the screen largely by means of "drawings" created on the computer screen. The actors portraying the superhero play largely in front of **blue or green screens**, the mise-en-scène created after the fact, when computer effects are laid in later. More and more, **motion capture** is being used so that human movements can be captured by a computer and then used to create animated figures. This should not suggest that superhero movies are less "real" than any other film, but rather to urge you to think about the level of fantasy that such films aim for. Most movies aim for the "reality effect," creating characters and worlds that we can imagine are close to our own or close to our fantasies. The superhero world is a fantasy space, in reality no space at all, except as it has been created by digital means.[7]

The superhero exists in a rarified atmosphere of frustrating and frustrated wish fulfillment. Perhaps we all fantasize that some well-meaning hero can take on the problems of the world and single-handedly solve them, through violence if necessary. Even more, we fantasize—mostly through comics and movies—about ruthless villains, who may be more interesting in their villainy than the hero they plot against. Make the villain pure, malicious evil, and the superhero conflicted about himself and his role in society, and the perfect formula is created for a translation from comic book to movie screen and a dramatic tension that finally supersedes the artificial means of its creation.

BATMAN

"Formula" is the key for understanding the superhero film (as it is for understanding so much of American cinema). We can see it at work in the first of the current Batman films, Tim Burton's *Batman* (Warner Bros., The Guber-Peters Company, PolyGram, 1989). The character, created by Bob Kane and Bill Finger, first appeared in comic books in the late 1930s and was the subject of a television series—which was very much a parody of the superhero—in the late 1960s. Batman came to the movie screen with Burton's film. Burton was previously known for small, eccentric films like *Pee-Wee's Big Adventure* (Warner Bros., Aspen Film Society, 1985), based on Paul Ruben's television character of a child-like man, and *Beetlejuice* (Geffen Co., Warner Bros., 1988). That movie, starring Michael Keaton as an antic homunculus, who takes great joy in the tricks of the dead, shows Burton's affinity to a surrealist and **expressionist** mise-en-scène. It is a cartoonish film, and indeed Burton is an animator as well as a live-action filmmaker. It was perhaps for all of these reasons, plus the commercial success of *Beetlejuice*, that persuaded Warner Bros. to let a relatively untested filmmaker direct a $35,000,000 blockbuster. Burton brought with him Michael Keaton, who played Beetlejuice, to be Batman, and Warren Skaaren, one of *Beetlejuice*'s writers, as well as composer Danny Elfman to work on the film. The result grossed over $400 million worldwide and spawned sequel after sequel.

One of the little known talents behind Burton's *Batman* was **production designer** Anton Furst, who had previously worked with Stanley Kubrick on *Full Metal Jacket* (Warner Bros, Natant, 1987). The mise-en-scène of *Batman* is dark and grim. Gotham City is a studio-created, expressionist nightmare of concrete shapes no actual city could contain. Made before the advent of CGI, the mise-en-scène of this *Batman* film is handmade, using **matte** paintings and **rotoscoped** animation. Burton and Furst create a place of fantasy and violence, and its strangeness is the ideal setting for a man in a bat suit attempting to fight evil and corruption. Burton's Batman is oppressed by his past and his class. He's out to avenge his parents' death and bring order to disorderly urban wilderness. His conflicts range from the mundane—his love for Vicki Vale (Kim Bassinger)—to his battle with the Joker, played with psychotic goofiness by Jack Nicholson. There are, as always in superhero movies, plenty of gadgets, explosions, car wrecks, and the inevitable battle to the finish.

THE DARK KNIGHT AND *THE DARK KNIGHT RISES*

When Christopher Nolan took over the Batman franchise, especially with *The Dark Knight* (Warner Bros., Legendary Pictures, Syncopy, DC Comics, 2008), our hero becomes much more morose and, in the hands of Christian Bale, more baleful, even guilty. Heath Ledger's Joker is more crazy, intense, and scary than Nicholson's, and the CGI mise-en-scène is less detailed and gloomy than what Furst created for Burton's film. But nothing has detracted from the popularity of Batman movies. *The Dark Knight* and *The Dark Knight Rises* (Christopher Nolan, Warner Bros., Legendary Pictures, DC Entertainment, Syncopy, 2012) have each grossed around half a billion dollars. The combination of monstrous villainy and a conflicted hero, battling

The superhero as superpsychotic. Rainn Wilson as The Bolt in *Super* (James Gunn, 2010).

within a morally compromised world, intrigues us as an alternative reality, reflecting our own, but spectacular enough to raise our imagination out of it.

The gaze at the damaged superhero, the man who should be perfect but suffers over his own flaws and inadequacies, seems unbreakable. We seem to have—or our movies seem to indicate that we have—a desire to look at all manner of damaged, dangerous, more than human or, equally as enthralling, less than human characters flying, leaping, or lurching around the screen. In addition to superheroes, vampires, zombies, the dead, the undead, the immortal, all seem to satisfy our desire to see ourselves reflected in ways more or less than we actually are. Or, given their vulnerability, just as we are.

SUPER

The superhero is ripe for parody. In 2010, the television actor Rainn Wilson, who played Dwight Shrute on the television series *The Office*, starred in the independent production, *Super* (James Gunn, This is That Productions, Ambush Entertainment, Crimson Bolt, IFC). Watching television, Wilson's character, Frank, has a religious vision and decides to be a superhero named "The Crimson Bolt." He makes himself a ridiculous costume, finds a young female "sidekick" (played by Ellen Page), and tries to bring a comic book life to the world. It is a disaster. The Bolt whacks people on the street with a wrench and gets his sidekick killed by a gunshot to the face by the drug mob that is his target (and that has taken his wife). *Super* is a grim, painful, comic film about a deluded, near psychotic loser. It carries the genre to its illogical conclusion, that superheroes are projections of the powerless wishing for power in a world that seems to deny that wish continually. We cannot avert our eyes from them, while they seem intent on averting their eyes from themselves. We take comic book superheroes seriously until that seriousness is reflected in the mirror of its own absurdity—or until we are ready to enjoy the absurd on its own cinematic terms.

SELECTED FILMOGRAPHY

Outrage, dir. Ida Lupino, The Filmmakers, RKO, 1950.

The Hitch-Hiker, dir. Ida Lupino, The Filmmakers, RKO, 1950.

The Bigamist, dir. Ida Lupino, The Filmmakers, RKO, 1953.

On Dangerous Ground, dir. Nicholas Ray, RKO, 1952.

American Graffiti, dir. George Lucas, Universal, 1973.

Saturday Night Fever, dir. John Badham, Robert Stigman Organization, Paramount, 1977

Superman, dir. Richard Donner, Warner Bros., 1978.

Norma Rae, dir. Martin Ritt, Fox, 1979.

Body Heat, dir. Lawrence Kasdan, The Ladd Co., Paramount, 1981.

Raiders of the Lost Ark, dir. Steven Spielberg, Paramount, Lukasfilm, 1981.

Fast Times at Ridgemont High, dir. Amy Heckerling, Universal, Refugee Films, 1982.

Trading Places, dir. John Landis, Cinema Group Ventures, Paramount, 1983.

Silkwood, dir. Mike Nichols, ABC Motion Pictures, Fox, 1983.

Desperately Seeking Susan, dir. Susan Seidelman, Orion, 1985.

Rambo: First Blood Part II, dir. George P. Cosmatos, Anabasis Investments, TriStar, 1985.

Ferris Bueller's Day Off, dir. John Hughes, Paramount, 1986.

Top Gun, dir. Tony Scott, Paramount, 1986.

Making Mr. Right, dir. Susan Seidelman, Orion, 1987.

Fatal Attraction, dir. Adrian Lyne, Paramount, 1987.

Beetlejuice, dir. Tim Burton, Geffen Co., Warner Bros., 1988.

Big, dir. Penny Marshall, Gracie Films, Fox, 1988.

Die Hard, dir. John McTiernan, Warner Bros., 1988.

Batman, dir. Tim Burton., Warner Bros., 1989.

Daughters of the Dust, dir. Julie Dash, American Playhouse, Geechee Girls, WMG Film, 1991.

Thelma and Louise, dir. Ridley Scott, Pathé, MGM, 1991.

A League of Their Own, dir. Penny Marshall, Columbia, Parkway Productions, 1992.

Basic Instinct, dir. Paul Verhoeven, Carolco Pictures, 1992.

The Dark Knight, dir. Christopher Nolan, Warner Bros., Legendary Pictures, 2008.

The Dark Knight Rises, dir. Christopher Nolan, Warner Bros., Legendary Pictures, 2012.

Super, dir. James Gunn, This is That Productions, Ambush Entertainment, Crimson Bolt, IFC, 2010.

SUGGESTIONS FOR FURTHER READING

Marcelline Block, ed., *Situating the Feminist Gaze and Spectatorship in Postwar Cinema* (Newcastle upon Tyne, UK: Cambridge Scholars, 2008).

Susan Jeffords, *Hard Bodies: Hollywood Masculinity in the Reagan Era* (New Brunswick, NJ: Rutgers University Press, 1994).

Laura Mulvey, "Visual Pleasure and the Narrative Cinema," in *Visual and Other Pleasures*, 2nd ed. (London, UK: Palgrave McMillan, 2009), 14–30.

Michael Rogin, *Ronald Reagan, the Movie* (Berkeley, CA: University of California Press, 1987).

Sue Thornham, *Feminist Film Theory: A Reader* (Edinburgh, UK: Edinburgh University Press, 1999).

Robin Wood, *Hollywood from Vietnam to Reagan—and Beyond* (New York, NY: Columbia University Press, 2003).

NOTES

1. Laura Mulvey, *Visual and Other Pleasures* (London, UK: Palgrave McMillan, 2009), 19.
2. See Lucy Fisher, "The Image of Women: The Optical Politics of Dames," *Film Quarterly*, vol. 30, no. 1 (Fall, 1976), 2–11.
3. A standard work on the homosocial is Eve Kosofsky Sedgwick, *Among Men: English Literature and Male Homosocial Desire* (New York, NY: Columbia University Press, 1985).
4. Justin Hall pointed out this trend toward the gaze at the male body.
5. Linda Williams, "When the Woman Looks," in Barry Keith Grant, ed., *Gender and the Horror Film* (Austin, TX: University of Texas Press, 1996), 32–33.
6. A full analysis of *Rambo* and *Die Hard* can be found in Robert Kolker, *A Cinema of Loneliness*, 4th ed. (New York, NY: Oxford University Press, 2011).
7. See Barthes, Roland. "The Reality Effect," *The Rustle of Language*, trans. Richard Howard. (Oxford, UK: Blackwell, 1986), 141–148.

CHAPTER 21

NEW TECHNOLOGIES (1950–PRESENT)

The modern superhero film is created in large part by digital special effects that began to be used in the late 1980s. Other technological changes also occurred during this time, not only in film production, but in reception as well—in the form of videotape and the DVD. This chapter traces the major technological shifts in filmmaking and film viewing over the past few decades.

AFTER READING THIS CHAPTER, YOU SHOULD UNDERSTAND:

- The history of home movie recording and playback devices.
- The effect on screen size of home video.
- Special effects.
- The history of CGI.
- The concept of "the reality effect."

YOU SHOULD BE ABLE TO:

- Consider the difference between seeing a movie at home or on a computer and seeing it in a theater.
- Understand the differences between CGI and earlier means of creating special effects.
- Try and determine where CGI is being used in a non–special effects film.
- Discuss how the digital revolution changes the ways in which films are made and received.

VIDEOTAPE, DVD, AND SCREEN SIZE

The 1980s were marked less by great movies than by technical changes in the availability of film that had long-lasting effects on filmmaking and film viewing. First came the videotape recorder. Introduced in 1975, this was an analog technology. That is, signals were recorded as magnetic waves on tape, analogous to the light waves that originated them. With each re-recording, the signal was degraded a little more. The image produced by videotape was poor to begin with and became worse over time or if the tape was copied.

This was one part of the problem. The technicians who oversaw the transfer of movies to tape decided that widescreen formats would provide an image for a small television screen that was too horizontally narrow, giving the appearance that the top and bottom of the image were cut off. This requires some history and explanation. When film adopted a **sound track** along the side of the **image track,** the size of the image was standardized at 1:1.133 or 4×3, that is, four units in height to three units in width. When the studios tried to counter television in the early 1950s they widened the width of the screen, hoping that a big screen would lure viewers away from the small screen of the TV. The result was a variety of widescreen formats: the huge screen of Cinerama, the 1:2.35 **anamorphic** image of **CinemaScope** and **Panavision,** and **"flat" widescreen** in which the image was cropped top and bottom, rendering a screen size of 1:1.66 or 1:1.88. By the mid-1950s, all films were made in one form of widescreen or another. But on videotape, the sides of the image were lopped off and magnified into a square format. In order to show the visual information on the lopped-off sides, the image was **panned and scanned,** resulting in odd movements across the frame. The result was that, as directors were beginning to understand and use the compositional properties of widescreen, the television audience was treated to parts of the image chosen by a technician in an optical lab.

Just as there were competing technologies during the coming of sound to film, there were competing videotape technologies. Sony developed a format called Betamax, which had a decent image quality but limited recording time. Another Japanese company, JVC, developed VHS "Video Home System," which had inferior image quality but could record up to 6 hours of programming. VHS won and became the standard. Sony also lost a lawsuit in which they claimed that videotaping programs violated copyright. The copyright issue would become prominent during the digital age, when copying media files became easy and the battle between those who owned content and those who believed it should be readily and freely available became quite fierce.

Despite degraded image quality and a panned and scanned frame, videotape had the important advantage of making movies portable. This caused an important change in viewing culture: people could buy or rent a movie and watch it at home at their convenience. The studios could rerelease films and market "director's cuts" of films, presumably restoring the movie to the original intent of its director after the theatrical release that reflected the cut of its producers. An archive of old films was created as well. A history of film was now available to consumers. This amounted to a new array of viewing possibilities and a new kind of control over viewing content. The viewer now had choices, not only about what to see, but when and how to see it. The studios had new powers: they could get more revenue from their films through video purchases and rental as well as from releasing their archival material on video.

New delivery media evolved quickly through the 1980s and 1990s. There was an intermediate format developed in the late 1970s called laserdisc, the size of a 12 inch long playing record. While still analog in its recording method, it allowed for chapter sequencing of a film and better image quality than VHS but no recording possibilities. Laserdiscs never went beyond a large niche market and were quickly succeeded by the DVD, introduced in the mid-1990s. Although a user couldn't record on them—at least not when they were first introduced—DVDs offered superior image quality because they were digital rather than analog. The image was sampled and translated as numerical zeros and ones, burned as pits into the DVD media, resulting, when played back, as a clean and well-resolved image that did not degrade when copied.

By the early 2000s, television sets began to evolve due to digital technologies. The cathode ray tube was replaced by flat LED (light-emitting diode), LCD (liquid crystal display), or plasma screens that produced a high-definition image—upping resolution to 1,080 lines of image information a second from the standard 480 lines. DVDs looked better on flat screens, and in the early 2000s, DVDs themselves began to be replaced by high-definition media. There was, again, a competition between formats, one called HD, backed by the Japanese electronics company, Toshiba; the other, Blu-ray, backed by Sony. After some back and forth, the movie studios backed the Blu-ray format, which is now the standard high-definition delivery method on disc. At the time of this writing, 3D technologies—which are a revival of a gimmick that Hollywood used to draw viewers away from television in the early 1950s—have made something of a comeback in both theatrical and home viewing. As in the 1950s, 3D requires glasses to view it—and a steep rise in the cost of tickets—and will probably have a brief existence as a novelty.

What we can understand from this brief history of delivery technologies is that movies seen at home have grown closer and closer to the experience of movies seen in a theater. Just as, beginning in the 1970s, the screens of movie theaters grew smaller with the advent of the mall multiplex, the screens at home began to grow larger and to present finer, higher definition resolution. This has affected movie attendance to a degree, but not as severely as might be imagined. Many people continue to enjoy the communal experience of the movie theater. The studios still depend on the initial income and the status of their product from its theatrical run—usually gauging the success or failure of a film on how much it makes during its first weekend in release.

SOUND

Along with the changes in screen size and the availability of home viewing came changes in sound reproduction. Two-channel stereophonic sound first came to music recordings on phonograph records in the late 1950s and to FM radio broadcasting in the 1960s. Film lagged slightly behind. Four-track **magnetic sound tracks** (as opposed to **optical tracks**) were available on prints of 20th Century Fox's CinemaScope biblical epic *The Robe* (Henry Koster, 1953) and six tracks of sound were available on the 70 mm prints of *Around the World in Eighty Days* (Michael Anderson, Michael Todd Co., Fox, 1956). The breakthrough occurred in 1977 with the first *Star Wars* film (George Lucas, Lucasfilm, Fox). Lucas used the Dolby Noise Reduction system—invented in the late 1960s by a man named Ray Dolby—that allowed for cleaner, noise-free sound reproduction. In the late 1970s, Kodak, RCA, and Dolby developed a method of putting a two-channel optical track on film, and slowly across the 1980s, filmmakers and film distributors adopted stereo sound.

Other sound systems were developed in the early 1990s that allowed for up to seven channels of sound that surrounded the auditorium (or the viewing room of a home theater system) with a sonic field. **Foley** recording, a process for capturing footsteps and other special sound effects, and **ADR**, or automated dialogue replacement (otherwise known as dubbing voices in postproduction), allows for the detailed creation of the sound design of a film. Listen closely to almost any contemporary film, and you will hear not only dialogue or music, but **ambient sound** carefully fashioned to create an aural as well as visual experience of the film.[1]

CGI

The technologies outlined above directly involve the way we as viewers view and hear film, particularly regarding where and how we view them. Another technology that began to be developed in the 1980s involved the way film was made, and it created a revolution in the means of production. Computer-generated imagery **(CGI)** started slowly. Stanley Kubrick used some computer graphics in *2001: A Space Odyssey* (and computer screens play a major role in the film's **mise-en-scène**), but in this film about computers and space travel made in the middle of the 1960s, most of the effects are made by old forms of model making and **optical printing**. During the 1980s, CGI began slowly and then in the 1990s rapidly took the place of conventional special effects and **process shots** in general. By the 2000s, some films (and not just animations) were made almost entirely in the computer.

To understand this, we need to go back in film history and note the fact that from its earliest days, filmmakers used special effects. Recall that *Uncle Josh at the Moving Picture Show* (Edwin S. Porter, 1902) and *The Great Train Robbery* (Edwin S. Porter, 1903) employed some kind of **matte** shots by means of which various elements of the shot were not made at the same time, but had parts of the shot matted in by means of an optical printer. Look back at the railway car sequence in *The Great Train Robbery* and notice how the scenery passing by the window looks a little out of place with the rest of the set. Most likely, the car and the action in it were filmed at one time with the window blacked (or blued or greened) out. Then, the unexposed film was placed in an optical printer (basically a camera and a projector) and the images of passing scenery were projected onto the unexposed film. With the two images perfectly matched, the developed film shows the railway car and the scenery going by out the window.

Various versions of these techniques have been used ever since to marry various elements of a shot together that would have been more expensive had they been done at one time. Of course, there were films that leaned heavily on special effects—*King Kong* (Merian C. Cooper, Ernest B. Schoedsack, RKO, 1933), for example. Even earlier, in Germany, Fritz Lang's science fiction film, *Metropolis* (1927), made full use of special effects to represent a city of the future, complete with a mad scientist who fabricates a robot before our eyes. These and other films made use of animation, matte shots, and **rear screen projection**—a technique most commonly used when the characters are in a car with the scenery going past behind them. Rear screen was also used when characters are seen walking on the street, on a treadmill, the background projected behind them—an indication of the studio's desire to keep all aspects of the production within their confines. CGI has taken the place of these techniques so that now all special effects, visible or not, are done by computer.

In the 1980s, CGI began appearing, appropriately, in science fiction. George Lucas's special effects company, Industrial Light and Magic (ILM), created a few minutes of computer-generated imagery for *Star Trek II: The Wrath of Khan* (Nicholas Meyer, Paramount, 1982). More extensive CGI was used for Disney's *Tron* (Steve Lisberger, Walt Disney Productions,1982). Since the action of this film takes place inside a computer, the effects were appropriately luminous in their representation of humans riding the circuitry of a machine. *Young Sherlock Holmes* (Barry Levinson, Amblin Entertainment, Paramount, 1985) was the first film in which a computer-animated figure—a knight who steps out of a stained glass window—interacted with human characters. ILM created the effect.

Computer-animated features grew apace in the 1980s, when Pixar, headed by computer graphics pioneer John Lasseter, was bought by Apple from George Lucas. Pixar made a number of computer-animated shorts in the 1980s, culminating in its feature film *Toy Story* in 1995. In 2006, the Disney Company bought Pixar, having already distributed its films, thereby joining a traditional animation company, which began making cartoons drawn by hand in the 1920s, with a new company that used computers to create limber, photorealistic characters and settings. Traditional animation was a painstaking process of painting characters and backgrounds on celluloid cells, each one advancing the movement of the characters a tiny bit. Computer animation is a no less painstaking process in which characters and movement are built up from wire frames to fully dressed and shaded figures, placed and moving in three-dimensional backgrounds.

The ultimate success of CGI came with the integration of computer-generated figures with live action. Computer graphics could now be used to replace traditional **process photography** and special effects. 1989 was the year in which both events were accomplished by Industrial Light and Magic. For *Indiana Jones and the Last Crusade* (Steven Spielberg, Paramount, Lucasfilm), ILM developed a means to scan the photographed image into a computer and then scan the manipulated image back onto film. James Cameron's *The Abyss* (Fox, Pacific Western, Lightstorm Entertainment,1989), essentially an underwater version of Spielberg's *E.T.*, featured a water creature that was entirely computer generated and integrated with the film's live action.

By the mid-1990s, CGI became ubiquitous, not only in movies that foregrounded special effects, but in any film where elements of a shot were added incrementally rather than being shot at the same time. By the 2000s, "live-action" figures, in films like *Avatar* (James Cameron, Fox, Dune Entertainment, Ingenious Film Partners, 2009), *Rise of the Planet of the Apes* (Rupert Wyatt, Fox, Dune Entertainment, Chernin Entertainment, 2011), and *Life of Pi* (Ang Lee, Fox 2000 Pictures, Dune Entertainment, Ingenious Media, 2012), were created by capturing and digitizing the motion of actual actors and then animating that motion in the computer, a modern version of **rotoscoping**, by means of which images of people in motion were painted over to appear as animations. In the case of *Life of Pi*, the tiger that is a prominent figure in the film is a digital creation. In addition, by the 2000s, more and more movies were being "filmed" with digital cameras, and all films, no matter what format they originate in, now go through a digital stage called the **digital intermediate**, where all the elements of the shot are put together and the color of the film is manipulated and the editing completed. In fact, cinematographers are asked to shoot "down the middle," without complicated lighting

Digital reality. Richard Parker, the tiger in Ang Lee's *Life of Pi* (2012), is a CGI creation made by the digital effects company Rhythm and Hues.

or color effects, because these can be added during the digitized phase, before the completed work is transferred back to film or to a digital format that is increasingly used to project a movie in a mall theater.[2]

THE "REALITY EFFECT"

All of this means that the culture of making and viewing a film has changed greatly since the beginnings of CGI in the 1980s. Some scholars have mourned the passing of celluloid-based cinema and the loss of a certain "reality effect" gained by photographing onto celluloid the world as it exists. The French critic André Bazin, writing in the 1950s, said the most valuable aspect of realist cinema is obtained when a director remains true to the temporal and spatial elements of the world before the camera. But even Bazin understood that "realism" is gained by formal manipulation. And even he would have to acknowledge that film from its beginnings relied on effects that were created by scenic painting and models that were married to the "live" action of the actors. Is the "reality effect" qualitatively different with digitally rendered effects? Certainly there is a perceptual difference that occurs when we watch the 3D digitally rendered characters in *Avatar*, and this difference makes the film closer to a cartoon than a live action drama. The collapsing and expanding worlds of *Inception* (Christopher Nolan, Warner Bros., Legendary Pictures, Syncopy, 2010) are presented as dreamscapes, interior fantasies, but in all such cases, these digital effects films are different only in the degree of detail when compared to the fantasy worlds created by film since the days of Georges Méliès.[3] As if to prove the point, Martin Scorsese made *Hugo* (Paramount, GK Films, Infinitum Nihil, 2011), a 3D, digital effects film about the world of Méliès. Scorsese's film celebrates the ability of film to create imaginary worlds, by whatever the technological means.

"Realism" is, after all, a relative term, and our response to cinematic realism shifts with the changes in film technologies and the ways in which we perceive and accept screen reality. The special effects of a 1950s science fiction film might look crude compared to a digitally engineered film made today. But the effects of the 1955 *The War of the Worlds* (Byron Haskin, Paramount) were as convincing—and remain quite remarkable—as those of Steven Spielberg's 2005 remake (Paramount, DreamWorks, Amblin Entertainment). However, something as simple as a rear screen projection, where the cutout of a car is placed in front of a screen on which is projected the passing landscape, looks blatantly fake to us today. We are used to seeing the image created when a camera is actually placed on the moving vehicle as the actors drive through traffic, delivering their lines.

Rear screen process shots have been replaced almost entirely by **blue or green screen** process shots, themselves an old technology, but now the backgrounds provided are digitally rendered. Unless we are looking at a special effects or superhero film, we take what we see as "real," just as an audience in previous decades took as real the rear screen projection of the road going by. In truth, we are able to adjust our expectations of what makes up movie realism, and these change as the technology changes. We base our expectations sometimes on the genre of the film, and we suspend disbelief in line with the desire to see effects that appear "real" in the context of those expectations. Watching *Inception*, we accept the "reality" of the dreamscapes that surround the characters. City streets rise up and fold around them. We marvel at the detail; we know that within the narrative of the film they are meant to be dreams; and we sit amazed at their presence, even as we acknowledge the technical achievement of their creation.

Yet our amazement at wide-screen, CGI spectacle may now be diminished when the image is transferred to the tiny screen of the smartphone or the slightly larger screen of a computer monitor or tablet. In the 1950s, screens grew to enormous sizes. In the 2000s, they have shrunk to the palm of one's hand. From the very beginning of film, we, as viewers, have been incredibly adaptable, embracing the cinematic image despite its size; eager to look, but now eager for the portability of the image. We are pleased to be amazed wherever we are.

SELECTED FILMOGRAPHY

The Robe, dir. Henry Koster, 20th Century Fox, 1953.

The War of the Worlds, dir. Byron Haskin, Paramount 1955.

Around the World in Eighty Days, dir. Michael Anderson, Michael Todd Co., Fox, 1956.

Star Trek: The Wrath of Khan, dir. Nicholas Meyer, Paramount 1982.

Tron, dir. Steve Lisberger, Walt Disney Productions, 1982.

Young Sherlock Holmes, dir. Barry Levinson, Amblin Entertainment, Paramount, 1985.

Indiana Jones and the Last Crusade, dir. Steven Spielberg, Lukasfilm, Paramount,1989.

The Abyss, dir. James Cameron, Fox, Pacific Western, Lightstorm Entertainment,1989.

Toy Story, dir. John Lasseter, Pixar Animation Studios, Walt Disney Pictures, 1995.

The War of the Worlds, dir. Steven Spielberg, Paramount, DreamWorks, Amblin Entertainment, 2005.

Avatar, dir. James Cameron, Fox, Dune Entertainment, Ingenious Film Partners, Lightstorm Entertainment, 2009.

Inception, dir. Christopher Nolan, Warner Bros., Legendary Pictures, Syncopy, 2010.

Rise of the Planet of the Apes, dir. Rupert Wyatt, Fox, Dune Entertainment, 2011.

Life of Pi, dir. Ang Lee, Fox 2000 Pictures, Dune Entertainment, Ingenious Media, 2012.

SUGGESTIONS FOR FURTHER READING

Rick Altman, ed. *Sound Theory, Sound Practice* (New York, NY: Routledge), 1992).

David A. Cook, *Lost Illusions: American Cinema in the Shadow of Watergate and Vietnam, 1970–1979, A History of the American Cinema*, vol. 9 (Berkeley, CA: University of California Press, 2000).

Lev Manovich, *The Language of New Media* (Cambridge, MA: MIT Press, 2001).

Stephen Prince, *A New Pot of Gold: Hollywood under the Electronic Rainbow, 1980–1989, History of the American Cinema*, vol. 10 (Berkeley, CA: University of California Press, 2000).

David Rodowick, *The Virtual Life of Film* (Cambridge, MA: Harvard University Press, 2007).

NOTES

1. Material for the discussion of sound in contemporary film is from David A. Cook, *Lost Illusions: American Cinema in the Shadow of Watergate and Vietnam, 1970–1979, A History of the American Cinema*, vol. 9 (Berkeley, CA: University of California Press, 2000), 386–393.
2. A timeline of CGI can be found at http://design.osu.edu/carlson/history/timeline.html
3. André Bazin's thoughts about realism in film can be found throughout the two volumes of *What Is Cinema?*, trans. Hugh Gray (Berkeley, CA: University of California Press, 1968, 1972). Roland Barthes's essay "The Reality Effect" is in *The Rustle of Language*, trans. Richard Howard (Oxford, UK: Blackwell, 1986), 141–148. A critical study of the digitalization of film can be found in David Rodowick, *The Virtual Life of Film* (Cambridge, MA: Harvard University Press, 2007).

CHAPTER 22

RISE OF THE MODERN DOCUMENTARY (1920–2014)

The documentary is as old as film itself and has gone through many changes in form and popularity. With the success of Michael Moore's *Fahrenheit 9/11* in 2004, documentary filmmaking gained a new lease on commercial viability. This chapter provides some historical background on documentaries and focuses on its modern incarnation, especially on those films whose subject is the Iraq and Afghanistan wars. Discussion of documentaries about conflict in the Middle East is contrasted with fiction films on the subject.

AFTER READING THIS CHAPTER, YOU SHOULD UNDERSTAND:

- What exactly constitutes documentary filmmaking and how it differs from fiction film.
- How documentary developed from the earliest period to the present.
- The increasing presence of the Maysles Brothers in their own documentaries.
- How *Gimme Shelter* accidentally reveals a crime.
- Advocacy filmmaking.
- How Errol Morris's documentaries differ from Michael Moore's.

YOU SHOULD BE ABLE TO:

- Focus on politically progressive documentaries and question why there are more of these than more conservative films.
- Define cinéma vérité.
- Understand how Michael Moore uses irony and sarcasm to make his political points.
- Look at a cross section of Iraq and Afghanistan war documentaries to find common threads.
- Discuss whether there is such a thing as an objective perspective where the presence of the filmmaker does not influence what he or she is filming.

THE EARLY DOCUMENTARY

From one perspective, all film is documentary film. Movies document feelings and ideas; they show us visions of how to live and die; they fabricate realistic, almost tactile worlds. Of course "fabricate" is the difference—or supposed difference—between fiction film and documentaries. Documentaries are meant to be records of actual events, recording the world as it is, capturing life as it happens as opposed to as it is staged. Film has been doing this since its beginnings. The earliest films from the Edison Company and from the Lumière brothers showed people and things in the world, in action, recorded as they occurred. *The Arrival of a Train at the Ciotat Station* (Lumière, 1895) was a signal event in early film, when the camera stood firmly on a station platform recording an incoming train. Even staged events like Edison's *The Kiss* (William Heise, 1896) documented the erotic potential of early film. Prize fights, real and staged, fire engines racing through the streets, films about exotic peoples, all made up subjects for the voracious eye of the new movie camera and its equally voracious audience.

THE MAN WITH THE MOVIE CAMERA, NANOOK OF THE NORTH, THE PLOW THAT BROKE THE PLAINS

We can imagine that, with its gluttony for images, early cinema was documenting its own novelty, which it shared with its audience, who reacted with delight at these recorded views of the world. Rather quickly, images of fictional stories and images of the world "as it is" became differentiated. The documentary film with which we are most familiar emerged in the 1920s in a variety of forms. Abroad, the revolutionary Russian filmmaker Dziga Vertov documented the daily life of the Soviet Union and in *The Man with the Movie Camera* (1929) recapitulated the fascination that the human eye has for images of the world at large. In the United States, Robert Flaherty made *Nanook of the North* (Les Frères Revillon, Pathé, 1922), a famous accounting of the lives of Inuit Eskimos, which is enlivened by staged sequences that nonetheless maintain a sense of life ongoing in front of the camera. During the 1930s, the US government funded a series of documentaries about life in the United States, including Pare Lorentz's poetic evocation of the Depression-era Dust Bowl, *The Plow That Broke the Plains* (Resettlement Administration, 1936). In addition to the government, the Workers Film and Photo League, a collective of progressive filmmakers, produced a number of documentaries, on the labor movement, for example, that were to the left of the social and political ideals of Franklin Delano Roosevelt's New Deal. As we noted in Chapter 12, the government once again took part in documentary film production under the direction of Frank Capra in the *Know Your Enemy* and *Why We Fight* series made during World War II.

Dziga Vertov's cameras absorb and are absorbed by the people in this early Soviet documentary, *The Man with the Movie Camera* (1929).

Images of the Dust Bowl. Pare Lorentz's *The Plow That Broke the Plains* (1936).

THE MAYSLES BROTHERS

CINÉMA VÉRITÉ AND *SALESMAN*

Documentary film went through a major transformation in the 1960s under the direction of such filmmakers as D. A. Pennebaker, Richard Leacock, and the brothers David and Albert Maysles, influenced by a movement in French film called **cinéma vérité**. Gone was the voice-over narrator of previous documentaries and, in its place, these new filmmakers allowed events to speak and act for themselves. The Maysles brothers's *Salesman* (Maysles Films, 1968) follows four Bible salesmen on their rounds in different parts of the country. The film gives the impression of a seamless narrative in which the four men talk to each other, visit prospective customers, all the while implying the sad aimlessness of their lives. That seamlessness is, of course, the result of careful editing and a sense of progression that could only be the result of an arrangement of the various sequences recorded by the Maysles, despite their attempts to erase their presence from the film. In other words, the *vérité* of *Salesman* is the result of careful editing. As in a fiction film, footage is manipulated in ways that create the illusion of seamlessness.

GIMME SHELTER AND *GREY GARDENS*

The "erasure" of the Maysles' presence did not last long. During the shooting of their documentary of the Rolling Stones' concert at Altamont, California, *Gimme Shelter* (Maysles Films, 1970), an audience member was stabbed to death by one of the Hell's Angels the Stones hired to keep order. At a crucial moment in the film, we see Mick Jagger and the Maysles brothers at an editing table, watching the footage of the melee. Jagger asks them to roll back on one portion of the footage; they slow it down, stop the action, and on the screen we see along with them a man pulling a gun and getting stabbed. The film documents itself making a documentary. By 1975, in their film *Grey Gardens* (Portrait Films), the brothers move directly into the action. The subjects of the film, a mother and daughter, relatives of Jacqueline Kennedy, who live in squalor in a fancy section of Long Island, talk to the Maysles directly, and from time to time, we see the filmmakers, at one point reflected in a mirror, filming the couple. The documentarist has become not a recorder of reality, but someone who changes reality by his or her presence. Some would argue that this is always

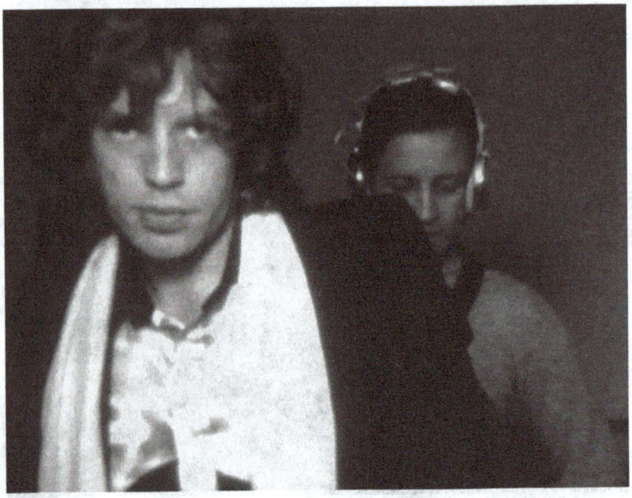

Mick Jagger and David Maysles in the grainy freeze frame that ends *Gimme Shelter* (David and Albert Maysles and Charlotte Zwerin, 1970) in which a member of the audience was killed.

the case, that whenever a camera is present, reality is transformed.

MICHAEL MOORE AND THE POLITICAL DOCUMENTARY

FAHRENHEIT 9/11

When the subject of the documentary is political, the presence of the filmmaker is very strong indeed, because this documentary form requires a strong point of view. The rebirth of the documentary in the early 21st century was deeply political, as filmmakers tried to come to terms with the war in Iraq and the problems of the George W. Bush Administration. A prime mover in the new political documentary is Michael Moore, whose *Fahrenheit 9/11* (Dog Eat Dog Films, Lionsgate, IFC, 2004) was the most commercially successful documentary ever made. Moore makes no pretense toward documentary objectivity or the illusions of ongoing reality advocated by cinéma vérité. Moore is at the center of his films, creating the persona of an ordinary guy in a baseball cap, amiably angry at the established order, working like a bulldog to corner individuals he thinks responsible for society's wrongs and making them respond or run away. Moore started with *Roger and Me* (Dog Eat Dog Films, Warner Bros., 1989), in which he pursues the then head of General Motors (GM), Roger Smith, to confront him with the decay of Moore's hometown of Flint, Michigan, which resulted from the closing of the town's GM plant.

Corporate and governmental irresponsibility are the main targets of Moore's work. His ability to find the most banal and absurd examples of terrible and stupid things is his great talent. At the beginning of *Bowling for Columbine* (Alliance Atlantis, Dog Eat Dog Productions, United Artists, 2002), his film about guns and the catastrophe of the 1999 Columbine high school shootings, he discovers a bank that gives away rifles when a new account is opened. He himself opens an account, gets his rifle, aims it in the bank office and asks, so innocently and knowingly, "Don't you think it's a little dangerous handing out guns in a bank?"

He finds not only ironies, but connections as well, deep connections between government and business, politics and profit, situations in which the poor lose and the rich gain. *Fahrenheit 9/11* takes as its opening premise that the first election of George W. Bush—an election that was determined by the Supreme Court—was fraudulent and that the early part of Bush's business and political career was tied to the

Michael Moore (right) attempts to convince a congressman to enlist his son in the Iraq war, *Fahrenheit 9/11* (2004).

Saudi Arabians and the Bin Laden family. (It was Osama Bin Laden who masterminded the 9/11 attacks.) This is not mere conspiracy theorizing. Moore pulls together documents, TV news footage, newspaper headlines, and interviews. He will even jokingly manipulate footage, as when he puts the heads of Bush's cabinet on the bodies of the characters of the television show *Bonanza*. Moore trades in absurdities—not his but the Bush government's reaction to 9/11. From spying on its own people to attacking a country, Iraq, that had nothing to do with 9/11, Moore discovers and gleefully expands upon the government's mistakes, misdeeds, and malfeasance. The Iraq war footage in *Fahrenheit 9/11* is particularly gruesome, and Moore takes full advantage of the horrors of war and the insensitivity of the government when he cuts between the wounded and the grieving to then Secretary of Defense Donald Rumsfeld, who is talking about the "humanity" that guides fighting the war. Amidst all this, Moore fearlessly pursues members of Congress on the street to convince them to enlist their own sons in the fight in Iraq.

THE CONTEMPORARY WAR DOCUMENTARY *RESTREPO*

Without doubt, *Fahrenheit 9/11* piles it on. It is unrelenting in its condemnation of Bush and the war. It is pitiless in its exposure of the suffering of the troops. It is advocacy filmmaking, satirical filmmaking, even, at times, sentimental filmmaking. But perhaps above all, it is angry filmmaking, and it caught the anger of a large part of the culture at the time. It opened the door to a resurgence of the documentary film, and a number of those new documentaries concerned the wars in Iraq and Afghanistan. Unlike Vietnam War films, fiction films about the Iraq war did not fare well commercially. Only Kathryn Bigelow's *The Hurt Locker* (Voltage Pictures, Grosvenor Park Media, Film Capital Europe Funds, 2008) made a mark with critics and filmgoers. It is somewhat ironic that one of the strongest fiction films about the war, a conventionally male enterprise, was made by a woman, but perhaps only a woman could enter a masculine world with a perception of its weaknesses. This story of an explosives specialist, driven by adrenaline and his own addiction to danger, is told with unrelenting force, indeed an auditory as well as a visually percussive force of gunfire and explosions. The very obsessiveness of its central character speaks to the madness of the conflict, and the lurking danger from bombs and shells, the shadowy dangers from all sides accurately describes the difficulty in seeing and naming an "enemy" in the conflict.

Documentary films of the Iraq and Afghanistan conflict focus less on the manic obsessiveness of individual soldiers and more on the daily grind of battle and its losses. *Restrepo* (Tim Hetherington, Sebastian Junger, Outpost Films, National Geographic Entertainment, 2010) follows a year in the life of a platoon

A soldier in Afghanistan grieves for a fallen comrade in *Restrepo* (Tim Hetherington, Sebastian Junger, 2010).

in an Afghanistan valley. It mixes interviews with the members of the platoon, held in tight close-up, with brilliantly sharp images of battle mixed with the day-to-day operations of housekeeping in the trenches, meetings with local Afghani elders, and occasionally just goofing around. The film is about as neutral in its point of view as a contemporary documentary can be. To be sure, the interviewees voice frustration and sadness. One mentions his suffering from post-traumatic stress disorder, and many grieve the death of Juan Restrepo, after whom they name their outpost, and for whom the film is named. The criticism of the war is implied rather than stated. The difficulties in communicating with the local population, the desperate fighting against the Taliban, the overriding sense of anxiety and dissatisfaction all serve to indicate the desperation of the Afghanistan war.

REDACTED

All of which is to say that, compared to Michael Moore's work, *Restrepo* is remarkably restrained and depends upon the viewer's understanding of the complexities and agonies of this particular conflict to fill in the spaces which, in the film itself, are filled with the daily activities of the troops and their words that recall their time in the field. *Restrepo* bears an interesting similarity to a fiction film about the Iraq conflict made a few years earlier, Brian De Palma's *Redacted* (The Film Farm, HDNet Films, Magnolia, 2007). De Palma attempts to create distance between the ugly events of the film, based on an actual incident—the rape and murder of an Iraqi girl by US troops—and the viewer by creating the *impression* of a documentary. The body of the film is told via the video being made by one of the troops. This is itself interrupted by a "documentary" made by a French film crew. There are further mediations made by people speaking via the Internet. As if the only way of understanding the horrors of the Iraq war is by getting enough distance from it, De Palma sets us apart from the conflict and the corruption of our own troops, filtering our gaze through various lenses. The fact is that we did get to understand the war only through the mediations of the news, and the government tried to control that as much as possible. De Palma attempts to bring us close by, paradoxically, creating a distance that allows us to understand more clearly what was going on.

The documentarists of the Middle Eastern conflicts create another paradox of mediation. Hetherington and Junger deliver extraordinary high-definition images of men at war and allow us to hear their own words about their experiences. But the film leaves us removed from the struggle; obviously because we are not there but only watching images. But on another level, the images, with some notable exceptions, do not communicate the sheer terror of combat. Rather, they present a dailiness of activity. I wonder if the filmmakers, like De Palma in his fiction film, felt that roaring combat footage, typical of films about earlier conflicts, bringing the viewer close to bloodiness and death, would blot out their intent with sensation? Perhaps more is to be learned by means of a calm, prolonged gaze than with the noise and horror of war.

ERROL MORRIS

THE FOG OF WAR, STANDARD OPERATING PROCEDURE, AND THE UNKNOWN KNOWN

An important practitioner of the patient, prolonged gaze is documentary filmmaker Errol Morris. He has made three war-related films, *The Fog of War: Eleven Lessons from the Life of Robert S. McNamara* (Sony Pictures Classics, Radical Media, SenArt Films, 2003); *Standard Operating Procedure* (Participant Media, Sony Pictures Classics, 2008); and *The Unknown Known*, (History Films, Radius-TWC, Moxie Pictures, Participant Media, 2014), a film about George W. Bush's Secretary of Defense, Donald Rumsfeld. His aesthetic in these films (and many others he has made) is to compose close-ups of his subjects and allow them to talk, sometimes fading to black and then back again in the midst of their talk, sometimes cutting to place them in a different side of the frame, and often intercutting their monologue with archival images, graphics, and reenactments created specifically for the film. The "talking head" is usually criticized in film and television as the least creative means of imparting information. But in Morris's hands, these create an intensity of expression and revelation. By allowing his subjects to talk, and carefully editing his footage, Morris in effect opens up his subjects or, more accurately, allows them to open themselves up before our eyes.

Standard Operating Procedure is about the horrors of Abu Ghraib, the prison where Americans tortured Iraqis, and the interviewees of the film are mostly the lower level soldiers who were responsible for horrible abuses of prisoners by Americans in that Iraqi jail. At one point, one of the subjects looks off camera at a photograph of American soldiers standing around a prisoner on the floor. He identifies the figures and goes on to say, "It was never an interrogation, the yelling was just for show, I believe." One by one, the subjects reveal the gruesomeness of the abuse and torture they visited on their prisoners—for show, for their own sometimes sadistic pleasure. At the center of the film is the story of a prisoner who died under torture. The interviewees coolly tell the story (one admits, "I kind of felt bad") and Morris intercuts ghostly reenactments of the event, which involved the soldiers and the CIA interrogators packing the body in ice, trying to hide it so as not to create a riot in the prison. At one point, one of the women soldiers tells her part in the story and Morris interrupts (as he occasionally does), reminding her that she got into trouble because of the photo taken with her and the corpse. And we see the picture, the woman in rubber gloves, pointing at and smiling over the body.

The film allows its participants to incrementally reveal the absurdities of the situation and attempt to absolve themselves of all blame for what occurred. "The fear of the truth silenced people." That is as close as one of the participants comes to an understanding of the situation. "Find a way to make it go away . . . sacrifice the little guys, that's how they cover it up." Morris shows an image of a prison hallway, filled with the detritus of shredded documents. Fortunately, the actual photographs of the abuses were not shredded—not all of them, at least. Some of the participants went to jail, though not the people who ordered the torture. "This war in Iraq, like Vietnam, will probably get remembered as the one time we were not the heroes, we were not the saviors. And these photographs will play a big part in that." So says one of the people interviewed. But he goes on to say that during war the "rules get fuzzy sometimes." The fog of war.

Morris's earlier film, *The Fog of War: Eleven Lessons from the Life of Robert S. McNamara* is in many ways more chilling than *Standard Operating Procedure*. The film is a kind of confessional for the man who was secretary of defense under the Kennedy and Johnson administrations from 1961 to 1968. He was, for all intents and purposes, the architect of the Vietnam War. Morris employs a wide variety of footage, from newsreels, to old documentaries, to staged visuals and montages. He unearths tape recordings of McNamara, Lyndon Johnson, even the commanders who doubted the accuracy of reports of the Gulf of Tonkin incident—the presumed torpedo attack by the North Vietnamese that led to our involvement in Vietnam. Some of these recordings voice McNamara's own hesitation about the government's commitment to total war, and in the present moment, at age 85 (he died at 93 in 2009), he sounds reasonably, coldly, distantly contrite. He admits that the Vietnam War, that cost 58,000 American and over a million Vietnamese deaths, was, essentially, a mistake. "How much evil must we do in order to do good?" McNamara asks at one point and goes on to claim that we must engage in evil "but minimize it." He refuses to answer Morris's question as to whether he feels guilty, though at the very beginning of the film, he says that any military commander will admit that he's made mistakes and killed people unnecessarily.

In the course of *The Fog of War* McNamara talks and talks. Morris's camera gazes at him, often at a canted angle, and between his words and the images that interrupt them, we gain a picture of a man who was at the center of a terrible and futile conflict, whose second thoughts do nothing to wipe out the "evil" that he did. *The Fog of War* epitomizes the way in which documentary filmmaking can elicit truths by stealth, by direct confrontation, by the measured intrusion of the filmmaker, by simply allowing the film's subject to reveal himself. There were many fiction films about the Vietnam War, from *Platoon* (Oliver Stone, Hemdale Film, 1986) to *Apocalypse Now* (Francis Ford Coppola, Zoetrope Studios, United Artists, 1979) to *Full Metal Jacket* (Stanley Kubrick, Warner Bros., 1987). But *The Fog of War* best indicates, in its quiet, deadly way, how entangled that war was in Cold War ideology and how its necessity was only apparent to the politicians and their servants of the moment.

No clarity is reached in *The Unknown Known*, where Donald Rumsfeld smiles and lies, twists language to suit his lack of knowledge or lack of desire to admit to what he doesn't want to be revealed. Morris tries to get clear responses from his subject through direct questions, through clips that contradict what the former Secretary of Defense says to him, but he does not have the luck he had with McNamara. Rumsfeld stands firm. He is proud of his career as a public servant, which spanned decades. He shows none of McNamara's contrition about Vietnam—"Some things work out, some things don't, that didn't . . . ," he says. Nor does he enlighten us about the Iraq war, which he oversaw. Rather, he barricades himself from Morris's probing with words. He talks and talks, obfuscates, and contradicts himself. Only Morris's use of clips of press conferences, of graphics, headlines, typewritten reproductions of historical events, and memos reveal the man, or at least the persona of the man, who attempts to talk and say nothing at the same time. "Wouldn't it have been better not to go there at all?" Morris asks about Iraq. "I guess time will tell," Rumsfeld answers and somewhat later gets a little choked up about visiting a wounded veteran. Time has told. Morris's film tells us.

The documentary is an extremely flexible form of cinematic storytelling. It can provide a window into events that seem to go on without the presence of the camera, even though the presence of the camera always changes the events it records. It can provide a platform for a deeply committed social or political voice to be heard, forcefully making its points through

Former Secretary of Defense Donald Rumsfeld in Errol Morris's *The Unknown Known* (2014).

carefully chosen images. Serious or mocking, funny or ironic, the documentary is cinema's way of getting at truths, even facts that fiction film, by the very nature of its creation of imaginative worlds, cannot manage directly. In the right hands, the subject of a documentary can open up—or at least be exposed—to reveal memories and emotions that have long been hidden and can speak if not truth at least an inquiry into the fog of reality.

SELECTED FILMOGRAPHY

Nanook of the North, dir. Robert Flaherty, Les Frères Revillon, Pathé, 1922.

The Man with the Movie Camera, dir. Dziga Vertov, U.S.S.R, 1929.

The Plow That Broke the Plains, dir. Pare Lorentz, Resettlement Administration, 1936.

Redacted, dir. Brian De Palma, The Film Farm, HDNet Films, Magnolia, 2007.

The Hurt Locker, dir. Kathryn Bigelow, Voltage Pictures, Grosvenor Park Media, Film Capital Europe Funds, 2008.

Restrepo, dirs. Tim Hetherington & Sebastian Junger, Outpost Films, National Geographic Entertainment, 2010.

David and Albert Maysles

Salesman, Maysles Films, 1968.

Gimme Shelter, Maysles Films, 1970.

Grey Gardens, Portrait Films, 1975.

Michael Moore

Roger and Me, Dog Eat Dog Films, Warner Bros., 1989.

Bowling for Columbine, Alliance Atlantis, Dog Eat Dog Productions, United Artists, 2002.

Fahrenheit 9/11, Dog Eat Dog Films, Lionsgate, IFC, 2004.

Errol Morris

The Fog of War: Eleven Lessons from the Life of Robert S. McNamara, Sony Pictures Classics, Radical Media, SenArt Films, 2003.

Standard Operating Procedure, Participant Media, Sony Pictures Classics, 2008.

The Unknown Known, History Films, Radius-TWC, Moxie Pictures, Participant Media, 2014.

SUGGESTIONS FOR FURTHER READING

Jack C. Ellis & Betsy A McLane, eds., *A New History of the Documentary Film* (New York, NY: Continuum International Publishing Group, 2005).

Barry Keith Grant & Jeannette Sloniowski, *Documenting the Documentary: Close Readings of Documentary Film and Video* (Detroit, MI: Wayne State University Press, 1998).

Bill Nichols, *Representing Reality: Issues and Concepts in Documentary* (Bloomington, IN: Indiana University Press, 1991).

———, *Introduction to Documentary* (Bloomington, IN: Indiana University Press, 2001).

CHAPTER 23

OUTSIDE HOLLYWOOD: STANLEY KUBRICK (1953–1999)

Stanley Kubrick stands as one of the most important contemporary filmmakers whose greatest films were made outside of Hollywood. His films are complex, deeply layered, and inimitable. He is a unique figure and the discussion of his films here provides a kind of mirror to the discussion of the early unique figure in American film, D. W. Griffith. What follows does not analyze every Kubrick film, but rather chooses a few for a close examination.

AFTER READING THIS CHAPTER, YOU SHOULD UNDERSTAND:

- What constitutes the Kubrick style.
- How the Cold War is interpreted in *Dr. Strangelove*.
- *2001: A Space Odyssey* as a culmination of 1950s science fiction and a preparation of the science fiction films of Spielberg and Lucas.
- The various aspects of "space" that Kubrick creates in *2001: A Space Odyssey*.
- The loss of human agency in Kubrick's films.
- A relationship between *Eyes Wide Shut* and F. W. Murnau's *Sunrise*.

YOU SHOULD BE ABLE TO:

- Compare Kubrick to Hitchcock and Welles.
- Define Kubrickian satire.
- Explore the notion that Kubrick's films exist on the border between wake and sleep.
- Discuss the relationship of Kubrick's war films with those of World War I and World War II.
- Observe the influences of *2001: A Space Odyssey* on the science fiction films that came after it.
- Compare the demands that Kubrick's films make on the viewer with Spielberg's films.
- Ask if Kubrick is, in the end, an American filmmaker.

THE LAST OF THE INDEPENDENTS

Stanley Kubrick is an anomaly in American film. Relatively early in his career, after having directed five films, he left the United States and did all his remaining work in England. He stayed in touch with American culture through films and the media. More unusual still, he worked alone, planning his films over long periods of careful, detailed research, and then using a relatively small crew to actually make the movie. By working away from Hollywood, he was free of the usual pressures of studio production. He produced his first two films, *Fear and Desire* (distributed by Joseph Burstyn, 1953) and *Killer's Kiss* (Minotaur Productions, United Artists, 1955) himself. He then joined forces with producer James B. Harris and made *The Killing* (Harris-Kubrick Productions, United Artists, 1956) under their own production company, and joined with the actor Kirk Douglas to make *Paths of Glory* (Bryna Productions, United Artists, 1957). He was called in by Douglas to replace Anthony Mann on the sword and sandal epic, *Spartacus* (Bryna Productions, Universal, 1960—the film that helped break the blacklist by recognizing Dalton Trumbo, who wrote the script.) It was his experience on that film, where he had little control, that caused him to leave Hollywood for good, setting up home and work in England.

Lolita (MGM, Seven Arts Productions, 1962) was produced by Harris, who helped set up *Dr. Strangelove: Or How I Stopped Worrying and Learned to Love the Bomb* (Columbia, Hawk Films, 1963), and then left to direct on his own. Kubrick produced *2001: A Space Odyssey* (MGM, Stanley Kubrick Productions, 1968) himself and afterward entered into an agreement with Warner Bros. that gave him complete freedom: they did not have to give advanced approval for a film; they accepted his budget (always small compared with Hollywood productions and given the high production values of his work); and they guaranteed distribution of the completed film. Later, his brother-in-law, Jan Harlan, became his producer, and in this protected environment, Kubrick made *A Clockwork Orange* (Warner Bros., Hawk Films, 1971), *Barry Lyndon* (Peregrine, Hawk Films, Warner Bros., 1975), *The Shining* (Warner Bros., Hawk Films, Peregrine, 1980), *Full Metal Jacket* (Natant, Stanley Kubrick Productions, Warner Bros., 1987), and *Eyes Wide Shut* (Hobby Films, Pole star, Stanley Kubrick Productions, Warner Bros. 1999).

KUBRICK, WELLES, AND HITCHCOCK

Kubrick's work covers the chronological range of film from the postwar 1950s to the end of the 20th century. He covers as well a range of genres: the gangster film, the war film, costume drama, domestic melodrama, horror, and science fiction. An independent filmmaker in all senses of the term, he nonetheless made films that, with few exceptions, were commercially successful. An interesting comparison can be made between Kubrick, Alfred Hitchcock, and Orson Welles. Hitchcock learned to work comfortably within the studio system, so comfortably, in fact that, when that system came apart, Hitchcock lost his creative edge. Like Hitchcock at his best, Kubrick made films that are accessible on one level at first viewing, but keep opening up new levels of meaning the more they are seen. Kubrick's films also have a formal precision that echoes Hitchcock's concern with the precise structure of his own films. But Kubrick's films are very different from Hitchcock's, whose obsession with the ways in which chaos and violence rain down upon unsuspecting characters infiltrates his work. Rather, Kubrick is interested in how individuals, often unwittingly, rain chaos and violence on themselves and others. Like Hitchcock, Kubrick calculates every shot composition, every edit, with a meticulous concern for detail. Like Welles, Kubrick operated outside of the studio system, though he did not have to scramble for funds to make his films the way Welles did. Despite that, Kubrick, like Welles, made relatively few films during his career, but those films, like Welles's, demonstrate a distinctive visual exuberance. Like Welles, Kubrick loves the moving camera and the large visual gesture. Unlike Welles, and like Hitchcock—at least in Hitchcock's 1950s period—Kubrick's films and their characters are, with rare exceptions, without sentimentality, without hope, without redemption. His gaze is cold, sometimes cruel, but always fascinated by the desperate struggles of the figures before his lens and ultimately our eyes.

This in itself puts Kubrick at odds with the continuum of American film. In the classic American style of filmmaking, in the foundational culture of film narratives, things must work out for the central characters. This was not only a function of the Production Code but grew out of a need for filmmakers to please their audience, to satisfy a desire for problems to be solved and transcended, for the perpetrators of evil and violence to come to a bad end. In short, to provide the kinds of closure generally unavailable to daily experience. Kubrick is uninterested in daily experience, in comfortable closure, in making his audience happy. What he is interested in is creating films whose complexities ironically mirror the most difficult, obdurate, wrong-headed, and deadly situations people and their institutions are able to get themselves into. These are films that challenge the viewer, make her uncomfortable, and demand attentiveness.

THE WAR FILMS: *FEAR AND DESIRE, PATHS OF GLORY, FULL METAL JACKET*

War was a favorite subject of Kubrick's, and he made three films about men in military conflict—perhaps four, if we count *Dr. Strangelove* as a film that contains battle footage and is about the ultimate war that ends the planet. His first—the first feature-length film he made—*Fear and Desire,* is a young filmmaker's meditation on war as an abstract state of mind. The war of *Fear and Desire* is unnamed, unlocalized; it takes place in "a country of the mind," according to the voice-over narrator. Here is Kubrick, the self-taught neophyte filmmaker experimenting with various techniques, trying out **Eisensteinian montage**, indulging in curious doublings so that the troops on one side are played by the same actors on the enemy side. In *Fear and Desire,* war is a tortured internal struggle; history is absent. Kubrick finds his historical grounding in *Paths of Glory,* set in France during World War I. In this film, the Kubrickian mindset is fully formed. *Paths of Glory* is an unrelentingly grim film that works like a doomsday machine toward a conclusion that would be unthinkable in a more conventional work. Its protagonist, Colonel Dax (Kirk Douglas) is caught in the rigid military machine, unable to save three soldiers (played by Ralph Meeker, Joseph Turkel, and Timothy Carey) accused of cowardice for refusing to partake in a suicide mission to take the impregnable enemy line. *Paths of Glory* is pitiless in its depiction of the grinding down of all moral and humane impulses. The three men receive a courts-martial in which their guilt is predetermined, despite Dax's pleas for understanding from a court of judges already fixed in their verdict. They are executed, cruelly and coldly. Kubrick's camera moves fluidly with Colonel Dax as he marches through the endless trenches that made up the geography of the First World War, as if he were in control of a situation over which he has no control whatsoever. The courts-martial sequence is filmed in carefully composed symmetrical compositions, the camera tracking low behind across the legs of the accused, Dax trapped

Col. Dax (Kirk Douglas) trapped between the men he is defending and the courts martial dead set on executing them in Stanley Kubrick's *Paths of Glory* (1957).

The confusion of war. Private Joker (Matthew Modine) wears a peace button and the words "Born to Kill" on his helmet in *Full Metal Jacket* (1987).

between them and the judges. Almost every composition speaks to the entrapment of the characters, the callousness of the high command, the impossibility of Dax's predicament as mediator between the generals and the doomed troops.

Kubrick's films are almost all concerned with men who erect institutions or actions that they lose control of and allow to turn on and trap them. His Vietnam War film, *Full Metal Jacket,* is no exception. The film is structured in two parts. In the first, the new recruits are mercilessly, viciously, and hilariously harangued by a foul-mouthed drill instructor (R. Lee Ermey), who unmans them, infantilizes them, attempts to diminish them into automaton fighting machines. He almost succeeds, until he is killed by the weakest member of the group (played by Vincent D'Onofrio), whose psychopathology blossoms under the treatment he receives, and commits suicide in turn. The second part of the film takes place "in country," and there the training that the men have received falls apart in the confusion of war. Lost and under attack, the platoon is painfully attacked by a female sniper. Having been unmanned by their training, they now are undone by a woman. Private Joker (Matthew Modine), a conflicted Marine, wearing a peace symbol on his uniform and the words "Born to Kill" on his helmet, finds his manhood through killing. He shoots the wounded sniper and the troops move out, singing the Mickey Mouse song.

Vietnam, for Kubrick, was a place that shrunk the human spirit. In *Apocalypse Now* (Francis Ford Coppola, Zoetrope Studios, United Artists, 1979), Vietnam is a theatrical stage on which an assemblage of strange characters acts out their rapid decline into insanity. Oliver Stone's *Platoon* (Cinema 86, Hemdale Film, 1986) created a Vietnam War that allowed its central character, Chris (Charlie Sheen), to come of age. He must choose between the conflicting forces of hardened strength represented by Sergeant Barnes (Tom Berenger) and the strong compassion of Sergeant Elias (Willem Dafoe). He walks out of the jungle a wiser person. Kubrick's Vietnam allows for no coming of age, no gaining of wisdom. Joker and his platoon can only wander blindly in a surreal landscape full of traps, culminating in their ambush by a female sniper. Throughout the film, women are the subjects of derision and crude profanities; that a woman is responsible for killing the men and proving Joker's macho bravura is a final irony. The "theater of war" is, for Kubrick, a theater of the absurd.

DR. STRANGELOVE AND THE COLD WAR

Where World War I movies celebrated the romantic interests of their soldiers, and World War II films focused on the cohesion of diverse members of a platoon, Kubrick's war films are about rigid control and painful dissolution, about the pain of submitting to the legalized slaughter that war is about. War, for

Kubrick, is a process of losing humanity, of becoming unmanned, not heroic, less than fully human. When Kubrick confronts the Cold War, he reconfigures all of this to make it appallingly funny. The rigid language of anti-Communism, the crazed institutionalizing of the arms race between the United States and the Soviet Union that marked the politics of the postwar period creates, in Kubrick's mind, a situation where the characters become caricatures, their actions exaggerated to the point of lunacy and menace, and events are taken out of their hands and the world is destroyed. *Dr. Strangelove* is a satire that exaggerates the character types and the lunatic discourse of the Cold War world. It is a direct assault on the assumptions that drove our cultural and military actions in the years following World War II.

Dr. Strangelove posits a variety of Cold War madness embodied in human figures who are crazy, monstrous, or simply stupid. General Jack D. Ripper (Sterling Hayden) thinks he is sapped of his vital bodily fluids when he makes love. A fundamentalist anti-Communist, he declares a one-man war by sending US bombers on their way to destroy the USSR. General Buck Turgidson (George C. Scott) calculates "World Targets in Megadeaths" and argues that society could prevail despite a nuclear catastrophe. A drunken Russian premier named Kissoff and the US president, Merkin Muffley (Peter Sellers), futilely attempt to communicate with each other in order to forestall the inevitable by arguing over the phone. Dr. Strangelove (Peter Sellers) himself, a crippled ghost of Nazism, rises from his wheelchair as death proclaims its dominion. Or its inevitability. In Kubrick's Cold War universe, both sides have created mutually assured destruction in the form of the "Doomsday Machine," which will blow them all up if either side uses atomic weapons. The total collapse of communication assures that one side, in this case the Americans, will bomb Russia, and, as the Americans in the war room argue about who will live in mine shafts in order to escape nuclear devastation, Dr. Strangelove stands, gives a Nazi salute, cries out "Mein Fuhrer, I can walk," and bombs destroy the world.

In the illogic of the Cold War, Kubrick discovers a crazed logic of tortured language and thinking, of communication that communicates nothing but each character's and each side's closed worldview, impervious to the realities of inevitable annihilation. *Dr. Strangelove* raised the ire of the right wing. After all, it pushed Cold War rhetoric so far that it and its practitioners are revealed as crazy. The film's satire did not bring an end to the Cold War, but, for those who paid attention, made it impossible for it to be taken seriously any longer.

Dr. Strangelove poses difficult questions. As a film of its moment, of the early 1960s, post Joseph McCarthy, but still saturated by Cold War rhetoric, it asks its audience to laugh away the grotesque and the self-destructive behavior of their politicians and military personnel. It maintains its power still, because the

The demented Nazi, Dr. Strangelove (Peter Sellers), comes to life as the world ends in Kubrick's *Dr. Strangelove. Or How I Stopped Worrying and Learned to Love the Bomb* (1963).

language of bloated belligerence remains part of the political and cultural discourse. But finally, what power does satire hold? We laugh as Major Kong (Slim Pickens) rides the H-bomb like a huge penis down to earth to start Armaggedon and shudder as Strangelove comes to life as the world comes to an end. But our laughter and schadenfreude is at our own expense. We put into power the very character types we are laughing at in Kubrick's film. The powerlessness, Kubrick seems to be saying, is our own.

HUMANS AND MACHINES: *2001: A SPACE ODYSSEY*

Dr. Strangelove was criticized on its appearance as Communist propaganda—as was any kind of statement that went against the prevailing anti-Communist ideology that held the culture in its grip. What the film does, in fact, is turn that ideology inside out and find it both hilarious and deadly at the same time. This kind of ironic stance is typical of Kubrick, who finds the deadly joke buried just below the surface of all human activity. Even when he casts his view to the future, as he did in *2001: A Space Odyssey*, he finds, as he did in *Dr. Strangelove*, that humans have given themselves over to their machines and have traded a sense of wonder for the banal operations necessary to find the origins of a fantastic object, a monolith seemingly planted on Earth and on the moon by alien intelligence. The computer they have built to aid them in their operations and their journey to the ends of the universe shows itself to be smarter than they, assumes a consciousness that turns to megalomania, and kills all the crew members but one.

2001 is one of the great speculative works of cinema. It asks if there is indeed such a thing as extraterrestrial life and, if so, does it control our future? Even more, it asks what happens when human beings have lost their imaginations, yielding their power to a machine. These two questions are interlocked, for they both posit the notion that human responsibility is not merely fragile but able to be entirely disowned. The visual impact of the film is enormous. Before digital special effects were available, Kubrick imagined—by means of models and matte paintings—an almost tactile sense of the details of what space travel and a voyage "beyond the infinite" might look like. We, as viewers, are in awe. The inhabitants of the film seem bored. Space travel, for them, is routine and numbing. We wonder at the ways in which Kubrick portrays weightlessness—things float and people walk upside down—but the characters in the film barely look up from their freeze-dried meals. In the flight to Jupiter, the two astronauts go about their tasks—jogging around the vast circular hall of spacecraft, receiving a birthday greeting, making sketches—while the rest of the crew is in state of hibernation, and the HAL 9000 computer runs the ship.

HAL fills the void left by the humans. In this film about space, Kubrick achieves a kind of spatial structure of action and response. The human characters seem to recede into the technologies of their own invention, functions of the screens and buttons and readouts that fill the screen that we, as viewers, look at in amazement. HAL emerges to fill the space vacated by the humans. The machine takes over, kills the hibernating astronauts, kills one of the working astronauts, Frank Poole (Gary Lockwood), and is finally lobotomized by Bowman (Keir Dullea) in the only show of emotion in the film. Bowman slowly removes HAL's memory modules, sending it spiraling in fear back to its primitive state. "I'm afraid, Dave . . . I can feel it . . . ," the computer cries. Bowman is cast out into an unknown realm, travelling through a wormhole in space, through alien landscapes, winding up in a kind of human cage in an indeterminate space, where he passes from youth to age to an encapsulated fetus circling the Earth.

I said that *2001* is a speculative film, meaning that it poses questions and presents enigmas that it refuses to answer. It is also a very slowly paced film, which puts it out of sync with most of American cinema that we are used to. It puts so much into its 141 minutes running time—from the "Dawn of Man" to "Jupiter and Beyond the Infinite"—and gives so little in the way of conclusiveness. It compresses time, most spectacularly in the edit from the bone that one of the hominids at the end of the "Dawn of Man" sequence throws in the air to a spacecraft travelling among the stars. It questions the power of human and artificial intelligence—HAL takes over the ship because it/he is the only one who knows the crew's mission, to find the source of the monoliths.

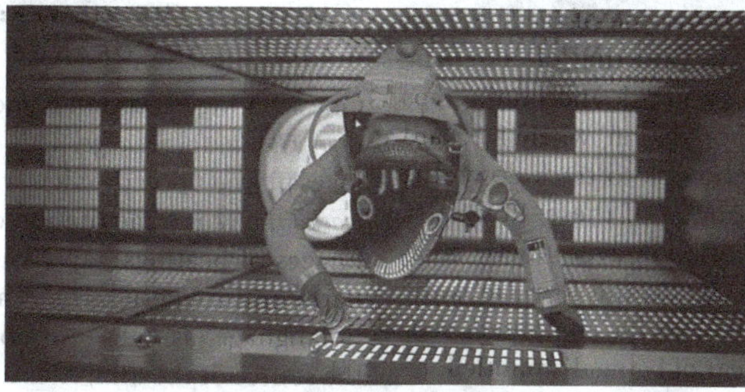

Dave (Keir Dullea) lobotomizes the computer HAL in Stanley Kubrick's *2001: A Space Odyssey* (1968).

The monoliths themselves are unexplained. Does Kubrick actually believe that humans evolved because of extraterrestrial influence, or are the monoliths symbols of change and rebirth? Is there a rebirth after all? Bowman passes through the stages of aging before his very eyes in the last sequence of the film that uncannily plays upon our expectations of **shot/reverse shot**. Each time Dave looks, he sees himself in an older state until, in the end he becomes a fetus who travels through the monolith and becomes a wandering object circling the Earth. This is a somewhat more optimistic ending than the atom bombs exploding at the end of *Dr. Strangelove*, but it does not clarify for us the meaning of the extraordinary image.

BLADE RUNNER

2001 has had the most influence of any of Kubrick's films. His complex, enigmatic vision of the future was taken up by the Russian filmmaker, Andrei Tarkovsky, whose *Solaris* (1982) is every bit as mysterious as its American forebearer. The **mise-en-scène** of Kubrick's *2001* can be seen in the detailed interiors and visions of space travel in the *Star Wars* films. We find the influence of HAL reincarnated in humanoid form in the "replicants" of Ridley Scott's *Blade Runner* (The Ladd Company, The Shaw Brothers, Warner Bros., 1982). But in fact HAL itself has had many antecedents. To understand this, we need to go back to the Frankenstein myth we discussed in Chapter 10. The dream of artificial machine intelligence is very old; and almost every time the dream is given body in fiction, the machines, whether in computer or humanoid form, use their intelligence and their consciousness to question their identity and, almost invariably, rebel against their makers. In Ridley Scott's film, the replicants, robots created to patrol space colonies where the well-to-do escape a dark, crowded, aging planet Earth, gain memory, consciousness, and a desire to outlive their

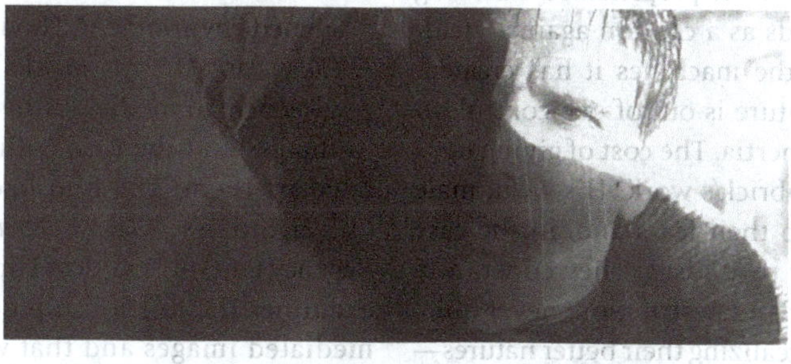

Dying replicant Roy Blatty (Rutger Hauer) and Deckard (Harrison Ford), his hunter, superimposed in Ridley Scott's *Blade Runner* (1982).

limited lifespan. The mise-en-scène of *Blade Runner* could not be more different than that of *2001*. The action takes place in a forever dark and raining Los Angeles, mostly Asian in population, where Deckard (Harrison Ford) is given the task to track down the rogue replicants. The strongest of these, Roy Batty (Rutger Hauer), is an emotional, even poetic creature, unafraid and brutal, gentle and lost. He is the humanoid version of HAL, with the computer's self-preserving instincts and fear of being dismantled.

AI: ARTIFICIAL INTELLIGENCE

HAL also turns up in very different form in Steven Spielberg's *AI: Artificial Intelligence* (Warner Bros., DreamWorks SKG, Amblin Entertainment, 2001). This is a film Kubrick wanted to make. He got as far as conceiving its production design and a preliminary script, but couldn't get a screenplay that pleased him. Before Kubrick's death he asked Spielberg to direct it, with Kubrick acting as producer. After Kubrick's death, Spielberg turned the film into his own version of science fiction as domestic and celestial melodrama. Here, artificial intelligence takes the form of a robot child, who seeks eternal love from the woman who adopts him. It is a touching film, richly imagined, but with a dose of sentimentality it would be hard to imagine Kubrick tolerating.

2001 was and continues to be a very popular film despite its enigmas and its refusal to answer the questions it poses. At the time of its release, it became a favorite of the late 1960s counterculture. The lightshow that represents Bowman's voyage to "Jupiter and Beyond the Infinite" was advertised as "The Ultimate Trip." A stoner movie. The film continues to hold its power, even after the year it prophesized has long since passed. *2001* stands as a caution against yielding human agency to the machines it has created, to believing that our future is out of our control, to simply succumbing to inertia. The cost of giving up is a constant theme in Kubrick's work. His weak male characters fall victim to their fears and, in the case of *The Shining*, to their psychoses. They constantly run in circles of despair and destruction, never quite meeting themselves, or realizing their better natures—if such exist at all in the Kubrickian universe.

A JOKE ON THE VIEWER: *A CLOCKWORK ORANGE*

One seeming exception is Alex (Malcolm McDowell) in *A Clockwork Orange*. This film is one of the great jokes played upon the viewer by a filmmaker. *A Clockwork Orange* is a meditation on violence told in bold images of beatings, rape, and abjection. Alex is our narrator throughout. His vitality, his imaginative use of language (as in the Anthony Burgess novel that is the source of the film, Alex and his "Droogs" speak a mixture of cockney English and Russian) place him at the center of our consciousness throughout the film. We wind up sympathizing with a killer and rapist. The film follows a perfect symmetrical arc, as Alex reaches the peak of his domination by the middle of the film and then descends after his capture and exposure to the "Ludovico Technique" that sensitizes him to violence so that he sickens whenever he is in a violent situation. At every point of this arc, Kubrick makes certain that we cheer Alex on when he is at his most powerful and feel sorry for him when he abases himself after his treatment. We wonder at how this poetic brute loves Beethoven and cringe when he becomes a political tool, restored to his previous violent self by the politicians who need him.

So many of Kubrick's films trap their male characters. *A Clockwork Orange* is a switch: it traps its viewers into a false and morally repugnant state in which we believe that, in the emotionally and aesthetically deadened world portrayed in the film, Alex's violence is an acceptable vitality and a sign of free will. In fact, it is our will that has failed, our notion of morality and kindness; our willingness to assume that violence is an adequate response to a deadened environment. Though set in the near future, *A Clockwork Orange* speaks to our own responses to violence, to media, to the ways in which we react to images and the ease with which we are manipulated by them. The film had a major influence on Oliver Stone's *Natural Born Killers* (Warner Bros., Regency Enterprises, Alcor Films, 1994), a film that also examines the relationship between violence and its mediated images and that we will look at again in Chapter 26.

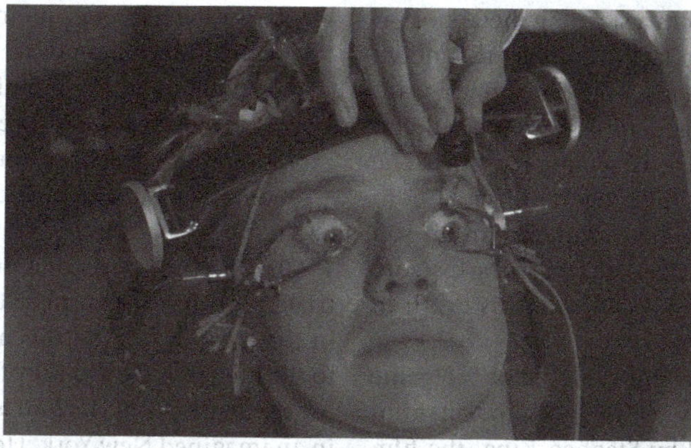

Alex (Malcolm McDowell) is forced to watch violent films in an attempt to desensitize him in *A Clockwork Orange* (1971).

GHOST STORY

Kubrick demands a great deal from his audience: an ability to read his complex images; to transverse the complicated turns of his narratives; to listen to the various voices at play in these narratives; to be alert to the ironies resulting from the often multiple perspectives Kubrick maintains in the course of a film. What, for example, are we to make of Jack Torrance's hallucinations in *The Shining*? Has he been overtaken by the ghosts of the Overlook Hotel? Is *The Shining* a ghost story at all, or is it rather a narrative of the collapse of patriarchy, of the inability of Jack (Jack Nicholson) to maintain domination over his little family isolated from the world? Jack is a drunk with pretensions to greatness. He thinks he is an author when all he can write over and over and over again is "All work and no play make Jack a dull boy." He thinks he is a lover and enters a mysterious room to find a nude young lady ready to embrace him. But once in an embrace, in a **reverse shot** she turns into a hideous old crone. He is instructed by the ghost of the hotel to "correct" his rebellious wife (played by Shelley Duvall), but she maintains the upper hand and his own child (Danny Lloyd) undoes him in the hotel's maze garden, leaving him a howling, frozen thing in the snow.

The real ghost of *The Shining* is the cankered spirit of patriarchy, the seemingly implacable gaze of male

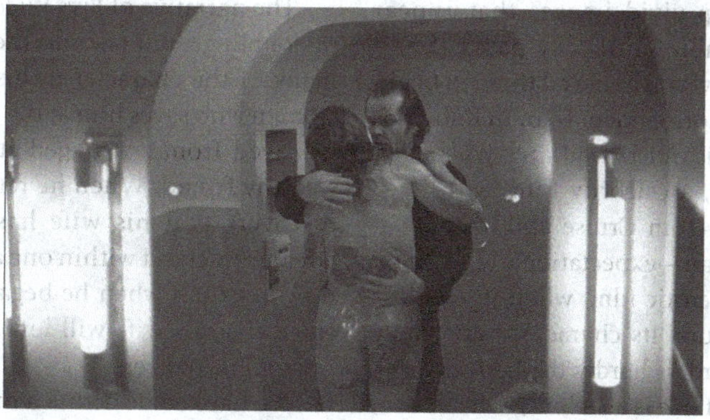

Jack Torrance (Jack Nicholson), who thought he was embracing a beautiful lady, sees a ghostly surprise in the mirror in *The Shining* (1980).

domination. Kubrick creates a startling metaphor for this in the moment when Jack overlooks the model of the hedge maze where his wife and son are wandering. Like a malevolent god, he peers down at them. But the power of his gaze is temporary only. The course of the film follows the process of Jack's undoing, an ironic oedipal narrative. Rather than his son following in Jack's footsteps, Jack pursues his son, who undoes his father, leading him to his death in the snow.

The Shining is an excellent example of the game Kubrick was able to play as an independent filmmaker. Based on a novel by Stephen King, the film had something of a readymade audience. As a horror film, it had yet another audience that loves that genre. It has created yet another audience of conspiracy theorists, who see all manner of coded messages hidden in the film. In the end, *The Shining* is especially about a filmmaker who could use the horror genre to probe more deeply into the heart of the culture of cankered masculinity, creating layers of complexity a viewer might discover, as in all of Kubrick's films, on subsequent viewings.

DREAM STORY

Kubrick can put us within the consciousness of his characters so that the world becomes a reflection of their own delusions. He creates, in many of his films, a kind of dreamlike mise-en-scène, or, more accurately, a hypnogogic mise-en-scène. The hypnogogic state occurs on the threshold of sleep, when the unconscious throws up vivid images that appear absolutely real and viable until they pass off and leave you wondering how you believed them to begin with. This is nowhere more evident than in Kubrick's last film, the widely misunderstood *Eyes Wide Shut.* Because it was, in part, a celebrity film, with huge stars (of the moment)—Tom Cruise and his wife at the time, Nicole Kidman—expectations were high. It was promoted as an erotic film, when in fact it is a film about erotic failure. Its characters, especially Tom Cruise's Bill Harford, is hardly the hero Cruise's fans had come to expect. He is a jealous, driven man, rendered powerless in the face of his wife's admission that she experienced sexual longings for a man she once saw when they were on vacation.

This admission puts Bill into a frenzy of self-doubt and sends him on an odyssey through the streets of New York in an attempt to discover or to prove or to assert his own sexuality. These streets are—with the exception of some **second unit** images shot on actual location—sets built in a studio in England. Kubrick had not been back to the United States since the late 1960s, and the streets that Bill wanders are an expatriate's dream of what his New York might look like in the late 1990s. And this adds another dimension to the film and to the place of Kubrick in this book on American film. Bill Harford is an imagined American in an imagined New York. He is, in many ways, stuck in Kubrick's imagination in which a fantastic vision is created of a world that never existed outside of the imagination. It is a cinematic imagination of an American expatriate filmmaker; and finally the unconscious of the film's very protagonist, who sees his world through the haze of his sexual insecurities.

That world is full of threat and promise, climaxing in an absurd orgy in which rich people in masks are sexually entertained by a ritual involving naked ladies and some kind of high priest, who puts them through their paces. Bill is the outsider to this spectacle, as he is to most of the characters and events he comes across in the course of his wanderings, as he is to his own life. He is caught as an intruder, unmasked, and—faced with that common fear among dreamers—told to get naked. He is saved by the intervention of one of the women (Julienne Davis), who later turns up dead.

The narrative of *Eyes Wide Shut* is constructed out of doublings: Bill takes to the streets twice; he meets many of the character in his wanderings twice; the woman who saves him at the orgy is the same woman he saved from a drugged stupor at the home of a wealthy friend. When he returns from the orgy, he discovers that his wife has dreamed of an orgy. Dreams intersect within one another, and Bill awakes no wiser than when he began. He wants to be reassured that his wife will love him forever. A promise impossible to keep.

We have come across a dream film earlier, in our discussion of Fritz Lang's noirish *The Woman in the Window* (Christie Coporation, International Pictures, RKO, 1944). There too the character entered an erotic

Bill Harford (Tom Cruise) in the orgy sequence of Stanley Kubrick's *Eyes Wide Shut* (1999).

universe and wound up committing murder. The murder in *Eyes Wide Shut* is not committed by Bill, whose spirit is already too constrained to do a violent act. He wanders awake in his sleep, trapped in his own confusions, misapprehensions, and chance. This is the state of so many of Kubrick's male characters. As far back as *The Killing*, Johnny Clay (Sterling Hayden) attempted to create a racetrack robbery so perfectly timed, so dependent on a foolproof plan, that it was doomed to failure, to the contingent, to events that could not be planned for. A flat tire, a yapping dog, a woman who could not keep the plans a secret. The robbery comes apart, Johnny is left helpless in the clutches of the police. Bill Harford is left helpless in the clutches of his unconscious and of the coincidences of the half-awake world in which he wanders—in a city no less fantastic in its own way than that in F. W. Murnau's *Sunrise* (Fox, 1927) that we looked at in Chapter 6. In his last film, Kubrick moved effortlessly from the external to the internal world and made it an **expressionist** odyssey of the unconscious.

Kubrick is so much out of the mainstream of American film production that he is, in the end, a filmmaker unto himself. His intellect was richer, his images and narratives more complex than almost any of his peers who remained within the Hollywood system of production and who are the main subjects of our study. He has no equals and his influence, outside of science fiction films, is negligible because his work in inimitable. But he *is* an American filmmaker, and his work has become part of the cultural unconscious.

SELECTED FILMOGRAPHY

Stanley Kubrick

Fear and Desire, distributed by Joseph Burstyn, 1953.

Killer's Kiss, Minotaur Productions, United Artists, 1955.

The Killing, Harris-Kubrick Productions, United Artists, 1956.

Paths of Glory, Bryna Productions, United Artists, 1957.

Spartacus, Bryna Productions, Universal, 1960.

Lolita, MGM, Seven Arts Productions, 1962.

Dr. Strangelove, or How I Learned to Stop Worrying and Love the Bomb, Columbia, Hawk Films, 1963.

2001: A Space Odyssey, MGM, Stanley Kubrick Productions, 1968.

A Clockwork Orange, Warner Bros., Hawk Films, 1971.

Barry Lyndon, Warner Bros., Peregrine, Hawk Films, 1975.

The Shining, Warner Bros., Hawk Films, Peregrine, 1980.

Full Metal Jacket, Natant, Stanley Kubrick Productions, Warner Bros., 1987.

Eyes Wide Shut, Hobby Films, Pole star, Stanley Kubrick Productions, Warner Bros., 1991.

Blade Runner, dir. Ridley Scott, Ladd Company, The, Shaw Brothers, Warner Bros., 1982.

A.I.: Artificial Intelligence, dir. Steven Spielberg, Warner Bros., DreamWorks SKG, Amblin Entertainment, 2001.

SUGGESTIONS FOR FURTHER READING

Michel Chion *Kubrick's Cinema Odyssey*, trans., Claudia Gorbman (London, UK: BFI Publishing, 2001).

———, *Eyes Wide Shut*, trans. Trista Selous (London, UK: British Film Institute, 2006).

Robert Kolker, ed. *Stanley Kubrick's 2001: A Space Odyssey: New Essays* (New York, NY: Oxford University Press, 2006).

James Naremore, *On Kubrick* (London, UK: British Film Institute Publishing, 2007).

Thomas Allen Nelson, *Kubrick: Inside a Film Artist's Maze* (Bloomington, IN: Indiana University Press, 2000).

Walker, Alexander, Sybil Taylor, & Ulrich Ruchti, *Stanley Kubrick, Director*, rev. and expanded. (New York, NY: Norton, 1999).

CHAPTER 24

THE NEW HOLLYWOOD AND AFTER: PART ONE (1967–2006)

The "New Hollywood" that emerged from the demise of the old studio system created a space for novel, unconventional filmmaking. The reemergence of the director created not only a new American cinema but a new audience and new ways of thinking about film. This chapter focuses on the films of Arthur Penn and Robert Altman.

AFTER READING THIS CHAPTER, YOU SHOULD UNDERSTAND:

- How the demise of the Production Code and the old studio system created space for novel, unconventional filmmaking.
- Which major directors emerged in the late 1960s and early 1970s and what the conditions were that made their work possible.
- How *Bonnie and Clyde* became a touchstone for "the New Hollywood" school of filmmaking and a reflection of the 1960s counterculture.
- The importance of Roger Corman and American International Pictures.
- The effect of the many assassinations during the 1960s on the countercultural films.
- The blockbuster.
- The influence of Robert Altman on the films of Paul Thomas Anderson.

YOU SHOULD BE ABLE TO:

- Identify the characteristics of the films of Arthur Penn and Robert Altman.
- Discuss the contributions of Peter Fonda, Dennis Hopper, and Sam Peckinpah to the New Hollywood movement.
- Speculate about the end of the Western genre.
- Discuss the explosion of film violence during this period and speculate on its effect on film viewing.

- Consider how Robert Altman reconfigures the Western in *McCabe and Mrs. Miller* as well as his reworking of the detective film, *The Long Goodbye*.
- Look at the variety of films that follow in the wake of Altman's *Short Cuts*, such as *Magnolia* (Paul Thomas Anderson, 1999) and *Crash* (Paul Haggis, 2004). What is the difference in approach to the multicharacter narrative and the emotional temperature of these films?

THE COLLAPSE OF THE CODE AND THE STUDIO SYSTEM AND THE RISE OF THE COUNTERCULTURE

The collapse of the Production Code and, even more important, the dissolution of the old studio system, left an opening for a new kind of film. A new class of directors emerged in the late 1960s and the 1970s, influenced by the experiments going on in European film, benefiting from the new studio heads, producers, and directors, who were looking for different kinds of films, and a young audience ready for films that spoke to them.

Morality was very much on the mind of these young men (and they were almost all men, though a few women producers appeared from time to time). They were concerned with the sometimes hypocritical moralism of the old Hollywood and the Production Code. They believed that film should reflect what people think, feel, and do rather than some ideal of morality, of crime and punishment, of redemption. They were against the Vietnam War, and some of them embraced the countercultural response to that war, a resistance tinged with a sense of hope and despair. More than anything, they were, most of them, young, and they wanted to make films for the young. Many of these new directors knew the history of film and, like their European counterparts, wanted to exploit that history, to respond to the films of the past and use them as the ground to build a cinema of the future. Theirs was a cinema of youth and the energy of exploration. It was a cinema of the director, who, for a brief time, held some power in Hollywood, for as long as their films made money.

ARTHUR PENN AND THE COUNTERCULTURE

BONNIE AND CLYDE

One of the films that changed Hollywood very nearly did not get made, almost got to be directed by a Frenchman, and once made was widely panned, pulled from distribution, and then rereleased to acclaim and a huge box office. *Bonnie and Clyde* (Arthur Penn, Warner Bros./Seven Arts, Tatira-Hiller Productions, 1967) originated in 1963 as a screenplay by Robert Benton and David Newman, two writers for *Esquire* magazine, who were deeply influenced by the early films of Jean-Luc Godard and François Truffaut, two of the best known members of the French New Wave. Not until Benton and Newman showed their script to actor Warren Beatty, who in turn showed it to Warner Bros., did it begin to gain traction. But just barely. The old guard at Warners couldn't make much sense of the script that idealized a group of 1930s gangsters, with a brutally violent ending, and the suggestion of a homosexual relationship between Clyde and another member of his outlaw gang. That part was removed (censorship was not entirely dead). Warners were also unhappy with the prospect of getting François Truffaut to direct the film, as the writers wanted. The writers and Beatty persisted, at one point inviting Jean-Luc Godard to take a look at the script, so intent were they to make a film that showed the influence of the New Wave. They wanted the open narrative style, the loose framing, and jagged editing that was energizing French cinema.

Truffaut and Godard turned down the film, and Beatty contacted Arthur Penn, who started his career as a director of live television dramas during the 1950s—the breeding ground of a number of young directors and actors. Penn had made three films, a Western about Billy the Kid called *The Left Handed Gun* (Haroll Productions, Warner Bros., 1958), in which Paul Newman played the legendary outlaw as a tormented adolescent; *The Miracle Worker* (Playfilm Productions, United Artists, 1962), a violent melodrama about the childhood of Helen Keller, a woman born deaf and blind; and *Mickey One* (Florin, Tatira, Columbia, 1965). This latter film, starring Warren Beatty, is an exciting, experimental work about a nightclub comic on the run from the mob. It is filmed and edited in a fractured style, very much in the manner of the French New Wave: imaginatively energetic, oblique, modernist. It foregrounds form over content and demonstrates an exuberance of style unlike most films being made at the time. Following the path of a nightclub comic escaping from the mob, *Mickey One* is occasionally absurdist in its juxtaposition of bizarre images and characters, and always surprising in its rapid changes of pace. It was a commercial and critical failure. Even its director disowned it.

Bonnie and Clyde finally came together with Warren Beatty and Faye Dunaway as its stars and Penn as its director.[1] The result was a film that broke many rules and spoke to a new audience ready for a cinema that defied conventions. The film takes place in the Depression-era Midwest, where two down and outers, Clyde Barrow, a convicted robber, and Bonnie Parker, a lost young woman, join in a robbing and killing spree. The country gangster/couple on the run film is a relatively old subgenre of the gangster film. It can be traced as far back as *You Only Live Once*, directed by the German émigré, Fritz Lang in 1937 (Walter Wanger Productions, United Artists). Its more recent antecedent is Joseph H. Lewis's *Gun Crazy* (coscripted by the blacklisted Dalton Trumbo, King Brothers Productions, United Artists, 1950). But *Bonnie and Clyde* goes far beyond its inheritance in joining the viewer closely to its protagonists and raising the amount and presence of bloody violence their actions incur, violence that eventually turns on them when they are shot to pieces, in slow motion, at film's end.

The film works by locking our gaze with Bonnie and Clyde early in the film. The looks they exchange with one another, as a bored Bonnie sees Clyde trying to hotwire her car, invites our eyes, and our emotions, to join with them, to accept them as adventurous, stylish, happy robbers who become folk heroes. Robbing, in the first part of the film, is a joyful experience and a poke at authority. As their exploits continue, as they are joined by Clyde's brother and his wife, the film turns darker, the police more menacing, the blood more copious. Violence and sexuality become blatantly linked as the film progresses. Clyde is impotent and, throughout the film, his gun becomes a substitute phallus, until he overcomes his own sexual reticence when he and Bonnie become cornered by the law and their notoriety. The more danger, the more sexual excitement. The element of sexual dysfunction and displacement, along with the way the film moves the viewer into close sympathy with the gangster, is a mark of how far and how quickly film was moving away from the Production Code and its insistence on retribution. When the "retribution" comes, it is overpowering.

The level of violence, especially the slow-motion slaughter of the main characters that brings the film

The escalation of screen violence as Bonnie and Clyde (Faye Dunaway and Warren Beatty) are gunned down at the end of Arthur Penn's *Bonnie and Clyde* (1967).

to an intense close was unlike anything seen in American film to date. Even *Psycho*'s shower scene—which was, after all, in black and white—could not have prepared the audience, drawn so closely to the film's characters, for so wrenching a sequence. The brutal end was not retribution in the old sense; rather, it elicits horror and sympathy, the latter emotion impermissible under the old code. Instead of Little Caesar groveling in self-pity as he is shot down by the police, Bonnie and Clyde reach the peak of their outlaw powers and their self-esteem when they are betrayed by one of their own gang. Clyde has even regained sexual potency. The violent end of the conventional screen gangster was inevitable. The excruciating end of Bonnie and Clyde is an assault on our senses and emotions.

Bonnie and Clyde became a touchstone film for a new generation of filmmakers and filmgoers. It spoke to the restlessness of the 1960s counterculture and their suspicion of authority. And it spoke to Hollywood. The film's success, despite all attempts of the studio and some critics to bury it, made the new studio executives and the critical community take notice. Pauline Kael, who was becoming an important critical voice in support of the New Hollywood, wrote a major review of the film for the *New Yorker* magazine, and this helped turn critical and popular opinion around.

ALICE'S RESTAURANT AND LITTLE BIG MAN

Arthur Penn worked into the early 1990s. He made two important films immediately following *Bonnie and Clyde. Alice's Restaurant* (Elkins Entertainment, Florin, United Artists, 1969) was based on the popular song by Arlo Guthrie (son of the famed folk singer, Woody Guthrie), a countercultural tale about a false arrest for littering, and *Little Big Man* (Cinema Center Films, Stockbridge-Hiller Productions, National General, 1970), a Western that held up Native Americans as both the heroes and the victims of Western expansion. *Little Big Man* was one of three films, including Sam Peckinpah's violent and moving *The Wild Bunch* (Warner Bros./Seven Arts, 1969) and Robert Altman's *McCabe and Mrs. Miller* (Warner Bros., David Foster Productions, 1971), a lyrical elegy to the myths of Western movies that effectively ended the Western as a viable genre. These three films constituted a rebuke to the myth of the West and manifest destiny of white expansion into the American frontier. More accurately, these films and the Vietnam War disabused American culture about the righteousness of violently interfering with another culture that they did not understand.

FOUR FRIENDS

Even while celebrating the counterculture, Arthur Penn was suspicious of it. Perhaps he picked up on the anxieties inherent in the antiwar movement and was not optimistic about its outcome. *Four Friends* (Geria Productions, Filmways, Florin, Cinema 77, Orion, 1981) is a rather sour look back on a decade that Penn now saw as one of emotional and intellectual confusion and loss. Where *Bonnie and Clyde* was both a reflection and an instigation of the rebelliousness of the late 1960s, *Four Friends* seems almost angry about the period—disappointed, perhaps. In one of the film's fine set pieces, the central character, Danilo (Craig Wasson), emerges from the hospital, having recovered from being wounded at a wedding where the bride was shot by her father. As he moves through the street, the sounds of the late 60s are magnified as various characters walk by, looked at by Penn with bemusement and some consternation. The period is now seen as faintly ridiculous, enormously violent, and, perhaps, a waste of energy.

NIGHT MOVES

Four Friends is an uneven film, an indication perhaps of a flagging imagination. A few years earlier, Penn made an extraordinary film that was not so much concerned with the counterculture as it was with the darkness of mood throughout the culture as a whole in the wake of the 1960s and the Watergate scandals of the early 1970s, scandals that resulted in the resignation of President Richard Nixon. *Night Moves* (Warner Bros., 1975) is a neonoir detective film about loss and powerlessness, a diminished sense of presence in the world. Here, the detective, Harry Moseby (Gene Hackman), goes through a grinding process of discovery that leads only to a series of betrayals and failures, leaving Harry stranded in a boat in the middle of the ocean, his job and his life unresolved. *Night Moves* is in the tradition of detective films like *The Big Sleep* (Howard Hawks, Warner Bros., 1946), though without that film's sense of humor or the detective's moral righteousness. It is a late modernist narrative of the diminished self in a world in which absolutely no one can be trusted. The film speaks to the feelings of cultural powerlessness of the decade, and to Penn's own feelings of exhaustion with the possibilities of change in the world at large. By the mid-1990s, he was finished with filmmaking and served for a time as director of the Actor's Studio and then as a producer of the television series *Law and Order*. He died in 2010.

THE GRADUATE, AMERICAN INTERNATIONAL PICTURES, AND *EASY RIDER*

THE GRADUATE

There were other films aimed at the "youth market" that did very well with a variety of audiences. Mike Nichols's *The Graduate* (Lawrence Turman, Embassy Pictures, 1967), appearing the same year as *Bonnie and Clyde*, was not nearly as daring in its formal structure, and was concerned with sexuality and its discontents rather than violent confrontations with a recalcitrant society. But its focus on a young man at odds with an adult world struck a similar chord as Penn's film. Dustin Hoffman's Ben is a lost soul caught in an arid middle-class environment. His affair with Mrs. Robinson (Anne Bancroft) and his love for her daughter Elaine (Katharine Ross) set up a tension of failure and desire that reverberated with a new, younger audience. The film's score by Simon and Garfunkel did much to enhance this appeal.

AIP AND *EASY RIDER*

Other films of the late 60s and early 70s set the tone for a changed American cinema culture. An important source for that change was an independent production company named American International Pictures (AIP). Started in the mid-1950s, its none too lofty goal was to produce cheap horror, science fiction, and exploitation films aimed at the thriving drive-in movie trade of the period. Its earliest films had titles like *The Undead* (AIP, 1957), *Sorority Girl* (Sunset Productions, AIP, 1957), *The Saga of the Viking Women and Their Voyage to the Waters of the Great Sea Serpent* (Malibu Productions, AIP, 1957), and *Teenage Caveman* (Malibu Productions, AIP, 1958). All of these films were directed by Roger Corman. Corman was not AIP's only director, but he became its most famous, going on in the 1960s to direct a series of excellent films based on stories by Edgar Allen Poe, especially his 1964 production, *The Masque of the Red Death* (Alta Vista Productions, AIP). But Corman had a different, more lasting influence on American film. He hired young aspiring actors, directors, and crew people to work quickly, for next to nothing in the way of salary, but to get a maximum of filmmaking experience. In 1966, he directed a biker film, *Wild Angels* (AIP), starring Peter Fonda. The next year, he made an LSD movie, *The Trip* (AIP), also with Peter Fonda and written by Jack Nicholson, who also did some of his early acting roles in Corman's films, such as *The Little Shop of Horrors* (Santa Clara Productions, 1960). Francis Ford Coppola directed his first film for Roger Corman, *Dementia 13* (Filmgroup Productions, AIP, 1963), and Martin Scorsese directed his second film, *Boxcar Bertha* (AIP, 1972), for him.

In 1968, Dennis Hopper, who had acted in various films, including Nicholas Ray's *Rebel without a Cause* (Warner Bros., 1955) and Corman's *The Trip*, brought an idea to AIP for a new biker movie. Hopper had a bad reputation in Hollywood as a crazy person, and the head of AIP turned him down. But some young producers at Columbia, Bert Schneider and Bob Rafelson, eager to ride the youth wave that made *Bonnie and Clyde* and *The Graduate* so popular, took on the project. The film was made with other Corman alumni: Hopper directed, Peter Fonda wrote the script, with an assist from Terry Southern; Hopper, Fonda, and Jack Nicholson played the main roles in the film.[2]

Easy Rider (Columbia, 1969) is a biker film with a difference. The production values are high: it was photographed by László Kovács, one of the great **cinematographers** of the period. The score is made up of existing rock music, a trend that was made popular by *The Graduate*. Most important, the film represents the cultural wars so prominent at the end of the 1960s. During their trip from LA to New Orleans

Rolling down the highway. The motorcycle film as generational statement. Wyatt, Billy, and George (Peter Fonda, Dennis Hopper, Jack Nicholson) in *Easy Rider* (Peter Fonda, Dennis Hopper, 1969).

with the money earned by selling a cache of cocaine, Wyatt (Fonda) and Billy (Hopper) come face to face with antihippie rednecks. They manage to reclaim Nicholson's tormented George Hanson, a civil rights lawyer in a backwater southern town, but he is killed, as are Wyatt and Billy, martyrs to free-living, pot-smoking hippiedom. This is rather straightforward as narrative lines go, but *Easy Rider* works against this line. It is something of a musical melodrama with violence, a choreography of motorcycles and the road they travel, LSD hallucinations, and the landscape of the American West, contrasting free spirits against the repressed, the angry, and the resentful.

Like *Bonnie and Clyde*, the film celebrates freedom by killing it. It was as if there was some deep-seated need on the part of the counterculture to see themselves as martyrs to their cause. Certainly the dominant culture did its best to marginalize them. President Richard Nixon called them "bums" as he escalated the Vietnam War. There were isolated attacks on hippies by construction workers and there were large-scale, brutal attacks on demonstrators by a police riot during the 1968 Democratic Convention in Chicago. This horrendous event served as the backdrop for the film *Medium Cool* (Haskell Wexler, H&J, Paramount, 1969). There were the murders of Kent State students by national guardsmen in 1970 and the string of assassinations across the decade: John F. Kennedy, Robert Kennedy, Martin Luther King, Malcolm X. Tear gas and death hung in the air. It is therefore no mystery that the moneymaking, youth-oriented films that marked the resurgence of Hollywood filmmaking during the late 1960s celebrated their audience while reminding them of their precarious standing in the dominant culture of the country.

It could be argued that *Easy Rider* takes a cheap shot. It brings us close to its three characters only to have them murdered. *Bonnie and Clyde* runs the same gamut, and this is typical of melodrama—working up our emotions and then working them up further by suddenly removing the characters from us. Traditional melodrama usually delivers its character a fatal disease (recall the 1939 Bette Davis vehicle, *Dark Victory*, discussed in Chapter 11 or *The Notebook* (Nick Cassavetes, New Line Cinema, Gran Via, Avery Pix, 2004) that we will discuss in Chapter 26). The violent deaths that end *Bonnie and Clyde* and *Easy Rider* draw from the melodramatic well and filter it through the contradictory currents of the late 1960s, the energy and despair that drove the culture and its films. The deaths of Bonnie, Clyde, Wyatt, Billy, and George are a curious kind of reaffirmation of a deep-seated anxiety about failure and a sense of martyrdom to the cause.

ROBERT ALTMAN

MASH

Within the culture of Hollywood, these films registered a sea change in the hierarchical structure of production. Taking their cue from the films coming

Robert Altman parodies Da Vinci's *The Last Supper* in *MASH* (1970).

from Europe, and the financial success of the films themselves, some studio producers were beginning to recognize the director as the formative, creative force in the filmmaking process. We may recall that, in the early history of American film, the director was a key figure, only to be reduced in status when the **producer system** came into play during the early 20s of the previous century. As the youth-oriented films made the studios a good deal of money, the directors of those films began to receive a great deal of attention.

Robert Altman was older than many of the filmmakers beginning their work in the late 1960s. He had done a great deal of television, made a compilation documentary (constructed mostly of still images) on James Dean (*The James Dean Story*, Warner Bros.) and a juvenile delinquent film, called, appropriately, *The Delinquents* (Imperial Productions, United Artists, both in 1957). He was not at the top of the list to direct *MASH* (Fox, 1970), but when he got the job, he turned the script by former blacklisted writer Ring Lardner, Jr. into a large canvas of antiwar high jinx in a field hospital in Korea. Though set during the Korean War, *MASH* was clearly about Vietnam, and the antiauthoritarian antics of the army surgeons fit the mood of the anti–Vietnam War sentiment sweeping the country. There was also something different about the look of *MASH*. Altman used a telephoto lens to shoot the film, and this resulted in a compression of space, a lack of depth that brought all action to the foreground. Within this crowded space, he used a zoom lens to move back and forth between characters, picking out a face in the crowd and then roving around to another as the surgeons joke around and play practical jokes on each other—Hawkeye Pierce (Donald Sutherland) and Trapper John (Elliott Gould) versus Frank Burns (Robert Duvall) and Hot Lips Houlihan (Sally Kellerman). The **soundtrack** is as busy as the **image track**, everyone talking at once, the camp loudspeaker continually squawking announcements and jokes—antiauthority and, unfortunately, sometimes antifemale.

ALTMAN AFTER *MASH*

MASH was a huge success and spawned the popular, long-running television series. This did not help Robert Altman because he made no money from the show, and he never again made as commercially successful a film as MASH. But he continued to work, making over 40 films (including television movies and series) in a career that lasted until his death in 2006. He continually bucked the changing tides of the Hollywood system, challenging film genres, experimenting with visual and narrative structures in films as varied as his elegiac Western, *McCabe and Mrs. Miller*; a serious parody of the detective film, *The Long Goodbye* (Lions Gate, MGM/United Artists, 1973); a sharp satire of the country music world, *Nashville* (ABC Entertainment, Paramount, 1975); a satire of contemporary Hollywood, *The Player* (Fine Line Features, Avenue Pictures, Spelling Entertainment, Addis Wechsler Pictures, 1992); a sardonic, multicharacter study of life in contemporary Los Angeles, *Short Cuts* (Fine Line Features, Sandcastle 5 Productions, Viacom Enterprises, 1993); and a faux-British country house drama, *Gosford Park* (USA Films, Capitol Films, Film Council, 2001). He made performance films, like his homage to ballet, *The Company* (Sony Pictures Classics, Capitol Films,

CP Medien AG, 2003), and, his last, a moving elegy about death and music, *A Prairie Home Companion* (Picturehouse Entertainment, GreeneStreet Films, River Road Entertainment, 2006).

MCCABE AND MRS. MILLER, THE WILD BUNCH, AND MORE ABOUT FILM VIOLENCE

Although the oldest of the group of new directors to emerge in the late 60s and 70s, Altman remained the one most dedicated to fighting the studios. He was able to convince producer after producer that he would make them as much money as *MASH*. None of his films did, but he moved artistically from strength to strength, developing an aesthetic that involved a deceptively gentle, probing camera that revealed characters at their worst, their most confused, their most lost. Many of his films played changes on established film genres, like *McCabe and Mrs. Miller*. I noted that the Western genre effectively came to a close in the early 1970s because of three films. Arthur Penn's *Little Big Man* reverses the Western polarity by depicting the Indians as the heroes of the West, the "human beings" struggling against the bumbling white men who will ultimately destroy them. Sam Peckinpah's *The Wild Bunch* is, in retrospect, and allegory of Vietnam. An aging band of outlaws joins forces with the Mexican army fighting revolutionaries. When they realize their error, they engage in a bloody shootout in which they are destroyed along with the Mexicans they attack. But as with so many of the films of this period, simple description does not express what this film is about, which is an elegy about the myth of the West, a lyrical, violent, visual poem of the passing of an old time and the films that mythologized it.

The Wild Bunch takes the violence of *Bonnie and Clyde* and increases it by some measure. Blood spurts like a fountain from gun wounds as men fall in slow-motion ballets of death. The result is visually entrancing, but at the same time raises the question about aestheticizing violence. Does a filmmaker have a moral obligation *not* to make violence attractive, or are filmgoers sophisticated enough to understand they are seeing an imaginative representation of violence and not an invitation to partake in it or become inured to it? Ever since *Psycho* (Alfred Hitchcock, Paramount, 1960), the level of violence in contemporary film has risen incrementally. The questions about the morality of its representation remain unanswered.

Like *The Wild Bunch*, Altman's *McCabe and Mrs. Miller* is an elegy about the myths of the "Old West." But Altman's film is less interested in the spectacles of the myth's fall than he is in taking apart the personalities the Western has created and the lies of history foisted by the genre. Altman depicts the Western "hero" as a bumbling gambler (Warren Beatty), who arrives at a half-built, cold, and rainy outpost to set up a whorehouse. This is not the open landscape of Ford's Monument Valley, but a closed, filthy, unpleasant location of suspicion and betrayal. McCabe's plans are compromised by the arrival of Mrs. Miller (Julie Christie), a tough-minded businesswoman, who is a far cry from the stereotyped school teacher from the East that populates many conventional Westerns. She takes over McCabe's business, builds an efficient house of prostitution, while he faces down the "bad guys," who turn out to be representatives of a mining company that will buy out the town,

Violent spectacles of death in Peckinpah's *The Wild Bunch* (1969).

Mrs. Miller (Julie Christie) pleads with McCabe (Warren Beatty) not to fight the business interests who want to buy out the town in Robert Altman's *McCabe and Mrs. Miller* (1971).

even over McCabe's dead body. Which is, in the end, what happens.

As interesting as is the story of *McCabe and Mrs. Miller*, the way its story is told is more interesting still. Altman was an innovator in visual style. He uses the **zoom lens** as a kind of probing instrument of perception, moving from a far shot to a close-up, picking up a face in the crowd, accenting a scene by means of a graceful zoom from one character to another. Along with the way he manipulates the **film stock** itself, suffusing it with a golden light, he creates a crowded, often melancholy **mise-en-scène**. With the addition of a busy soundtrack, where characters talk at cross purposes with one another, and a lyrical music track made up of songs by Leonard Cohen, Altman displays a kind of sadness over the loss of the Western genre at the same time that he attacks it by exposing its contradictions and downright lies. McCabe is not the famous gunslinger that townspeople think he is, nor the lover he wants to be. Mrs. Miller rebuffs him, and when he goes after the gunman that the mining company sends in to take over the town, the townspeople get distracted by a fire in the church they have up to this time completely ignored. McCabe kills the gunmen and dies in the snow as Altman, playing on the editing tradition started in the early silent era, cuts between him, the gunmen, the townspeople fighting the fire, and Mrs. Miller, who withdraws to the warm security of an opium den. A conventional editing structure, alternating space and actions occurring at the same time, is used to create an unconventional take on a traditional genre.

NASHVILLE AND *SECRET HONOR*

Nashville is probably Altman's best-known film after *MASH*. Its huge cast of characters and their interlocking stories create a complex narrative about the foibles and politics of the country and western scene. The film is satirical and unrelenting in its attack on hypocrisy and passivity, two of Altman's favorite targets. *Nashville* is a film not only about country and western songs (the film's actors wrote most of their own music), but about celebrity, assassination, and the willingness of people to worship at the feet of phonies. The film ends in an open-air concert where a singer is shot down. The crowd joins in a song "You may say that I ain't free/But it don't worry me." It is an anthem and a state of mind that Altman saw as rampant across American culture in the wake of Watergate and the administration of Richard Nixon as the counterculture faded. Later, Altman made a film about Nixon himself called *Secret Honor* (Sandcastle 5 Productions, 1984), essentially a one-man show in which actor Philip Baker Hall creates a profane, paranoid, resentful, angry, belligerent version of that benighted president. The large canvas of *Nashville* and the small stage of *Secret Honor* both speak to the confusions inherent in the culture in the post-Watergate period, expressed by Altman in a spirit of anger and bemusement.

SHORT CUTS

Altman continued on an independent path. He broke with Hollywood filmmaking for almost a decade in the 1980s, making, with his own production company,

Sandcastle 5 Productions, and his own studio, Lions Gate (not to be confused with the contemporary production house, Lionsgate), small films based on theatrical works like *Come Back to the Five and Dime, Jimmy Dean, Jimmy Dean* (Sandcastle 5 Productions, Viacom Enterprises, 1982). In 1992, he made a surprise comeback with a satire on Hollywood morality (or lack thereof), *The Player*. He continued with a variety of films, most notably the aforementioned *Short Cuts*, based on stories by the short story author Raymond Carver. *Short Cuts* expands the multicharacter canvas of *Nashville* and is one of the most misanthropic films ever made. It contains no sympathetic characters, only a steady, quiet onslaught of resentment and anger, of misunderstandings, of acting out and reacting to wrongs real and imagined. *Short Cuts* is a kind of disaster film. Beginning with an infestation of insects and ending with an earthquake, it relates the very human disasters inherent in lack of trust, in sexual panic, in the generally squelched and attenuated lives of middle-class couples in contemporary Los Angeles.

Short Cuts is focused on female vulnerability, signified by the number of women in the film who are seen naked and whose nudity becomes a source of anger and resentment on the part of the film's men. Most notorious are the sequences of the fishermen, who discover the partially clothed body of a woman under the water where they are out for their sport. One of the men urinates on the body. They refuse to report their discovery until after they have finished their fishing trip. In another sequence, Marian Wyman (Julianne Moore), standing half naked before her husband, must listen to his verbal outrage over an affair that occurred 2 years ago. Marian is a painter, mostly of nude women. She feels and represents the immediacy of the body and suffers over its exposure to her husband's rage. Rage expressed or suppressed is shared by many of *Short Cuts*'s characters. Bill Bush (Robert Downey, Jr.), a makeup artist, paints his wife's face with bruises and gets so turned on that he fakes beating her by smashing his arm into a pillow above her head. In the film's penultimate sequence, real violence is committed against a woman. While on a picnic with their wives, Bill and his friend Jerry (Chris Penn) pick up two girls in Griffith Park. Jerry, who throughout the film quietly seethes over his wife's job as a telephone sex worker, picks up a rock and smashes one of the girls in the head. An earthquake ensues, as if nature itself was rebelling against this outrage.

MAGNOLIA

Short Cuts is an uncompromising film, often painful to watch, the interlocking lives of its characters serving only to emphasize the interlocking visitations of pain and misunderstanding. It has had an extraordinary influence on other filmmakers, who found the narrative of multiple characters meeting by coincidence in Los Angeles irresistible. Paul Thomas Anderson, who has created a number of important films, including *There Will Be Blood* (Mirimax, Ghoulardi, Paramount Vantage, 2007) and *The Master* (Annapurna Pictures, Ghoulardi Film Company, Weinstein Company, 2012), made his own version of *Short Cuts* in 1999. *Magnolia* (Ghoulardi, New Line Cinema) raises the temperature of its predecessor. Almost all of the film's characters not only suffer but act out their suffering loudly against one another. Pain and misunderstanding, some downright cruelty, and very small acts of contrition play across this large melodramatic canvas of people at odds with themselves and their world—which ends with an apocalyptic shower of frogs from the sky.

In *Magnolia,* Anderson makes a more serious, melodramatic film than Altman, who even in a film as grim as *Short Cuts* finds, if not humor, at least a sense of the absurdity in the situations he creates. Humanity as well. I said that *Short Cuts* is a misanthropic film. But, as sharp as his satire is and as cutting his approach to established Hollywood genres, Altman maintains a deeply human connection with the characters who people his films and the self-defeating situations in which they so often find themselves. In addition, he stands as a major figure in the Hollywood new wave. He was defiantly independent of the studios, yet able to get financing for an enormous variety of films. While some filmmakers attempt to imitate his style of filmmaking, few can conduct a career as productive, varied, and culturally attuned as his.

SELECTED FILMOGRAPHY

Arthur Penn

The Left Handed Gun, Haroll Productions, Warner Bros., 1958.

The Miracle Worker, Playfilm Productions, United Artists, 1962.

Mickey One, Florin, Tatira, Columbia, 1965.

Bonnie and Clyde, Warner Bros./Seven Arts, Tatira-Hiller Productions, 1967.

Alice's Restaurant, Elkins Entertainment, Florin, United Artists, 1969.

Little Big Man, Cinema Center Films, Stockbridge-Hiller Productions, National General, 1970.

Night Moves, Warner Bros., 1975.

Four Friends, Geria Productions, Filmways, Florin, Cinema 77, Orion, 1981.

Robert Altman

(Note that this is a small fraction of the films directed by Altman)

MASH, Fox, 1970.

McCabe and Mrs. Miller, Warner Bros., David Foster Productions, 1971.

The Long Goodbye, Lions Gate, MGM/United Artists, 1973.

Nashville, ABC Entertainment, Paramount, 1975.

Come Back to the Five and Dime, Jimmy Dean, Jimmy Dean, Sandcastle 5 Productions, Viacom Enterprises, 1982.

The Player, Fine Line Features, Avenue Pictures, Spelling Entertainment, Addis Wechsler Pictures, 1992.

Short Cuts, Fine Line Features, Sandcastle 5 Productions, Viacom Enterprises, 1993.

The Company, Sony Picture Classics, Capitol Films, CP Medien AG, 2003.

A Prairie Home Companion, Picturehouse Entertainment, GreeneStreet Films, River Road Entertainment, 2006.

Easy Rider, dir. Dennis Hopper, Columbia, 1967.

The Graduate, dir. Mike Nichols, Lawrence Turman, Embassy Pictures, 1967.

Medium Cool, dir. Haskell Wexler, H&J, Paramount, 1969.

The Wild Bunch, dir. Sam Peckinpah, Warner Bros./Seven Arts 1969.

Magnolia, dir. Paul Thomas Anderson, Ghoulardi, New Line Cinema, 1999.

Roger Corman

The Little Shop of Horrors, Santa Clara Productions, 1960.

The Masque of the Red Death, Alta Vista Productions, AIP 1964.

Wild Angels, AIP, 1966.

The Trip, AIP, 1967.

SUGGESTIONS FOR FURTHER READING

Peter Biskind, *Easy Riders, Raging Bulls: How the Sex-Drugs-and the Rock 'n' Roll Generation Saved Hollywood* (New York, NY: Simon and Schuster, 1998).

Diane Jacobs, *Hollywood Renaissance* (Cranbury, NJ: A. S. Barnes & Co., 1977).

Mark Harris, *Pictures at a Revolution: Five Movies and the Birth of the New Hollywood* (New York, NY: Penguin Press, 2008).

Robert Kolker, *A Cinema of Loneliness*, 4th ed. (New York, NY: Oxford University Press, 2011).

Jon Lewis, ed. *The New American Cinema* (Durham, NC: Duke University Press, 1998).

James Monaco, *American Film Now* (New York, NY: Oxford University Press, 1979).

Stephen Prince, *Savage Cinema: Sam Peckinpah and the Rise of Ultraviolent Movies* (Austin, TX: University of Texas Press, 1998).

Robert T. Self, *Robert Altman's Subliminal Reality* (Minneapolis, MN: University of Minneapolis Press, 2002).

NOTES

1. A thorough discussion of the production of *Bonnie and Clyde* is in Mark Harris, *Pictures at a Revolution: Five Movies and the Birth of the New Hollywood* (New York, NY: Penguin Press, 2008).
2. Production information on *Easy Rider* can be found in Peter Biskind, *Easy Riders, Raging Bulls: How the Sex-Drugs-and Rock'n' Roll Generation Saved Hollywood* (New York, NY: Simon and Schuster, 1998), 61–75.

CHAPTER 25

THE NEW HOLLYWOOD AND AFTER: PART TWO (1972–2011)

We continue investigating the work of some of the filmmakers—Francis Ford Coppola, Steven Spielberg, and Martin Scorsese—who were part of the revival of Hollywood film in the late 1960s and the early 1970s.

AFTER READING THIS CHAPTER, YOU SHOULD UNDERSTAND:

- How *The Godfather* and *Jaws* became the most popular films of the period.
- How Francis Ford Coppola mixed intimate filmmaking with large-scale productions.
- What is distinct in the style and content of Steven Spielberg's films and how he alternated "entertainments" with more serious subjects.
- How Spielberg creates a response from his audience.
- How Martin Scorsese moved from an experimental filmmaker to a popular director and alternated documentaries with feature films.

YOU SHOULD BE ABLE TO:

- Recognize the stylistic attributes of films of Coppola, Spielberg, and Scorsese.
- Distinguish between the gangster films of Martin Scorsese and Francis Ford Coppola.
- Discuss the use of point of view in cinema.
- Compare the careers of Francis Ford Coppola and Steven Spielberg.
- Discuss how Scorsese's documentaries differ from his fiction films.
- Discuss how *Mean Streets*, *Goodfellas*, and *The Godfather* films compare to the gangster films of the 1930s.
- Account for the rise and fall of "the director as superstar."

FRANCIS FORD COPPOLA

Robert Altman's *MASH* was a huge success, but not nearly as huge as two films that appeared within a few years of each other in the early and mid-1970s and which, however briefly, solidified the place of the director as star of the production. The films were Francis Ford Coppola's *The Godfather* (Paramount, Alfran Productions, 1972) and Steven Spielberg's *Jaws* (Zanuck/Brown Productions, Universal, 1975). In both cases, the directors surprised everyone—perhaps even themselves—with the success of their blockbusters. Coppola was one of the new breed of filmmakers who went to film school. The Hollywood tradition was that a director worked his way through the ranks; now, in the late 1960s, there emerged new directorial talent schooled in film history, coming to filmmaking with their own ideas based on the films they had seen and learned from, experienced in the universe of cinema. Coppola worked for a time for Roger Corman, making a horror film for him, *Dementia 13* (Filmgroup Productions, AIP, 1963). He went on to make other small-budget films: *You're a Big Boy Now* (Seven Arts, Warner Bros., 1966), *The Rain People* (American Zoetrope, Warner Bros./Seven Arts, 1969), and a big studio musical, *Finian's Rainbow* (Warner Bros./Seven Arts, 1968). He also did screenwriting, winning an Academy Award for his script for *Patton* (Franklin J. Schaffner, Fox, 1970—a rather conventional war film made in the same year and by the same studio as Robert Altman's *MASH*). He set up his own production company, American Zoetrope, in San Francisco, hoping it would become an alternative to what he saw as the suffocating production system of southern California. But his big break came when Paramount chose him to direct *The Godfather*, perhaps because Coppola was an Italian American.[1]

THE GODFATHER

What is most remarkable about *The Godfather* and *Jaws* is the subtle and effective ways in which they take cinematic conventions and rework them, creating films that, although they are, in the case of *Jaws*, based on the monster film—something like *The Creature from the Black Lagoon* (Jack Arnold, Universal, 1954)—and the gangster film in the case of *The Godfather*. The two young directors successfully reinvented the genres and our response to them. Response is a key to their success, as it was to *Bonnie and Clyde*. It is as if Coppola and Spielberg carefully constructed audience response within their films so that we, as viewers, are assured to react in exactly the way the filmmakers want us to. *The Godfather*, for example, does not begin with a standard **establishing shot**, which would locate the viewer in the visual and geographical space of the film—a view of the New York skyline, for example—before editing into the narrative proper begins. Instead, the film begins in darkness with only the face of an unknown character visible, as he pleads for vengeance for his violated daughter. The camera slowly tracks back until the figure of Don Corleone (Marlon Brando) comes into

The Brando gesture in the opening sequence of Francis Ford Coppola's *The Godfather* (1972). Compare with the image of Brando in Chapter 18.

view. He too is surrounded by darkness, cradling a cat in his lap. His character is inflected with some gestures common to Brando's performance style: a small wave of his hand, a brush of his fingers on his cheek.

We are at the wedding ceremony of the Don's daughter, a time when favors are asked of the Godfather. Coppola contrasts the dark inner sanctum of Don Corleone's office with the bright family celebration outside. As viewers, we are privileged to this inner world, where violent acts are planned and the family is protected. This is the duality that works throughout the film. The idea of a closely knit family structure continually threatened by rival mobs whipsaws us, tests our loyalties, but ultimately keeps us on the side of the Corleone's, at least until Don Corleone dies and his son Michael (Al Pacino) ascends to power.

Michael represents the transition from the family-operated business, where the Don made people an offer they couldn't refuse, to a more cold-blooded, business operation. This process was common to many gangster films from the late 1940s on, when the lone gangster was forced to become part of a larger organization or be left out in the violent cold. The idea of the Mafia as the big business of crime was irresistible to a culture weaned on the gangster film. The lone gangster is a threatening and threatened figure. The Mafia is a large, invincible organization, an outlaw corporation working at the corrupt heart of the society. Don Corleone's operation is a family business. At the beginning of *The Godfather*, Don Corleone's violence was large but personal—when the movie producer, Woltz (John Marley), refuses to employ the Don's godson, he wakes up to find the severed head of his favorite horse under his sheets. When Michael takes power, his ruthlessness is acted out on a grand scale, climaxed by the **montage** of murder and baptism—or better, baptism by murder. Michael stands as godfather to his sister's baby while his minions murder his rivals. The montage follows the precepts laid down by the Russian filmmaker Sergei Eisenstein, who held that the emotional and intellectual power of a film lay in the way shots were put together in often shocking ways. Cuts from the priest's hands on Connie's (Talia Shire) baby are matched to the movements of the gang as they prepare to murder the rivals. "Do you renounce Satan?" the priest asks. "I do renounce him," Michael responds, and we see a man in Las Vegas get shot through the eye. "Will you be baptized?" the priest asks, and there is a montage of murdered bodies.

Michael is not quite a satanic figure, but he is cold and calculating, and the film ends with the audience being shut out of the inner sanctum into which they were welcomed at the beginning. His wife, Kay (Diane Keaton), sits outside the office, while Michael's men swear fealty to him, kissing his ring. One of them shuts the door and we are left in the darkness that began the film, though this time without a privileged view into the workings of the mob. We are played with in the course of the film, our desire for the protective family countered by the realization that "protection," in this case, entails vengeful violence. As with *Bonnie and Clyde*, we are presented with a fragile intimacy that is rudely shattered. Unlike *Bonnie and Clyde*, *The Godfather* is not loosely structured, and our relationship to its characters is not as close. The film is somewhat operatic in its stately set pieces: carefully composed and shot, a purposeful unfolding of events meant to invite and shock, holding us simultaneously close and at a distance.

It is interesting to note that *The Godfather* appeared just before the Watergate crisis—the break-in by Republican operatives into the offices of the Democratic Party, an event that ultimately led to the resignation of President Richard M. Nixon in 1974—was beginning to gain considerable traction. We can speculate that some of the attraction of Coppola's film occurred from its taking corruption as a given and portraying a family that, for a while at least, protects its members from the very corruption they are a part of. *The Godfather* is a film about security and its vulnerabilities; it plays on our desire for the one and fears of the other. It is, in short, not only a film whose violence forms part of its attraction, but that holds out the hope that violence can be committed as part of the process of protection and security. This is a strange contradiction, but for a culture vulnerable at the time because of the irresponsibility of its leaders, suspecting a deep-seated corruption in the very seat of power, a potent one and which led to the film's enormous popularity.

THE CONVERSATION

Coppola's future as a filmmaker was not as auspicious as its start. In fact, he flamed out. Between the *Godfather* Parts One and Two, Coppola made an extraordinary small film called *The Conversation* (Directors Company, The Coppola Company, American Zoetrope, Paramount, 1974). A surveillance expert, Harry Caul (Gene Hackman), believes he has overheard a murder plot. The film follows Harry's slow descent into paranoia as he himself becomes (he believes) the object of surveillance. The film ends with his tearing his apartment to pieces in an attempt to find a hidden microphone. This film is as intense as *The Godfather* films are broad, as detailed in small gestures and large consequences as the two large films that surround it are broad and operatic. Like Arthur Penn's *Night Moves*, made a year later and also starring Gene Hackman as a character—a detective in this case—also named Harry, it is a late modernist work that tells of reduced individual agency in a world too large, too abstract to control. It is a film of intense paranoia—something of a popular subject for films in a decade of failed government and seeming universal spying on citizens—told in small gestures about a small man made smaller by his own fears.

COPPOLA AND THE VIETNAM WAR FILM *APOCALYPSE NOW*

Films about the Vietnam War are very different from those of World War I or II. Tormented figures rather than great combat heroes haunt them. They are films of loss and learning, of jungle rot and crazed violence rather than redemption through battle. Coppola's Vietnam War film, *Apocalypse Now* (Zoetrope Studios, United Artists, 1979), was a film made in such chaos that it drained the imaginative resources of its director. Based on Joseph Conrad's story, *Heart of Darkness*, it is a vision of Vietnam as the hellish nightmare that it was, exaggerated to a surrealist pitch. Captain Willard (Martin Sheen) travels up river to find the rogue Colonel Kurtz (Marlon Brando). The deeper he moves through the jungle, the more bizarre and out of control things become. Soldiers are without leaders; scantily clad women arrive in a helicopter as part of a stage show in the middle of a battle zone. Kurtz's compound has reverted to primitive tribalism. The film equates the Vietnam War to a reversion to our most destructive, anarchic instincts. And, in a way, the structure and content of the film echo its production, which itself got crazier and more out of control in the Philippine jungle where it was filmed the longer it went on.

Apocalypse Now is one of the great Vietnam War films and one of the more interesting war films in Hollywood history. While it may have undone Coppola as a filmmaker, it stands as a mad and grandiloquent piece of filmmaking, imperfect but powerful in its depiction of war as a destroyer of men and their moral structures. It is full of great set pieces, concluding with the appearance of Marlon Brando's Kurtz—enormous, bald, dark, and threatening. Like the first *Godfather*, it ends with an **Eisensteinian montage** as Kurtz's tribe hacks an animal to pieces as Willard hacks Kurtz to death.

Entering the heart of darkness. Francis Ford Coppola's *Apocalypse Now* (1979).

STEVEN SPIELBERG

Coppola went on to make other films, including the ill-conceived and ill-fated *Godfather Part III* (Paramount, Zoetrope Studios, 1990), but he has never matched his earlier successes. Steven Spielberg, on the other hand, grew in stature and in filmmaking talent as his career expanded from an amateur moviemaker as a youngster to one of the most recognized directors in American cinema. By the late 1960s, he was working at Universal studios, directing television series and making a competent movie for television, *Duel* (Universal, 1971), which was released as a theatrical feature in Europe. *Duel* is about a man being pursued by a monster truck; it is the visual and narrative template for *Jaws*—an unstoppable monster on the attack. He made a couple-on-the-run movie, *The Sugarland Express* (Universal, Zanuck/Brown Productions 1974), and then directed *Jaws*, that, like *The Godfather*, was one of the biggest moneymakers of its time and changed the way films were released.

Of all the filmmakers who started as part of the "New Hollywood" movement in the 1970s, Steven Spielberg's career has been the most successful—certainly from a commercial point of view. During the 1980s and 1990s, he was at the center of American moviemaking. Not only did he direct almost one film a year, but he produced other directors' films as well. With producers Jeffrey Katzenberg and David Geffen, he set up a production company, DreamWorks SKG, which produced films, television series, and cable programs. DreamWorks SKG changed hands in 2008, and Spielberg remains part of the new DreamWorks in partnership with a large holding company in India. DreamWorks now releases their films through the Disney Company.[2] In addition to DreamWorks, Spielberg and Producers Kathleen Kennedy and Frank Marshall run a production company called Amblin Entertainment.

JAWS

Spielberg is in the enviable position of owning the means of production along with his equally enviable talent to create large cinematic narratives and individual scenes within those narratives that seal the viewer's attention, tying them emotionally to what is happening to the characters. In effect, Spielberg makes the viewer something like a character in the film. The trick is in the composition of his shots, the editing, and in the setting. Spielberg is, for example, much taken with the middle-class suburban family. In many of his films, it forms the core out of which adventure spins. The pull of family and job can be seen in the composition of shots in *Jaws*. Chief Brody takes up his job and settles his family in the seaside resort of Amity. When he receives a phone call reporting the shark attack, Spielberg frames Brody forward and to the right of the frame, while his family is in **soft focus** behind him. It is from this family that Brody is called to face the larger, public issues of the shark attack. The tension between family and official duty creates the larger tensions of the film, which draws us away from the domestic scene to the struggle of three men against a sea monster.

Formally, *Jaws* works differently than *The Godfather*. Its editing patterns throughout are more rapid and rhythmical. Much of the film takes place out of doors, as befits a movie about the beach, the ocean, and their unexpected dangers. The way it plays with the spectator is different as well. We are asked to identify with Chief of Police Brody (Roy Scheider), who carries the burden of protecting his beachfront town from the predations of the shark and the town elders who, despite the dangers, don't want to frighten away the tourist trade. Spielberg is often very crafty in the ways he manipulates audience attention and allegiance, weaving our gaze between a number of characters and, in the case of *Jaws*, animals. Every time the shark is about to attack, Spielberg cuts to a shot from the creature's point of view, accompanied by composer John Williams' thrumming bass fiddle score. The fear factor is in effect attached to the thing that creates the fear. We see what the predator sees, but the result is not that we identify with it; rather, we identify with its threat.

This rapid shifting of points of view keeps us locked into the narrative structure of *Jaws*. When Brody is sitting on the beach, keeping a close lookout, his view is blocked by passersby, and, like him, we keep straining for a closer view. Each time someone passes in front of him, Spielberg cuts to a closer view of Brody looking, heightening the tension. When he

"We're gonna need a bigger boat!" Quint (Robert Shaw), Brody (Roy Scheider), and Hooper (Richard Dreyfuss) spot the killer shark in Steven Spielberg's *Jaws* (1975).

finally sees a shark attack, Spielberg executes the camera movement that Hitchcock used in *Vertigo* (Paramount, 1958): a track in one direction with a zoom in the opposite, creating the impression that space is collapsing around Brody, heightening our own fear and expectation. This Hitchcockian play on the viewer's knowledge of what is to come, her waiting to see how it will manifest itself and then being startled or frightened when it does constitutes the formal tissue of *Jaws* and Spielberg's other films. Touching upon, heightening, and resonating with his viewers' fears and aspirations is the key to the Spielberg style.

The connection to Brody becomes redirected with the arrival of marine biologist Matt Hooper (Richard Dreyfuss) and the old shark hunter, Quint (Robert Shaw). When the three of them join forces, the film turns into a buddy movie in which the men must learn to work together to defeat their common enemy. Yet even together, Spielberg carefully marks differences between the three men. Quint, the old man of the sea, is too much a representative of times past; his snarling ways don't quite fit into the modern setting of efficient battle. He gets eaten by the shark. Hooper, the rich young scientist, is too much the intellectual, too young and cocky. When the crunch comes, he hides out in fear, while Brody, the working family man of the people, defeats the monster.

Like *The Godfather*, *Jaws* responds to the politics of the day. Film scholar Stephen Heath noted that *Jaws* was released "in the summer of America's final year in Vietnam," and that its three main characters act out a ritual of "destruction and conscience and manliness and menace and just-doing-the-job."[3] At the time of Vietnam, Watergate, and the collapse of the Nixon presidency, the spectacle of a cover-up, the desire of the town fathers to suppress the reality of the shark attacks would have a special resonance. The "manliness . . . and just-doing-the-job" of the three shark hunters provided a kind of surrogate victory over the forces of corruption. Meanwhile, the shark, that reincarnation of the movie monster from hell, provided enough fright to keep nervous people from going into the water.

CLOSE ENCOUNTERS OF THE THIRD KIND

Sometimes, one family has to be dissolved and a new one formed. Roy Neary (Richard Dreyfuss) has to leave his family in *Close Encounters of the Third Kind* (Columbia, EMI Films, Julia Phillips and Michael Phillips Productions, 1977) because they cannot deal with his obsession with the location of an alien landing. He creates a new family by running off with Jillian (Melinda Dillon), whose son has been abducted by the visitors from space. At the landing site, Roy is welcomed into yet another family, that of the aliens themselves. *Close Encounters* plays a major variation on the science fiction genre so prevalent in the 1950s. As we've seen, that decade's paranoia infiltrated its films, and visitors from outer space were almost invariably hostile. The army was needed to discover ways of destroying them. The paranoia of the 1970s seemed to work in the opposite direction. Upset and disillusioned with the politics of the decade, the culture looked elsewhere for redemption—or so

Spielberg wagered—and he made a science fiction film in which the army helps the aliens to come down and welcome earthlings to a new world. The childlike Roy Neary joins the family of space children under the paternal gaze of their leader.

Close Encounters is, in an unintended way, something of a scary film. It tells us that we will be better off, more open to excitement, to salvation, by looking upward toward alien worlds. The film provokes a childlike innocence of wonder and yearning that absolves us from earthly responsibility. It promises escape from the earthly into the welcoming arms of a strange but welcoming patriarchy. The film offers the promise of regression to childhood by leaving the untidy responsibilities of daily life on Earth.

E.T. AND *WAR OF THE WORLDS*

The suburban family is at the core of the narrative of *E.T.: The Extra-Terrestrial* (Universal, Amblin Entertainment, 1982). Elliott (Henry Thomas) must create acceptance for E.T. from his nonbelieving, single-parent family. The alien becomes a surrogate friend, father, and guide until a human father figure, the scientist Keys (Peter Coyote), takes its place. For Spielberg, the family is both inviolate and violated at the same time. But its violation almost always results in the reformation of the family in an alternative form. Where *Close Encounters* promised happiness beyond the Earth, *E.T.* offers the possibility of otherworldly intervention into the life of a lonely child, another version of the recreation of the domestic scene. There is a deep vein of sentimentality at work here, a play upon almost any viewer's desire for the security and comfort of family, a concept created as much by movies as by the realities of daily life. We saw it at work in the mafia world of *The Godfather* and we see it again in the yearnings for friendship and protection in *E.T.*

In Spielberg's early science fiction films, the reorientation of family is the result of an urge to move beyond the earthly domestic group to something unknown yet somehow more exciting and promising. Only in his remake of the 1953 film, *War of the Worlds* (Paramount, DreamWorks SKG, Amblin Entertainment, 2005), does he see the aliens as profoundly threatening. But even in this film, with its echoes of 9/11 in its depiction of hellish destruction, Spielberg focuses on the family and the trek of Ray Ferrier (Tom Cruise) to reunite with his wife and redeem his fatherhood in the face of a world cataclysm. The enormity of destruction is countered by the small, painful movements of Ray to reach his wife; gigantic alien machines prove no match for the persistence of the human instinct for survival. The bloodsucking aliens are undone not only by human pathogens to which they have no resistance, but by the resistance and resiliency of the common man, a conclusion very much in line with traditional Hollywood narratives.

SCHINDLER'S LIST

Spielberg is in the enviable situation of being able to alter his output every few years. He seeds his production of popular, spectacular entertainments with works that take on large historical subjects: race in *The Color Purple* (Amblin Entertainment, Guber Peters Co., Warner Bros., 1985) and *Amistad* (DreamWorks SKG, HBO, 1997); war in *Saving Private Ryan* (Amblin Entertainment, DreamWorks SKG, Paramount, 1998); American history in *Lincoln* (20th Century Fox, Imagine Entertainment, Amblin Entertainment, DreamWorks SKG, 2012); and perhaps most daringly, the Nazi extermination of the Jews in *Schindler's List* (Universal, Amblin Entertainment, 1993). It has been said that it is impossible to represent the horrors of the Holocaust because no image, no narrative can adequately express the horrific reality of one people, the Germans, attempting to wipe another, the Jews, off the face of Europe. Despite this warning, there have been a few films that have tried to narrate this most awful of political, racial crimes, ranging from fictional treatments to documentaries. Spielberg's attempt is a curious mixture of historical representation and Spielbergian sentiment. He constructs a narrative made of opposing figures. On the one side is Amon Goeth (Ralph Fiennes), a bloodthirsty Nazi who rapes and murders at will. He is an embodied idea of the most monstrous Nazi one can imagine. On the other is Oskar Schindler (Liam Neeson), a German who becomes convinced that he should save as many Jews

Nazi examining a Jewish woman in a concentration camp in Spielberg's *Schindler's List* (1993).

from the gas ovens as possible. In the middle is Itzhak Stern (Ben Kingsley), who works for Schindler and becomes his connection to the Jews Schindler tries to save.

Schindler's List is in many ways an uncompromising film. Its stark black and white images, the portrayal of the terror faced by the Nazi's victims is immediate and almost unrelenting. "Almost" is the key term. Spielberg seems unable to completely shake off the sentimentality of the saving family, in this case figured in the paternal Schindler, who in reality managed to save only a relatively small number of people. Spielberg attempts to cut the enormity of the Holocaust down to manageable size. He must do this in order to make a manageable film. But in so doing, he runs the risk of trivializing and sometimes sensationalizing his subject. There is a particularly troubling sequence in which a group of women in Auschwitz are stripped, have their heads shaved, and are sent into the shower. Spielberg's camera lingers over their naked bodies and terrified faces, looking through a peephole like a voyeur. The "shower" in a German concentration camp was Zyklon B gas; but in this imagined sequence, the women are not killed and the shower is not gas, but water. The sequence seems created to bring the audience to a pitch of anxiety and then suddenly relieve it. But such manipulation seems out of place in this film, which threatens to fall victim to its director's overwhelming need to find salvation and a saving figure amidst the most hopeless circumstances.[4]

MUNICH

But there is a moment, one film, in which the ameliorating instinct, Spielberg's need for a saving father figure, is squelched for something more complex and ambiguous. *Munich* (DreamWorks SKG, Amblin Entertainment, Universal, 2005) is the most serious and complex film that Spielberg has made to date. It concerns the actions taken by the state of Israel to avenge the murder of Israeli athletes at the 1972 Munich Olympic Games. The film raises complex moral issues about terrorism, state-sponsored murder, and about the dangers visited on the team chosen to hunt down the presumed murderers of the athletes. This team becomes a kind of surrogate family, led by Avner (Eric Bana), who, in the midst of their murderous activities, cooks enormous meals for the group. Within their dangerous fields of operation, an all-male domesticity becomes a place of refuge, though they fall away one by one, murdered or blown up. For their information about the terrorists, the group depends on a shadowy family that sells it—betrayal for profit. This family is headed by a man known as "Papa" (Michael Lonsdale), who befriends Avner, becoming a surrogate but untrustworthy father figure in an increasingly paranoid landscape, where threats blossom into reality and Avner is ultimately left alone to confront demons real and imagined.

The family in *Munich* finally offers no protection. Though Avner returns to his wife and child at film's end, he is alienated from domestic calm by the fears and paranoia created by his work as a counterterrorist assassin. He is left out in the cold by his government and all but undone by his uneasiness. Terrorism becomes internalized, not only an external threat, but a gnawing discomfort and wariness, a discomfort with ordinary life. The film ends with an image of the Twin Towers of the World Trade Center, a reminder of the tenuousness of living in a dangerous world over which control is tenuous at best, and probably impossible.

Munich is the only film in which Spielberg's optimism flags. But we must admit that it is that very optimism, Spielberg's belief that some kind of family or family surrogate will make right the most difficult circumstances, that makes his films so attractive. This, combined with his talent for assuring that the viewer's gaze is firmly stitched into his narrative, has served to maintain his popularity over the many decades of his filmmaking career. Of all the contemporary filmmakers we have discussed, he has maintained the elevated status of a commercially and critically appreciated figure. His films seem in touch with an audience's desire for pleasure. When he does not deliver this pleasure, as was the case in *Munich*, the films do not fare as well. But despite the occasional lapse, Spielberg remains the best-known filmmaker in the United States, a kind of cultural icon of pleasurable moviemaking—at once a calmer of fears, a teacher of history, an entertainer.

MARTIN SCORSESE

WHO'S THAT KNOCKING AT MY DOOR?

One of the most important auteurs to emerge in the late 1960s and early 1970s is Martin Scorsese. Scorsese came to Hollywood out of New York University's film school, where he made a number of short films and a feature called *Who's That Knocking at My Door?* (Trimod Films, 1967). This is an experimental work, shot on the streets of New York. Its rough and tumble view of its central character, J.R. (Harvey Keitel), has a kind of improvisational quality, a trying out not only of character, but of how characters can be seen on the screen. It has much in common with the films of an important independent filmmaker, John Cassavetes, whose 1959 film, *Shadows* (Lion International), a semi-improvised work about race relations in New York, filmed on the run in the streets, with the camera acting almost like another character, racing after the actors, circling and capturing them, nervous and jittery like a jazz performance. Like Cassavetes, Scorsese is taken with street life, with the doings of knockabout friends, who are filmed in a handheld black and white style. J.R. and his girlfriend (Zina Bethune) talk about movies—Scorsese's lifelong obsession—while the film itself plays with the way movies are seen. Shots are cut in a **nonlinear** fashion, flashing backward and forward; long **lap dissolves** and silent footage are mixed into this playful, yet serious film about life on the streets and a character deeply conflicted and damaged by his sexuality.

Who's That Knocking on My Door? stands somewhere between a student and a commercial film. It indicates the kinds of experimentation Scorsese will attempt in his later films, but it doesn't yet zero in on the world of small-time hoods that will be the subjects of many of the films to come. He had to go to school with Roger Corman and AIP to get a feel for commercial filmmaking. *Boxcar Bertha* (1972) is not a particularly noteworthy film, but it gave Scorsese some idea of studio production, at least under the particular low-budget pressures that Corman provided. When Warner Bros. decided to back *Mean Streets* (Warner Bros., Taplin, Perry, Scorsese Productions, 1973), Scorsese was able to break out and create a film that was both commercial and experimental, a rethinking of *Who's That Knocking on My Door?*, a riff on street life in New York's Little Italy, and an announcement of an important new filmmaking talent.

MEAN STREETS

Like *Who's That Knocking?*, *Mean Streets* also has an improvisational feel, although it is carefully scripted. Harvey Keitel returns, this time as Charlie, a young man of the streets, with aspirations to be a petty Mafioso, and a need to take care of Johnny Boy, a slightly mad, very impetuous young man played by Robert De Niro, in the first of eight films he would make with Scorsese. Under Scorsese's direction, De Niro is all nervous energy, a time bomb waiting to go off. In fact, the first we see of him in *Mean Streets*, he tosses a bomb into a mailbox and watches it explode.

Throughout the film, he continually knocks Charlie off balance. He owes money, he starts fights, he is responsible for a violent outburst of gunfire that gets him shot in the neck and wounds Charlie and his girlfriend, Teresa (Amy Robinson). Violence is always at the surface in *Mean Streets*. Aggressive language—Scorsese and screenwriter Mardik Martin create a kind of poetic imitation of New Yorkese—and aggressive fists and guns are ready to go off at the fraction of a moment's notice. It is a hellish world, full of camaraderie and danger.

Early in the film, Charlie is in church and in voice-over (actually Scorsese's voice) he ruminates about sin and redemption, about the pain of Hell. "The pain of Hell has two sides," he says, after he passes a finger over the flame of a votive candle: "The kind you can touch with your hand. The kind you can feel in your heart. Your soul, the spiritual side, and you know, the worst of the two is the spiritual." At the point where Charlie speaks about his soul, Scorsese has cut to the interior of the bar where Charlie and his friends hang out. It is lit in dark red. The camera tracks in slow motion along the bar as the Rolling Stones sing "Tell Me" on the soundtrack. The use of a rock soundtrack and slow motion will become trademarks of Scorsese's style. Slow motion becomes a representation for Scorsese of a disturbed perception. Whenever a character is in distress, is anxious or aggressive or apprehensive, Scorsese will give him a slow-motion point of view. The music echoes the characters' moods and locates them in time, since the tunes Scorsese selects are contemporary to the time during which the film is taking place.

With the introduction of Johnny Boy, Charlie says to himself, "We talk about penance and you send this through the door. Well, we play by your rules, don't we? Well, don't we?" The camera moves quickly to him and Scorsese cuts to his point of view as Johnny Boy walks down the bar in slow motion, the Stones this time singing "Jumping Jack Flash" on the soundtrack. *Mean Streets* continues this pattern of rapid action, agitated cutting, and the attempts of Charlie to find stability amidst a group of unstable petty crooks. He winds up wounded in body and soul.

Mean Streets was made almost simultaneously with Coppola's two Godfather films (the second of which has Robert De Niro playing a young Vito Corleone). But the films could not be more different in style and in their representations of gangsters. Scorsese's style in *Mean Streets* is loose and open; it borrows from the feel of the streets of Italian **neorealism** and Cassavetes's *Shadows*. The dialogue is rapid and profane and the stakes seem ridiculously low. Where Coppola's mobsters are involved in deep-seated political corruption, Scorsese's are proscribed by the streets of Manhattan's Little Italy, their neighborhood which is changing before their eyes. They are petty hoods whose victims are mostly themselves. They aim low and miss.

TAXI DRIVER

Throughout his films, Scorsese creates a dynamic **mise-en-scène**, a space for his camera to probe and roam, to experiment with the ways in which film sees and recreates the world. Or the ways in which a character sees it. *Taxi Driver* (Columbia, Bill/Phillips, Italo/Judeo Productions, 1976) is one of the few films that create a consistent first-person **point of view**. That is, a film that creates a world that represents the point of view of its main character. You may recall that Orson Welles's idea for his first film was a first-person adaptation of Joseph Conrad's *Heart of Darkness* (that story, written in 1902, later formed the basis of Coppola's *Apocalypse Now*). He quickly discovered that it was not possible to present a film literally through the eyes of a character. How did Scorsese succeed where Welles failed? Partly by having his main character, Travis Bickle (Robert De Niro), on screen in almost every sequence. We are, therefore, present in and to his consciousness. Even when he is not present, as in the grim sequence in which the pimp, Sport (Harvey Keitel), dances with his child prostitute, Iris (Jodie Foster), he punctures the scene as Scorsese cuts to a shot of Travis in a shooting range, firing his gun as if at the viewer.

His consciousness is present to us, and we see the world he inhabits. Travis sees only the darkness, the bleak dregs of the city, peopled by prostitutes, dopers, and brawlers. He is a creature of the night and its darkness impresses itself on his brain. He attempts to enter the daylight world when he comes on to the blonde and attractive campaign worker, Betsy

"You talkin' to me?" Travis (Robert De Niro) goes crazy tough in Martin Scorsese's *Taxi Driver* (1976).

(Cybill Shepherd) and invites her on a date. He takes her to a Times Square porn movie. She flees in disgust and in a following scene, we see Travis on the phone to Betsy in a deserted office building. As he talks to her, facing the wall, his back to us, the camera slowly tracks to the right, coming to rest on the empty corridor leading to the street. There seems to be no motivation for this shot, except as it represents the emptiness of Travis's mind. It becomes one of many sequences which present Travis as a kind of blank slate onto which is impressed the darkness and violence around him. There is a chilling sequence in which Travis picks up a fare played by Scorsese himself. The passenger, appropriately, acts as Travis's director, bringing him to an apartment building where his wife is having an affair. In an explosion of racist vulgarisms, the passenger tells Travis the violence he will do to his wife. It is a further step toward Travis's mental unraveling.

Travis explodes at the end of the film in one of the most violent sequences in a postcode, post *Bonnie and Clyde*, post *Wild Bunch* decade. Travis decides to save the child prostitute Iris, killing Sport and two other people in an eruption of bloodletting. He is Ethan Edwards from *The Searchers*, saving Debbie from the Indians; he is Norman Bates from *Psycho*, deeply insane, acting out of sociopathic impulse. But he becomes a hero. Because one of the people he kills is a Mafioso, the press treats his bloodbath as an act of bravery. The joke is on us. A psychotic individual becomes a local celebrity.

Taxi Driver is very much a film of its moment: a consummation of film violence in the 1970s, a vision of the mad Vietnam veteran (Travis says he was in the marines, if we can believe him), a swipe at politics (Travis's first target is a banal presidential candidate), a vision of contemporary New York as a place from hell. It is also a film with a great deal of narrative and visual experimentation, incorporating ideas from the **French New Wave** and, in its careful framing, from Hitchcock, inviting its audience to engage, with Scorsese, in challenging and exhilarating filmmaking. In that respect, it transcends its moment, remaining a film of enormous cinematic energy and invention.

SCORSESE AND THE URGE FOR SUCCESS

RAGING BULL

After *Taxi Driver*, Martin Scorsese continued to find his cinematic footing. Perhaps, more appropriately, he continued to find his commercial footing, trying out various genres, moving in and out of his comfort zone and aiming more and more at a larger audience. *Raging Bull* (Chartoff-Winkler Productions, United Aartists, 1980) is a landmark film for Scorsese. It emerges from the boxing genre, during a period when Sylvester Stallone's *Rocky* films had set a standard of the hard-charging, working-class hero, who fights the most difficult opponents to an unexpected victory. The first *Rocky* (Chartoff-Winkler Productions, United Artists),

Blood flows as Jake La Motta (Robert De Niro) takes punishment in the ring in Scorsese's *Raging Bull* (1980).

directed by John G. Avildson and starring Sylvester Stallone, appeared in 1976, and was a huge success.

Raging Bull is the anti-*Rocky*. Jake LaMotta (Robert De Niro), is a working-class boxer, but, unlike Rocky, he is the definition of an unheroic character. He is crude, stupid, and pathologically jealous. The film, like *Taxi Driver*, assumes Jake's point of view much of the time and sees the world as a kind of slow-motion train wreck of forces that Jake allows to overtake him. The boxing sequences are especially grueling, with a soundtrack of animal sounds and screaming fans, of slow-motion brutality, and blood spurting from wounds. Jake is brutal and masochistic. He takes punishment both in and outside of the ring.

Raging Bull is also a film about show business, about boxing as a display of the beaten body to the public and of Jake LaMotta's changing body on display to the viewers of the film. From lean fighter to obese performer in second-rate nightclubs, Jake's body is a screen on which Scorsese projects brutality, self-indulgence, and self-hatred, qualities he carries over to his film about Jesus Christ, *The Last Temptation of Christ* (Universal, Cineplex Odeon Films, 1988). The film created an outcry from the religious community because of its depiction of Christ (played by Willem Dafoe) as more human than divine, in fact struggling against his divinity with a desire for normal domesticity.

GOODFELLAS

So many of Scorsese's films involve a struggle with the self, with the law, with "normal" society as a whole. He is infatuated by outlaws, whether petty crooks in *Mean Streets* and *Goodfellas* (Warner Bros., 1990), or eccentric millionaires like Howard Hughes (played by Leonardo DiCaprio) in *The Aviator* (Forward Pass, Appian Way, IMF Internationale Medien und Film GmbH & Co. 3. Produktions KG, Miramax, Warner Bros., 2004), or the excesses of Wall Street stock traders in *The Wolf of Wall Street* (Paramount Pictures, Red Granite Pictures, Appian Way, 2013). *Goodfellas* is perhaps the perfect Scorsese gangster film. Played with an energy that derives from all the gangster films he has known and loved, Scorsese makes this film a homage and a tribute. He recalls the scene from *Little Caesar* (Mervyn LeRoy, Warner Bros., First National, 1931) where Rico is introduced to his new gangster pals, the camera circling around the table as each one catches the camera's eye in recognition. Here, Henry Hill (Ray Liotta) introduces us to his pals, and the camera circles around, each one nodding in recognition as it passes by.

As in *Mean Streets*, Scorsese has something of a split affinity to his gangster characters. He is enthralled by their energy and camaraderie, while at the same time he horrifies us with their brutality. There is a lunge toward success by Henry Hill and his companions and a constant threat to that success by their own internal entanglements and betrayals. Hill is a force of urban nature, pushing his way up the ranks, and Scorsese's camera shares and communicates this push, as in the extraordinary 4-minute take of Henry and his fiancé Karen (Lorraine Bracco) moving through the backdoor, the corridors, the kitchen, and into the main floor of the Copa Cabana nightclub as the Shirelles sing "And Then He Kissed Me" on the soundtrack. This is the kind of camera strategy that calls attention to itself—which is precisely the point. *Goodfellas* is not simply another gangster film, but a film about gangster films; a film that wants us as viewers to recognize the artifice of the genre while we enjoy its brutal vitality. It is so self-reflective that, by the end of the film, when Henry gives up his friends to the FBI, he literally walks out of the scene and addresses us directly, first in the courtroom and at the end when, looking out at us from his home in the witness protection program, he tells us that he is now just a schnook like everybody else. The film ends with a homage to Edwin S. Porter's *The Great Train Robbery* (Edison, 1903)—a shot of Tommy (Joe Pesci) shooting his gun at the camera. We are taken in on the joke, as deadly as that joke might be.

THE DOCUMENTARIES

Scorsese uses direct address in his nonfiction films, including documentaries that show a special interest in movies (not surprisingly, since film makes up the storehouse of Scorsese's imagination) and rock music (again not surprising, since the soundtrack of most of his films is made up of popular music and rock 'n' roll). Two long-form documentaries, *A Personal Journey with Martin Scorsese through American Movies* (British Film Institute, Miramax, 1995) and *My Voyage to Italy* (Pasa Doble Film, Media Trade, Cappa Production, Miramax, 2001) cover the history of American and postwar Italian film by means of carefully chosen clips and smart, insightful commentary that links the clips to one another and to Scorsese's own work.

The music documentaries vary. There are rock concert films like *The Last Waltz* (FM Productions, UA, 1978) which documents the last concert by The Band and *Shine a Light* (Paramount Classics, Concert Productions International, Shangri-La, 2008) that records a performance by the Rolling Stones. In each case, Scorsese applies the same energy of vision that he uses in his fiction films, capturing the rhythm of the music with camera movement and precise editing. He has also made "personality" documentaries: *No Direction Home: Bob Dylan* (Thirteen/WNET, 2005) and *George Harrison: Living in the Material World* (Grove Street Productions, HBO, 2011), which combine interviews with performance footage that interrogate the artists' life and times.

No matter what the form or genre Scorsese chooses, and despite the fact that he has moved from 1970s maverick auteur to a mainstream Hollywood director, he maintains an interest in film as a provocative medium, as a force for seeing the world and creating characters whose energies may be self-destructive, but who at least have a driving vitality and who, like their creator, want to impress that vitality on their world. "I don't want to be a product of my environment," says Jack Nicholson's Frank Costello in *The Departed* (Warner Bros., Plan B Entertainment, Initial Entertainment Group (IEG), 2006), "I want my environment to be a product of me." In Scorsese's case he is himself a product of his environment, and that is the environment of film, which he celebrates in every movie he makes, no more so than in *Hugo* (Paramount, GK Films, Infinitum Nihil, 2011), which, on the face of it, is a complete departure for Scorsese. Shot in 3D, it is a fantasy about a boy who lives in a Paris railroad station and keeps its clocks. But more than that, it is about the birth of cinema and one of its pioneers, the French fantasist, Georges Méliès (played by Ben Kingsley). With this film, Scorsese continues his urge to experiment—it is the most interesting use of 3D filmmaking to date—and a continuing reminder that Scorsese, like so many of his "New Hollywood" contemporaries, grew up with and remained influenced by the universe of cinema.

MICHAEL CIMINO, THE END OF UNITED ARTISTS, THE END OF THE AUTEUR

For a relatively short time, and in only a few instances, Hollywood gave up the producer system that was formed in the early 1920s and ceded some limited power back to the director. As long as this paid off, as long as Francis Ford Coppola, Steven Spielberg, George Lucas, or William Friedkin (*The Exorcist*, Warner Bros., Hoya Productions, 1973) made films that made huge amounts of money, the studios were satisfied that the director might be given some creative freedom. When that freedom, however circumscribed, created not a great film but a financial disaster, the director as "auteur," the director with control over the film, came, with a few exceptions, to an end.

THE DEER HUNTER AND *HEAVEN'S GATE*

Michael Cimino directed *The Deer Hunter* for Universal and EMI in 1978. It is a somewhat different kind of Vietnam War film that concentrates on a group of working-class male friends before, during, and after their tour of duty. Unlike Coppola's *Apocalypse Now*, released the following year, *The Deer Hunter* focuses more on its characters than on the violent landscape of the war. It is a long, painstakingly detailed work. The sequence in which one of the characters plays Russian roulette is especially grueling. It was a very popular film. So much so, that when Cimino came to United Artists with his next film, a Western called *Heaven's Gate* (1980), they gave him free reign. The production went wildly over budget and schedule, and its extravagant production became fodder for the press. The film was doomed even before UA released it in its 3 1/2 hour version. It was such a critical and commercial failure that the studio pulled it and rereleased it in a shorter version. But the damage was done. United Artists had bankrupted itself because of this film, and the company that was formed in 1919 by Charlie Chaplin, Douglas Fairbanks, Mary Pickford, and D. W. Griffith, and which by this time was owned by a car rental company, was sold off and essentially ended. The other studios and their holding companies resumed their control of production and the time of the director, with a few exceptions like Altman, Scorsese, Spielberg, Kubrick, and a few more recent figures, like Paul Thomas Anderson, was over.

SELECTED FILMOGRAPHY

Steven Spielberg

Duel, Universal, 1971.

Jaws, Zanuck/Brown Productions, Universal, 1975.

Close Encounters of the Third Kind, EMI Films, Julia Phillips and Michael Phillips Productions, Columbia, 1977.

E.T.: The Extra-Terrestrial, Universal, Amblin Entertainment, 1982.

The Color Purple, Amblin Entertainment, Guber Peters Co., Warner Bros., 1985.

Schindler's List, Universal, Amblin Entertainment, 1993.

Amistad, DreamWorks SKG, HBO, 1997.

Saving Private Ryan, Amblin Entertainment, DreamWorks SKG, Paramount, 1998.

War of the Worlds, Paramount, DreamWorks SKG, Amblin Entertainment, 2005.

Munich, DreamWorks SKG, Amblin Entertainment, Universal, 2005.

Lincoln, 20th Century Fox, Imagine Entertainment, Amblin Entertainment, DreamWorks SKG, 2012.

Francis Ford Coppola

You're a Big Boy Now, Seven Arts, Warner Bros., 1966.

The Rain People, American Zoetrope, Warner Bros./Seven Arts, 1969.

The Godfather, Paramount, Alfran Productions, 1972.

The Conversation, Directors Company, The Coppola Company, American Zoetrope, Paramount, 1974.

The Godfather II, Paramount, The Coppola Company, 1974.

Apocalypse Now, Zoetrope Studios, UA, 1979.

Martin Scorsese

Who's That Knocking at My Door? Trimod Films, 1967.

Mean Streets, Warner Bros., Taplin, Perry, Scorsese Productions, 1973.

Taxi Driver, Columbia, Bill/Phillips, Italo/Judeo Productions, 1976.

The Last Waltz, FM Productions, UA, 1978.

Raging Bull, UA, Chartoff-Winkler Productions, 1980.

The Last Temptation of Christ, Universal, Cineplex Odeon Films, 1988.

Goodfellas, Warner Bros., 1990.

A Personal Journey with Martin Scorsese through American Movies, British Film Institute, Miramax, 1995.

My Voyage to Italy, Pasa Doble Film, Miramax, 2001.

The Aviator, Forward Pass, Appian Way, IMF Internationale Medien und Film GmbH & Co. 3. Produktions KG, Miramax, Warner Bros., 2004.

The Departed, Warner Bros., Plan B Entertainment, Initial Entertainment Group (IEG), 2006.

Shine a Light, Paramount Classics, Concert Productions International, Shangri-La, 2008.

Hugo, Paramount, GK Films, Infinitum Nihil, 2011.
The Wolf of Wall Street, Paramount Pictures, Red Granite Pictures, Appian Way, 2013.

Michael Cimino

The Deer Hunter, Universal, EMI, 1978.
Heaven's Gate, United Artists, 1980.
Shadows, dir. John Cassavetes, Lion International, 1958.
The Exorcist, dir., William Friedkin, Warner Bros., Hoya Productions, 1973.

SUGGESTIONS FOR FURTHER READING

Lester D. Friedman, *Citizen Spielberg* (Urbana, IL: University of Illinois Press, 2006).
Jon Lewis, *Whom God Wishes to Destroy: Francis Coppola and the New Hollywood* (Durham, NC: Duke University Press, 1995).
———, *The Godfather* (London, UK: Palgrave Macmillan, 2010).
Lesley Stern, *The Scorsese Connection* (Bloomington, IN: Indiana University Press, 1995).
Michael Henry Wilson, *Scorsese on Scorsese* (Paris, FR: Cahiers du cinema, 2011).

NOTES

1. See Peter Biskind, *Easy Riders, Raging Bulls: How the Sex-Drugs-and Rock 'n' Roll Generation Saved Hollywood* (New York, NY: Simon and Schuster, 1998), 142.
2. See Michael Cieply & Brooks Barnes, "A Studio's Real-Life Drama," *The New York Times* (January 30, 2012), B1.
3. Stephen Heath, "*Jaws*, Ideology, and Film Theory," in *Movies and Methods*, II, ed. Bill Nicholls (Berkeley, CA: University of California Press, 1985), 511. A more detailed analysis of the film is in Kolker, *A Cinema of Loneliness*, 4th ed. (New York, NY: Oxford University Press, 2011).
4. For a discussion of the problems inherent in *Schindler's List*, see Sara Horowitz, "But Is It Good for the Jews? Spielberg's Schindler and the Aesthetics of Atrocity," in *Spielberg's Holocaust*, ed. Yosefa Loshitzky (Bloomington, IN: University of Indiana Press: 1997), 119–139.

CHAPTER 26

AMERICAN FILM IN THE 1990s AND 2000s

Our discussion of the "new Hollywood" led us to an examination of contemporary American film by way of the work of some key directors. In this chapter we consider some recent filmmakers and films of the 1990s and 2000s to understand where American filmmaking is trending today and, at the same time, go a bit further back to review the history of African Americans in contemporary film in order to bring that strain in American film up to date.

AFTER READING THIS CHAPTER, YOU SHOULD UNDERSTAND:

- The role and history of independent filmmaking.
- Modernism, postmodernism, and the work of Quentin Tarantino and Oliver Stone.
- The comedies of Judd Apatow.
- The complexities of David Fincher's *Fight Club*.
- Contemporary versions of the genres of comedy, the thriller, melodrama, as well as films that do not fit into generic categories.
- The recent history of African American filmmaking.
- American film's strength in its variety.
- The various trends moving across the field of current American film.

YOU SHOULD BE ABLE TO:

- Identify and discuss trends of contemporary film and compare them with films of the past.
- Clearly define different genres and how they are modified (or not) over the course of film history.
- Critically examine the revenge films of Quentin Tarantino.
- Discuss the treatment of race in current American film.
- Discover other African American directors beyond those mentioned here.
- Examine the various genres currently popular in American film.
- Decide whether the characters in Tyler Perry's films are stereotypes or authentic representations of the African American experience.

MULTIPLE SCREENS

Categorizing and analyzing where American film is during this long period of the present is a complex task. We are still so close to the 1990s, not to mention the current century, that it is difficult to spot trends and make pronouncements about the state of culture and the cultures of film in particular. There are a few certainties, especially in the technological arena. "Film," as we noted in Chapter 22, is quickly disappearing in its old form as a celluloid ribbon of images running through a projector. Digital recording and projecting systems are taking its place. So are the locations where film is seen. Theater attendance is down. The flat screen TV, the computer screen, the iPad, even the tiny smartphone screen have become alternatives to the movie theater. On the business side, the big studios have retracted to a degree, producing somewhat fewer films and almost always in collaboration with smaller production companies so that costs and risks are shared down the line. Look at the credits of any current film and note the number of production companies and producers involved—or at the list of production companies following the title and director in this book.

In what follows, we will attempt to pull together a few of the threads of contemporary cinema in order to discover, if not patterns, at least some points of interest between which connections can begin to be made.

INDEPENDENT CINEMA

> When you talk about movies, you also need to talk about money. There are few more dolorous domains than the American movie business, a fraught realm that has at times, almost inexplicably, produced astonishing works of art often despite the industry's greed and worst impulses. And as tough as it is to get any movie made, it's even more difficult to produce and distribute genuinely original, nongeneric, non-groupthink work, which is one reason the big studios are now largely in the recycling business (*Iron Man 3* and the regurgitated like). American independent cinema is a confusing, contradictory and maybe useless designation. Who, after all, is independent? Yet it used to seem like both a refuge and a promise, a place where art and industry were on equal terms.
>
> —MANOHLA DARGIS[1]

"Independent" cinema has become increasingly difficult to define. Originally, it referred to films made on small budgets outside of the studio system. Independent productions have been around since the formation of the studios. Samuel Goldwyn set himself up as an independent producer around the time that his name became part of one of the biggest studios in the old Hollywood, Metro-Goldwyn-Mayer. He was, in fact, never a part of MGM when that company was formed. United Artists was formed in 1919 to distribute independently made films. Since then, small production companies came and went and continue to come and go across the history of American cinema. The contemporary independent movement might be traced back to the films of John Cassavetes, whose *Shadows* (Lion International, 1959) was made on the streets of New York for very little money. Shot in 16 mm, the film is rough and seemingly improvised (although there was a script that formed the basis for the film). Intimately close to its characters, who work out their romantic and racial issues, the film picks up the rhythm of unrehearsed dialogue, and it looks like it was shot on the fly with an immediacy and passion that is the hallmark of all of Cassavetes' work. Independent of the studios, Cassavetes forged a style that became deeply influential, especially on the work of Martin Scorsese.

Independent filmmaking was the focus of the Utah/US Film Festival, which began in Salt Lake City in 1978. A few years later, in 1985, actor Robert Redford took over directorship of the festival, which had moved to Park City, Utah, and renamed it "Sundance." A showcase for small-budget films, it remained a quiet venue for filmmakers who were off the beaten track, working away from the major studios. That is until Steven Soderbergh's *Sex, Lies and Videotape* (Outlaw Productions, Miramax) set off a bidding war among distributors at Sundance in 1989. It was picked up for distribution by a small company called Miramax, run by Bob and Harvey Weinstein. Through careful marketing and control of release patterns—carefully building positive reviews and word of mouth so that it could be successfully opened in more and more cities—the film earned $25 million, largely because of its sexual content. The film set a pattern for many of its successors in the independent movement, focusing less on action than on quiet dialogue between its male and female characters, in this case interspersed with intimate sexual encounters with the added enticement of voyeurism. While Soderbergh went on to direct big-budget films, such as the *Ocean's Eleven, Twelve,* and *Thirteen* series (Warner Bros., 2001, 2004, 2007), his original independent film led to a small subgenre of independent filmmaking dubbed **"mumblecore,"** defined by critic David Denby as movies

> made by buddies, casual and serious lovers, and networks of friends, and they're about college-educated men and women who aren't driven by ideas or by passions or even by a desire to make their way in the world. Neither rebels nor bohemians, they remain stuck in a limbo of semi-genteel, moderately hip poverty, though some of the films end with a lurch into the working world. The actors (almost always nonprofessionals) rarely say what they mean; a lot of the time, they don't know what they mean.[2]

Sex, Lies and Videotape is more upscale and has higher production values than the mumblecore that followed it and it served to put "independent" cinema on the map. Mumblecore covers a small patch of filmmaking that includes (among many others) such titles as Andrew Bujalski's 16 mm film, *Funny Ha Ha* (Goodbye Cruel Releasing, 2003) to Miranda July's *The Future* (GND Productions, Haut et Court, Match Factory, Medianboard Berlin-Brandenburg, Razor Film Production, Roadside Attractions, 2011) and Noah Baumbach's *Frances Ha* (RT Features, Pine District Pictures, Scott Rudin Productions, ITC, 2012). July's film (and it is important to note that low-budget independent film does provide an opportunity for women directors) contains all the slow, aimless dialogue typical of mumblecore with the added bonus of narration supplied by a cat with an injured paw, suffering from existential angst. Its grating, simpering voice is supplied by July herself, who also plays one of the main characters in the film. Baumbach's *Frances Ha* almost takes David Demby's description of mumblecore as its scenario. A young woman who wishes to be a dancer, despite her lack of talent, moves without emotional anchor or sense of commitment or purpose. She is a kind of blank slate, acting on whims, unattached, upheld, and saved by her own guileless innocence. The film moves at a leisurely pace and invites the viewer to a gentle identification with its characters.

Certainly not all independent films qualify as mumblecore. The early films of Ramin Bahrani, *Man Push Cart* (Noruz Films, Flip Side Film, Films Philos, 2005) and *Chop Shop* (Muskat Filmed Properties, Noruz Films (I), Big Beach Films, 2008) are subdued studies of people in the city—a food cart operator in the first film, children running around the auto repair shops in a Queens, New York, neighborhood in the latter. *Chop Shop* owes a great deal to **Italian neorealism** in its leisurely, nonjudgmental observation of children—played by nonprofessionals—wandering the streets. Like many independents. Bahrani has gone on to direct bigger budget movies. His 2012 film, *At Any Price* (Black Bear Pictures, Treehouse Pictures, Killer Films, Sony Pictures Classics) is a subtle film that builds intriguing dramatic conflict out of the life of a desperate seed salesman, played by Dennis Quaid. Bahrani uses the setting of farm country to provide some insight into lives at odds with their environment and their own uncertain aspirations.

An audience certainly exists for the dialogue-driven films of independent cinema, filled with somewhat awkward pauses and editing patterns that, while they don't go against the rules of Hollywood continuity cutting, are more leisurely, less likely to push the viewer forward through story than to linger on the characters' uncertainties. Such an audience was strong enough that, for a time, the major studios formed "independent" distribution units in an attempt to target this relatively small but loyal demographic. Many of these units are gone (a few, such as Fox Searchlight and Sony Pictures Classics, are still active, though the latter focuses more on distribution of foreign films), and as the studios have become more distribution centers rather than originators of projects, it could be said that many films today, high or low budget, are "independent" to a certain extent. Almost any production has to put together its funding from small, "independent" backers, with the studios providing distribution. Quiet, dialogue-centered films continue to get made, a fact that indicates that there will always be an audience for alternatives to the usually loud, action-oriented fare of the major studios.

POSTMODERN FILMMAKING: QUENTIN TARANTINO AND OLIVER STONE

During its peak in the late 1980s and early 1990s, Miramax was one of the most successful of the independent production companies and distributors, and one of their most successful films was Quentin Tarantino's *Pulp Fiction* (A Band Apart, Jersey Films, Miramax, 1994). The film is important not only as a successful independent production but as a manifestation of an interesting movement in cinema's perception of itself: an inward-looking movement that valued popular culture, joking references to other movies, and a narrative that playfully breaks the linear movement we are most used to in watching film. The movement was given a name: postmodernism.

I have been arguing that film has had a peculiar relationship to the modernist movement that began early in the 20th century when film was in its own early stages. To summarize some of the points made earlier: modernity takes as a given that the world is a disorderly, uncontrollable place, and that subjective experience is contingent, unpredictable. There is no dependable center; no secure place of rest. Modernist art takes this chaos as a starting point and gives it form, often by examining the structures of art itself. Painting, for example, becomes less interested in portraits and landscapes, in representing the world around it, and more interested in the quality of color and shape on canvas—and so we have abstract art. Modernist art across the disciplines becomes a refuge from the chaos of modernity and celebrates itself by foregrounding its form and acknowledging the universe of art by allusions to other works of art. We have seen that at the end of Martin Scorsese's *Goodfellas* (Warner Bros., 1990), there is a shot of Tommy (Joe Pesci) pointing his gun at the audience and firing. With this, Scorsese alludes to the last shot of Edwin S. Porter's 1903 film, *The Great Train Robbery*, and thereby links his film to the history of cinematic violence. Some modernist art—abstract painting, for example—may appear to be untidy, but it comforts itself and excites its viewers by referring to its own imaginative rigor and its relationship with other works of the imagination.

The paradox is that film, born of modernity, largely sets itself up as modernity's antidote. The deeply sentimental, conservative nature of so much of American film is an act of assurance, a refuge against the turmoil of modernity and, unlike so much modernist art, has created a form that renders itself invisible. Therefore, it is of great interest when a film comes along that, like modernist art, seems conscious of its own form, calling attention to itself beyond its plot, allowing us to peek into the forms that create meaning. *Citizen Kane* (Orson Welles, RKO, 1941) is such a film, with its overlapping narrative and point of view fractured through the perceptions of its various characters; its use of deep focus, a technique only available to the camera lens, rendering images that we could see only with the cinematic eye. Alfred Hitchcock's *Vertigo* (Paramount, 1958) takes the modernist's perspective of diminished human agency in a world that cannot be controlled, despite its character's attempt to do so. All of Stanley Kubrick's films speak to the issues of contingency and loss, of worlds that spin away from individual control. These are modernism's themes.

PULP FICTION

In *Pulp Fiction*, Tarantino calls upon some elements of modernism: the film plays games with the linear narrative progression that we are so comfortable with in conventional film narratives. It starts with the same sequence that it ends with, the diner robbery by Pumpkin and Honey Bunny (Tim Roth and Amanda Plummer). Then it picks up Vincent and Jules (John Travolta and Samuel L. Jackson), doing a job for Marcellus Wallace (Ving Rhames). It later takes up the story of the boxer, Butch Coolidge (Bruce Willis), who kills Vincent in the toilet midway through the film. But then, returning to the sequence early in the film, Vincent is still alive as he and Jules seek help for cleaning up their car after Vincent accidently shoots a man in the backseat after going over a bump in the road. The film's final joke occurs when the film returns to its opening sequence, and Vincent comes out

Bloodied. Jules (Samuel L. Jackson) and Vincent (John Travolta) have accidentally shot a passenger after going over a bump in the road. Postmodern violence in Quentin Tarantino's *Pulp Fiction* (1994).

of the diner bathroom as Jules talks Pumpkin and Honey Bunny out of their robbery.

What takes *Pulp Fiction* from modernism to postmodernism is its utter lack of seriousness in its references to other films. Its offhanded violence and rapid-fire dialogue draw on Martin Scorsese's *Mean Streets* (Warner Bros., Taplin, Perry, Scorsese Productions, 1973). The complex, overlapping time schemes of its various narratives refer to Stanley Kubrick's *The Killing* (Harris-Kubrick Productions, United Artists, 1956). Its rough-hewn, trash-talking gangsterism looks back at the films of Samuel Fuller. This is all playful pastiche as opposed to serious allusion. *Pulp Fiction* is intensely unserious, and this carries the danger of leaving a bad taste. There is so much dialogue and so much violence that we might expect some payoff, some insight. But it is the nature of the postmodern not to pay off. The insight provided by the film is its own glossy, jokey surface. Postmodernism does not seek to order a disordered world through the structure of art, nor does it particularly want to reflect this disorder. It simply reflects an almost carefree playfulness, in Tarantino's case in face of the amount of violence that explodes in the course of the film.

Miramax, as an independent production and distribution company, did not last very long after *Pulp Fiction*. Bob and Harvey Weinstein were bought out by Disney in 1993—in effect, making *Pulp Fiction* a Disney film—and they left the company (which was eventually sold to an investment firm) in 2005. They started up their own company again but have so far not met with quite the success of *Pulp Fiction*. Quentin Tarantino continued his explorations of the postmodern style, recently with a curious World War II film, *Inglourious Basterds* (Universal, The Weinstein Company, A Band Apart, 2009), which fantasizes a group of Jewish soldiers scalping Nazis and killing Hitler and his High Command in a movie house. The jokiness of the film flies in the face of and makes light of history, but it follows Tarantino's obsession with revenge in films like his two *Kill Bill* volumes (A Band Apart, Miramax, 2003, 2004) and *Death Proof* (Dimension Films, Trouble Maker Studios, The Weinstein Company, Rodriquez International Pictures, 2007). *Django Unchained* (Weinstein Company, Columbia Pictures, 2012) takes the revenge motif further, this time setting it in the pre–Civil War South, where a freed slave seeks to save his still enslaved wife. Full of violent set pieces, including a slave being torn apart by dogs, alluding to the operatic "spaghetti Westerns" of the Italian filmmaker Sergio Leone, mixing a composed score with contemporary pop music, the film plays a dangerous game. Like *Inglourious Basterds*, Tarantino works fast and loose with a dreadful historical moment. He wants the viewer to have fun; he wants us to cheer at the revenge Django takes on slaveholders; he risks trivializing the desperation of slavery in the interest of a joking spectacle laid over a serious subject.

NATURAL BORN KILLERS

An interesting comparison to *Pulp Fiction* is a film based on a story by Tarantino and a screenplay written

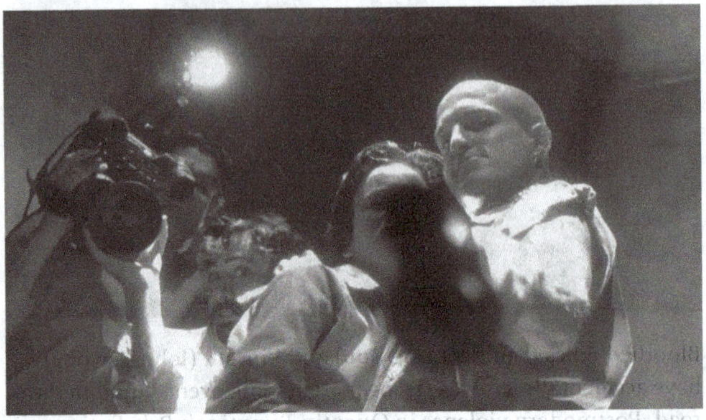

Violence and the media. Micky (Woody Harrelson), Mallory (Juliette Lewis behind the rifle), and Wayne Gayle (Robert Downey, Jr., next to the camera) in Oliver Stone's *Natural Born Killers* (1994).

by David Veloz, Richard Rutowski, and Oliver Stone and directed by Stone. *Natural Born Killers* (Warner Bros., Regency Enterprises, Alcor Films, 1994) is a mad, violent road movie about a couple of serial killers, played by Woody Harrelson and Juliette Lewis, who leave a trail of mayhem across the Southwest and are made famous by the press and a trashy television show. The film is designed, literally, to throw the viewer off kilter. Almost every shot in *Natural Born Killers* is canted off center. These compositions and the film's crazed editing style give it a hallucinatory quality. Its nonstop violence is like an assault on our senses. The film alludes directly to *Bonnie and Clyde* (Arthur Penn, Warner Bros. Seven Arts, Tatira-Hiller Productions, 1967) and *A Clockwork Orange* (Stanley Kubrick, Warner Bros., Hawk Films, 1971), and much like Kubrick's film takes violence as a subject to investigate as well as flaunt. Stone attempts to explore how violence is mediated, that is, how we understand it not as it is, but how the media represent it. He plays with viewer response, sliding perception back and forth, bringing us close to the violence and then pushing us away to look at it wide-eyed. This is a difficult game for a filmmaker to play. Hurling so many violent images at the audience can run the risk of diverting attention from a more serious theme. *Natural Born Killers* did not succeed with some viewers, who condemned its violence, but it succeeds as both critique and play with the violent images we seem to love to see on the screen.

JFK

Earlier, Stone made an even more controversial film, a profoundly political film on the assassination of President John F. Kennedy, *JFK* (Warner Bros., Canal+, Regency Enterprises, 1991). Stone's *JFK* is the rare example of a contemporary film that not only takes politics as its subject, but became the subject of politics—more accurately, political scorn by critics who considered it to be the work of a conspiracy theorist. It was a cinematic phenomenon that was either embraced or despised. What it is in fact is an assault of images that creates an alternative narrative about the assassination of the 35th president, an event that shook American culture to its core. For many people, the official line that the assassination was caused by a single shooter was too simple, too insufficient a response to such an enormous event. Stone's film posits that the answer wasn't simple and therefore makes his answers complex and interrogatory. He asks that we interrogate our own perception of the images we see on the screen, images so dense with information, cut so rapidly, that they demand reviewing a second or third time. Both *JFK* and *Natural Born Killers* actively engage in perceptual play; they challenge our complacency with the stable image, the invisible cutting of classical Hollywood cinema, and the easy morality of redemption that so many films offer us. They demand careful attention.

The modernist urge present in Stone's films of the early 1990s did not last long. His work tended to become somewhat more conventional in form, though he continues to make films that look closely at the culture, taking on professional football in *Any Given Sunday* (Warner Bros., Ixtlan, Donners' Company, 1999); the events of 9/11 in *World Trade Center* (Paramount, Double Feature Films, Intermedia Films, 2006); the financial crisis in *Wall Street* (Twentieth Century Fox Film Corporation, American Entertainment Partners L.P., Amercent Films, 1987) and its sequel, *Wall Street: Money Never Sleeps* (Edward Pressman Film, Fox, 2010); and even the Mexican drug trade in *Savages* (Ixtlan, Onda Entertainment, Relativity Media, Universal, 2012). He has also made documentaries on the leftist movements in Latin America. No matter his subject, whether the Vietnam War in *Platoon* (Cinema 86, Hemdale Film, Orion, 1986) or a 10-episode alternative history of the United States for cable television (*The Untold History of the United States* (Ixtlan Productions, Showtime, 2012–2013), Stone's films remain engaged with the history of the time in which they are made. They create an interesting contrast to the work of Quentin Tarantino—the contrast of high seriousness with a recognition of violence as an inescapable element of modernity versus violence as cinematic playfulness.

JUDD APATOW

TALLADEGA NIGHTS: THE BALLAD OF RICKY BOBBY

On the opposite pole to Oliver Stone's serious, politically controversial films are the spiritedly funny films by director and producer Judd Apatow. Unlike, for example, Woody Allen's restrained, self-deprecating comedies, Apatow's movies are bright, raunchy, and inevitably rated 'R' "for language and crude sexual humor throughout." Apatow got his start in television, where he produced such 1990s cult series as *The Larry Sanders Show* and *Freaks and Geeks*. Actors Seth Rogen and Jason Segel moved with Apatow from TV into feature film production, and along with Jonah Hill and occasionally Will Ferrell or Steve Carell in starring roles, he has created, directed, or produced some of the funniest and lightly relevant films in current cinema. *Talladega Nights: The Ballad of Ricky Bobby* (Adam McKay, Columbia, Relativity Media, Apatow Productions, 2006) stands among the best, even somewhat complex films in the Apatow collection (he produced the film; Ferrell and McKay wrote it; McKay directed it) as well as the most politically curious.

The film satirizes the very audience it seems to be aimed at: Southern Nascar racing fans, folks mostly conservative and sensitive about their culture. What's more, the film was made at the height (or depth) of the George W. Bush Administration, and it makes fun of the pieties and excesses of that time. It makes fun as well of the Hollywood culture of **product placement** (sometimes called "embedded marketing") that allows silent advertising to appear in films through the prominent display of brand-named products. But Apatow's films are rarely silent about anything. The film's jokes about product placement are a joke on Nascar itself, whose cars and drivers are festooned with the names of their sponsors. Of course, while it makes fun of product placement, there is no doubt that the products placed in the film helped fund the movie. So, when Ricky's wife, Carly (Leslie Bibb), calls the family for dinner, yelling that she's been "slavin' over this for hours," the camera moves across a table covered with Domino's Pizza, Wonder Bread, Coca Cola, Taco Bell, the names of which Ricky (Will Ferrell) repeats in his blessing to the "Baby Jesus." The blessing starts a fugue around the dinner table about what to call Jesus, and ends with Ricky thanking Jesus for all the money he's made. Even evangelical Christianity is not spared from the film's good-natured joking.

At the top of his game, Ricky is challenged by a French race car driver—a gay French race car driver. The French had voiced strong opposition to George W. Bush's invasion of Iraq in 2003. As an absurd gesture of displeasure, some congressmen moved to change the name of french fries in government cafeterias to "freedom fries." In the 2004 presidential race, when John Kerry unsuccessfully challenged George Bush for his second term as president, he was derided by the opposition as being "French." Therefore, the introduction of Sacha Baron Cohen's Jean Girard as a gay Frenchman does a double play on the Francophobia and homophobia of the right. Cohen's performance is so broad and silly that the joke is easy to

Ricky Bobby (Will Ferrell) and Jean Girard (Sacha Baron Cohen) share an intimate moment on the Nascar track in *Talladega Nights: The Ballad of Ricky Bobby* (Adam McKay, 2006).

take—like everything in the film, it goes so over the top that it returns as a gentle poke of fun that doesn't give offense. Finally, to make certain no offence is given, the film is wrapped in an oedipal narrative about a father and son—Ricky and his good-for-nothing dad (Gary Cole)—who reconcile by film's end.

But the end of the film does not completely finish its satire. In a rare postcredit sequence (it is a good idea to sit through the credits to see who is responsible for what in the film you just watched and perhaps be surprised by a bonus), we see Ricky's grandmother (Jane Lynch), who has tamed his two wild boys, Walker (Houston Tumlin) and Texas Ranger (Grayson Russell). They are lying together reading, of all things, William Faulkner's complex, modernist story, *The Bear*. "So what do you think that story was about?" asks Grandma. Texas Ranger pipes up: "Doesn't the bear symbolize the Old South and the new dog the encroaching industrialization of the North?" "Duh," says Walker, "But the question is, should the reader feel relief or sadness at the passing of the Old South?" "Yeah, how 'bout both?" asks Grandma. "Oh, I get it! Moral ambiguity, the hallmark of all 20th century American fiction." "Great analysis, Walker," his brother responds. This antic film ends with a little seminar on modernist American fiction and a reflexive commentary on the film's own ambiguous relationship to its subject, which it takes seriously and not seriously at the same time. This may not quite constitute moral ambiguity, but just enough ambiguity to keep *Talladega Nights* hilarious but with a satirical edge at the same time.

The films Judd Apatow produces or directs always have an edge, but it is usually the edge of raunch—and sometimes over that edge. The toilet jokes in *Bridesmaids* (Paul Feig, Universal, Relativity Media, Apatow Productions, 2011) are really gross, more so than the penis jokes in some of the other Apatow productions that tend to center on male friendships. But the grossness humanizes his characters and brings to the screen the language and the actions of ordinary people, at least ordinary people of a certain young age and gender. The films of the Apatow school are deeply felt and modestly sentimental, refreshing in their forthrightness and silliness about the body and its functions. They celebrate the closeness of male friends and in *Bridesmaids* female friendships as well. They make jokes about the cultures of the past, as in the satire of 1960s communal life, *Wanderlust* (David Wain, Apatow Productions, Relativity Media, 2012) and the present, as in *This Is 40* (Judd Apatow, Apatow Productions, Universal, 2012), but are firmly rooted in the contemporary world where they turn cultural uncertainties and anxieties upside down and—unlike melodrama—solvable through friendship and laughs and jokes about the body.

DAVID FINCHER

As we have seen from the very beginning of its history, the body is the central focus of the cinematic gaze. What the body does and what is done to it is the subject of many films, especially those whose concern is violence and sexuality, evident in so much of contemporary American film. Hitchcock's *Psycho* (Paramount, 1960), Arthur Penn's *Bonnie and Clyde*, and Sam Peckinpah's *The Wild Bunch* (Warner Bros./Seven Arts, 1969) started the contemporary escalation of violent films in which the body was beaten up, stabbed, shot, and generally abused in a very bloody fashion. Certainly, the proximity of the Vietnam War as it was mediated on television spurred filmmakers and audiences to represent and accept more and more gruesome screen violence. As we noted, Oliver Stone reflected on the ubiquity of violence and the ways in which it is mediated in *Natural Born Killers*. One film, David Fincher's *Fight Club* (Fox, 2000, Regency, Linson Films, 1999), looked at violence as a sadomasochistic expression of self-hatred, resentment, and powerlessness.

Along with Oliver Stone, Fincher is one of the most important new directors to appear since the "new Hollywood" movement. His films are marked by an eye for detail and an expressive **mise-en-scène** that pays attention to the spaces that surround his characters and helps define them. The dark, rainy gloom of *Seven* (Cecchi Gori Pictures, New Line Cinema, 1995) along with the tight compositions that confine his characters create the atmosphere of dread that surrounds the hunt for a serial killer. Fincher is one of the pioneers in digital filmmaking and special effects. From *Zodiac* (Paramount, Warner Bros., Phoenix Pictures, 2007) on, he has filmed using digital cameras, and in *The Curious Case of Benjamin Button* (Warner Bros., Paramount, Kennedy/Marshall Company, 2008)—a narrative about a man aging backward—he seamlessly placed Brad Pitt's head on the body of an aged man. In *The Social Network* (Columbia, Relativity Media, 2010), he was able to find the right balance of close-up and movement to express screenwriter Aaron Sorkin's rapid-fire dialogue in a film about the creation of disembodiment—the virtual world of Facebook. *Fight Club* is about a different kind of body, that of young men who hurt themselves and each other in order to feel something. In the dark, dank recesses of the city, these men gather to fight each other, using their physical pain to express and give relief to their emotional pain and feelings of impotence in the world.

FIGHT CLUB

In comparison, the characters of Judd Apatow's films take their diminished status as a given and work with it in comic mode. Adam Sandler's character, George Simmons, in *Funny People* (Judd Apatow, Universal, Columbia, Relativity Media, Apatow Productions, 2009), a famous comic who believes he has a fatal disease, spends the film bemoaning his fate as well as fighting against his fears with a narcissistic, needy wit. The characters of *Fight Club* are narcissists tied up in knots; they need attention and cannot find it without violent means. They can only be untied by splitting their personalities figuratively and literally. The "narrator" of the film—the nameless character played by Edward Norton—is the rational and repressed half of Brad Pitt's Tyler Durden. They struggle with each other throughout the film in a fruitless attempt to integrate their personalities, just as their followers struggle to separate their daily existence from their nocturnal lives as fist fighters and terrorists. *Fight Club* is a film about disintegration, of a falling of will and reason into meanness and brutality. There are grim undertones of neofascism here, as Tyler organizes his disaffected colleagues into black-shirted mobs out to terrorize the city. There is as well a premonition of 9/11 in the blowing up of corporate skyscrapers that ends the film.

The disaffected men of *Fight Club* are the opposites of the superheroes celebrated in some other films we have looked at. They are unheroic and weak. Whatever strength they possess is aimed toward causing each other pain and then outward through acts of terrorism. But even here, the nightmare quality of the film allows us to question whether the bombing of the city that ends the film has actually occurred or is some fantasy of a broken mind. Tyler and the Narrator are one and the same. The Narrator shoots himself in the mouth and Tyler dies. The towers come down. The film flickers in the projector—one of Tyler's jobs is a projectionist, and he splices obscene images into the film he is showing. A few frames of the image of a penis appear. The film ends with an internal reference to itself as an artifact, a film shuddering on the screen, and an image of a masculinity that is failed.

Male aggression. A scene of masochistic fist fighting in David Fincher's *Fight Club* (1999).

Fincher is at some pains to emphasize the artifice of his film, to reflect on its existence as a cinematic fiction. But his attempt at modernist irony may not have been strong enough, given the fact that some young men took the macho posing of the film seriously and started actual fight clubs. The somewhat stunted young men of Judd Apatow's films never take themselves very seriously, or at least are so represented that we cannot take them seriously ourselves. That is the nature of comedy. And here is an interesting problem: American film in general does not want us to take it seriously. After all, it is only entertainment. When it does get too serious, too close to the bone, as in the various Iraq War films we have looked at, audiences tend to ignore it. When it gets brutal, as with *Fight Club*, some people take it the wrong way, as something to emulate. When it presents a vague metaphysical urge, as does Terrence Malick's *The Tree of Life* (Cottonwood Pictures, River Road Entertainment, Brace Cove Productions, Fox Searchlight, 2011), where a domestic melodrama is distended with images of the creation of the world, some people stand in awe. It sometimes seems as if it is difficult for contemporary American film and its audience to find an appropriate footing. But that may in the last analysis be its strength, creating films that are all over the place in terms of content and style, films that are often *inappropriate*, gross, violent, sentimental, but sometimes serious and even difficult.

A STUDY IN CONTRASTS

Given this mixture of styles and genres, I want to consider four different films to illustrate these conflicting and vibrant forces in contemporary American cinema. One, a comedy, went somewhat unappreciated during its run, *Dinner for Schmucks* (Jay Roach, Paramount, DreamWorks, Spyglass Entertainment, 2010). The second is a melodrama about youth and old age, *The Notebook* (Nick Cassavetes, New Line Cinema, Gran Via, Avery Pix, 2004). The third is a glossy thriller, *The Bourne Identity* (Doug Liman, Universal, The Kennedy/Marshall Company, Hypnotic, 2002). The fourth is a difficult, often painful film about the entanglements of the United States with the Middle East, *Syriana* (Stephen Gaghan, Warner Bros., Participant Productions, 2005).

DINNER FOR SCHMUCKS

Dinner for Schmucks is an elaboration on a French film made in 1998 by Francis Veber. The premise is simple: a group of businessmen invite people they consider to be morons to their weekly dinner in order to make fun of them. The elaboration is more interesting. Tim (Paul Rudd, an actor who has become all but ubiquitous in contemporary comedy) works for a private equity company of ruthless high fliers, one of whose jobs is to acquire companies and fire their workers. The top members of the firm, so full of themselves, collect eccentrics and oddballs, whom they proceed to belittle. Even before the financial collapse of 2008, the overbearing corporation became the butt of many films, both comic and serious. The evil corporation has had a long history in American film, and this reflects the ambivalence in the culture as a whole toward the rich and powerful. We have seen this played out in Frank Capra's films of the 1930s, where an upright individual can correct the dangers of out-of-control capitalism. We can see it in any number of films where individuals are pursued by large corporate concerns and singlehandedly reveal their wrongdoings or, in the case of a film like *Silkwood* (ABC Motion Pictures, Fox, 1983), discussed in Chapter 20, become its victim. Even contemporary science fiction, in particular the *Alien* series—*Alien* (Ridley Scott, Brandywine Productions, Fox, 1979); *Aliens* (James Cameron, Fox, Brandywine Productions, SLM Production Group 1986); *Alien*^{3} (David Fincher's first feature film, Fox, Brandywine Productions, 1992)—base at least part of their narrative on the premise of an evil corporation allowing the monster to survive in order to use it as a weapon. James Cameron's *Avatar* (Fox, Lightstorm Entertainment, Ingenious Films, 2009) portrays a harmonious distant world at risk because a corporation wants to exploit its resources.

In a comedy film, corporate excess is guaranteed to be punished, and its careless practitioners shown up as venal and foolish. In *Dinner for Schmucks*, corporate hard-heartedness leads to the meeting up of the film's two main characters, the corporate man, Tim, and the idiot savant, Barry (Steve Carell). Barry causes all kinds of mischief—not the least of which is getting Tim to lose his girlfriend and then mixed up with the IRS and its local nutty, hypnotist manager, Therman Murch (Zach Galifianakis). But the necessity of this kind of comedy is to prove that simple-mindedness is really a manifestation of a good heart and a simple cleverness. The fool is a venerable figure in literature as well as cinema: he acts as a kind of absorptive and reflective figure, exposing the flaws of society by speaking and acting out in all apparent innocence. He is stupid and harmless, wise and honest.

Barry is an artist as well as a fool. He makes whimsical pictures and dioramas using dead mice. He is contrasted with the pretentious modern artist Kieren (Jemaine Clement). It is in Barry's simplicity that his and Tim's redemption—an event that is almost required in any American movie, serious or comic—lies. When the dinner finally occurs, with not only Barry but an entire collection of oddballs present, chaos ensues. A blind man takes a sword to the crowd; a phony art collector loses a finger to a vulture; the boss's house catches fire. Of course, it is the corporate types who are proved to be the schmucks. Barry teaches Tim what real friends are; Tim teaches Barry to have courage. The two artists become collaborators. Barry, of course, gets his girl back. Everyone learns they can live their dreams.

This narrative is nicely indicative of American film today. Nevermind whether the film is as goofy as *Dinner for Schmucks*, it is still all but inevitable, with relatively few important exceptions, in a comedy or a melodrama that the main character will learn a lesson, that he or she will be taught to search their innermost selves to find the truth, find their true love, and that the rich and powerful will get their comeuppance. This is not, of course, the narrative of

Barry (Steve Carell) shows off his diorama of stuffed mice in *Dinner for Schmucks* (Jay Roach, 2010).

our lives, which tend to be somewhat more complex, but the narrative we want to be told about our lives. We are used to it, acculturated to it; we desire it. And film, being a commercial entity, will try its best to meet and satisfy our desires in order to gain our trust and our patronage.

THE NOTEBOOK

Melodrama must work to gain our trust, even though the process might seem effortless as we are watching it. Because it is based on a rising and falling graph of emotions, on coincidences of love found, lost, found again, on the ravages of disease and death, we must allow it to take care of our response. Because it does all the work, melodrama requires more passivity than other genres precisely because we are asked to give ourselves over to its sea change of feelings. Because melodrama demands an emotional response that is, in a sense, separate from the content of any individual melodramatic film—or perhaps because the content melodramatic film remains so stable—the genre has changed little over the years.

The Notebook is in many ways a close relative of *Dark Victory* (Edmond Goulding, Warner Bros., 1939), a film we discussed in Chapter 11. There, Bette Davis's wealthy Judith slowly succumbs to blindness and finally death, while keeping the seriousness of her condition from her doctor husband. In *The Notebook*, Allie is a rich young woman (played by Rachel McAdams) who, in her old age, succumbs to Alzheimer's disease. Unlike *Dark Victory*, we do not see the decline, but its result, as the old Allie (Gena Rowlands) sits in a nursing home being read to about her past by her husband Duke (James Garner), the old incarnation of her lover, Noah (Ryan Gosling). We discover that the notebook being read was written by Allie herself. The melodramatic irony lies in the fact that, as a young woman, Allie had trouble recognizing Noah's undying love. As a demented elderly woman, she once again cannot recognize her faithful husband.

As Cassavetes (the son of the director of *Shadows*, John Cassavetes; Gena Rowlands is his mother) cuts back and forth between youth and old age, the emphasis falls on the constancy of love, despite the obstacles put in its path—class difference, the active resistance of Allie's parents (her mother hides Noah's letters, her disapproving father wears a handlebar moustache like a silent film villain), the ups and downs of their turbulent romance, the final, brief reconciliation and recognition of each other in old age, and, inevitably, their death. Happiness, pain, and dying—pushed and accented by swelling, yearning music—remain the essentials of melodrama now as in the past. These conventions encapsulate lifetimes in 2 hours, and we willingly give ourselves over to the impossible concentration and coincidence of events. Melodrama is more than life; it is rather a cinematic life unto itself that projects, protects, and engorges our emotions.

THE BOURNE IDENTITY

The trust demanded by the thriller film is of a different order than that of comedy or melodrama. Comedy

Transcendent love—in death. James Garner and Gena Rolands as the adult Noah and Allie in the quiet melodramatic end to *The Notebook* (Nick Cassavetes, 2004).

Jason Bourne fires away at his pursuers while leaping off a stairwell. Matt Damon in *The Bourne Identity* (Doug Liman, 2002).

asks us to accept and laugh at the absurdities of the world; melodrama asks of us to experience the yearning desire of fictional characters. The thriller asks us to assent to the absurdities of chases, shootings, escapes, beatings, threats, assassinations, stabbings, explosions, of people falling into water, into fire, of incalculable damage to objects and especially to bodies. These bodies are incredibly resilient, made so by the tricks of editing and CGI. A thriller is the ultimate escape machine, an engine to drive us out of our comfortable space into a cinematically contrived space of action and invincible bodies (contrived, yet specific: action thrillers often include date, time, and place stamps to locate us and move the action forward). The invincible hero is particularly interesting in *The Bourne Identity* and its sequels.

Jason Bourne (Matt Damon) is a scaled-down version of the superhero. He is close to a mechanical fighting machine—in fact, he is called that by his "handler." He is a distant relative of Rambo, able to deliver knockout blows to any number of assailants in an attempt to work through the enigma of who he is and why he is being pursued. His pursuer is, of course, the CIA, a villainous organization even more omnipresent than the evil corporation in films of this genre. The CIA (at least the version of it that exists in film) is out to maintain its reputation, even when, almost inevitably, it loses control of a rogue agent. Bourne is not merely "rogue," but unaware of why the agency is pursuing him. The driving principles of *The Bourne Identity,* and many thrillers like it, are identity and pursuit—finding out who the hero really is and why people are after him. Therefore, beyond the pleasure of over-the-top action and violence that keeps the rhythms of a thriller in forward motion is the sublimation of fears about governmental powers beyond our control—in a word, paranoia. Bourne becomes a kind of every/superman, always in danger, always able to escape danger through sheer physical prowess. He proves that the machinations of the CIA are no match for his cunning, and he refuses to be used. As viewers, we allow ourselves to be used by the driving force of the film. It is, as with melodrama, a willing giving over of our emotions, in this case to the tumbling energies of someone who could not exist outside of his genre.

SYRIANA

The identity/chase/political thriller provides considerable release, if nothing else than for the rollercoaster ride it brings to a satisfactory conclusion. But what if a satisfactory conclusion is not reached? What if the usual fulfillment of narrative desire provided by most films is frustrated? It is a rare occurrence (though we have seen it across that large group of films called film noir, which spoke to other, darker desires), and rarer still when a film takes on an overtly political slant.

Syriana appeared in 2005, 4 years after 9/11 and well into the Iraq conflict. It was a time of great confusion and misunderstanding, especially of Islam and the Middle East. That same year, Steven Spielberg released *Munich* (DreamWorks SKG, Universal, Amblin Entertainment), a film about the killing of Israeli athletes at the 1972 Olympics and the Israeli hunt for their murderers. *Munich* is an extraordinarily complex film for Spielberg, for it questions the very moral structure of revenge and the toll it takes on those who would engage in state-sponsored murder. Although *Munich* contains flashbacks to the Munich massacre, it is otherwise told in straightforward linear fashion, following the string of murders committed by the Israeli team in search of revenge. Not so with *Syriana*, whose narrative structure is as complicated as the turmoil and politics of the Middle East itself. Numerous threads are interwoven during the course of the film. To protect themselves against Chinese incursion into their business, two oil companies create a questionable merger to form a giant corporation with operations in the Persian Gulf. One result is that many Islamic workers are fired, leading to their disaffection and anger. One Pakistani young man joins a madrassa and ends up committing a terrorist act. Bob Barnes (George Clooney), a CIA agent who refuses to play by the rules, becomes embroiled in Middle-Eastern intrigue that ultimately gets him horribly tortured and finally targeted for destruction by his own agency, which has been using him for their own ends. The US government commits a terrorist act on one of its own and again we find the CIA constructed as an evil entity. Matt Damon plays a financial broker. His son is accidentally killed while attending a party thrown in Switzerland by a Middle-Eastern country. He attempts to cover his grief by helping the Westernized son of a Middle-Eastern emir (Alexander Siddig). He chooses the wrong side, the wrong son, the other target, along with Barnes, of the CIA's drone attack.

The details of these and yet other narrative threads are woven in exquisite detail and with a sometimes maddening lack of transition or clear explanation. There is an unusual coolness to the film's emotional temperature (with the exception of the horrible scene of torture). Gaghan, the director and screenwriter, wants the viewer to remain intellectually engaged and somewhat puzzled by the intricate connections between the individuals and groups working through the mistakes, the corruption, and the opaqueness of Middle-Eastern affairs and our government's inability to see clearly through it all. His images are striking, the interactions of his characters and the seemingly bottomless treachery of governments and individuals deeply troubling. "Corruption is our protection. Corruption keeps us safe and warm. . . . Corruption is why we win," says one character in the film's most overtly cynical outburst. And because of that, the wrong choices are made and the wrong people are hurt.

It would be an easy way out to say that most American film lies somewhere between the complexities of *Syriana* and the silliness of *Dinner for Shmucks*; but the spectrum sometimes seems to fall toward the shmuck side. There is a share of melodramatic cinema that carries an earnestly serious tone, though too often that tone is conveyed in films of family dysfunction or blighted romance. There are violent thrillers and bloody horror films that substitute loud noises or grotesque violence for genuine fright or thrills. In the end, the great variety of contemporary American film can seem somewhat constrained, lacking the urge toward visual and formal experimentation, playing it safe. But what our four films—*Dinner for Schmucks*, *The Notebook*, *The Bourne Identity*, and *Syriana*—indicate is that old genres can be refreshed and that there

CIA agent Bob Barnes (George Clooney) walks away from an exploding car bomb in Stephen Gaghan's *Syriana* (2005).

remain some small possibilities for formal experiment. The nonlinear form of *Syriana* was attempted in other films at the time, such as *Babel* (Alejandro González Iñárritu, Paramount Vantage, Anonymous Content, Zeta Film, Central Films, 2006), and they can trace their lineage as far back as *Citizen Kane*. *Syriana*'s confrontation with the politics of the moment is not entirely neglected in American cinema.

In fact, *Syriana* joins those anticorporation, anti-CIA thrillers that are political in the way they address power and its abuse. Some, like George Clooney's film about newscaster Edward R. Murrow's attack on Senator Joseph McCarthy, *Good Night and Good Luck* (Warner Independent Pictures, 2929 Productions, Participant Productions, 2005), offer the hope of overcoming political wrongdoing. Many simply take governmental agencies, especially the CIA, or big corporations, as insuperable enemies of the individual. Liberal or conservative, these films at least engage the world at large. They may be fanciful and exaggerated, but they recognize that melodrama can be created beyond the confines of a pair of lovers and a dysfunctional family.

Comedy and melodrama, the two opposing super genres of film ("super" in the sense that most subgenres are varieties of comedy or melodrama) speak to the conflicting poles of our own experience: the desire to find the world ridiculous and the inevitable recognition of its tremendous sadness. With this we are back to the matter of reception, of how we respond to films and our wide-ranging capacity to react to their variety. Filmmakers depend on this; they know that the appetite for variety is wide and that their own capacity for providing for that appetite is somewhat limited by their own imaginations and the commercial demands placed upon them. That is one reason for the seeming lack of variety in output. Too much demand, too little cinematic imagination to meet it, too much commercial pressure. But perhaps enough variety to keep movies interesting.

IN PRAISE OF DIVERSITY

There is a paradox here. If we complain about the lack of variety in much of contemporary American film, we must at the same time applaud its diversity. By that I mean not only the diversity of genres, which is great, but the diversity of characters. More and more we see gay characters appearing in film without derision or without a major fuss being made about their sexual orientation. African American characters have become part of the mix of people we see on the screen, and some films are even brave enough to represent mixed-race romance. None of this came any easier to film than it did to the culture at large. And despite the presence of African American characters, it is as rare to find an African American director as it is a woman in the same capacity.

BLAXPLOITATION

SHAFT AND SWEET SWEETBACK'S BAADASSSSS SONG

To understand the history of contemporary representation of African Americans in film, we need to look back a few decades. There was a brief period in the 1970s when a few African American filmmakers directed films that were called "Blaxploitation." As if in response to the absence of black heroic figures, these films—such as *Shaft* (Gordon Parks, MGM, Shaft Productions Ltd., 1971), and the independently produced *Sweet Sweetback's Baadasssss Song* (Melvin Van Peebles, Yeah, Inc., Cinemation Industries, 1971)—created characters that start with stereotypes and step them up a few notches. *Sweet Sweetback*, a film made in the spirit of the Black Power movement of the time, is "dedicated to all the Brothers and Sisters who had enough of the Man." Shot in a ragged, rapidly cut style, with multiple exposures and distorted images, the film comes close to avant-garde pornography in its attempt to portray a strong, silent black character. Sweetback, played by Van Peebles, is a male prostitute, who, saving the life of a Black Panther, goes on the run after beating two cops in what becomes a black road movie. On the road, he gains the help of other African Americans and a white motorcycle gang as the police chase him down. He finally finds safety in Mexico. In this film, the outlaw becomes a representative of righteous strength, his power emerges from his outrageousness and defiance. *Shaft* is more conventionally filmed than *Sweet Sweetback*, and creates its character, played by Richard Roundtree, as a black superhero, a private investigator, working parallel to the cops to break up a Mafia ring.

The black superhero. Richard Roundtree as *Shaft* (Gordon Parks, 1971).

In both films, the black hero is tough and resilient, a wish-fulfillment character of resistance and strength: stronger, sexier, angrier than African Americans had been allowed to be—when they were allowed to be at all—in mainstream Hollywood film. Women too were part of the Blaxploitation movement. The actress Pam Grier, for example, starred in a number of films, such as *Foxy Brown* (Jack Hill, American International Pictures, 1974), in which she took the role of avenging hero. Quentin Tarantino paid homage to these films in *Jackie Brown* (Miramax, A Band Apart, Lawrence Bender Productions, 1997).

It was not since the 1950s and a film like *No Way Out* (Joseph L. Mankiewicz, Fox, 1950) that African American characters asserted themselves as they do in these films. In *No Way Out*, there is a black uprising against a bigoted white community, an uprising the film sees as justified. While there were many films in the 1950s that took a liberal view of integration, none were as radical as *No Way Out* (see Chapter 15). In the 1970s, there was the hope of creating a strong black identity, separate from whites, self-sufficient, and, when necessary, violent. The various Black Power movements were more radical than the integrationist policies of liberal America, and they scared much of white society. *Sweet Sweetback*, in particular, played upon this fear by creating a character on the margins even of African American culture: silent and sullen, profoundly sexualized, fighting "the Man." The movement both in the culture and in the film did not last long. Some leaders of the various Black Power factions were murdered, others moved on to quieter work in the mainstream civil rights movement. Black filmmaking went on to represent other aspects of the African American experience with different kinds of heroes. Most African American filmmakers, like the women directors who thrived in the 1980s, eventually disappeared as white male-dominated Hollywood regained—perhaps "maintained" is more accurate—its control.

SPIKE LEE

SHE'S GOTTA HAVE IT AND *DO THE RIGHT THING*

In a sense, the Blaxploitation movement was a parody of the Black Power movement that was occurring in the United States in the late 1960s and early 1970s. The heroes of the films were too over the top—a case, perhaps, of overcompensation. A somewhat cooler approach was needed to comment on race and racism. Spike Lee, an NYU film school graduate, came to prominence with an independent film about a sexually liberated woman, who plays off three men to her delight and their frustration. *She's Gotta Have It* (40 Acres & A Mule Filmworks, Island Pictures, 1986) is a long way from the Blaxploitation films of the early 1970s. Gentle, direct, self-aware—the characters often address the camera—the film offers a decidedly nonheroic, even ordinary representation of African American life while at the same time praising the open sexuality of its main character.

Racial tension boils over into the streets in Spike Lee's *Do the Right Thing* (1989).

Lee went on to make a number of powerful films about the black experience. *Do the Right Thing* (Universal, 40 Acres & A Mule Filmworks, 1989) is already a more polished and detailed film than *She's Gotta Have It.* In the harsh yellow-red tint of a hot summer's day, Lee's film examines the racial interactions of one small Brooklyn neighborhood, all black with the exception of a white-owned pizza shop and a Korean grocery. In one startling sequence, Lee tracks swiftly into one individual after another—Mookie, played by Lee himself; Pino (John Turturro); a cop; a Korean shop owner—each one spewing a string of racial epithets, ending with the local radio disk jockey (Samuel L. Jackson), yelling that "you need to cool that shit out!" But things do not cool out. They get hotter and hotter. Antagonisms between the people in the neighborhood, antagonisms between the racist Pino and his father, Sal (Danny Aiello), grow until an uprising occurs. Sal destroys the boom box of one of his customers, leading to a full-scale fight. The cops kill a man. Mookie throws a garbage can through the window of Sal's Pizzeria. The crowd tears it apart and sets it on fire. The pictures of white celebrities on the restaurant wall that had so offended the community go up in flames. The strains of the rap song "Fight the Power" accompany the devastation. But Lee is not offering simple responses to complex issues. The film ends with two epigraphs, one by Martin Luther King proclaiming nonviolence, the second by Malcolm X suggesting that violence is necessary as a means of self-defense. A photograph of the two leaders, together, smiling, follows. The issue of racial tension, as in the culture itself, is left unresolved. The film holds closely to that irresolution, denying simple answers.

Lee has been one of the most visible and prolific of African American filmmakers. Perhaps his best is his extraordinary biography of Malcolm X (Warner Bros., Largo International N.V., JVC Entertainment Networks, 40 Acres & A Mule, 1992), in which Denzel Washington plays the controversial civil rights leader, who was assassinated in 1965. Since then, Lee has mixed television production with feature films, including a multipart HBO documentary on the lasting effects on the black poor of New Orleans in the wake of hurricane Katrina, *When the Levees Broke: A Requiem in Four Acts* (HBO Documentary Films, 40 Acres & A Mule Filmworks, 2006). He mixes small, personal films, like *Red Hook Summer* (40 Acres & A Mule Filmworks, Variance Films, 2012), with more commercial productions, like his remake of a violent South Korean film, *Old Boy* (Good Universe, Vertigo Entertainment, 40 Acres & A Mule Filmworks, 2013). He remains an important figure of African American independent filmmaking that can be traced all the way back to Oscar Micheaux.

TYLER PERRY

As happened with women, opportunities for African American directors have diminished—with the exception of Spike Lee and Tyler Perry, and recent films by Lee Daniels and the British director, Steve McQueen. Perry has established himself as a one-person, independent filmmaking operation. He has his own studio in Atlanta. He writes plays and writes and directs movies that have a large following across black and white audiences. Perry's films offer a sharp contrast to the Blaxploitation films of the 1970s and the complex interrogation of racial issues offered by Lee. It could be argued that they represent a post–civil rights attitude toward race where blackness is a given and attention can be turned to how everyday life is lived in the African American community without the pressures of racism bearing down. Alternatively, Perry's films can be read as a sentimentalizing, some would argue a stereotyping of African American life, focusing on relatively comfortable middle- and lower middle-class people, working through pains of intimacy and family struggles. To me, the films comfortably navigate between these poles.

A slight hint of the ghetto infiltrates Perry's films in the character of Madea, played by Perry in drag, the tough-talking matriarch with a gun. She is a modern version of the "mammy" figure that populates literary and cinematic fiction—we see her in Scarlett O'Hara's Mammy (Hattie McDaniel) in *Gone with the Wind* (MGM, Victor Fleming, George Cukor, Sam Wood, 1939). But unlike the traditional "Mammy," Madea is a self-sufficient, gun-toting adult who takes charge of impossible situations, albeit by ridiculous, comic means. In the Perry universe, she is the guardian of the African American family and its children.

TYLER PERRY'S I CAN DO BAD ALL BY MYSELF

Tyler Perry's I Can Do Bad All by Myself (Lionsgate, Tyler Perry Studios, 2009) is a good example of Perry's work: a disrupted family; a selfish, alcoholic nightclub singer, April (Taraji P. Henson), whose life has taken a bad turn; children who have lost their mother to drugs; a villainous adulterer (Brian White); Madea, full of energy and malapropisms, who teaches the children to pray; and a Latino, Sandino (Adam Rodriquez), who helps April to redeem herself through a life of responsibility and religion. Gladys Knight sings an uplifting song. A preacher offers an uplifting sermon and sings to his congregation. The film ends with the marriage of April and Sandino and a block party with black and white participants. The closing song, "You can't hold a good woman down. . . . You're not alone," is a far cry from the song "Fight the Power" that accompanies the racial tensions and destruction of the block in *Do the Right Thing*.

The melodramatic impulse of all this is fleshed out with a colorful mise-en-scène and an earnestness on the part of all concerned that belies the sentimentality inherent in this and most of Perry's films—or at least makes the sentimentality heartfelt and, to use a tricky word, *authentic*. Can sentimentality be authentic? Sentimentality is usually thought of as unearned emotion, that is, emotion pumped up by the fictional events of a film. But Perry seems to earn the emotionality of his films by a sense of commitment to the characters and their lives in a spirit of optimism, certainly a rare quality in contemporary film. In contrast to *The Help* (Tate Taylor, Touchstone Pictures, DreamWorks SKG, Reliance Entertainment, Imagenation Abu Dhabi, 2011) or even *Lee Daniel The Butler* (Follow Through Productions, Salamander Pictures, AI-Film, 2013), films that seem to be as much about salvaging white guilt as portraying an ugly aspect of the southern black experience, in the case of *The Help*, or the Civil Rights movement and the endurance of African Americans in *The Butler*. The dark seriousness of Steve McQueen's *12 Years a Slave* (Regency Enterprises, River Road Entertainment, Plan B Entertainment, Fox, 2013) takes melodrama to a peak of painfulness. It is so grueling in its depiction of the everyday brutalities of slavery that it threatens to overwhelm the viewer with horror and disgust. Tyler Perry's films do not overwhelm. They emerge out of contemporary middle-class black experience, sugarcoating it a bit, playing to his audience, and steeped in optimism. His melodramatics are not as severe as the films of Oscar Micheaux; and the movement in his films from bad situations to the characters' redemption may be a bit too facile. But in watching his films there is pleasure, an emotion not to be taken lightly when much of contemporary cinema seems to play to anxiety rather than its opposite.

In the end, pleasure is key and is multifaceted. Without it, we would not want to watch movies at all. The fact that pleasure is derived from a variety of genres that keep renewing themselves, from films as diverse as *Django Unchained* and *I Can Do Bad All By*

Celebration in the streets in *Tyler Perry's I Can Do Bad All by Myself* (2009).

Tyler Perry as Madea, the tough-talking matriarch in *I Can Do Bad All by Myself*.

Myself, from loud-noise horror films to Judd Apatow comedies, indicates yet another kind of diversity. Most of us like all kinds of movies and are open to the various kinds of pleasure they provide—fright, outrageous violence, tearful sentimentality, raucous, vulgar comedy, even anxiety; perhaps, on occasion, complexity. From film's beginnings to the present, we like to look at a variety of stories. The desire to look is met with the ongoing effort of filmmakers to fulfill that desire—a complex process that makes up the cultures of American film.

SELECTED FILMOGRAPHY

Shaft, dir. Gordon Parks, Shaft Productions Ltd., MGM, 1971.

Sweet Sweetback's Baadasssss Song, dir. Melvin Van Peebles, Yeah, Inc., Cinemation Industries, 1971.

Foxy Brown, dir. Jack Hill, American International Pictures, 1997.

Alien, dir. Ridley Scott, Fox, Brandywine Productions, 1979.

Aliens, dir. James Cameron, Fox, Brandywine Productions, SLM Production Group, 1986.

Sex, Lies and Videotape, dir. Steven Soderbergh, Outlaw Productions, Miramax, 1989.

The Bourne Identity, dir. Doug Liman, The Kennedy/Marshall Company, Hypnotic, 2002.

Ocean's Eleven, Twelve, and *Thirteen*, dir. Steven Soderbergh, Warner Bros., 2001, 2004, 2007.

Funny Ha Ha, dir. Andrew Bujalski, Goodbye Cruel Releasing, 2003.

The Notebook, dir. Nick Cassavetes, New Line Cinema, Gran Via, Avery Pix, 2004.

Good Night and Good Luck, dir. George Clooney, Warner Independent Pictures, 2929 Productions, Participant Productions, 2005.

Syriana, dir. Stephen Gaghan, Warner Bros., Participant Productions, 2005.

Man Push Cart, dir. Ramin Bahrani, Noruz Films, Flip Side Film, Films Philos, 2005.

Chop Shop, dir. Ramin Bahrani, Muskat Filmed Properties, Noruz Films (I), Big Beach Films, 2008.

At Any Price, dir. Ramin Bahrani, Black Bear Pictures, Treehouse Pictures, Killer Films, Sony Pictures Classics, 2012.

Talladega Nights: The Ballad of Ricky Bobby, dir. Adam McKay, Columbia, Relativity Media, Apatow Productions, 2006.

Tyler Perry's I Can Do Bad All by Myself, dir. Tyler Perry, Lionsgate, Tyler Perry Studios, 2009.

Funny People, dir. Judd Apatow, Universal, Columbia, Relativity Media, 2009.

Dinner for Schmucks, dir. Jay Roach, Paramount, DreamWorks, Spyglass Entertainment, 2010.

Bridesmaids, dir. Paul Feig, Universal, Relativity Media, Apatow Productions, 2011.

The Future, dir. Miranda July, GND Productions, Haut et Court, Match Factory, Medianboard Berlin-Brandenburg, Razor Film Produktion, Roadside Attractions, 2011.

The Help, dir. Tate Taylor, Touchstone Pictures, DreamWorks SKG, Reliance Entertainment, Imagenation Abu Dhabi, 2011.

Wanderlust, dir. David Wain, Apatow Productions, Relativity Media, 2012.

This Is 40, dir. Judd Apatow, Apatow Productions, Universal, 2012.

Frances Ha, dir. Noah Baumbach, RT Features, Pine District Pictures, Scott Rudin Productions, ITC, 2012.

Lee Daniel, The Butler, dir., Lee Daniels, Follow Through Productions, Salamander Pictures, AI-Film, 2013.

12 Years a Slave, dir. Steve McQueen, Regency Enterprises, River Road Entertainment, Plan B Entertainment, Film4, Fox, 2013.

Quentin Tarantino

Pulp Fiction, A Band Apart, Jersey Films, Miramax, 1994.

Inglourious Basterds, Universal, The Weinstein Company, A Band Apart, 2009.

Kill Bill, Vols. I & II A Band Apart, Miramax, 2003, 2004.

Death Proof, Dimension Films, Trouble Maker Studios, The Weinstein Company, Rodriquez International Pictures, 2007.

Django Unchained, Weinstein Company, Columbia Pictures, 2012.

Oliver Stone

Platoon, Cinema 86, Hemdale Film, Orion, 1986.

JFK, Warner Bros., Canal+, Regency Enterprises, 1991.

Natural Born Killers, Warner Bros., Regency Enterprises, Alcor Films, 1994.

Any Given Sunday, Warner Bros., Ixtlan, Donners' Company, 1999.

World Trade Center, Paramount, Double Feature Films, Intermedia Films, 2006.

Wall Street: Money Never Sleeps, Edward Pressman Film, Dune Entertainment, Fox, 2010.

Savages, Ixtlan, Onda Entertainment, Relativity Media, Universal, 2012.

The Untold History of the United States, Ixtlan Productions, Showtime, 2112–2013.

David Fincher

Alien[3], Fox, Brandywine Production, 1992.

Seven, Cecchi Gori Pictures, New Line Cinema, 1995.

Fight Club, Fox, Regency, Linson Films, 1999.

Zodiac, Paramount, Warner Bros., Phoenix Pictures, 2007.

The Curious Case of Benjamin Button, Warner Bros., Paramount, Kennedy/Marshall Company, 2008.

The Social Network, Columbia, Relativity Media, 2010.

Spike Lee

She's Gotta Have It, 40 Acres & A Mule Filmworks, Island Pictures, 1986.

Do the Right Thing, Universal, 40 Acres & A Mule Filmworks, 1989.

Malcolm X, Warner Bros., Largo International N.V., JVC Entertainment Networks, 40 Acres & A Mule, 1992.

When the Levees Broke: A Requiem in Four Acts, HBO Documentary Films, 40 Acres & A Mule Filmworks, 2006.

Red Hook Summer, 40 Acres & A Mule Filmworks, Variance Films, 2012.

SUGGESTIONS FOR FURTHER READING

Manthia Diawara, *Black American Cinema: Aesthetics and Spectatorship* (New York, NY: Routledge, 1993).

Novotny Lawrence, *Blaxploitation Films of the 1970s: Blackness and Genre* (New York, NY: Routledge, 2008).

John Lewis, ed., *The End of Cinema as We Know It: American Film in the Nineties* (New York, NY: New York University Press, 2001).

Steve Neale, *Genre and Contemporary Hollywood* (London, UK: British Film Institute, 2002).

Janet Staiger, *Interpreting Film: Studies in the Historical Reception of American Cinema* (Princeton, NJ: Princeton University Press, 1992).

Linda Ruth Williams & Michael Hammond, eds., *Contemporary American Cinema* (Maidenhead, Berkshire, England: Open University Press, McGraw-Hill, 2006).

NOTES

1. "As Indies Explode, an Appeal for Sanity: Flooding Theaters Isn't Good for Filmmakers or Filmgoers," *The New York Times* (January 12, 2014), AR1.
2. David Denby, "Youthquake: Mumblecore Movies," *The New Yorker* (March 16, 2009), 114. A history of Sundance by Benjamin Craig can be found at http://www.sundanceguide.net/basics/history/.

GLOSSARY

ADR Automated dialogue replacement, also known as looping or dubbing, is the way dialogue is added to a film in postproduction.

AMBIENT SOUND All the background noises on the soundtrack that are neither dialogue nor music.

ANAMORPHIC A process that squeezes the image onto a 35 mm or 65 mm strip of film and when unsqueezed by a special lens on the projector creates an image of 2.35:1 or wider.

AUTEUR THEORY The concept that holds the director as the main creative engine of a film.

BACKLIGHT Used to separate the character from the background.

BLOCK BOOKING During the studio period, this was the process of forcing theater owners to show all the releases of the studio in order to get their major films.

BLUE OR GREEN SCREEN The background that will drop out when computer imagery is **matted** into the shot.

CGI Computer-generated imagery.

CINEMASCOPE The **anamorphic** process developed by 20th Century Fox in 1953.

CINEMATOGRAPHER The individual responsible for lighting the film, choosing the appropriate lenses, and, in collaboration with the **director** and **production designer**, establishing the general look of a film. Also called the director of photography or DP.

CINÉMA VÉRITÉ A form of documentary that does away with voice-over narration and the obtrusive camera, allowing the people and events to speak for themselves as if the camera were not present.

CLASSICAL HOLLYWOOD STYLE The reigning style of American filmmaking that emphasizes story over form and attempts to make form invisible. It includes elements such as the **over-the-shoulder** dialogue style, **shot-reverse shot**, **continuity editing**, and a **narrative** arc that is linear and results in the resolution of conflict.

CLOSE-UP A shot usually encompassing the face of a character.

COMPOSER Unlike a conventional composer, the writing of music for a film is done in small increments or "music cues" that accompany specific moments and moods.

CONTINUITY EDITING At the heart of the **classical Hollywood style** is the cutting together of shots of dialogue and action so that the editing itself becomes invisible.

CRANE The camera on a large mechanism that moves it up in the air to achieve a high-angle shot or down from a high shot to a close-up.

DEEP FOCUS OR DEPTH OF FIELD All characters and elements in a shot, from foreground to background, are in focus.

DEFOCUS The camera goes out of focus on a character or scene.

DIGITAL INTERMEDIATE Before editing, film is transferred to a digital file, where the color is manipulated and editing is done.

DIRECTOR During the studio period, the director was a contract employee, who was responsible for translating the screenplay to film. Today, some directors have more control over the entire production.

DISSOLVE One shot fades out at the same time as the following shot fades in.

DOCUMENTARY A film that alleges to capture events that would have occurred even if the filmmaker were not present. A nonfiction film.

DOLLY SHOT The camera moving on its supporting mechanism, or dolly.

EDITOR Puts together the pieces of film created during the shooting stage. During the studio period, the editor worked mainly with the film's producer. Today the director takes a greater part in the editing process.

EISENSTEINIAN OR RUSSIAN MONTAGE The technique of Russian filmmaker Sergei Eisenstein that emphasizes the rapid collision of shots to create an effect greater than the shots by themselves.

ESTABLISHING SHOT The first shot of a film or its sequences that locates the viewer in a particular place. See also **Master Shot**.

EYELINE MATCH Making certain that a character is looking in the same direction from shot to shot.

FADE OUT The image fades to black.

FAR SHOT A shot taken at some distance from the characters.

FICTION FILM An imaginative story. A **narrative** of made-up events.

FILL LIGHT Used to control shadows.

FILM STOCK Refers to the kind of film being used, especially the "speed" of the film, or how much light is required for an adequate exposure.

FLAT WIDE SCREEN Created by masking the top and bottom of the image rather than using an **anamorphic** lens.

FOLEY Named after Jack Foley, the Foley design is part of the sound effects added to a film in postproduction.

FORCED PERSPECTIVE A way of constructing a set that creates the illusion of depth on the two-dimensional plane of the motion picture screen.

FORDISM Henry Ford developed the assembly line to manufacture automobiles. The term refers to the process in which each worker knows one part of the manufacturing process and repeats the same action over and over as the assembly line moves by.

FRENCH NEW WAVE A movement in the late 1950s and throughout the 1960s of film critics turned filmmakers who investigated and experimented with the formal properties of their medium. They included Jean-Luc Godard, François Truffaut, Jacques Rivette, Claude Chabrol, and Eric Rohmer.

GAFFER The head lighting electrician.

GAZE The "look" of one character to another and the look of the viewer toward the characters on screen.

GENRE A *type* of film made up of specific narrative and thematic conventions, such as the Western, the gangster film, science fiction, romantic comedy, etc.

GERMAN EXPRESSIONISM An early 20th-century aesthetic movement across the arts that emphasized disturbed emotional states reflected in the **mise-en-scène** that surrounded the characters.

HIGH-KEY LIGHTING Even, bright lighting across the shot.

IMAGE TRACK The series of images printed on the celluloid ribbon of conventional film.

INTERTEXTUALITY The cross-referencing of one work within another so that one film carries, in effect, a conversation with another.

INTERTITLE The written dialogue or description interrupting the images of a silent film.

IRIS SHOT A silent film convention of opening a scene with a pinpoint of light that expands to fill the screen or closing it with the shot contracting to black.

ITALIAN NEOREALISM A post–World War II movement that took filmmakers out of the studio and onto the streets to film largely non-professional characters struggling in the poverty of postwar Europe.

JUMP CUT Leaps in small amounts of time created when a continuous action is edited to remove continuity. The cinematic equivalent of ellipses.

KEY LIGHT The light that illuminates the face of an actor. You can see the reflection of the key light in the eyes of an actor during a **close-up**.

LAP DISSOLVE One image fades out while at the same time the following image fades in.

MAGNETIC TRACK As opposed to an **optical track**, the sound is contained on a magnetic strip running along the side of the film.

MASTER SHOT This establishes the space of the scene. Once established, the filmmaker can then begin editing shots within this space without confusing the audience. See **Establishing Shot**.

MATTE SHOT As opposed to a **rear screen projection**, actors perform in front of a **blue or green screen**, which is dropped out when the elements of the background are added later.

MIDSHOT Characters composed usually from the midsection of the body to the head.

MISE-EN-SCÈNE The entirety of the visual space of the film, including lighting, production design, camera placement and movement, and use of color or black and white.

MONTAGE The dynamic collision of shots, usually associated with the Russian filmmaker Sergei Eisenstein, but now used to describe any rapidly edited sequence.

MOTION CAPTURE The contemporary version of **rotoscoping**. Sensors are placed on an actor, whose movements are captured by computer and then animated.

MOVIEOLA This was the machine used to edit film, making it possible to cut sequences and arrange them in the order necessary to create film's narrative structure. Now obsolete because of digital editing.

MULTIPLE EXPOSURE A single strip of undeveloped film is exposed to different images.

MUMBLECORE Low-budget, independent film, focusing on the romantic entanglements of (usually) 20 year olds. Emphasis is on low-key dialogue.

MUSIC AND EFFECTS TRACK That part of the soundtrack that includes the music and ambient sounds that are recorded separately from the dialogue.

NARRATIVE The telling of the film's story. As opposed to plot, which abstracts a story from the film, the narrative is made up of character development, shot composition, editing, the perspective from which the story is told, the temporal events that communicate what the film is about.

90-DEGREE SHOT The camera is placed in a position directly in front of the characters. This placement is discouraged in the **classical Hollywood style**.

NONLINEAR NARRATIVE Breaks chronological continuity by means of flashbacks and forwards, or by mixing up sequences without attention to strict continuity.

180-DEGREE LINE OR RULE The convention that a camera cannot cross to the other side of an imaginary line across a scene in the belief that this would create the impression that the characters had flipped positions.

OPTICAL PRINTING Projecting one piece of film onto another that has not been developed enables a filmmaker to build images in layers.

OPTICAL TRACK A soundtrack printed as a variable clear strip alongside of the **image track**.

OVER-THE-SHOULDER DIALOGUE SEQUENCE A typical dialogue sequence is edited so that the camera jumps from a shot over the shoulder of one character to over the shoulder of the other character, back and forth for the duration of the sequence.

PAN Not a bad review, but rather the pivoting of the camera right or left.

PANAVISION The **anamorphic** process that followed **CinemaScope**.

PANNED AND SCANNED When widescreen films were shown on television or on videotape, the sides were cut off and the image blown up to a square shape. An **optical printer** was used to move around the frame to show what had been left out.

PARALLEL EDITING Alternating scenes that may be happening at the same time but at different places.

POINT OF VIEW A shot representing what a character sees. Point of view can also refer to the perspective of the **narrative** as a whole.

PROCESS SHOT Any shot in a film which involves **special effects**, where parts of the shot are added at different stages of the production. A car placed in front of a **rear screen projection** of moving scenery is an example of a process shot.

PRODUCER During the studio period, the producer was in charge of the entire production. Today, there are multiple producers, each one responsible for some the film's funding and organization. The process by means of which the producer guides a film from beginning to end is known as the **Producer system.**

PRODUCT PLACEMENT Brand-name products visible in the film that constitute a paid advertisement for that product. Also called "embedded marketing."

PRODUCTION DESIGNER Chooses and creates the elements of the various sets that reflect the time period and the taste of the characters in the film. A good production designer adds to the visual coherence of a film.

REAR SCREEN PROJECTION A moving image projected behind the characters while the shot is being made. Most often used when photographing the characters in a car meant to be moving down the road.

REVERSE SHOT When a character looks at something and then there is a cut to what is being looked at, that shot is a reverse of the previous. See **shot-reverse shot.**

ROTOSCOPING Tracing over footage of actual actors to create the effect of animation.

ROUGH CUT An early assemblage of footage that precedes the final editing.

SCREENWRITER One of usually a number of people responsible for the script of a film.

SECOND UNIT A self-contained production unit, often working on location, that films material that will be used in the main feature.

SHOT-REVERSE SHOT The basic structure of American filmmaking in which a character looks and there is a cut to what the character is looking at. Also applies to the **over-the-shoulder** style of a dialogue sequence.

SOFT FOCUS The opposite of **deep focus**: the foreground is in focus while the background is not.

SOUND-ON-FILM When the soundtrack is printed alongside of the **image track.**

SOUNDTRACK That part of the celluloid strip that contains the information for reproducing sound.

SPECIAL EFFECTS Visual elements added to the shot, such as computer-generated images of explosions.

STANDARD (OR ACADEMY) RATIO The size of the image from shortly after the coming of sound until the 1950s: 4×3 or 1.33.1, four units in width to three units in height.

TAYLORISM Named after Frederick Taylor, who, at the turn of the 20th century, developed ways to measure the time and motion of factory production in order to get the most out of workers.

TECHNICOLOR A proprietary process (that is, owned by the Technicolor company) in which the color spectrum was filtered into red, green, and blue light and photographed in black and white on three separate negatives. These strips were then dyed to take up the colors to which they were exposed and printed to create a color positive. The process was ended in the early 1950s.

TEXTUALITY The complex interweaving of narrative, characters, and cinematic devices that make up a film.

THREE-POINT LIGHTING The standard lighting of a shot employing a **key light, backlight,** and **fill light.**

TRACKING SHOT The entire camera and its supporting mechanism moving forward, backward, or sideways. Often, the supporting mechanism is literally set on tracks.

TWO SHOT Two characters in a shot.

VERTICAL INTEGRATION In the history of film, this refers to the fact that the studios owned the theaters in which their films were shown—ownership from production down to distribution.

WIPE A silent film technique in which one shot pushes the preceding shot away across the screen.

ZOOM LENS Made up of elements that when moved change the focal length of the lens from wide angle to telephoto and back.

INDEX

N

O

X

Y

Z

Thus, the legend of Umi, in a condensed form, can stand as the theme against which a few select variations can be set.

The Legend of Umi

It is said that Umi was a part chief because his mother, Akahiakulana, was not a chiefess, although his father, Liloa, was a very high chief, whose genealogy could be traced to the very beginning of all things. So it is that Umi was high on his father's side, but very humble on his mother's side. But in tracing out the origin of Akahiakulana, his mother, it is found that she must have been of very high blood, for her name appears in the genealogical tree of the Kings.

Liloa, the father of Umi, King of Hawaii had as his first wife Piena who bore Umi's older half-brother Hakau.

After having dedicated a temple at Kokohalile, Liloa goes to bathe in a stream where he sees Akahiakulana. Seeing how beautiful she is Liloa seduces her. After living with her a short while, Liloa sees that she is pregnant and asks her "Who is your father?" Akahiakulana answers, "Kuleanakupiko." Liloa then says, "you are a cousin of mine?" She replies "Maybe so." Liloa then leaves but before doing so he tells Akahiakulana that if she has a son to name him Umi and send him to him. He leaves behind his malo, niho-palaoa, and war club for Umi so that he can recognize him.

Umi grows up in his mother's household, thinking her husband is his father. Finally after mistreatment of Umi by the husband, Akahiakulana says, "Stop. You can not treat Umi in this fashion for he is not your son but that of Liloa."

She then sends Umi off to join his real father giving him the things Liloa had left behind and having two friends to go with him. Umi finds the court, climbs over the wall, and sits down on his father's lap. Just as the guards start to seize him, Umi produces the malo and Liloa recognizes him as his son. All goes well except with Hakau, Umi's older step-brother, who is absolutely furious at his father's recognition of Umi.

At Liloa's death, Hakau is willed all the lands of Hawaii, but Umi is left the temples and the gods to care for. Umi therefore lives under Hakau as dependent but in a high position. While thus living, Hakau shows great hatred for Umi in many ways. If Umi took Hakau's surf board, Hakau would become angry and say to Umi, "You must not use my surfboard because your mother is not a chiefess; the same with my loin cloth." Finally after much abuse, Umi leaves court with his two followers. They go off and live secretly with a common family, taking wives.

During the aku season, people begin seeing the frequent appearance of a rainbow on the cliff. Kaoluloku, a high priest who lives in this area also sees the rainbow and wonders at its appearance. Being of a class well versed in ancient lore, he realizes this is the sign of a true chief and knowing of Umi's disappearance, follows the rainbow. He takes Umi and his two followers with him and helps Umi to raise an army. With the army, Umi is able to overthrow his half-brother who is hated by all and becomes the King of Hawaii.[33]

Reduced to the barest outline, the story concerns the gaining of rank, the fall from that rank, and the subsequent regaining of that rank. A slight variation of this theme is found in the legend of Kila.

The Legend of Kila

Kila the new King of Hawaii, is despised by his brothers who plot against him. They suggest that they all go to another island in order to bury the bones of

have enough power to gain the material to have a cloak made, or if they could, their cloaks were smaller and made with less valuable feathers.

These cloaks and capes were worn either on formal ceremonial occasions or in battle. During these important occasions, one's approximate political position in the *ali'i* was visually expressed. Both the size and color of the cloak demonstrated to all classes the political power of an individual chief. By the protection it afforded during battle, it was a very real object that guarded a man's life according to his value in the social hierarchy. A fanciful version of the death of Captain Cook, painted by George Carter c. 1783, illustrates this hieratic scale (Fig. 5). Three men face Cook in the right foreground. Each one wears a cloak. The figure which plunges a dagger into Cook's back wears a full-length yellow cloak. A second figure is placed closer to the viewer and bends forward to thrust a spear into Cook's abdomen. He is less elegantly clothed, minus the first figure's helmet and necklace, and wears a smaller red cloak. The third figure kneels in the foreground and looks up at Cook. He wears a shoulder cape composed of white and long green feathers (the least valuable of all feathers used). The slain Hawaiian sprawled at the feet of Cook is without any cloak at all.

Figure 5 *The Death of Captain Cook* by George Carter. Oil on fabric, c. 1783. Bishop Museum, Honolulu.

The early European explorers understood the size and color of the cloak as indicating the proper order of Hawaiian chiefs just as it is rendered through scale and position by Carter in order to indicate this social order for his western audience through the visual keys that they understood. From these early descriptions and later writings by the Hawaiians themselves, we can explain the material value of these cloaks and the symbolic value they had as signifiers of rank. But while a materialist analysis reveals the political significance of the cloak's size and the type of feather used, it does not explain the term *'ahu 'ula* itself. Nor does it explain the ubiquitous crescent shape and/or design which was used equally on the smallest cape as on the largest cloak, or why the feathers were collected during the second tribute levy. To get at these issues, we must work at them from a different angle. We must seek the levels at which the cloak was transfigured from a material property to a symbolic unit by identifying the cultural codes that gave it meaning.

As has been said, the *ali'i* represented not only a politically ranked group of overlords but also a sacred class of people who, if they were not gods incarnate, were at the very least their relatives. In this aspect, the *ali'i* were thought to be accompanied by various signs and attributes, both real and mythical, of which the *'ahu 'ula* was a combination of both. We have already seen that the signification of the real occurs at the material level of the cloak's size and color, but we have also found no trace of its mythical signification at that level. In fact, the striking contradiction between the term for the cloak (*'ahu 'ula*—red cloak) and the fact that the most desired color was yellow demands recognition that there are several levels of signification at work.

At one level the term *'ahu 'ula* referred to red, the royal color. This association derived from the pan-Polynesian tradition of red as a royal signifier. Moreover, it seems very likely that historically Hawaiian cloaks were totally red before the time when there was sufficient surplus labour to use some of it in gathering the much scarcer yellow feathers. None the less, when the preference for yellow feathers over red ones occurred, the generic term for the cloak was not changed.[22] The concept of red still held greater cultural signification than the merely materially important yellow. In this context it is important to note that red was also associated with the rainbow, another royal sign. The rainbow marked either the coming of a chief or the unknown presence of one. The relation between red, rainbow, and feather cloak is not arbitrarily drawn. Their close connection is demonstrated by linguistic evidence from the closely related Polynesian languages of Maori and Tahitian.

In Maori, the language of New Zealand, the word for feather cloak, *kahukura*, also signifies both the name of the god in the rainbow and simply the rainbow.[23] In Tahitian the word for feather cape, *tohura*, also means "peace of the rainbow." These two words are related as is *kulelulu* in Hawaiian which belongs to the same phylum and means "bending" or "arching of the rainbow."[24] Unlike the Maori and Tahitian terms however, *kulelulu* does not also signify a feather cloak. However, *kulelulu* is linguistically related to *'ahu 'ula*, but this ancient relation is mitigated by the rare use of the word *kulelulu* in Hawaii. When

referring to the rainbow that heralds a Hawaiian chief's presence, the words *pi'o-o-ke-anuene*, "arch of a rainbow," or simply *pi'o* are used instead.[25]

It would seem, then, that at some point in Hawaiian history the connection between rainbow and feather cloak as expressed by the linguistic relation between the words *'ahu 'ula* and *kulelulu* became obscured by the shift to the use of the terms *pi'o-o-ke-anuene* or *pi'o* to signify the rainbow.

Regardless of the fact that *'ahu 'ula* and *pi'o* are linguistically unrelated, Hawaiian nomenclature and chants sometimes recall the ancient connection between the cloak and the rainbow. For example, one chant sung before going into battle is phrased as follows:

> Komo ku i Kono 'ahu 'ula
> (Ku is putting on his feather cloak)
> Ka wela o kan na i Ka lani
> (the rainbow ((stands)) in the heaven).[26]

A further suggestion that the *'ahu 'ula* was at least unconsciously conceived of as a *rainbow* lies in the *kahili*. The *kahili* was a large feather standard used to denote the royal presence and is presumed to have derived from a feather fly whisk.[27] Its antiquity, however, is suspect, and its use became conspicuous only during the period of the nineteenth-century Hawaiian monarchy,[28] that is, after the dissolution of the *ahu ali'i*, the breaking of the *kapus*, and the cessation of the widespread usage of the *'ahu 'ula*. The word *kahili* means either "a feather standard symbol of the *ali'i*" or "a segment of a rainbow standing like a shaft."[29]

Here the feather symbol of royalty and the sign of a rainbow were fused in a time of social and cultural upheaval and confusion, as if to preserve the association that was merely implied by the *'ahu 'ula*. The *'ahu 'ula* and the *kahili* have shared properties that make this connection more secure. Both were the exclusive property of the *ali'i*, both were made of feathers, and both touched the back of the *ali'i* (the *'ahu 'ula* covered the back; the *kahili* was originally used to brush it).[30] This last point is the most significant when it is realized that the back of the *ali'i* was taboo.[31]

It seems certain then that the *'ahu 'ula* was at least tacitly conceived of as a rainbow and that its arched shape was linked to, or even inspired, the shape and design of the cloak. Yet, this metaphor does not fully explain why the *ali'i* restricted the cloak's design almost exclusively to the crescent nor does it explain the disjunction between two meanings of the Hawaiian words for cloak and rainbow. Both the Tahitians and the Maori used the same word for feather cloak and rainbow; yet, neither culture used the arching form of the rainbow in the design of their cloaks. For these questions to be answered, the distinct significance of the rainbow in Hawaiian society must be determined. And, because the rainbow is a mythical attribute that can identify the presence of a chief, we must turn to the actual legends and myths in which it occurs.

The legend of Umi is one of the most often told legends of Hawaii,[32] and it is also the key myth in the group under analysis. It is not the intention here to discuss all the variations and transformations the set entails, but rather to show how it derives its social meaning from the social structures of Hawaiian culture their father. Kila is abandoned on the island of Waipo and the brothers return home telling their mother that Kila was eaten by a shark. Kila falls asleep on the beach and is awakened by the people by Waipo. He tells them his story and is taken back to the home of one of the chiefs.

During the first part of Kila's life on Waipo, he lives under the chief as a servant doing everything he is told to do. His constant labours consist of farming and cooking of the food for his masters. He lives this way for three years. At times, he is told to bring firewood from the top of the cliff and would climb to the top of Puaahuku. During one of his climbs, he is seen by a priest, who lives in the temple of the Pakaalana, by means of the constant appearance of a rainbow that hangs over the cliff. Upon seeing the sign, the priest determines to find out if this is the sign of a high chief. But he is unable to see the sign every day for Kila doesn't always go to the top of the cliff.

Shortly after this Kila is accused by his master of breaking Kapus, but Kila is innocent of the charge so he flees in order to save himself. He runs to the temple of Pakaalana, a place where violators of any Kapu could be saved. As he enters the temple, the priest again notices the rainbow he had seen before. Upon seeing this sign he speaks to Kunaka, the king of Waipo, saying, "You must take that boy as your son. That boy is no commoner, he is a high chief."[34]

It would seem at first glance that these hero tales are told in a straightforward manner with as little exaggeration and the supernatural as possible. Both situations are set up, however, as impossible from an Hawaiian viewpoint and thus have significance beyond the history they recount. In the legend of Umi, a contradiction is immediately introduced which the whole myth tries to resolve. It is said that his mother is a commoner, but her genealogy is related to prove her pedigree. Umi is acknowledged by his father but his half-brother refuses to acknowledge him because of the supposedly low position of his mother. Umi is forced to flee from the secular court and live as commoner. It is only through the sign of the rainbow that a priest versed in sacred matters is able to aid Umi in regaining his rightful rank.

Similarly, Kila is driven away from court, and when he recites his pedigree to those who find him, they choose to ignore it. This is highly improper conduct for Hawaiians who, as has been mentioned, maintained their social distinctions by genealogy recorded in their name chants. Thus, like Umi's rank, Kila's rank is ignored by means of a contradiction which is resolved in the myth. Again, it is through a rainbow that a priest who is wise in sacred things is able to help the hero regain his rightful rank. The rainbow is the sign that is able to properly distinguish the amorphous position of the hero, and its recognition does not come from the secular body who have already chosen to deny the hero's rightful rank, but from the sacred side of Hawaiian culture.

A third myth brings the meaning into better focus.

The Legend of Elio

Elio was the runner for Kakaalaneo, King of all Maui. It was his duty to fetch awa fish for the King. Once on his way back, he met on the road Kaahuali (the spirit of the royal cloak), a spirit, who asked for some fish. Elio answered, "Take the hairs on your behind for the fish and your urine for water." When Kaahuali heard this he chased Elio. This happened on three different occasions so that he finally changed his course. On his new course he met a

> beautiful woman named Kanikaniaula. She invited him into the house and he accepted. She was really a spirit of a high chiefess who coming to Maui married a commoner. When she came to Maui she brought along with her from Hawaii a feather cape which was the insignia of a very high chief but which she had hidden upon her death, nor had she alluded to her rank. After Elio talked to her husband and found out she was dead, he undertook to restore her and succeeded. She then asked him what she could do to repay him. "Shall it be myself?" Elio answered that he would take nothing in payment but he wished her to become the wife of his lord. She said "yes" but first made him take the cloak to his master. At seeing the cape the husband of Kanikaniula realized for the first time that she was a chiefess. Because Elio was detained, Kakaalaneo was furious and had an umu (oven) started in readiness for Elio. When Elio returned wearing the cape, he was immediately captured and thrown into the fire. However the king saw something beautiful on Elio's back and called to his men, "seize him." Elio was pulled from the fire but the cloak was ripped to shreds. Elio had but a small piece and Kakaalaneo asked, "Where did you get such a beautiful thing?" Elio answered, "This was the cause of my delay. Kanikaniaula, a very handsome woman was dead and I brought her back to life again. I told her that you are to be her husband." Elio went to fetch Kanikaniaula who had just returned from Hawaii with some chiefs, their servants and with feather capes. She stood before Kakaalaneo and they dwelt together as husband and wife. After a short while she conceived a child.[35]

A first reading of this myth would seem to put it outside the set, but a closer one reveals that it maintains structurally the same pattern set up by the first two. The heroine, Kanikaniaula, falls from rank and with help regains it, in this case doubly so because she is also dead. Elio, a runner, discovers her and restores both her life and rank as a high chiefess. Unlike the first two myths, the helping figure is neither a priest, nor is he led to the hero by a rainbow. But, Elio is no ordinary runner. He is able to outrun a spirit and bring the dead back to life. He is therefore placed outside the realm of normal men and has the capacity to put right that which is out of order. As such, he occupies the same mediating position as the two priests in the Umi and Kila legends. They are all equally the element which rectifies an imbalance, the ideal of which is represented by a rainbow in the Umi and Kila myths. Elio, however, is not drawn to the situation by a rainbow but by the spirit of the *'ahu 'ula*. It forces him out of his normal running course to where he finds Kanikaniaula. Still Elio does not recognize that she is a chiefess because she has hidden the fact. It is not until she pulls out her cloak that her rank as an *ali'i* is revealed to Elio and her commoner husband. Her restitution to that rank is aided further by the cloak. For when Elio is about to be killed, he is pulled out of the fire only so that the king can see the cloak she has given him. This enables Elio to tell his story resulting in the marriage of Kanikaniaula and Kakaalaneo. The cloak therefore takes the signifying position which enables the conflict to be recognized and resolved and the ambiguities to be stabilized in the same manner as the rainbow in the first two myths does. That the cloak and the rainbow occupy the same signifying position is shown by the fact that although feather cloaks were not supposedly known on the island until Kanikaniaula brought them, Elio immediately recognized it as an incontrovertible sign of a high chief. Thus there is an inner connection between the rainbow and the *'ahu 'ula* that goes beyond mere metaphor.

It is the Umi legend that allows this last connection to become clear. Umi's whole conflict revolves round the uncertainty of his mother's rank. Even though it is vigorously denied at the outset of the narrative, there would be no story if the position of his mother were not unclear. And it must be his mother's rank that is questioned because it is the female principle in Hawaiian thought that has an ambiguous position in the hierarchical and ritual systems.[36] Umi cannot claim the prerogatives of the *ali'i* so long as there is such a doubt. The whole structure of the *ali'i* was based on a pure genealogy that gave it its sacred nature, of which the ultimate expression was the child of a brother-sister marriage, called *pi'o*. Such a union was conceived of as "a thing bent on itself" as in "the arc of a rainbow."[37] It was this expression that marked off the chiefly class from the commoners through claim of direct descent from ancestral gods. It is not surprising, therefore, that such a union was not practiced between the *maka 'ainana* and was considered incestuous by them. In fact, missionaries even had difficulty converting the common class because of their Western tolerance for first cousin marriages.[38] Yet, for the *ali'i*, this was the second most sacred form of marriage carrying the general name *nui pi'o* and more specifically *hoi'i* or "return." Both titles indicate "bent" or "curved" as does the name of the third most preferred marriage, *naha*.[39] Thus, the kin relations that gave Hawaiian royalty their unique status, the status that is in doubt in the case of Umi, were signified by words meaning "curved" and even more specifically, "the arching of a rainbow."

Both Umi and Kila are unquestionably recognized as members of the *ali'i* by the sign of a rainbow arching over them, and the word used to express that natural phenomenon is *pi'o*. By transformation within the Umi group, the *'ahu 'ula* comes also to stand equally for that sign. Both are the single clear unquestioned sign that defines their rank but which needs to be recognized by someone versed in sacred matters. This does not mean that Umi, Kila, or Kanikaniaula are actually offspring of a brother-sister marriage. Rather, just as the *pi'o* offspring represent the source of *mana* or sacredness for all of the chiefs, the rainbow and the *'ahu 'ula* were the sign of the inalienable position in Hawaiian society of the beholder of that *mana*. The *pi'o* marriage was the ordering device around which the *ali'i* was structured, and the rainbow and the *'ahu 'ula* were the signifiers of that order in the myths just described. They are the same things, the metonymical element that stands for the whole.

The *'ahu 'ula* in myth and reality therefore was a symbol of royalty, a prerogative of the *ali'i*. It was the shape of the cloak and its position in the legend of Elio that provided for the key to unlock the meaning of that symbol. On one level, it shared the properties of the *pi'o* and the rainbow, expressing by its curved elements the fixed and definite position of the *ali'i*. On another, its crescent shape and design were part of a coordinated whole and expressed a system of marriage around which a whole culture was organized. As something restricted to only the *ali'i*, it expressed visually the dual aspect of the class. Its size and color marked the wealth and power of the individual, and the crescent shape and design marked the wearer as a member of a group based on sacred descent.

We can understand finally that the geometric crescent design of Hawaiian cloaks was not due to an arbitrary change in the lining, nor was it simply due to the cloak's ancient pan-Polynesian relation to the rainbow. Rather, it was because the crescent of the rainbow, expressed by the term *pi'o*, was used by Hawaiian royalty to represent the ideal kin relation that ideologically separated them from the peasants. But this does not explain why the rainbow and the crescent-shaped cloak were chosen as signs for this concept. Of course, early in Hawaiian history it is very likely that the feather cloak and the rainbow were conceptually related as royal signs and were both called *kulelulu*, *'ahu 'ula*, or a third linguistically related term. This was a cultural inheritance from Hawaii's pre-migratory state. However, as Hawaiian culture developed its unique social structure, some of these old signs were enhanced with new signification. Such a shift in codes was especially necessary for the most cataclysmic of all Hawaiian social change: the change from a prohibition of incestuous marriage to that of raising it to the highest and most sacred form of human relations. It was a change almost unprecedented in cultural history. To achieve such a reversal, old codes of signification were simply no longer adequate.

The cloak and the rainbow were just some of the many old royal signs that could have been used to signify this order. Their selection for the signification of the new order, however, was not arbitrary. Rather, it was contingent on the replacement of the word *kulelulu* by the word *pi'o* to now signify both the rainbow and the divine offspring of an heretofore incestuous marriage. Words related to *kulelulu* in Maori, Tahitian, and Mangarevan all signify either a royal red cape and/or rainbow, and as such are consistent with their common origin.[40] These terms, however, including *kulelulu* did not have any meanings that would have any reference to incest. *Pi'o* did.

Pi'o in almost all other Polynesian languages is only nominally related to the rainbow, meaning "physically crooked," "curved" or "arched." But associated to these physical/natural meanings is the cultural one: "wrong in the moral sense."[41] It is this pan-Polynesian meaning of the word that made it necessary for its adoption by the Hawaiians for their new most sacred form of marriage. Almost universally the prohibition of this type of union is the sign of the transition from nature to culture. The logic is therefore consistent: if the unacceptable now becomes desired, then the signifier of that unacceptability, if still to be used, must now signify the desired. What is more morally wrong in almost all human societies than a brother/sister marriage, what is potentially more culturally chaotic? This certainly was the case in all other Polynesian societies, all of which shared a close ancestry with Hawaii. In Hawaii, however, incest in a politically restricted sense became morally correct.

Therefore in Hawaiian, *pi'o* came to have new meanings: "superior," "highest," "highest grade of chief," "to cohabit as a brother and a sister." Concomitantly, the meaning of "twisted," "crooked," and "awry" was unraveled to now signify the smooth arc of the rainbow and thereby linked it with the ancient sign of royalty. At the same time *pi'o* also retained its negative connotation by signifying "confused mind" or "to reduce to servitude." Such a dichotomy was necessary for a social system in which classes were conceptually separated into those who still maintained the strict laws of the prohibition of incest and were those in servitude, and those who transcended this cultural boundary and were the rulers. *Pi'o* replaced the word *kulelulu* as the common word for rainbow not because of its association with a rainbow but because it could convey more precisely the new order of Hawaiian society.

As Hawaiian culture shifted to this new order, the cloak, already related metaphorically to the rainbow, took a new shape and design. The important element was not the rainbow per se, but the crescent. In this sense, it did not matter that the crescent was inverted as it is on the cloak. Its presence simply marked the new form of sanctity on an object that already functioned as a royal sign. As such, the term *'ahu 'ula* was not changed. It was not necessary or desired. In fact, as the material value of the cloak became judged by the amount of yellow it contained, it was important to also maintain the original essence of the cloak as a sacred entity expressed by the term *'ahu 'ula*. The crescent design on the cloak, unique to Polynesian design, was sufficient to signify the unique social order that had brought it into being.

Hawaiian culture underwent one last momentous change. With the coming of the Europeans in 1778, traditional Hawaiian culture was again altered cataclysmically. The sanctity of the chiefs dissolved in 1810 when the traditional religious order was overturned by the breaking of the taboos. But the ideological restructuring of Hawaii did not mean the political undoing of the chiefs. Rather, it laid bare the class system that had been masked through the pretension to rule through divine right but which had been maintained through material wealth and military power.

At the time of Cook's arrival, the Islands were divided into four kingdoms ruled by rival chiefs who were frequently at war with each other. Within twelve years, Kamehameha I, a minor chief in 1778, had conquered all his rivals, a success which depended on his ability to win the aid of the British and, more importantly to obtain their weapons. With this chain of events, the nature of Hawaiian leadership was altered radically and irrevocably. As I. Goldman points out so succinctly:

> Hawaiian chiefs took immediate advantage of the new post-European order to enrich themselves at the expense of commoners. They took legal title to the land, and they engaged in the profitable sandal trade, to the serious detriment of food production. The European commercial tradition is evident. Maori chiefs in similar circumstances fought against land appropriation. Hawaiian history points to a remarkable degree of convergence between the interests of the chiefs and the European powers. Both saw virtue in power and in the growth of the state.[42]

With the dissolution of the sacred power of the ruling class and their emphasis on material power, we can understand the design and color of one last cloak (Fig. 6). The underlying base of material power, now given complete freedom, finds its expression in the cloak made for Kamehameha I. It is composed almost entirely of the yellow Mamo feathers with just a few red Iwi feathers on the border of the neck. It is one of a kind. In 1839, only fifty-one years after the arrival of Cook, it was valued at one million dollars.[43] This, of course, is a western material value placed on an Hawaiian object, but such a value system spoke to a

Figure 6
'Ahu 'ula (Kamehameha cloak).
Bishop Museum, Honolulu.

new social order. This solid yellow cloak expresses the breakdown of the traditional dual structure. The prominent colored crescent design that signified the social organizing element of the nobility is gone, given away, as it were, by Kamehameha to Vancouver. Instead, the amassing of so many precious yellow feathers speaks only of the material wealth now used to claim rule.

NOTES

1. E.H. Bryan, *Ancient Hawaiian Life*, Honolulu, 1939, p. 70.
2. W. Brigham, *Hawaiian Feather Work*, Honolulu, 1899, p.4.
3. This passage comes from Vancouver's diary as quoted in ibid., p.7.
4. Brigham, op. cit., p. 52.
5. P. Buck, "The Local Evolution of Hawaiian Feather Capes and Cloaks," *Journal of the Polynesian Society*, vol. 53, 1944, pp. 1-16.
6. Ibid., and P. Buck, *The Arts and Crafts of Hawaii*, Honolulu, 1957, p. 227.
7. E. Handy, *Ancient Hawaiian Civilization*, Vermont, 1965, p. 40.
8. Ibid.
9. By the time of Cook's arrival such genealogies stretched back more than thirty-eight generations. The chiefs of Maui and Hawaii generally traced their ancestry to Ulu, and those from Kauai and Oahu from Nanaula, M. Beckwith, *Hawaiian Mythology*, New Haven, 1940, p. 293.
10. A. Fornander, *Hawaiian Antiquities and Folklore*, vol. IV, Honolulu, 1916-17, pp. 61-2.

11. This order of sanctity of the ruling class is found in the concept of taboo. As is common to all Polynesia, taboo meant a general pattern of avoidance. But in Hawaii, it had a second, unique meaning to the particular prerogatives of demanding both obeisance and freedom from obeisance, see I. Goldman, *Ancient Polynesian Society,* Chicago, 1970, pp. 216-17.
12. The *makihiki* was a four-month period when men, women, and chiefs rested and abstained from work. Neither were the usual religious festivals observed during this time. The *makahiki* period began in *Ikuwa* (October) and continued through *Kaelo* (January). It was a time of religious observances and tribute paying, D. Malo, *Hawaiian Antiquities,* Honolulu, 1958 (1898), pp. 61-2.
13. Beckwith, op. cit. (1940), p. 378.
14. For the origins of the *kauwa*, see Malo, op. cit., p. 70.
15. Ibid., p. 60.
16. Buck, op. cit., p. 218.
17. Malo, op. cit., p. 77.
18. Ibid.
19. Ibid., p. 146.
20. Malo, op. cit., p. 77.
21. W. Rice, *Hawaiian Legends*, Honolulu, 1923, p. 53.
22. Buck, op. cit., p. 217.
23. E. Tregear, *The Maori-Polynesian Comparative Dictionary*, The Hague, 1969 (1891), p. 114.
24. Ibid., and L. Andrews, *A Dictionary of the Hawaiian Language*, Honolulu, 1865, p. 312.
25. A. Fornander, *Hawaiian Antiquities and Folklore,* vol. IV, Honolulu, 1916-17, p. 188.
26. A. Fornander, *An Account of the Polynesian Race,* vol. II, London, 1880, p. 394.
27. Brigham, op. cit. (1899), p. 14.
28. Buck, op. cit. (1957), note 12 by the editor, p. 578.
29. M. Pukui and S. Elbert, *Hawaiian English Dictionary*, 1957, p. 105.
30. A. Fornander, *Hawaiian Antiquities and Folklore*, vol. V, Honolulu, 1918-19, p. 61.
31. M. Pukui, S. Elbert, and E. Mookini, *Place Names of Hawaii*, Honolulu, 1974, p. 261.
32. Beckwith, op. cit. (1940), p. 391.
33. The myth of Umi and the two myths which follow it have been condensed from those recorded by Fornander. Ibid., pp. 178-88.
34. Ibid., pp. 130-4.
35. Ibid., pp. 482-6.
36. Valerio Valeri, *Kingship and Sacrifice Ritual and Society in Ancient Hawaii*, trans. Paul Wissing. Chicago: University of Chicago Press, 1985, pp. 18-19.
37. Malo, op. cit., p. 54 and Pukui and Elbert, op. cit., p. 238.
38. Beckwith, op. cit. (1951), p. 13.
39. Pukui and Elbert, op. cit., pp. 70 and 238.
40. Tregaer, op. cit.
41. Ibid., p. 337.
42. Goldman, op. cit., p. 203.
43. Brigham, op. cit. (1899), p. 58.

12

The Weight of My Name Is a Mountain of Blankets

Potlatch Ceremonies

Stanley Walens

The peoples of the Northwest Coast lived along a stretch of rugged coast some 1,200 miles long, from Yakutat Bay in Alaska southward to the northwest corner of Washington state. Wherever the ceaseless action of the sea eroded a protected beach out of the cliffs which rise hundreds of feet above the water, or wherever the action of tide or torrent deposited a sheltered strip of sand, they built their villages, a thin wedge of humanity between the forces of the sea and the darkness of the forest (Fig. 1). There they developed a unique culture whose beauty and vibrancy never cease to amaze those who learn about it.

The dramatic, powerful, and complex ceremonies—called potlatches—of these peoples are among the most spectacular in North America. Potlatches were involved with the maintenance and orderly transfer of rank and power and the distribution of wealth that was an essential part of the responsibilities of a person of rank. The amount of wealth that was distributed at a potlatch could be tremendous and might take years of hard work and judicious saving to amass. At one Kwakiutl potlatch the chief not only fed several hundred guests during the two-week-long ceremony but distributed to them 18,000 Hudson's Bay blankets (which cost $.50 each), 700 carved silver bracelets, a dozen canoes valued at 3,000 blankets each, sewing machines, outboard motors, pots and pans, clothing, hundreds of sacks of flour, sugar, fruit, and other food, a large amount of cash, and a copper worth 12,000 blankets. At some potlatches, chiefs gave away everything they owned, even the boards with which the walls and roofs of their houses were built.

Reprinted from *Celebration, Studies in Festivity and Ritual*, edited by Victor Turner, Washington, D.C.: Smithsonian Institution Press, 1982, pages 178-189 with permission of the author and publisher.

Figure 1 The Haida village of Skidegate, late 19th century.

It must be realized, however, that, whether a great amount or a small amount of wealth was distributed—and potlatches of the splendor just described were by far the exception—the peoples of the coast had a well-defined philosophy about the nature of wealth and the necessity of giving it away. Furthermore, if we look at potlatches in terms of profit and loss we miss the very basis on which they were predicated: it was the purpose of the potlatch, not to make a profit, but to lose wealth for the benefit of others, to obtain spiritual purity through philanthropy. It was not enough just to distribute wealth; it was important that it be distributed in the correct way. It was not extravagance that they admired, it was the ability to distribute great amounts of wealth to everyone according to their rank and station.

The distribution of wealth had its foundation in the cosmology of the Northwest Coast Indians. Like other North American Indian groups, they envisioned the world as a place of constant flux and motion, like a great river ceaselessly flowing. Those features of the world which seemed permanent—the mountains, the inlets and fjords, and the beaches—were created by Raven to give people a place from which to observe the world in motion. To distribute one's wealth was to be in harmony with the world's flux, to contribute to this cosmic motion.

Every Northwest Coast group had a myth about how the world as we know it came into existence, about how generosity, reciprocity, sacrifice, and moral responsibility were first created. Perhaps the most famous of these is the story (found in different versions) about how Raven stole the sun. At the beginning of time, the sun, like all the world's treasures, had been kept in a box by a man. Raven, through magical means, impregnated the daughter of this man and was born to the man as his grandson. The joy Raven brought to the old man was so great that when Raven asked for the man's possessions as playthings, they were given to him one by one. Finally Raven asked for the sun as a plaything, and as soon as he got it he changed from a boy into his true form and flew away with the sun in his beak. The sun was hot and burned Raven's feathers, turning them from their primal white into their present black; Raven dropped the sun in the sky, where it can be seen today, a great treasure for the entire world.

In this myth is encapsulated the entire moral basis of generosity and exchange in Northwest Coast society. Raven presents the first gift—he gives himself as a child, the greatest of all treasures. His grandfather reciprocates by giving Raven (though not altogether willingly) those treasures he had previously kept only for himself and which now benefit everyone. Raven gives himself as a sacrifice for the world, sacrificing his beauty for the benefit of the rest of the world. Raven's black feathers now remind us that we are part of that covenant, that we must give, must sacrifice. Nothing—not wealth, not beauty, not power, not status, not life itself—can be kept. Everything must be given away. Indeed, as in the myth, it is to one's descendants that everything a person owns must and will be given.

The pattern of food and wealth distribution at a potlatch was necessitated by the particular nature of the Northwest Coast environment. The Northwest Coast was a land uniquely rich in natural resources. The forests grew as densely and luxuriantly as those of the tropics, providing the Indians with the materials they needed for their homes, their canoes, the baskets and boxes in which they stored their food and material possessions, their clothing and their sacred objects. The animals of the forest—bear, deer, elk, mountain goats, and so forth—were part of the Northwest Coast larder, but it was fishing and sea-mammal hunting which formed the basis of the Northwest Coast economy. Salmon could be found in virtually every stream along the coast and provided the staple food of the native diet, but cod, halibut, herring, candlefish, octopus, and a score of other varieties of fish, as well as sea mammals and shellfish, were also important.

However, though food was plentiful, the rugged topography of the Northwest Coast limited the number of places where human access to food was possible. There were only a limited number of places where a person might stand to spear passing fish, only a limited number of river mouths with geography that was conducive to effective fishing with nets, only a limited number of shallow spots along streams where it was possible to set up weirs. Furthermore, the abundance of any given animal varied from season to season, year to year, and area to area, although these fluctuations were somewhat offset by the methods of food preservation which allowed the Indians to stockpile large amounts of dried fish.

The limited number of spots where food could be collected required the Indians to develop an economic system which combined the most efficient gathering of food by a small number of people with a widespread distribution of the food. The division of the tribe into small units, which was necessary for efficient resource exploitation, was achieved by making the composite household an autonomous economic, political, and ceremonial unit. A household might consist of twenty to forty people, related by membership in a common lineage or clan; a village might consist of eight to ten households. The ownership of resources resided in a household head who was often the head of the lineage or clan as well, and under whose aegis the members of a household worked together to gather resources at places that belonged to their clan (Fig. 2).

On the household heads—often called chiefs—fell the responsibility of organizing not only the collecting and distributing of food but a large number of ceremonial and religious responsibilities as well. As executor of his clan's estate, the chief had the responsibility of displaying the rituals of his clan and distributing its wealth. It was the chief who decided what dances must be performed and by whom, when to place a new totem pole (which by its images recapitulated an important myth of his clan's past), when new songs or prayers must be composed, a new mask carved, or a potlatch given. The chief stood as representative of his clan, as ambassador both to other human groups and to the animals as well.

A household's rights of access to resources were jealously guarded and formed an important part of the patrimony a chief passed down to his heirs. Indeed, a great deal of the public ceremony in Northwest Coast society centered around the establishing or maintenance of the legitimacy of a chief's claims to resources, the acting out of his ritual and spiritual responsibilities toward both

Figure 2
Tlingit people in ceremonial potlatch costume, Sitka, Alaska, 1904.

the animals being collected and the humans to whom they are being given as food, and the orderly succession of a chief's heirs to his rank and to the responsibilities attendant upon that rank.

It is not surprising, then, that the peoples of the coast saw their world as one where myriad forces were at work, all influencing food, and humans' ability to obtain food. Every animal, every human, every clan, had its own needs, its own demands, its own hunger. All these conflicting needs and demands needed to be balanced against one another, to be directed for the greatest mutual benefit. It was through ritual that this balance was obtained, that the competitive forces which could have brought about the destruction of the universe were tamed. It was a delicate balance; the slightest misweighing could send the world back into the chaos of selfishness and conflict from which Raven had delivered mankind. The judicious balancing of one's needs against one's obligations was a difficult and complex task.

Indeed mutual dependence—the idea that one's life was securely in the hands of others—was so important an idea that some tribes made a religious proscription against any clan's performing some of the most important rites of passage of its own members. Among the Tlingit and Haida, for example, members of each moiety (half the tribe) were solely responsible for the birth and funeral ceremonies, the housebuilding and pole raising, of the other moiety. Thus only through cooperation of the entire tribe could the proper succession to rank be accomplished, and the order of the world maintained.

Potlatches occurred at all points of social stress, wherever society might fall apart because of some change. At these times, the order and control of the ceremony, with its reassertion of mutual dependence, was meant to reestablish the order and control of the universe as a whole. Northwest Coast peoples were so aware of their central role in maintaining world order that their very names for themselves—"Providing Smoke for the World," "People of the Raven," "First People"—signify the centrality of ritual in their lives.

Perhaps the clearest demonstration of the Northwest Coast idea that human sociality and morality tame the potentially destructive forces of the universe can be found in the Hamatsa (Cannibal) ritual among the Kwakiutl. Here an initiate into the Hamatsa society returned to the world of humans after a sojourn in the world of the spirit-being, Man Eater. Man Eater was a symbol of the endpoint of time and the ultimate destruction of the universe; he was a black hole of hunger, the power of his desire pulling everything toward a final dissolution. The Hamatsa initiate threatened to bring this destruction to the human world to which he had returned. He was tamed only when his fellow humans pledged to uphold the covenants they had made with the animals and the spirit-beings and to provide these beings with the requisite sacrifices of their wealth and possessions. Indeed, since wealth was an agreement to sacrifice oneself during one's lifetime and to provide the spirit-beings with a properly treated body upon one's death, a person who owed his life to others also owed them his death.

The idea of death as sacrifice, and wealth as a symbol of death, lies at the basis of Northwest Coast religion. Like many other Native American peoples, the peoples of the Northwest Coast believed that success in hunting was achieved not only by technical mastery of hunting skills but by the maintenance of a ritual relationship between a hunter and his prey. This relationship placed humans and animals in a web of mutual dependency: humans survived only because animals sacrificed themselves for human welfare, in return for which humans treated animals' bodies with respect and performed rituals which insured the reincarnation of the animals. Knowledge of these rituals and possession of the songs, dances, prayers, and paraphernalia which comprised them were the most precious treasures of Northwest Coast culture. It was through performing these rituals and distributing to other people some of the food which one had obtained that the social and political status of a chief and his associates was legitimized. No event of importance in a person's life occurred without the accompaniment of a ceremonial in which a person displayed, performed, validated, and revitalized in a public display the all-important ritual links between himself and his animal benefactors.

It was in myth that these covenants between humans and animals were set forth. Myths are sacred narratives of how things became as they are, of how chaos became cosmos, of how amorality became morality, of how human beings came into existence and came to accept the burden of moral responsibility and sacrifice placed upon them. Myths provide paradigms and structures for living; they present mysteries which put people into direct contact with the powerful forces of the cosmos.

Every aspect of Northwest Coast life was imbued with myth and with ceremony—the representation of myth through motion. The display of a family's or individuals's myths, of mythically bestowed treasures, rights, statuses, and wealth, and the portrayal of a group's ancestral heritage, were inextricable parts of every social occasion. No meal began without the recital of a myth or sacred song, no feast could be held without the ritual acknowledgment of the beneficence of the animals upon which one was dependent, no change in status could occur without the revalidation of the myths about how that status came to exist. The moral person, in telling the myths of his family's past, indicated that he had accepted the burden of that past.

The celebration of the glory of a clan's mytho-historic heritage can be found everywhere in Northwest Coast life. Every object of ritual importance—canoes, boxes, bowls, houses, poles, chairs, clothing, spoons, bracelets—is decorated with images of the clan's mythic ancestors, with depictions of incidents in the clan's history, with images of the cosmos and of man's place within it. In some tribes, even people's bodies were tattooed with images of the clan's ancestral spirit-beings. These images, called crests by anthropologists, were symbols of the beings from whom a clan traced its origin and the origin of its possessions.

Any object which had been decorated with a crest was imbued with the vital forces of the spirit world and was considered to be alive. The spirits could act through these objects; these objects acted as pathways for power to travel from the spirit world to the human world. Because of the power they possessed and controlled, these objects were important parts of rituals and were used to contain and direct power in the ritual.

The right to wear or display these crests, to perform rituals relating to them, and even to pronounce their names, was a highly valued prerogative. Many of these images, as befits an image that deals with the transformation of the mythic world into the modern world, display symbols of change and transformation, mingling human and animal forms in ways which show that the two are manifestations of each other, locked in an inextricable mesh of social relations and ritual responsibilities, of shared identities and destinies. Through the display of crests, Northwest Coast ceremonies provided for the expansion of the self and the group beyond their social boundaries and in doing so linked humans to each other and to the vital forces of the cosmos. Rituals demonstrate the place and purpose of human action in the universe as a whole. Rituals make opposites equivalent: a local house becomes the entire universe, a human becomes a cosmic being, the the past of myth becomes manifest in the rituals of the present.

This expansion of the self and the group to equivalence with the cosmos is achieved by the close identification of individuals with their ancestors and with the spirit-beings whom they portray in dance and embody in this world. In Northwest Coast thought, a person is only one component of a complex being which consists of that person's body, the person's sacred name, a spirit-being's body, and a composite soul shared by human and spirit-being together. The sharing of a single soul enables a human to manifest his spirit self simply by changing his visage and the appearance of his body. In order to become a spirit-being, then, a person merely brings the cosmic power of the spirits into his house and then puts on a mask depicting the spirit-being. Then, with the ordered poetry of speech and dance, he carves out of space and time the ordered beauty of the cosmos.

The shared representations of self and transformation are an important aspect of Northwest Coast crest design. Depictions of an animal or spirit-being show the human soul residing in the being's chest, or between the ears as if it were a frontlet (a forehead mask). Indeed, humans wore frontlets on ritual occasions when they were not to be transformed into a spirit-being but still needed to represent the nascent spirit component of their rank. The boxes in which treasures were stored often show images of transformation and the mingled identities of spirit-beings and humans. This constant representation of transformation is not surprising once we realize that these items were meant to recapitulate myths and that myths are about transformations.

The shared identities and transformations of the self which are so essential a part of Northwest Coast thought and ritual are depicted in several ways. On totem poles and house posts, which recapitulate key myths of a clan's past, transformations may be represented merely by a linear progression of images, or by a complex interweaving of the bodily parts of the different figures as they change from one to another. Some tribes used mechanical masks that can be opened and closed to conceal or reveal the altered identities of a single being (Fig. 3).

Transformation is frequently shown by depicting different aspects of a single identity on the opposite sides of an object. For example, a Haida box in the Smithsonian collection shows the spirit-being Cirrus Clouds on one face of the box and the spirit-being Eagle on the other. The shared human soul of the two spirits is shown in both its spirit form, located beneath the mouths of the

Figure 3 Kwakiutl mechanical transformation mask, partially open. The mask depicts the head of a raven, flying scavenger, inside that of a wolf, a land-based predator. An image of the wolf, painted in relief, is visible on the inside of the outer case.

spirit-beings, and its human form, represented in profile to either side of the faces of the two spirit-beings. On the sides of this box, the Bear crest of the clan is represented in its two forms as well, first as animal and then as human.

The way in which symbolic oppositions are obviated through ritual is well shown by this Haida box. Cirrus Clouds and Eagle are opposite to each other in that Cirrus Clouds are the prevalent clouds of the Northwest Coast summer, and Eagle, who flies in cumulus clouds, is the lord of the winter sky. Eagle and Cirrus Clouds stand in mutual opposition to Bear, who is a land creature most active in the summer, and to humans, who are land creatures whose rituals are more frequent in the winter. All these oppositions, these separate identities, are linked into a single coherent entity, all their differences obviated and combined into a box for the storing of powerful sacred objects.

Another way in which transformation of the self is shown is through the static depiction of the very moment of equilibrium between the two components of the self. One of the most striking examples of this type of image is found on a frontlet on which the human identity of Eagle is seen emerging from the bird's chest at the same moment as Eagle is losing his avian identity (Fig. 4). Eagle's face has already become humanoid, and the beaky avian component of the self is represented as a tongue about to be pulled into Eagle's mouth. As the wearer of this frontlet moved and danced, firelight reflecting off the haliotis shells surrounding the image threw different parts of the image into shadow or light so that it would seem constantly to change.

Perhaps the most cogent image of transformation occurs on the Raven rattle (Fig. 5). Here we see Raven carrying a dead man toward the afterlife on his back.

Figure 4
A chief's frontlet, probably Haida but collected among the Kwakiutl, showing the instant of transformation when all the component identities of a single being are in equilibrium.

The man's vital force, seen as a red bridge like a tongue, has been captured by a frog, a symbol of life, which is itself being captured by a crane, the symbol of death. In the Raven's beak is a small red object representing both the sun, which was Raven's gift to mankind, and the man's soul, which is man's reciprocal gift to the spirits. On the belly of Raven is the face of the shared soul of Raven and mankind, its beak recurved into its own mouth in a cogent symbol of the cycle of reincarnation. The use of the Raven rattle in ritual not only reaffirms mankind's covenant with Raven, but through its intertwined images of life, death, and the cycle of rebirth, the rattle directs these vast forces in a specific cyclic pattern of transformation.

One of the most important images of the autocosmic self in Northwest Coast ritual is found in coppers. These plaques were one of the most treasured of ritual possessions, and their exchange, sale, and sometimes destruction at potlatches were events of the greatest significance. Through their symbolism, coppers link man to the entire universe. Their shape recapitulates that of the body and soul

Figure 5 Haida raven rattle, used by chiefs and high-ranking members of the community to punctuate their speech and actions.

of a being, making equivalent the body of the chief, the body politic of his clan, and the bodies and souls of all the animals which the clan has captured. The color of the copper symbolizes the red of salmon flesh on which mankind survives; the menstrual blood which is a mother's first gift to her unborn children; the color of the sun, which was Raven's first gift to mankind; and the fire by which man both cooks his food as the myths require him to and burns his wealth and his corpses so that they become food for the spirit-beings.

The chief was the representative of his house, and his person was the nexus by which the many varied components, both spirit and human, which comprise his own and his group's identity, became united. The way in which this was achieved in ritual was evidenced by the chiefs' ceremonial costumes. Every piece of a chief's clothing and adornment—from frontlet or crest hat, downward through facial painting, jewelry, yokes and collars, robes and tunics, kilts and leggings—might be decorated with a crest design. The vertical serialization of these images turned the chief into a living analogue of a totem pole, encapsulating his and his clan's ancestral heritage. At ceremonials, where the chief stood as symbol of his house, the carved speaker's staff he held, which symbolized his authority, was analogous to the house's totem pole, from which the house derived its authority.

One item of chief's costume—the Chilkat Tlingit blanket (Fig. 6), a ceremonial robe adopted by many other Northwest Coast tribes—provides perhaps the clearest example of the portrayal of the chief as avatar of both the human and spirit components of a single identity. These blankets show, in highly stylized form, the image of a crest animal as if it were on a box, and as if the four sides and lid of the box had been flattened into a single plane. A person wearing such a blanket became analogous to a treasure stored in a box. The sharing of a single soul by both crest animal and human was indicated by placing the image of the blanket's soul—seen as a humanoid face in the center of the blanket, which represented the lid of the box—over the place in the human chest where the human soul resides. When a chief wearing a Chilkat blanket is seen from the front, then, we see his social, human self, with his nascent spirit identity shown by the image on his frontlet or crest hat; from the chief's rear we see only his supernatural alter ego, which has its human identity depicted as a frontlet between its ears. Thus, as a chief wearing such a blanket moves and turns, he is continually being transformed before our eyes.

Through transformation the participants in the Northwest Coast ritual became more than just individuals, and the dimensions of their actions transcended the limitations of everyday space and time. Each chief became the representative of his house and his house's spiritual authority, linked to the ancestral past by costume and to cosmic forces by paraphernalia such as Raven rattles and speaker's staffs. The careful placement of hosts and guests on mats around the room reproduced the geographical distribution of the world's villages—the social map recapitulating the cosmic map. The ceremonial house itself stood for the universe as a whole, its various rooms differentiating the various parts of the world, its vertical beams representing the axis mundi which links the human realm to the spirit realm, its great horizontal beam standing for the vault

Figure 6 Chilkat blanket, Tlingit, Alaska. The Chilkat blanket takes its name from the Tlingit subgroup responsible for its popularization through trade. For high ranking Haida and Tlingit, a complete ceremonial outfit included tunic, apron, and leggings, often woven in the Chilkat style, as well as frontlet, clan hat, and Raven rattle or staff.

of the sky and the Milky Way. Thus, once the universe was contracted to the size of the ceremonial house whose boundaries had been expanded until they were coterminous with the entire universe, the actions of distribution that occurred at feasts recapitulated the process of distribution at a cosmic level.

In short, then, the potlatch was not, as it has so often been described, just a prestige contest. Analysis of the details of potlatches shows, on the evidence of the emphasis on protocol and the careful enactment of myths and dances, that the structure of potlatches and feasts was intended to recapitulate the structure of the universe as a whole. The moral person, in telling the myths of his family's past and in distributing the wealth of which he was merely temporary custodian, indicated that he had accepted the burden of that past, the burden of the covenant which says that he must dance, sing the sacred songs, give away his material possessions and even, ultimately, his very life for the benefit of other beings. The moral person dedicated his life, in some ways sacrificed himself–through his wealth, which was the symbol of his self—for the benefit of others, just as animals sacrificed themselves for the benefit of mankind. Northwest Coast ceremonies celebrated the relevance of the past to the actions of the present; they linked the political and social structure of the group to the innermost spiritual values of the members of the group, especially that of self-sacrifice, as expressed and refracted through cosmology; and they presented, in a cohesive poetic statement, the universal conflicts and dilemmas of human life and the nature and purpose of human existence.

PART FOUR

PASSAGES
ARTS OF FESTIVAL, RITUAL, AND INITIATION

Lee Anne Wilson

Festivals, celebrations, rituals, initiations—all make use of art objects to display status and wealth, communicate ideas and concepts, manifest cosmic order and world views, protect the community from evil forces, and ensure or restore balance between the human and supernatural realms. Most of the articles in this section see these activities as passages or times of transition from one state of being to another. For example, the articles by Barbara L. Moulard (*Form, Function and Interpretation of Mimbres Ceramic Hemispheric Vessels,* page 259) and Suzanne Preston Blier (*The Dance of Death: Notes on the Architecture and Staging of Tamberma Funeral Performances,* page 275) discuss how funerals mark the passage from life to death, from this world to the realm of the ancestors, while the articles by Ruth B. Phillips (*Masking in Mende Society Initiation Rituals,* page 231), Anita J. Glaze (*Woman Power and Art in a Senufo Village,* page 217) and Warren d'Azevedo (*Mask Makers and Myth in Western Liberia,* page 111) examine the way puberty rites mark the transition from childhood to adulthood (see also Foss 1979). Some societies even have ceremonies that mark the transition from non-person to person, especially important in areas where high infant mortality rates result in babies not being considered fully human until they reach a less fragile age. In his article on the Odwira festival Herbert M. Cole (*The Art of Festival in Ghana,* page 201) points out that festivals often involve the entire village and commemorate such important transitions as the passage of the seasons and the yearly agricultural cycle, during the course of which political hierarchies, social relationships, and family ties are strengthened and renewed. Examining the seemingly static form of Australian aboriginal paintings, Howard Morphy (*On Representing Ancestral Beings,* page 245) discusses how Yolngu artists use two-dimensional painted images to suggest ongoing transformational relationships between past and present, ancestral beings and humans, myth and ceremony.

In all of these contexts art plays an important part, although the art forms may not be considered "art" from a more ethnocentric European-oriented point of view. Indeed, both object and process are often of equal importance and encode not only important religious, but also social, and even political (see Chapter four) concepts. In many cultures, the process of the ritual itself often becomes the art form. Indeed, in some societies, the process is as important, if not more so, than the object itself. For example, the Ibo of Nigeria build houses (called *mbari*) filled with life-size figures made from mud that may take large numbers of villagers several years to complete (see Cole 1982, 1984). Ultimately, however, it is the act of creating the *mbari* that pleases and feeds the gods. The structures themselves are allowed to decay back to the earth from which they were made. Among the Navajo of the American Southwest, elaborate dry paintings (sand paintings) are created using crushed minerals, ground corn, or other powdered materials only to be destroyed as an important part of the ritual restoration of harmony and balance essential to the well-being of both individuals and universe alike (Witherspoon 1977). These and other ceremonies are accompanied by singing, dancing, and feasting—all ephemeral and non-permanent art forms which can not be collected and hung on a museum wall. Indeed, these often ignored ephemera are often so essential to the proper completion and success of the ritual that the ritual cannot be conducted without them (see Adams 1986).

While Esther Pasztory (1982) has argued that these basically ephemeral art forms belong more truly to the realm of theater than art, Herbert Cole (*The Art of Festival in Ghana*, page 201) suggests that the multivalent, multivocal aspect of these ceremonies is itself an art form, one that can not be defined or characterized by traditional definitions of art objects. Indeed, the "art object" here is a constantly moving, constantly changing panoply of color, sound, smell, and even taste that is impossible to absorb all at once. It is precisely this impossibility that makes these rituals so powerful and causes them to be repeated in the same format over and over again. Repetition may reinforce tradition, but it (repetition) is also necessary in such richly endowed ceremonies simply because one person can not see or partake of the entirety of the ceremony in any *one* performance.

While not all rituals are rites of passage in the strict sense defined by Van Gennep (1960:166), Victor and Edith Turner have pointed out that Van Gennep's three basic phases (separation, transition, and incorporation) can be applied to most ritual celebrations (see Victor and Edith Turner 1982:202ff). In this sense, Navajo sand paintings represent the transition from disharmony to balance (illness to health), while the Odwira festival relates to the agricultural cycle (planting to harvesting, seed to fruit), life cycle (birth to death), and leadership cycle (ruler to ruler), and the Ibo *mbari* depicts the transformation of clay from mud sculptures to food for the gods and back to earth (life to death to rebirth).

Virtually all passages or transitions from one place or state to another are regarded as frightening experiences fraught with hidden dangers. The here and now is a known quantity, but what lies ahead in either time or space is unknown and therefore dangerous and frightening. In particular, the individual passing through this unknown territory himself becomes unknown, existing outside the normal space-time continuum in a kind of limbo, neither here nor yet there, no longer child but not yet adult, not sick but not yet well, no longer out of balance with the spiritual world but not yet in balance with the real world. Indeed, this liminal state is dangerous not only to the individual passing through, but also to the entire village. Some way must be found to alleviate this dangerous state of transition. It is at times like these that rituals, elaborate, detailed, circumscribed, and circumspect, each carefully fitted to a specific transition, serve to temper the danger and fear of these liminal states.

Some transitions are universal passages that all must go through (child to adult, life to death), while others are passages of choice such as marriage or initiation into a particular group or society. Still other passages are undertaken only by select individuals who have undergone rigorous training sessions to prepare them for the dangers they will encounter on their voluntary journeys through the unknown. Throughout much of the circumpolar region, central and southeastern Asia, and the new world, this particular individual is known as the *shaman*.

Healer, visionary, controller of the weather, and master of game animals, the shaman is ultimately responsible for the well-being of the group usually through direct contact with the supernatural, the unknown realm. Indeed, it is the shaman's continued contact with the supernatural that sets him or her apart from other individuals for the shaman lives most of his life in a liminal state. Neither and both here and there, the shaman draws power from a series of oppositions. Like the mythic supernaturals that inhabit the other realm, the shaman is man and animal, old and young, male and female, human and supernatural, civilized and wild (see Jonaitis 1978, 1982). And like other rituals, those of the shaman have both permanent and ephemeral aspects including storytelling, dancing, singing and drumming, props and costumes, and even audience participation.

Rituals have an extremely important place in all societies, serving to link the unknown with the known, provide assurances in times of distress, ensure safe passage from one state to another, and mark important points of transition. While the rituals themselves may make use of a number of permanent objects such as carved wooden figures and masks or pottery bowls, other aspects are more ephemeral like the multimedia extravaganza of the Akuapem Odwira festival in Ghana (Cole). If we are to understand and appreciate these art forms fully, we must suspend our biases and look at the whole process of art from construction to destruction and not ignore the great feast of festivity that encompasses ritual art.

BIBLIOGRAPHY

Note: In addition to references cited in the text, this bibliography also includes a sampling of related works on ritual arts.

Adams, Monni. 1986. "Women and Masks among the Western Wè of Ivory Coast," *African Arts*, vol. 19(2), pp.46-55, 90.

Bishop, Joyce M. 1982. "Ephemeral Art in Context," in *Fiestas of San Juan Nuevo, Ceremonial Art from Michoacan, Mexico. Albuquerque: University of New Mexico, Maxwell Museum of Anthropology, pp.49-57.*

Brett-Smith, Sarah. 1982. "Symbolic Blood: Cloths for Excised Women," *Res*, No. 3, pp.15-31. Cambridge: Harvard University, Peabody Museum of Archaeology and Ethnology.

Cole, Herbert M. 1970. *African Arts of Transformation. Santa Barbara: The Art Galleries, University of California, Santa Barbara.*

——, 1982. *Mbari: Art and Life among the Owerri Igbo.* Bloomington: University of Indiana Press.

Cole, Herbert M. and Chike C. Aniakor. 1984. *Igbo Arts: Community and Cosmos*. Los Angeles: Museum of Cultural History, University of California.

Drewal, Margaret Thompson and Henry John Drewal. 1983. "An Ifa Diviner's Shrine in Ijebuland," *African Arts*, vol. 16(2), pp.60-67.

Fenton, William N. 1987. *The False Faces of the Iroquois*. Norman: University of Oklahoma Press.

Foss, Susan Moore. 1979. "She Who Sits as King," *African Arts*, vol. 12(2), pp.45-50, 90.

Furst, Peter. 1973/74. "The Roots and Continuities of Shamanism," *Stones, Bones and Skin: Ritual and Shamanic Art, Artscanada*, vol. 30(5/6), pp.33-60.

Gebhart-Sayer, A. 1985. "The Geometric Designs of the Shipibo-Conibo in Ritual Context," *The Journal of Latin American Lore*, vol. 11(2), pp.143-175.

Jonaitis, Aldona. 1982. "Sacred Art and Spiritual Power: An Analysis of Tlingit Shaman's Masks," from *Native North American Art History: Selected Readings*, edited by Zena Pearlstone Mathews and Aldona Jonaitis. Palo Alto: Peek Publications, pp.119-136.

——, 1978. "Reconciliation of Complementary Opposites: The Yakut Shaman Costume," *Anthropology*, May, pp.61-66.

Lincoln, Louise. 1987. *Assemblage of Spirits: Idea and Image in New Ireland. New York: George Braziller in association with the Minneapolis Institute of Arts.*

Nunley, John W. and Judith Bettelheim. 1988. *Caribbean Festival Arts: Each and Every Bit of Difference.* Seattle and London: The Saint Louis Art Museum in association with the University of Washington Press.

Office of Folklife Programs and Renwick Gallery. 1982. *Celebration: A World of Art and Ritual. Washington, D.C.: Smithsonian Institution Press.*

Ortiz, Alfonso. 1972. "Ritual Drama in the Pueblo World View," from *New Perspectives on the Pueblos*, edited by Alfonso Ortiz. Albuquerque: University of New Mexico Press, School of American Research, pp.135-161.

Pasztory, Esther. 1982. "Shamanism and North American Indian Art," from *Native North American Art History: Selected Readings*, edited by Zena Pearlstone Mathews and Aldona Jonaitis. Palo Alto: Peek Publications, pp.7-30.

Strathern, Andrew and Marilyn Strathern. 1971. *Self-Decoration in Mount Hagen. Toronto: University of Toronto Press.*

Thompson, Robert F. 1978. "The Grand Detroit *N'Kondi*," *Detroit Institute of Arts Bulletin*, vol. 56(4), pp.206-221.

Turner, Victor, editor. 1982. *Celebration, Studies in Festivity and Ritual.* Washington, D.C.: Smithsonian Institution Press.

van Gennep, Arnold. 1960. *The Rites of Passage. Translated by Monika B. Vizedom and Gabrielle L. Caffee from the 1909 French edition. Chicago: University of Chicago Press.*

Witherspoon, Gary. 1977. *Language and Art in the Navajo Universe*. Ann Arbor: The University of Michigan Press.

13

The Art of Festival in Ghana

Herbert M. Cole

Many festivals in Ghana are "total works of art" (*Gesamtkunstwerke*). They commonly involve countless minor artistic forms and actions (i.e., songs, dances, sculptures, etc.) which can be seen as distinct, but whose separate nature is subsumed in such festivals by the impact of the whole, a continuous and unified event often of surpassing beauty and rich cultural significance. This paper is an examination of the artistic principles manifest in such festivals, and will discuss the relationship of parts to one another and to the unified whole. It will conclude with an interpretation of festival art and meaning.

First a definition: a festival is a relatively rare climactic event in the life of any community. It is bounded by a definite beginning and end, and is unified thereby, as well as in being set apart from and above daily life. Its structure is built up on a core or armature of ritual. The festival brings about a suspension of ordinary time, a transformation of ordinary space, a formalization of ordinary behavior. It is as if a community becomes a stage set and its people actors with a battery of seldom-seen props and costumes. Meals become feasts, and greetings, normally simple, become ceremonies. Although dependent upon life-sustaining rituals, the festival is an elaborated and stylized phenomenon which far surpasses ritual necessity. It often becomes the social, ritual, and political apotheosis of community life in a year. At festival time one level of reality—the common and everyday—gives way to another, a more intense, symbolic, and expressive level of reality.

Many festivals in Ghana occupy five days or a week; others are compressed into one or two days. Whatever the duration, they are events of great complexity,

Reprinted in abridged form from *African Arts*, Vol. 8(3):12-23, 60-62, 90, 1975 with permission of the author and publisher.

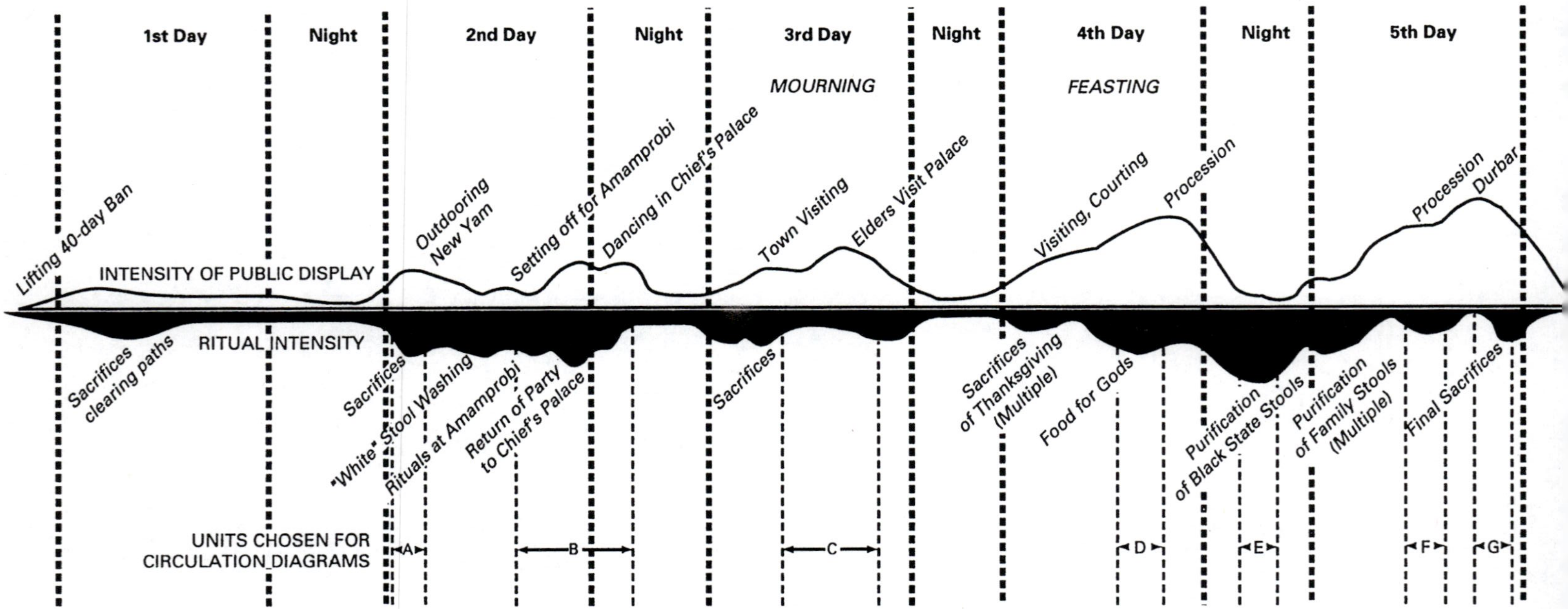

Figure 1 Schematic energy flow of Odwira at Akropong.

and often confusion, especially for an outsider. They invoke all available artistic media orchestrated to a common purpose at once spiritual and serious, playful and entertaining. It is in their nature to be meaningful on several levels and difficult to understand, though enjoyable even without a full understanding. They are affecting and appealing experiences to a child and a wise local priest or farmer or chief, to an educated accountant returned home for the celebration and to a stranger. The well-staged festival brings everyone into its ambience. These characteristics and others they share with more conventional works of art. Indeed, the same vocabulary used in describing or analyzing a sculpture, musical composition, or drama can be applied with equal validity to festivals. They have boundaries (i.e., "frames"), compositions and rhythms: patterns, textures, tonality, themes, and contrasts. Motifs and variations occur within acts and scenes, tempos and moods are established leading to climax and resolution.

ODWIRA IN AKROPONG

To amplify these ideas let us turn to a specific festival held annually by the Akuapem peoples in Akropong, seat of the paramount chief of some 55,000 Akuapem (Kwamena-Poh 1973:3). This is Odwira, and it embraces several related purposes: thanksgiving; eating New Yam; sacrificing to ancestors and other deities; purifying the king and his people for a New Year; mourning the deaths of the past year; reaffirming political loyalties and allegiances, reestablishing the military order and social ties, and proclaiming the unity of a state organization. This rich, multi-leveled content is reflected in the structures and composition of the five-day event, and tends to characterize most festivals. Both artistic forms and their meanings in festivals are often so numerous, layered and overlapping that they are seldom if ever fully intelligible from any single vantage point. At least fourteen distinct ceremonies occur during the five days, some simultaneously; no single participant or observer would or could be present at all times.

To aid in visualizing the shape of the whole festival, I have reduced it to a schematic and interpretive form, a diagram of "energy flow" as I was able to observe or reconstruct from native accounts (Fig. 1). Two complementary types of behavior are graphed: below the center time-line is my view of the flow of ritual intensity in ceremonies either public or private; above the time-line, the intensity and elaboration of public display and spectacle. As may be observed in the diagram, "ritual intensity" and "display elaboration" are sometimes discontinuous, sometimes simultaneous and interdependent. Together they form what may be called an "energy system" which ultimately calls upon virtually all the ritual and artistic resources of the Akuapem state. The development of several Western art forms—ballet or opera, for example—could be charted along a time-line in an analogous manner.

The festival proper begins with the clearing of paths from various points to the state capital and festival site, Akropong, so "the gods may come and eat." The event ends five days later, after a magnificent procession, with a grandiose formal gathering during which chiefs revalidate political ties and make final sacrifices. The five-day period is shaped by a rhythmic ebbing and flooding of energy, with a crescendo building to the climax of the final day. This schematic expression of time flow can be supplemented and cross-cut by another type of diagram, shown here in series (Figs. 2A-2G), in which the spaces of the town and circulation through them may be visualized at selected periods of time from a bird's-eye view. Again simplified, these space/circulation patterns make graphic both the *formal* character of different events and the *contrast* of one activity to another. The specific events, somewhat arbitrarily chosen, are several of the more important private and public phases of the festival's development. The symbols on them are explained in the key, and each phase is identified by a letter on the lower part of the time-energy flow chart. It is useful, I think, to give an abbreviated account of the main events of the five-day festival period.

Synopsis of Odwira

As if to prepare the community for an extraordinary event, priests impose a ban on drumming, dancing, and mourning forty days prior to Odwira. On Sunday before the Monday when the festival truly starts, one of the royal executioners (a clan that now has a largely ceremonial role, with police functions) shoots a gun into the air to lift the ban (Kamena-Poh 1973:150).

Monday. After preparatory sacrifices, pathways are cleared from and within Akropong to shrines, to the royal graveyard some miles distant, and to villages subject to the paramount chief of the Akuapem state. This "path-clearing" has a more symbolic than practical value, especially in these days of greater commerce and mobility; lines of communication to ancestors, gods, and other men are opened that all may reaffirm the integrity of life under their living head of state.

Tuesday. After paths are cleared, the new agricultural year is officially opened. The yam crop, the yield of ancestral lands, is introduced to the gods and people by the town's senior elder. The "outdooring" of New Yam (Fig. 2A) involves both non-public sacrifices and public display, the latter being a community-wide announcement of the former, including a kind of mock battle or race, when young men compete in kicking pieces of New Yam through the main street of Akropong. Little music and no dancing attend this unusual "procession," and its general tone is more athletic and martial than artistic or stately. At most, two or three hundred people are involved as participants and audience, and the spatial foci are first the house of the oldest living man in Akropong, and then a several-hundred-yard-long section of the town's main street. Clothing is for the most part non-distinctive.

Later the same morning an essentially private ceremony is held in one of the palace courtyards. This is the "washing of 'white' state stools" (Fig. 3). It should be mentioned that for Akan peoples, stools mean far more than mere supports for the body; a person's soul is identified with his stool, and stools thus serve varied ceremonial functions. Those of particularly important dead leaders are ritually blackened, then enshrined, whereupon they serve as ancestral symbols. Five finely carved old stools, some made around 1850 or before, are carried out

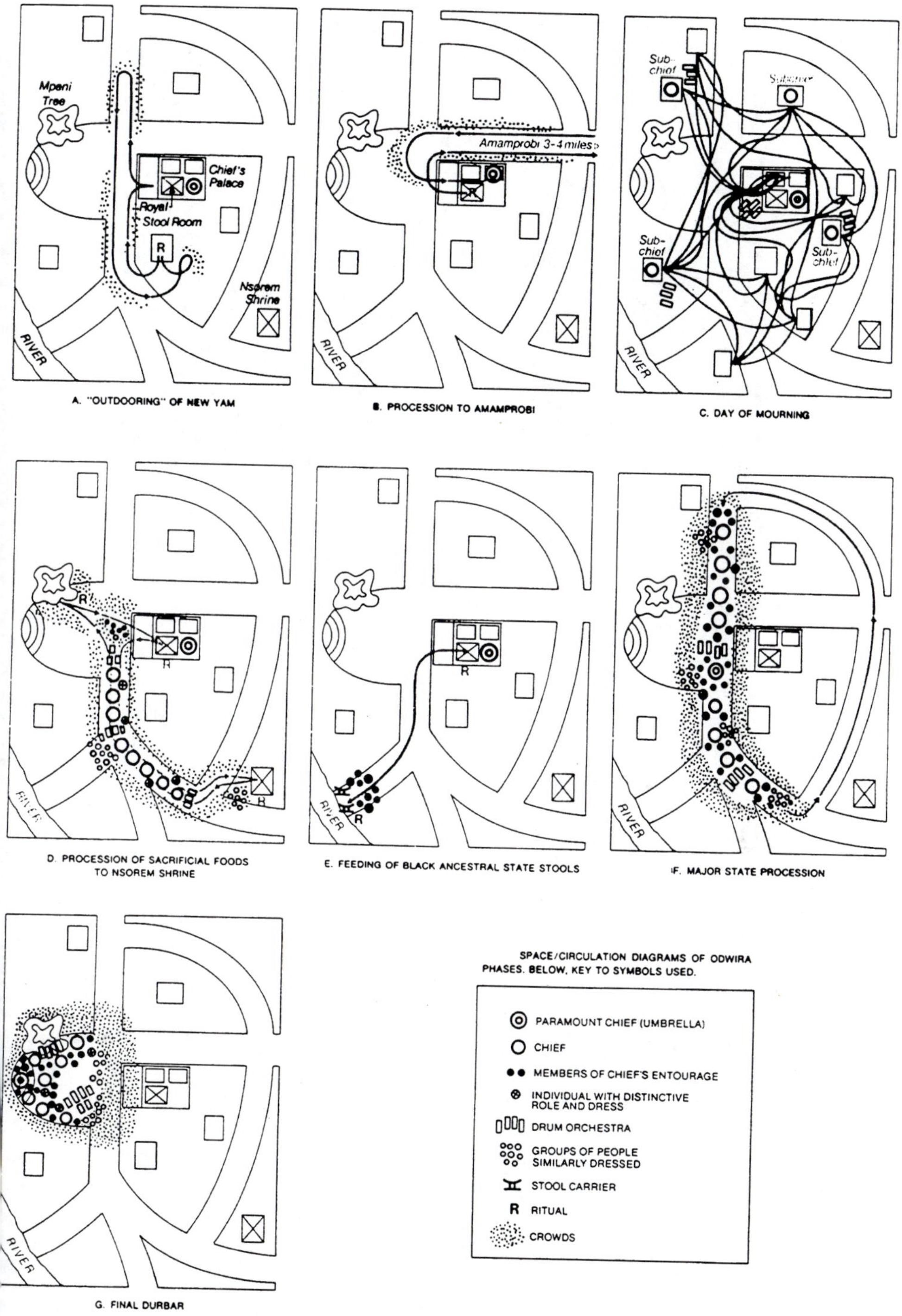

Figure 2 Space/circulation diagrams of Odwira phases.

Figure 3 Ceremonial washing of "white" state stools, Akropong.

by attendants and literally washed and cleaned in large brass basins with certain leaves and medicines mixed with water. Libations are poured, and clearly the stools are purified, although since they are domestic royal heirlooms rather than ancestral symbols (i.e. "black stools"), the rite is neither secret nor as ritually intense as later stool ceremonies. Nevertheless, few observers were present.

The next event (Fig. 2B)—the procession of priests to the royal mausoleum at Amamprobi, three or four miles distant—begins quietly but distinctively. A solemn tone is set by mournful, measured beats on the executioner's drum, a remarkable piece, carved in relief and covered with intricate brass repoussé. A group of twelve to fifteen people, carrying sacrificial materials and leading a sheep (also for sacrifice), walk to the mausoleum. The group is led by the chief of the state executioners and includes the more important priests of the state (and town). I was barred from the rite itself (though not from the departure or return of the party), but was told that offerings were made at the graves of royal ancestors, and that a purifying, strengthening mixture was prepared from perpetual medicines at this site. This medicine and other paraphernalia, called "Odwira," recalls state history because Amamprobi was the original Akuapem capital (ca. 1731) where sacred state symbols are kept. Brought to the current capital and king, these items and their corresponding rituals represent the purification and perpetuation of the state.

The rather triumphant return of this party draws crowds into the streets. Drumming and some spontaneous dancing converge on the small group as it brings the sacred Odwira medicine to the chief in his palace. In mourning costume the chief receives the party, and aided by the majestic state *frontomfrom* drums, much dancing ensues (Fig. 4). The distinctive reds and blacks of mourning are appropriate dress for all in attendance at this crowded reception in the largest of palace courtyards.

Figure 4 Women dancing before chief in mourning dress, Cape Coast.

Wednesday. The third day is devoted to public and private mourning. As the diagram (Fig. 2C) shows, there is much visiting throughout the town, with circulation patterns diffuse and random rather than strongly focussed. The activities of this day are repeated by all family heads and involve countless libations, prayers, and speeches remembering those who have died during the previous year. The mood is serious but festive, for Akan mourning involves much drumming, dancing, and drinking. Important elders, still in mourning costume, visit the paramount chief in the afternoon to pay him homage and to honor deceased members of the royal family.

Thursday. A similar pattern of intercompound visiting occurs during the fourth day, given over to feasting. This is a time of thanksgiving for life and health, a day on which townspeople promenade throughout Akropong in their best attire to show off the blessings they have received. Traditionally, too, this is a day of courting and making engagements. Family meetings are held to decide upon issues involving all its scattered members, whose attendance is all but mandatory. In many Ghanaian festivals such feasts are dramatized in two particular ways. The first is the construction of special cooking hearths in public spaces adjacent to family compounds, in contrast to everyday sites inside. Such hearths are often artistically constructed at the beginning of a festival and ceremonially destroyed at its end. The second, logically, is the preparation, ceremonious eating and distribution, to ancestors, passersby and the entire extended family, of distinctive and especially rich foods that are commonly not eaten during the rest of the year. Such a focus on feasts, reiterated often during the festival period, is a universal aspect of such events, as the etymology of the English word "festival" suggests.

By now the town is full of returned sons and daughters working and living elsewhere, and the atmosphere is buoyant and festive. The first of the week's two major processions occurs that afternoon, when young female representatives of all the chiefs carry sacrificial foods to a major shrine, Nsorem, on the outskirts of the town (Figs. 2D,5). The gods are honored and thanked and placated with these offerings, made by priests with a restricted audience inside the walled shrine. Crowds of people attracted by the colorful procession wait outside the enclosure; many dance and sing spontaneously to pass the time before the procession returns over its original route to the main plaza of Akropong opposite the king's palace. Further sacrifices are made at the impressive sacred tree there, *mpeni*, and still others are performed later and privately in the palace stool room.

This large procession included the "sacrificial entourages" of some fifteen chiefs, each party made visible by its sheltering umbrella (Fig. 5). Seven or eight musical groups took part and hundreds of people both lined the streets and followed entourages of their choice, the women often fanning with their "covercloths" and thereby cooling and praising the heavily-laden food carriers, who occasionally stumbled, possessed by the spirits they were chosen to serve. Adding complexity and textural richness to the prescribed processional order and its core of essential participants, the "audience"—now onlookers, now active participants—lent an air of informality and bustling interaction with the main actors. A considerable amount of unexpected, unprogrammed action—dance, gesture, song, and other random activity—marked this procession, a contrast to the more formalized and larger procession of chiefs the next day.

Thursday night. The dramatic peak of ritual intensity followed this procession in the darkness of late evening, night and early morning, when the highly sacred state and royal "black" ancestral stools were washed in the waters of the local stream (Fig. 2E). As I was not present during this time I will quote a colleague, Patricia Crane, who recorded her impressions of the event though she also was barred from the ritual itself:" . . . The brilliance of display, the boisterousness [of previous events] were suddenly held in check by total silence,

Figure 5 Major procession of sacrificial food to Nsorem on Thursday at Akropong.

lack of movement, and non-visibility. For one evening out of the year there was an actual physical separation of the living and the dead, a spatial reversal. When the ancestral spirits are taken out of their shrine [the royal stool room], living inhabitants of Akropong must remain inside their homes. The noise of daily living ceased, giving way to the silence of the spirit." At 9 p.m. a gong player moved through the town warning people to return home and extinguish lights. By ten o'clock it was eerily still and dark and the only sounds were executioners running and bombing rocks on the tin roofs of houses where occasional lights still burned. After half an hour, total silence and total darkness. Some hours later, perhaps 3 a.m., the blackened ancestral stools were taken by a priestly delegation to the stream, ceremonially washed, thereby purified, then "fed" with the blood of a sacrificial sheep. About 4 a.m. the paramount chief greeted the returning stools and their entourage. Two shots were fired to announce that individual family stools should then be purified, and the royal ancestors—black stools—returned to their sanctuary.

Friday. Begun with solemn and exclusively private rites, the fifth day blossoms later with a crescendo of dramatic public display and political panoply. The week's most majestic procession is mounted about noon (Fig. 2F). Colorful, gold-bedecked chiefs parade through the major town streets, hedged about by richly embellished members of their entourages. This procession was not held at Akropong during the Odwira I witnessed (1972) because the paramount chief was sick, but doubtless it would have been similar to others I have witnessed. Participants dress according to office or rank, in multiple variations on the theme of ceremonial finery. The procession reveals the splendor of displayed political power and wealth in stately movement. A thunderous drum or horn orchestra follows nearly every chief, while each entourage vies with the next in grandeur, elegance, and the size of its following. Scores of gold-leafed swords, staffs, flywhisks, and umbrella tops compete with sumptuous cloths, patterned bodies, elegant hairstyles, and luxurious gold and bead jewelry. Swaying, twirling umbrellas mark chiefs, linguists and swordbearers, and some chiefs are borne aloft in stately palanquins, expressing their superiority (Fig. 6). Royalty and common people are bound together, however, by exaltation and common purpose. The display—activated by drum rhythms, horn blasts and song, made expressive by gesture and dance—captivates, entertains and dazzles; all townspeople, commoner and chief, old and young, are swept into its aura, caught by its majesty. But its multiple meanings are by no means lost. The social order is manifest in the dress and behavior of all participants, whether onlookers or actors.

The procession is in turn measured and orderly or wildly active, transported by vibrant dances, as commanded by drummers. The parade ends at the main town plaza, opposite the chief's palace, where chiefs and nobles sit in state, their king and paramount centered at the highest position under his double umbrella, with lesser chiefs and officials carefully placed according to tradition and rank (Figs. 2G, 7).

If the procession is the active, *popular* event which maximizes the public visibility of royalty and allied groups (i.e., priests, warriors, executioner clan, voluntary associations, musical bands and so forth) and which stimulates the "audience" to become participants, then the hierarchically disposed and sedentary durbar is the cool and formal *political* event which binds the state into a cohesive unit. Sociopolitical display (the procession) terminates in real but nonetheless symbolic transactions between chiefs on behalf of their people (the durbar). Oaths are sworn, speeches given, and drinks are distributed to important people. Formal behavior prevails. Being spatially focussed (Fig. 7) rather than circulating through a mile or more of town streets amid thousands of people, the durbar reaches a smaller public–despite the large size of the plaza and the attendant crowds–and energy focusses on reciprocal expressions of loyalty and allegiance among the chiefs in the state organization. Yet these interchanges–expressed in speeches, prayers, dances, gestures and drummed proverbs–represent the solidarity of the renewed, purified state and its leaders, supported on the one hand by ancestral and other spiritual sanctions and on the other by the people at large. "The edges of the years have met," runs a local New Year's maxim, and the cosmos, embracing all Akuapem people, is renewed and thus ready for the trials and triumphs of the year now beginning.

FORM AND CONTENT

Clearly one cannot separate the significance and content of such a festival from the complex orchestration of artistic media marshalled to express and reinforce

Figure 6
Paramount chiefs dance in their palanquins, creating dramatic peaks in festival processions. The decorated chief's niece, here partially enveloped in his robe, also gestures and dances, adding visual richness to the scene at Abeadze Dominase.

such meanings. Indeed the multiplicity of art forms and processes supports the many levels and types of content. Such intricate interweavings of artistic patterns emphasize the importance and depth of the event, as well as present the onlooker/analyst with a profusion of elements and structures. In short, the festival is a complicated and often subtle art form. The fact that a festival may occupy several days rather than a few hours, like the performed arts in our culture, detracts not at all from its flow and unity in the minds of local people. In African ideas of time, events can be interrupted (e.g. by sleep) and discontinuous but still linked in purpose and therefore whole. The very length of such a work of art indeed serves to underscore its uniqueness in the ceremonial calendar and thus its centrality in the life of the community.

Structural Elements

Certain structural elements that cross-cut both phases of the festival and its component arts (i.e., music, sculpture, dance, etc.) can be seen as devices which unify the entire event. Hierarchy, repetition, and variation are among the more important. Each of these, too, can be visualized both synchronically and diachronically. Thus a visible *hierarchy* of participants is clearly expressed in the formal seating of chiefs and others at the final durbar (Fig. 7). The double umbrella of the paramount chief is the apex of a pyramid comprised

Figure 7
Chiefs and nobles massed for the Odwira festival durbar at Akropong Akuapem in southern Ghana. The king is all but hidden under his double umbrella. In the foreground appears a gold-leafed carved wooden stool, an elephant, symbolic of the strength and power of the Akuapem state.

of lesser chiefs and their entourages; this entire structure in turn rests upon the broad foundation provided by the people at large, the "supporting audience." To this synchronic view, however, must be added the "hierarchy of activities" during the five-day period, the apex being the final procession and durbar, the crowning events in a mounting flood of energy and intensity—both of artistry and of meaning. The "energy flow" diagram can thus be taken as a diachronic view of hierarchy.

Many other hieratic structures are present, too, as might be expected in a socio-political organization such as that of the Akuapem in which a strong centralized leader is supported by varied levels of more or less specialized roles and groups. Thus the majestic spatial hierarchy of the durbar scene is echoed, in miniature, by that of a single chief seated or walking under his umbrella with his linguist and other members of his small entourage (Fig. 8). The larger, "linear" hierarchy of a state procession is made up of a linked series of smaller hieratic groups, individual chiefs and their parties, with varied ancillary individuals and groups forming the "sub-base" and the vast audience the base itself. The identities and distribution of main actors in an analogous New Year's festival procession (in Awutu) was accurately recorded.

The principle of repetition follows logically, since each layer in a hierarchy, save the top, is composed of repeated or similar elements of varied character. Repetition, moreover, may be a still more fundamental component of festival

Figure 8
A sub-chief under his royal umbrella with his small entourage. They are preceded by two "linguists," traditional spokesmen for a chief, who carry gold-covered wooden staffs of office topped by sculptured proverbs.

structure than hierarchy. Virtually everything is repeated on different levels: rituals, including prayers, libations, sacrifices, and honorific gestures; musical performances; dance; isolable sculptures such as golden staffs, stools, swords and other items; processions; feasting; assemblies and speeches; ceremonial dress, jewelry, body painting and hairstyling. Public events are repetitious, as are private ones; spatial and temporal patterns recur throughout the week and a good many events are repeated simultaneously in scores of family compounds throughout the town (Fig. 2C). Clearly, too, repetitions in visual patterns and artistic processes are expressions of content, that is, they reflect the socio-political and spiritual realities of a complex state and social organization, including the needs of ordinary people to act out their support of the power structure.

All such repetitions, moreover, involve the principle of *variation* to greater or lesser degrees. No two chiefs or priests dress or embellish themselves identically nor do their entourages include exactly the same numbers of people or the same decorations. Chiefs and many other participants wear different "costumes" for as many different occasions. No two orchestras among the twelve or more present are the same either in make-up or in the musical pieces played. A number of men may dance in series to praise the king, but each dancing style is of course individual. Examples could be multiplied. Spatial and temporal variations and contrasts are of greater importance still in establishing the rhythmic progress of festival development. A plaza is now empty, then filled; one procession is small and another large; circulation is now random, later focussed along a prescribed route; one day is for mourning, the next for feasting. And in any one event, especially a major public one, there are dozens of individuals or groups whose personal ornamentations and actions are distinctive, thereby providing a visible means of distinguishing among roles. Visual, auditory, and kinetic variations are nearly impossible to count and document at a major event such as a state procession. The onlooker would have to be in a dozen places at once with eyes in the back of his head. If slides or videotape recordings are made from a distance, then of course individual variations are lost, though the textural richness and artistic depth and multiplicity of the whole are recorded fairly well, and its unity is apparent.

When repetitions and variations are multiplied, as they so often are in a festival, the principle of *elaboration* comes into play. Sights and sounds and motions, nearly all of which are stylized and thus removed from their daily counterparts, proliferate and thereby give an impression of enormous wealth and diversity. Like much of the music heard, the festival itself is polymelodic and polyrhythmic. The fabric of the whole comes from the complex interweaving of literally hundreds of disparate threads—elements that overlap, change, merge, move, and rest. The *ensemble* principle—a whole comprised of interrelating parts—is present in nearly all festivals.

Pars pro toto

Yet our interest in the whole should not obscure the significance of each element, however small, for it is often a microcosm, as well as being necessary to the existence of the whole. In this regard we may briefly consider what Allegra Fuller Snyder (1972) calls "the dance symbol." Whether a single dance gesture made by one person or an entire performance by many, dance often symbolizes and supports a people's world view. Akuapem (and much African) dancing does just that. A dancer who rolls his arms inward, then stretches his right arm out to the end beats of the music, is saying: "If you bind me with cords, I shall break them to pieces" (Nketia 1963: 160n). Dozens of similarly meaningful gestures are made by both performers and their audience during the course of a dance (Fig. 9). Festival dancing to state orchestras can refer to historical events, reinforce ritual actions, express the subservience of a sub-chief, the grief of mourners or the ferocity of a warrior. There would, of course, be no dance without music, and with neither of those arts present it is difficult to conceive of a festival at all. Professor Snyder believes that the dancer, internally, experiences "transformation," through which he "experientially builds a bridge between physical reality and conceptual reality" (1972:221). The dancer becomes something more, or "other" than his ordinary self. Though his actions are of course real, he has created an illusion. Many other minor acts and arts could be cited to reinforce this point. A chief's linguist with his sculptured staff serves both to separate that chief from his audience and link him to it. The chief understands very well the voice of the visitor; the linguist is thus an essential (ideological) but unnecessary (practical) intermediary. He is at once minor in any transaction but most significant in expressing the *nature* of the transaction. He is somehow real but at the same time illusory.

Figure 9 An elder dancing in palace, Tuesday afternoon, Akropong.

Illusion and Transformation

The festival too is simultaneously real and illusionistic: a transformation of the lives and spaces of a town for the brief duration of the ceremonial period. With ordinary life suspended, the community acts out its ultimate concerns. Yet the actors play *themselves*, validating and communicating their own traditional and up-dated ideas of what is important in the world. The people are also their own patrons, ordering a work of art necessary to their existence, a work that is executed communally by the very same "artists," that is the patrons! The shrines, and the foods fed to gods and ancestors, too, are real. We can ask if the gods really *eat* only if we ask if a Catholic priest really changes wine to the blood of Christ.

The "play element" is very much present, as it is in all ritual, contributing to the transformation and the illusion embodied in the festival (Huizinga 1950). Both *recreation* and *display* are important characteristics of such events, and those words, broken down, reinforce ideas of both play and illusion, a central aspect of play; "re-*creation*" suggests the cosmic renewal of the New Year, while "dis*play*," emphasizes the special, conventionalized character of festival activity, which stands apart from normal behavior. "Re-*presentation*" stresses the creation, again, of a particular cosmic event, "when the edges of the years meet," when New Yam, a kind of eucharist, is presented to the gods and the people. Despite the varied non-spiritual embellishments of the festival, it remains a sacred performance rooted in and dependent upon ritual. Thus the festival, a *holiday*, is also a "*holy* day," when gods and ancestors are invited to partake in this blessing which people may enjoy only through their beneficence. And, as Huizinga says, " . . . with the end of play [festival/ritual] its effect is not lost; rather it continues to shed its radiance on the ordinary world outside, a wholesome influence working security, order and prosperity for the whole community until the sacred play-season comes round again" (1950:14).

CONCLUSION

The artistic impact of a festival stems not from isolated artistic forms or actions but from the formally orchestrated interaction of all the aesthetic resources of a community. A varied and rhythmic interplay of smaller and larger events establishes a directed flow of energy which engulfs the people and transports them—through the mystery of ritual, the majesty of power and the magnificence of display—to a transcendent plane. Serious play builds an illusion of the world more controlled and more perfect than men actually find it. The festival is thus relief and catharsis and hope, a spatial and temporal pocket in workaday lives; people in the richest of clothes eat the richest of foods and turn talking into prayer and song, walking into dance. The stylized artistry of transient festival life points up the essentially non-artistic character of constant daily behavior. With work and other normal activities suspended, people transform their community into an intensified idealized world of communion among gods and men. Peace and order prevail, and the atmosphere is charged with promise.

Life and art interpenetrate, creating a dynamic interplay, a dialogue between reality and illusion, man and god, form and meaning. Returning to Odwira in Akropong, we can visualize these tensions through the metaphor of "call and response":

- dancers respond to the urgent call of drumming;
- food-carrying messengers respond, swaying and bending to the calls of spirits possessing them;
- women, cooling and praising with fanning cloths, respond to the call of these spiritually-laden messengers;
- sub-chiefs respond to the political call of their paramount;
- the festival itself is a response to the call of spiritual and social renewal.

Life itself, throughout the year, is a spacious 360-day round of meaningful social and spiritual activities. But humdrum and ordinary daily life needs to be recharged and renewed. The formalized and charged atmosphere of the five festival days works this revitalization, isolating and dramatizing life's meanings in artistic form. Expressive acts, in the festival, *become* symbols of life and beget still more artistry, and multiple works of art cascade together through the week, climaxing at the durbar.

The artistic energy system of the unified whole stems from man's need to construct a symbolic and idealized world, a model capable of crystalizing and dramatizing those aspects of life which, in any given community, are so crucial to its health and continuity. It is clear that no work of art, other than a festival, is equal to the task of projecting all these meanings in virtually simultaneous form. Festivals, then, are the most important and complex and beautiful works of art in southern Ghana.

BIBLIOGRAPHY

Coomaraswamy, Ananda K. 1956. *Christian and Oriental Philosophy of Art.* New York.

Kwamena-Poh, M.A. 1973. *Government and Politics in the Akuapem 1730-1850.* Longman, London.

Kyerematen, A.A.Y. 1964. *Panoply of Ghana.* Praeger, New York.

Langer, Suzanne K. 1953. *Feeling and Form.* Scribners, New York.

Huizinga, Johan. 1950. *Homo Ludens: A Study of the Play Element in Culture.* Beacon Press.

Nketia, J.H. Kwabena. 1962. *African Music in Ghana.* Northwestern University Press, Evanston.

Nketia, J.H. Kwabena. 1963. *Drumming in Akan Communities of Ghana.* Nelson, London.

Nketia, J.H. Kwabena. 1965. *Ghana–Music, Dance and Drama.* University of Ghana, Legon.

Snyder, Allegra Fuller. 1972. "The Dance Symbol" in *The Dimensions of Dance Research; Anthropology and Dance.* Cord, New York (mimeographed copy).

14

Woman Power and Art in a Senufo Village

Anita J. Glaze

The theme of Woman in all its variations, including the important mother-and-child image, is widespread and constant in African art—an observation that is hardly new. The difficulty is that endless catalogues of African sculpture have tended to note the theme without coming to grips with the dynamics of its setting in a particular place and time, and thereby have risked doing an immense disservice to the richly divergent aspirations and achievements of the Black African cultures concerned. Somehow, the vital involvement of African women in some of the very institutions which have sustained great art traditions (e.g. divine kingships, initiation societies, divination cults) has often remained obscure behind such facile expressions as "fertility figure" or even "Queen Mother." Quite apart from consideration of the impressive contributions of African women in such creative fields as personal ornamentation, textiles, and pottery, it would seem time to take a closer look into women's roles in all those spheres of aesthetic expression that are integral to the structures of social, political and spiritual authority in the community.

This paper is based on research conducted in a cluster of Kufuru villages in Ivory Coast. The Senufo generally apply the designation "Kufuru" to an area that begins about twenty kilometers to the southwest of Korhogo in north-central Ivory Coast and which historically seems to have extended as far south as the Bou River. The area is a rich mixture of distinct dialect and occupational sub-groups. The Kufulo, a farmer group speaking a Central Senari dialect closely related to Tyebara, frequently constitute a minority group in the Kufuru area except in a number of villages in the transitional zone which begins just north of Guiembe.

Reprinted in abridged form from *African Arts*, Vol. 8,(3):24-29, 64-68, 90, 1975 with permission of the author and publisher.

The major artisan group is the blacksmiths, the *Fönöbele* (*bele* is the plural ending), whose dialect seems much the same as Kufulo except for certain ritual and technological vocabularies. Women in this group are known especially for fine basketry and matmaking. Other artisan groups present are the *Kpëëbele*, of which the men are brasscasters and the women pottery specialists; the *Tyelibele*, the leatherworkers group; and the *Kulebele*, the sculpture specialists. Weaving is a thriving art practiced by the men of three groups: the brasscasters, the non-Senufo Dyula ("our Dyula," ancient settlements as opposed to the "stranger Dyula," a more recent influx), and a blacksmith group of problematic origin called the *Tyedunbele*, whose women are reputed to create the finest pottery in the entire central Senufo area. The dominant population, especially in the southern half of the Kufuru region, is Fodonon. This is a farmer group speaking Fodörö, a Senari dialect which is virtually incomprehensible to Central Senari speakers but which, according to Fodonon informants, has much in common with the Gbönzoro and Tagwana dialects to the southeast.

The Fodonon are a most fascinating member of the Senufo language family, known to the Senufo for their traditional rainmaker specialists (*n'dàáfölö*) and for their ancient and widely renowned society of healing specialists (*Nöökariga*, recognized by their brass insignia rings with the bushcow head motif). In the context of this paper, of particular note is *Tyekpa*, a women's organization and concept, apparently unique to the Fodonon group, which in the Kufuru villages has become a stimulus for some exciting developments in the arts. Despite the relatively recent political ties with Korhogo (Tyebara, French, and Ivoirien, in that order), oral tradition collected in the Kufuru region, linguistic data, and continuing kinship and ritual ties all indicate that the strongest historical relationships are with the groups to the west, the south, and the southeast. An average village of about 1,500 people comprises perhaps as many as six or seven distinct sub-groups called *katiolo*, briefly defined as residential and cooperative work units having dominant ties to a particular matrilineage or lineage segment (*narigba* or *nërëge*).

From the literature one would think that Senufo art is essentially a man's world, for apart from passing references to the Sandogo women's "divination" society, by far the larger proportion of discussions of Senufo art has centered around the Poro society, usually described as a "men's society." With a few important exceptions, it is true that the more dramatic contexts of the arts, such as masquerade performances, are at one level men's business. Yet even in the area of spectacle and aesthetic display certain women's activities must be included, as anyone would agree who has witnessed a Fodonon women's society (*Tyekpa*) funeral performance (Figs. 1, 2, 3) where even the virtuoso drummers are women, or an all-night consultation with a Tagwana diviner (*Sando*) who, to the beat of drum and rattle, is possessed by spirits visually manifested in the sculptures that one by one become her dancing partners. The real point, however, is that a disproportionate attention to outward spectacle may lead to a serious misunderstanding of the active, if less outwardly visible, roles of women in both Poro and Sandogo, the two institutions that are the chief patrons of the arts.

Figure 1 Members of four Tyekpa groups (four Fodonon villages represented by sculpture). Funeral of "mother of Tyekpa," Solo Soro. Males in photo are members of dead woman's lineage; they will have to undergo purification ritual for having come so close to the "children of Poro" figures. Fodonon group, July 1970.

Figure 2
Tyekpa society virtuoso drummers providing the beat for beautiful songs that use a secret language to insult the men by offering scathing comments on their behavior.

Figure 3
Tyekpa figure of nursing mother with navel motif.Commemorative sculptures such as this one praise the courage and endurance of women. Funeral of "Mother of Tyekpa," Solo Soro. Fodonon group, July 1970.

A telescopic vision that, understandably, focuses on the visual excitement of masquerades in a Senufo funeral ritual is apt to miss the elder women standing unobtrusively at the periphery of the ritual arena; yet it is the very presence of these Sandogo leaders that both validates and adds power to the ritual itself. Poro and Sandogo work together to meet problems and ensure the continuity of the group; however, in the Senufo system, women are ultimately more responsible than men for seeking the goodwill and blessings of the supernatural world–the Deity, the Ancestors, and the bush spirits. The evidence suggests that as the activities of these two institutions move toward a more critical relationship with the supernatural and spiritual world, the more secretive the objects and events become, and the greater is the role of women (real or mythological).

Within the framework of Senufo culture as represented in a typical Kufuru area village, it will be the purpose of this paper to indicate briefly the range and depth of women's involvement with those aesthetic forms and events that communicate, control, and create power in both the temporal and supernatural senses of the word. To avoid possible misunderstanding of what exactly is meant by "woman power" in the Senufo context, let it be noted at the outset that in Senufo thought, all powers and positions rest ultimately on supernatural authority. There is rarely a question here of women usurping male authority; if anything, the opposite can be said to be historically the case, as the Senufo have come increasingly under the impact of both Islamic and Western pressures, particularly in the Tyebara dialect area in the immediate environs of Korhogo. It would be a travesty of the Senufo world-view to diminish in any way the legitimate authority of the male in the socio-political order. Rather, to speak of "woman power" is an attempt to restore to discussions of Senufo culture that desired balance of male and female components which will be seen to constitute a basic tenet of Senufo ideology.

A dearth of information regarding Senufo kinship structures has been a serious barrier to understanding more fully the woman's role in their culture. For instance, as recently as 1967, in Murdock's *Ethnographic Atlas*, the Senufo are purported to be patrilineal, yet it is clear that they are predominantly matrilineal in character and that the true head of the men's society is a woman. A high degree of matrilineality in the Kufuru area was evident in the number and kind of rights, status, obligations, and property that were said to pass through the mother's line. Even to those families and groups that have shifted to a patrilineal system under increasing Islamic and Western influences, the matrilineage seems to retain an ideological significance not readily dismissed. Of course, it does not necessarily follow that in a matrilineal succession all types of power lie in the hands of the women, since authority is commonly delegated to the mother's brother and other males on the maternal side of the family. The fact remains that a consideration of the critical importance of the matrilineage illuminates several problematic categories of Senufo masquerades and sculpture. A deep respect for women, particularly the elder leadership, is expressed in traditional Senufo culture not only in their art but in a great number of formal gestures and honors paid to them within various structured, living art situations, such as the formal gesture of homage a young initiate of blacksmith-Poro junior grade offers a woman elder of his lineage at the time of *Kwöörö* initiation. Attired in the masquerade that celebrates his advancement in Poro (*Kwööbele Kodöli* mask), the initiate places his hands on the woman's shoulders in a gesture which both honors her status and also suggests a drawing of sustenance and protection from one who can secure ancestral blessings. That is, the masquerader by this action is making a non-verbal statement concerning the role of women elders as mediators with the ancestors.

Another example of ritual which places male-female role interaction in the context of aesthetic forms is *Lango*, essentially a young men's dance paying homage to women elders. *Lango*, an ancient Fodonon dance tradition with songs, is performed only at the funeral celebrations of important Fodonon women elders. A strong vibrant dance, *Lango* is characterized by vigorous boot stamps that ring the stacks of iron bell anklets, the crack of metal-ringed whips, and the hot rhythms of a barrel drum and hand gongs. As the dance column moves swiftly through the village paths and courtyards, a few young women who sing "strong" intersect and support the male dancers. Thus *Lango* honors elder women, is danced by young men, who are themselves encouraged and strengthened by the support of young women. This basic pattern typifies the flow of male-female interaction in the considerably more complex setting of Poro.

The Kufuru data indicate that a kind of balance of power between the male and female sectors of the community is achieved within the formats of both the Poro and Sandogo organizations. Significantly, the mere presence of both a men's society and a women's society is by no means the critical aspect of balance. This would be far too static an image to portray what is in reality an ingeniously graded series of structured opportunities for dynamic interaction between male and female sectors.

A close examination reveals that the institution of Poro itself is a vital channel for the interaction of male and female sectors of the community at a surprising number of age group levels, and that indeed the role of the female is intrinsic to the functions and continuity of Poro. So critical is the woman's part in Poro that her presence is absolutely necessary in the founding of a new *sinzinga* organization. The initial ritual act that creates and dedicates the *sinzinga* is performed by a man and a woman acting together. The male *sinzingafölö*, or chief of the sacred grove, succeeds to the title through the maternal line–a nephew rather than a son. The elder woman's title is nërëjaö, head of the lineage segment concerned, and she is generally the oldest sister of the uncle of the new *sinzingafölö*. Moreover, it is the *nërëjaö* who is considered the chief head of Poro–a staggering fact in the light of our previous conception of the so-called men's society. However since the woman cannot kill, that is, risk contamination with sacrificial blood, or play the Poro drums (having lost this right in the mythological past), she gives these jobs to her brothers or nephews.

In its role as the principal center of male religious and social instruction and as the basic framework for the male political leadership, the Poro can most certainly be termed a men's society. Uninitiated women along with junior boys and children are excluded from participation in many Poro activities, out of a concern, above all, for their protection from powerful supernatural forces. At the same time, secrecy is an important psychological factor in the institutionalization of male and female members of Senufo society, a principle that extends as well to establishing identity with a particular ethnic group or age group. Although the terms "men's," "secret," and "initiation" society all convey important facts of Poro, Poro is also a "society of the sacred grove," an epithet that at least has the advantage of not entirely excluding the integrated activities of girls and women and that draws attention to the *sinzinga*.

Poro is above all an organization designed to maintain the right relationships with the Deity and the Ancestors. The most important ancestor is the woman who was head of the founding matrilineage of each *sinzinga*, the greater ideological weight of Ancestress over Ancestor being neatly expressed in the larger proportions of the female in the vast majority of male and female couples, the primary category of figure sculpture used by Poro and Sandogo (Fig. 4). A village will have a number of *sinzinga* organizations, all linked ultimately to matrilineal kin groups whose ancestors had settled there. The *zingböhö*, literally "the big one," is the title given the principal *sinzinga*, that of the founding lineage in the village. It is so unusual for a man to join his father's *sinzinga* instead of his uncle's (mother's eldest brother) group that the phenomenon is remarked upon in the secret name that will be given to the initiate upon completion of the final phase of Poro instruction and service (*tyologo*).

I can think of no single expression in Senufo language which better communicates the ideological core of woman power or more intimately touches

Figure 4
Primordial couple. Funeral for a champion cultivator. The female figure is slightly larger; the male wears a champion cultivator hat. Kufulo group. March 1970.

the very heart of their religious thought than the phrase, "at our Mother's work." A literal translation from a local modification of Senari used as a "secret language" by Poro initiates, this phrase forms the nucleus of a combination formal greeting/secret password used wherever members are engaged in the affairs of Poro, especially within the sacred precincts of the *sinzinga*, or sacred grove. The words refer to the initiated Senufo's status as a child of divinity conceived of as being distinctly on the distaff side and under whose control human activity finds wisdom, creativity, and order. Thought of in human terms as Ancient Mother, Màlëëö (or Kàtyelëëö) is considered to have her *katiolo*–her home and seat of authority–in the *sinzinga*, the very nexus of divine and temporal authority in the Senufo village. As has been noted earlier, *katiolo* in the everyday sense of the word is a work group having dominant ties to a particular matrilineage or lineage segment (*narigba* or *nërëge*).

The sacred requirement that a woman be the true head of Poro follows with perfect logic and consistency from the basic premises of Senufo thought concerning the nature of deity and family, that is, of cosmological and social order. The involvement of women in Poro would also seem to be an institutionalized expression of the deeply rooted concept of twinship in Senufo cosmogony.

Central to Senufo religion is the concept of a bipartite deity called Kòlotyölöö in its aspect of divine creator, and Màlëëö or Kàtyelëëö in its aspect of protective, nurturing being. As suggested above, Ancient Woman (or Mother) works at the level of village life primarily through the institution of the sacred grove and attendant Poro members. The secret names of certain of the Poro's most sacred equipment (such as the most important drum and mask types) refer directly or indirectly to Ancient Woman. Although justice and punishment are concerns of both facets of the deity, it is primarily Ancient Woman who deals with crimes that threaten the well-being of the community. Suspected murderers or thieves, for example, would traditionally come before the instruments of Ancient Woman for trial.

More importantly, the members of Poro are entrusted under the authority and validation of Ancient Woman to maintain community order by means of a complex system of education, designed to help shape the intellect, moral character, and skills of each succeeding generation and age set. Although I will not go into detail here about the levels of initiation in Poro, suffice it to say that the appropriate age groups of young girls are intimately involved at every major stage of training, and in the ordeals, advancement rituals and celebrations. For example, in the Fodonon sub-group, girls are included in *Tiga*, the "language of the dead." During arduous three-month long sessions, they learn by memory and song the secret language of Poro ritual and are excluded only from certain sessions dealing with secret terms available solely to men and older initiated women. It should also be noted that women past menopause undergo a special initiation into full Poro membership.

The creator god (Kòlotyölöö) is seen as a wholly good but relatively remote Being responsible for the original Creation and for "bringing forth." There is some evidence to suggest that Kòlotyölöö was originally considered female in nature (*työlöö wii*, for example, means "woman" or "wife" in Tyebara) although present usage suggests a more neuter or even a paternal image. According to elder informants, Kòlotyölöö is non-visible and difficult to approach without the help of *Yirigefölö* (literally owner or chief of "creating, making, bringing forth") or *Nyëhënë* ("sky" or "light"), two corollary manifestations which mean essentially the same thing as creator god. The basic difference is that *Yirigefölö* and *Nyëhënë* are material objects intended as visual aids for worship, supplication, and sacrifices. As one elder explained, "*Yirigefölö* is a thing one sees to help pray to Kòlotyölöö."

These objects are often highly aesthetic. The *Yirigefölö* is usually expressed sculpturally as a miniature adobe house, significantly positioned next to the beautiful large water jar a woman is given at marriage and which is the central feature in the outside chamber of her house. The miniature house is usually built upon the advice of a Sando diviner as part of her prescription in meeting a particular domestic crisis. The Yirigefölö shrine frequently contains some of the small cast brass charms which are directly related to consultation with a diviner and which are inherited through the maternal line. Similarly, a family leader and head of a compound builds an adobe Nyëhënë altar in the courtyard, shaped like a truncated cone with a python motif in relief. The altar is often crowned with a pottery bowl containing the brass and wood sculpture associated with Sando divination. Foo (wii) or python, messenger of the spirits, is first in the hierarchy of symbols of power used by the diviner. Brass and iron figures and ornaments which relate to lesser spirits than Kòlotyölöö, particularly the unpredictable and potentially dangerous *madebele* or bush spirits, frequently complete the total gestalt of *Nyëlënë*. With these more immediate, material manifestations of God, we have come full circle again to the crucial involvement of women, in this case the diviners. Neither male nor female leadership would make a single important decision or ritual act of importance without consulting one *Sando* (a diviner of a certain category) or even a dozen *Sandobele* (plural) whose assistance as intermediaries with the supernatural world is considered indispensable.

Sandogo, the association of *Sandobele*, is a dual level institution which includes a branch of divination specialists but whose primary concern is with family relationships. The Sandogo members' greatest responsibility is safeguarding the purity of the matrilineage; their activities include, for example, administering penalties in cases of adultery or unsanctioned pre-marital behavior on the part of males from other lineages. A Sandogo village membership is composed of representatives from every matrilineal segment (*narigba* or *nërëge*), most of whom are designated by ancestral diviners who communicate with the living diviners by means of the *Sando* technique. (The entire socio-aesthetic process of *Sando* divination is a fascinating topic demanding a detailed analysis beyond the scope of this brief paper.) Under certain circumstances, men can be trained as diviners; however, it should be noted that this skill is always considered an inheritance through the maternal line. In short, not all *Sandobele* are diviners or, for that matter, women. As in the case of the Poro "men's" society, to say that Sandogo is a "women's" or a "divination" society is useful but oversimplified. Unlike the *Tyekpa* society, which parallels the Poro society in its emphasis on prestigious visual display for large audiences in funeral and initiation rituals, the sphere of Sandogo is more an inner, closed arena where the individual grapples with daily problems and his relationship with the unknown. In the small consultation chamber of the diviner, an atmosphere of supernatural power is created by a glittering, intentionally bewildering display of visual forms, but on a miniature scale suitable to the intimate private relationship of diviner and client. Here, too, prestige is enhanced by the aesthetic merits of the visual setting; in some ways, artistic elaboration of equipment and office decor is a direct index of the diviner's skills and popularity (Fig. 6). The contrast of a public versus a private world is therefore reflected in the very dimensions of figure sculpture used by Poro and *Tyekpa* (two to three feet high) and that which forms part of the *Sando's* equipment (averaging six to eight inches).

Among the various spirits that communicate through the mediation powers of a *Sando* diviner are Twins, *Ng'àábele*. Spirits of twins could be considered a highly specialized subdivision of the ancestors (*Kùubele*, the dead ones), although living twins are also given special treatment. Belief in the supernatural properties of twins is a widespread phenomenon in West African cultures. Twins play an important role in the Creation narratives of Sudanic cultures, the Dogon apparently having the most elaborate development of the theme, and the Senufo are clearly part of the same broadly based tradition. The Senufo explain the tremendous significance of twins, as follows:

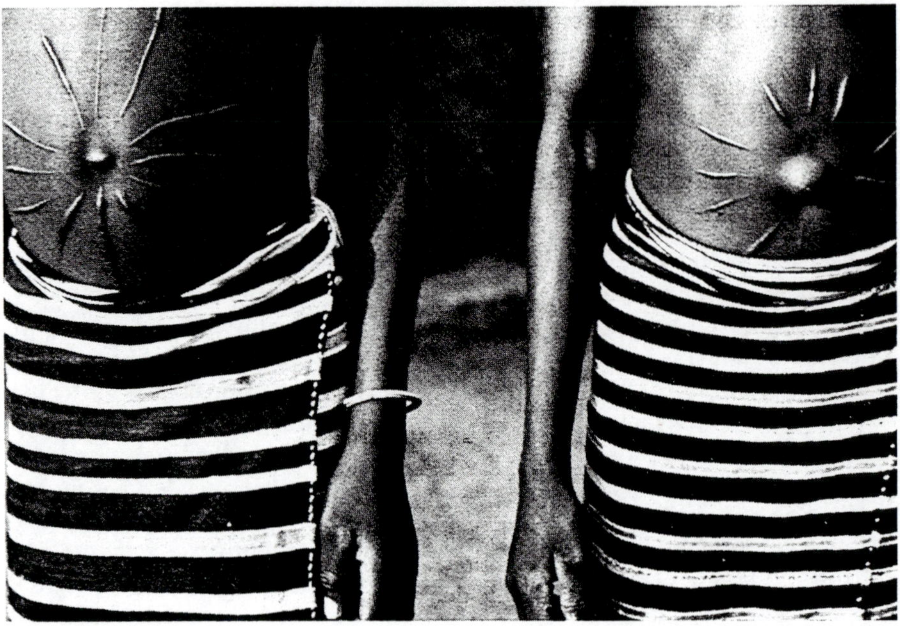

Figure 5 Two young blacksmith girls of marriageable age, showing the navel design motif. Kufuru area, 1970.

"When Kòlotyölöö created the first man and woman (they became man and wife). When the woman conceived for the first time, she gave birth to a boy and a girl who were twins. So it was that twins were the first children born to man."

The Senufo believe that twins possess a supernatural power that can be a potential force for good or bad. Thus, attitudes towards twins are ambivalent: twin spirits are considered dangerous, and yet, if properly approached, can bring about desirable results.

Given this brief segment of the Senufo Creation narrative and their concept of power as having a supernatural base, it seems reasonable to conclude that twins are thought to possess more inherent power because they have closer ties with the supernatural world than ordinary people. To be right, however, this twinness must have the sexual balance indicated in the text: the birth of two girls or two boys, or the death of one twin, is feared as a potential source of great misfortune, evil and death.

The criterion of balance as an ideal quality is also expressed in the concern for absolutely equal treatment of the twins. Jealousy on the part of one twin (living or dead) caused by unequal treatment is a constant danger to the health and life of the family bound by twin ritual. For instance, food offerings placed in the twin shrine must not be unequal in size or quality. For this reason, the Senufo have developed an elaborate set of rules of behavior toward twins and ritual precautions to be followed by the appropriate relatives, which include the wearing of cast brass rings, bracelets and amulets bearing twin motifs. The aesthetic quality

Figure 6
Insignia of Sando official, including a tiny calabash rattle and bracelets of cowrie shells and pythons.

of a brass twin bracelet, for example, goes far towards pleasing twins and warding off further malevolent acts. *Sando* diviners will blame any misfortune that befalls the family on its failure to meet the ritual requirements; thus, twin births are not welcome.

There is some evidence that the related twinship and Ancient Woman concept is succinctly articulated in the carved linear design that ornaments the female navel. By the age of puberty, every young girl has permanently drawn on her abdomen a design that is at once a synthesis of the Creation myth and a promise of her future role as wife and mother in the matrilineage (Fig. 5). Called *kû̠nööng'àádya* ("navel of mother," "woman of twins," or "female twin"), this highly abstract design is one of the two most important scarification motifs in Senufo personal art. Long familiar to students and collectors of Senufo sculpture, the basic design is a configuration of four sets of three (or four) lines grouped into fan-shaped units which radiate from the navel in a composition of two intersecting pairs or "twins" (Fig. 3). One pair has an exact parallel in the three lines that fan out from the corner of each side of the mouth, an elemental motif carved on every child, male and female ("face scars," *yegi kàbaara*, a generic description). In the non-verbal language of body decoration, the pair ornamenting the mouth proclaims, "I am a Senufo person," and perhaps, "child of the original twins." The choice of placement is in itself significant: a major aim of

Poro is to teach control of self, a quality found in the ideal Senufo man and woman; Poro sayings indicate that control of the mouth is necessary to self-control. This quality of inner control and reserve is expressed above all in the large-scale figures that commemorate the first couple (Fig. 4). When the same design units that identify one as a Senufo form part of the navel design, they are called *ng'àádya piipele tāari*, which translates roughly as "female twin, three little marks." The two pairs cross at the navel. Philosophy reduced to a few abstract lines, this design is a celebration of the Senufo woman as matrix of life, guardian of matrilineal and village continuity. Implicit in the design is the balanced interaction of two twinned parts, reminiscent of the first man and woman (or *ng'àámbele*, their children). The projecting peg-like navel, remnant of the umbilical cord, is a constant reminder of the ancestral mothers reaching back to Ancient Woman. Among Kufuru young people, a short, convex navel is a criterion of both male and female physical beauty, as is again clearly reflected in Senufo sculptural idealizations of the human form. As the navel is the nucleus of the body design, so the *Narifölö* or *Nërëjaö* (head of the matrilineage) is the center axis of family organization, and so Màlëëö, Ancient Woman, is the ideological axis of the sacred forest society and village order.

The *Tyekpa*, literally, "women's poro" ("women's secret society"), or "women's society," appears to be in effect a declaration of ritual independence on the part of Fodonon women. Unlike the Sandogo women's society, which complements and is integrated with the functions of the Poro Society in a pattern characteristic of all Senufo groups, the *Tyekpa* presents direct and striking parallels with the Fodonon men's Pondo, including such details as specific gestures and movement patterns in the funeral ritual which exactly mirror the patterns of the men's masquerade performances. For example, the parturition stance which the Pondo ancestor mask assumes over the body of an elder member and which symbolically marks the beginning of new life as spirit is also used in *Tyekpa* ritual (Fig. 1). Like the Poro society practices, the most sacred and truly powerful *Tyekpa* objects are less noticeably visible–their significance camouflaged from the understanding of non-initiates–than the more aesthetically exciting large sculptures.

The intimate relationship of sculpture and dance in African art is generally associated exclusively with the category of masks, yet this is by no means always the case. The *Tyekpa* funeral ritual is a marvelous example of figure sculpture being given a mysterious vitality in a multi-media theater of music, dance and poetry. Raised above the heads of the *Tyekpa* members, the sculptures progress in a dignified manner with large and measured movements, their restrained energy expressed at intervals in counterpoint motions of quick, vital twists. The dance is centered around a long, elegantly carved three-legged drum, played by women musicians whose artistry rivals that of the men.

The following narratives relate the origin of the Fodonon men's Poro (Pondo or Kpa-) and women's Poro (*Tyekpa*). "Poro" as used in the two narratives below refers not only to the secret society organization as a whole but especially to its sacred paraphernalia such as drums, figure sculpture, and masquerades, a usage that is common practice in Senufo conversational idiom.

THE ORIGIN OF PONDO

In the beginning, Pondo was with the women. If you hear *màlëëö* or *kàtyelëëö* (the Ancient Woman), this is to remind us that the first Poro belonged to the women and was not with the men.

The men prepared food and pounded yam. When the men finished preparing the meals of pounded yam, the women would come out of the sacred forest of Poro to take the food. But the men were forbidden to see (the secret things of) Poro. If the women came out (dressed in Poro), the men had to hide, leaving the dishes of food outside the house.

Then the Creator God *(Kòlotyölöö)* said, "No, I cannot leave Poro with the women—they are too wicked and sinful." So he seized the Poro and gave it to the men. The men were too tired and thin. They had to hide while the women ate.

THE ORIGIN OF TYEKPA

The first person to do Poro in (Senufo) country was an elder woman who went to the stream to look for *kobi* (used to make a strong soap). When the woman entered the woods by the stream, she saw some *madenyûdö* (chief of the *madebele*, a hairy-headed bush spirit). The bush spirits were drumming a *Tyekpa* dance. She stopped and looked: "This thing is too beautiful!" So the bush spirits asked, "What are you doing here? You must take Poro and go with it; that is what you want—we are tired of it."

When they let the woman return to the village, the *madebele* told her, "You must go have carved spirit figures in wood and you must also make Poro as you saw us do."

When the old woman came to the village, she fell sick. Her family went to see a *Sande*. They consulted with the Sandogo. The diviners found that the kind of thing she had seen among the *madebele*, this same thing she should do. So then the women had made some "little children of Poro" (i.e. figure carvings) and they had them carved of wood. So they did all that the old woman had seen among the *madebele*. That was the beginning of *Tyekpa*.

A first point to be noted is the textual reference to the aesthetic enjoyment associated with things of Poro. The woman looked at the bush spirits' Poro and found it "too beautiful!" Also of interest is the suggested source of creative beauty—the bush spirits, creatures of the supernatural world. Senufo sculptors and graphic artists say that the bush spirits inspire them in dreams.

However, the major theme that emerges clearly in the narrative is one of tension between male and female roles, a conflict requiring supernatural intervention. As expressed in the creation theme of the primordial couple and the twins, issue of the first procreation, the Senufo philosophic ideal is a balance between male and female. This balance is a precarious one, however, and the text relating the origin of Pondo reveals that the real situation can become distorted through human weakness and abuses of power. So it came about that in ancient times Senufo women lost certain privileges and aesthetic pleasures of Poro because of their "wickedness" (*fu̱behefölö*: "Owner" of breaking a sacred restriction; ugliness; blindness). The myth teaches that power may be used for good or evil, a constant theme in Senufo oral literature. Persons who break the laws of Ancient Mother and the Ancestors, and those who appropriate supernatural power for anti-social purposes, the witches, are an ever-present threat to the equilibrium of self, family, the village. The dynamic interaction of female and male leadership in both Poro and Sandogo engages the Senufo in what is ultimately the most important level of interaction, that of man and spirit. In the context of these two institutions, aesthetic form and performance become part of the vital process whereby conflicts and tensions which threaten equilibrium are harmonized and resolved.

15

Masking in Mende Sande Society Initiation Rituals

Ruth B. Phillips

Public masquerades constitute extremely important symbolic forms among the Mende of Sierra Leone. Masquerades are a means of mediating between the secret Societies which dominate Mende social life and the general community. Through masking performances the public is kept informed of important events which occur in the secret domain and is allowed carefully limited participation in the experience of Society members. The masquerades make visible the powerful "medicines" (*haleisia*) of the secret Societies without revealing their essential mystery. Maskers personify and dramatize the powers of the "medicines" and exact respect and tribute from the spectators. At the same time, participants and audience are drawn into a common experience, which is aesthetically heightened by techniques of theatre, dance, music, and the plastic arts. The resultant feeling of unity and harmony helps to overcome the threat of disunity implicit in the division of the community into separate secret factions.

The masquerade of the women's Society, the Sande, is of special ritual and artistic interest (Figure 1). The Sande masker, the *sowei* (pl. *Soweisia*, commonly referred to by the Sherbro term, *bundu*) is the most artistically elaborated of the Mende mask types. It is also the only documented mask in Africa worn by women. Although the cultural role and general features of the Sande Society have been described, precise information about the ritual context of its public masking performances has not yet been made available.[1] An examination of the ritual context of Sande masking provides essential background for the understanding of the *sowei* mask as an art form and illustrates the role of masquerades in Mende life.

Reprinted in abridged form from *Africa*, Vol. 48(3):265-276, 1978 with permission of the author and publisher.

Figure 1 Sowei masker with attendants. Njahindama village, Kakua Chiefdom Bo district.

The Sande Society is one of a number of associations which regulate conduct and perform special services in Mende life and whose activities are kept secret from non-members. Sande, one of the most important, is a women's Society entrusted with the education of young girls. Traditionally this included all the ritual knowledge and many of the practical skills women needed throughout life and paralleled the training given to young men by the Poro Society. Proper attitudes towards their future husbands, sexual behavior, childbearing, and rearing were all expounded to young girls during Sande initiation. For non-urban Mende, membership in the Society remains an essential precondition to marriage and acceptance as a responsible adult woman.[2] At puberty, or in past years sometimes earlier, girls are taken from their families to the Society enclosure or "bush," built especially for each new session just outside the village. There, segregated from the rest of the village, they are instructed by officials of the Society, and traditionally circumcision—excision of the clitoris—is performed. Formerly the girls remained initiates for several years, interrupting formal Sande sessions with periods of normal activity amongst their families. During the whole period, however, sexual relations were forbidden and severe penalties were exacted from those who broke this rule. Initiates were instructed to avoid men they encountered outside the village by passing quickly by without speech or contact. Thus one important function of Sande was to protect the virginity of girls until the completion of their training as responsible adults, and the close of the initiation period was traditionally followed by marriage. Now the initiation period is usually shortened to a period of months or even weeks, often timed so that the major ceremonies take place during school vacations.

After the initial period of seclusion following clitoridectomy is over, Sande initiates return to the village during the day to perform chores for their families and for the Sande leaders. As in Poro initiation the girls have been given new names by which they are addressed for the rest of their lives. On request groups of initiates may come out from time to time to perform the special dances they have been taught in the bush. In the past this was one of the finest entertainments a chief could provide for important visitors. Instruction in singing is also an important part of Sande training and provides women with a repertoire of songs which are used on special occasions throughout their lives. Professor Little also points out that Sande training, which includes the performance of many chores for the older women, is designed to inculcate values of modesty, diligence, and respect for one's seniors.

The importance of Sande membership does not stop with the instruction of the young. Membership in both Sande and Poro continues to be a strong bond among adults, enabling these Societies to act as central institutions exerting considerable economic and political power in Mende life. Little has stressed the parallel ritual functions of Poro and Sande. These are indeed striking, yet the structural implications of initiation into the two Societies cannot coincide exactly because the position of women in a predominantly patrilineal and virilocal society is fundamentally different from that of men. Girls are initiated into the Sande Society in the town of their birth and early childhood, although they may later leave to marry men from other villages. Furthermore, girls are usually entrusted to a Sande group attached to the patrilineal lineage group. The strong bonds which are formed with other initiates and the older women who have been their preceptresses thus reinforce loyalty to the descent group and to the childhood community. These bonds offset the ties which are formed through marriage and increase, in a sense, the options available to a woman. Throughout her life a woman remains a member of the Sande group into which she was initiated. Those who marry out of the village may return to it in old age as respected elders of the Society.

The higher offices of the Sande Society are titles inherited through the patrilineal descent groups, preferably from mother to eldest daughter or younger sister. Since the normal Mende custom of marrying out of the descent group would thus result in control over Sande leaving the family, descent groups controlling the Society discard the usual prohibition against marriage between paternal first cousins in order to retain possession of Sande titles and medicines. When necessary the family may also appoint a woman who is related by marriage rather than blood to high Sande rank, or they may recall a blood relative who has married out and gone to another town. Each Sande group is led by one or more Soweisia who have custody of the *sande* "medicine" and the *sowei* masks. Though a woman of lesser rank may own a *sowei* mask, it must be kept for her by the Society head in a special enclosure called the *kunde* together with the *sande* "medicine" and other masks. In a large town there are usually several Sande groups which will join forces to initiate new members, although each girl is attached to a particular group and pays fees to its officials. One amongst the Soweisia in a town will be chosen as the supreme head and has the title of Sande Wa Jowei (big Sande Sowei) or Sowo Kindei (keeper of the *kunde*). She is assisted by the Nyande Jowei (the beautiful Sowei) who can act for her and by one or more Ndogbo Jowei (bush Sowei), responsible for "begging" the bush from the chief for Sande sessions. Other administrative and financial duties, such as collecting fees from the initiates' families and preparing food and water for them, are carried out by the Ligbɛisia, (sing. Ligba), the next rank of Sande officials. These are in turn subdivided into Ligba Wa (big Ligba) and Ligba Wulo (small Ligba). To dance with the *sowei* mask or to act as its attendant, a woman must be of Ligba rank. The ordinary members of the Society are known as *sande nyahei* (Sande wife), the initiates as *gbomogboi*, and non-members as *kpowa*.

Mende terminology provides useful clues to the identity of the Sande masker. The Mende do not have a separate word for "mask" itself, for to distinguish the costume from the human being who wears it, or the headpiece from the rest of the costume, would contradict the notion that a masked figure is an *ngafa*, a spirit. The Mende recognize different types of *ngafa*. There is the *ngafa* in each person which survives after death and goes to join the ancestral spirits. There are spirits which live in the bush and in rivers and which can appear to human beings in different guises. These spirits must be treated with great cleverness lest their trickery bring disaster, but they can also be made to bestow riches and knowledge on their human correspondents. A third category of spirits, those connected with the secret Societies, reveal to the leaders of the Societies through dreams the locations and uses of special herbs or other substances imbued with supernatural power. Each chapter of a secret Society must possess such "medicine" or *hale*, which legitimizes its activities and gives it power. The Society as a whole is known by the name of its *hale*: thus the *hale* of the Sande Society is *sande*, of the Njayei Society, *njayei*, and so on. The *sande* is collected in rivers where the Society *ngafa* is found, and a woman who dreams of *sande* or of the *ngafa* must be initiated as a Society official if she does not already hold office.

The Sande masker, as we have seen, bears the same title as the highest rank in the Society, Sowei. This title gives an extra dimension to the masker's identity. Like the other secret society masquerades, she is both *hale* and *ngafa*, a personification of the Society medicine and an embodiment of its particular spirit. But unlike the other Mende masquerades the Sande masker is also given the same title as the human leaders of the Society. This title can be translated as "expert," indicating that she is expert in the secret knowledge and wisdom of Sande. To distinguish the *sowei* masker from the other Soweisia and also to characterize her particular role in the Society the masker is usually referred to as *ndoli jowei*, the dancing Sowei. The choice of this term is significant, for dancing is a key part of the masquerade. Thus, though the Mende say that it is theoretically possible to hold Sande initiation without a *sowei* masker, since the possession of *sande* is the only essential for the efficacy of the session, in practice it is felt that the masking performance adds so much to the ceremonies that the rare village Society which has no *sowei* masker of its own will go to great lengths to borrow one or more from neighboring villages. Dancing, if not essential in ritual terms, is necessary to provide the festive mood appropriate to the completion of the several stages of initiation, and it is *ndoli jowei* who provides the focus for the celebration. Without dancing, in the words of one Mende man, "the town will not be lively," for dancing "demonstrates its well-being."

During Sande initiation *ndoli jowei* is seen in public at three key moments in the initiation period. Her appearances serve to announce to the families of the initiates and to the public that certain stages of initiation have been successfully accomplished and that preparations and donations of food and money must be made by the village. The first of these appearances occurs two or three days after the girls have been taken to the bush and circumcised and is known as *yaya gbɛ gbi* or simply *yaya* (they hunt *yaya*). The *ndoli jowei* comes into town with a group of Sande women while the new initiates remain secluded in the bush. This is a time of danger, for the initiates are still recovering from circumcision and the families of the girls have not previously had news of them. The women "come out to tell men they've initiated people into Sande," it is explained, and "they rush around the town waving leaves and taking food and things they need which don't belong to them." The *ndoli jowei* does not dance on this occasion, as it is not yet time for celebration, but her presence is a visible reminder of the powerful medicine which has been invoked by the Sande session and which legitimizes the lawless behavior of the women on this occasion.

In some villages of the central (Sewa) Mende the *ndoli jowei* also comes out at a minor feast which occurs a week or so later called *kpɛtɛ gbula yombo le* (to make the mud of the swamp mushy) or *sowo mba yili gbi* (the cooking of the Sowei's rice). On this occasion the Soweisia collect supplies for a special dish to be eaten by them and by the girls in the bush. In most towns where the *ndoli jowei* appears at this time she does not dance, and the occasion may be used to announce the date for the imminent *gani* celebration.

One evening, about two weeks after *yaya, ndoli jowei* comes out again. The Soweisia announce that the new initiates will be brought to town for the first time the next day, and to celebrate the event *ndoli jowei* dances through the night (Figure 2). Contributions of rice, oil, fish, and money are collected from the initiates' families and the Soweisia prepare *gani*, a special dish containing "medicinal" herbs which they take into the Sande bush for the initiates. Portions are also distributed to the girls' relatives, as it is held to be beneficial to partake of the food. After eating the *gani* the initiates come into town wearing headcloths tied in a special way around their waists and a necklace (*gbali*) on which is strung an animal horn or bell, cowrie shells, and a leopard's tooth, the ancient symbol of the well-born. White clay (*wuji*) is rubbed on their faces and they wear ropes of beads around their waists. The girls dress in this way until the end of the initiation period as a visible reminder of their special status–and a warning to men to keep their distance. The reappearance of the initiates in town is known either as *gani* or as *ndahiti* (they are ready). "They come to deliver greetings to their families," one informant explained, and from this time on they spend their days in the village and return to the Sande bush to sleep at night. Despite the

Figure 2 *Ndoli Jowei* dancing, Gofor village, Makpele Chiefdom, Pujehun District.

joyous atmosphere of the *gani* celebration, the demeanor of the initiates is solemn and they are led forth in an orderly row under the supervision of the Soweis. *Ndoli jowei* accompanies them and dances are performed both by the maskers and the initiates.

The final release of the girls from the initiation session is known as *ti sande gbua* (they pull *sande*) which, these days, usually occurs one or two months after *gani*. The night before the "pulling" begins the Soweisia cut branches of leaves (*ta tifei lo gbia*) and the initiates are collected from the houses of their families and brought together in a special round enclosure built near the house of the Sande Wa Jowei called the *gumi*. The girls are dressed all in white—white clay is rubbed on their upper torsos and faces and they wear white wrappers and headties. The Soweisia, too, wear white headties on this as on other ritual occasions the significance of which is explained as "unity." The initiates remain in the *gumi* for three days, while final preparations are made for their release, and each night there is dancing by the *ndoli joweisia* known as the *ja wa* (big *ja*, or Sande dance). New clothes and finery are collected for the initiates during this time and the final payments are made to the Society. When arrangements have been completed the Sowei march around the village carrying the *kunde*, the *sande* medicine contained in a rectangular box draped in white cloth. This is one of the rare occasions on which the *kunde* is seen in public. The *ndoli jowei* is not present since the *sande* and the masker do not appear together as their combined powers would be too powerful to control. On the following morning the initiates are led by the *ndoli jowei* to be ritually washed at the river, dwelling place of the Sande *ngafa*. The special protection extended to them by the *sande* is removed or "pulled" and they are released from the prohibitions of the period of initiation. The white clay is washed from their faces and, according to traditional practice, their skin is rubbed with oil to make it gleam attractively. They are dressed in the finest clothes their parents are able to buy or borrow and, in the past, they were decked with heavy silver jewelry. Today European clothes and make-up are often worn and umbrellas may replace the traditional canopy of country cloths under which the new Sande members are escorted to the town (Figure 3).

During the washing ceremony the *ndoli jowei* again disappears because she may not be present together with the Sande *ngafa* who is being invoked at the riverside. The masker comes back, however, to lead the procession of richly dressed initiates, Sande officials dressed in white robes and headties, and older women carrying branches of leaves back to the town meeting place, the *bari*. There the Sande graduates are seated in state and are feasted and made much

Figure 3 Sande girls dressed in traditional style at the "Pulling" celebrations completing their initiation. Kenema Gbangbma village, Fakunya Chiefdom, Moyamba District.

of for several days. At the close of the celebration they either go to their appointed bridegrooms or, these days, return to school. *Ndoli jowei*, having presented the girls to their parents, disappears until the next Sande session. "She will almost cry," it is said, "at being dismissed from her post, and appears angry as she goes away."

The *gani* and *ti sande gbua* ceremonies are the highpoints of Sande initiation and they are conducted in much the same way all over Mendeland. There is considerable variation, however, in the occasions on which *ndoli jowei* appears between the start of the initiation session and the initiates' first appearance in town. In Kailahun District among the eastern Mende, *ndoli jowei* parades around town on the day the girls first enter the Sande bush, but the *yaya* rite is not observed. The ceremony is called *sande wa gbii* (they all go to Sande) or *kpowa gowi* (non-initiate path). The attendants of *ndoli jowei* announce what has taken place but there is no dancing. In the Gola/Mende area, the *ndoli jowei* comes out on the evening before the start of initiation to celebrate the "buying of the bush" (*ndogbo wu ma wo le*) and a small dance is held. Instead of the *yaya* or *kpɛtɛ gbula yombo le* appearances of the Sewa Mende, here the *ndoli jowei* comes out again seven days after initiation to announce that the girls are "under the water" and demands contributions of money for the buying of fire and rice. There is no dance for, as at *yaya*, the time has not yet come to celebrate. This occasion is known as *ngombu yeya le* (buying the fire). In the Vai/Mende area the first appearance of *ndoli jowei* occurs about two weeks after the start of initiation to celebrate the completion of the first stage of initiation and to beg food from the initiates' families. This is known in Vai as *bo maɛ* (we have done it) and the Mende translation is given as *kpɛtɛ gbula yombo lɛ*, although the event is observed differently in the Vai/Mende area than among the Sewa Mende since a small dance is held.

Ndoli jowei is often referred to as the "tutelary spirit" of the Sande Society since her public appearances occur primarily during Sande initiation and because, as we have said, she bears the title of a Society leader. During Sande initiation her appearances tell the community that specific stages of initiation have been successfully completed, and they act as the focus for public celebration. *Ndoli jowei* also appears, however, on certain other occasions when her presence is a means of impressing on the community the unity and strength of the female corporate body. Thus the Sande Society expresses its respect for the chieftaincy by causing *ndoli jowei* to dance with the other masked *haleisia* at the crowning of a Paramount Chief or the funeral of a prominent man. She may also dance if another chief or high government official visits the town. That the participation of *ndoli jowei* on such occasions has specifically political significance is made evident by the fact that on purely festive occasions, such as Christmas and the end of Ramadan, when many masked *haleisia* come out to dance, *ndoli jowei* does not appear.

In past years *ndoli jowei* also came out to bring to justice an offender against Sande laws, such as a man who has spied on the Sande bush or had sexual relations with an initiate. In such cases the offender is pointed out by the Sande masker and led to the chief, who imposes the punishment demanded by the Society.

Depending on the offense this might involve initiation into the Society at great expense or a substantial fine and ritual "washing."

The Sande masker must also come out if a Sowei or an important Ligba dies. On such an occasion it is the *ndoli jowei* rather than members of the family who "pulls the cry" for the deceased, walking around the house of the dead woman with her attendant Ligbɛisia in attitudes of mourning and announcing the death. Since men may not see the body of a dead Sowei they first prepare the grave and then retire, allowing the Sande women to conduct the burial. The *ndoli jowei*, hands on her head, leads the procession to the grave. If a three or seven-day ceremony is held for the dead woman, the *ndoli jowei* will again appear and dance.

Lastly, a small dance may be held when a new *sowei* mask is "initiated" into the Society, for, since the *ndoli jowei* is a leader of the Sande group, she too must undergo the ceremonies a woman would go through. Masks are frequently acquired by women who at first lack the status and money to have them initiated. Such a mask is known as *kpowa jowei* (uninitiated mask) and although it may be danced with at Sande celebrations it lacks the supernatural power of a true *sowei* mask. The ceremony of initiation may be held at any time and is called *ti kpia ngiti ya* (they bring it outside). The other *ndoli joweisia* in the town bring the new masker outside and present her after the owners of the new mask have paid a fee of money, rice, oil, fish, and a goat to the owners of the old masks. A gun is shot off and the new *ndoli jowei* is taken to call on the chief and important men of the town. Feasting and dancing follow.

The dancing performances of the *ndoli jowei* follow the same general pattern as the other secret Society masquerades. The *ndoli jowei* emerges from the Society enclosure or from a house, depending on the occasion, and she is accompanied by a Ligba who carries a straw mat which is draped over the masker's lap when she is seated and which may also be used to screen her if she wishes to rearrange her costume. Her attendant calls out the masker's personal name in a short wailing chant to introduce her to the crowd and warn of her presence as they approach. The *ndoli jowei* wears, in addition to the black helmet mask, one or more capes of blackened palm fiber around her neck and waist and under this a shirt, pair of trousers, and shoes which cover the masker's skin completely. Traditionally these clothes should be black as well, but today garments of other dark colors are occasionally worn and tennis shoes are not uncommon. She carries a switch in one hand with which she gestures, and bells are tied to her costume which jingle when she moves. The costume, like those of other maskers, includes various traditional herbal charms encased in *fritambo* or sheep's horns, as well as Moslem amulets folded into leather or cloth packets. These are intended to increase the masker's powers and afford protection from witchcraft.

A group of Sande women accompanies the dancing, singing and rhythmically shaking *segbura* (gourds filled with seeds encased in a netting sewn with more seeds), and they are joined by men beating the *sangbei* and slit *kili* drums. If there are a number of *ndoli joweisia* each dances in turn for short periods of time. The dancer faces the drummers and does not move far in the course of the dance. The Mende characterize the dancing of *ndoli jowei* as "tight" and "awkward" (*kamo loongo*), and value the quickness and intricacy of the footwork. The dancer moves her feet in a rapid series of steps capable of much individual variation. The raffia capes flare out and swirl in wide circles with the dipping and turning of the dancer. As at other dancing performances the audience forms a wide circle around the dancer and shows its appreciation at the end of each performance by means of gifts of money. There is humor, too as *ndoli jowei* assumes playful, spirited, or restless attitudes which her attendants must control, often by presenting her with more money.

The use of dramatic mime is an important part of the *ndoli jowei's* performance and her behavior, as we have seen, varies according to the occasion which calls her forth. At *yaya* while the new initiates are still in a precarious state, her wild rush around the town with the Sande women demonstrates the power which has been released by the opening of the Sande session and the care with which it must be controlled. At the death of a Sowei her behavior dramatizes the grief of the Society. On occasions of rejoicing, such as *gani*, "pulling," the crowning of a Paramount Chief, or the visit of an important personage, *ndoli jowei* dances because dancing creates an atmosphere of infectious happiness and harmony. As one man expressed it "dancing is what [we] do to forget about death." And the dancing of the Society masker is felt to be both the spark necessary to set off general rejoicing and also the highlight of the celebration.

In addition to the *ndoli jowei* there are two other minor women's masquerades which add greatly to the texture and enjoyment of Sande entertainments. These are the *gonde* masker described as *ngengema jowei*, the "funny Sowei," and the satirical masker *samawa*. They often appear on the periphery of the performances of *ndoli jowei*; and the humor of *gonde* in particular is heightened by her juxtaposition with the object of her parody. Like the male *gongoli*, *gonde* is not a real *hale* but a clown-like figure which overturns all the conventions and decorum proper to *ndoli jowei* (Figures 4, 5). Her costume is a pastiche of rags and tatters, and she is hung about with all sorts of junk—rusty old tin cans, shells, and other discarded fragments. Like *gongoli* too, she represents the anti-aesthetic, purposely reversing the normal criteria of beauty. Because *ndoli jowei* is always in black, *gonde* wears any color; because the *ndoli jowei's* headpiece is always beautifully blackened, polished and intact, and surrounded by a full raffia cape, *gonde's* mask is weathered, broken, daubed with paint, and possessed of only the wispiest raffia. The headpiece of the *gonde* is, in fact, often an old *sowei* mask discarded because of insect damage or breakage. When the headpiece is carved specifically to be *gonde* the workmanship is crude and the features made to look grotesque. Most upsetting of all to the approved behavior of a masked *hale*, *gonde's* face and body are often left half-uncovered by her disarray. One song about *gonde* goes, "*gonde* is shameless, she's not ashamed to show her face," and she may actually push her mask up a she dances to reveal even more of her head. *Gonde* is also shameless in going right up to people and asking for money despite her utter unworthiness, rather than waiting in a dignified manner for people to present whatever gifts they might want to give her. This angers *ndoli jowei* (who, people explain, wants all the money for herself) and, to the amusement of the crowd she will try to chase the *gonde* away.

Figure 4 An obstreperous Gondei masker is pushed back by Sande Society officials. Ngiyehun Village, Luawa Chiefdom, Kailahun District.

The *samawa* masquerade makes use not only of parody but of satire, and the masker's costume changes depending on her object. *Samawa* wears no headpiece but face paint, exaggerated clothing and the appropriate appended objects. In one version the *samawa's* face was painted with black and white spots to represent leprosy, a strip of fur was tied around her chin as a beard, and she was dressed in dirty rags. A big bulge under the front of her costume represented a swelling of the scrotum, and she hobbled about leaning on a stick like a cripple. All these deformities, she sang, would afflict any man who disobeys Sande rules, and she interrupted her song with bursts of loud raucous laughter. Another interpretation of *samawa* in a nearby village satirized Moslem "learned men." She scribbled away with a crab's claw and "divined" people's fortunes with a collection of old shells and pieces of broken toys. In her kit she carried many pairs of spectacles for her "reading" which she constantly put on and off, and she wore a necklace of bones which she kissed and touched to her forehead in imitation of Moslem prayer beads. She also had a collection of horns and bones slung over her back to "dance with," satirizing the *wudi* worn by the male *falui* and *goboi* maskers. She wore mismatched shoes and an old battered straw hat, which she proclaimed were her "badges of office" in the Poro Society. Although the *samawa* masquerade is not nearly so widespread as *gonde* (which is found in nearly every village that has sowei masks), it is probably quite old and may have been borrowed from neighboring peoples.

Gonde and *samawa* are, in different ways, good examples of Turner's dictum that: "Cognitively, nothing underlines regularity so well as absurdity or paradox.

Figure 5 Gondei masker and crowd at Mende Kelema village, Luawa Chiefdom, Kailahun District

Emotionally nothing satisfies as much as extravagant or temporarily permitted illicit behavior" (1969: 176). *Gonde*, through her absurdity, serves not only to reinforce the dignity and transcendent power of *ndoli jowei*. *Samawa* in her graphic representation of the ills which befall offenders against Sande demonstrates the helplessness of men before the power of *sande*, and her open satire is itself made possible by the position of power she occupies as a member of Sande. The weakness of men, normally more powerful than women, is thus shown up in a temporary assumption of supremacy by women during Sande Society masquerades. Issues fundamental to the very survival of the group are at stake, for the Mende believe that male impotence results from transgressions against Sande, just as female barrenness is caused by the breaking of Poro laws. In laughing at these "comic" maskers, then, one is also laughing at the folly of ignoring the principles of right conduct. Thus, through comic and serious masquerades the Sande Society provides the public with periodic reminders of its teachings and powers. And equally important, its masking performances afford occasions for community-wide celebrations of the successful application of these powers and teachings as each new group of young women enters into Sande.

NOTES

1. Kenneth Little's publications on Mende ethnography are fundamental to this study and, indeed, to all work on the Mende. For this reason I have not felt it necessary to provide detailed citations. For the Sande Society his account is less satisfactory than for the Poro and this is where the present study, it is hoped, can make a contribution.
2. My findings contradict Richards' statement that membership in Sande has become less important in recent years (1974: 279). In fact, the sporadic challenge of reformist and iconoclastic Islamic groups in this century has been met by the formation of Mori Jande, or Moslem Sande chapters. Although modified by the loss of masking traditions and other pagan features these reformed Sande groups thrive, often side by side with traditional Sande chapters.

REFERENCES

Alldridge, T.J. 1901. *The Sherbro and Its Hinterland*, London: Macmillan.

——. 1910. *A Transformed Colony*, London: Seeley.

Caine, Augustus Feweh. 1959. *A Study and Comparison of the West African Bush School and the Southern Sotho Circumcision School*, Northwestern University, M.A. Thesis.

D'Azevedo, Warren. 1973. "Mask Makers and Myth in Western Liberia," in *Primitive Art and Society*, ed. Anthony Forge, London: Oxford University Press.

Hoffer, Carol P. 1972. "Mende and Sherbro Women in High Office," *Canadian Journal of African Studies*, vol. 6(2), pp.151-164.

Little, Kenneth. 1949. "The Role of the secret society in cultural specialization," *American Anthropologist*, vol. 51, pp.199-212.

——. 1951. *The Mende of Sierra Leone*, London: Routledge and Kegan Paul.

Richards, J.V.O. 1974. "The Sande: a Socio-cultural Organization in the Mende Community in Sierra Leone." *Baessler-Archiv*, vol. 22(2), pp.265-281.

Turner, Victor. 1969. *The Ritual Process, Structure and Anti-Structure*. London.

16

On Representing Ancestral Beings

Howard Morphy

INTRODUCTION

The Yolngu are an Aboriginal people who live in eastern Arnhem Land, a coastal region of northern Australia. Until the 1940s the Yolngu were hunters and gatherers leading a semi-nomadic life in a rich natural environment. More recently, as a consequence of European colonization, Yolngu life has been in many respects transformed, with people spending much of the year in larger settlements that are, to a considerable extent, integrated within the political and economic life of the wider Australian society. However, the Yolngu still retain considerable cultural and political autonomy, and many Yolngu continue to practice a predominantly hunter-gatherer way of life. Indeed, in the past decade, with the increasing return of people to their traditional lands to live in small "outstation" communities and the granting of land rights under Australian law, a new impetus has been given to the maintenance and development of a distinctively Yolngu way of life. To the outsider, nowhere do continuities with the past seem stronger than in the case of the rich and varied artistic life of contemporary Yolngu.

From the Yolngu perspective, art mediates between the Ancestral Past, or Dreaming, when the form of the land was created by the actions of mythical Ancestral Beings, and the present. Art is an extension of the Ancestral Past into the present and one of the main ways in which ideas or information about the Ancestral Past is transmitted from one human generation to the next. The Ancestral Past is never directly experienced, in that no human beings living today were present when the Ancestral events took place. Rather, an understanding of

Reprinted in abridged form from *Animals into Art* edited by Howard Morphy, London: Unwin Hyman, 1989, pages 144-160 with permission of the author and publisher.

the Ancestral Past is developed through representations and encodings in art and ceremony. Such understandings may be converted by the imagination into feelings of participation in the Ancestral Past, when stimulated by certain events or induced by periods of reflection. In this chapter, however, I am not so much concerned with these inner states as with the nature of the information transmitted, with the ways in which Ancestral Beings are represented in the art and the kinds of images and understanding of the Ancestral Past that it is possible for the individual to develop.

SOME GENERAL CHARACTERISTICS OF ANCESTRAL BEINGS

Before considering the ways in which Ancestral Beings are encoded in paintings, it will be helpful to consider some general characteristics of Ancestral Beings and the Ancestral Past to see the kind of characteristics and properties that might be portrayed in the art.

The Ancestral Past (*wangarr*) is a complex concept precisely because it is both cut off from the present yet at the same time interpenetrates it. The Ancestral Past existed before human beings, yet extends into the present. Some myths refer to a time before human beings existed, when Ancestral Beings journeyed across the Earth and through their actions created the form of the landscape. They dug in the ground and wells were formed, they stuck their digging sticks in the ground and trees grew up, they bled and great deposits of red ochre were formed. Some Ancestral Beings were able to transform themselves as well, from human to animal form, from animate to inanimate object, and back again. Some Ancestral Beings had forms that were not unlike creatures living today, though differing in their scale and capacities. They had the form of animals such as crocodiles and sharks, albeit crocodiles and sharks that could talk, travel underground, and transform parts of their bodies into features of the landscape. Other Ancestral Beings had forms that, though connected to existing objects, seem at first to be further removed from everyday reality. They may be said to be inanimate objects such as rocks or mangrove trees, but as rocks they could move, talk, think, and behave just like an animate being. Indeed, in some cases it is hard to conceive of the Ancestral Beings having any comprehensible unitary form, because either we consider it intrinsically a part of something else, as in the case of the Cough Ancestor, or we consider it to be a complex phenomenon of many parts rather than a unitary being, as in the case of the Flood Ancestor. In short, almost anything can be the focal form for a Yolngu Ancestral Being. The image of an Ancestral Being is constructed out of properties of the object, animal, or abstract concept concerned, though not absolutely constrained by it.

At all times, Ancestral Beings interacted with things that are today part of the real world: they caught fish or hunted wallaby, lit fires, and threw spears. While creating the real world, they were at the same time part of it. Later on in the creative period Ancestral Beings interacted with human beings; they gave birth to them, gave them language, and instituted correct social and religious practices for them to follow. The subsequent occupation of the land by human groups was conditional on them performing the ceremonies and passing on the sacred law that commemorated the Ancestral creativity. The Ancestral Beings who interacted most with the founding human ancestors of the respective clans tended to be the most human in form and characteristics. They are often presented as intermediaries between human beings and those Ancestral Beings with more fantastic and imaginary attributes. However, although it is tempting to divide the Ancestral past in to temporal zones, it would be misleading, since the events seldom follow sequentially as in ordinary time, and often seem out of phase with one another. Indeed, from a certain perspective Ancestral events have not really ended. They continue to be created again anew through the performance of ceremonies. The Ancestral Beings continue to intervene in everyday life through the process of spirit conception and through the transference of spiritual power from one generation to the next, and in many respects the Ancestral Past is better conceived as a dimension of the present, rather than as a period distant in time (see Morphy 1984, Ch. 2).

SYSTEMS OF REPRESENTATION

Yolngu art employs two very different systems of representation or ways of encoding meaning, and the majority of paintings involve a combination of both systems. One system is iconic and figurative, the other system is non-iconic and geometric. The iconic system represents objects by producing an image that is intended to look like the object concerned, while the non-iconic system operates in a more abstract way by encoding meanings in particular combinations of geometric motifs. The questions thus arise as to whether we can see the possible form of Ancestral Beings in figurative representations, and in what ways, if any, the geometric art functions to build up or create images of Ancestral Beings. Do the Yolngu use the figurative system to portray the Ancestor in the act of transformation, and, if not, in what ways are the transformational properties of Ancestral Beings encoded in paintings?

PAINTINGS AS SELF-REPRESENTATIONS

Before trying to answer these questions, it must be noted that paintings are not simply representations of Ancestral Beings, but are themselves creations of, and manifestations of, the Ancestral Past. Paintings are said by Yolngu to be Ancestral in origin and simply handed on from one generation to the next, though we shall see that exactly what this means is somewhat problematical.

The Yolngu paintings that I am primarily concerned with are ones that can be referred to as *mardayin miny'tji* or "sacred paintings." Paintings of this category form the majority of paintings that Yolngu produce, though paint is used with purely decorative intent on everyday material culture objects, and today some paintings which are not derived from the "sacred" category are produced for sale. Indeed, I later refer to one of the latter types of painting, that is paintings which, although not "sacred paintings," represent mythical events that are traditionally presented in the form of "camp stories" or moral fables.

Mardayin miny'tji are Ancestral (*mardayin, wangarr*) in two senses: first, they are designs which were created by Ancestral actions and handed on to the ancestors of the human social groups who today own them; and, secondly, they encode meanings about the Ancestral past, about the "Dreamtime" events and the resulting creation of the landscape. The same component of a painting may perform both functions. For example, one design element in Gumatj clan paintings is a pattern of linked diamonds. According to myth, the design originated when it was burnt into an Ancestral clap stick as a bush fire passed through a ceremonial ground. The design was then reproduced on the chests of the Ancestral Beings as they subsequently danced on the ground. The design thus originated in Ancestral times and when it is produced today reproduces the Ancestral events–it is a form from the Ancestral Past that is continually recreated. Yet the design is at the same time a sign of the event, and refers to the fire and the origin of the design. Particular details of the design can encode more specific meanings, especially when it is produced in an elaborated form. The diamonds may be infilled in different colours (in red, white, yellow, and black) and these in turn may refer to different aspects of the fire (to flames, ash, smoke, and burnt wood). The diamond design is likely to be only one component of a *mardayin miny'tji*, and other components will encode or refer to other details of the same mythic event. The same fire that burnt the clap stick was spread by a quail who flew with burning sticks in its beak, and elsewhere the fire forced a bandicoot to hide in a hollow log while the flames swept by. The episodes may be represented either by a figurative representation of the quail or bandicoot, or by a geometric element that, in the context of the particular painting, encodes an associated meaning. The bandicoot in the hollow log may, for example, be represented by a rectangular figure with a diamond pattern on it. It is not just the diamond pattern that is said by Yolngu to be an Ancestral form, but the whole painting, including figurative representations or signs that elaborate on its meaning. The whole painting will be said to have been handed on to the founding ancestors of the owning groups by one of the Ancestral Beings associated with the land. The Ancestor may be a different one from the one involved in the origin of the design (see Morphy 1977a, Ch.4). In the example given, one Ancestral Being or set of Ancestral Beings may have been involved with the events that resulted in the origin of the diamond design, and another Ancestral Being in contact with those events may have handed the design, in the form of a body painting, on to the first human group occupying the land. The painting is thus of Ancestral origin and designation. However, one must add a note of qualification to this discussion. What the Yolngu mean when they say a painting is of Ancestral origin is not that every element of the form of the painting is as it was in the Ancestral Past, rather they mean that every part of the painting is produced by an Ancestral template which prescribes the possible content of the painting and which contains elements such as the diamond design which originated through Ancestral action. In a sense they could mean nothing else, for the paintings are what the Ancestral Past is measured by, rather than vice versa–the designs are both part of the events of the past and a record of those events, they are essentially reflexive images that refer to their own creation and which create their own value.

THE ENCODING OF ANCESTRAL BEINGS: FIGURATIVE REPRESENTATIONS

Most often, when an Ancestral Being is represented in figurative form, it is represented in a single unambiguous form only—the form by which it is usually characterized. If it is usually referred to as a goanna, then it will be represented as a goanna (Fig. 1): if it is thought of as primarily human in form, then it will be represented by a human figure. Transformational aspects of the Ancestor are usually *not* represented figuratively. There are no part-snake/part-emu/part-crocodile representations as there are, for example, in western Arnhem Land (*Kumeimku*) art. However, in myth and song many Ancestral Beings are referred to as existing in different states, in particular in the form of an animal, a human, a feature of the environment, and a sacred object (cf. Munn 1965). These different manifestations of the Ancestral Being may all be represented figuratively (though rarely in the case of a natural feature). Representations which combine features of two or more states occur very rarely.

An Ancestral Being may be represented in the same painting as a fish and a human being, but is unlikely to be represented by a composite figure that is part human and part fish. In the case of Ancestral Beings of fantastic form, such as trees that move and stones that talk, then such aspects of their form are never represented figuratively.

Similar considerations apply to transformational acts—there are no figurative reproductions of the landscape undergoing transformation. The acts that

Figure 1
A painting by Roy Dardanga Marika of the ancestral goanna at Yalangbara. (Photo courtesy of the Australian National University.)

resulted in the transformations are sometimes represented, but they are represented as if they were acts in the natural world. For example, an Ancestral Being in human form may be represented digging a well in the ground with a digging stick. Eventually, the well concerned was transformed into a lake and the digging stick became a tree, but these transformations are not represented. Similarly, representations of Ancestral Beings in animal form focus on the animal as a natural species rather than as a transforming agent and, indeed, represent it in a passive mode. For example, the Crocodile Ancestor is usually represented from above, stretched out, and is said to be lying on the river bank or basking in the water. The goanna in Dhuwa moiety paintings is shown in a similar mode, and is said to be lying on the sand dunes in the sun. On the whole, the animal manifestations are not incorporated into scenes which relate to their land-transforming actions, they are simply rather static portraits of the animal concerned.

In most *mardayin* paintings the figurative content is limited to one or two representations of animals or objects, the remainder of the painting consisting of geometric elements. However, in some categories of paintings humans and animals are represented organized into scenes that refer to events or stories. These paintings are generally referred to as "hunting stories," and they relate to public phases of ceremonies, to almost secular myths, and to the content of public songs (Fig. 2).

Figure 2
A painting by Wuyulwuy of the Marrakulu clan who died in 1974. The painting represents a female Ancestral Being hunting a kangaroo through the forests of eastern Arnhem Land. At one level the designs represent rocks in country. (Photograph courtesy of Australian National University.)

Scenes Involving Figurative Representations

For heuristic purposes I have defined three distinct types of scenes that are represented in Yolngu art. Although not exhaustive, these types cover the majority of paintings in which figurative representations are organized into scenes.

Scene type 1. People taking part in a ceremony. These typically show people taking part in a ceremony by dancing or acting at a ceremonial ground, manufacturing ceremonial objects, or performing various parts of a mortuary ritual. Occasionally, paintings containing such scenes may also represent spiritual or mythical aspects of the respective ceremony. A painting of a mortuary ritual may represent, in one of its sections, a scene from the land of the dead, in which figures are shown acting as spirits in the afterworld. The precise interpretation of a particular scene of a ritual is often impossible without the artist's guidance. Even if the scene is clearly of a mortuary ritual, the artist could have intended it to be a mortuary ritual performed by human beings or a mortuary ritual performed in the Ancestral Past. In a society in which the present shades into the Ancestral Past, interpretation is never going to be simple.

Scene type 2. Episodic representations of myths. Since the late 1950s, Yolngu at Yirrkala have produced paintings which illustrate in segments a series of episodes of myths. In particular, these paintings were developed by artists of three clans: Mawalang of the Rirratjingu clan, Munggurrawuy of the Gumatj clan, and Narritjin of the Manggalili clan. Perhaps the best known of these are Mawalang's paintings of the Djan'kawu mythology and Narritjin's paintings of the Djert (eagle) and Bamapama (trickster) stories. Narritjin's paintings represent semi-secular myths, which concern events which are not located in the Ancestral Past but which involved transformational events and have locational referents. Figure 3 illustrates a painting of the Bamapama story. It is in paintings of this type that figurative representations of the act of transformation sometimes occur. In the case of the Djert paintings, for example, which refer to a myth in which an angry child was gradually transformed into a sea eagle during a temper tantrum, part-human part-bird figures are sometimes produced. Djert and Bamapama are moral tales told to children as examples of the consequences of breaching moral norms or behaving badly—they are also very much a form of entertainment.

Scene type 3. Hunting and manufacturing scenes. These are the most common scenes represented figuratively. They consist of people hunting a wallaby with spears (see Fig. 2), people in a boat harpooning dugong, or people manufacturing a rope for hunting turtle. Again depending on context, the scene may refer to a mythic event or represent human beings going about their lives. As Ancestral Beings frequently carried out the same everyday actions as living people, a hunting scene quite often has a mythological referent. Dharlwangu clan paintings often show people fishing at a fish trap. In this case the fish trap was an Ancestral creation at Gaarngarn in Dharlwangu country, resulting from an

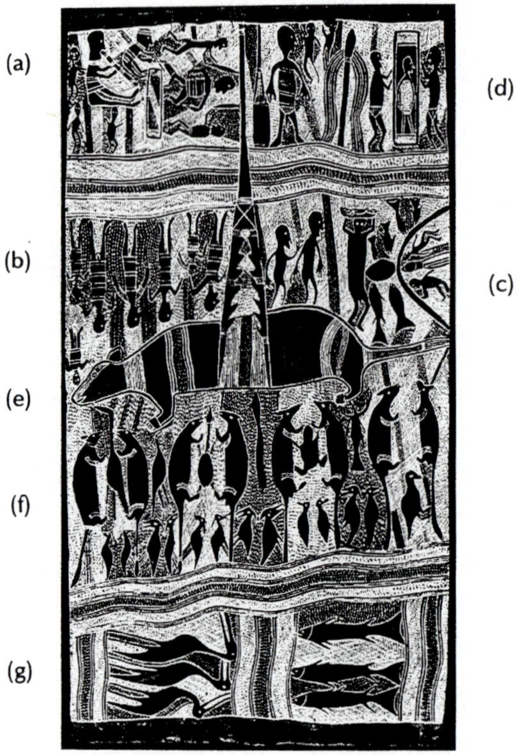

Figure 3 A painting by Narritjin Maymuru of the Manggalili clan who died in 1982. The painting represents the story of Bamapama, a trickster Ancestral Being. Bamapama (see Warner 1958, p. 545 *et seq.* Groger-Wurm 1973, p. 124), was sent to collect young men for a ceremony. He went to a nearby settlement (a), but asked for young girls instead of boys. He challenged them to a race, saying that only the fastest one would be selected for the ceremony (b). One girl, his classificatory sister, raced ahead of the rest, and eventually she and Bamapama were alone. They rested to fish at a lake, and Bamapama sent her to collect firewood. While she was away, he inserted a fish bone in his foot, and on her return said that they would have to camp the night because he was lame. They built a hut with a fire in the centre (c). In the night he threw stones onto the roof, and frightened her by saying that the sound was made by a sorcerer. She moved over to his side, whereupon he raped her, killing her with his large penis. He hid her body in a bark container and returned to her camp (a). When the people found out what had happened, they started to beat him (a). He became wild, and began to spear dogs(e) and vegetable food (d), that is, things that people do not normally spear. After a while, everything began to change. All the people turned into the animal species that were totems to their clan (f) and (g), and returned to their own clan territories. Finally, a great flood came and covered the area where the events took place. (Photograph: Australian National University.)

Ancestral transformation, and the fish trap is manifest today as a rocky bar across the river. The figurative representations usually give no clue as to the Ancestral significance of the events depicted and do not show the transformations that occurred. They portray the Ancestral Beings as if they were ordinary people taking part in everyday activities.

THE ENCODING OF ANCESTRAL BEINGS IN THE GEOMETRIC ART

How then are Ancestral Beings, in particular the fantastic and transformation aspects of them, encoded in paintings if they are not represented figuratively? The answers to this question are multiple and have already partly been given: where they are represented in paintings they are present indirectly in the relationships between sets of paintings, they are alluded to in the content of the paintings, and they are encoded in the geometric art. The characteristic of each of those means of representation is that they are indirect, and the message is dependent on knowledge of the code and even on foreknowledge of what is encoded—meaning is not (if it ever is) internal to the painting.

As we have argued already in the case of diamond designs, geometric patterns are themselves often thought to be transformations of the Ancestral Beings. To take another example, the design of the Manggalili clan represents marks left by the ebb and flow of the tide on the body of an Ancestral Being as he lay dead on the beach, cast up by the sea. The design painted as the background in a sacred painting refers to and recreates that transforming event in which the design was etched into the Ancestor's body. Yet the meaning of the design, and hence the concept of the Ancestral Being, is filled out by its connection to myth and song and through the metaphors contained within them. Although here is not the place to explore Yolngu symbolism, the image of the tide mark in the sand is a key symbol to the Yolngu of the ephemeral nature of people—for the marks wash away with every subsequent tide. The tide itself is the great cleanser of the beach, washing debris out to sea. The particular clan design and the myth of the body on the beach is associated with mortuary rituals and with the removal of pollution associated with death. The concept of the Ancestral Being consists partly of the core metaphors associated with them. The transitory patterns of the sand on the beach transformed into permanent form on the body of the Ancestral Being provide the focal point for metaphors about the impermanence of life.

Frequently, sacred paintings have no obvious figurative component and various aspects of the Ancestral Being concerned are encoded in different geometric elements. A characteristic of the geometric art is that it is multivalent and the same element may encode a number of different meanings. Figure 4 is of a painting by Dula Ngurruwutthun of the Munyuku clan. The painting represents the Wild Honey Ancestor at an inland place of paperbark lagoons. The diamond pattern has some relationship with the Gumatj pattern discussed earlier, since it, too, is associated with fire. In this case, however, fire is an attribute of the Wild Honey Ancestor rather than the core Ancestral Being of the painting. At one level of interpretation the diamonds represent the cells of the hive, the cross-hatching signifies different components of the hive, the grubs, the honey, the pollen, and the bees; the cross-bars that bisect some of the diamonds represent small sticks that are found in the hive; while the dots within the circles represent the bees swarming from the entrance of the hive.

At another level, elements of the design signify attributes of the fires lit by hunters who collected the wild honey: the white cross-hatching is the smoke, the red is sparks, and the white dots ash. At another level still, the diamond pattern represents the sparkling fresh water as it flows beside the flowering paperbark trees, the trees in which the honey is found. The other components of the painting have associated meanings: the central figure represents the trunk of a paperbark tree, and the two lateral figures represent the hive and its entrance. These all have an iconic aspect in that they represent similarly shaped ceremonial objects. However, as the objects themselves are largely non-iconic representations of Ancestral Beings, the iconicity is arguable. Indeed, it is misunderstanding the nature of the Wild Honey Ancestor to think of it as being able to be represented figuratively. For the Ancestor is an abstract concept that consists of all those things associated with wild honey: the hive, the bees, the trees and flowers, the flood-water, and the season. All of those things in turn have components—the tree has branches, roots, leaves, bark, and so on, the hive has cells, honey, bees, grubs, and pollen—and all of the components have their own connotations. Many of them are taken up in songs about the Wild Honey Ancestor, others are the

Figure 4
A painting by Dula Ngurruwutthun of the Munyuku clan representing the Wild Honey Ancestor at Mandjawuy. (Photo courtesy of Australian National University.)

product of individual experience and depend on the subject's relationship to the Ancestral Being. But from another perspective, the Wild Honey Ancestor is an entity rather than an amorphous complex of associated traits, for it has a name and a journey, and places that it has created, and manifestations in the form of paintings, sacred objects, and transformations of the landscape. Figurative representations could encode its components by representing the bees, trees, flowers, hunters, and so on separately but it seems that the multivalency of the geometric art creates the possibility of an individual grasping it as a whole. And as a collectively acknowledged manifestation of the Ancestor it does, of course, represent itself.

This same potentiality of the geometric art for multivalency enables paintings to encode transformational aspects of Ancestral Beings and Ancestral events. Elsewhere I have argued that it is productive to think that there is a template underlying each set of Yolngu sacred paintings, which in effect generates their surface form (Morphy 1977a). The template consists of a set of positions which exist in a fixed relationship one with another, at each of which a series of meanings is encoded. Depending on which of the respective set of meanings is focused on, the surface picture changes. A hypothetical example should clarify what I mean. A particular template has two loci, (a) and (b). At locus (a) the meanings well, lake, and vagina are encoded. At locus (b) the meanings digging stick, river, and penis are encoded. There are clearly a number of possible pictures that combinations of those sequences could generate. Three of them would be a river flowing into a lake, a digging stick being used to dig a well, and a penis going into a vagina. The three stories may all be interconnected as events in the same mythic sequence:

> A Kangaroo Ancestor was digging a well with a digging stick. When he finished, a female wallaby bent down to drink the fresh water, and the kangaroo seized his opportunity to have sexual intercourse with her. The semen flowed out of her body and into the waterhole. Today a river flows into the lake at that place and the kangaroo's penis was transformed into a digging stick which can be seen as a great log beside the lake.

Now, as well as generating a whole series of pictures depicting the various events, the template could be represented by a single multivalent design. In this design the meanings at locus (a) are represented by the circle and the meanings at locus (b) are represented by a straight line, to produce a familiar component of Yolngu clan designs. In this way, the transformational events are encoded in a single motif without being directly represented. The geometric motif gives priority to no one meaning but allows all to be active. This is precisely how Ancestral transformations are encoded in Yolngu paintings, by marking the positions where they occur rather than by directly representing them.

DISCUSSION: THE NATURE OF THE BEING

How do we explain the way in which Ancestral Beings are represented in Yolngu art, in particular the lack of figurative representation of transformational events and of the fantastic aspects of their beings? I think that the answer involves two issues: the nature of the Beings themselves and the system of knowledge of which they are a part. The first I have largely dealt with already.

Yolngu Ancestral Beings are highly complex concepts that cannot be said to have a single image. When they are represented by a single image then that image is misleading, often deliberately so. As I argued in the case of the Wild Honey Ancestor, the Ancestor consists of that whole complex of things to do with wild honey. Yolngu do not have a single image of it but acquire an emergent and, in part, connotative understanding of it over time. The geometric design as a manifestation of the Ancestral Being is structured to encode those developing understandings.

Moreover, Ancestral Beings are really inseparable from the concept of totemism and the process of myth. They are not discrete separable objects with defined boundaries, but just as they transform the world they are, in turn, in a constant state of transformation. Representations of Ancestral Beings involve the whole way in which objects of the environment are used by the Yolngu as components of a semiotic system. The Wild Honey Ancestor gains its meaning through the connotations of its parts and through the symbolism, actively created, of fire, water, and honey (of red, white, and yellow), and also through its associations with particular clans and countries. Over time it can absorb some more components or leave some behind, it can follow new routes across the land, transforming itself anew into the landscape and becoming the emblem of new groups. Images of the Ancestral Beings must be continually changing as the system is used over time. But the geometric art can remain the same while the concept changes, because of the distance between form and content and because of its multivalency (see Morphy 1980). Its detailed meaning can change while it remains a fixed image associated with the Ancestor, a timeless manifestation. Even in cases where the Ancestor is associated with a characteristic human or animal form, the Ancestor cannot be fully represented by a single fixed image. The Crocodile Ancestor is a case in point. The crocodile in paintings is frequently presented figuratively with a background pattern of diamonds, representing fire. In myth the crocodile grew out of fire. He was sleeping in his bark hut when it was set fire to by his wife, the blue-tongued lizard. The crocodile fled, with the burning bark from the hut torturing his body, and dived into the sea to cool off, leaving the fire burning beneath the waves. The serrated back of the crocodile is the ragged bark burnt into his skin, and the pattern of the scales is the product of blistering. But what was the form of the crocodile during these events, what was his shape before they occurred, and how does the fire burn beneath the waves? The crocodile in the painting is a sign for the Crocodile Ancestor, not a representation of it.

Coming Into Being

Yolngu art is incorporated in a system of revelatory knowledge in which one learns more and more about the connections between things as one goes through the system. It is not so much that aspects of Ancestral Beings are secret, though indeed some are, as the fact that they are presented in parts spread over a long period of time. One part will be presented in one ceremony, another in a later one: one aspect will be represented in a dance, a different one in a painting, and so on. At whatever stage one first encounters an Ancestral Being, one encounters a part not a whole, the whole only emerges later. Thus, the Ancestral transformations from one state to another are separated out in time and space. The myth is never enacted as a whole, the connections are made retrospectively, the transformations are not supposed to be seen but to be revealed. The geometric art integrates well within this system. It gives priority to no one transformation, to no one meaning, it enables all the parts to be encoded in a concealed way and their connections to be subsequently revealed. In other words, the template is a template for transformation. If we return to our example of the circle and line we will be able to see how this works.

A person may get to know "Kangaroo Lake" by walking around it as a child. He is shown the lake and the stream that flows into it which is called "digging-stick creek." Later when he is shown the circle and line design on the painting he is told it represents the lake with the stream flowing into it. On a subsequent occasion in a ceremony, a dancer acting the Kangaroo Ancestor digs a circle in the ground with his digging stick and marks a line leading into that circle. The connection is made, the lake is called Kangaroo Lake because it was created by the kangaroo digging a well that was subsequently transformed into a lake. But some things still puzzle the child about the lake. Why is the water cloudy white and why do women avoid bathing in it? Later he hears about a further transformation and the true origin of the lake's water, created from the sperm of the Ancestral Kangaroo as it flowed into the water hole. It is then he is told of a second name of the lake, "wallaby vulva."

In this way a series of transformations get encoded in the form of a single design, which cumulatively encodes Ancestral events.

CONCLUSION

Figurative representations in Yolngu art are not intended to represent the mythical form of the Ancestral Beings—they are signs of the natural objects that are incorporated into totemic discourse; organized in scenes, they represent events in the ordinary world, hunting and gathering, and taking part in ceremonies. The only transformational images (humans changing into animals and so on) concern fantastic events associated with "actual" human beings in "fables" and moral tales—paintings with such images are recent innovations. On the whole, transformations are encoded in the geometric art enabling individuals to develop their own concepts of the Ancestral events, enabling the images to be psychologically satisfying and to maintain their power—they are condensation symbols which, although they allude to the form of the Ancestral Beings and refer to a time of transformation when everything was possible, do so without directly presenting the event in a phantasmagorical way. However, all is not freedom. At the same time the geometric art—the sacred paintings—consists of relatively fixed forms, belief in their Ancestral origins is collective, meanings are encoded in them in a structured and systematic way, and interpretation of them is constrained by their incorporation in a hierarchical system of knowledge. In Giddens's terms (1979) they are the ideal medium for structuration, they are socially transmitted forms associated with collective ideas about a particular Ancestral Being acted out in ritual and acquired in everyday life, yet they also allow individual perceptions and understandings of the object to vary within limits and with respect to individual experience. The collective design does not give the lie to that experience but absorbs it, and may even transmit it while maintaining the illusion of continuity. Subtle shifts of form, meaning, and ownership go unnoticed in a timeless universe with no recorded history.

REFERENCES

Berndt, R.M. (ed.) 1964. *Australian Aboriginal art.* Sydney: Ure Smith.

Giddens, A. 1979. *Central problems in social theory: action, structure and contradiction in social analysis.* London: Macmillan.

Groger-Wurm, H. 1973. *Australian Aboriginal bark paintings and their mythological interpretations.* Vol. 1: Eastern Arnhem Land. Canberra: Australian Institute of Aboriginal Studies.

Morphy, H. 1977a. *Too many meanings.* Unpublished PhD thesis, Australian National University, Canberra.

Morphy, H. 1977b. "Yingapungapu: bark painting as sand sculpture." In *Form in indigenous art,* P.J. Ucko (ed.), 205-9. Canberra: Australian Institute of Aboriginal Studies.

Morphy, H. 1980. "What circles look like." *Canberra Anthropology* 3, 17-36.

Morphy, H. 1984. *Journey to the crocodiles nest.* Canberra: Australian Institute of Aboriginal Studies.

Munn, N.M. 1965. "The transformation of subjects into objects in Warlbiri and Pitjantjanjara myth." In *Australian Aboriginal anthropology.* R. M. Berndt (ed.). Nedlands: University of Western Australia Press.

Munn, N.M. 1966. "Visual categories: an approach to the study of representational systems." *American Anthropologist* 68, 936-50.

Munn, N.M. 1973. *Warlbiri iconography.* Ithaca: Cornell University Press.

Warner, W.L. 1958. *A Black Civilization.* Chicago: Harper and Row.

Form, Function and Interpretation of Mimbres Ceramic Hemispheric Vessels

Barbara L. Moulard

An understanding of the cultural and historical context of an art form is crucial to an understanding of its meaning. Two aspects of cultural context that are often not synthesized into interpretations of prehistoric North American Indian art are the process by which an art object was made and its utility in the culture. Due to the lack of written records for ancient cultures, these are often not well understood. This paper briefly examines the process of manufacture, the form and the function of Mimbres painted ceramics in order to determine what, if any, relationship these have to the designs painted on the interiors of the bowls. The meanings inferred in this study for the Mimbres hemispheric ceramic form are derived largely by ethnographic analogy using data from historic and contemporary Pueblo Indian cultures.

The Mimbres evolved from early Mogollon cultures and flourished in Southwestern New Mexico around AD 1000 but by the end of the twelfth century the culture was dispersed and the region was taken over by the intrusive Casas Grandes culture from the south and later Salado peoples from the west. However, the Mimbres culture appears to have been closely related economically and ideologically with the Anasazi that inhabited the region to the north of the Mimbres area. There is a clear chronological development of Anasazi culture into historic times represented by contemporary Pueblo societies of Northern Arizona and New Mexico. When compared sociologically, economically and geographically the Mimbres and the Pueblos cultures are strikingly similar; and several ethnographic sources for the Pueblos testify to their conservative nature and the tenacity by which they have held on to their traditional social and religious

Reprinted in abridged form from *Phøebus 4*, edited by Anthony Lacey Gully, Tempe: Arizona State University, 1985, pages 86-98 with permission of the author and publisher.

institutions. The Mimbres archaeologist, Dr. Steven A. LeBlanc, recognized the similarities between these temporally disparate cultures. LeBlanc feels that "there is little need to suspect a direct relationship between the prehistoric Mimbres and the historic Hopi; the Hopi certainly shared a broad common history and similar adaptation to the Southwest environment."[1] He uses close ethnographic analogy to interpret the plant, food procurement and food processing, and to a great extent the social organization of the Mimbres. Following the same methods, ethnographic analogy can be used to establish the ideological context in which Mimbres art was created.

Any discussion of traditional fine arts incorporates an analysis of the process by which the object was made as well as its original physical context. Generally speaking, most interpretations of Mimbres ceramic art have viewed the painted images separately from the object on which they appear[2] either by reproducing the image without the ceramic background[3] or by discussing the compositions without relating them to the form.[4] The significance of the use of the form as a vehicle for the paintings has never been examined. This is due in large part to the fact that ceramics have been relegated by scholars and writers to utilitarian use while the images often seem to have other than secular meaning. As J. J. Brody states in a discussion of Mimbres painted pottery:

> The utility of the vessels on which Mimbres paintings were made is obvious. They were containers for food, water, ritual objects, and a great variety of other things, and many were ultimately used as mortuary offerings. The utility of the paintings is not so easily assumed or demonstrated. They have little or no relation to vessel use, and they underline the proposition that the function of a utilitarian object should not be confused with the decoration on it. A picture is not a pot; they mean different things, are used for different purposes, and function in different ways for different ends.[5]

Granted, it is most likely that the hemispheric vessel was thought of, and used, by the prehistoric Mimbres as a bowl. Archaeologically it has been shown that many of the painted wares exhibit use either from interior scraping or exterior scorching. However, the majority of these painted hemispheric vessels as well as plain brownware and blackware hemispheric vessels survive today because of their placement in graves. Harriet S. Cosgrove and Cornelius B. Cosgrove noted the predominance of hemispheric vessels in graves and stated that:

> The prevailing custom, so nearly universal in the Mimbres country that it must have some religious significance, was to invert over the skull a single bowl...the arrangement, when there was more than one in the grave, had been either to nest the bowls over the head, or to invert one over the skull and the other on the body or at one side.[6]

It becomes clear that the Mimbres had a preference for the hemispheric vessel as mortuary furniture. As suggested by the Cosgroves, it would appear that the form, or at least the act of placing the bowl over the head of the deceased, had significance for the Mimbres. However mundane these objects appear to be, it would be negligent to disregard their form, function and process of manufacture in an investigation of the images that appear on them.

The Mimbres differentiated between paintedwares, plainwares and corrugatedwares and other utilitarian vessels. Storage jars and cooking vessels were left unslipped and often coils were not scraped but were textured to create a corrugated surface which enhanced heat retention.[7] The paintedwares had relatively soft friable white kaolin clay slipped interiors. Well-preserved examples retain a carefully patinated surface suggesting their preparation for use as food bowls. Some show unmistakable interior surface damage and many exhibit staining from organic material. However, a case can be made for the assertion that the function of the form in the living culture and the function of the form as a mortuary offering were mutually exclusive and that the latter was anticipated and equally as significant for the Mimbres as the former.

Mogollon black-on-white ceramics were traded outside the Mimbres area. They are found at Snake-town and Hohokam sites in the Tucson Basin of Arizona and at Paquimé to list a few occurrences. However, these make up a small percentage of intrusive pottery at these sites and are usually the Three Circle Phase, boldface style of pottery painting. Classic Mimbres black-on-white and polychrome, especially those with representational decoration, rarely found their way outside the Mimbres area and appear to have been concentrated in the Mimbres and upper Gila River drainages. While the more generalized geometric designs on hemispheric vessels may have crossed cultural lines the more pictorial style evidently remained within the Mimbres boundaries[8] suggesting that the latter were held in high esteem by the Mimbres and even may have been made exclusively for their own use.

The economic use of the hemispheric painted vessel seems to have been limited. Few similar compositions are found and no two are exactly alike suggesting that painted vessels were kept or taken out of circulation before images could be memorized by different artists. Instead, similarities in compositions, subject matter and themes suggest a shared ideology rather than a knowledge of specific prototypic images (Fig. 1, 2).

Many of these painted vessels exhibit no sign of wear and are in such good condition that it is felt that they were either handled with extreme care or were disposed of shortly after their manufacture. Many of these are poorly fired and warped, and thus ill-suited for utilitarian purposes. As Clara Lee Tanner points out:

> Seemingly, these [Mimbres] potters were not too careful when they fired their wares, for many dark firing clouds appear and frequently bowls are misshapen. This carelessness may indicate that the vessels were not made for utility purposes but rather, were explicitly and perhaps hurriedly produced for burials.[9]

This is not a case against the utility of the form as a bowl but a suggestion that their use as such may have been temporary and that the form also functioned and had meaning in a funerary rite and that in some cases this was a primary concern of the ceramist at the time of manufacture.

The actual use of the bowl is not as easily demonstrated as may be assumed or expected. There is very little data available about the function of the hemis-

Figure 1 Classic Mimbres black-on-white ceramic hemispheric vessel with a nine figure procession scene, ca. AD 1000 to 1150. Upper Gila River region, New Mexico. H: 10 x 22 cm. Private collection, Photo copyright 1982 John Bigelow Taylor.

pheric bowl outside its use in Mimbres burials. There is no certainty that they were used for food, water, ceremonial containers or anything else however likely this would appear. As Brody points out, "these painted vessels may have been made and used for other purposes, but in the end they were buried and the art became a mortuary one."[10] If the paintings are the mortuary art and the hemispheric form of the ceramics is of little consequence to their meaning or purpose, then one may expect that over the six or seven generations of Mimbres ceramic production, the form would flatten out to afford a surface more conducive to painting. Shallow painted bowls do exist from the Mimbres area. These however, tend to be the Boldface variety. Although exact dating is problematic for Mimbres ceramics it has been established that the Boldface style predates the Classic Mimbres style and probably continued into the later period to fall into disuse in the last quarter of the eleventh century. If this development is true, then if anything, the form of the hemispheric vessels does not seem simply one of practicality. Other ceramic forms such as ollas, ladles, seed jars and on rare occurrences effigy figures were painted and placed in graves. These are few and exceedingly scarce when compared to the number of painted hemispheric vessels retrieved from Mimbres burials. Other contemporaneous prehistoric cultures, such as the Hohokam, utilized a much wider range of painted vessel

Figure 2 Classic Mimbres black-on-white ceramic hemispheric vessel with an eight figure procession scene, ca. AD 1000 to 1150. Mimbres River valley region, New Mexico. H: 11.4 x 24.7 cm. Private collection, Photo copyright 1982 John Bigelow Taylor.

forms than did the Mimbres. Up until the close of the Classic Mimbres Period ceramic phase, the bowl form was the preferred funerary offering and the preferred surface for painted decoration even though it created technical and compositional problems for the artist. The tenacity for the form was due to preference, not to an ignorance of alternatives.

Stylistic analysis suggests that the hemispheric form is as much a part of the artistic statement as the painted image. Distorted, warped bowls were painted as if they were hemispheric (Figure 3). Great care was taken even with complicated narratives, which may have been more successfully rendered on a flat surface, to adjust the pictorial and illusionistic subject matter to the concave surface of the bowl. Concerning this aspect of the art form Brody points out that "everything followed from the basic premise that paint was applied to the surface of the vessel as a sort of skin, hugging it and adjusting its two-dimensionality to the three-dimensional reality of the space enclosed by the vessel."[11]

A pot is not a picture but a pot is not a pot when it is no longer treated like a pot. On rare occasions the form of a utilitarian object may be lifted from its pedestrian role to be transferred to another in which it transcends its original meaning. There are thousands of different Mimbres painted images that are found on similarly shaped, thin walled ceramics. These paintings may be thought

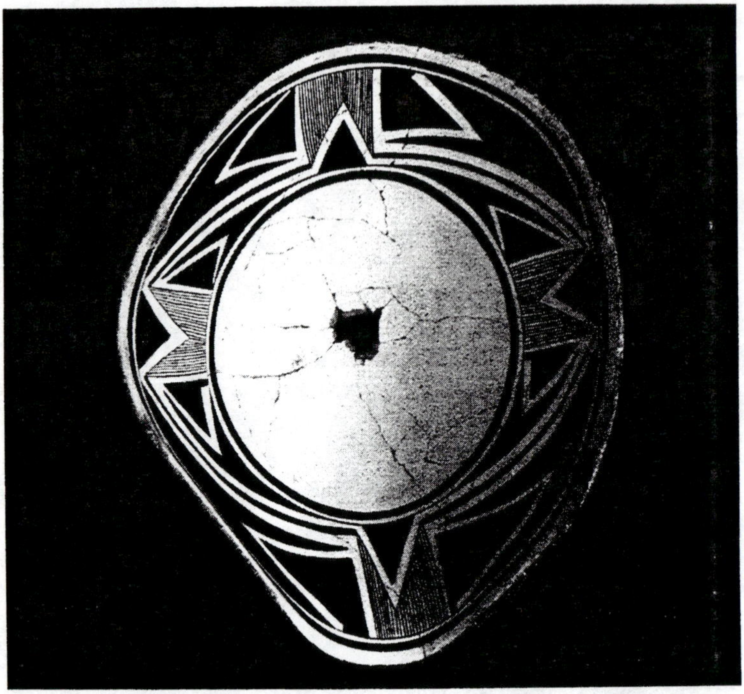

Figure 3 Classic Mimbres Black-on-white ceramic (warped) hemispheric vessel with a quartered geometric rim band, ca. AD 1000 to 1150. Mimbres River Valley region, New Mexico. H: 12 x 19 x 26 cm. Private collection, Photograph copyright 1982 John Bigelow Taylor.

of as subsets or constituent parts of the total three dimensional art object. The meaning of the ceramic form and the meaning of the painting may be different but they are inextricably related due to their ultimate use as burial offerings in which they function in a similar manner for similar ends.

The synergistic nature of this Mimbres form and painting have been obscured by time and a history that lacks precise written documentation. However, when these aspects are examined in light of archaeological data they yield information about themselves and the context in which they functioned. This context is the basic determining factor which shapes our point of view toward the ceramic art and its significance in the culture. For the Mimbres painted hemispheric vessels, context is its dissident use in graves; for the majority of Mimbres painted images, context is their appearance on the white slipped interiors of these bowls. A complete understanding of the painted images may never be possible, but any interpretation of the images should begin with an attempt to answer the question, "Why a pot?" and then a second question, "Why a broken pot?"

The above-ground use of the ceramic form may be negligible as a consideration for its role in the burial tradition of the Mimbres. Regardless of its pre-burial functions, its use in a burial context gives us a certain information about its meaning. As funerary offerings they were not containers for food or other objects. Their application was curiously unbowl-like. Generally, a single bowl was inverted over the head of the deceased as either a tightly fitting skull cap or as a covering for the face. Where there was more than one bowl associated with a body, these were often nested over the head (Figure 4). In cremations, an atypical mortuary custom for the Mimbres, three different uses of these ceramic forms were employed: The remains of the dead were gathered and placed under an inverted bowl; the cremated remains were placed in a bowl with an inverted bowl resting over the top of it; the cremated remains were placed in a seed jar and a hemispheric vessel was placed over the top of the former.

The prevailing custom during the Mimbres burial rite appears to have been the sacrifice of the bowl at the time of interment by knocking a hole in the center of the form. In instances of nesting, the bowl not directly in contact with the dead was sometimes, but not often, left intact. Likewise, in cremations the containers of the dead were left whole while the inverted cover was usually perforated. If the hemispheric vessel functioned as a container, then it was as a container of the dead, not for the dead.

But the idea of container may have to be discarded altogether in light of the fact that not only were most of the bowls inverted at the time of burial, they were also broken. They were either indiscriminately smashed or, more often, care was taken to punch or peck a hole in the center of the apex of the curve of the inverted bowl (Figure 5). The continuous coil method of construction aided in this second manner of breaking ceramics.

Unlike most of the prehistoric ceramics found in the Southwest region which started with a molded or pinched base on which coils were attached, the Mimbres ceramic bowls, for the most part, were constructed with a continuous coil from base to rim. When struck by an object at the center, bowls broke easily along contacts between coils.[12] The technique of manufacture aided this aspect

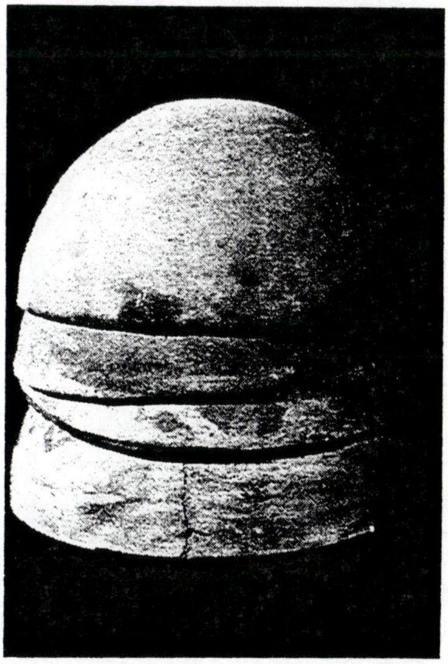

Figure 4
Four nested Mimbres bowls (assembled).
Photograph by Barbara L. Moulard, 1982.

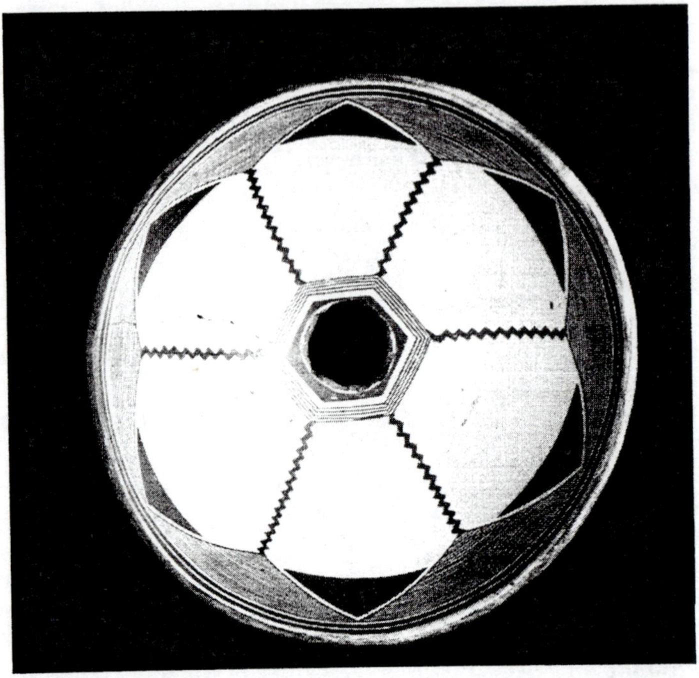

Figure 5 Classic Mimbres black-on-white ceramic hemispheric vessel with a geometric composition and a carefully cut "kill hole," circa AD 1000 to 1150. Mimbres River Valley region, New Mexico. H: 17 x 25 cm Private collection, Photograph copyright 1982 John Bigelow Taylor.

of the mortuary use of the ceramic vessel. In addition, since the breakage of the form was deliberate, it must be considered part of the total art process involved in Mimbres painted hemispheric ceramics.

Painted bowls that occur in burials are generally inverted either over the top of the head, the face, or the cremated remains of the dead. This inversion creates a dome shaped object (Figure 6). Most of these domes were penetrated at the top, forming an oculus-like aperture. The form in the living culture may have been a utilitarian food bowl but when it was placed with the dead it had a different, virtually opposing, connotation; the former was a closed basin container; the latter was an opened dome enclosure. Such dualities for a single object are not rare in the philosophies of the ethnographic people of the Southwest. The meaning of the perforated dome and its association with death can only be inferred from a review of the historic Pueblos ethnographic data.

The idea of the sky being a penetrable dome enclosure is a dominant image in emergence mythology from the Western Pueblos. An unmistakable association for the form was recorded by Ruth L. Bunzel from the Zuni who state that "the sky (*a'po'yan-e,* stone cover), solid in substance, rests upon the earth like an inverted bowl";[13] there are breaks or a passage in the cover, if you pass through, you reach the home of the Eagle People.[14] Texts recorded at Third Mesa, Hopi relate that a variety of birds and/or plants were grown, "to pierce the dome of

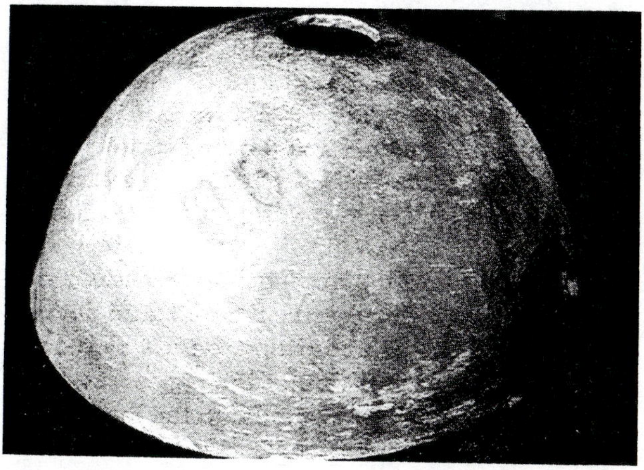

Figure 6 Inverted Mimbres bowl, or dome-shaped object. Photograph by Barbara L. Moulard, 1982.

their [the Hopi Underworld] sky"[15] so that the people trapped in the Underworld could emerge from the below to this world.[16] The same is virtually true for the mythology recorded at Zuni, except that there were four worlds to be traversed and the people emerged from the Underworld with the aid of the twin sons of Sun.[17] An emergence myth recorded by Matthew W. Stirling at Acoma Pueblo has the surface of the earth being penetrated from the below by a pine tree, the hole enlarged for the passage of the people by Badger and the circumference of the hole plastered permanently by Locust.[18] These emergence myths explain the existence of the Pueblo race and revolve around the ancestors of these people who are associated with the past and the dead.

Emergence mythology and subsequent migration mythology of the Pueblos defines the prehistory of the culture before their arrival at their present location and the realm of the spirit world. Before emergence, mortality was not known to the race. Shortly after emergence the first death occurs and the dead person is witnessed by the newly emerged people as having returned back through the hole of emergence to the realm of the spirits of the dead or Underworld. Through mythological passages, death and the afterlife are explained and described. When the Pueblo ancestors are invoked during Kachina ceremonies at the Pueblos, the process begins in the kiva[19] at the mouth of the *sipa'pu,* the hole on the kiva floor that leads to the Underworld and that remains covered when invocations are not taking place. Thus the *sipa'pu* is symbolic of, or functions in a similar manner as, the original hole of emergence; it is a passageway between two realms.

Because of its similarity in form to the description of the Pueblos Underworld "dome of the sky" and *sipa' pu* hole of emergence, it seems plausible to suggest that the Mimbres domed shaped ceramic form with a hole in the center represents a barrier between worlds and the break in it is a passage between two worlds and that the form carries connotations of a Mimbres notion of an Underworld realm of the dead. In the case of the Mimbres burial rite, the movement appears to be one between lower and upper worlds. Nested Mimbres bowls in burials may suggest the layering of worlds as described in the Zuni myth. The contemporary Puebloans believe that the dead, in the form of a "breath body," which issues from the mouth of the deceased, pass from the Underworld to the Upperworld by means of a "ladder" left in the grave, to return to the corporeal community in the form of rain or Kachina ancestral spirits. If the Mimbres had a similar belief, then a punctured dome would represent the boundaries between the two worlds and the means of exiting from one to the other.

Another association that the Mimbres funerary practices may have had with contemporary Pueblo thought is the placement of the dead under house floors. Throughout all periods of Mimbres occupation, burials, flexed or semi-flexed, were placed under floors and occupation of the house was often continued. Although infants who have not been initiated into the Pueblo community are sometimes buried under house floors at some pueblo villages, in the Pueblos there is a universal fear of the immediate dead and they are usually taken outside the living area of the village for burial. However, it is believed that the dead go to the two storied house of *Masau'u*, the Pueblo deity of death.[20] The grave is the entrance to his house which is visualized as being constructed like those of the living and dying is thought of as a returning to the earlier house. In this way the floor of the Mimbres' house may also represent a barrier between the house of the dead and the house of the living.

Finally, the process by which ceramics were made and treated in the Mimbres culture and the funerary rite may have been a metaphor for the human dead. The way in which ceramics are made is not unlike the process by which the surface of the earth was formed in mythology or the process that a Puebloan undergoes to become an adult member of the community. In several transcriptions of Pueblo mythology the people emerge to a wet, soft, muddy land that is unformed, but through various methods and the aid of supernatural beings the land is made dry and hard. As the people continue on their migration to the center of their world (where they now live) they receive gifts and knowledge along the way which make them culturally complete by the end of their quest. Likewise, in many of the Pueblos there is a notion that before persons are initiated into the society, between the ages of seven and twelve, they are not truly formed. Small children that die before this time are not buried in the same manner as adults for it is thought that they are still linked to the spirit world and can be reborn. This is described by Don Talayesva in connection with the death of his child:

> We place no cotton on its face and did not bury it in the regular cemetery, for we wished the child to return shortly. Everyone knows that if a baby dies, a young mother may bear the same child again, but of opposite sex.[21]

Ortiz in his monograph on Tewa culture describes this notion clearly in his definition of the Tewa word *ochu* (moist, green and unripe) and *seh t'a* (dry, hardened and ripe). At the time of the people's emergence to this world the land was *ochu* and later became *seh t'a*.[22] In a similar manner uninitiated youths under the age of six or seven are thought of as being *ochu* and after initiation become *seh t'a*. This notion is shared by several other Pueblo groups. After each major rite of passage the Puebloan becomes closer to being complete. At death the person joins his ancestors and enters a different state of being.

The process of forming a Mimbres vessel goes through a similar transformation. Dry clay was gathered and filtered and cleaned with water, tempered with fine grain volcanic ash and then kneaded until the proper level of plasticity was achieved. During the cleansing process the clay is in a soft, wet and uncontrollable stage; through the tempering and kneading process the clay is made manageable. Next, the base of the bowl was formed by either a continuous coil or a basal pat was formed by pressing a small amount of clay into a mold or form. Coils were added to this tapering gradually upwards and outwards from the center. The greenware vessel was allowed to dry slowly to a leathery state and then it was scraped smooth to obliterate and bind the coils. It was then ready to receive painted decoration. Up until this time and indeed until the time of firing the vessel could have been broken down and returned to its original state possibly to be used again. After the white kaolin slip had been applied to the surface and any decoration made from iron ore pigments had been applied the greenware vessel was left to completely dry. After this the vessel was ready to be fired. In this process the clay form became hard ceramic and was ready for use in the community. At the time of a burial rite of a Mimbreño a vessel was ceremonially killed by either punching a hole in it or breaking it; this rendered it unfunctional and it was returned to the ground from which it came but in an altered state.

Like the member in the Pueblo community the ceramic form progresses through a series of events from a moist or green state in which it may return unchanged to nature, to a dry hard state and finally, to a non-functional state and returned to the earth. This analogy between the social growth of humans and the process of ceramic manufacture may be reflected in the Tewa custom of giving small children or infants a bowl which they are to keep throughout their lives.

It is difficult to assess the importance the manufacture of ceramic vessels held for the prehistoric Mimbres. Even today pottery making is done in reverence to and with aid of a supernatural figure known as Clay Woman, who "gives her flesh" to the Puebloan potter.[23] It was an industry that probably took place year round in most Mimbres sites, although certain parts of the process may have been seasonal. The complete process of gathering, mixing, creating the form, its use and its destruction was likely to have been a constantly observed transformation. That this process was consciously thought of as a metaphor for a similar human life process is impossible to prove but the ubiquitous use of ceramics as mortuary furnishings as well as the historic mythic comparison certainly brings it into the realm of possibilities.

Through the use of ethnographic analogy it is apparent that the Mimbres hemispheric ceramic form has several layers of meaning. The process of manufacture of the ceramics may have been analogous to either or both the mythic evolution of the surface of the earth and the development of the individual Mimbreño. The form of the rounded bowl may have performed a necessary utilitarian function during its life span in the culture; however, the hemispheric form was used symbolically in the Mimbres funerary rite to represent the barrier between two worlds: the Underworld and the Upperworld. The act of breaking the vessel created a passageway between these two worlds. Thus, the domed shaped form with the hole in the top of it became a symbol in the Mimbres burial rite for death and emergence into the spiritual world. It is within this ideological context that the painted images found on the interior surfaces of these vessels should be examined.

NOTES

1. Steven A. LeBlanc, *The Mimbres People: Ancient Pueblo Painters of the American Southwest*, (London, 1983), p. 119.
2. The exceptions are stylistic studies in which the basic form is considered in relationship to how it effects the structural elements of painted design. For example see: J. J. Brody, *Mimbres Painted Pottery*, (Albuquerque, 1977), pp. 131-200.
3. For examples see: Fred Kabotie, *Designs from the ancient Mimbreños with a Hopi interpretation*, (Flagstaff, 1949); O. T. Snodgrass, *Realistic art and times of the Mimbres Indians*, (El Paso, 1975); and Pat Carr, "Mimbres mythology," *University of Texas Southwestern Studies Monograph* 56, Austin, 1979).
4. For examples see: Jesse Walter Fewkes, "Designs on prehistoric pottery from the Mimbres valley, New Mexico," *Smithsonian Miscellaneous Collections* 74(6), (Washington, D.C., 1923); and Fewkes, "Additional designs on prehistoric Mimbres pottery," *Smithsonian Miscellaneous Collections* 76 (8), (Washington, D.C., 1924).
5. Brody, *Mimbres Painted Pottery*, p. 211.
6. Harriet S. Cosgrove and Cornelius B. Cosgrove, "The Swarts Ruin: A typical Mimbres site in southwestern New Mexico," *Papers of the Peabody Museum of American Archaeology and Ethnology* 15(1), (Cambridge, 1932), p. 28.
7. Brody, *Mimbres Painted Pottery*, p. 128.
8. Steven A. LeBlanc, "Temporal change in Mogollon ceramics," In *Southwestern ceramics: A comparative review*, ed. Albert A. Schroder, *The Arizona Archaeologist*, 15 (Phoenix, 1982), pp. 119-122.
9. Clara Lee Tanner, *Prehistoric Southwestern Craft Art* (Tucson, 1976), p. 114.
10. J. J. Brody, "Mimbres art: Sidetracked on the trail of a Mexican connection," *American Indian Art*, 2(4) (Scottsdale, 1977), p. 29.
11. Brody, *Mimbres Painted Pottery*, p. 138.
12. Cosgrove and Cosgrove, *Papers of the Peabody Museum of Archaeology and Ethnology* 15(1), p. 73.
13. Ruth L. Bunzel, "Introduction to Zuni ceremonialism," *Bureau of American Ethnology, Annual Report* 47, (Washington,DC, 1932). p. 487.
14. Ruth L. Bunzel, "Zuni tales," *Publications of the American Ethnological Society* 15, (Washington, D.C., 1933), p. 225.
15. Leo Simmon, editor, *Sun Chief: The Autobiography of a Hopi Indian*, (New Haven, 1942), p. 418.
16. H.R. Voth, "The traditions of the Hopi," *Fieldiana* 8, (Chicago, 1905), p. 10.
17. Ruth Benedict, *Zuni Mythology*, (New York, 1935), vol. 1, pp. 2-3.
18. Mathew W. Stirling, "Origin myth of Acoma and other records," *Bureau of American Ethnology, Bulletin* 135, (Washington, D.C., 1942), pp. 1-2.
19. Kivas are semi-subterranean structures that are generally entered from a hatch way in the roof and a ladder. They are primarily used by men.
20. A.M. Stephen, "Hopi Journal of Alexander M. Stephen," edited by E.C. Parsons, *Columbia University Contributions to Anthropology* 23, (New York, 1936) vol. 1, p. 151.
21. Simmon, *Sun Chief: The Autobiography of a Hopi Indian*, p. 271.
22. A. Ortiz, *The Tewa World: Space, time and becoming in a Pueblo Society*, (Chicago, 1969), p. 16.
23. E.C. Parsons, *Pueblo Indian Religion*, (Chicago, 1939), vol. 1 pp. 195-196.

PART FIVE

SHELTER AS SYMBOL

USES AND MEANINGS OF ARCHITECTURAL SPACE

Lee Anne Wilson

Privacy, protection, and security—these are just a few of the reasons for the construction of living places that range from simple and temporary brush structures to elaborate building of wood, stone, or adobe erected in permanent, carefully planned towns. Indeed the diversity of human solutions to the problem of shelter is amazing. The choice of materials, type of decoration, orientation and location of structure, and degree of permanence are all variables that reflect the group's response to their environment.

However, buildings are built not only to provide people with protection from the elements and privacy from their neighbors, but also to provide palaces for rulers, communal gathering places for political activity, and sacred space for ritual celebration. For example, among the tribes of Africa where a divine or semi-divine king (see Part Three) is the paramount ruler, elaborate palaces with courtyards, audience halls, ceremonial chambers, and even mausoleums serve to reenforce and reiterate the sacred power of the ruler. In other areas where a council of elders provides the ruling force, the men's council house becomes the seat of government where political debates are held, laws made and enforced, and judgments carried out (for example, see Brachear 1974 and Huet 1988 on the Dogon).

In Oceania, the men's house often provides an arena for social, political, and ritual activities including debates, discussion of effective leadership, organization of communal activities, production of ritual objects, and rehearsals of songs, dances, and other ceremonial activities. These buildings are generally regarded as the sole province of the men. Women are prohibited from entering and sometimes even from walking near by. Yet the interior of the men's house is often regarded as the belly or womb of a woman and, during puberty rites, the young boys are reborn as adult men by their passage through the womb of the men's house. In fact, in many areas the men's house has both male and female sexual characteristics contained within its framework. In addition, the men's house is either characterized as representing the body of an ancestor or the place where the ancestors come to visit, and ancestors are both male and female (see Fraser 1968), thus reconciling an essential male/female dichotomy in a manner that suggests the combining rather than the separating of the sexes.

In societies where separate ritual or ceremonial buildings are important, they are frequently distinguished from ordinary dwellings by unusual size or shape, special decoration, and specific location or orientation. For example among the Pueblo Indians of the American Southwest, a special structure known as the *kiva* is the locus of much ritual activity. As discussed in Amos Rapoport's article (*The Pueblo and Hogan: A Cross-cultural Comparison of Two Responses to an Environment*, page 308), the *kiva*, descended from prehistoric pit houses, is generally differentiated from the rest of Pueblo architecture by its subterranean or semi-subterranean location, round shape, painted wall murals, and special furnishings including benches, altars, looms, and storage facilities for ritual paraphernalia (see also Bunting 1976, Hawley 1950).

In addition to the specific buildings already mentioned, individual dwellings are often designed to reflect such important concepts as family lineage, community standing, social status, ritual ability, individual or family wealth, and even professional occupation. For example, among the Indians of the coastal Pacific Northwest, painted house fronts or carved entrance poles reflected the ancestral lineage, communal status, and wealth of the resident family, while designs painted on some Plains Indian tipis reflected ownership of ritual bundles, exploits in battle, and family status (see Fraser 1968, Brasser 1979, Lowie 1954).

In addition, the actual shape of both individual structures and village settlements frequently conveys important information. For example, two basic shapes of structures and village plans are found throughout the world–round and rectangular (or square)–with the shape often conveying significant meaning in its own right. For example, among the Dogon the basic dwelling as well as the men's council house or *toguna* is rectangular, while the women's menstrual hut is round. These particular shapes reflect the Dogon belief in the essential complementary duality of all things: round or spiral forms depict deities, creation myths, and the supernatural realm, while square, rectangular, or linear designs reflect cultivated fields, woven cloth, and the human world (Brachear 1974; see also DeMott 1974). In other societies, round or square dwellings may relate directly to that society's view of the cosmos. For example, among the Great Plains tribes of North America, the circle is thought to be the only form in harmony with nature, so both dwelling and camp circle (group of up to a thousand tipis) take this shape as do other ritually charged objects such as shields.

Not only do the shape of buildings and village plans reflect concepts essential to their inhabitants, but they are often intimately linked to the entire life cycle. For example, among the Tamberma of Northern Ghana, the house and village becomes a backdrop that delineates and shapes space much as the various passages of a Tamberma individual's life demarcate and define time (Blier, *The Dance of Death: Notes on the Architecture and Staging of Tamberma Funeral Performances*, page 275, and 1987). In this sense, the stage-set-like aspect of the Tamberma house can be compared to that of the shaman's tent of the nomadic Evenk of Siberia. For the

Evenk, this special ritual structure reflects not only the cosmos but also the shaman's journey through that cosmos (Anisimov 1963).

Buildings are rarely constructed solely for shelter. This becomes obvious when structures from a wide variety of cultures are closely examined. While protection from the actual environment may be necessary for physical survival, humans do not live by shelter alone. Larger concerns about life and death, world view, cosmic images, roles of the sexes, and the relationship of the human realm to that of the supernatural also affect building size, shape, form, function, and location. Not only do individual buildings reflect these concerns but so do village layouts, often visually depicting the relations between the sexes, images of the cosmos, and human links both to the ancestors and the supernatural realm.

BIBLIOGRAPHY

Note: In addition to references cited in the text, this bibliography also includes a sampling of related works on architecture.

Anisimov, A.F. 1963. "The Shaman's Tent of the Evenks and the Origin of the Shamanistic Rite," in *Studies in Siberian Shamanism*, edited by H.N. Michael. Arctic Institute of North America, *Anthropology of the North*, Translations from Russian Sources, No. 4. Toronto: University of Toronto Press, pp.84-123.

Blier, Suzanne Preston. 1987. *The Anatomy of Architecture: Ontology and Metaphor in Batammaliba Architectural Expression*. New York: Cambridge University Press.

Brachear, Robert. 1974. "Men's House/Women's House," in *African Art as Philosophy*, edited by Douglas Fraser. New York: Interbook, Inc., pp.76-83.

Brasser, Ted J. 1979. "Pedigree of Hugging Bear Tipi in the Blackfoot Camp," *American Indian Art Magazine*, vol. 5(1), pp.32-39.

Bunting, Bainbridge. 1976. "Architecture of the Indian Epochs," in *Early Architecture in New Mexico*, by Bainbridge Bunting. Albuquerque: University of New Mexico, pp.16-51.

Courtney-Clark, Margaret. 1986. *Ndebele: The Art of an African Tribe*. New York: Rizzoli.

——. 1990. *African Canvas: The Art of West African Women*. New York: Rizzoli.

De Mott, Barbara. 1974. "Spiral/Checkerboard," "The Spiral," "The Spiral and the Checkerboard in Dogon Ritual Life," "The Checkerboard," in *African Art as Philosophy*, edited by Douglas Fraser. New York: Interbook, pp.13-19.

Fernandez, James. 1977. *Fang Architectonics*, Working Papers in the Traditional Arts, Vol. 1. Philadelphia: Institute for the Study of Human Issues.

Fraser, Douglas. 1968. *Village Planning in the Primitive World*. New York: George Braziller.

Guidoni, Enrico. 1975. *Primitive Architecture*. New York: Harry N. Abrams, Inc.

Hawley, Florence. 1950. "Big Kivas, Little Kivas, and Moiety Houses," *Southwestern Journal of Anthropology*, vol. 6(3), pp.286-303.

Huet, Jean-Christophe. 1988. "The *Togu na* of Tenyu Ireli," *African Arts*, vol. 21(4), pp.34-37, 91.

Kernot, Bernie. 1983. "The Meeting House in Contemporary New Zealand," in *Art and Artists of Oceania*, edited by Sidney M. Mead and Bernie Kernot. Palmerston, New Zealand: The Dunmore Press, pp.181-197.

Kirtland, Louise and Deborah Wettlaufer. 1973. "Religious Architecture," in *Dimensions of Polynesia*, edited by Jehanne Teilhet. San Diego: Fine Arts Gallery of San Diego, 1973, pp.38-47.

Lowie, Robert H. 1963. "Settlement and Dwellings of Plains Indians," in *Indians of the Plains* by Robert H. Lowie. Garden City: The Natural History Press (reprinted in *Native North American Art History: Selected Readings*, edited by Zena Pearlstone Mathews and Aldona Jonaitis. Palo Alto: Peek Publications, 1982), pp.227-234.

MacDonald, George F. 1983. *Haida Monumental Art*. Vancouver: University of British Columbia Press.

Nabokov, Peter and Robert Easton. 1989. *Native American Architecture*. Oxford and New York: Oxford University Press.

Oliver, Paul. 1987. *Dwellings: The House across the World*. Austin: University of Texas Press.

——. 1971. *Shelter in Africa.* New York: Praeger.

Oliver, Paul, editor. 1977. *Shelter, Sign, & Symbol.* Woodstock, New York: The Overlook Press.

Oliver, Paul, editor. 1969. *Shelter and Society: Studies in Vernacular Architecture.* New York: Praeger.

Prussin, Labelle. 1974. "An Introduction to Indigenous African Architecture," *Journal of the Society of Architectural Historians*, vol. 33, pp.183-205.

——. 1969. *Architecture in Northern Ghana: A Study of Forms and Functions.* Berkeley and Los Angeles: University of California Press.

Rapoport, Amos. 1969. *House Form and Culture.* Englewood Cliffs, New Jersey: Foundations of Cultural Geography Series, Prentice-Hall, Inc.

Rudofsky, Bernard. 1977. *The Prodigious Builders: Notes toward a Natural History of Architecture with Special Regard to Those Species That Are Traditionally Neglected or Downright Ignored.* New York and London: Harcourt Brace Jovanovich.

——. 1964. *Architecture without Architects: A Short Introduction to Non-Pedigreed Architecture.* Garden City, New York: Doubleday & Company, Inc.

Scully, Vincent. 1972. "Men and Nature in Pueblo Architecture," in *American Indian Art: Form and Tradition*, Walker Art Center exhibition catalogue. New York: E.P. Dutton & Co., Inc., pp.34-41.

——. 1975. *Pueblo, Mountain, Village, Dance.* New York: The Viking Press.

18

The Dance of Death

Notes on the Architecture and Staging of Tamberma Funeral Performances[1]

Suzanne Preston Blier

The Tamberma of northern Togo stage elaborate funeral performances called *Tibenti* ("The Dance of Drums") to honor their deceased male and female elders. These funerary productions follow the same dramatic format each time they are performed. They are presented by a group of artists who act out specific roles in front of and for the benefit of a critical audience, which often numbers several hundred. Because of the significant factor of the audience, and because of the emphatic (if sometimes obscure) "story" being told, performances of this type are set apart from standard Tamberma religious ritual. This distinction is further supported by the essential role in the funeral of designated casts, specific stages, coordinated lighting, dramatic timing, and associated criticism. In addition, according to one Tamberma elder, the principal design features of the traditional Tamberma two-story house (Figs. 1, 2) are defined by the crucial role that the house potentially plays as a theatre. He explains the differences between the houses of the Tamberma and those of their neighbors, the Lamba, vis-à-vis the differing dramaturgical needs of these two groups. "As the Lamba do not perform their funerals in the same way as the Tamberma perform them, the architecture of the two should not be the same."

In this light, it may be useful to discuss the Tamberma funeral from a dramaturgical perspective. As proposed by Kenneth Burke (1941, 1945, 1952), such a model can be applied to the analysis of symbolic action in both social process and literary form. It can also be appropriate, as here, in describing the complex architectural contexts and the symbolism of a funeral cycle. Appropriately, in the course of its multi-year structure and division into actlike segments, the

Reprinted in abridged form from *Res*, No. 2, Cambridge, MA: Peabody Museum of Archaeology & Ethnology, Harvard University, 1981, pages 107-143 with permission of the author and publisher.

Figure 1 View of Tamberma house from back. House owner and architect: Atchana. Village of Koufitoukou. August 28, 1977.

funeral is viewed by the Tamberma as a type of "play." As one elder explained to me. "In *Tibenti* [the funeral cycle] one 'plays' the deceased." Because of the inclusion of both actual and figurative action, these performances also conform to the wider concept of play as it has been discussed by Huizinga (1938, p. 15).

My treatment of the Tamberma funeral performance is structured around a greatly abbreviated synopsis of its main events (see chart, Blier, 1981) in which the multiple dimensions of the traditional drama will be described through the articulation of its settings. Aspects that will be discussed within the context of each funeral segment include the use of the traditional house as a performance theatre, the delineation and symbolism of specific staging areas, the selection and meanings of special forms of theatrical lighting, the employment of stage scenery (and related props, cues, and musical accompaniment), and the principal role of casts, patronage, criticism, and symbolic action in the performance.

THE PERSON SLEEPS

Every Tamberma funeral play begins with a prologue made up of scenes collectively called "The Person Sleeps" (*Onitiloua*). This preliminary act is a private one taking place on the day of death. It has as its main concerns: the announcement

Figure 2 Facade of Tamberma house. House owner: Tiefieti. Architect: Atchana. Village of Koufitoukou. January 28, 1977.

of the death, the determination of the cause of death, the construction of the tomb, the preparation of the deceased for burial, and the burial itself. Drawing examples from this prologue segment, I will discuss here two central dramaturgical features in the funeral. These include the choice of stages used in the performance and dramatic structuration.

Stages and Dramatic Structuration

Each traditional Tamberma two-story house contains a number of areas that function as stages during the funeral performance (see Figs. 3, 4). These stages derive their form from the actual rooms, alcoves, and wall areas of the house.

Figure 3
Diagram of house funeral stages: (a) house portal stages (upper and lower); (b) male and female wall stages; (c) male and female granary overhang stages; (d) taboté hole stages (upper and lower).

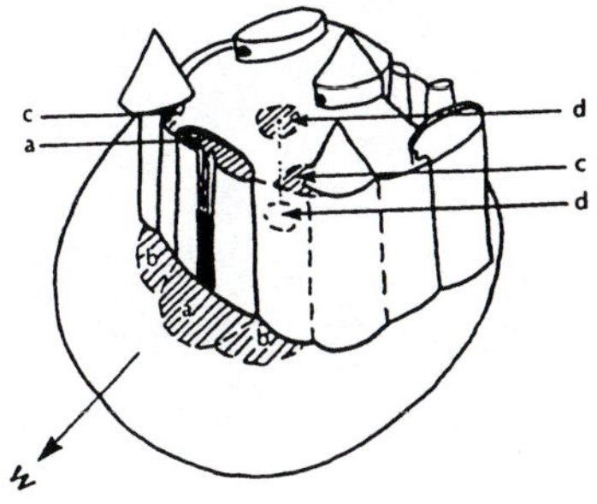

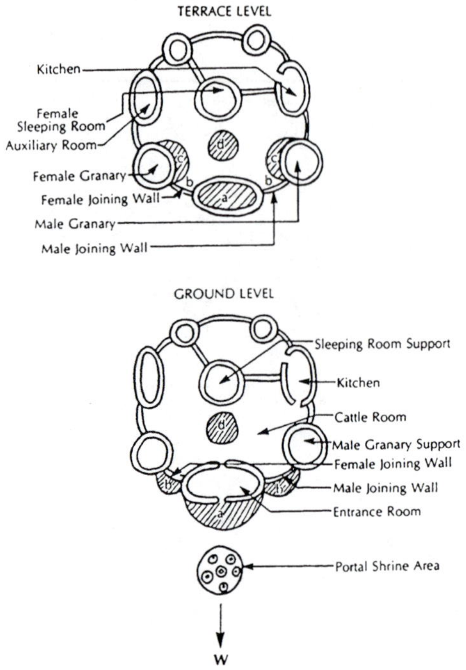

Figure 4
Diagram of house funeral stages: (a) house portal stages (upper and lower); (b) male and female wall stages; (c) male and female granary overhang stages; (d) taboté hole stages (upper and lower).

Figure 5 Funeral musicians playing on upper portal stage. Village of Lissani. April 29, 1977. (Note quivers and poles covered with money displayed on facade. Funeral drums are being played in foregraound.)

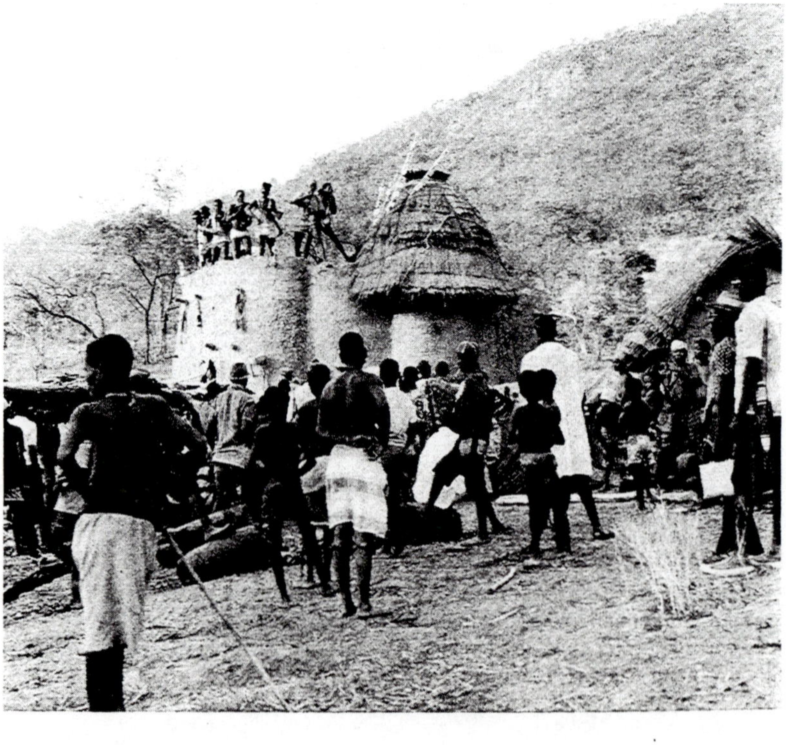

Viewing places fan out around each stage, either inside the house itself or out-of-doors within the perimeters of the circular landscaped yard. The most public scenes of the funeral are enacted on those stages seen from the largest viewing areas. These are generally located either on the entrance roof or outside the house along the front of its western facade (Fig. 5). Other stages, which are reserved for private or semiprivate funeral action sequences, have more limited viewing facilities, usually inside the house or on its terrace.

In the funeral, certain scenes are always performed on certain staging areas. The choice of a particular stage for a given scene is important, for the symbolism associated with each is often central in conveying the principal theme of any related action. In "The Person Sleeps," consistencies in the symbolism and choice of funeral staging locales are clear. The two "portal" stages (the entrance roof and the entryway), for example, are usually employed for those scenes concerned with the ontology of death. In the course of prologue action, the relationship between doorways (the means of architectural transition) and death (the moment of life's transition) can be seen both in the frequent use of the deceased's front door as a mortuary stretcher and in the role of the deceased's house portal in funeral divinations to determine the cause of death. Similar symbolism is displayed in the ceremonial grinding of millet on the mortuary house doorstep before the departure for the cemetery (Fig. 6). This prologue grinding action is explained as a reference to the recent death, specifically to the fact that the departed elder will no longer need earthly sustenance. The marking of a miniature tomb in front of the deceased's portal further defines the reality of death, for it foreshadows the construction of the tomb, which follows at the cemetery.

Other forms of staging symbolism come into play in prologue actions performed on the two house *taboté* areas. The *taboté* stages circle the ceremonial hole (called *taboté*), which pierces through the house in the middle of its main

Figure 6
Grinding millet on doorstep at funeral. Village of Lissani. April 29, 1977.

terrace. During the funeral, the upper and lower *taboté* stages, which are defined by this hole, find use primarily in scenes of spirit transition. This staging symbolism is based on the role that the *taboté* plays during house religious ceremonies. In these, the *taboté* hole is frequently identified as a means of spirit passage, i.e., as a vertical axis from the house center to the heavens. In the course of the funeral prologue, perhaps the most significant example of *taboté* transition symbolism is found in the taking of the deceased's stone *taboté* cover from its normal position on the house terrace to the cemetery where the stone will serve as the tomb closure (Fig. 7). The transporting of this stone from one funeral stage to another effectively marks the transition of the deceased and his (her) soul from the community of the living to the community of the dead. Similarly, in the later "turning-over" (*bita*) ceremony of the next act, the now coverless *taboté* hole at the deceased's house is used to signal the transition that the elder's soul makes in its upward flight from this world to the world of the ancestor spirits in the sky. Likewise, in the following act ("The Afternoon Dance") this same hole is used as a transitional means when grooming materials are passed down through it so that the deceased (represented by a baobab wood carving on the interior) can be prepared for the soul's final voyage to the world of the dead.

The four remaining funeral stages, i.e., the areas adjoining the raised male and female granaries and the adjacent male and female joining walls, reflect other concerns in staging. These four stages are generally reserved for sequences glorifying the deceased. Male stages (on the south side of the house) are used in scenes that praise deceased men: female stages (on the north side of the house) are for those scenes honoring women. The linking of these four stages with the deceased's honor finds support in the frequent association of these areas with a person's identity and wealth in life: the granary usually defines an elder's economic wealth; the adjoining wall area often incorporates his or her sacred

Figure 7
Placing house taboté stone over tomb hole after burial. Village of Koufitoukou. September 25, 1977.

wealth (related religious shrines). In "The Person Sleeps" the honorific symbolism of these stages is clear, for it is here where the deceased (or a surrogate figure) will lie in state to receive gifts and songs of praise before the burial (Fig. 8). In later funeral acts, these four stages similarly serve as the backdrops for much of the honorific scenery and props (cloths, quivers, money, etc.) which are intended to display the considerable wealth and status of the deceased elder in the community (Figs. 5, 9).

Like staging, prescribed forms of dramatic structure also are clearly manifested in this preliminary funeral segment. One can see, for instance, the use of such theatrical structuring techniques as symbolic foreshadowing in the delimitation of a miniature tomb in front of the house door before the elders leave for the cemetery to build the actual tomb. This miniature tomb likewise foreshadows the sequence of action followed in every subsequent act, for in each, the tomb becomes the central structuring element for the play action as a whole. The use of synecdoche is similarly conveyed in "The Person Sleeps." In this and in later funeral acts, the house is generally seen to represent its deceased owner (as a container represents its contents) through its dress (scenery) and ritual use. As one Tamberma elder has noted, at the funeral "we [speak of the house and] say that it is a man and it is dead. . . . We call the house *takoukyèta* (the dead house)."

THE DANCE OF DRUMS

The next act of the funeral, called *Tibenti* or "The Dance of Drums," incorporates a separate grouping of dramatic scenes. These are either presented the evening following the prologue or, more commonly, they are postponed until the festival months of January through April. The action of "The Dance of Drums" centers around a number of generally sober and serious scenes associated with the loss

Figure 8
Women singing mourning songs beside wooden figure representing deceased (figure is positioned under straw of granary overhang). Village of Lissani, April 29, 1977.

Figure 9
Mortuary house dressed in funerary cloths. Cowrie and bead strand hangs from portal. Possessions of deceased beside door. Village of Koufitoukou. August 20, 1977.

of the family elder. This act is concerned with publicly mourning the loss, with reinitiating the deceased into the various religious associations of the village, and finally with turning out his or her soul so that it will leave for the world of the ancestors. Special forms of theatrical lighting and dramaturgical choreography are important elements in this as in other play segments.

Theatrical Lighting

Prescribed forms of lighting are assured in the funeral, both through the timing of scenes to coincide with particular day- or night-light qualities (as defined vis-à-vis the positioning of the sun or moon) and through the concomitant use of fixed, precisely oriented stages for each dramatic sequence. The common employment of special festival months (January through April) and the universal orientation of Tamberma houses toward the west, also means that the directionality of light—the angle of the sun and moon—remains relatively constant for each funeral drama. The choice of late winter for most funeral performances is significant because during this period the usually tall and thick millet crop that surrounds Tamberma houses is cut to a short stubble. This allows a maximum amount of light to reach the house stages, and provides the assembled audience with both a cleared seating area and an unobstructed view of the front house stages. In addition, food is relatively abundant at this time. Furthermore, because there is a general ease from farm work during this period, there is time to complete the considerable preparations required before the performance can take place.

As with performance staging, certain qualities of natural light are frequently employed in the funeral to reinforce the symbolism and aesthetic values of the dramatic action. Dusk and dawn, the times marking the termination and beginning of day and night, for example, are generally reserved for those funeral action sequences that are linked to beginning and end. "The Dance of Drums" itself climaxes with the dawn-lit "turning-over" (*bita*) ceremony on the house entrance roof. At the beginning of this dramatic climax, as dawn is seen to approach, the funeral cast and audience leave the warmth of the house interior, where they had been participating in initiation songs, dances, and related action sequences throughout the night. Meanwhile, two funeral performers climb to the top of the entrance roof, appearing dramatically silhouetted against the rich backdrop of the just-awakening eastern sky. During the funerals of elder men, these two cast members cut the male (south) house horn and allow it to drop to the ground along with the deceased's bow, quiver, and leather bag. Immediately following this action, in the funerals of both men and women, the appropriate male and female granary cover is turned over on its head—a *bita* action viewed as a public sign that the elder's life has ended, that life itself has been reversed. At this early hour, the faces and props of the performers on the entrance roof are still very much obscured by the blackness of night surrounding them, but their actions, framed by the blue and red light of dawn are dramatically distinct. The parallel light qualities at dusk have similar importance in the funeral, especially for the joyful terminations and inception scenes like the gift-giving sequence at the climax of the next act ("The Afternoon Dance," Fig. 10), or the children's cereal feast at the conclusion of the third play segment ("The Feast of the Dead").

The broadly defined periods of noon and midnight have still other symbolic and aesthetic roles in Tamberma funeral dramas. These light periods are frequently identified by the Tamberma with the paths or "stations" of the sun and moon across the sky. Accordingly, in the funeral, noon and midnight are generally reserved for scenes of process or life passage. During "The Dance of Drums" and the following "Afternoon Dance," the light associated with noon and midnight finds primary use in the processual scenes of initiation. In these action

Figure 10
Tossing down cowries and agricultural produce from the house entrance roof onto the mortuary stretcher. Women fan the stretcher with skins and a covered basket. Village of Koufitoukou. October 27, 1977.

segments, the mortuary house walls and carved baobab figure are sequentially tapped with initiatory *sacra* as a means of reinitiating the deceased into the various associations that he or she had known in life. Supplementary lighting is frequently used for both the noon and midnight scenes: burning brands and bonfires provide illumination and visual emphasis for somber nighttime actions: the house doorways and windows serve as interior light shafts during the day.

The contrasting midmorning and afternoon light periods (roughly between 9:00 and 10:30 A.M. and between 3:00 and 4:30 P.M.) are generally associated with scenes of communication, particularly between human beings and the spirit world. Midmorning and midafternoon are ordinarily identified by the Tamberma as the times when the ancestors most frequently descend to earth. In the funeral, afternoon sunlight likewise is used for the principal ancestor communication scenes (generally offerings) associated with the ancestral spirits who are said to come to earth to witness and participate in the funeral festivities. This same light period provides an appropriate theatrical backdrop for the dramatic processions back to the house once the cemetery action has terminated (Fig. 11). Such processions include an orchestra of horn and flute players, whose music is said to represent appropriately the voices of the returning ancestors. Mortuary divinations, the formalized communication between the deceased and his or her descendants to determine the cause of death, similarly take place during midmorning or afternoon, as does the climax sequence in the play's epilogue ("The Reenactment") when the deceased's spirit is called back to earth to serve as a family ancestor.

Dramaturgical Choreography

Dramaturgical choreography or prescribed configurations of movement are also of importance in the funeral performance. These delineated movement patterns

Figure 11
Funeral procession from the cemetary to the mortuary house. Village of Koutanliakou. March 4, 1977.

have significance both visually, in directing the eye of the audience in a particular manner, and symbolically, by helping to define the content of particular play segments. In Tamberma drama, choreographic movements of the type discussed here replace many of the spoken lines or dialogue central to Western theatre.

Four linear modes of choreographic movement can be distinguished in the funeral: the circle; the horizontal line; the downward line; and the reversal line. The most commonly employed of these dramatic lines is the circle, a movement pattern that circumscribes forms and delimits their perimeters, thereby reinforcing the spatial identity associated with each. In the funeral, circular lines are formed as clockwise movement patterns when linked to women, but are counterclockwise motion sequences when employed for men. Like the form of the house itself, circular movement in the funeral is generally used to suggest themes of gathering together or containment. Thus, when the house (or surrogate body) is circled and "tapped" in the initiation sequences of "The Dance of Drums" and "The Afternoon Dance," this is seen to assure the placement of the initiatory deity inside the interior of the house and, by extension, inside the body of the deceased elder. Similarly, in the play prologue, when the body is carried in a circle around the perimeter of the house before being brought to the cemetery, this "line" is said to call together the house ancestors so that they will come to the cemetery for the ceremonies to be performed there. At the end of every cemetery scene, the tomb itself is circled. According to one elder, in this circling, one is silently calling the name of the first village ancestor and asking him to unite all the ancestors to come back to the house for the rites that follow. Another circular pattern, the one made around a calabash and basket in front of the door and later at the cemetery to delimit the form of the tomb, also suggests containment, as exemplified in the definition of the chamber that will eventually hold the deceased.

Another key choreographic form in funeral performances is a horizontal one. This is often used in the play as a means of uniting time, place, and persons. The funeral parade from the cemetery represents one such horizontal line (Fig. 11). It unites the ancestors, village inhabitants, and present cast of characters, bringing the action from the tomb to the house. This linear mode is essentially a profile one: a pattern of movement intended to be seen from the side. It is a visual device that pulls the eye both to the place where the line originated and to the place where it is going.

The two final choreographic patterns used in Tamberma funeral performances include a distinct downward motion, which is used to suggest separation, and a reversal or turning-over motion, called *bita*, which is employed to allude to death (the reversal of life). Both of these lines are clearly shown in the climax scene of this act. At this time, in a man's funeral the male house horn and the deceased's possessions are dropped to the ground in a downward line. This is said to force the spirit of the dead person to separate itself from the house. During this same climax scene, the deceased person's house granary cap is turned over onto its head–a motion of reversal signaling that life has ended.

Both of these choreographed motions also have significant visual import. The reversal line emphasizes the silhouettes of images, since in turning things on their heads one is forced to see them as independent shapes having a particular quality and dimension devoid of normal cognitive or functional associations. In contrast, the downward line visually points up the purely frontal aspect of a given form. Appropriately, in the funeral this line is most often employed on the upper portal stage in the center of the house facade.

THE AFTERNOON DANCE

The second act of the funeral, called "The Afternoon Dance" (*Koubenyouakou*), begins at about noon on the day following "The Dance of Drums." Through its multiple scenes, the major actions of the preceding evening are repeated, but the overall emphasis is shifted from one of sorrow to one of joy for the deceased. This act, in its repeated action sequences, focuses on the reinitiation of the deceased and the exuberant send-off for his or her soul. These scenes serve to glorify the deceased and to honor his or her family. The act climaxes with a vibrant dance and a shower of food and money for the deceased's voyage to the other world (Fig. 10). These riches are dropped onto the mortuary stretcher from the upper portal stage at dusk. The *fabenfé* drumbeat accompanying this action emphasizes the theme of voyage and transition at this time.

Scenery and Props

In this, as in other acts, scenery is an important means of reinforcing the dramatic sequences. When we arrive at the house of the deceased, we are immediately aware that this will be a drama concerning death. The appropriate granary cover has been turned on its head (Fig. 5), and the deceased's essential worldly possessions are grouped together on the corresponding male or female side of

Figure 12
Funeral "props" and scenery lined up along mortuary house facade. From left to right: hoes, stretcher, hoe blades, house door, bow/quiver/sack assemblage (behind door), woman's initiation basket, and lance. Goat skins are attached to the wall above these objects. Village of Koutanliakou. March 4, 1977.

the entrance (Figs. 9, 12). We also see that three funeral drums have been positioned together in front of the same house area (Fig. 5). The presence of these drums reinforces one of the funeral's central themes, a vibrant "dance of death" choreographed to the rhythm of drums.

Most of the additional scenery elements that make up this stage set express the honor due to the deceased (Figs. 5, 9, 12). Imported cloths, fresh animal skins, cowrie (shell money) strands, and money draped on poles are displayed on the granaries, male and female joining walls, and upper portal terrace to symbolize the wealth of the deceased. Bows, quivers, hoes, and agricultural produce are similarly amassed along the facade (or interior) to show the deceased's hunting and farming talents. Forked sticks, flutes, and a man's initiation headdress recall an elder's membership in *Lifoni*, the initiation society for men. Lances, chicken cages, horned headdresses, bells, and condiment baskets define association with the women's initiation cycle, *Likuntili*.

Props taken primarily from the scenery compositions also have an important part in many Tamberma funeral segments. Thus, in the second act, when the action shifts to the house after the semiprivate meal at the cemetery, hoes are taken from the facade scenery arrangements to serve as props for persons representing the deceased man's adversaries. These hoes are used to shovel dirt and weeds onto the house as a means of insulting the deceased. The same props are later taken up by young men representing the deceased's *Lifoni* "brothers" as they plow a circle around the house to praise the elder's lifelong work. The lance and antelope headdress similarly become props for a performer portraying the deceased's "elder daughter" as she runs to meet the returning funeral parade. The animal-skin wall coverings, the condiment basket, and again the initiation headdress function as props when they are taken to fan the surrogate body as food and praise are rained onto it (Fig. 10). . . .

Play Aesthetics

The various members of the funeral cast contribute as artists to the play's overall aesthetic image through their carefully choreographed movement patterns and through their use of the house facade for arrangements of scenery. Such compositions are each aimed at "enhancing the beauty of the house," as one elder explained.

A variety of aesthetic factors are taken into consideration by these artists during the performance. The criteria used are similar to aesthetic factors that are important in other Tamberma art forms, particularly architecture. The first is visibility, e.g., each part or element of the composition or movement sequence must be clear and thoroughly "readable." For this reason, the musical instruments, hoes, quivers, cloths, and skins arranged on the facade are carefully placed so that the distinct features of each will be seen (Figs. 5, 9, 12). Vessels, similarly, are often turned on their sides so that the top opening and interior surfaces will be open to view. Visibility is also an important characteristic in the choreographed funeral movements. In these, slow and deliberate actions are emphasized so that none of the essential elements will be missed.

The second aesthetic principle found in the funeral play is one stressing the repetition of forms within the whole so that each motif will be clearly defined. Repetition becomes an important factor both in scenery compositions (like the multiples of hoes, cloths, quivers, and flutes used in the facade arrangements) and in the structuration of the overall funeral cycle (emphasizing multiple repeated segments and action modes). Another aesthetic consideration in the funeral is framing, which can be observed in the parade paths that carefully encircle and thus give emphasis to the forms or spaces they circumscribe (the tomb, the cemetery, the house, etc.). In scenery compositions, the use of framing is evident in the choice of plain background spaces to set off the scenery compositions and assemblages.

Balance of mood, theme, and action also is important. Thus each funeral play contrasts periods of relative activity with periods of comparative calm; somber actions are alternated with joyful ones; day scenes are followed by night scenes. Likewise, scenery compositions carefully balance the diverse colors, forms, compositions, and textures of their various elements so that this juxtaposing will provide greater interest. A similar concern can be seen in the repeated use of multiple levels of space in the funeral play, both for staging areas and with respect to the movement sequences and scenery compositions associated with each.

Criticism

Critical reaction to the funeral performance shows a concern for these aesthetic criteria as well as for other dramaturgical factors such as the size of the production, the wealth of scenery, the number of people in attendance, the "script" interpretation, and the intensity of the drama. Because funeral productions often have several scenes occurring simultaneously on different stages for different audiences, an appraisal is usually formulated independently, according to the role and place of each viewer. Nonetheless, an overall criticism is generally made as well.

Funerals with few actors, props, or sparse scenery are said to be dull and joyless by young and old alike. Such was the case with one funeral performed in the middle of the rainy season when there was no time for an elaborate performance. A funeral for a dead baobab tree (which had been "sponsored" by a village ancestor) during the same period was similarly viewed as uninteresting. Its purpose was solely to fulfill a ritual requirement. On the other hand, funerals with an abundance of stage scenery, an extensive cast, a large audience, and vibrant action are discussed for many years.

THE FEAST OF THE DEAD

"The Feast [Cereal] of the Dead" (*Boukoukia*), the third funeral segment, takes place on the day following "The Afternoon Dance." It provides the setting for payment of the various funeral expenses. The most important participants in this act are the relatives of the deceased. In "The Feast of the Dead," the deceased's maternal relatives receive large quantities of food (cooked cereal and fresh meat) from the ultimate patrons of the funeral play, the paternal family of the late elder. This is in recognition of the role of the maternal relatives as corporate mothers. Appropriate portions of meat and cereal are also set aside in this act for the Earth priest, "the guardians of death," the musicians, and others who played significant parts in the funeral production.

Performance Payment

"The Feast of the Dead" climaxes at dusk with the offering of multiple balls of cooked cereal (presented on a winnowing tray) to family children standing in front of the door on the house's lower portal staging area. This action is seen as a direct reference to the finality of death (the deceased no longer requires food) and to the potential for future life (new children) since the necessary payment (the funeral) has been provided. This feast has particular importance because for the Tamberma food and eating are common metaphors for life. Such an association between food (the principal means of payment) and regeneration is suggested in funeral songs . . . in which the house serves as a symbol of the great loss. . . .

Significantly, the broad concept of payment that is so strongly emphasized in this act also provides one of the principal structuring devices for the funeral play as a whole. In each act there is an inherent theme of payment. The first two acts incorporate dance presentations, the third centers around food, the fourth focuses on drink. This formal sequence–dance, food, drink–also is followed in other Tamberma sacrifices as payment to a particular spirit or deity. Thus the dance defines the motion of sacrifice; feast is the offering; and drink is the gift making it sacrosanct.

THE DRINK OF THE DEAD

In the preceding sections, we have discussed several key themes important to the development of the funeral's central story. "The Person Sleeps" begins by announcing the recent death; "The Dance of Drums" brusquely sends away the deceased's soul; "The Afternoon Dance" serves to honor this spirit on its trip to the world of the dead; and "The Feast of the Dead" provides payment for his or her life. The next act, "The Drink of the Dead" (*Bakouna*), which takes place usually three days later, can be viewed as aimed primarily at encouraging the deceased to return and bring forth children in the families of his or her descendants. The stress on rebirth in this act is emphasized in various songs of the funeral. [For] example, the metaphor of a poorly kept house suggests the plight of families who are without offspring because of the failure of ancestors to return and sponsor young. . . .

Symbolic Action

The importance of life renewal in this fourth act brings us to the question of symbolic action and its role in the theatrical structure of the funeral. A series of symbolic actions are central in this act as a means of assuring the future pregnancy of young women of the house so that the life recently lost will be replaced. With this in mind, during "The Drink of the Dead" segment, the deceased's married daughters and daughters-in-law are asked to stand in the center of the house cattle room on the lower *taboté* stage, facing west into the late afternoon sun. Here, on the spot where they will eventually bear children, a family aunt smooths butter (an allusion to fatness and fertility) on their small toes (metaphors for children).

Other types of regeneration found in symbolic action during this act document the Tamberma theory of conception, a theory deriving ultimately from the Tamberma account of creation. According to this legend, when the earth and sky originally separated, the first Tamberma male ancestors who were living on earth fell ill and died. Immediately after, their wives became pregnant and soon bore children. Death accordingly was necessary for new life to spring forth. Symbolic actions that allude to this death-birth relationship are numerous. In one scene of this act, an adversary of the deceased man is asked to shoot an arrow through the late elder's quiver, which is placed against the portal. This action (which also occasionally occurs in the prior "Afternoon Dance") is seen not only to injure his pride, but also to establish publicly the death of the deceased so that new life will soon follow in the family.

During a parallel segment of a woman's funeral, the shooting of the quiver is often replaced by the destruction of ten to fifteen calabash bowls in front of the door. These vessels, assembled by the female guardians of death on the entrance roof, are important Tamberma symbols for marriage and the procreative powers of women. They are dropped from the roof and are then trampled on by the men standing below. In addition to this dramatic destruction, there often follows a competition between the family of the woman's parents and the family of her husband to see who will catch and retain her closed condiment basket after it has been dropped from the terrace roof. The family that is successful in keeping this basket is said ultimately to receive the deceased woman's aid in bringing forth children. In this context, the closed condiment basket (like the calabash) suggests her womb, just as the adversary's arrow alludes to the deceased man's part in the reproductive process.

Related symbolic action takes place at the cemetery as the living son and daughter of the deceased (or persons representing them) complete the tomb "terrace" (Fig. 14). Their participation in this construction is said to assure that future children will be strong architects and house plasterers. The talent is thought to pass from the late elder to the descendants at the tomb.

The path followed by the funeral musicians from the cemetery to the house, then through its stages (Fig. 13), also has symbolic importance. It is intended to show the soul of the deceased the road it should take in coming back to form the new child. In this and in other acts, the flute and voice songs of these musicians are aimed at encouraging the deceased to return quickly through their praise of his (or her) hunting, farming, and child-producing qualities. To make the point clearer, the assemblage of the deceased's personal possessions (*tinanti*)–the eating and cooking vessels (Fig. 9), shoulder bag, condiment basket, walking stick, quiver, and bow–as well as the cords, roots, and baskets associated with the funeral are placed beside the door. Because of the distinguishing personal "dirt,"

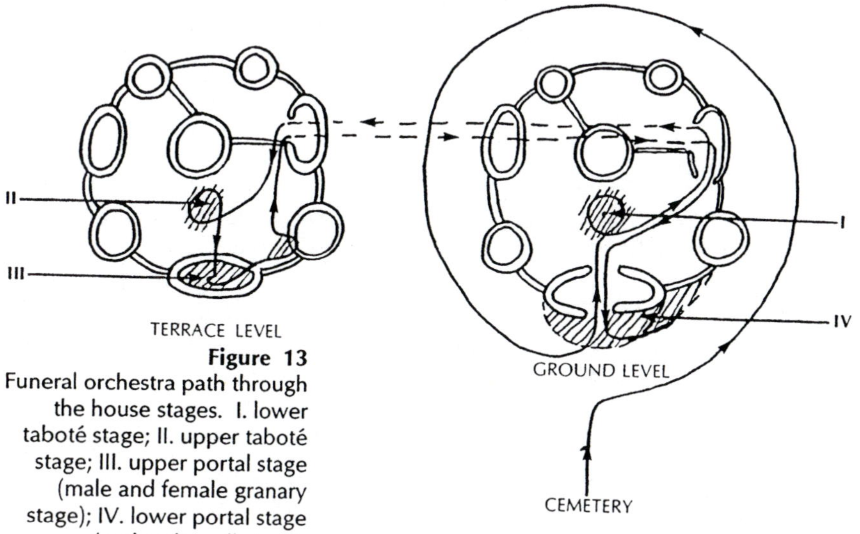

Figure 13
Funeral orchestra path through the house stages. I. lower taboté stage; II. upper taboté stage; III. upper portal stage (male and female granary stage); IV. lower portal stage (and male wall stage).

or essence, found in them, they are said to assure that the ancestor will return to the correct house.

Symbolic action linked to regeneration is also important in the various initiation sequences in the funeral. These initiations are intended to make certain that the resulting children will be acquainted with the associated initiation deities and therefore will not suffer from fright and possible death at meeting them later for the first time. Thus a priest explains the ceremonial red and white or black and white dotted forms which are painted on a corpse before burial.

Figure 14
Plastering the tomb terrace. Note upper rounded surface of the overturned water jar and west-facing "portal" of the tomb. Village of Koufitoukou. October 31, 1977.

> When a man dies, you do *Lifoni* [men's initiation] to him again—that which he did before he died. And when he brings out a child, the child will know that. If you do not do this, when he dies, the child will refuse [to be initiated] . . . the child will die.

As a reinforcement of this idea, several Tamberma elders have suggested that the funeral play as a whole is structured around the men's and women's initiation cycle. This is defined not only by the rituals and ordering of the various funeral sequences, but also through the use of house scenery to recall the image of the novices as they emerge from initiation rites (Fig. 15). As one priest explained, "Dressing the house with funeral cloths is like dressing the novices at *Lifoni*" (men's initiation). In the final public rites of initiation, rich cloths are draped over the shoulders of the male and female novices (like those draped over the upper stories of the funeral house) (Fig. 9), cowries are hung around their necks and waists (like those placed around the portal), and horned headdresses are placed on their heads (paralleling the earthen horns on the center of the entrance roof). Through symbolic action, the house is thus reinitiated to represent and nurture its new youth (future offspring).

Figure 15 *Lifoni* initiates carrying bows, quivers, leather sacks, and whips. Cloth streamers are suspended from their straw hats. Village of Kounadokou. May 15, 1977.

THE REENACTMENT

"The Reenactment" (*Likou*) is the funeral epilogue. It takes place a year or two after the main funeral sections described above, and serves both to summarily repeat the events of the preceding acts and to terminate the mourning period through various multivillage parades, mock battles, vibrant drum tatoos, and contests of power. The end of the mourning period is defined through the casting away of the deceased's assembled portal possessions (*tinanti*) at the crossroads. When combined with another late afternoon crossroad and portal scene, which entices the deceased's soul back to the house with food and drink, and the subsequent construction of an ancestor shrine (*liboloni*) beside the door, this effectively reincorporates the deceased—who now is an ancestor—into the house. As the funeral epilogue, "The Reenactment" is an appropriate play segment for closing observations on the importance of theatre in Tamberma architectural design.

Architecture and Theatre

It is clear that a dramaturgical analysis offers much to our understanding of Tamberma architecture with respect to its structure, symbolism, and use. Important factors or architectural design are determined by the potential need within each house for precise staging and performance areas. Theatrical factors also influence house landscaping and orientation. For this reason the front yard is designed as an expansive area that can seat large audiences. The western alignment of Tamberma houses assures a consistency of lighting for theatrical effect and symbolism. Numerous decorative and structural elements in the house likewise are built with their theatrical use in mind: the earthen house "horn" can be "cut," the granary covers can be turned on their heads, the door can be removed and used as a stretcher.

Architectural criticism also takes into account the important use of the house as a theatre. Of the houses I saw completed in 1977, one was criticized because its incorrect room placement would adversely affect the amount and direction of interior light for the performance. Another was derided because its misplaced roof supports would greatly impair interior funeral dances. An admonishment heard during a different ceremony ("He says his terrace is not solid, so dance less, and do it . . . slowly") suggests that the quality of the performance itself may be threatened when structural standards in Tamberma architecture are not maintained. Finally, the dramaturgical use of the house helps to make certain the maintenance of high overall aesthetic qualities in architecture, so that the dramas presented at these house theatres will have a consistent and visually powerful staging. Appropriately, therefore, many Tamberma men, as they approach the age of Tibenti (i.e., their sixties) commission a grand, more spacious house within the traditional mode. Such men are, in essence, designing the theatres that will be used for their own funerals.

NOTES

1. Background information on the Tamberma may help to place them in the broader African perspective. The Tamberma (or Batammariba, as they call themselves) are a traditional Voltaic people living in the remote Atacora Mountains of present-day Togo and Benin. They remain generally isolated from the broader influences of both Christianity and Islam. Paul Mercier (1949, 1953, 1954, 1968) provides considerable cultural information on the eastern Tamberma, whom he refers to variously as Somba and as Betammadibe. Leo Frobenius earlier published (1913) information on the eastern Tamberma near Tapounté. K. Kourouma (1954) has provided a brief description of a Somba/Tamberma burial. The Tamberma houses, where these funerals take place, are occupied by individual, generally nuclear, patrilineal family groups (average house size, five persons). These houses stand twenty to thirty feet in diameter and are usually fifteen to twenty feet in height.

BIBLIOGRAPHY

Adedji, Joel A. 1966. "The Place of Drama in Yoruba Religious Observance," *Odù*, no. 3, pp. 88-94.

——. 1969. "Traditional Yoruba Theater," *African Arts/Arts d'Afrique*, vol. 3, no. 1, pp. 60-63.

Blier, Suzanne Preston. 1980. African Art as Theatre: The Mount Collection. Exhibition Catalogue, Vassar College, Poughkeepsie, N.Y.

——. 1981. "Architecture of the Tamberma (Togo)." Ph.D. dissertation, Columbia University.

Burke, Kenneth. 1941. *The Philosophy of Literary Form*. Baton Rouge, La.

——. 1945. *A Grammar of Motives*. New York.

——. 1952. *A Rhetoric of Motives*. New York.

Cardinall, A. W. [1920]. *The Natives of the Northern Territories of the Gold Coast*. New York.

——. 1921. "Customs at Death of King of Dagomba," *Man*, no.52 (June), pp. 89-91.

Charles, Lucile. 1948. "Regeneration through Drama at Death," *Journal of American Folklore*, vol. 61, pp. 151-174.

Clark, J.P. 1966. "Aspects of Nigerian Drama," *Nigeria*, vol. 89, pp. 118-126.

Delafosse, Maurice. 1909. "Le Peuple Siena ou Sénoufo," *Revue des Études Ethnographiques et Sociologiques*, vol. 2, pp. 1-21.

——. 1916. "Contribution à l'Étude du Théâtre Chez les Noirs," *Bulletin de Comité d'Études Historiques et Scientifique de l'Afrique Occidentale Francaise*, pp. 352-355.

Dhlomo, H. 1939. "Nature and Variety of Tribal Drama," *Bantu Studies*, vol. 13, pp. 33-48.

Enekwe, Ossie Onuora. 1976. "Theatre in Nigeria: The Modern vs. the Traditional," *Yale/Theatre*, vol. 8, no. 1, pp. 62-67.

Finnegan, Ruth. 1970. *Oral Literature in Africa*. London.

Fortes, Meyer. 1949. *The Web of Kinship among the Tallensi*. London.

Frobenius, Leo. 1913. *Und Afrika Sprach*, vol. 3 (Unter den Unsträflichen Athiopien). Berlin.

Froelich, J. C., P. Alexandre, and R. Cornevin. 1963. *Les Populations du Nord-Togo*. Institut International Africain, Paris.

Glaze, Anita. 1981. *Art and Death in a Senufo Village*. Bloomington, Indiana.

Goody. Jack [John R.]. 1962. *Death, Property and the Ancestors: A Study of the Mortuary Customs of the Lodagaa of West Africa*. Stanford, Calif.

Graham-White, Anthony. 1967. "A Bibliography of African Drama," *Afro-Asian Theatre Bulletin*, vol. 3, pp. 10-22.

——. 1970. "Ritual and Drama in Africa," *Educational Theatre Journal*, vol. 22, no. 4, pp. 339-349.

——. 1974. *The Drama of Black Africa*. New York.

——. 1976. "The Characteristics of Traditional Drama," *Yale/Theatre*, vol. 8, no. 1, pp. 11-24.

Griaule, Marcel. 1933. "Le Chasseur du 20 Octobre," *Minotaure*, no. 2, pp. 31-44.

Griaule. M., and G. Dieterlen. 1942. "La Mort Chez le Kouroumba," *Journal de la Société des Africanistes*, vol. 12, pp. 9-24.

Guébhard, Paul. 1911. "Notes Contributives à l'Étude de la Religion: Des Moeurs et des Coutumes des Bobo du Cercle de Koury (Soudan Français)," *Revue d'Ethnographie et de Sociologie*, vol. 2, pp. [125]-145.

Holas, Bohumil. 1966. *Les Sénoufo (y Compris les Minianka)*. Monographies Ethnologiques Africaines. Institut International Africain, Paris.

Huizinga, Johan. 1938. *Homo Ludens: A Study of the Play Element in Culture*. London. Reprint 1950.

Jeffreys, M. D. W. 1951. "The Ekong Players," *Eastern Anthropologist*, vol. 5, no. 1, pp. 41-48.

Jones, G. I. 1945. "Masked Plays of Southeastern Nigeria," *Geographical Magazine*, vol. 18, no. 5, pp. 190-199.

Kirby, E. T. 1974. "Indigenous African Theatre," *The Drama Review*, vol. 18, no. 4, pp. 22-35.

Kourouma, K. 1953. "Un Enterrement Somba à Natitingou," *Notes Africaines*, no. 59 (July), pp. 81-82.

Labouret, Henri, and Moussa Travélé. 1928. "Le Théâtre Mandingue (Soudan Français)," *Africa*, vol. 1, no. 1, pp. 73-97.

Lane, Michael. 1958. "The Auku-Ahwa and Aku-Mago Post Burial Rites of the Jukun Peoples of Northern Nigeria," *African Music*, vol. 2, no. 2, pp. 29-32.

Mercier, Paul. 1949. "Conceptions d'Orientation Chez les Bètàmmaribè," *Notes Africaines*, no. 41 (January), pp. 9-10.

——. 1953. "L'Habitat et l'Occupation de la Terre Chez les 'Somba,'" *Bulletin de l'Institut Français d'Afrique Noire*, vol. 15, no. 2, pp. 798-817.

——. 1954. "L'Habitation à Étage dans l'Atakora," *Études Dahoméennes*, vol. 11, pp. 30-78.

——. 1968. *Tradition, Changement, Histoire: Les "Somba" du Dahomey Septrional*. Paris.

Messenger, J. 1962. "Anang [Ibibio] Art, Drama, and Social Control," *African Studies Bulletin*, vol. 5, no. 2, pp 29-35.

Murray, Kenneth C. 1939. "Dances and Plays," *Nigeria*, vol. 19, pp. 214-218.

Ottenberg, Simon. 1973. "Afikpo Masquerades: Audience and Performance," *African Arts*, vol. 6, no. 4, pp. 33-35, 94-95.

——. 1975. *Masked Rituals of Afikpo*. Seattle.

Ouedraogo, Joseph. 1950. "Les Funérailles en Pays Mossi," *Bulletin de l'Institut Français d'Afrique Noire*, vol. 12, pp. 441-455.

Povey, John. 1976. "The Mwondo Theatre of Zaire," *Yale/Theatre*, vol. 8, no. 1, pp. 49-54.

Rattray, R. S. 1932. *The Tribes of the Ashanti Hinterland*. London.

Ridgeway, William. 1915. *The Dramas and Dramatic Dances of Non-European Races, in Special Reference to the Origin of Greek Tragedy*. Cambridge, Eng., New York, 1964.

Roy, Christopher. 1979. "Mossi Masks and Crests." Ph.D. dissertation, Indiana University.

Traoré, Bakary. [1958]. *Le Théâtre Négro-Africain et ses Fonctions Sociales*. Paris.

19

Dutch Galleons and South Nias Palaces

Jerome A. Feldman

In the southern part of the island of Nias, Indonesia, domestic architecture has assumed a complexity and scale totally unexpected in such a tiny, isolated part of the world. Given that Nias society is highly aristocratic, it is easy to understand that the houses of village rulers would be more impressive than the rest. Few would imagine, however, that a chief's house such as the one standing in Bawömataluo village would be twenty meters tall and rest upon more than one hundred pillars, each a meter thick, and that the entire edifice would be constructed of interlocking pieces of polished hardwoods (see Feldman 1979). One wonders how this architectural tradition evolved in a culture area of less than seven hundred square miles.

The true answer to this question will probably never be known. The absence of firm written and oral documentation precludes a definitive architectural history. The aim, therefore, of such an historical investigation is not to prove, but to probe, utilizing whatever relevant evidence is available, toward a plausible explanation. The conclusions of such an undertaking must be tentative but may establish a foundation for future research.

MOTIVATIONS FOR ARCHITECTURAL CHANGE IN THE HISTORY OF SOUTH NIAS

The indigenous inhabitants of Nias island agree that the culture began in Central Nias in an area called Gomo. Since the names of the founding rulers of Gomo are known in both North and South Nias, it is probable that a stratified, aristocratic society had already formed in Central Nias before the cultures

Reprinted in abridged form from *Res*, No. 7/8, Cambridge, MA: Peabody Museum of Archaeology & Ethnology, Harvard University, 1984, pages 21-32 with permission of the author and publisher.

dispersed. Genealogies collected in South Nias are quite consistent, and it appears that the migration from Central Nias took place approximately nineteen or twenty generations ago. The longest probable span for a ruler's average tenure is approximately thirty-five to forty years. This would mean that South Nias was not settled prior to the late twelfth century. Since rulers held their position for life, and tended to live long, a short estimate of rule would be twenty years, implying settlement of the South by the sixteenth century. Therefore the southern region was probably settled by the present line of rulers some time between the twelfth and sixteenth centuries. The absence of a modern archaeology of the island precludes dating by any other source at this time.

Although nothing survives of the architectural tradition of Gomo at the time of these migrations, it is possible to make some presumptions concerning its characteristics. Utilizing ethnographic analogy, our best guess as to the design of the ancient Central Nias chief's house is the plan that was in use when these houses were first documented. Although there have been changes throughout the centuries, in Central Nias there is a distinct type of house that shares certain features with both North and South Nias.

The Central Nias house is a rectangular structure composed, as are those in the other regions of the island, of three vertical sections (Fig. 1). The bottom section consists entirely of pillars. These are grouped into two types, the vertical

Figure 1 Chief's house from Central Nias. Photo: Greg Moore 1975.

ehomo and the oblique *driwa*, or *diwa*. *Driwa* usually meet at a point to form a V-shape or sometimes will cross to form an X. The X form is the style found in North Nias, while the V is found exclusively in the South. Thus certain elements of northern and southern designs are found in the central part of the island. *Driwa* frequently run across the house as well as in front and back. In Central and North Nias the first row of pillars in the front of the house is the *ehomo*; in the South the first row consists of *driwa*.

Above this section is the dwelling area, which is divided front and back into communal and private sections, respectively. The communal section contains most of the sculpture in the house as well as a special inner pillar called *lauwo ba gazi*, which has an animal head and a disc at its top. The facade of the center section consists of a single step projection corresponding to a seat that runs across the front of the house on the interior. Above this projection there is a trellis window, which is used when viewing the village square. On the exterior there are often carvings of composite monster heads at the edges and center. In addition there are often vertical supports running from the area just above the pillars to the base of the thatch.

The roof section consists of a high ridge pole and a graceful curving roof line. Characteristically, all well-made Nias houses have a flap in the roof to allow light and air to circulate. In Central Nias there would be one or two flaps in the front and back.

The villagers in the southern part of the island must have brought with them the traditions and arts of the central region. Often the older South Nias villages bear the names of the previous Gomo locations. Villages such as Lahusa and Orahili can be found in both areas. There is even a Gomo River in South Nias, named after its Central Nias counterpart. This type of house, therefore, is the best guess as to the architectural notions the settlers of South Nias would have brought with them. Sometime after the arrival in the South, villages were founded, and presumably constructed in a manner similar to those of the homeland in Central Nias.

Slavery was found in all regions of Nias, but it is clear from the historical record that it achieved extraordinary proportions in South Nias at an early period. In the early seventeenth century it is known that Aceh, under its leader, Iskandar Muda, led an attack on Nias in order to monopolize the slave trade (Lombard 1967:94, 197). An even earlier report by the French admiral Beaulieu mentions an active trade with the port of Baros in Sumatra (1664-1666: II, 98). By 1822 the British reported that 1,500 slaves per year were being exported out of the port of Teluk Dalam, South Nias (Anon. 1822: 10). This trade resulted in the accumulation of enormous amounts of wealth in the hands of the rulers of the region.

Wealth poured into a society in which displays of wealth and ostentation were very important. There was a strict two-tiered class system (slaves were not considered part of society) in Nias. One's rank within this system was determined by staging an expensive and dramatic series of feasts. Produced in connection with these feasts were vertical stone monuments, gold ornaments, or a house of a design and scale befitting the status attained by giving the banquet and distributing wealth.

As the feasting system operated, it created not only the need for memorials, but the necessity to elaborate upon the basic forms that the memorials had. In South Nias, for example, by giving a *fa'ulu* feast, one qualified for a vertical stone memorial (*batu wa'ulu*). Small *batu wa'ulu* were fairly common in South Nias, but if one gave an especially elaborate feast, a huge and ornate stone was designed and erected. The two tall stones in front of the *omo sebua* in Bawömataluo are a good example of this (Fig. 2).

Architecture in South Nias formed the climax of the feasting system. If the village rulers could trade a large number of slaves for wealth, especially gold, which could be distributed in feasts, they would qualify for especially elaborate houses, and the highest prestige. The increase in wealth over a long period of time would result in the expectation that the South Nias chief's house should become more elaborate than the Central Nias prototype. Hence the motivation would be established for a new basic design for the *omo sebua* in the southern part of the island. The architects of these buildings would be searching for, or at least be open to, new ideas.

THE ARRIVAL OF ORNATE DUTCH SHIPS

The earliest evidence we have of an intensified slave trade comes from the beginning of the seventeenth century, and it might therefore be reasonable to presume that the desire for and receptivity to new architectural ideas would have developed by 1700. This coincides with a period of time when journeys by ships of the Dutch East India Company between the Netherlands, South Africa, and Indonesia reached their historical peak (Hall 1964:304-309). Written evidence of contact with Nias was presented by Schröder, but it cannot be proven whether other contacts had occurred (Schröder 1917: I, 309-313, II, pl. CXIII-CXVII). Informants on Nias claim that there were many such early contacts with galleons,

Figure 2
The *omo sebua* at Bawömataluo, South Nias. Schröder 1917: fig 117.

and they point out that in every South Nias chief's house there are sets of chains hanging from the rafters that were taken from these ships.

The fact that Dutch ships could be captured is also corroborated by evidence in Dutch accounts. In 1856 during a Dutch incursion into Lagundi Bay, a lieutenant Donleben and part of his crew were cut off from their ship by a well-organized action on the part of the Niassers. Under the direction of "radja Wadoea" (probably Siduhu, another name for Laowo, at that time the ruler of the powerful village of Orahili), the inhabitants formed two divisions. One was stationed on the beach, and the other opposite Donleben in the bush (Anon. 1860:333). Donleben managed to get back to his ship, but the incident demonstrates that the claims made by the contemporary Niassers concerning their ability to capture ships may be true.

Even if no ship were ever captured, it is clear that Niassers would have been keen observers of any ships that would have anchored offshore. The galleons of the early eighteenth century were indeed impressive. Their sterns were elaborately carved and gilded, and often major European artists were commissioned to do the work. In Nias society gold is associated with feasting and royalty and is important enough for that color itself to attract attention.

CULTURAL ASSIMILATION IN SOUTH NIAS

In order to understand how foreign elements such as the sterns of Dutch galleons could be utilized as artistic models in Nias, it would be best to examine the assimilation process in other instances that can easily be proven. The gun, for example, was first introduced into South Nias in the mid-nineteenth century. By the early 1880s guns were being manufactured in Bawömataluo and other villages (Thomas 1882:95). These rifles were quite different from their European prototypes. The barrels were thickened and silver stripes were inlaid into the barrels. Rifle butts were carved with floral designs. In fact the European rifle was converted into a form that matched the Nias sword. The stripes on the sword and rifle are a reference to the tiger, an animal that does not exist on the island of Nias, but which has been incorporated into the culture to metaphorically symbolize the qualities of a great ruler (Feldman 1983: 152-153).

The chair is another element that was put to use in a peculiarly Nias way. In the traditional context, horizontal stones in the village square, called *darodaro*, are used as seats for ancestors and living dignitaries during formal oratory (*orahu*). The term *darodaro* is also used to describe the seat for an ancestor image inside a house. In certain villages, notably Bawömataluo and Hilizihönö, a chair (*darodaro*) is carved on the wall; the ancestor figure does not sit on the chair, however, but upon a stool on top of the chair. The chair then is used as the Niasser would use a horizontal stone, which also bears the name *darodaro*. In fact a person of high rank, such as a priestess, would often sit upon a stool atop a stone *darodaro*.

In Bawömataluo there is also an example of a Dutch ship that was used in a distinctly Nias way. On the wall of the chief's house is a carving, which Schröder dubbed the "Dutch Cruiser" (Fig. 3). The ship is modeled after a combination steam and sail vessel similar to those which appeared in the mid-nineteenth

Figure 3 Carving of the "Dutch Cruiser," left wall of the chief's house, Bawömataluo. 1974.

century. The two large cannons indicate that it is a warship; the uniformed Dutchmen on the deck identify it as Dutch. A vessel closely matching this description—the *Reiner Claussen*—was used by the Dutch in 1863 to attack the South Nias village of Orahili (Anon. 1863:8). During the attack the Dutch burned Orahili, and the inhabitants were denied a permanent village until 1878 when they founded Bawömataluo (Schröder 1917:731). It is very likely that it is the *Reiner Claussen* that is depicted in this carving.

The Niassers totally transformed this ship to fit their needs. They made it into a carving on a wall opposite the ancestral altar. In this position it becomes a symbol of the living Nias society, as opposed to the dead ancestors. The figures aboard the ship are depicted capturing two large fish, while below a crocodile catches a small fish. An analogy is intended between the crocodile and nature, and the ship and society. Society is highly productive, whereas the yields of nature, or nonsociety, are meager.

It is clear that within the indigenous tradition, foreign elements must be transformed into usable Nias cultural items. Despite these transformations, influences are clearly recognizable. If Dutch galleons were a source for the South Nias architectural tradition, one should not expect an exact copy of the galleons, but rather that the structural ideas and decorative forms would be put to a distinctly Nias pattern and mode of use.

DESIGN ELEMENTS FOUND ON DUTCH GALLEONS OF THE EARLY EIGHTEENTH CENTURY AND SOUTH NIAS PALACES

Schröder was the first to publish the observation that the facades of South Nias houses resemble the designs of old European ships' sterns (1917: 118). A comparison of a number of different ship sterns reveals that Dutch ships at the beginning of the eighteenth century show the closest relationship. Ship builders' models and artistic engravings give a detailed picture of the appearance of these ships.

A model in the Museum of Fine Arts in Boston of the East Indiaman *Valkenisse* is an excellent example of the type of ship that resembles the South Nias chief's house facade. The actual ship was launched in 1716 in Zeeland, the Netherlands. The 1,150-ton vessel was equipped at Zeeland and made its first voyage for Batavia from the port of Rammekens on July 11, 1717 (Bruijn, Gaastra, and Schöffer 1979: II, 338). It is estimated that the ship was 161 feet long and had a beam of approximately 42.5 feet (Anderson 1932: 163). The vessel made seven voyages to Indonesia over a period of twenty-three years. The last official voyage was in 1733 under captain Elias Moenix arriving in Batavia on January 21, 1734. There are no accounts of the *Valkenisse* for the next six years, but it is reported to have been wrecked at Bantam in 1740 (Bruijn, Gaastra, and Schöfer 1979: II, 430-431). It would be tempting to assume that during its six years in Indonesian waters, the ship stopped at Nias, but there is no direct evidence.

The stern of this ship has many elements in common with the facade of the South Nias *omo sebua*. Both have step-like projections that result in a cantilever consisting of two steps and a trellis window that runs across the facade (Figs. 1, 7). Evidently the Rococo curving lines of the Dutch ship did not appeal to the Nias architects, but many of the other elements may have. Below the trellis window in both cases are curved pieces of wood that stretch in front of the facade projections. In the center of the *Valkenisse*, just below the trellis window, is a carved lion (Fig. 4). In the same position on the *omo sebua* is the *lasara* monster. Two more monsters adorn the sides (Fig. 2). In the old *omo sebua* from Hilimondregeraya, now in the Copenhagen National Museum, the *lasara* also have four legs and a curving tail similar to the *Valkenisse* (Fig. 5). Below the trellis window on the ship is a band of carved curvilinear ornament. On the chief's house this area is reserved for designs that are painted over shallow relief carving. At the village of Hilinawalö Mazingö there is a design in this area that resembles the style of carving on the ship (Fig. 6). Between the curving vertical wooden pieces of the ship and below the carved panels just described, there are coiled foliage designs with vertical plants arising from the center (Fig. 4). These are repeated in each of the eight bays. A very similar design consisting of coiled ferns with vertical plant elements appears in the same position in each of the eight bays on the *omo sebua* (Fig. 7).

Although there are variations in the facades of *omo sebua* and in the sterns of East Indiamen, the type of elements, their position, and their design are very consistent. These designs are complex and arbitrary, which, as Douglas Fraser pointed out, diminishes the chance of accidental similarity (1966: 36).

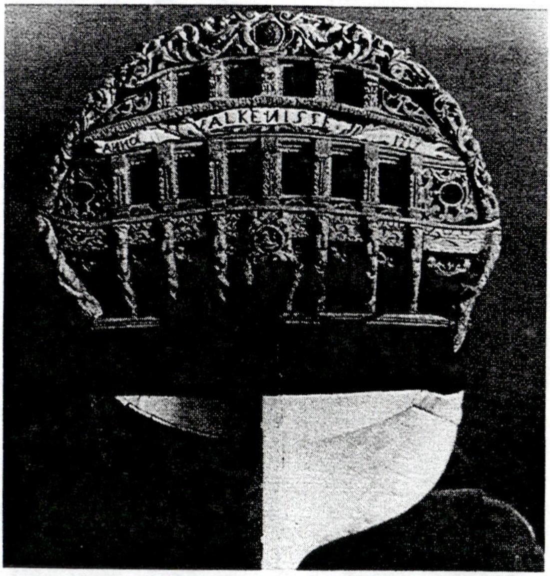

Figure 4
Stern of ship model of the *Valkenisse*. Courtesy of the Museum of Fine Arts, Boston.

Many of these elements also appear on Central Nias *omo sebua*, but in a very different form. The curved wooden strips start lower on the facade and proceed in front and over the trellis window. The stepped facade usually consists of only one step. The *lasara* monster is very plain and geometric as opposed to the more

Figure 5 *Lasara* monster from the chief's house at Hilimondregeraya village (detail). Danish National Museum. Courtesy of Dr. Agner Møller.

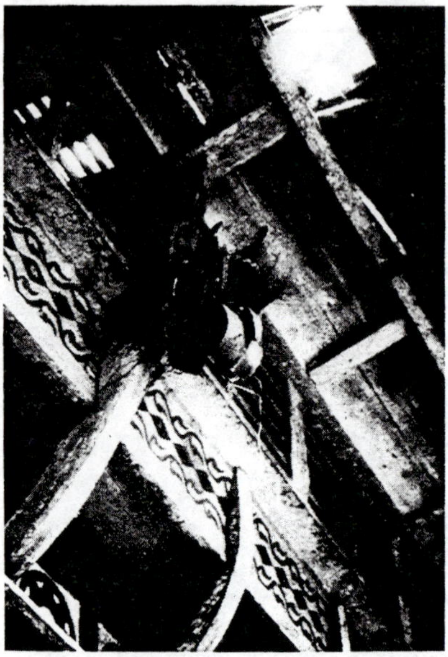

Figure 6
Detail of the facade of the *omo sebua* at Hilinawalö Mazingö. 1974.

Figure 7 Facade of the *omo sebua* at Bawömataluo showing coiled fern designs. 1974.

ornate *lasara* of South Nias and the Dutch lion. There are no coiled ferns in similar positions on the Central Nias house (Fig. 1). The style of the Central Nias *omo sebua* does not have the refinement found in the South and on the galleons. It appears that the facades of South Nias *omo sebua* more closely resemble the Dutch galleons than they do their Central Nias counterparts.

On the interior of a South Nias chief's house there are some elements that may have a distant connection to the structure of Dutch galleons. The floor of the house has several levels: high in the front, it reaches its lowest point in the center and rises to the highest level in the back. In Dutch galleons the deck levels are not identical to those of South Nias, but they do follow the same pattern. In Central Nias the floor is level with seats at the front and back. There are four decorative posts on the interior of the South Nias *omo sebua* that serve not as structural supports but as display pieces for great sculptures. The form of these posts derives from stone monuments in Central Nias, but their proliferation in the house may have been inspired by masts. At the rear of the house in Bawömataluo, at the center of the highest level, there is a carved loop that has no explanation in Nias culture, but which resembles a cleat, or a place for tying rigging. The comparisons on the interior of the house are much less apparent than those on the facade, but again these details do not appear in Central Nias houses.

The cultural meanings of the *omo sebua* have nothing to do with its resemblance to ships. According to informants, ship symbolism and metaphors are limited to coffins, horizontal stones, pallets, and direct depictions of ships. The house is a metaphor of the cosmos and may also represent an ancestor (Feldman 1979). The resemblance between the *omo sebua* and ships (which some Niassers recognize) is purely formal and derives from artistic sources.

The Spread of "Galleon Style" Facades into Commoners' Houses in the Twentieth Century

In the oldest photographs taken in South Nias the commoner's house (*omo hada*) is quite different from the way it appears today. In Figure 8, the facade of the left *omo hada* is almost identical to the style used in Central Nias (Fig. 1), while the newer house on the right has extra steps in the facade and the vertical curved elements are done as they are on the *omo sebua* and galleon. The house type at the left is no longer seen in South Nias, and its old age at the time of the photograph (c. 1900) can be detected by the existence of temporary props of the kind used to salvage houses that are about to collapse. The house on the right is typical of modern *omo hada*. *Omo hada* are not permitted to have *lasara*.

It is apparent that the changes that were made to the *omo sebua* are filtering down to the commoner's house. The *omo hada* shows clearly the genesis of the modern house from its Central Nias prototype. The direction of this change is toward the designs found on early-seventeenth-century Dutch galleons.

The evidence shows that economic pressure from increased wealth, combined with a cultural need for ostentation, could have resulted in new house forms for the chiefs of South Nias. The timing of the increase in wealth and the

Figure 8
Detail of a photo showing old and new types of *omo hada*. Photo: W.L. Abbott, c. 1900. Smithsonian Institution glass neg. #52.3.

arrival of ornate Dutch galleons, as well as the establishment of a process for assimilating foreign motifs, made it possible for the architects to make innovations. The complex clustering of similar motifs in similar positions argues strongly in favor of the hypothesis that the sterns of Dutch galleons were formal models for the facades of South Nias *omo sebua*. The process of change from Central Nias prototypes is illustrated in the commoners' houses in the early twentieth century.

BIBLIOGRAPHY

Anderson, R. C. 1932. "Models of Dutch East Indiamen, 1716-1725." *The Mariner's Mirror* 18: 160-167.

Anon. 1822. "Short Notices Concerning the Island of Pulo Nias from Observations Made During a Visit to the Island in 1822." *Malayan Miscellanies* 2, no. 8: 1-18.

——. 1860. "Een Nederlandisch etablissement te Lagoendi." *Tijdschrift voor Nederlandisch Indie* 22:331-349.

——. 1863. *Javsche Courant*, no. 54 (July 1863): 7-10.

Barbier, J-P. 1976. "Un monument en pierre de l'ile Nias." *Bulletin annuel du Musée d'Ethnographie de la ville de Genève*, no. 19:9-36.

Beaulieu, A. de. 1664/66. *Relations de l'estat présent du commerce des Hollandais et des Portugais dans les Indes Orientales; mémoires du voyage aux Indes Orientales du Général Beaulieu.* In Thevenot, M., *Relations de divers voyages curieux, qui n'ont point été publiées ou qui ont été traduites d'Hacluyt, de Purchas et d'autres voyageurs, anglois, hollandais, portugais, allemands, espagnols et de quelques persans, arabes, et autres auteurs orientaux* 2: 1-128. Paris.

Boer, D.W.N. de. 1920. "Het Niassche Huis," *Mededeelingen van het Encyclopaedisch Bureau betreffende de Buitengewesten* 25. Batavia.

Borgers, W.C. 1936. "Nias - the Island of Gold." *Travel* (London), vol.67:23-25, 48.

Bruijn, J.R., Gaastra, F.S., and Schöffer, I. 1979. *Dutch-Asiatic Shipping in the 17th and 18th Centuries* 2, 3, The Hague.

DeGroot, I., and Vorstman, R. 1980. *Sailing Ships: Prints by Dutch Masters from the Sixteenth to the Nineteenth Century*. New York.

Feldman, J.A. 1979. "The House as World in Bawömataluo, South Nias." In Bruner, E., and Becker, J., *Art, Ritual and Society in Indonesia*. Athens.

——. 1983. "The High Tiger in South Nias, Indonesia." *Empirical Studies in the Arts*, vol. 1 (2): 143-156.

Fraser, D. 1966. *The Many Faces of Primitive Art*. Englewood Cliffs.
Hall, D.G.E. 1964. *A History of Southeast Asia*. London.
Heine-Geldern, R.F. 1961. "Survivance de motifs de l'ancien art bouddhique de l'Inde dans l'ile de Nias." *Artibus Asiae*, vol. 24, nos. 3-4:299-306.
Lombard, D. 1967. "Le Sultanat d'Atjéh au temps d'Iskandar Muda 1607-1636." *Publications de L'Ecole Française D'Extrême Orient* 61. Paris.
Nieuwenhuis, R. 1961. *Tempo Dulu*. Amsterdam.
Schröder, E.E.W. Gs. 1917. *Nias, ethnographische, geographische en historische aanteekeningen en studien*, 2 vols. Leiden.
van Rees, W.A. 1866. *De Pionniers der Beschaving in Neêrlands Indië, verhall eenige Krijstogten op de Buitengewesten*. Arnhem.

20

The Pueblo and the Hogan

A Cross-Cultural Comparison of Two Responses to an Environment

Amos Rapoport

INTRODUCTION

Primitive and vernacular architecture, in addition to its intrinsic value, offers the most obvious and relevant material for the study of the relative importance of different forces on the development and character of built form. A cross-cultural study of such material suggests that generally, for any given situation, climate, site and constraints of materials and technology will modify, but not determine, the form of the dwelling. That form will be primarily the result of a choice among possible alternatives. This choice reflects an image of an ideal life expressed through socio-cultural forces in the broadest sense, which are, therefore, far more important than physical forces in the generation of form. This I have demonstrated elsewhere, giving it a more general, theoretical formulation and suggesting that this is the only way of accounting for the great variety of built forms.[1]

The south-western United States present a particularly striking set of conditions for a specific case study of this hypothesis. Not only is the physical setting very uniform but it is powerful in its impact on man. It is a land of sage-brush, buttes and mesas; pine covered mountains and fantastic rock forms in brilliant colours seen against a vivid blue sky with towering clouds. The average elevation is between 5,500 and 6,500 feet and the land does not support many people, being generally arid or semi-arid with flowing water rare, and rains

Reprinted in abridged form from *Shelter and Society*, edited by Paul Oliver, London: Design Yearbook Ltd., Barrie and Rockliff, 1969 pages 66-79 with permission of the author.

uncertain. The growing season is short and killing frosts and storms frequent. Even so, the area has been inhabited for a long time and the numerous cultures in it have been studied in great detail.

In this paper I shall compare the built environment of two such cultures: the Pueblo Indians and the Navajo.

THE PUEBLO

The term "*pueblo*" (Spanish for town) has been used generically for a large variety of ancient and modern cliff-dwellings, mesa-top villages and plains villages, as well as for many tribal and language groupings–Hopi, Zuñi, Tewa and others. This generic use is possible because all these settlements and tribes have common characteristics. They are composed of people with the same economic base, social structure, personality type and religion living in similar houses in similar settings.

All the present Pueblo inhabitants are descendants of Pueblo people who once covered a much larger area of the south-west and who preserve that ancient culture almost in its aboriginal purity, in spite of centuries of contact and conflict with the white man. The Hopi particularly have resisted pressures towards acculturation and possibly show the pre-Columbian culture in its purest form. Much of what is said, therefore, will be based on Hopi material, supplemented as necessary by material from the Zuñi, Tewa and others.

The south-west has been settled since the end of the last Ice Age. The first permanent settlements date from the beginning of the Christian era, when the Basketmakers lived in round pit-houses which, by A.D. 700, tended to become oval. Between A.D. 700 and 1300 the area developed the Pueblo culture combining basketmaker background with new ideas, both local and borrowed, but showing a continuity of development through several stages from the pithouse to the pueblo. During the developmental stage (A.D. 700-1100) various forms were tried: subterranean, semi-subterranean and rectangular surface houses grouped in small pueblo-like settlements. The classic phase, beginning around A.D. 1100, was marked by many multi-storey pueblos of hundreds of rooms (such as Mesa Verde, Chaco Canyon, Pueblo Bonito and others) (Fig. 1), and ended during the great twenty-two year drought of A.D. 1276-1299. By 1300 many pueblos were deserted and Navajo raids became a problem. Many survivors fled to the Hopi area which was relatively better-off than most. The historic Pueblo period dates from the coming of the Spaniards in 1540. They reached the Hopi area in 1629 and between 1650 and 1680 there were a number of bloody revolts. The Navajo raids, which became worse after the waning of Spanish power, ended when they were conquered by Kit Carson in 1864, although the Navajo gradually acquired a good deal of Hopi land, leading to over-use and erosion. Unlike the Navajo, the Hopi and other Pueblo groups have decreased in size since the coming of the white man, and the Hopi today number between four and five thousand.

Throughout this development the people lived in the same area, with similar climate and using similar sites; their agricultural economy, based on irrigation, was unchanged until the coming of the Spaniards. Yet, in spite of this constancy,

Figure 1 Ancient Pueblo cliff dwelling. Oak Tree House, Mesa Verde, Arizona.

the dwellings underwent the changes described. After the arrival of the Spaniards, and then the Americans, many aspects of material life changed, yet the dwellings changed little.

The Pueblo as Dwelling

Whatever their specific form, all pueblos have a great deal in common and are the most characteristic feature of pueblo life. They consist of rooms with thick mud or stone walls arranged in closely-built, extremely compact, multi-storey, flat-roofed, terraced, clustered groups, with passages penetrating the pueblo mass. These clusters are additive and express a highly organized social life through their complex community architecture, so different from individual dwellings. Although the form of the cluster may vary, it is always arranged around an open space, also varying in form, with the plaza generally preferred, which expresses the importance of dance ceremonies. These courts may contain ovens for baking bread for fiestas but, particularly in the older pueblos, they contain the sacred rooms, or Kivas, which are an essential part of the pueblo (Figs. 2, 3).

These rooms are a social and work-room for the men, a council chamber and, most important, the scene of sacred observances. They were traditionally subterranean, a factor of such importance that even on rocky sites depressions were used to ensure that the Kivas were sunk below the surface. This form is clearly related to the pithouse and was entered by a ladder in the roof, although modern Kivas, except in Taos and the Hopi Towns, are above ground. Kivas may

Figure 2 Taos Pueblo, view of kivas and ovens.

be either rectangular or round and tend to be more carefully orientated than the houses. The southern part of the floor where observers sat was raised above the northern part where the fire-pit and the *Sipapu* were located. The Sipapu is the sacred "place of emergence," an opening in the floor symbolising the link with the lower world from whence mankind emerged. Along the walls of the north part were compartments for sacred objects.

Because of the limited materials and techniques used in their construction, and their relationship to the landscape, all pueblos have a specific visual character. They look as though they were an inevitable part of the landscape and are always related to the rather dramatic mesa formations in form and colour, thus being somewhat difficult to see (Fig. 4). It is this quality which most impressed the Spaniards, and Joseph Ives who described them in 1861. They have changed little since then, as a comparison of Hopi towns today with the 19th century drawings of Stephen or Mindeleff will show.

The external wall traditionally had no openings and lower rooms were reached by ladders and a trap in the first flat roof. Successive storeys were set back and upper rooms were entered through doors off the roofs. These roofs were—and are—used for sitting and sleeping, winnowing grain, drying chili and the like. Houses were made up of rooms measuring 6-8 ft. x 8-12 ft. which had small doors and were often arranged three deep with inner rooms used for storage (Fig. 5). They were floored in mud or stone and had few furnishings other than fireplaces and bin metates for grinding corn. The fireplaces, as well as roof drains and chimneys, were all different (Fig. 6).

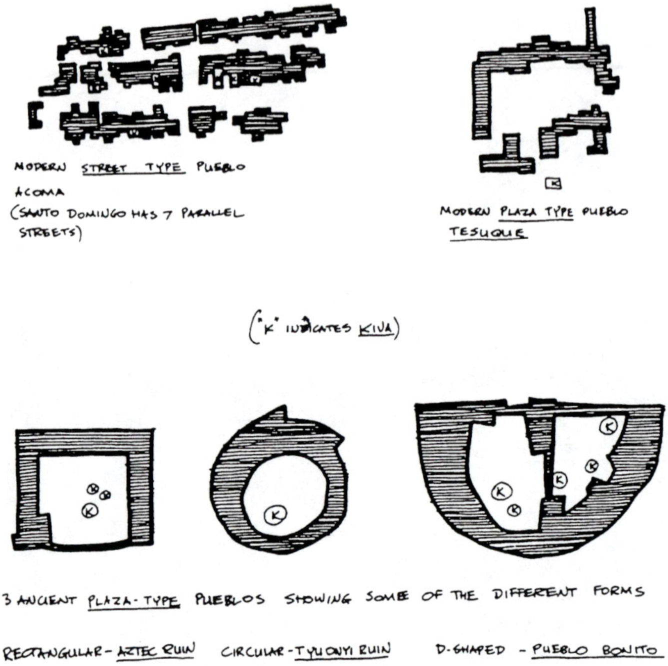

Figure 3 Drawing of various types of Pueblo forms.

Walls were thick; the Hopi build in roughly dressed stone laid in mud, the other Pueblos in mud. Prior to the coming of the Spaniards the latter built with tamped mud laid in form-work very much like modern concrete. The first major modification of technique was the adoption of adobe block from the Spaniards, but this did not change the form of either the room or the pueblo. Roofs and floors above the ground are of tamped earth or clay on close-set poles, brushwood and grass, laid on peeled log beams set in the walls. The beams were often brought great distances and were therefore precious; they had to be used full length so as to be re-usable elsewhere. As a result, beam ends often projected beyond the walls, creating one of the most characteristic visual features of the pueblo. Small spans were used, with rooms added, even though large spans were known and used in Kivas. Walls externally were plastered and internally plastered or stuccoed, whitewashed with fine white clay or decorated in colour, often in patterns similar to those on blankets.

Climatically the compact nature of the pueblo provides maximum volume with minimum surface area, mutual shading of surfaces and a vast mass, with the resultant high time-lag of the building fabric; thus the building works extremely well both in summer and winter. In fact, Stephen mentions that cabins used in the 19th century were much less comfortable than the Hopi dwellings. Both Kivas and dwellings, at least among the Hopi, were heated with soft coal which was mined for the purpose. Roofs and courts were used for living and there were also brush shelters in the fields very much like the Navajo summer hogan (described

Figure 4 Taos Pueblo.

below). Ventilation was poor, but this may have been partly deliberate; in a number of pueblos windows are kept closed when women give birth, and today many refuse to use hospitals because of open windows. Babies were gradually weaned to fresh air.[2] Sanitation generally was poor; Hopi pueblos were only cleaned before public ceremonies, and good health was greatly aided by the dry air and strong sun of the area.

The Pueblo and the Culture

Since Pueblo culture, like that of most pre-industrial peoples, is highly integrated, with religion, symbolism and mythology closely linked to the social organization

Figure 5 Ideal section through Pueblo terrace.

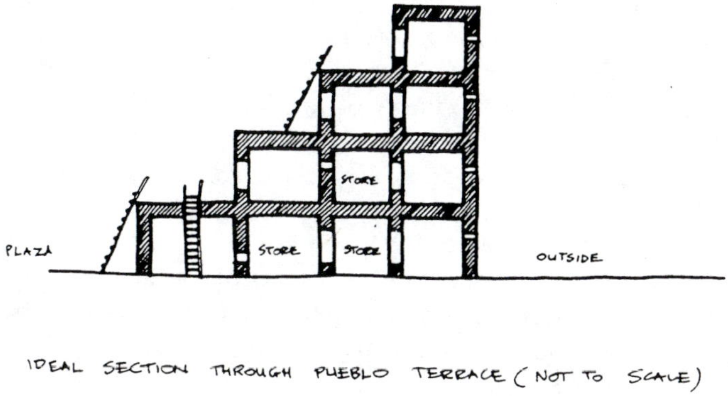

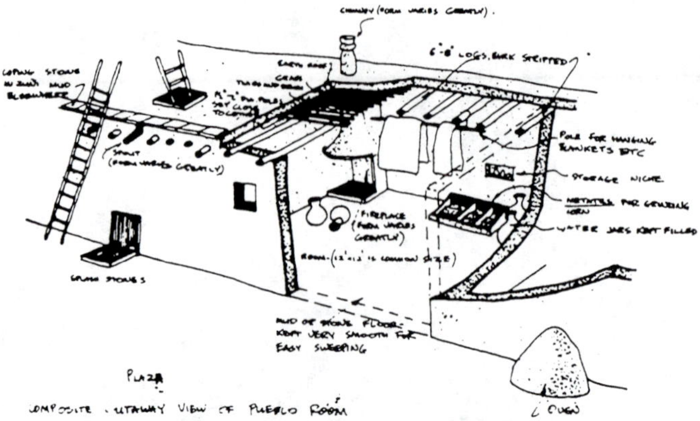

Figure 6 Composite cut-away view of Pueblo room.

and everyday life, even a superficial understanding of these aspects which reflect their world view, will greatly help towards an understanding of the pueblo as a form. It must be stressed that both the pueblo and the culture are too complex for a simple one-to-one correspondence and the insights will be more on the conceptual level.

Pueblo culture is characterized by close links with the environment which enable it to be in a self-regulatory ecological balance with that environment. Pueblo religion generally stresses a harmonious universe where nature, gods, plants, animals and men are all interdependent. Their mutual welfare depends on a reciprocal system of obligations and ceremonials. These ensure the preservation of the whole world and its peace, happiness and prosperity. Since the ceremonies keep the sun rising and preserve all life, as well as the pueblo, they have cosmological significance and all participants acquire dignity.

The cycle of rituals, related to the seasons, affects the order between man and nature and is directed towards the protection and conservation of life. For example, a hunted animal is propitiated; one apologizes to it explaining that it is being killed only because of great need. One never kills more than is needed and every part of the animal must be used. Similarly, only the number of plants needed is picked; the first plant of the type sought is never picked: an offering is placed before it and others sought.

This world view is reflected in every aspect of traditional Pueblo culture and gives meaning to behaviour and institutions. A special type of personality results to which a "balanced character" has been attributed. "Hopi" means good, peaceful, happy; these are the ideals of the followers of the "Hopi Way" who regard white men as restless, uneasy and mad.[3] Art, mythology and ceremonial express the same world view, in symbolic and formal ways, and their various elements only have meaning in relation to the total pattern. It is my argument that the pueblo similarly reflects this world view.

The form of the pueblo, which has been explained on the basis of defence, climate and construction can also be understood in symbolic terms. It defines a sacred "place" and is built to protect the sacred room at the centre and enclose the dance ground; it has close links to the religion which is an essential part of the life of the people. The sun and other deities are closely concerned with house life. Prayer sticks are laid over the central roof-beam to "strengthen" and "feed" the house, and new houses are consecrated, the same ceremonies being used for the house and the Kiva. Although the Kiva is the main centre of ceremonial activity, the house is also used for religious ritual; while the Kiva itself, as we have seen, is an early form of the house.

The close link between dwelling and land expressed in the resemblance of the pueblo to a land-form seems to reflect the overall harmony of man and nature. The house is sacred, and so is the whole landscape and everything in it. Corn was more than a food, it was a symbol of life, and corn growing was regarded as a religious activity. Among the Tewa, for example, the greater part of religion centres around corn and, by extension, around agriculture in general. This attitude must influence the form of the pueblo and particularly its siting and relationship to the land; it helps to explain why the pueblo seems such an inevitable part of its surroundings.

Sun movement and solstices are extremely important, being related to ceremonial cycles. The pueblo is carefully orientated: it is related both to mountains ("Life comes from the mountains"[4]) and to the six cardinal points and the sacred directions of East and North. The very choice of site may have cultural connotations; in the same area of the Verde valley of New Mexico the Hohokam built on the flat or on terraces while the Sinagua, who followed them, built on hills and mesas (never on terraces left by the Hohokam).

Whorf points out that language expresses the world view and influences the manner in which the world is understood. In addition to studying the link of language to many manifestations of culture, he specifically demonstrates the relationship between Hopi language and architecture. For example, space for the Hopi has no objective existence: it is a subjective mental realm. Space is "inner" and related to the heart of things, to the vertical dimension and to its poles–Zenith and underground–which form an *inner* axis. While the Hopi have many words for parts of buildings, there is a remarkable absence of terms for interior, three-dimensional space. The word which is given as the equivalent of "room" is very different from other building terms and one cannot, for instance, say "my room." The word, which is related to Pueblo names such as Oraibi, is rather a locator, similar to "here," "above" or "North." A hollow space is not an object, but objects are located within that space. Most building terms denote solid or rigid masses, perforations through such masses or definitely bounded areas on them. The Hopi also lack terms for the various specialized buildings which they have. The occupancy of a space is not identified with the building in which it is housed; both the occupancy and the spot where it takes place are simply called the building. These two main aspects of Hopi linguistics seem to correspond to the reality of the pueblo. The various parts of the pueblo are merged within the total form, while the small room becomes a location within the mass of the building and there is no attempt to increase its size–i.e. the space which it encloses.

The Pueblo and Social Organization

Pueblo life is minutely but flexibly regulated by a complex socio-religious organization which requires a compact, communal form of settlement for effectiveness. The physical form was an essential part of the social control mechanism which relied on diffuse group pressure—gossip, ridicule and accusations of witch-craft—and self-regulatory, internalized controls, rather than on physical coersion (which is abhorred).

The social organization is based on a female-centred kinship and clan system, the mother's house being a man's real home even after his marriage. The household, consisting of a woman, her husband and unmarried children, married daughters and their families, is the important economic and social unit. This grouping usually occupies a set of adjoining rooms near the mother's house, placed side by side or atop one another; new contiguous rooms are built to accommodate the growth of the household. It seems that clans had traditionally been spatially localized, but this was no longer the case even in the 1880's. In each clan, however, one house is the traditional, permanent ancestral clan home, where sacred property is kept; the leaders are the clan mother and her brother. The clan owns the springs, gardens and land; houses, stores and the like are owned by women, while men own the livestock, fruit trees, tools, personal effects and ceremonial objects.

Women could easily have dominated such a system, but this would have been at odds with the harmony of the Pueblo world view. The female-centred kinship system is therefore balanced by a male-centred ceremonial system. Religious leadership is given to men and performed by secret groups whose members do not belong to the clan but join voluntarily. The degree of religious specialization varies but is generally low. Also, while the specific task definition may vary in different pueblos, men's and women's roles are also sharply divided. Weaving, for example, is done by men, pottery by women; men build and repair houses while women do the plastering and replastering. This balance between the kinship and ceremonial groups gives men and women comparable status by institutionalizing their complementary biological functions. It gives strength and durability to Hopi pueblo organization and reflects the consistency, balance and harmony of their world view.

Traditional Pueblo leadership, combining religious and social functions, is unsought, self-effacing and opposed to singling out individuals for praise and special recognition. Emphasis is on responsibility for tribal welfare, not on the prestige of the office. Prestige is a function of the complete assumption of the expected role and whole-hearted participation in the culture. The social system, therefore, seems to be the world view at the emotional and behavioural level.

The social organization and personality type have both been described as internalized and leading to complexity within quite definite boundaries. This seems to correspond to the way in which the form of the pueblo is achieved by internalized controls, producing an overall form with individual variations and giving picturesque visual qualities. The harmony and unity of the pueblo reflect the world view and social organization, while the form in turn helps the social control mechanisms to operate. The truly communal nature of the dwelling, where even the flat roof is not separated by partitions but is regarded as common ground, like the plaza, reflects the egalitarian society where all individuals are treated alike. Each family has an identical house and there are no palaces, since personal prestige and prerogative are rejected. The importance of the sacred space, the symbolism of orientation and harmonious relation to the land and landscape, all reflect the religious vision of the people. All these features help to explain the form of the Pueblo—not by a one-to-one correspondence but through a fundamental insight into the way of life.

The Pueblo and Modern Life

The white man upset the ecological balance of Pueblo culture and its environment, and started the "crisis of culture." Yet the Hopi, and some other Pueblo groups, kept their culture alive under the new conditions more than almost any other Indian group and showed remarkable cultural stability; by 1950 there were only two per cent Christians among them. The Hopi managed to escape the impact of white culture in fundamental ways and the neglect of these symbolic and spiritual values has resulted in the failure of a number of well-meant administrative efforts. The Hopi have adopted new traits and have not resisted change at the periphery of the culture. They accepted improved farming, the horse which gave them mobility, sheep which improved the economic base, and fruit trees. Yet they were very tenacious concerning intangible values and their way of life, which included their dwellings.

Not that the dwelling was unchanged. As early as 1888 Stephen notes the use of iron roofs.[5] Adobe was adopted shortly after the coming of the Spaniards; then windows, doors and chimneys were adopted; but neither these changes, nor other new techniques which the Indian saw, had a major impact on the basic form. In fact Pueblo forms influenced most buildings in the area.

The essential space organization of the Pueblo, its "community of residence," which is the key to the social and political organization, remained unchanged, although American teachers, traders and missionaries had an impact and the return of World War II veterans accelerated the introduction of new ideas, attitudes and needs. As a result, changes are now occurring in the world view and way of life, and are leading to the beginning of a scattering of houses in certain pueblos. For example, the new houses at San Ildefonso are separated from one another and are of one storey, although they still surround a plaza and have a Kiva. This, and the fact that as early as the 1880's Mindeleff speaks of the scattering of houses, suggests that the process may still be slow. But such major changes of a people's dwellings, when they do occur, only come with fundamental changes in the way of life and world view; technical and material changes alone rarely have that effect.

THE HOGAN

The Navajo are now the largest and most successful Indian tribe in the United States, numbering 90,000. The origins of their culture are very complex, but both the Navajo and the related Apache seem to be of northern Athabascan origin and their migration 2,000 miles to the south-west took many centuries. Although Navajo archaeology is difficult, the route of their wanderings has been explored to some extent. Many Hogan sites have been found in Utah and Colorado dating from A.D. 1000 while the earliest hogan in New Mexico, at Governador, dates from A.D. 1540.

The history of the Navajo is that of a comparatively simple culture enriched by contact with other tribes, especially the Pueblos, who in Navajo lore appear to be wealthy and sophisticated with awesome powers of religious ceremonial. Contact with Pueblos changed the Navajo economic base from foraging and hunting to agriculture, which they had adopted by the 17th century, and enriched their ritual life. They adopted tools and techniques from both the Pueblos and the white man (meeting the Spanish in 1540 and the Americans in 1864), thus changing their economic base once again. Through all this, however, they remained true to their own culture, including their house which is a northern Athabascan type common in the north generally. It has a conical frame of poles covered with the material available–hides, bark, branches or leaves. During the migratory period the hogan changed little, but when the Navajo reached the south-west and settled there, a whole series of gradual changes took place in response to the new materials available and the warmer, drier climate. Mainly, the frame became stronger, the brush covering was more carefully placed and the thick mud coating became standard, with straw mixed in to make it tighter and more permanent. The Navajo did not, however, adopt the Pueblo form even when, in the 17th century, large groups of Pueblo Indians, fleeing the Spanish, lived among the Navajo for many years. In spite of their close familiarity with the multi-storey, flat-roofed adobe and stone villages, they retained the hogan of which several types exist (Fig. 7).

The forked stick hogan is the oldest (Fig. 8). Five logs, 10-12 ft. long are placed on the ground radiating out from a central point, with two pointing east and the others in the other cardinal directions. The circle described is marked and the ground within levelled. The north, south and west poles are raised and interlocked and the apex bound. The spaces between the two east poles, which lean on the others, form the smoke-hole and the doorway. The frame is covered with sticks and branches and plastered with mud.

The earth-covered hogan, originally possibly a ceremonial form, was coming into use as a dwelling by the 1870's. Four heavy crotched posts form a 20 ft. square. The main log frame receives cribbing for the roof and branches are leaned against the frame to form a rough circle, the whole being covered with mud and earth.

The six-sided hogan is currently the most widely used (Fig. 9). It too, was originally a ceremonial form, although it has been suggested that it was first built of discarded railroad ties in the 1880's. The availability of ties certainly helped in its adoption, as did the availability of steel tools for notching the logs. The frame is similar to that of the earth-covered hogan. Around it a six-sided log cabin is built with log walls notched at the corners. The roof cribbing is built inwards to form a beehive shaped roof with a central smoke-hole. The framework may be

Figure 7 Types of Navajo hogans.

Figure 8 Navajo forked-stick adobe hogan.

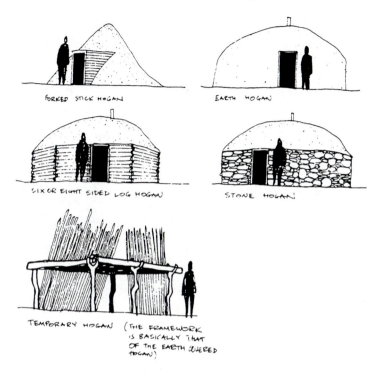

Figure 9 Six-sided log hogan.

omitted for more space; the form may be eight-sided or the corners may be rounded off.

The stone hogan is uncommon, but when it occurs the form reverts to circular while the summer hogan is basically a brush shelter arranged around a frame to give shade. In sheep camps a brush windbreak often sufficed.

Hogans rarely occur singly and tend to cluster. Even sheep camps have a corral for animals as well as windbreaks or tents. Usually two or more matrilinearly related families live in proximity with at least one hogan for each biological family. A group may link three generations and consist of four to six hogans, sheep corrals, storage structures and shades, all loosely grouped. Frequently a ceremonial hogan or sweathouse (a small replica of a forked-stick hogan without a smoke-hole) will be hidden away close by. Even an isolated family will build two or more hogans, using one mainly for storage. Most families have more than one permanent establishment although there is always one main location. A family with 1,000 sheep may have five or six separate clusters of dwellings, and most have at least a summer and winter hogan some distance apart. One dwelling is always near the fields so that crops may be planted, protected and harvested. In all cases when old buildings are destroyed or abandoned, new ones are built near by—no further than half a mile away.

Within the hogan the roof structure, odd corners and the low part of the walls are used for storage, so that all available space is used effectively. When heavy or bulky furniture is used, which is rare, it is kept in supplementary cabins rather than in the hogan. Whenever weather permits, the area around the hogan is used for living or working; in the summer some or all may sleep outside. Whether indoors or out, eating takes place from common bowls on blankets, skins or oilcloth spread on the ground. Normally the whole family eats together, but when two sittings are needed, due to the size of the group, the men and boys will eat first and the women later.

Many observers have commented that the hogan is more comfortable in both summer and winter than white homesteaders' cabins; they are easier to keep cool in summer and to heat in winter. The central fire not only heats all parts of the dwelling, but allows a greater number of people to sit or sleep around it than in white men's houses. Ventilation tends to be poor by our standards and, while hogans vary in cleanliness, the main environmental problem is the presence of lice. These can become so bad that new hogans may have to be built just to escape them (Fig. 10).

The Hogan and the Culture

The hogan cannot be understood without reference to Navajo religion; while both show Pueblo influences they are basically pre-migration in origin. The hogan is a sacred space separated from the usually profane, and often hostile, world. Although the sweat-house, open only to men, is a very important ritual building, the rites which place the Navajo in tune with the Holy People take place in the hogan at least once every six months. The sacred drypainting (sandpainting) always takes place inside the hogan even if a specially large one needs to be built.

Figure 10 Construction of forked-stick and earth-covered hogans..

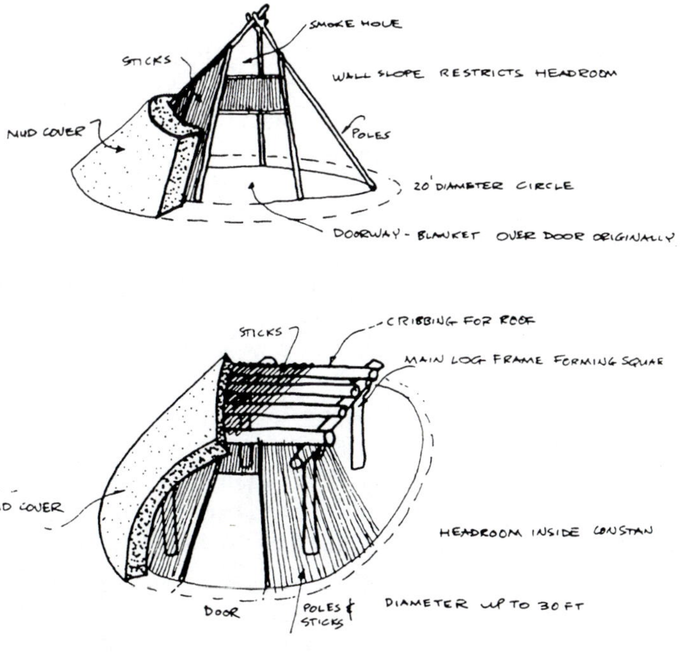

The hogan is more than a place in which to live: it occupies a central place in the sacred world of the Navajo. For them, as for most pre-industrial people, religion is a central concern. Navajo men spend up to one third of their productive time, and women up to one fifth, on religious activities and twenty per cent of family income is devoted to religion.[6] At the same time the Navajo have no word for religion, the breaking up of life into economic, social and religious aspects is as foreign to them as to most pre-industrial people. There is a basic oneness to the Navajo world view which may partly account for the observation that the Navajo move smoothly, with flowing gestures and sustained circular motion rather than with the angular, staccato movements typical of white cultures.[7]

The hogan also has a mythological base. The prototype was built by the Holy People out of turquoise, white shell, abalone shell and jet, corresponding to the four principal sacred colours–turquoise, white, yellow and black–while the hogan of the first man was built of sheets of sunbeam and rainbow. The hogan is always consecrated to ensure long life and happiness to the occupants, the main ceremony being the House Blessing Way. This speaks of beauty radiating from the hogan in all directions and also refers to the supremacy of the woman in the hogan, reflected in the symbolism of the structure: the east pole is the Earth Woman, the west the Water Woman, the south the Mountain Woman and the north the Corn Woman. The principal deity is also female: Changing Woman.

Because of the sacred prototypes, the hogan should conform to the original model. This attitude, generally typical of primitive building, discourages change, and when any changes occur the basics–round form, eastward orientation of the entry and internal arrangement–are retained. The sun (husband of Changing Woman) is very important in Navajo religion and the east orientation of the door assures that it will receive the first blessing of the rising sun. The position of objects and people in the hogan, and all seating arrangements, are strictly laid down. While this helps to accommodate the maximum number of people and objects in an orderly fashion within a small space, the main basis of the arrangement is symbolic rather than functional. The hogan is divided into spheres reflecting the important directions of east, south, west, north, zenith and nadir which are associated with sacred colours. Each part of the hogan is sacred and the House Blessing Way names many parts: the rear corner, centre, fireside, side corners, doorway and surroundings of the hogan. The all pervasive sun symbolism is seen in the "sunrise path" inside the hogan along which people must move. Women are always on the south side, men on the north. The male head of the family and important visitors, such as the officiating medicine-man, face the doorway. The bodies of the dead must be removed through a hole in the north wall. It is significant that all forms of the hogan have this identical arrangement.

Every daily act is affected by religion, helping man control the threatening supernatural forces in the Universe, which is seen as a dangerous place. This control is achieved through the orderly repetition of ritual acts in a fixed rhythm without climax. As a result there are complex restrictions on the simplest activities which affect the design of the dwelling and enable the sacred nature of the dwelling space to be seen as a safe refuge.

Hogans are carefully sited so as not to interfere with the rights of others in respect of grazing and water. For example they are located "near water," about two or three miles away rather than adjacent to it and timber is never cut within one mile of someone else's dwelling. The hogan must not intrude upon the landscape of which it is a part, but must blend with it and be inconspicuous. The care with which the land is treated reflects both the attitude to nature, which is regarded as more powerful than man so that man must adapt to it, and also the importance of the land and landscape. Navajo legends, for example, refer to four sacred mountains, at least one of which is always visible everywhere in Navajo country. When the Navajo were exiled during the wars with the Americans, one of the main deprivations was being away from the vivid landscape which they prize so highly. Shrines are placed on many natural features where events of great mythological significance are thought to have occurred and much of the landscape is, therefore, sacred. This is reflected in agricultural patterns, corn being planted in spirals starting in the centre.

The Hogan and Social Organization

The world view of the Navajo is also reflected in their social organization which, in turn, is related to the hogan. "Navajo" is a Spanish word, they refer to themselves as *Diné* (The People). Each individual among them has a strong sense of belonging with the others who speak the same language, and a strong sense of alienation from the rest of humanity. Within the group there is a strong sense of duty towards relatives and a distrust of non-relatives. The most severely condemned offences and personality traits are those which threaten the peaceful working together of the people; morality is practical rather than abstract or divine.

While the individual is always seen as a member of a larger group, he still retains personal integrity and identity; even children have a right to personal property. The basic social and economic unit is the biological family of which the man is formally the head. Women, however, are influential, descent is traced through the mother and the man lives with his wife's people. In cases of polygamy, each wife with her children will have her own hogan. If the wives are related the dwellings will be close, if they are not the dwelling may be distant.

Relatives are so important that ideal behaviour is defined in terms of acting as though everyone were a relative. Consequently, beyond the biological and extended family, there are other groups the members of which are regarded as "relations." There is the "outfit" which covers a wider circle than the extended family and is more fluid. The members of the outfit regularly cooperate for ceremonial and other purposes but, while the family live within at least shouting distance of each other, an "outfit" may cover many square miles. There are also clans and linked clans which were originally based on locality and played an important role in social control and mutual help. Their effect is also to link biologically unrelated people. A person is related to both his father's and mother's clan and can't marry into either. Many biological families, with the support of these groups, are able to live apart as independent units. There are also unattached people, such as the aged, crippled or childless. If these cannot live in the hogan of one of the biological families they will have their own house, provided they are able to take care of themselves, or have a child living with them to help.

Some tasks are sex-typed and people are embarrassed to perform tasks associated with the other sex. Women do household tasks and weaving, men cut wood; men build corrals and houses while women assist in chinking and plastering the hogan. In economic cooperation people retain both economic and other individuality. Since men live with their wife's family and continue economic and ceremonial activities in their mother's family, they have dual allegiance which is a source of strain and conflict in Navajo social organization.

Some things are communally owned: no individual can own timber, water or salt-bush. Farm and range "belong" to the family through "inherited use ownership." Although the ideal personality traits among the Navajo are similar to those of the Pueblo, there is more acquisitiveness and property is highly prized, although its accumulation stops when one is "well off."

The Navajo are highly sensitive to body exposure and privacy in the hogan is difficult. They do not, therefore, undress when they go to sleep, excretion takes place in hiding outside and sex relations in the dark. When most of the family are away on a trading, ceremonial or work trip, the lone remaining person takes advantage of the privacy to take a bath or have a complete change of clothes. The Navajo like occasions which bring people together–ceremonies, chants, hunts and fairs. They love having a good time, play games in and around the hogan and love singing, believing that it is important in keeping peace with the Holy People. Wit, humour and repartee, whimsy and teasing in conversation are highly prized.

The greater degree of individuality in all areas of life, the greater acquisitiveness and aggressiveness, and the rather looser social organization seem to find a clear reflection in the more individual nature of the dwelling, and the more shifting and changeable social groupings, showing once again a clear correspondence between the dwelling and social organization–both reflections of the world view.

The Hogan and Modern Life

Before their contact with Pueblo Indians and the white man, Navajo artefacts, construction techniques and crafts were rather simple in comparison with other American Indian groups. After this contact they quickly adopted a number of tools and the crafts of pottery, weaving and silversmithing. The Navajo are adaptable and rapidly absorb material elements from other cultures without losing the essence of their own tradition. These traditions did change, however. The horse and saddle increased mobility and enabled more frequent visits to ceremonials and the like and also enabled more distant hogans to be supplied, leading to changes in the social relationships within the tribe. The introduction of sheep gave saleable wealth leading to a trading economy which in turn created certain new goals, values, social stratification and prestige hierarchy. But, while most Indians who accept as many white material objects as the Navajo have done, tended to abandon their customs and become degraded "Poor Whites," the Navajo have retained their way of life and religion. They seem to have a capacity to fit new techniques and tools into their image of the ideal life.

As early as 1885, R. W. Schufeldt described three hogans built in successive years as changing from the forked stick type, through an intermediate form with vertical walls on the north and west, to a cabin with vertical walls and pitched roof. Yet even today the hogan is still the most common dwelling and some conservative areas still use the forked stick hogan. The change was slow for a number of reasons. Western houses are more expensive in material and need special carpentry skills still lacking; the hogan is climatically more comfortable and, most important, curing chants can only be carried out in the hogan. Since few Navajo, including most nominal Christians, have abandoned their religion, and the hogan is an essential part of that religion, even those who live in white style cabins must have one. As ceremonials at the moment seem more frequent than for many years past, it is likely that the hogan will survive.

The twenty thousand Navajos who returned from military service or war industries after World War II greatly increased the dissemination of white ideas. Many Navajo now want separate rooms and seem increasingly to expect American-type houses, a trend encouraged by the tribal government. Thus the change to the Western house, when it does occur, is due to changes in the way of life. Previously neither environmental pressures nor the new economic base, new tools, materials or technology changed the form of the dwelling. When new materials were used, or Pueblo culture had its impact, the circular form, orientation and internal organization remained unchanged. These forms are reflections of an ideal and change much more slowly than material elements.

Among the innovations adopted as early as the 1880's was the covered wagon which provided a home on wheels enabling a whole family to attend ceremonies and fairs. Today the pickup truck has become the new mobile home; it, and the canvas tent, have replaced the temporary brush shelters of the sheepherders much more rapidly and thoroughly than the hogan has been replaced—because the temporary shelters have no mythological and symbolic bases. A number of well meant government efforts have failed through a failure to understand the cultural bases of Navajo life. For example, the stock reduction programme, meant to help overgrazing, failed, because it stressed material aspects and neglected the role of herds as symbols of prestige and the ideal life. Cultural factors, values, goals and world view must be examined in order to understand the validity of any problem—including the dwelling.

THE PUEBLO AND THE HOGAN

Both the hogan and the pueblo occupy the same physical environment. They are built by people with a similar economic and technological base, who have been in contact for hundreds of years and have profoundly influenced each other and who have both been affected by Spanish and American contact. It would, therefore, appear that the key to the great differences in the built forms is *choice*–and that this choice depends on what people regard as important, that is, on the world view expressed in social organization, religion and ritual.

The purpose of Navajo ritual is basically to restore harmony within the individual, and between the individual and other people or super-natural forces. The basic theme of almost all Pueblo ritual, on the other hand, is to restore harmony in the whole universe.[8] Navajo language leads to sharply defined categories, the filing away of things in tight little categories and tends to lead to differences rather than similarities being noticed.[9] The Pueblo Indians stress the continuity of life and death, the relationship between the living and the dead whereas the Navajo fear and abhor death and the dead.

All these differences in world view help to account not only for many specifics of life and culture but the different forms of dwelling. In this light we can better understand the pueblo, which is *always* a basically communal building housing a group, while the hogan, although often grouped, is basically an individual family dwelling and may be on its own.

Pueblo thought regards any individual as a comparatively incidental part of an intricate, codified equilibrium of forces. The Navajo are a group of individuals who, in the absence of such a codified world view, present a unified front through myth, ritual and symbol. Yet, unlike the white man, both groups share a systemic view of the world, thinking in wholes rather than in the analytical way of Western culture, with its lack of connectivity. This, and the very real similarities of some aspects of ritual and world view account for some similarities in attitudes to the built environment. For example, both groups respect nature and try not to intrude on the landscape, but, while the Navajo try to fit the hogan to the site, they lack the highly developed and "codified" Pueblo view of the relationship of man to the land and the Universe.

Although the Navajo have been quicker to abandon old ways and more willing to adopt new techniques than the Pueblo, both groups have adopted some new materials, doors, windows and chimneys, while retaining the essential form and space organization of the dwelling. Among the Navajo, furniture may be kept in a modern cabin next to the hogan; in a pueblo modern beds, a dresser, a mail order trunk, linoleum on the floor and pictures and photographs on the wall may be found–but the intrinsic nature of both remains unchanged. Even today a person's roof in a pueblo is regarded as a public space. Since the dwelling is more than a material object, being closely linked to the world view and the expected relationships with other men and gods, it is retained and its form guarded.

Without examining Navajo and Pueblo art, it has been held that the Hopi work inwards from the periphery while the Navajo work from the centre out. We have seen how, in the House Blessing Way, the Navajo speak of the hogan radiating beauty outwards and how they plant corn in spirals starting in the centre. Conversely, the pueblo is inward turning: it clearly defines domains and protects the sacred space by turning to the court.

The importance of the court is shown by the case of the Tewa Pueblo of San Ildefonso. Originally it had one plaza, on a site dating back to 1696. After a dispute, new houses were built–with a second plaza; the new faction needed a plaza as a focus. The importance of this space may partly reflect the importance of dance rituals and ceremonial games for which they provide an essential setting.

The differences in the pattern of pueblo and hogan have significant social consequences which partly explain the greater receptivity of the Navajo to modernization. This was clearly shown when, after World War II, returning Navajo and Zuñi veterans brought back new ideas. The Navajo, with their more dispersed pattern of settlement, were better able to accept innovation because such innovation only affected the single household and did not disrupt the community. Among the Zuñi, and undoubtedly among other Pueblo groups where the settlement pattern is compact and communal, any innovation would have affected the whole community. As a result, innovation was resisted much more strongly and the social controls were both stronger and more effective.[10] The physical form in this case was an aid to other tendencies and was still operating as an aid to social control.

What of the future? Are we to expect that the built forms of the Navajo and Pueblo Indians will begin to resemble each other–both tending towards the American norm? I would suggest that this is unlikely. In the south-west there are two other traditions which coexist in the same environment. On either side of the border between Mexico and the United States we find major differences in man-made landscape, townscape and built form which reflect differing world views and choices among the possibilities available. The processes which have created different responses to environment are still operating, although, admittedly, the differences are becoming smaller. The long survival of cultural differences elsewhere in the United States, and their revival, suggests that different responses will continue. There will be changes in built form due, not to new technology and materials, but to new ways of life and changing world views. But it is likely, and I for one hope, that both life styles and built forms–the future equivalents of the pueblo and the hogan–will preserve their differences and continue to bring richness and beauty to the south-west.

NOTES

1. Amos Rapoport: *House Form and Culture*. Englewood Cliffs, New Jersey, Prentice-Hall, 1969.
2. W. Whitman: *The Pueblo Indians of San Ildefonso*. New York, Columbia University Press, 1947. pp. 31-32
3. C.G. Jung: *Memories, Dreams, Reflections*. London, Routledge & Kegan Paul, 1963. p. 233.
4. Ibid.
5. A.M. Stephen: *Hopi Journal* (ed. E. C. Parsons). New York, Columbia University Press, 1936. p. 284.
6. C. Kluckhohn and D. Leighton: *The Navaho*. Garden City, New York, Doubleday Anchor Book, 1962. p. 226.
7. Flora Bailey cited Kluckhohn, *op. cit.* p. 86.
8. Kluckhohn, *op. cit.* p. 239.
9. Ibid. pp. 271-276.
10. Personal communication from Professor Laura Nader, Department of Anthropology, University of California, Berkeley.

BIBLIOGRAPHY

General

MORGAN, Lewis H. 1881. *Houses and House Life of the American Aborigines*. Republished University of Chicago Press, Chicago, 1965.

RAPOPORT, Amos. 1969. *House Form and Culture*. Prentice-Hall, Englewood Cliffs, New Jersey.

Pueblo

MINDELEFF, Victor. 1891. *A Study of Pueblo Architecture: Tusayan and Cibola*. Eighth Annual Report, 1886-7. Smithsonian Institution, Bureau of American Ethnology, Government Printing Office, Washington D.C.

STEPHEN, A.M. 1891. *Pueblo Architecture*, Eighth Annual Report, 1886-7. Smithsonian Institution, Bureau of American Ethnology, Government Printing Office, Washington D.C.

——. 1936. *Hopi Journal*, (ed. E.C. Parsons). Columbia University Press, New York.

STUBBS, Stanley A. 1950. *A Bird's-eye View of the Pueblos*. University of Oklahoma Press, Norman.

WHITMAN, W. 1947. *The Pueblo Indians of San Ildefonso: a Changing Culture*. Columbia University Press, New York.

Navajo

CORBETT, John M. 1940. "Navajo house types." *El Palacio* (Santa Fe), Vol. XLVII, pp. 97-107.

KLUCKHOHN, Clyde and LEIGHTON, Dorothea. 1962. *The Navaho*. Doubleday Anchor Book, The American Museum of Natural History, Garden City, New York.

MINDELEFF, Cosmos. 1897. *Navaho Houses*, 17th Annual Report, Part 2. Smithsonian Institution, Bureau of American Ethnology, Washington D.C.

SHUFEDT, R.W. "The evolution of house building among Navajo Indians," Proceedings of the U.S. National Museum, Vol. XV, pp. 279-282.

PART SIX

CONTINUITY AND CHANGE IN FOURTH WORLD ARTS

Janet Catherine Berlo

All too often, the popular impression of tribal societies is of a romanticized, "pristine" world that was somehow ruined by modern European or American culture. Museums and educational institutions sometimes foster this impression. Nineteenth-century American Indian, Oceanic, and African artifacts are often highlighted in exhibits, while contemporary arts are ignored. Courses on ethnographic arts often focus on the past rather than the present, codifying tribal styles or style regions, rather than examining the dynamic interrelationships both *within* the tribal world and *between* the Fourth World and modern industrial society. Yet in the last two decades, scholars have increasingly come to see that trade, contact, and even colonialism can be looked at in a number of ways. It is far too simplistic to invoke a uni-dimensional model in which change in tribal arts inevitably means deterioration, and contact with outsiders serves only to sully traditional arts. We can also look at arts of acculturation as a strategy by which cultures maintain their own dynamic momentum, choosing from a wealth of new materials, ideas, and ideologies to construct an identity that is appropriate for them at a particular historical moment.

To recognize this is not to minimize the horrific effects of colonialism: in some regions entire ethnic groups were wiped out, or zealous missionaries extirpated religious and cultural values in an effort to promote Christianity. The transatlantic slave trade of the 17th to the 19th centuries ripped millions of Africans from their cultures and transported them into servitude in the Americas. In Australia, the Americas, and many parts of Africa, native peoples were deprived of their ancestral lands and reduced to conditions of poverty and servitude. In the late 20th century in some nations, this has translated into welfare dependency.

In this section, the article by Bol (*Lakota Beaded Costumes of the Early Reservation Era*, page 363) chronicles some of the tragedies of the colonialist process on the Great Plains of North America, while simultaneously showing that even in the midst of the worst adversity, many peoples continued to make art. Indeed, in a time of rapidly shifting cultural values, art often becomes the focus of ethnic identity, maintaining some values even in the midst of sweeping societal change. Wade's article (*Straddling the Cultural Fence: The Conflict for Ethnic Artists within Pueblo Societies*, page 371) demonstrates how societies work out their own coping mechanisms for dealing with change. In the case of the potters of San Ildefonso Pueblo in New Mexico, their response to an art market that was greedy for pots signed by the famous Maria Martinez was to have Maria mold or sign pots belonging to others. The rise of a prosperous group of artists' families led to factionalism, and even changed the face of politics in the community.

No culture is static, nor is any art tradition. Both change or else they die. Art metamorphoses to meet ever-changing social needs, as all the articles in this section demonstrate. Contact *between* indigenous cultures gave rise to many developments in artistic and social systems long before the colonial era (see King, *Tradition in Native American Art*, page 374). In the Pacific, this is apparent in the interrelationships between various Polynesian societies, in which sea-going peoples brought ideas and objects with them on their travels. In Africa, contacts among the ancient Ife and Benin kingdoms of Nigeria led to the introduction of complex brass-casting technologies to the royal artists of the Benin court by the 16th century (see Ben-Amos 1980).

Artistic traditions can be infused with new life and alter their directions in a number of ways. New materials, new markets, and new iconographies are among the most common changes affecting ethnic art styles. When Portuguese explorers reached the coastal cities of Sierra Leone at the end of the 15th century, they were impressed with the elegant work of Sapi ivory carvers. Within a few years, these ivory carvers were making new objects with a mixed African/European iconography for the export trade. These objects were imported to Europe, where Valentim Fernandes wrote in Portugal around 1510 that "in Sierra Leone the men are very ingenious, and they make ivory objects that are wonderful to see, namely saltcellars, spoons, and dagger-hilts" (Bassani and Fagg 1988:60).

Aboriginal artists in the central desert of Australia have been painting scenes of their ceremonial songs and stories for thousands of years, sometimes on rock walls, on their own bodies, on bark, or in the sand. Today these same images are painted on canvases with acrylic paints, and sold in art galleries in New York, Sydney, and St. Louis to a new art market. Tradition still dictates that the rights to paint particular designs are the properties of certain individuals, and this ownership of visual properties must not be transgressed (see Sutton 1988). The Yoruba of Nigeria still carve *ibeji* figures to commemorate the death of twins, who hold a special place in the Yoruba family and in religious belief. In addition, the modern technique of photography can serve a traditional purpose, when photographers take duplicate pictures of a living child in commemoration of his dead sibling (see Sprague 1978).

As an example of new iconographies, the religious cult of the water spirit "Mammy Wata" is widespread in Cross River State, Nigeria. It got its initial impetus about 50 years ago when a local carver saw a German illustration of a female snake charmer and replicated this vivid image in a wood carving. Today Mammy Wata is widespread in the art and religious iconography of the region (see Salmons 1977), for it fits in well with indigenous beliefs about the powers of women, snakes, and water spirits.

In the 1990s, we talk about living in a "multicultural society." We listen to musical styles—rap, hip-hop, salsa, jazz—that are regional variants of African rhythms disseminated first by the slave trade and more recently by the international music community. We wear ethnic garb woven or sewn by people in Bolivia, Panama, Ghana, or the Philippines. Members of Fourth World societies participate in this multiculturalism as well. John Nunley's essay (*Purity and Pollution in Freetown Masked Performance*, page 333) outlines the multicultural strands of one contemporary masking society in Sierra Leone, called Ode-lay. Drawn from Yoruba sources in Nigeria, Ode-lay was introduced to the distant country of Sierra Leone through 19th century ethnic migrations. Today it combines costumes of ancestral Yoruba deities as well as contemporary dress such as sneakers, jeans, and t-shirts. As modern urban masqueraders, Ode-lay bands must cope with fund-raising, obtaining permits from the police, and distributing flyers through the mail.

In the 1990s, black residents of New Orleans, Brooklyn, Toronto, and London put on lavish Carnival festivals in which costumes derive from African, Caribbean, and even American Indian prototypes—not to mention the imagery gleaned from other aspects of global popular culture such as cartoons and science fiction (see Nunley and Bettelheim 1988). Contemporary Native American artists experiment in their art with a rich, multicultural mixture that reflects their ethnicity and their dialogue with modern international art movements, politics, feminism, ecology, and other issues (see DeMott and Milburn 1989; Hammond and Smith 1985; Ingberman 1990; Wade and Strickland 1981).

As visionary social planner Buckminster Fuller remarked in the 1960s, the world is truly a "global village" in which technology and communication systems have linked us all, and no one is left untouched. Art has been perhaps the most powerful of such communication systems, and it will continue to be, as Fourth World peoples extend their traditions into the 21st century.

BIBLIOGRAPHY

Bassani, Ezio and William B. Fagg. 1988. *Africa in the Renaissance: Art in Ivory*. New York: The Center for African Art and Prestel-Verlag.

Ben-Amos, Paula. 1980. *The Art of Benin*. London: Thames and Hudson.

Blackman, Margaret B. 1976. "Creativity in Acculturation: Art, Architecture, and Ceremony from the Northwest Coast," *Ethnohistory*, vol. 23(4): pp.387-413.

Coe, Ralph T. 1986. *Lost and Found Traditions: Native American Art 1965-1985*. Seattle: University of Washington Press.

DeMott, Barbara and Maureen Milburn. 1989. *Beyond the Revival: Contemporary Northwest Coast Native Art*. Vancouver: Scott Gallery, Emily Carr College of Art.

Hammond, Harmony and Jaune Quick-To-See Smith. 1985. *Women of Sweetgrass, Cedar and Sage: Contemporary Art by Native American Women*. New York: American Indian Community House.

Hammond, Joyce D. 1986. *Tifaifai and Quilts of Polynesia*. Honolulu: University of Hawaii Press.

Ingberman, Jeanette, ed. 1990. *Hachivi Edgar Heap of Birds: Claim Your Color*. New York: Exit Art.

Nunley, John and Judith Bettelheim. 1988. *Caribbean Festival Arts: each and every bit of difference*. St. Louis: St. Louis Art Museum.

Salmons, Jill. 1977. "Mammy Wata," *African Arts*, vol. 10(3), pp.8-15.

Sciascia, Piri. 1984. "As the Old Net Piles Up on Shore, the New Net Goes Fishing," in *Te Maori: Maori Art from New Zealand Collections*, edited by Sidney M. Meade. New York: Abrams Press, pp.156-166.

Sprague, Stephen F. 1978. “Yoruba Photography: How the Yoruba See Themselves,” *African Arts*, vol. 12(1), pp.52-59.

Sutton, Peter, ed. 1988. *Dreamings: the Art of Aboriginal Australia*. New York: George Braziller Inc.

Wade, Edwin L. and Rennard Strickland. 1981. *Magic Images: Contemporary Native American Art*. Tulsa: The Philbrook Art Center.

21

Purity and Pollution in Freetown Masked Performance

John Nunley

Police in Big Clash with Masqueraders
Bloody Mary Arrested

As the feast of Eid-Ul-Adha was celebrated yesterday, Freetown was not without its incidents of drama.

It was a test of strength and will power between the police and masqueraders who went out to defy the ban on street performing.

As the defiance continued police pounced.

Scores of arrests were made and heavily armed policemen patrolled the streets the whole of the day

The mask of the popular "Bloody Mary" devil was seized by police at Fergusson Street as the group masqueraded in the street.

As the devil was grabbed, the followers fled.

Along Mountain Cut and Kroo Town Road, Siaka Stevens Street and Campbell Street, dancers were out as early as Monday night, the eve of the holiday.

Much alcohol flowed as the night progressed and in the morning the streets were a sea of broken bottles.

The police were put on the alert and the war of Wills began.

And yesterday, by midday, teargass [sic] was used at a number of points.

We Yone, 23 November 1977

Confrontation—the power of one Ode-lay masking society of Sierra Leone against another, the government, or the police—extends from the aesthetic/spiritual realm into everyday reality, where violence often goes along with successful performances. Ode-lay groups such as Firestone, Rainbow, Bloody Mary, Civilian

Reprinted from *The Drama Review*, Vol. 38(2):102-122 with permission of the author and publisher.

Rule, and Juju Wata have grown up in the tough urban environment of Freetown and have claimed the streets for masked performances. The success of these performances depends both on their location in the streets and on the risk of danger. In contrast, an unsuccessful masked performance by the Firestone group in 1977 was restricted to a given area by government permit. It was apparent that what ordinarily occurred outside this area—namely in the streets—was missing in this instance. The location and the risk are both essential to successful performance, as well as potential causes of violence.

Ode-lay originated in the Yoruba masking societies of Nigeria, introduced to Sierra Leone from 1807 to the middle of the century. Yoruba culture—its music, masked performances, religion, and medicine—played a central role in a long-standing political dialectic which currently manifests itself in the relationship between the Ode-lay groups and the Sierra Leone government (Peterson 1969:44-47). The government often depends on the political patronage of masked societies, yet it is fearful of the aesthetic intensity generated by their processions.

Hunting masks are the prototype of Ode-lay. They consist of *eri* (a horned headdress); *asho* (a loose-fitting smock and baggy pantaloonlike pants); and the most powerful part of the costume, *hampa* (a vestlike garment worn over the smock) (Fig. 1). The hampa may be covered with a variety of materials including wooden spoons, tortoise shells, and small gourds studded with quills that protect the maskers from witches. Dried and gutted sea porcupines stuffed with leaves containing medicinal properties are placed on the back of the hampa to help maintain its shape, and mirrors are attached to the garment so that attendants can see the reflections of witches. Also attached are bushbuck horns dipped in poison, wooden combs, monkey and dog skulls, empty pasteboard shotgun cartridge casings, and cowrie-lined red cloth sacks filled with medicine.

The Hunting costume honors Ogun, the deity of hunters, who was introduced to the colony by repatriated slaves, sixty thousand in all, most of whom were Yoruba. With horror and evangelical frustration, missionaries describe the

Figure 1
Hampa and eri of a hunting society mask. (Photo by Jerry Kobylecky.)

appearances of Ogun in his Hunting costumes. Traditional Hunting associations formed a solid institution which helped establish the Yoruba Creole class as the cultural elite of the then British colony.

Throughout the pre-World War II era, native sons applied for and were denied membership in the Yoruba Hunting societies. For this reason, during the mid-1940s the so-called Alikali maskers formed their own groups based on Hunting Society traditions. About 1950, Michael Banton photographed one Alikali group at the west end of Freetown. The performer is surrounded by participants in paramilitary dress. A few of them hold up a banner. The formation of the group and its militant posture strongly resemble the present-day Ode-lay society masquerades.

The 1978 Easter Monday outing of Juju Wata at Hastings exemplified a successful Ode-lay performance. Their objective was to establish a strong reputation for devil processions on the east side of Freetown. Since most of its members were Internal Security Unit troops (ISU), some of whom were trained in Cuba, it was important that they stage a successful masked performance. The fancy aesthetic of the costumes was intended to complement the fierce reputation of the ISU. Ode-lay representatives from nearby towns were invited.

Sometime during the preceding night, a sacrifice of uncooked rice in a bowl of water, a bottle of rum, and a 45 rpm record in its paper sleeve (symbolizing the record-breaking beauty of the devil), were spread before the assembled costume (Fig. 2). With more early-morning sacrifices, members drank rum from a glass offered by the society's female officer called the mammy queen.

At 8:30 AM, a bush mask which had been used the previous year caroled through the town to announce the procession of the Juju Wata "devil" (Krio term for maskers). The bush devil costume was decorated with porcupine quills and hunter's raffia, displaying a few fancy materials like the hunter's costume (Fig. 3), but the headpiece was much more elaborate. The procession moved from house to house until noon to the accompaniment of snapping sounds of rhythm sticks similar to those used by the Hunting societies.

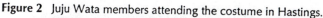

Figure 2 Juju Wata members attending the costume in Hastings.

By 1:00 PM most of the Juju Wata Society members and their girlfriends had gathered around the house of the *agba* (society leader). The women wore long uniform dresses of brown print; their hair was decorated with cowrie shells to complement the fancy mask. A flag carrier paraded up and down the road with a town crier who rang an assembly bell to announce the procession. The men wore jeans and printed T-shirts which bore the name of the group along with a variety of designs and slogans. The air was charged with excitement. At the shrine enclosure several members in *ashoebi* (society dress) and tennis shoes, along with the mammy queen in black satin pants and blouse, served portions of rum in the bottlecap. Other members carried phonograph records in honor of the event. Several broke 78 rpm discs hung from a flagpole. Meanwhile, the group's sponsors paced back and forth waiting to begin.

Expectation and tension mounted as word spread that the Bantus Mailo Jazz Band would not play until it received a cash advance. This is a method often employed by bands to guarantee payment. After reaching a compromise, the Juju Wata leader signaled the jazz band that the devil was prepared to dance. As the band struck up the first notes, the masker crashed through the mat enclosure, dancing for a few moments before he was carefully led down a hill and across the rocky path of an old rail bed. On the opposite side of the rail bed, women, flag carriers, the Bantus Mailo Jazz Band, and society members moved toward the devil. The music and singing intensified as the crowd and masking party converged.

Once the two groups met, the procession turned toward the home of the society's financial sponsor, where the devil danced for several minutes.Then the group departed for the homes of other important society members and townspeople. At 2:00 PM the party made its way to the village headman, who made a contribution to the society and gave a speech lauding the beauty and restraint of the procession. The procession then returned to the agba's house to change dancers and refresh the musicians. An hour later the Juju Wata group was prepared to play until the late evening. By 10:00 PM the jazz band and the society members were exhausted. Returning to the agba's residence for rice, meat sauce, and drink, the band jammed through the early morning while several society members played the mouth organ, triangle, and *mbira* (the so-called African thumb piano)–a jam session the group called "back off."

The Juju Wata performance met the expectations of its members and, indeed, all of Hastings. The village headman requested that he be considered a grand patron for the society's next performance. As the celebration was a record breaker, the agba smashed numerous discs at several points along the procession route (Fig. 4).

In contrast, the 1977 Firestone Society performance was a failure. At that time the Ode-lay society claimed about 90 members and over 3,000 supporters who gathered annually for Eid Ul-Adha at the end of Ramadan in order to attract Muslims. The head of the group, *ashigba*, maintains the shrine of Ogun, the Yoruba deity of war. The power and danger of Ogun, as conceived by the Yoruba, have effortlessly lent themselves to an urban toughness and concern for militancy expressed in Ode-lay masked performances.

When the government rejected Ode-lay requests for public permits for Eid Ul-Adha in November, Firestone selected the first week of December of that year to present their devils *off* the street. The main Firestone costume was built in the same three-part construction as the Hunting costume previously described, though the headpiece was strikingly different (Fig. 5). Yet despite the expertise of the artist who made it and the aesthetic quality and completeness of his creation, Ode-lay maskers must be placed at risk to be successful. The performance must be dangerous.

Restricted to a confined and private space, the performance failed to reach its potential intensity, and the disappointing first night resulted in the cancellation of the remaining presentations. Roger Abrahams's theory of enactment helps explain what went wrong (1977:80). He defines enactment as any cultural event that brings people together to employ multivocal and polyvalent signs and symbols to heighten ritual experience. Such enactments may include performances, games, rituals, and festivities. These four components are interpenetrating, as, for example, the coin toss and national anthem *rituals* in the *game* of football. In Ode-lay, the masked *performance* may be interrupted by the *play* of the *kaka* (shit) devil mask who mocks the main performance. Overlap is also evidenced in the post-masking *festivities* when members *play* at kung fu.

Abrahams notes that these four components are highly stylized, each marked, or framed, to foreground the form and movement of the participants (1977:98). With the appropriate frames and their most effective editing, the organizers of Ode-lay enactments have at their disposal a mechanism for structuring masked performances in order to heighten individual experience.

Figure 3 Juju Wata bush devil featuring a snake carrying a female image known as Mammy Wata.

Figure 4 Juju Wata performance, Hastings.

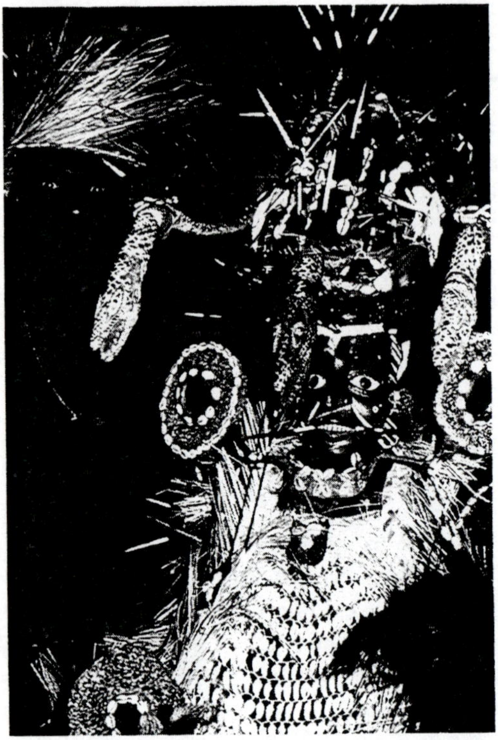

Figure 5
A Firestone devil costume.

By identifying the frames of Ode-lay enactment and by assigning affective significance to each one, successful performances may be compared with the failed Firestone event. From several successful Ode-lay performances, I developed a list of primary sequential frames.

1. *Officers of the society meet and select the days for masking.* In the larger group, celebrations occur at fixed times of the year, such as New Years, Muslim and Christian holidays, and political celebrations such as Independence Day. In special circumstances, a group will "pull" its devils for elections and political demonstrations. Performances have also been staged to challenge other masking societies.
2. *A permit is requested from the police.* This is one of the most difficult tasks set before Ode-lay societies. Their officers decide which political contacts to use for obtaining permits. Occasionally a politician will visit a group and give a progress report. The police will invite society leaders to headquarters to discuss permits in general. Rarely, society members will lobby with leading politicians on this issue.
3. *The general membership meets to collect funds.* This event occasions mistrust among members. Questions of how much to raise, what each member should pay, and how the group's leaders spend the money are a source of tension. Sometimes challenges and accusations result in physical confrontation.
4. *Styles of costumes are discussed and selected at a special meeting.* The minutes of one Ode-lay society shown to me by G.T. Coker of Paddle Society indicated vigorous debate over the type of headpiece, cloth, and other applied materials. In some cases the intent of a particular performance determines the style. The first time Bloody Mary took to the streets, the society decided that because it was on a mission of revenge the style should be fierce, similar to Hunting society maskers, with horns

and other animal parts and a bag-cloth asho. On other occasions, when violence is not the expressed goal, fancy costumes are made (Shaft 1978).

5. *Several officials visit the artist while he works on the commission.* At the first meeting, society officers may present a drawing or illustration of the kind of costume they want. It can be an elaborately detailed rendering of the headpiece or a chromolith featuring such images as Hindu deities (Fig. 6). These sessions are private and held in hushed voices.
6. *The artifacts are collected from the artist a week or so before the public display.* Usually this frame is performed late at night under the protection of darkness. The delegation arrives in an automobile and takes the costume to a protected space
7. *A mailo jazz band is selected at one of the meetings.* The term "mailo" (milo) derives from mailo gin, a locally distilled beverage with an alcoholic content high enough to render it as "hot" as mailo's musical inventor, Dr. Olu of Freetown, who assembled the first group in the 1960s. Mailo ensembles include a bass box drum, *sangbai* (single-headed drums), *keling* (a wooden slit gong), and *agoogoo* (a double metal gong often carried on the waist and struck with wooden mallets). Such ensembles are capable of making or breaking the masked performance–if the music lacks the appropriate rhythm and tempo the dancer will perform poorly. The explosive staccato rhythms and hypnotic ostenato beats establish the tempo for the dancing. Mailo music compels dancers to move pell-mell down the streets with an unpredictability that ensures risk and danger for anyone unexpectedly confronting a masker. With dance steps such as "Pole to Pole," the masker nearly crashes into one telephone pole after another; "Banga Banga" confronts moving vehicles straight on; and "Gutter Anse" trips along the deep trench gutters paralleling the streets. Everyone is poised for action. Nothing is safe, and surprise predicates danger.
8. *A flyer announcing the society program and crediting its organizers is prepared at a party the night before the performance and then distributed by mail* (Fig. 7). Its prose style, a Krio-English mix, helps set the participants' expectations.
9. *Sacrifices to the dead are offered at the local cemetery the morning of the performance.* Sacrifices of kola nut, rum, and uncooked rice are offered to the costume, which is positioned on a mortar some Ode-lay members associate with Shango, the Yoruba deity of thunder and lightning. On one Bloody Mary visit to the cemetery, Johnny Shaft, an important society member, and a couple of *jeweni* (medicine men) aroused two spirits. The first one, according to Shaft, was evil and manifested by a forceful

Figure 6
Drawing of an Ode-lay headpiece from Lumley Beach outside Freetown.

Potential Potential Potential
Heavy Heavy Heavy
Na We Yes

We say life is a mission, and we are after that mission.
The Super Heavy
Mission Bloody Mary
will be OUT again in Full Festac swing
On the 11th November 1978
We have been lying low in the Wilderness for-a-long long time and now we are Coming Back on the scene with our Tondo Tondo Dancing

WHAT HAS BEEN IS WHAT WILL BE. AND WHAT HAS BEEN DONE IS WHAT WILL BE DONE:
SO BROTHERS AND SISTERS LET THE IRONY OF ALL THAT HAS PASSED BE A LESSON TO ONE AND ALL.
LET ALL GRIEVANCES SUBSIDE AND PEACE ABIDE
LET ILL FEELINGS BE ERASED, AND POSITIVE VIBRATION REIGN.

Mission Mary: Say any good Hustler must some how try to keep on his Guard and realize that real is ofen.

So hustle with every mustle and make the show funky. We gonna portray the cultural heritage of our papa's land, so lets join hands together and make the Carnival Hectic.

Remember we say to you Goodness is a Benediction,
Padlock all the Bad Mouth so Peace must Prevail.
Mission Mary Mission Mary Mission Mary

AGBA WONTI (Jr.)
Sec Gen. MOMOH "C"
PUBLICITY MAN MR. T

Figure 7
Mission Bloody Mary flyer announcing a performance.

wind. The other was a Muslim man wrapped in white cloth with his thumbs and big toes tied in submission to Allah. The spirits were asked to prevent those "funny arguments" and fighting that occur before the masker appears in order to ensure that the performance would be peaceful.

10. *On the morning of the festival there is a parade (caroling) of a fancy mask or a bush devil.* After a sacrifice of kola nuts and rum, this devil and several society members proceed through the town collecting money to buy food and drink for the main masker. Children spread the word in their neighborhoods.
11. *Women prepare food.* Not all societies allow women to participate in the festivities, but in such groups as Juju Wata the wives and girlfriends of society leaders prepare ground-nut soup, sauces, rice, and fish stews for the final entertainment at the end of the day.
12. *Members dress in the fashion predetermined at society meetings.* In some groups, men choose stenciled T-shirts, jeans, and sneakers, while in others they select more elaborate costumes such as brown army uniforms and red berets accented with stripes of red ribbon over the shoulders and on the cuffs. Invited women participants purchase cloth for making long dresses and carefully fitted, wraparound gowns. Hairstyles and head wraps are also specified.
13. *Alcohol and marijuana are consumed from early morning.* Drinking among the membership may vary somewhat, from formal toasting with a specified beverage to sparingly distributed liquor in the bottle cap. Drinks include Remy Martin, champagne, Sierra Leone factory-bottled gin, mailo, and various beers and soft drinks. Marijuana is rolled in large quantities in six-inch paper wrappers occasionally seasoned or cured with rum, the favorite drink of Hunters.
14. *The* soweh (*or* saweh: *medicine*) *is applied to the costume.* Within the confines of the mat enclosure the medicine man, the agba (head of the society), and invited guests

spread soweh over the costume. Meanwhile, attendants carefully check the costume to determine if all its parts are securely attached and in place.

15. *Reception of the mailo jazz band(s) usually involves heated debate over the amount of payment and its method of dispersal.* In a Seaside Firestone festival the mailo jazz band waited nearby an outdoor bar for cash payment before agreeing to play. Messages went back and forth between the agba and the band's leader, building tension among the general membership. Resolving the dilemma, the band approached the shrine, urging the devil to dance. Finally, at a distance of a few yards, the masker could no longer resist the mailo sound and burst out of the mat enclosure. The two forces—aural and visual—were consummated.
16. *Members and maskers are doused with soweh from this point throughout the performance.* To receive the medicine, members move to form an inner circle where society strongmen protect the devil.
17. *The masked dancer is replaced in the costume three or four times.* These are very dangerous moments because both the costume and dancer are stripped of their "covers" and are thus susceptible to the malevolent acts of diviners and competing societies. The masked dancers, known as the *onifakun,* are selected at the group's meetings. After strengthening their own medicine with sacrifices, the performers are closely watched to see if their dancing is correct and if any part of their body becomes exposed as a result of their athletic actions.
18. *The society encounters and confronts competing groups and the police.* With colorful, yet accurate description the press covers the conflict. One *Sunday We Yone* article entitled "Bloody Mary Under Arrest" (11 December 1978:I) describes the group's encounter with Firestone:

> Also involved in the gunshot incident was one Oram Moses of 15 Wellington Road, Kissy Mess-mess, who was treated and discharged at Connaught [hospital]. The incident which led to the arrest of the "Bloody Mary" was a fight at Krootown Road involving a rival masquerade group known as "Firestone."
>
> Earlier, the two groups had engaged in a battle along Siaka Stevens Street. In the fighting along Saika [sic] Street, the situation got so desperate that supporters of the "Bloody Mary" were reported to have boarded a taxi and give [sic] chase to supporters of a rival group when in a bid to avoid trouble, they decided to leave in taxis.

19. *The mask is retired at the society settlement.* The dancers and supporters funnel through the small threshold of the shrine where a few members assist the dancer with removing the costume.
20. *The members eat and recount the day's events.* During this time, mailo or recorded music entertains members. Younger boys play around and practice martial arts, including kung fu. Courtship also occurs.
21. *Press coverage is read.* Throughout the week members living in and near the society headquarters collect news articles about themselves. Bloody Mary members sit around Johnny Shaft, who recites them with dramatic verve, at times slapping the paper with his fingers to stress a particularly exciting episode with the police or another society. The press reports reaffirm the aggressive character of the Ode-lay societies while fostering the fierce aesthetic of its maskers.
22. *Confiscated costumes and jailed members are retrieved.* Society leaders make frequent trips to their local police stations to request the return of their devils, asking how police can arrest a spirit or whether they have the right to interfere with something that is sacred. Frequently members will seek the advice and cooperation of politicians.

Compared with this ideal scenario, the Firestone celebration of 1977 lacked several frames, including 16-18 and 20-22. Just as notes missed in a song or unexpected gaps in a melody leave listeners questioning its legitimacy as song, missing frames of the Firestone performance left participants unconvinced of its enactment as enactment. There are intrinsic qualities in each missing frame which account for the affective failure of the Firestone event. These inherent qualities are explained with reference to Mary Douglas's work on purity, danger, and social pollution (1966) and Gregory Bateson's on play and fantasy (1972).

Douglas introduces a primary assumption: "Rituals work upon the body politic through the symbolic medium of the physical body" (1966:128). In the Sierra Leone case, the symbolic notions essential to the body ritual were located primarily in the missing frames, and therefore these notions were not manifest in the Firestone masked performance or its body politic, and vice versa.

Douglas identifies four types of social pollution which inspire body ritual: (1) pollution which presses on external boundaries; (2) pollution which transgresses internal lines of a system; (3) danger in the margin of lines; and (4) danger from internal contradiction–i.e., basic postulates denied by others (1966:122).

Ode-lay as well as Hunting society members express fear and anxiety especially over the first two kinds of pollution. These shared anxieties are expressed in individual body ritual, projected onto the masker, and passed on to the body politic. Hunters and Ode-lay members fear *fangay* (harmful medicines which cause skin rashes, scabs, and other skin disorders) on what Douglas calls external boundaries. Skin pollution is countered by soweh, a Mende-derived, creolized term for medicine.

The other major pollutant feared by members is medicine that penetrates the stomach or, in Douglas's terms, internal boundaries. Stories and practices related to the stomach and medicine abound. From the day an initiate joins a society he must take the *oogun* (medicine) of his group and swear to maintain its secret. Should he reveal the secret, his belly would swell and kill him seven days after his initiation. Related to this stomach anxiety are stories in the newspapers and in neighborhood gossip pointing to lethal stomach poisoning by witches. One of the most powerful Yoruba-descended diviners in Sierra Leone once described how the repatriated slaves carried medicines in their stomachs on ships (Brown 1978). Hunters and Ode-lay members believe that the stomach is vulnerable: although it contains the purity of society medicine, it can swell and eventually kill its carrier if he should pollute that medicine by revealing its secret or by taking other medicine. In short, body rituals in the urban societies of Freetown pertain to purity and pollution of the skin and stomach.

The soweh man applies medicine to members' skin for protection against fangay pollution. As if by analogy, he uses a broom applicator to sweep clean the polluting agent. Hats, shoes, and long pants also protect the participants' skin. To safeguard the stomach, members eat and drink sacrifices prior to performance.

These body rituals, if provided the proper framing, are projected onto the masker, especially through parts of the costume: the asho, eri, and hampa. The asho covers the entire body except the head, which is protected by the horned eri. As an additional layer, the asho protects the skin. The most powerful part of the costume, the vestlike hampa contains medicines which protect the dancer's stomach area. Like newly initiated members who consume the society's medicine and forever carry it in their stomachs, the masked dancer likewise carries the medicine in his hampa. The masker's skin and stomach must be inviolate to impurities inflicted by outside sources.

The empty shells, sea porcupine bodies, skulls, tortoise shell, shotgun casings, horns, and small sacks which make up the Seaside Firestone Ode-lay costume are all filled with medicine. Like the stomach, they are medicine containers. Maskers and society members are homologically served from these containers with carved ladles which hang on the back of the hampa.

Only two of the eight missing frames in the Firestone celebration—the morning parade and the postmortem news reports—were not directly related to concerns about pollution. It is the street processions that provide participants the opportunity to apply medicines for protection from malevolent diviners and members of competing societies. The government's refusal to grant procession permits preempted this option, preventing the necessary intensity for achieving the desired heightened experience.

Though societies abhor pollution, they are bound to it by paradox. Purity cannot be defined without knowing impurity in the same way that a feast cannot be appreciated unless the daily menu of a particular society is known (Abrahams 1977:105). In rituals, games, performances, and festivities, participants can attain the purity of heightened experience only by becoming susceptible to pollution. Taking the mask to the streets provides the necessary susceptibility.

Moreover, the concept of individual pollution is projected onto the masker and the body politic. The Ode-lay procession suggests an anthropomorphic formation which expresses individual fear of the two pollutions. At the head of the procession the flautist, or flagman, directs the masked dancer through the streets. He is the eyes and ears of the dancer. Second is the *bila* man who, with carved gun or stick in hand, protects the masked dancer. He is its hands. The masked spirit itself symbolizes the stomach of the procession with the large, medicine-filled hampa. Members protect the stomach (hampa) by forming a semicircle around the masker. These participants are fully dressed in ashoebi (society dress), which collectively constitutes the social skin of the body politic.

Denied the fear-inspiring aesthetic experience which accelerates as it moves in a reverberating manner from individual concerns to those of the masker and the body politic, Firestone members could not project their personal concerns about pollution and its dialectical partner, purity, onto the group or the masker. One explanation for the participants' inability to identify with the Firestone performance concerns the types of communication available *off the streets*. Play, threat, and histrionic behavior are based on the dancers' ability to communicate by recognizing signals and map-territory distinctions. Occasionally during these periods signals go unrecognized. When this happens play changes to mood-sign behavior and nip becomes bite. Bateson comments:

> [T]he discrimination between map and territory is always liable to break down and (for example) the ritual blows of peace-making (among the Andaman Islanders) are always liable to be mistaken for the "real" blows of combat. In this event, the peace-making ceremony becomes a battle (1972:182).

Ritual may be mistaken for the real thing and with that reality another kind of heightened experience is obtained by the participants.

In the region where art, magic, and religion overlap, humans have evolved the metaphor that is meant. To see how the "metaphor that is meant" comes into play, Bateson provides a useful classification of messages. In the message he calls the mood-sign, the parties are nonreflective during the message-sending phase. If they exhibit biting behavior face to face they take real action and bite. Here the map and territory are the same. The second message simulates the mood-sign and, by exhibiting a set of behaviors called play, the nip instead of the bite results. The remaining type of message allows the receiver to discriminate between, or to equate mood-signs and those which resemble them. The third message asks the question: Is this play? The equivocation introduced by this question allows the Ode-lay participants, in this case, to confirm the "metaphor is meant" and its resultant potent experience (see Bateson 1972:189).

At times playful Ode-lay behavior turns to the mood-sign. Then nip will become bite and people get hurt. The confusion of nip and bite is seen in the relationship between Ode-lay groups and the police. Whereas members may parade with a coffin in front of police, playfully warning them not to interfere with its procession, the taunting of law enforcers may result in their use of tear gas, or more, to stop the play. In this instance the police equate map and territory. In the failed Firestone event, the absence of particular frames preempted the third type of message. Without it, map and territory could not be equated; therefore, the real metaphor and the heightened experience that results from it were denied (see Bateson 1972:191).

The labile nature of Ode-lay signaling or message-sending during street processions is the axis on which its affective success turns. The "metaphor that is meant" creates excitement and nonanalytical Gestalt perception of the enactment. In successful Ode-lay masked performances, members become the masked spirit; the spirit becomes the membership; the spirit becomes the medicine. The achieved aesthetic diminishes the participant's sense of being separate. "We are Ogun," "We are the god of Iron," "We are inviolate," are pronouncements that express that collectively. It is as if to say, "Our external and internal boundaries are pure and protected in the collective purity of the body politic." At this juncture Bateson's words are appropriate: "here we can recognize an attempt to deny the difference between map and territory, and to get back to the absolute innocence of communication by means of pure mood-signs" (1972:183).

Unlike Firestone, the Juju Wata and Seaside Firestone performances were able to *take it to the streets*, therefore achieving success (Fig. 8). By masking in the streets, societies such as Juju Wata risk spiritual and physical pollution of each member, masker, and the rest of the group–i.e., the body politic. By experiencing all of the frames they achieve ritual purity. The excitement generated by the masked dancers breaking through the mat enclosures onto the public streets, the sacrificing along the routes, the vulnerable changing of the dancers, and the performing before important personages on route all add to the ritual intensity.

In Ode-lay masked performances, the open air and the streets provide a wide variety of contrasting qualities of texture, color, motion, and sound. The

Juju Wata costume featured an electric-blue, female face-mask with red lips. The mask was surrounded by soft, fuzzy, shiny, hard, and dull materials in pink, red, gold, and yellow. Such surfaces reflect the intense, direct African sunlight and actively engage the retinas of participants, no doubt modifying everyday perception. At the same time, shouts, screams, keening, song, footsteps, bells, and mailo jazz establish a cacophony of sound on the streets. These aural elements impact qualities of action, thus inspiring carefully studied musical steps, circle dancing, marching, rushing, and the general success of performance. The complexity of sound and costume helps determine everyone's body movement. At certain times during the procession leaders such as the bila man jump with spread legs while holding their guns or staffs straight. At the height of their ascent they draw their feet together and execute a scissor kick, returning to earth with both feet together. Countering the weight of the jump, they squat to the ground in a shock-absorbing action. Other members of the group maintain fixed expressions: mouths open in a circular shape with tension focused on the muscles connected to the lips, eyes cast downward. Since the qualities of these performances frequently appear as oppositions I speculate that there is something about oscillation between polarities that excites human beings.

Figure 8 Seaside Firestone devil in the street.

Firestone members attributed the failure of their performance to the government's refusal to grant permits. They did not explain the disappointing celebration in terms of purity, danger, pollution, mood-sign and the "metaphor as meant," or qualities of opposition; however, they did sense that what was lacking had to do with masking in the streets.

The All Peoples' Congress (APC) has wisely established a patronage system which includes the major Yoruba secret societies and the Ode-lay groups. It has done so to strengthen the positions of party members. In the case of young men's societies it has used this system to keep a close watch on a potential breeding ground for political radicalism. Ode-lay associations like Firestone, Bloody Mary, and Paddle have demonstrated for the APC on election and nomination days and in 1978 for the referendum to declare the one-party state, instituted in April of that year. With such active Ode-lay support, why do government officials insist on controlling the movements of the maskers by permit? Mistrust prevails on both sides. During the Ode-lay masked performances, societies support their patron, yet the affective experience they obtain extends beyond the political realm and into the religious and sacred. Such ambiguity is not well-tolerated by governing institutions that rule by establishing clearly defined roles, governing departments, and the black-and-white letter of the law. Ode-lay performance expresses a worldview whose foundation was established well before the advent of institutionalized religions and nation states.

REFERENCES

Abrahams, Roger. 1977. "Toward an Enactment-centered Theory of Folklore." In *Frontiers of Folklore*, edited by W. Bascom, 79-120. West Boulder, CO: Westview Press.

Bateson, Gregory. 1972. *Steps to an Ecology of Mind*. San Francisco: Chandler Publishing.

Brown, David Nelson. 1978. Personal communication.

Douglas, Mary. 1966. *Purity and Danger*. London: Routledge and Kegan Paul.

Nunley, John. 1987. *Moving with the Face of the Devil: Art and Politics in Urban West Africa*. Urbana and Chicago: University of Illinois Press.

Peterson, John. 1969. *Province of Freedom: A History of Sierra Leone, 1787-1870*. London: Faber and Faber.

Shaft, Johnny. 1978. Personal communication.

22

Tradition in Native American Art

J.C.H. King

INTRODUCTION

All cultural systems exist in a constant state of change, brought about both by internal and external forces. If societies change continually, often as a result of foreign influence, then the concept of tradition in culture and art cannot be viewed as absolute. Instead, it must be seen as a relative term, used, for instance, to compare one situation or object with another, or to describe an art object with respect to a given corpus of related material. As such, it is a heuristic device, inseparable from the equal but opposing idea of nontraditional art. Tradition, which the *Oxford English Dictionary* defines as "something that has prevailed from generation to generation," is also a highly emotive term, used in many contexts to validate not only art objects but also political and cultural ideas. Used in this way, it is not an objective idea, and therefore is not necessarily useful in scientific investigation. However, because it appears such a simple and clear-cut term, suited to an infinite number of situations, it has become a "semantic booby trap" (Brody 1971:59).

Everybody has an idea of what "tradition" means. However, few address the limitations of this concept, whose general use often raises more problems than it solves. While the various uses of the concept may be defined either explicitly or implicitly through context, they cannot be applied rigorously as art historical tools any more than they can be employed as instruments for scientific analysis.

Reprinted in abridged form from *The Arts of the North American Indian: Native Traditions in Evolution*, edited by Edwin L. Wade, New York: Hudson Hills Press, 1986, pages 64-92 with permission of the author and publisher.

THE CONCEPT OF TRADITION AS BASED ON TECHNIQUE AND MATERIALS, FORM AND FUNCTION, SYMBOL AND MEANING

Traditionalism within a material culture complex can arise through a variety of different means, all of which are dependent on time-persistent elements within each tradition. Traditionalism can be based on technique and materials, and identification by these two criteria is relatively straightforward. Pottery, carving techniques, and embroidery, to take three separate areas, are easily defined, and can be related to the vast body of materials in museum collections. Technology varies within traditions. The use of metal tools and metal needles, for example, altered Woodlands carving, quillwork, and moosehair embroidery (Figures 1, 2). However, the techniques themselves need not alter, so that the coiled and twined basketry traditions in the Southwest, California, and the Northwest Coast survive, using the same techniques found in the most ancient examples of basketry. The persistence of materials is more complex, in part because Euro-American trade goods came to be substituted for their aboriginal American counterparts, such

Figure 1 Mirror and Case. Crow, c. 1880. Philbrook Art Center, Tulsa. Gift of Mr. Mark Dunlop. 78.8. This glass mirror was undoubtedly acquired through trade and then mouunted by its native owner in a wooden protective frame and encased in a bag of native-tanned skin, richly embellished with trade beads and yarn. This Crow mirror is an example of a European object thoroughly incorporated into a Native American aesthetic context.

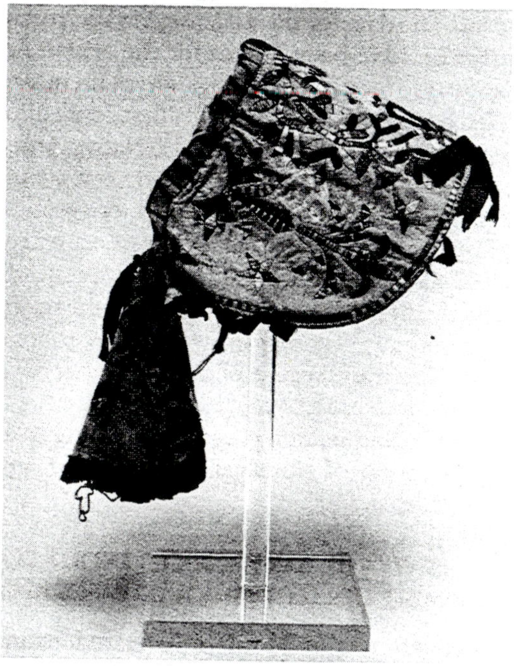

Figure 2
Bonnet. Santee Sioux, c. 1890. Quillwork on hide, plaid fabric lining, ribbon. Philbrook Art Center, Tulsa, Elizabeth Cole Butler Collection, 82.1.38. This hide bonnet is a direct translation of the 19th century headgear worn by American frontier women. The distinctive angular floral motifs favored by the Santee are their interpretation of the more fluid curvilinear designs and embroidery compositions found among the natives of the Great Lakes region, who in turn had absorbed these influences from the French-Canadian Metis trappers.

as wool yarn for goat wool on the Northwest Coast, beads for porcupine quills, and wool cloth for skin. However, as in all the elements that go to make up any particular material culture tradition, the change in technique or tools and the substitution or addition of foreign materials do not necessarily alter the total traditional aspect of an object.

Traditionalism can also be evaluated (inevitably with some subjectivity or ethnocentrism) through discussion of changes of form and function and through alterations in the symbolic value, either of the object itself or of the symbols with which it is decorated. The study of traditionalism in motifs and realistic symbols is a very complex subject, to a large extent because of our inadequate historical knowledge.

Certain basic ideas about the origin of conventionalized designs should be mentioned because they underscore the paucity of our understanding of traditionalism in symbol and meaning. Although not always appreciated by contemporary students of Native American art, this traditionalism and Indianism were and are perhaps the most important aspects of art for its makers. Conventional designs arise in three ways. They can derive from or relate to the technical basis of the artifact. Northwest Coast carving, coiled and twined basketry, and southwestern weaving all utilize the qualities of the materials and techniques for aesthetic purposes. The simple introduction of lines of even adze work on Northwest totem poles, and the alternation of different materials in single stitches and the blocks of color, enable basket weavers and carvers to build up designs without symbolic intent. Similarly, Navajo textiles, through the use of different weft colors, can effect striking designs without suggesting any specific symbolic intention. The data for the meaning of much conventional design is absent today and may also have been absent for the Native American; in these cases, we are predisposed to look for meanings where no meaning may actually exist. Second, and related to this, is the possibility that conventional designs were provided with meanings after their creation by the Native American artist. This makes it very hard to define what is traditional and what is not traditional in Indian art, even in a vulgar, day-to-day manner. Third, conventionalized design may originate in the deliberate attempt by an artist to associate a realistic form, whether sculptural or two-dimensional, with another aesthetic tradition, and then reproduce the design in the new technique. In this case, the reproduced motif or realistic subject matter frequently becomes less realistic or more conventionalized in the second tradition. The transference of design may occur with a change in traditionalism, or may not. Two examples of the former are the translation of sacred Navajo Yei designs from sand paintings used for healing to secular rugs woven for sale, and the reproduction of shamans in wood and argillite by Haida carvers of the Northwest Coast.

THE NECESSITY FOR BASING IDEAS ABOUT TRADITION ON AVAILABLE COLLECTIONS AND INFORMATION

The appreciation of Indian art and the understanding of traditionalism in Indian art depend on the collections available for study. Most of the principal North American collections of Indian artifacts were created between 1860 and 1930, in large museums in eastern and central North America. It is inevitable, therefore, that most of the standards by which traditionalism in Indian art is judged depend upon these collections for purposes of definition and comparison. The late nineteenth and early twentieth centuries, however, saw enormous upheaval in Indian North America. During this period, formerly independent tribes were confined to reservations. The Dawes Act of 1887 proposed converting Indians into American citizens by allotting 160 acres to each head of household. The final military battles between Plains Indians and the United States Government were fought. In Canada the potlatch–the important Northwest Coast Indian feast at which goods and money were distributed–was banned by an 1884 law. And ironically, this was the peak period of collecting. As a result, the most traumatic period in Native American history has provided the material basis for the definition of what is traditional and what is not. Basketry, beaded costume, and carving from this time exist in such large quantities that they are used as a general, though often unstated, yardstick by which the unconscious standards of traditionalism are set.

Similar problems occur in the examination of art traditions within an archaeological context. Archaeological collections are characterized by the sparseness of prehistoric remains and the fact that most artifacts come from burial or ceremonial sites. When collections of objects from the distant past are suddenly fleshed out, it is due to the addition of artifacts preserved under either the most arid or the most humid conditions. The Anasazi and Puebloan traditions of the Southwest are illuminated in this way by a few finds of material which include extraordinary basketry, superb cotton textiles, and painted wood ceremonial artifacts, including masks (Coe 1976:203; Vivian et al. 1978). In Florida, the sites of Key Marco and Fort Center have produced evidence of woodworking traditions with artistic qualities, particularly realism, that equal those of anything we know from the historic period (Gilliland 1975; Sears 1982). Most of this material, however, whether from wet or dry sites, is of ceremonial significance. In this respect, the high proportion of archaeological artifacts of great artistic quality is paralleled by that of early museum collections, which often concentrated on acquiring the beautiful and unique rather than the implements of everyday life.

When an artifact is viewed, the beholder selects a personal frame of reference for it. Sometimes information necessary for understanding an object's symbolic content may still be available from present-day followers of ancient traditions. This is particularly true for Puebloans in the American Southwest, and for cultures in the Northwest Coast and Arctic. But among other traditions, especially those of eastern North America, no ethnographic data exist to illuminate the ancient past. Appreciation of Puebloan architecture and recognition of the central importance of the kiva—a circular ceremonial room still used today—is a relatively straightforward matter. An understanding of the ancient Serpent Mound, or comprehension of the significance of the mounds in Mound City, both in Ohio, is very different. While both the Ohio sites derive from archaeological traditions related to historic cultures, the use of ethnographic parallels is insufficient as a basis for explanation. Instead, an archaeological and ethnographic explanation may need to be imported from general sources to help us interpret the great wealth of art objects recovered from Adena and Hopewellian burial sites. On the other hand, in the southeastern United States, Mesoamerican influences are fundamental to an explanation of the late prehistoric architecture of the Mississippian traditions of sites such as Etowah and Cahokia. The basis for appreciation of prehistoric North American artifacts is, however, often aesthetic, historical, and archaeological, rather than cultural.

There are many categories of Indian art for which ethnographic explanations are incomplete or nonexistent. The significance of porcupine-quill decoration on early historic Woodlands artifacts, of the engraved designs on Beothuk antler pendants, of the painted designs on the skin coats of the Central and Eastern Subarctic are not known. This does not mean that we cannot define them as an art tradition, but merely that we can only say that they derive from Indian traditions which we comprehend on the basis of technology, and fragmentary ethnographic data.

Reliance on the techniques which define categories of objects as a means of grouping and defining art traditions is a further reason for emphasizing the limitations of the concept of traditional art. Examples of this are provided by the atlatl, or throwing stick, and the toggle harpoon, a harpoon point which detaches from the foreshaft; both are common from prehistoric times. The atlatl was employed over much of North America. In historic times it was used principally in the Arctic and Northwest Coast, and in most areas it was hardly decorated at all. Among the East Greenland Eskimo, however, throwing sticks were and still are decorated with small, applied three-dimensional ivory carvings of mammals. In Alaska, the Aleut and Pacific Eskimo decorated throwing sticks with beads and inlaid ivory figures; the Pacific Eskimo also carved their throwing sticks with figures of sea otters, often highly abstract. There can be no general explanation for the varying embellishment of these things, and the cultural symbolism must remain relative to the traditions from which they spring. On the Northwest Coast, the few Tlingit throwing sticks that survive are carved with the crests of the people of high status who owned them, rather than with the animals that were hunted. Similarly, the toggle harpoon was decorated by only a few groups, such as the Makah and the Nuu-chah-nulth (Nootka) on the Northwest Coast. Their whaling harpoons, owned by the chiefs of high status (the only people permitted to hunt whales), were sometimes decorated on the barbs with crests. As these two technologies spread throughout the Arctic and Northwest Coast, we must assume that their symbolic significance varied and evolved within cultures and from one culture or group of people to the next. In the Arctic they were associated with subsistence activities; on the Northwest Coast, with the crests of chiefs. There is no reason to assume that an Indian art tradition will survive transference from one culture to the next with its symbolic, rather than physical form intact. It may be that as technologies or techniques such as those used in quill embroidery on skin and birchbark, or in false embroidery on twined baskets, were transferred from one location to another, their aesthetic content was adapted in meaning and, thus embellished, they began a new life in a new culture.

TRADITION, TRADE, AND EXCHANGE

Another break in tradition occurs when artifacts created within one tribe or culture are transferred by exchange, trade, or war to another. This can occur at many levels. At the most basic level, alteration of meaning takes place when a raw material travels from its place of origin. We can assume that this occurred for the wide variety of materials, such as copper, sharks' teeth, and marine shells, that were traded extensively in precontact times. Examples of altered symbolism of raw materials are rather rare in ethnographic literature, and most are confined to variants on the same kinds of material. Catlinite, the red claystone mined by the Santee at Pipestone, Minnesota, occurs in various colors. The Santee preferred the pure red stone for their own pipe bowls and traded the speckled or apparently less pure stone to other tribes. At a different level, we may assume that artifacts traded on the Northwest Coast, such as bentwood boxes and canoes made by the Haida and traded on the mainland for *oolachen* grease, altered in symbolic significance upon transfer to their new owners, the various Nishga- and Gitksan-speaking peoples.

Indian art traditions cannot, even when viewed as a whole, within a totally Indian context, be seen as discrete entities that develop independently. At every stage of transfer, raw materials and finished artifacts that were traded or captured in war, and even whole ceremonies, could be transformed symbolically or physically by their integration into indigenous art traditions. Another agent of change was the creative force of individuals who originated symbolic meanings through personal or social experience, and adapted and created art forms. Part of the unstated basis for using the binary opposition of "traditional" and "nontraditional" in analyzing Indian cultures is the assumption that individuality was not significant. While it is difficult to appreciate the importance of an individual's work in changing art traditions in precontact times, it becomes increasingly clear, in fields such as basketry and Northwest Coast carving, that individuality must have played a highly significant role in the adaptation of art traditions in the late nineteenth and early twentieth centuries, the period of maximum collection of Indian artifacts (see Holm, chapter 3). For example, there was a relatively small number of carvers of argillite among the Haida in the early nineteenth century; nevertheless, within a few decades, especially after the devastating smallpox epidemics of the middle of the century, a thriving souvenir industry developed, involving sizable numbers of carvers. In another case, the Micmac of Nova Scotia are known for the carving of pipe bowls, yet it seems likely that a single carver was responsible for all the finely finished bowls embellished with figures of mammals, perhaps of totemic significance, and geometric designs including the double-curve motif. Because of their great beauty, the pipes of this one artisan have come to epitomize Micmac carving traditions (Figure 3). Through the creation of this ideal type, our perception of Micmac art has been distorted; we could even say it has been falsified, since artifacts appearing superficially to be traditional were in fact transitional, having mostly been sold or given to Euro-Americans rather than used indigenously.

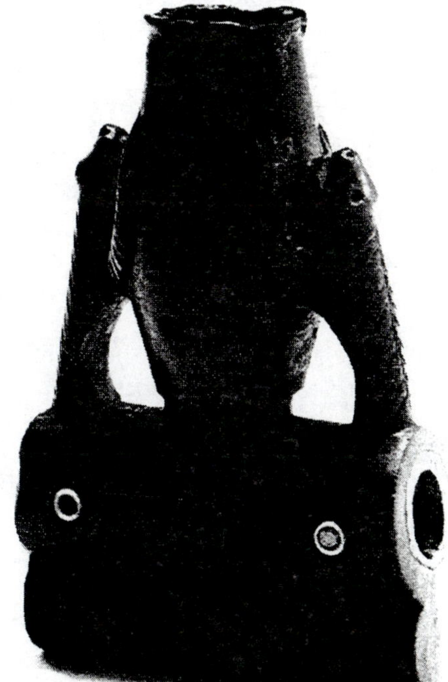

Figure 3
Pipe bowl. Micmac. Late 1800s. Carved slate. Philbrook Art Center, Tulsa, Elizabeth Cole Butler collection, L82.1.378. Pipe bowls of wood and stone elaborately decorated with realistic and mythic creatures incorporate geometric compositions that recall the decorative woodcarving styles of the early Dutch, German, and Swedish immigrants.

TRADITION AS AFFECTED BY EARLY CONTACT WITH EURO-AMERICAN CULTURE

The question of what is traditional and what is not becomes even more complex when the overwhelming influence of the European and Euro-American colonization of North America is taken into account. The central problem here is that many artifacts commonly regarded as nontraditional are in fact nontraditional only in use. As we have seen, raw materials, finished artifacts, and ceremonial complexes were commonly transferred among indigenous groups in precontact times. The question is then whether or not the contact between European and Indian society was of a different nature, and so rendered European influences on Indian art different in some way from other influences. The concept of the "nontraditional" is a value-laden judgment. It reflects stereotyped ideas about Indians and expectations of the art appropriate to noble savages untainted by Western society, which in turn altered (if it did not devastate) their ideal products. The extent to which Indian material culture complexes, and therefore art traditions, internalize Western technology and ideas provides a standard against which it is possible to judge the extent of foreign influence. But this judgment is, in the end, of no use since it is based on unworkable ideal types of what Indians should be in order to be traditional, and these ideal types, like that of the Noble Savage, depend on the imposition of Western standards on Indian art. As with the description of the precontact era, that of the postcontact can be divided into a series of situations in which different kinds of non-Indian influences are brought to bear. Sometimes these influences relate to simple technologies, such as the tools that were acquired in trade from the earliest years of European contact and which wrought immediate, radical changes upon material culture and art. Sometimes these influences brought with them whole technological complexes which had a more profound effect than mere tools; an example of this is the arrival of the horse, which radically altered the subsistence base of Plains society, and ultimately revolutionized Plains art (Ewers 1955). Sometimes Western trade introduced new materials whose acquisition influenced art without necessarily altering the form of artifacts or their symbolic content; the most significant of these trade items were beads, paints and dyes, wool cloth and silk ribbon, and metals such as silver and copper, which were used for decoration and ceremonial artifacts. At a more fundamental level, Western intrusion into Indian society produced social and political responses which, although resulting from the colonization of North America, did not necessarily incorporate Euro-American ideas. Movements such as the traditionalist Midewiwin cult of the Western Great Lakes, and the Ghost Dance and Native American Church of the Plains produced ceremonial art that was new and in a sense nontraditional, but which in fact had its roots in ancient Indian society.

Finally, there are two more superficial levels at which Euro-American society affected Indian art. The first is the adoption or adaptation of European design and its incorporation into Indian art. The second is the development of art forms, in basketry, embroidery, and carving, designed for Euro-American purchase but using Indian techniques and symbolism. The adoption by Indians of apparently

European media should also be included, since this again obscures any clear division between traditional and nontraditional art (Figure 4).

The European and Euro-American colonization of North America also provided new materials through trade, which affected art and so in a sense made it less traditional. The fur trade, for instance, made wool cloth widely available to replace the skins and furs that were acquired for disposal in the east, and in Europe and Asia. Whereas skins had often been painted and decorated with moosehair and porcupine-quill embroidery, cloth was more often decorated with

Figure 4 Necklace, probably Santo Domingo Pueblo. 1880-90. Coral, turquoise, silver. Thomas Gilcrease Institute of American History and Art, Tulsa, 8437.1408. The double-barred cross is a native modification of the Spanish form given to the Puebloans by the Franciscan fathers of New Spain. Puebloans associated the cross not so much with Christianity, but with the ancient fertility symbol of the dragonfly that adorns kiva murals and sacred medicine bowls.

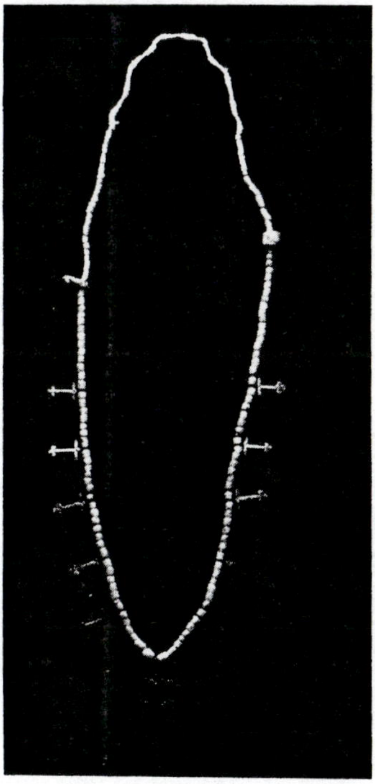

Figure 5 Coat. Oto. Late 1800s. Floral beadwork on wool. Philbrook Art Center, Tulsa, George M. Tredway Collection, TR 30. Although it was collected among the Osage, and identified as a bride's coat, the distinctive motifs beaded on this European-cut frock coat suggest an Oto origin. The bisymmetrically-divided fleur-de-lis and the three-petaled flowers suggest French influence.

glass beads from Italy and Bohemia (Figure 5), also provided by the fur trade. Many other substitutions occurred over time; for instance, the replacement of bone, antler, and shell ornaments by silver ones. These apparently simple changes produced artifacts which were still primarily used by Indians within Indian society, and yet by their very nature seem to be nontraditional (Figure 3). A slightly different effect occurred with the appearance of specifically European versions of Indian tools.

A separate series of incorporations occurs when non-Indian designs are taken for Indian use. The preeminent example of this is the use of European floral motifs and designs in Woodlands and Subarctic beadwork and moosehair embroidery (Figure 6). In the eighteenth century, Quebec religious orders such as the Ursuline nuns taught Indian girls to embroider in European techniques. This seems to have been in part the origin of the floral styles which appeared in the nineteenth century. Other styles perhaps came from the patterns commonly used by nineteenth-century Euro-American women in embroidery. Still, a certain proportion, mostly the more abstract designs, were certainly indigenous to native groups. The influence of French religious orders is, however, more complex and more interesting than the mere transferal of techniques and designs to Indians suggests. Because of shortages of European materials such as silk in Canada in the eighteenth century, French-Canadian nuns used Indian materials such as porcupine quills and moosehair. These materials were then incorporated into a syncretic art form, which was then taught back to the indigenous people from whom it had in part been learnt. The center of this work was the community of Lorette, which had been founded for Christian Huron dispersed from their original homeland in Ontario during the seventeenth-century wars with the Iroquois over access to fur sources (Brasser 1976:42-43; Morissonneau 1978). By

Figure 6 Saddle. Cree, c. 1900. Beadwork, hide, yarn. Philbrook Art Center, Tulsa, Elizabeth Cole Butler Collection L82.1.393. The Cree pad saddle was a direct adaptation of European military riding gear, beautifully illustrating a fusion of Native American and European aesthetic ideals.

the beginning of the nineteenth century, the Lorette Huron were producing large quantities of skin moccasins ornamented with floral embroidery in moosehair, as well as birchbark souvenir artifacts, such as boxes, trays, fans, and napkin rings decorated with figurative scenes of Indian life designed to appeal to visitors and tourists. It is reasonable to say that by the middle of the nineteenth century these were characteristic of the Huron, and so in a sense were traditional Huron artifacts, even though their beginnings were extremely complex, and by no means entirely Indian in origin or design.

TRADITION AND COMMERCIALIZATION

So far we have discussed the Indian acquisition of tools, techniques, materials, and design elements. More interesting, perhaps, are the occasions when Indians learned new technologies that used new materials and new aesthetics. An example of Indian adoption of outside influences is provided by the development of Navajo textiles in the Southwest. The Navajo had come south within the last millennium, separating from the main body of Athapaskan-speaking peoples in the Central and Western Subarctic. In the seventeenth century they were not weavers. However, after the expulsion of the Spanish during the Pueblo Revolt and the subsequent Spanish reconquest of the Southwest in the late seventeenth century, they obtained weaving technology, probably from the Hopi, and began to weave wool and to herd sheep.

Few Navajo textiles survive from before the middle of the nineteenth century. Most of those that exist are simple in design and consist largely of bold compositions of stripes in natural brown, white and deep indigo. In the middle of the nineteenth century, and especially after the effective military defeat of the Navajo in the 1860s by the United States, the aesthetics of Navajo textiles began to undergo a series of far-reaching changes. In particular, geometric stepped designs, probably of Mexican origin, came to be used on blankets woven for Indian use. Increasing American influence brought other significant changes, especially after the arrival of railways in the 1880s. Rugs for use in American homes came to be the primary textile form, and designs began to incorporate foreign motifs, particularly from Mexican Saltillo serapes, with their vivid stepped and wedge-edged geometric designs. These designs, known as Eye Dazzlers, are visually mobile and highly detailed, contrasting with the strong, simple designs of the earliest known blankets. At the same time, new dyes were introduced, and aniline dyes came to be more important than the old and more traditional colors, including the imported indigo. Newly introduced yarns began to replace ancient natural yarns; some were raveled from imported cloth, others purchased from eastern North America, for instance from Germantown, Pennsylvania, whose name is now synonymous with non-Navajo yarns of the late nineteenth century. These influences on Navajo textiles were absorbed without non-Navajo intervention. After a period of decline in textile quality at the end of the nineteenth century, a succession of Euro-American traders became involved in the development of technical quality and the introduction of new patterns and designs outside the Navajo repertoire. Traders such as J.B. Moore acquired trading posts and set about improving the quality of wool and dyeing. From 1897, when he purchased the trading post which he renamed Crystal, Moore tried to promote Navajo textiles through refinements not only in quality but also in design and motifs. Some of these, such as the swastika or "whirling logs" design, which derived from Navajo sand paintings, were traditional (Rodee 1981:19-24); others were new. Moore was also instrumental in introducing the Oriental design principles of Caucasian rugs, particularly that of a border design with a central pattern, to Navajo weavers. This was in line with his avowed intent of making Navajo textiles more commercial, in this case by making them competitive in design with imported Asian rugs. Perhaps the most significant design alteration to Navajo weaving was, however, the introduction of religious designs, particularly from sand paintings or dry paintings, in the form of Yeis, the supernatural figures portrayed in the paintings. While this idea had begun in the nineteenth century, it only developed into a substantial tradition with the work of Hosteen Klah, an important medicine man from near Newcomb, New Mexico, during the 1920s and 1930s. This introduction of religious material into an art form made entirely for commercial purposes is perhaps a direct parallel to the Haida introduction of shamans and shamanistic rituals into the subject matter of argillite carving. The Navajo still feel uneasy about the sacrilegious aspect of this tradition (Rodee 1981:103-104).

Aesthetic and ceremonial traditions may respond to acculturation differently, even within the same community or tribe. Material culture traditions concerned with subsistence activities are often the first to disappear, particularly when these depend on very time-consuming manufacture, such as the basketry artifacts used, for instance, in the gathering of nuts or acorns. An example of this is provided by the twined basketry traditions of the Panamint Shoshone, a Central-Numic-speaking people of southeastern California. The Panamint live in an exceptionally arid area around Death and Panamint valleys, so that much food traditionally came from the mountains above the valleys. The most important food resource was the pine nut, although acorns and mesquite beans were also very significant. Twined willow baskets were made in forms for use as water ollas, winnowing and parching trays, and conical carrying and seed baskets. Basketry hats and cradles were also made. Coiled basketry, on the other hand, although comparatively finer, continued to be made in larger quantities as a tourist art after twined basketry had ceased to be necessary for purely subsistence purposes (Figure 7).

Panamint coiled baskets usually have a three-rod foundation, often of willow, but also including sumac and grass. The withes are cut in winter and prepared with a knife. The coiling element, also of willow, incorporates decorative sections of baltic rush, a light brown alkali bulrush, dark brown devil's claw, and the inner root of the joshua tree or tree yucca, which is red-brown. In the nineteenth century it is likely that all baskets were made with geometric designs for ceremonial usage. In this century, with tourist and other non-Indian activity in Panamint lands, figurative designs were included that appear to be of Euro-American derivation. These designs consist of lizards, birds, butterflies, and conventionalized animal and floral patterns. The favored and more traditional

Figure 7 Basket. Sarah Hunter. Panamint, c. 1930-40. Willow, martynia, tree yucca root. Philbrook Art Center, Tulsa, Clark Field Collection, BA 616. This Panamint fancy basket, made for sale, is traditional in medium and technique, but adapted to a changing life style and a changed relationship to the Euro-American world.

geometric designs included vertical rows of triangles and diamonds touching each other. Perhaps the most significant change, however, was technological. Whereas, aboriginally, stone knives had been used to shape basketry elements, punctured tin lids, through which the withes were drawn, came to be used for fancy baskets. This permitted quicker production of raw materials and consequently also of what had traditionally been the basketwork of highest status (Kirk 1952; Steward 1941:333-339). On the Northwest Coast, among the Nuu-chah-nulth people of West Vancouver Island and the Makah of Washington, slightly different adaptations were made in the production of twined fancy baskets sold as souvenirs. Metal tools were introduced; parts of razor blades were used in specialized knives to produce uniform widths of grass. Figurative designs had always been a feature of basketry, particularly on the whaling hats worn by chiefs. In the nineteenth century, traditional and nontraditional motifs came to be used in large numbers on baskets made for sale (Figure 8). More unusual is the alteration in the pattern of use of particular species of grass, which occurred in this century. Most of the fine white grass used on basket exteriors was obtained in Washington and traded to Vancouver Island. With less aboriginal trade and the decline of labor opportunities in Washington, the Nuu-chah-nulth began to use more easily prepared but less fine local grasses. In this way, not only were they able to continue their souvenir art when the supply of grass declined, but they were also able to increase productivity because of the use of more easily worked materials. In no sense, however, can this substitution, or that of metal blades for knives, be regarded as altering the traditionalism of the twined souvenir baskets still produced in large numbers today. Indian artifacts, even

Figure 8
Basket with lid. Nootka, c. 1930–50. Cedar bark, grasses. Thomas Gilcrease Institute of American History and Art, Tulsa, 7137.579. Trinket baskets like this one were probably adapted from forms of imported ceramic jars. To fully Anglicize their appeal, the baskets were woven with American designs such as the eagle clutching arrows.

when created for sale, contain clues about change, information about diachronic processes of which they are part, and evidence that the easy division of art into traditional and nontraditional categories is misleading.

A good example of this confusion is provided by the souvenir art of the Haida, argillite carving. In the nineteenth century, the Haida of British Columbia created a new smoking pipe, a dish form, and other objects of carved shale. These were all made for sale to Europeans and other non-Indians. It is commonly assumed, although scholars know otherwise, that argillite carving played no part in indigenous Haida art. A recent exhibition of argillite carving was entitled "Pipes that Won't Smoke, Coal that Won't Burn," even though the first argillite pipes probably were carved for smoking, and other artifacts such as shaman's charms were also carved for native use (Sheehan 1981). The confusion stems in part from the mistaken notion that the Haida suddenly started to carve shale souvenirs that had no reference to their indigenous culture. Compounding the error is the isolation of argillite carving from other forms of souvenir creation, particularly the carving of wood artifacts, whether pipes, bowls, or figures; and the too exclusive association of argillite carving with the Haida, even though numbers of pipes were also carved by the Kwakiutl and others on Vancouver Island, of shale taken from local coal mines. Haida argillite carving should be seen in the context of a wide range of artistic phenomena on the Northwest Coast which occurred as reactions to the European colonization of Indian peoples. If native art is seen in the context of its political and cultural situation, then the need to distinguish "traditional" from "nontraditional" art disappears and is replaced by a more subtle understanding of the way in which art traditions emerge, flourish, and decay within the context of Indian society, whether or not they are influenced by white cultures during the process.

In a common usage, the word "traditional" is applied to artifacts that were meant wholly for native use, as opposed to those that were not. By this definition, an artifact may be entirely traditional in technique and symbolic content, and nontraditional only in that it was sold rather than used. This simplistic definition avoids consideration of the political and economic context in which art objects are produced, and without which we cannot say art exists. Haida argillite is an apparently nontraditional art form because it was made for sale, and very often included Euro-American motifs which were non-Haida. But because it fully represents in a more general manner Haida society at a time of devastating change, it is very much part of the complex whole of Haida society of which art was and is an aspect. The "nontraditional" label in this, as in most other cases, derives from the most common Euro-American affectation, that of pretending that Indians and other native peoples somehow cease to exist, or at least lose their souls, if they employ white man's materials or symbols, or create art to sell to the white man. White society does not accept Indian society as it exists at any one time: it is a part of this denial of Indian existence to denigrate postcontact adaptations in art and material culture as nontraditional.

THE EFFECT OF WHITE INSTITUTIONS ON NATIVE AMERICAN TRADITIONS IN THE MODERN PERIOD

More extreme forms of Euro-American influence occurred in the middle of this century, with the institutional fostering of Indian art, either with or without the financial and other support of the federal government. Perhaps the most successful and best-known examples of the institutional fostering of native arts occurred among the Inuit or Eskimo in Canada during the 1940s and early 1950s. The initial interest in Eskimo sculpture was stimulated by a Canadian artist, James Houston, who purchased carvings in the Port Harrison-Povungnetuk regions while on a painting trip to the Arctic in 1948. Houston's collection attracted the interest and material help of the Canadian Handicrafts Guild, the Hudson's Bay Company, the Anglican Arctic Diocese, and eventually the Canadian government. These institutions, for diverse reasons both artistic and economic, helped stimulate the emergence of a full-fledged Inuit school in the 1950s (Swinton 1972:123-126). In all of this, James Houston's charismatic presence acted as a catalyst. In some sense, then, the white impact upon this art form may be considered nontraditional, particularly in terms of the kinds of artifacts produced, which were non-utilitarian sculptures created for sale outside the community. Additionally, while most Inuit men were carvers, stone carving, the principal medium for this work, was a minor tradition more or less confined to the production of stone lamps and cooking pots. However, the easy label of "nontraditionalism" as applied to Inuit sculpture and graphic productions, distorts their context and, because of Euro-American prejudices, even taints the art as somehow non-Inuit. The reasons for this label are similar to those identified in the rejection of other apparently nontraditional art forms as non-native. And, as in other cases, it again implies a refusal to accept that the Inuit, like other native North Americans, have kept many aspects of their culture at a time of extreme economic and political change. The retention of many aspects of subsistence traditions, family networks, and linguistic and oral traditions are three basic attributes of the artistic context without which specific sculptures representing these traditions cannot be viewed.

The use of the words "traditional" and "nontraditional" suggests a black-and-white situation, when reality is much subtler. The maintenance of native traditions provides an unbroken continuity which is often hard for the Euro-American to perceive.

TRADITIONALISM IN INDIAN ART AS A COMPLEX AND SUBTLE PHENOMENON

Traditionalism, then, is not an attribute that can be easily identified in Indian art. Specific traits, whether technical or aesthetic, whether derived from new materials or a new social and political context, may develop in an ancient society without rendering its art nontraditional. Indian art must be made by Indians, but in all other attributes it can only be defined as Indian and traditional by the maker or beholder. To compartmentalize Indian art artificially as "traditional" or "nontraditional" is to deny the continuity of Indian society by specifying a particular point at which it breaks from the past. To do this is to idealize precontact societies and to imply that in adopting Euro-American ideas, materials, and markets, Indian societies are absorbed. The crucial term in Indian art is "Indian"; without it, Indian art has no existence, whatever the apparent traditionalism of the artifacts to the European or American beholder.

BIBLIOGRAPHY

Brasser, Ted J. 1976. *"Bo'jou, Neejee!" Profiles of Canadian Indian Art.* Ottawa: National Museum of Man, National Museums of Canada.

Brody, J.J. 1971. *Indian Painters and White Patrons.* Albuquerque: University of New Mexico Press.

Coe, Ralph T. 1976. *Sacred Circles: Two Thousand Years of North American Indian Art.* London: Arts Council of Great Britain.

Ewers, John C. 1955. "The Horse in Blackfoot Indian Culture." *Bureau of American Ethnology Bulletin* 159. Washington, D.C.

Gilliland, Marion Spjut. 1975. *The Material Culture of Key Marco Florida.* Gainesville: The University Presses of Florida.

Kirk, Ruth E. 1952. "Panamint Basketry—a Dying Art." *The Masterkey*, vol. 26(3), pp.76-86.

Morissonneau, Christian. 1978. "Huron of Lorette." Pp. 389-393 in *Handbook of North American Indians 15, Northeast.* Bruce G. Trigger, ed., William C. Sturtevant, general ed. Washington, D.C.: Smithsonian Institution.

Sears, William H. 1982. *Fort Center: An Archeological Site in the Lake Okeechobee Basin.* Gainesville: University Presses of Florida.

Sheehan, Carol. 1981. *Pipes That Won't Smoke, Coal That Won't Burn: Haida Sculpture in Argillite.* Calgary, Alberta: Glenbow Museum.

Steward, Julian H. 1941. "Culture Element Distributions: XIII Nevada Shoshone." *University of California Publications in Anthropological Records*, 4:201-359. Berkeley.

Swinton, George. 1972. *Sculpture of the Eskimo.* Toronto: McClelland and Stewart.

Vivian, R. Gwinn, Dulce Dodgen, and Gayle Hartman. 1978. "Wooden Ritual Artifacts from Chaco Canyon, New Mexico." *Anthropological Papers of the University of Arizona 32.*

23

Lakota Beaded Costumes of the Early Reservation Era

Marsha Clift Bol

Although generally unrecognized, a flowering of the beaded costume of the Lakota, also known as the Teton or Western Sioux, occurred during the early reservation period of the late nineteenth and early twentieth centuries. How might we account for such an artistic burst of energy given the extreme stress and severe societal disruption which these people were encountering during this time period? For a fuller understanding of the ingredients of this efflorescence it is necessary to examine the role of costume in the prior period.

The Lakota costume occupied a central position in pre-reservation Sioux society. It functioned as a form of graphic rather than verbal communication in reinforcing the roles and positions of its societal members. For the Lakota male, costume was an important avenue for conveying success and fame as a warrior, as well as gaining honor and prestige through the wearing of fine apparel. Symbols of achievements, painted in the representational style by the warrior, and the geometric decoration quilled and beaded by his wife and female relatives on his shirts, leggings, and moccasins, communicated his skills and prowess to the rest of his society. Fine clothing was a highly prized gift which reinforced his position as a generous man by serving as an important exchange item in the institution of the giveaway.

It was the Lakota woman who produced the majority of the clothing required by her husband, brothers, and children. Skill in beadwork and quill work provided an avenue of reflected prestige both for herself and her family. So highly prized were the feminine virtues of industry and artistic skill that they were institutionalized as societies and guilds.

Reprinted from *Phøebus 4*, edited by Anthony Lacey Gully, Tempe: Arizona State University, 1985, pages 70-77 with permission of the author and publisher.

Large allotments of time were necessary in order to accomplish the manufacture of these costumes. In order to accommodate art, an extraordinary division of labor occurred between a daughter of child-bearing age and her mother (or mother-in-law). As reported by Mirsky, until the mother was very old, past seventy, she continued to help her daughter by caring for the small children and doing much of the heavy labor. Mirsky states:

> During this period the daughter takes over the pleasanter, sedentary tasks of porcupine work, while the mother tans the hides, or the daughter does the fancywork on pair after pair of moccasins while her mother sews the soles on and finishes them. If a daughter of 35 tans the skins while her mother does porcupine quillwork, people will say, "She tans hides at her age!" "She is still doing embroidery!"[1]

Lakota clothing functions as a personal identifier as evidenced by the following statement: "Borrowing of anything is permissible and common, but not personal apparel or ornaments . . . They make fun of someone who wears even her mother's shawl . . . 'That family lends each other shawls, you cannot tell one individual from another'. . ."[2] Lakota costume also acted as a collective identifier, in much the same way as the description by Bogatyrev in his discussion of folk costumes, of the ethnic pride of the group in wearing what he terms "our costume."[3] In short, as the Lakota entered the reservation era, they were wearing clothing which served as both a personal identifier and a group identifier.

In the final decades of the nineteenth century, a rapid succession of historical events fostered a breakdown of Sioux society. In 1868, the large Sioux Reservation was established in western South Dakota. The Battle of Little Big Horn in 1876 brought the defeat of Custer and with it the white retaliatory campaign which spelled the final military defeat for the Sioux. At that point the majority of the Sioux moved onto the reservation. In 1881 the U.S. government prohibited the holding of the Sun Dance henceforth; and the last great buffalo hunt was held in 1882, the final buffalo killed by a Lakota in 1883.

The cumulative effect of these events was staggering. Whereas "in 1880 the political, social, and religious structure of the Teton Sioux remained largely intact," the decade following ushered in an era of profound stress.[4] Many Lakota institutions could not withstand such drastic change. Warfare, one of the primary activities of the men, was no longer possible. As a result war societies ceased to function, and the principal means of attaining prestige, rank, and wealth vanished. The tribal economy collapsed with the disappearance of the buffalo. Without the buffalo, traditional diet and the materials for many objects of material culture perished, as did another means for the Sioux hunter-warrior to gain recognition. The religious framework was vastly weakened with the ban on the Sun Dance. As MacGregor notes:

> This prohibition of the Sun Dance took away not only much of the security which religion gave to the people but also the public regarding and sanctioning of social life and social institutions. The ending of this reinforcement of the Dakota custom and the instruction of the young people by observation

> and participation contributed greatly to the weakening of social controls and the crumbling of Dakota culture.[5]

In the wake of these combined losses, additional pressures were brought to bear by the U.S. government which replaced buffalo with rations and farming implements, substituted Christianity and missionaries for the Sun Dance, and replaced Lakota chiefs with government agents.

The combination of these events was particularly devastating for the Lakota male. Luther Standing Bear, a Lakota chief, records: "It was as if a runner suddenly felt the ground beneath his feet disappear, leaving him off balance and plunging over a precipice."[6] The male role had been completely undermined leaving him stripped of his function as protector and provider and with no means for achieving cultural approval through warrior status and hunting prowess.

It is therefore not surprising that the Ghost Dance, which provided hope for return of the old life was a powerful attraction in 1889. "Wounded Knee drove home the impossibility of escape from white subjugation."[7] Lakota men, experiencing tremendous despair, often resorted to non-productivity, apathy, and alcohol. Ella Deloria states:

> It was they [Lakota men] who suffered the most from the enforced change, whether they realized it or not. It was their life primarily that was wrecked; it was their exclusive occupation that was abruptly ended. The women could go right on bearing children and rearing them. They could cook, feed their families, set up and strike camp unaided, pack and unpack when on a trip. Even embroidery, exclusively a woman's art, was not cut off suddenly . . . The man was the tragic figure . . . And so he sat by the hour indifferent and inactive, watching—perhaps envying—his wife as she went right on working at the same essential role of woman.[8]

Thus it was left to Lakota women to maintain the cultural traditions, as has been confirmed in a 1960 study on the Pine Ridge and Rosebud reservations by an economist and a social-clinical psychologist, Hagan and Shaw who found:

> Their [women's] transition to life as captives in the reservations allowed them to carry into the new way of life their old roles of mother and wife as private affairs, left untouched for a long period after the men lost their special function of dealing with problems outside the family and the group. As they [the women] came to acquire more autonomy as the persons responsible for the maintenance and support of family life, they became even freer to continue to raise their children as they were taught children should be raised. The traditional values held by the older people reinforced the role of the mother as a cultural refuge where Sioux practices could be kept alive beyond the reach of external suppression. That refuge became increasingly more crucial as children had to be surrendered to white schools at a younger age.[9]

The Lakota woman continued to follow the pathway of industry and arts. As in pre-reservation days, the costumes which she manufactured acted as a contribution to her family and her society. She had to confront, however, two new conditions: 1) the vacancy left by her masculine counter-part for achieving and maintaining group identity, and 2) the everpresent threat of white assimilation.

Lakota women responded to this changed situation by creating some of the most elaborate beaded costumes in Lakota history, which are characterized by increased complexity of pattern, complete beading of items, incorporation of new forms, and inclusion of the pictorial image in the repertoire. Increased complexity of pattern after 1875 has been noted by Lyford.[10] It was during this time that the Lakota developed beadwork patterns distinctively their own, which are characterized by delicate, nervous line, and complex compositions constructed of geometric elements, particularly triangles, forked lines, and terraces.[11] (Figure 1)

In addition to complexity of design, a tendency to bead items completely was initiated during the reservation period.

Pohrt, one of the few to note this change, states:

> The artistic appeal of a particular item seems, in part, to have been determined by the number of square inches of beadwork used. A tendency to bead objects completely may be seen on examples of every item the Sioux produced at this time . . . The ultimate examples of this aestheticism are completely beaded dresses. The sheer weight of the glass beads would have made wearing of these dresses an unpleasant experience.[12]

Figure 1 Lakota beaded saddle blanket, late 19th century. Maxwell Museum of Anthropology, University of New Mexico.

Many of these beaded dresses were made for young Lakota girls (Figure 2). Certainly wearing-comfort and practicality were not the thoughts uppermost in the minds of the makers. It must be remembered, however, that it was the children who were the particular target of assimilation through education. In the late nineteenth century, the U.S. government, in an all-out effort to expeditiously assimilate the Indian into white society, mandated the wearing of white clothing by Indian school children. As Standing Bear recalls: "At Carlisle the transforming, the 'civilizing' process began. It began with clothes. Never . . . could we be civilized while wearing moccasins and blankets."[13] By creating particularly fine traditional clothing for her children, a mother found one vehicle to combat the threat of assimilation (Figure 3).

The item which became the foremost symbol of ethnic identity was the beaded moccasin, whose longevity outlasted all other items. Here again the Lakota woman, during the reservation period, took the opportunity not only to fully bead the upper moccasin but the sole as well, eschewing practicality in favor of elaboration.

Lacking buckskin, a basic material in the pre-reservation period, the Lakota craftswoman incorporated new materials and new forms into her repertoire, without sacrificing the integrity of her art. She had long before recognized the opportunities available with white man's goods, for instance, glass beads which were found particularly appealing. For her husband and her sons she developed

Figure 2
Lakota girl in fully beaded dress.
Smithsonian Institution National Anthropological Archives, Neg. No. 54,662.

Figure 3
Lakota girl. Colorado Historical Society, No. 188WPA.

a unique amalgamation of the white man's cloth vest, available as an annuity good, which was either beaded fully so that none of the cloth remained visible or recreated in cowhide and beads.[14] (Figure 4)

The fully-beaded vest served as a successful union of a new form with a traditional style of decoration which allowed for placing one foot into the white man's world while continuing the Sioux traditions. The vest may also have functioned as a filter in the manner that Deveraux has suggested in his discussion of the nature and functions of art; that is, that art may make outside influences safe to confront by translating them into a culturally acceptable form.[15] The form found special favor with those who traveled with the Wild West shows and around the turn of the century with the newly-emergent Sioux cowboy.

The introduction of pictorial imagery into beadwork is found particularly on vests and pipebags, both items owned by men. Representational forms traditionally were the exclusive prerogative of the Lakota male, strictly enforced by the sexual division of labor.[16] One of the new conditions facing the Lakota female, however, was the vacancy left by the lack of masculine fulfillment of role in art as well as other endeavors. A possible explanation for the assumption of the pictorial style by the Sioux woman may have been in an endeavor to maintain the tradition of recording heroic events as well as traditional Sioux life through her own medium of beadwork. Wissler described a boy's pictorially beaded vest

Figure 4
Lakota man from Rosebud Reservation with pictorial beaded vest and quillwork tie, c. 1904. Smithsonian Institution National Anthropological Archives, Neg. No. T-15, 322.

as the object of military decoration and "claimed to reflect the deeds of the family," a task formerly performed by painted clothing decorated by male artists.[17]

A further indication of the significant role which costume continued to play in the reservation era was the adoption and use of the Ghost Dance dress in 1889. The costume of the Ghost Dance assumed the function of a form of rebellion against the usage of white products, and as a powerful source of protection from the enemy, in this case, military bullets.

Although the Ghost Dance costume quickly proved inadequate to the task, the beaded costume continued to be produced into the 1920s. Severe societal disruption, rather than signaling the eclipse of an art form, was responded to by Lakota women with an intensification of the beaded costume. The traditional Lakota use of costume as a form of protection and cultural identification was a vehicle employed in the endeavor to contend with the external threat of assimilation and the internal threat of societal breakdown.

NOTES

1. Jeanette Mirsky, "The Dakota," Margaret Mead, ed., *Cooperation and Competition Among Primitive Peoples* (New York: McGraw-Hill, 1937), p. 297.
2. Ibid., p. 426.
3. Ibid., p. 96.
4. Robert M. Utley, *The Lasts Days of the Sioux Nation* (New Haven: Yale Univ. Press, 1983), p. 21.
5. Gordon MacGregor, *Warriors Without Weapons: A Study of the Society and Personality Development of the Pine Ridge Sioux* (Chicago: Univ. of Chicago Press, 1946), p. 91.
6. Luther Standing Bear, *Land of the Spotted Eagle* (Boston: Houghton-Mifflin, 1933), p. 177.

7. MacGregor, *Warriors Without Weapons: A Study of the Society and Personality Development of the Pine Ridge Sioux* (Chicago: Univ. of Chicago Press, 1946), p. 33.
8. Ella Deloria, *Speaking of Indians* (New York: Friendship Press, 1944), pp. 95-96.
9. Everett E. Hagan & Louis C. Shaw, *The Sioux on the Reservations: The American Colonial Problem* (Cambridge: M.I.T Press, 1960), pp. 10-18.
10. Carrie A. Lyford, *Quill and Beadwork of the Western Sioux* (Lawrence, KS: Haskell Institute Press, 1940), p. 71.
11. Ibid., p. 67.
12. Richard A. Pohrt, *The American Indian and the American Flag* (Flint, MI: Flint Institute of Arts Press, 1975), p. 9.
13. Standing Bear, *Land of the Spotted Eagle*, p. 232.
14. Mrs. D. B. Dyer, *Fort Reno or Picturesque Cheyenne and Arrapahoe Army Life, Before the Opening of Oklahoma* (New York: G.W. Dillingham, 1896), p. 50.
15. George Deveraux, "Art and Mythology: A General Theory," Carol F. Jopling, ed., *Art and Aesthetics in Primitive Societies* (New York: E. P. Dutton, 1971), pp. 203-6.
16. Lyford, *Quill and Beadwork of the Western Sioux*, p. 12.
17. Clark Wissler, *Decorative Art of the Sioux Indians*, American Museum of Natural History Bulletin, XVIII:321-78.

24

Straddling the Cultural Fence

The Conflict for Ethnic Artists within Pueblo Societies

Edwin L. Wade

The market for American Indian arts and crafts has had a serious psychological effect on native artists and on their families and fellow community members. The participating artist introduces an alien, disruptive force into his native community in the form of Westernized beliefs, ideas, and values. His influence has radically changed the very nature of native art and has redefined the role and importance of the native artist in his community. The transition has been difficult. Community backlash against such artists can best be characterized as violent and unrelenting. Many have been the object of vicious gossip, witchcraft accusations, and social ostracism. Some have even been banned from their native villages or threatened with loss of life. The source of the controversy lies in the fundamental differences between mainstream and Native American world views. Two Southwestern Indian attitudes that cause particularly bitter conflict when challenged are man's relation to the supernatural, and what constitutes "a good man" within an egalitarian society.

MERCHANDISING THE GODS

A continual source of conflict between traditional Southwestern Indian ethos and the commercial art market has been the painting of ceremonial dances and the sale and display of sacred ceremonial items outside the native community. To understand why this conflict has been so intense, one must look to the Navajo and Pueblo conceptions of man's role in the universe.

For these Southwestern Indians, the universe is a place where all beings—men and supernaturals alike—are mutually dependent for survival. Man relies

Reprinted from *The Arts of the North American Indian*, edited by Edwin L. Wade, New York: Hudson Hills Press, 1986, pages 243-254 with permission of the author and publisher.

on the benign intentions of supernaturals, who determine whether his crops will grow and his people remain free from disease. At best, the supernaturals are seen as indifferent to man's plight; at worst they are vengeful. The Navajo feel that the balance could shift at any moment, and indifference become malevolence. Man must supplicate the spiritual beings through prayer and ritual, in order to persuade them to bring harmony to the earth. At the same time, spiritual beings such as the Yeis among the Navajo and the Pueblo Katcinas are equally dependent upon man. These beings have an overpowering need to be praised and worshiped. Bunzel (1932:489) noted that "the great divinity, the sun, and all the lesser divinities, the Katcinas, the rain-makers, the beast gods, the war gods, and the ancients, must be reminded that man is dependent upon their generosity; and that they, in turn, derive sustenance and joy from man's companionship."

The Puebloans, and especially the Hopi, believe that one man alone cannot fulfill the needs of the supernaturals. Performing the elaborate seasonal ceremonies–the Shalako, Niman, Summer Corn Dance, Mixed Animal Dance, and Buffalo Dance–requires the cooperation of an entire village. These ceremonies express communal gratitude for past favors while they petition for future abundance and the general well-being of the community.

At the root of Pueblo religion, then, is an intense belief that cosmic and earthly disharmony is caused by a failure of man's collective efforts to appease the supernaturals. Every villager, child or adult, observer or dancer, is expected to focus positive thoughts upon the ritual performances and to banish negative thoughts from consciousness. In light of this all-encompassing injunction, a failure of the collective can only result from the failure of an individual. In the marginal existence of the small-scale Pueblo farmer, there are inevitable dry years, untimely frosts, and other natural disasters. Rather than question the effectiveness of their religion, the Puebloans view such misfortunes as a consequence of antisocial behavior.

For Puebloans, one extremely offensive antisocial act has been the use of ceremonial dances in Indian paintings meant for sale to non-Indians. Though the artist may not have intended insult, such paintings have frequently been interpreted by traditionalists as an affront to the supernaturals. The commercial exploitation of sacred Pueblo rituals was the one negative thought, the selfish individualistic act, that could destroy the sanctity of the ritual.

Accusations have been harsh. The Hopi painters who illustrated J. Walter Fewkes's 1903 volume on Hopi Katcinas, for example, were labeled witches, and their paintings were considered instruments of sorcery. At Hopi and Zuñi, a witch is a "two-heart," a parasitic creature who preys upon the life force of others. A witch is a chaotic element that upsets the balance of all natural phenomena, and consequently disrupts the sacred dance ceremonials. An accusation of witchcraft is no minor charge; in Pueblo society, it is one of the few offenses that can invoke the death penalty.

Extremely bitter conflict arose over the painting of Katcina performances and the sale of Katcina masks and dance costumes. The explanation for this hostile reaction lies again in the communal nature of Puebloan religion. An individual does not own a ceremony or any of the paraphernalia used in its production. The seasonal dances, initiation rites, curing rituals, and other secret kiva ceremonies belong to the lineage groups, cults, or medicine societies whose members may inherit the right to care for a mask and to wear it in a ceremony. As Ruth Benedict (1934:71) notes, Katcina masks "are owned and cared for . . . by family lines in the same houses that have cared for them . . . since the beginning of the world." Sacred art is never privately owned in the non-Indian sense of that phrase. An individual has no right to sell it, dispose of it, or even to show it indiscriminately.

More than for their importance as religious heirlooms, Katcina masks, god images, and fetishes are valued for their intrinsic spiritual life force, an extension of the supernatural being represented by the object.

> The use of masks is surrounded by special taboos. One must never try on a mask when not participating in a ceremony, else one will die. . . . If one is incontinent during a katcina ceremony the mask will choke him or stick to his face (Bunzel 1965:443).

Respect for the life force of the Katcina mask is in fact so strong that a priest is required to feed the mask. Cornmeal is placed around its mouth, or a bowl of food placed before it; the being within then consumes the spirit of the food. The priest also grooms the mask, repainting it if the earth paints show wear, and replacing feathers that are ragged or missing. If the mask can no longer be renewed, it must be ceremonially retired in a ritual that sends the Katcina spirit home with many blessings and expressions of gratitude.

Beginning in the 1890s, a number of Katcina masks and other sacred objects were sold or traded to museums and private collectors. The spirits that dwell in these objects have not, in most cases, been "sent home." The Puebloans feel that these spirits are being starved and abused, that they are prisoners, and that all the benefits they might have brought the community are locked up with them. This abridgment of ethical responsibility toward the sacred by museums and collectors is an extremely serious problem and will continue as a source of controversy until Native American religious sensitivities are acknowledged.

The demand for the clandestine acquisition of sacred art objects has been so great, and the objects so hard to obtain, that many Indian artist have produced facsimiles and inexact, crude replicas. Commercial Katcina dolls are derived from the semisacred *tihu;* the Zuñi prayer-meal bowls that are offered for sale are commonly miniaturized, less elaborate versions of kiva step bowls (Figures 1, 2). Cardboard ice-cream cartons have been used as the foundations for fake Katcina masks. The commercial sale of these objects has only been accepted to a limited degree by the Puebloans. Objects reproduced with inexact fidelity are more likely to be allowed to be sold. The Katcina mask, however, is held in such reverence that even the ice-cream-carton replicas are considered profanities. Hopi and Zuñi, the only two pueblos that have actively produced nonsacred Katcina dolls, have been the most lenient in interpreting what can be commercialized. The depiction of Katcinas, Katcina performances, or kiva rituals is strictly forbidden among the Rio Grande pueblos; consequently, their commercial artists interpret minor ceremonial themes involving the public dances. Never are masked beings portrayed.

Figure 1
Santa Clara polychrome jar. Artist Lois Gutierrez (1948–). Philbrook Art Center, Tulsa, 81.6.3. Recent work by this artist imitates the form and some of the designs common to the sacred kiva jars of the Tewa Pueblos. Though the imitation of sacred forms and designs has been practiced over the last 60 years, the traditional religious practitioners of the Pueblos still feel an uneasiness when confronted with such vessels made for sale.

Figure 2 Zuñi ceremonial bowl, c. 1939. Philbrook Art Center, Tulsa. Clark Field Collection, PO 216. In the late 19th century, stepped-terrace bowls became common in Pueblo ceremonialism. Cornmeal mixed with turquoise was placed in the center of the bowl. These sacred objects excited the interest of white collectors and an illicit market for the contraband objects developed. By the 1920s, the Zuñi theocracy realized their inability to control this market, so they elected to allow commercial potters to produce inexact, unconsecrated facsimiles of medicine bowls for sale.

Acceptance of the commercialization of Navajo and Pueblo sacred arts is coming slowly, but only after much dissent and violence and the passing of generations of Southwestern Indians.

SERVING TWO MASTERS

The question of acceptable imagery is not the only source of friction between a contemporary Indian artist and his tribal group. An equally bitter, if more subtle, conflict is set up by his assumption of the role of "Indian artist" in a world dominated by non-Indians. The superstar image of a celebrated Native American artist conflicts with the Southwestern Indian definition of a good man in several ways.

The issue partly revolves around success. Success in mainstream American society is measured in terms of money, publicity, and prestige—precisely the commodities that arouse suspicion and distrust in the artist's home community when accorded him by the commercial Indian-art market. By obtaining the non-Indian earmarks of success, a Pueblo artist jeopardizes his ability to succeed as a tribal member, a "good man," in the context of his own group. The question is whether a man can succeed simultaneously in two worlds that define goodness and success differently.

Since the end of the 1970s, increasing numbers of Indians of all tribal extractions have attempted to assimilate into mainstream American culture. A common pattern has been to pursue a new urban life for a year or so, then for various reasons to return to the reservation and its values and customs. The Indian artist can thereby maintain a home on the reservation while also earning money and recognition from the public. In so doing, he remains under the close scrutiny of his neighbors and must conform to the image of a good man prescribed by his society, while at the same time playing the role of a sophisticated, Westernized art-market participant.

Residents of the pueblos have a clear conception of what constitutes appropriate and inappropriate behavior. The Zuñi image of a good man is typical:

> The ceremonious Zuñi place a high value on inoffensiveness and sobriety. They deplore an authoritative manner and strongly disapprove of aggressiveness and qualities of leadership. A man who manifests such traits is suspect as a witch . . . and would formerly have been hung up from the ceiling by his wrists or thumbs until he confessed. . . .
>
> Individualistic qualities are held in low esteem in the collectivized culture of Zuñi, where the maintenance of oneness with the universe is believed to depend on the subordination of individual ambition for the benefit of the group, lest the supernatural powers look with disfavor upon Zuñi and withhold their blessing (Spencer and Jennings 1965:318).

The Indian artist who gains notoriety, who might be interviewed on television, appear at gallery openings in white buckskin and turquoise, and have droves of Anglo patrons parked outside his house, is seen by his fellows as having all the qualities a good man does not possess. Although a good Puebloan should not be boastful, Margaret Gutierrez, a Santa Clara potter, says, "today our pottery is the finest and most beautifully worked pottery in the world, and it is known the world over" (Maxwell 1974:44). A good Puebloan holds individualistic qualities in low esteem, but Dextra Q. Nampeyo, from Hopi, says, "I want to keep my pottery unique" (Maxwell 1974:36). A good Puebloan is unselfish, cooperative, and kind to his fellow community members (Aberle 1951:16); nevertheless, one of Nampeyo's granddaughters says that the designs she and the other Nampeyo descendants use are theirs, and not free to be used by others. They have established a kind of copyright by publishing in papers that these designs are theirs (Collins 1974).

The conflict is intensified by success, in the non-Indian meaning of the term. The average craftsman is generally viewed by his community as humble and modest. As long as he remains faceless and nameless, his behavior will not be contradictory to the Puebloan image of a good man. But for some artists such anonymity is neither possible nor desirable. Their patrons know them by name and favor them over other craftsmen in the pueblo. To remain so favored, these artists must assert themselves and promote their work.

In traditional Puebloan society, the role of artist has carried little prestige. A woman shaping a well-formed pot, with pleasing designs, could at most expect the praise of her neighbors. Another potter might admire her wares, or discuss their designs with her. Decoration of utilitarian pottery during the historic Pueblo period was not critical to the welfare or survival of the society. Although men's production of sacred arts was crucial to the spiritual survival of the community, the demand for these arts was never great enough to warrant a class of professional artists.

One pursuit, however, was critical to survival: to be a successful farmer. Farming was the only legitimate full-time undertaking. Politics, the priesthood, art, war-making: all were part-time pursuits. Moreover, an individual could not aspire to leadership until proving to his community that he was a good man, a contributor to the general welfare. He had to be a good farmer. His own vitality was caught up inextricably with the vitality of his fields. Tall cornstalks and bright yellow, trumpet-shaped squash blossoms symbolized his right to be recognized as a productive Puebloan. Although today's agriculture only supplements the Pueblo economy, farming remains an important obligation every man must meet.

A Pueblo artist still must tend his fields. Even in the 1970s, an Indian artist who decided to straddle the cultural fence had to convince his elders that he had not "sold out" to the non-Indian world. He had to make his crops grow—close to a full-time job in summer— and yet find time to make and market his art.

Methods for coping with this problem were devised as early as the 1930s by several prominent commercial artists of San Ildefonso. When painters like Awa Tsireh (Alfonso Roybal), Julian Martinez, Wo Peen, and Oqwa Pi were absent from the pueblo for long periods of time, they hired Spanish American laborers to tend their fields (Soil Conservation Service 1935:51-52). When sales slumped, the hired labor was laid off and artists resumed traditional economic roles. One observer noted in 1935, "the bottom has dropped out of painting. The three principal painters [of San Ildefonso] are cultivating their fields this year" (Soil

Conservation Service 1935:52). Women artists encountering similar problems developed similar solutions. A Pueblo woman's first calling is to be a conscientious housekeeper, wife, and mother. With the increasing need for cash income, however, women began to spend more time digging clay, and shaping, painting, and firing their pots. But Maria Martinez's career as a potter soared while her reputation as a good housekeeper remained unblemished; she employed Spanish American women to perform her household duties.

The Puebloans are in many ways frightened of change; and the commercial artist who succeeds in the Anglo world instigates social change, even if he or she juggles both the old and the new with exceeding agility. The extent to which Indian artists are capable of instituting radical—and even permanent—change in their communities is clearly illustrated in the events that occurred at San Ildefonso between 1900 and the late 1930s.

The story begins in the 1880s, when the first tourist pottery (San Ildefonso polychrome) was manufactured. By 1900 there was a husband-and-wife team specializing in pottery for the tourist market. Florentino Montoya painted the pots and his wife, Martina, shaped, polished, and fired them. The success of this couple inspired other such alliances. Ten years later, the name of Crescencio Martinez was well known to Indian art collectors. He decorated the pottery made by his mother, wife, and sister (Figure 3). Among other famous husband-and-wife teams were Julian and Maria Martinez, and Juan Cruz Roybal and Tonita Martinez Roybal (Figure 4; Chapman and Harlow 1970:25-27).

Pottery-making emerged as the most profitable profession for a San Ildefonso woman. Between 1910 and 1915 many more women joined the profession (Figure 5). A number of men who had worked with their wives in the manufacture of pottery turned to painting on paper to supplement their incomes, but it

Figure 3
Crecensio Martinez (1879–1918) and his wife Anna Montoya Martinez (1885–196?) at San Ildefonso Pueblo with Charles Wakefield Cadman, c. 1915

Figure 4 Juan Cruz (1887–?) and Tonita Roybal (1892–1945) at San Ildefonso Pueblo, c. 1935.

always ran a poor second to their wives' occupation. In the 1920s, when black-on-black ware had replaced the older polychrome and black-on-red traditions, there was not enough pottery to meet the demand. The team effort concept cut down at least some of the time required to finish a piece, and importation of Cochiti slip made a further contribution to the volume of pots turned out. Even the perfection of black-on-black tourist ware was a step in this direction, since it used less elaborate designs on smaller pieces.

These innovations changed San Ildefonso pottery to such an extent that the 1920s end product bore almost no resemblance to its progenitor of the 1880s. But if there were any cries of illegitimacy, they came from outsiders and not from the pueblo. Changes in a secular art tradition, no matter how drastic, do not seem to distress Puebloans. What did distress them was that ambition and the lure of the dollar were urging their potters toward increasingly unorthodox behavior.

Maria Martinez stands out from this group of potters as the most forceful and inventive. Her boldness led her to buy her neighbors' unfinished pots, complete them, and sell them under her own name (Whitman 1947:105). She polished slip so meticulously that it became a black mirror, and her pleasing pots sold much more dearly than did the work of other potters. Resentment toward Maria grew quickly. She had challenged the egalitarian nature of Pueblo society; she could make more money because she was more skilled. Other San Ildefonsans began to realize that a pot or painting signed by a "better" artist brought more money:

Figure 5 San Ildefonso women making pottery on the lawn of the Palace of the Governors in Santa Fe, c. 1919. From left to right: Maria Martinez, Anna, unidentified, and Ramona.

> Adam Martinez (the son of Maria and Julian) makes naïve paintings for his parents' shop that are signed "Julian." On being asked why Adam did not sign his own paintings, Santana, Adam's wife, said: "Because they would not sell" (Soil Conservation Service 1935:51-52).

Meanwhile, the profit motive spawned even greater inventiveness. By the end of the 1920s, Maria had employed several relatives to assist in stages of pottery-making. The economic advantages of mass production became evident, and as the 1930s began, the experiment expanded into a full-scale cottage industry:

> At Maria's and in other houses in the pueblo, specialized workers have been developed who regularly "slip" and polish the pots and, in some cases, mould them. Sometimes, as at Maria's, the group is a family group: a daughter-in-law, a husband's niece, a dependent sister, or others. These workers, if paid, Maria says receive $1.00 per day . . . with other employers, less successful, they are paid with wheat or corn. Where family dependents are not available, the poor regularly work for the rich in San Ildefonso potterymaking (Soil Conservation Service 1935:68).

At the height of the factory system, certain employees were responsible even for signing the artist's name on the bottom of the vessel: "The signature of the pot, made by the woman who applies the slip, is nevertheless 'Maria and Julian.' Dionicia, a young relative, was observed making these signatures as she worked.

On inquiry Maria said: 'The pot is mine. . . . I moulded this pot'" (Soil Conservation Service 1935:68).

The overwhelming financial success of the major San Ildefonso artists introduced much more than just new production techniques. Two revolutionary changes in the structure of the society occurred. First, the buying and selling of labor became a permanent part of the pueblo's internal economy. Second, as the hiring of poorer community members became common, two economic classes grew out of a formerly egalitarian system.

As San Ildefonsan pottery production increased, the next step was marketing. The Fred Harvey bus tours inadvertently provided the new method of distribution by faithfully stopping at the doors of Maria, Antonita, and other prominent potters, so that tourists could meet these celebrated Indians in person. This steady, dependable flow of buyers soon led to the creation of small home retail shops. Porches and living rooms were stocked with baskets from Jicarilla Apache, White Mountain Apache, and Ute, and with silverwork and textiles from the Navajo and Hopi (Soil Conservation Service 1935:57; Burton 1936:69).

Other Indian groups were anxious to deal with the San Ildefonsans, since they offered cash, rather than goods, in trade. No other Indian group in the United States had developed such entrepreneurial skills. A comparison with Tesuque Pueblo illustrates this point. Like most other Puebloans in the 1930s, the Tesuque poorly understood the concept of wholesaling, assuming it meant merely selling their materials to a trader. While San Ildefonsans usually required wholesale buyers to purchase fifteen to twenty pieces, Tesuque potters sold any quantity the trader would buy. Furthermore, they exchanged their pottery for groceries instead of cash. When a potter became desperate for food, she lowered her prices, allowing a trader to fill all his needs to the exclusion of the rest of the village. This meant, in effect, that if one woman had groceries for the week, her competitors went hungry (Soil Conservation Service 1935:55).

In a small community, where everyone is a relative or friend, nothing could be worse than competition for food. Tesuque's farmlands had been essentially depleted; there was almost no wage work available. Selling pottery meant survival, but it also meant turning on one's neighbor. The Tesuque were acting against the Pueblo concept of a good community member: instead of promoting the common good, they were ruthlessly undercutting each other. Resentment and hostility riddled the pueblo.

Although by contrast the San Ildefonsans applied Western economic principles to salvage a dying economy, no amount of financial security could change the fact that they too were experiencing serious social problems. The artist's stampede to claim a corner of the market was trampling traditional values and attitudes. "The pot now symbolized not the connection of the potter with the deep spring of Indian life, but her connection with the white life" (Soil Conservation Service 1935:105-106) and all the Pandora's box of troubles that entailed.

The most predictable outcome of this newfound surplus was jealousy and rivalry among potters. As one observer commented:

> Feelings have grown to such a pitch that women will not visit one another lest they be suspect of trying to spy on the number of pots their rivals may have or be accused of stealing designs. And women say jealously of one another, "She works night and day on her pottery" (Whitman 1947:106).

This competitiveness became generalized as an intense rivalry between the two halves of San Ildefonso Pueblo, the North and South plazas, which deepened as the economic gap between the two widened. Non-Indian patrons began to take sides. Friends of the South Plaza, such as Ina Cassidy, accused the North Plaza supporters of discriminating against the other half of the pueblo. They felt Rose Gonzales and Susannah Aguilar were being slighted by leaders of the Santa Fe Indian Fair. The South Plaza patrons were equally vocal, accusing Maria Martinez and Antonita Roybal of an unfair monopoly of the fair (Soil Conservation Service 1935:81).

What the North Plaza women won in wealth and prestige, the men lost in morale. Women potters became the heads of households, bought the family groceries, and paid the bills. Although a number of men helped their wives or other female relatives to design and paint pottery, it was the women's names that were associated with the work. With the exception of Julian Martinez, none co-signed pots they painted. This reversal of roles resulted in feelings of worthlessness and failure on the part of the men. Some sold their own paintings for extra cash, but this income was never substantial. Up until 1937, painters could expect to earn a maximum of nine hundred dollars in a good year, whereas the better potters made close to two thousand dollars a year as early as the 1920s (Brody 1971:88).

The incidence of alcoholism among men of the North Plaza rose markedly during this period (Soil Conservation Service 1935:85). By 1930 the level of alcoholism in the pueblo had seriously handicapped the smooth internal workings of the society, and women became the heads of households in an even truer sense.

> This was evident on San Antonio Day—a day on which the returned school children are supposed to be brought into the spirit of the ceremonies. In a charming bower on the plaza, Maria and her sisters sat in beauteous raiment, watching with inner pain and devastation the debacle of the men. According to a reliable informant, the two male dancers and the entire chorus save one man (Romando Vigil) were drunk by evening and "lying in the ditch" (Soil Conservation Service 1935:85).

A pueblo can function only in a limited way without male authority figures. Religious and political leadership traditionally belonged to men; a woman could not be governor, *cacique*, or priest. Men had little chance in the 1930s to regain their roles as economic providers, but it was feasible for them to recapture their political and religious standing. Some women, such as Maria Martinez, began to push their husbands into sobriety and encourage them to take more interest in community affairs. Along with moral support, these women could provide the money needed to sponsor events such as weddings, dance ceremonies, and initiations. Taking on the costly responsibility of providing feasts for up to a hundred people, and financing wedding garments and dance costumes, brought great admiration and respect to the donor. Drawing on his wife's ample income, Julian Martinez was able to support community events generously. This show of goodwill enabled him to overcome his unfavorable reputation as a problem drinker. In fact, by 1940, he had so thoroughly regained the respect of the pueblo that he was elected governor.

Julian's ascension is a case in point, illustrating further the social changes wrought directly or indirectly by the flourishing art of San Ildefonso pottery-making (Figure 6). His recovery of standing in the community would never have occurred even one generation earlier. In traditional San Ildefonso society, once a man brought shame upon his house, he could never qualify for a position of leadership, whatever his change of heart. However, by the time Julian was named governor, this had changed (Marriott 1948:267). The San Ildefonso coup d'état of 1925 was instrumental in establishing many new ground rules for the attainment of political power and leadership. The North Plaza faction, dominated by wealthy women artists and their families, had seized control of the pueblo from the poor farmers of the South Plaza, whose legitimate rule no longer had economic support. As the pueblo's future was dependent on the continued monetary support of the wealthy arts-and-crafts-producing families, the South Plaza had no choice but to capitulate to the new regime, which has remained unchallenged to the present.

Figure 6
Julian Martinez firing pottery, c. 1940.

The power struggle at San Ildefonso was facilitated by the commercial artists' close association with Anglo patrons and dealers. Through this association they gained financial independence from the rest of the village. As their economic reliance on fellow community members diminished, they began to make their own decisions and run their own affairs. When the non-art-producing families came to rely on the artists for the financial support of the pueblo, the artists' dictates inevitably were accepted. After the coup, it became important for political leaders, especially the governor of the pueblo, to have a good rapport with the white society. One of the governor's main functions was to act as a liaison between his community and the outside world. There could be no more logical candidate for this role than a commercial artist. When the North Plaza took over, they placed artists or members of art-producing families in key political positions: The new governor, Sotero Montoya, appointed as his assistants Julian Martinez and Juan Cruz Roybal, a pottery decorator. Richard Martinez became War Chief and Alfonso Roybal and Romando Vigil assisted him in his duties. All three were painters. Julian Martinez then became governor in 1940 and his son, Popovi Da, a potter, was elected to the office a decade later.

With the defeat of the South Plaza leadership, most of the North Plaza men abandoned their careers as painters and devoted their time to politics. Their wives continued to make pottery, pay the bills, and buy the groceries. But the men had a sense of purpose in their lives now; they had a reason for devoutly taking part in the religious ceremonies—and for remaining sober.

The role of the Indian artist has been totally redefined by the commercial Indian art market. Once the artist produced exclusively for the needs of his own community, but today he is almost solely concerned with the demands of white patrons. Commercial artists have to be striving, competitive, individualistic, and self-motivating. Unfortunately, these are exactly the qualities discouraged in many traditional Southwest Indian societies. Resistance to the acculturative influence of the commercial artist has followed a uniform pattern. Native community members resent the artist's newly acquired social mobility and wealth. As soon as the artist's superiority in marketing his personal talent and outstripping others financially has been proven, they view him as a threat to the egalitarian nature of their society.

Initially, native communities, and especially the Puebloans, used threats and physical coercion to suppress the commercial artist. Yet realizing that the extinction of their traditional economies is inevitable, they have slowly relaxed this pressure and have reluctantly begun to accept the ethnic-art market, with all its threatening influences, as their new source of subsistence.

BIBLIOGRAPHY

Aberle, David F. 1951. *The Psychosocial Analysis of a Hopi Life-History*. Berkeley: University of California Press.

Benedict, Ruth. 1934. *Patterns of Culture*. Boston and New York: Houghton Mifflin.

Brody, J.J. 1971. *Indian Painters & White Patrons*. Albuquerque: University of New Mexico Press.

Bunzel, Ruth L. 1932. "Introduction to Zuñi Ceremonialism." Pp. 467-544 in *Forty-Seventh Annual Report of the Bureau of American Ethnology, 1929-1930*. Washington, D.C.

——. 1965. "The Nature of Katcinas." Pp. 442-444 in *Reader in Comparative Religion. An Anthropological Approach*, William A. Lessa and Evon Z. Vogt, eds. New York, Evanston, and London: Harper and Row.

Burton, Henrietta K. 1936. *The Re-establishment of the Indians in Their Pueblo Life through the Revival of Their Traditional Crafts*. New York: Teachers College, Columbia University.

Chapman, Kenneth M. and Francis H. Harlow. 1970. *The Pottery of San Ildefonso Pueblo*. Albuquerque: University of New Mexico Press.

Collins, John E. 1974. *Nampeyo, Hopi Potter: Her Artistry and Her Legacy*. Flagstaff, Arizona: Northland Press.

Marriott, Alice. 1948. *Maria: the Potter of San Ildefonso*. Norman: University of Oklahoma Press.

——.1956. "The Trade Guild of the Southern Cheyenne Women." 1956 *Bulletin of the Oklahoma Anthropological Society* 4:19-27.

Maxwell Museum of Anthropology. 1974. *Seven Families in Pueblo Pottery*. Albuquerque: University of New Mexico Press.

Soil Conservation Service. 1935. *Tewa Basin Study: vol. 1: The Indian Pueblos*. Albuquerque: Soil Conservation Service.

Spencer, Robert F. and Jesse D. Jennings. 1965. *The Native Americans*. New York: Harper and Row.

Whitman, William. 1947. *The Pueblo Indians of San Ildefonso*. New York: Columbia University Press.

INDEX